The Only Three Questions That Count

The Only Three Questions That Count

Investing by Knowing What Others Don't

KENNETH L. FISHER

WITH JENNIFER CHOU

AND LARA HOFFMANS

FOREWORD BY JAMES J. CRAMER

John Wiley & Sons, Inc.

CONTENTS

ACKNOWLEDGMENTS

This book originally sprang from interactions between literary agent Jeff Herman and me. Jeff was eager for me to do a book since I hadn't done one in so many years. I had the concept but wasn't keen on the energy and time commitment necessary to complete a work of this size. Having done three books before I knew it would be a lot of work. Jeff kept at me, persuading me he would sell my book and publishers would receive it well and others would help me. He provided a lot of motivation. Many would tell you he is the best book agent in America today and I don't disagree. If you're thinking of writing a book, I encourage you to read his books: *Write the Perfect Book Proposal: 10 That Sold and Why*, and *Jeff Herman's Guide to Book Publishers, Editors, & Literary Agents, 2007*. He really is as good as it gets.

Then I recruited Lara Hoffmans and Jennifer Chou. Lara had been an investment counselor in my firm's client services group dispensing advice to more than 100 clients having had a prior background in the industry. But before that she had a background in writing. Jennifer had worked for seven years in our research group primarily doing capital markets research for either me or Andrew Teufel. We came to terms. Jennifer would be responsible for the data and visuals and fact checking and Lara would rough out the book. Working from meetings discussing what we would cover, we created an outline that point by point and item by item Lara turned into a very rough draft while Jennifer started cranking out data. Then I started editing and changing. After an edit Lara would clean it up, edit my edits, and we would look at it again.

But the data burden was too great. There is a mass of data in this book and statistics behind the data. And a lot of visuals—120 in all—and all data-laden.

So my firm's research department pulled out the stops. Jill Hitchcock, Group Vice President, Research, assigned Elizabeth Anathan, a long-time employee, to oversee a crew to work with Jennifer in data and fact checking. Ultimately, there was a lot more data and facts checked than ended up in the book and that took a lot of effort from Jared Brenner, Mark Christy, Jason Dorrier, John Hertzer, Greg Miramontes, David Watts, and Rose Zarrinpar. I appreciate all their work because without them it would have been impossible to put together the mass of material that my words describe. In effect, they set up a process to cross-check their cross-checking so little would get lost in the process. I particularly appreciate Elizabeth's organization of all of this and David Watts, who has done a lot of work with me in the past doing visuals, putting up with my increased angst as we got close to the end and I got nervous.

Speaking of data, I would be remiss not to thank the following data providers: Bryan Taylor and Global Financial Data, Thomson Financial Datastream, Standard & Poor's, Bloomberg, and Ibbotson Analyst, without whose contributions to the investment community, we may not have conducted our studies and research both for this book specifically and over the years leading up to it. The quality and scope of market data get better every year, allowing us to continue expanding our work and create new capital markets technology. Very importantly for readers, there is appendix material provided courtesy of Global Financial Data that I don't believe general book readers have ever been able to access before. I must thank *Forbes*—four of my columns are used in the book and were reprinted by permission of *Forbes* magazine, *Forbes* 2006. While I write them, they do belong thereafter to *Forbes*.

As the book began to take shape and after I'd done one complete edit, I passed parts of it on to various people for comments. Meir Statman is the Glen Klimek professor of finance at Santa Clara University. Meir has been a friend for 22 years and we've done a lot of behavioral finance research for a long time and published a handful of scholarly research papers together. He and I are very different. He is the academic. I am the practitioner. We often agree and often disagree which is why our work together has been fruitful. But this time we weren't working together. Meir is very clear that this book isn't his cup of tea. It is too much, too edgy, and too assertive, and in many ways and places Meir simply disagrees with me. But it's my book, not Meir's and despite our many disagreements we're friends and the book is vastly better for his criticisms as I adapted parts of it in many ways to accommodate some of his disagreements with my assertions.

I'm always appreciative of interactions with Jeff Silk and Andrew Teufel. I've worked with Jeff since 1983. He is Vice Chairman of Fisher Investments and, with Andrew Teufel, the three of us make all portfolio management decisions at my firm. Andrew, one of the firm's three co-presidents to whom the 850-plus employee force reports through Group Vice Presidents, has been with the firm a decade and is the brightest young person it's ever been my pleasure to work with. Both Jeff's and Andrew's comments helped, and particularly Jeff had major impact on changing Chapter 5. Justin Arbuckle, who runs our institutional group at my firm, also offered criticisms that changed my tone in a number of areas.

Grover Wickersham put a lot of effort into editing drafts. On planes, at night at home, in London, in Canada, in the Bay Area. Wherever he was, he was editing everything from big ideas down to copy editing. Grover is a securities lawyer by background, having once upon a time been Los Angeles Branch Chief of the Securities and Exchange Commission. In his role as a practitioner, he has edited a lot of prospectuses. He said this was a lot more fun by comparison. I'm indebted. He also runs an investment advisory business and is Chairman of the Purisima Funds.

Obviously I'm indebted to my friend Jim Cramer for his very nice Foreword. Where a guy like Jim finds time only the Lord knows—except Jim has a lot more energy than most people. Others whose encouragement and help are appreciated include Pierson Clair and Thomas Grüner. From Thomas, who runs a money management firm of some note in Germany, I got an instant offer to have the book translated and published in Germany, and so it will be by the very same firm he suggested.

Ultimately, before submitting the manuscript I did five complete edits of every chapter and a sixth on three of them. While I am deeply indebted to Lara and Jennifer for their exhaustive work in organizing and laying out the book and drafting and data—in the end my fingerprints are all over it and all errors and inadequacies are mine.

The time I put into those edits came directly from time I otherwise owe my wife of 36 years. I appreciate her tolerance, devotion, and love as always. Finally, I acknowledge that without the input from my father, Philip A. Fisher, I never would have moved as a youth in the direction of capital markets. He loved stocks from the time he was 21 in 1928 until he died in 2004 at 96. I wish he could have lived to see this book and I dedicate it to his memory.

FOREWORD

Ken Fisher has quietly built an empire based on a simple precept: make as much money as possible over time with the least amount of risk because that's what the customer deserves, and deep down, it's what we all want. Nobody's better than Ken. That's not some crazy hyperbole. He actually is the best. My agent's going to kill me for saying all of this. Ken and I are competitors, what am I doing praising his product? What kind of capitalist am I? First off, Ken's a good friend, but that's not what matters to you. What matters to you is simple: Ken can make you money. I believe that reading his book may be the single best thing you could do this year to make yourself a better investor. Let me be totally honest with you; right now I run a charitable trust with all kinds of restrictions, but if I were allowed to have my own money managed, I'd hand it over to Ken without a second thought. I'm only telling you this because I'm unhealthily honest and because I want to make you money—Ken can help with that.

After reading this book all the way through in one sitting because I couldn't put it down (which I really don't have the time to do), I realized something. In this book, Ken has just turned the entire world of investing upside down. He's taken every myth, every useless, silly belief that most of the professionals ruin themselves with, and he's not only refuted them, which after all is just an assertion, but actually proved them wrong. And he does better than that because in this book he teaches you how to do that yourself.

I'll admit he ruffled a few of my feathers when he pretty clearly demonstrated that a couple of the things I believe aren't strictly—how do I say this—true. But that's his point, it's his goal, it's his job. It's how he will make you a better investor.

Before I say what I'm about to, let me just tell you that Ken and I have radically divergent views about running money. I pick stocks and I think I'm pretty good at it. Ken tells me that is a sucker's game. I'm quickly trying to pull some numbers together and use his own methods to show him otherwise, but that could take a while. I'm no relativist, especially when it comes to money, but I do know there's more than one way to skin a cat. I also know Ken's way works really, really well. Despite our different approaches, I believe that this is the single most rigorous, intelligent, comprehensive, and useful book about investing that I've had the good fortune to read in my decades-long romance with the market.

If you own stocks, or if you're just getting started, if you're a pro or an amateur, this book is for you. As Ken aptly points out: Most pros, at least on the mutual fund side of things, could do their jobs a lot better, so maybe it's not useful to talk about professionals and amateurs. The point is that everyone wants to make money. Everyone wants to generate returns that beat the market, or whatever index you feel most comfortable snuggling up to and competing with. All of you want this, and I'm willing to bet most of you don't know how.

You might think you've got it figured out. Maybe you've gotten lucky for the past few years. Let me be straight with you: You probably need some help. There are thousands of mistakes individuals make with their money each and every day. If you want to put your money to work for you, you should do yourself a favor and read this book. I've been in the game for over twenty-five years, and *The Only Three Questions That Count* taught me a thing or ten about investing. I am probably the most shamelessly self-promotional man on television, and I'm telling you, for the next few hours, stop listening to me and listen to Ken. If you're one of my detractors, you don't need me to tell you that Ken Fisher's got a strategy, or set of strategies, that look nothing like my own. And even though we disagree on some points, I still think he's the greatest—not that he's a great guy, although he is—but he's a great investor.

Now when it comes to the fundamental premise of this book—it's Ken's book, I'm not going to give anything important away—I agree with Ken completely. Good investors need to know how to innovate if they want to stay good investors. And when you take a position in a stock or a sector or an entire country, you're either right or you're wrong. If you're right, then you win and you make money. If you're wrong . . . you get the point. There will always be winners and losers in the market; for you to win somebody else almost always has to lose. Ken isn't trying to tell you how to be right, not at first. You'd better know how to walk before you run. This book gives you a system, an approach, a method that seems intuitive when you read it, but in reality it is far from how most people approach the market. It's a way of thinking about the market that, once you master it, will make you an infinitely better investor. Ken knows that you need to be right if you want to win, and he knows how to be right— I've seen his performance, and I've read his columns. And now he's teaching you how to take his scientific approach to investing and use it to make yourself a richer person, in money if not necessarily in spirit.

You don't need to be a genius to use Ken's advice—you don't even need to be that clever. You don't have to know much about anything, and I mean that, other than how to read to make good use of this book. Ken teaches you everything you need to know to make use of what he calls "the only three questions that matter." He's right about them, and it's good that he's writing about them. In a way, this book is the great equalizer: It takes professionals to task and raises up amateurs to where the pros are supposed to be because nothing the pros know or think they know really matters. Trust me, I've been one. There's an old saying, "God created men, but Sam Colt made them equal." I don't know who's responsible for creating most modern investors, but I know it is Ken Fisher who'll make them equal. Or maybe not so equal—some investors are more equal than others, and that's the camp Ken will put you in, if you listen to his years of accumulated wisdom. And don't take my word for it; let's go for some objectivity. You don't get to be number 297, where Ken is currently stationed, on the *Forbes 400*, unless you know what you're doing, unless you know something other people don't know.

When you write a book about investing, you're always staring straight into the abyss. No matter how tempting money is, it's hard to read through most of the books on the subject. They're boring, they're beyond boring, and they're better than a couple of Valium if you're looking to get some sleep. Forget about the fact that most books on the subject are just plain wrong. Even the stuff that's right doesn't get processed because it's dull. Ken knows all this. He's been writing books a heck of a lot longer than I have and it shows. Before you can teach anyone anything, you need to grab his or her attention. Sometimes I've been accused of going a little bit too far in this area, but I'm an extremist.

Even if you don't care at all about investing, even if you don't have a penny to your name, or if you've got trillions of pennies, and either way don't care about money, you still might want to pick up this book. It's engaging, it's entertaining, and yeah, it's even funny. It is compulsively readable. Sure, it's erudite, sure it's got charts and graphs and—gasp—references to academic literature, but that's the point. Investing hasn't become a science yet, but Ken's trying to get us there. Don't be scared by the graphics, or the academics for that matter, because Ken knows how to filter all this information. It's all about making things that seem daunting and impossible turn into things that seem pretty simple and easy to do. Ken's a master of that transformation.

The Only Three Questions That Count is a great book. It could be the kind of book that entirely changes the face of investing from here on out, although most fund managers are too set in their ways for that to happen, but it's not a book about picking stocks. It's not about finding what's hot. It's not about day trading. It's not about anything that usually gets lumped into the "sexy" category of investing. And you know what, if I've learned anything from being a money manager, or from dispensing advice through various media for years, it's that sexy rarely works. You want to know what works? Do like Ken and run the numbers, do some basic statistics, and then you'll know what works.

You could go through Ken's columns, you could look at his record, you could look at the sheer amount of money he's managing—$30 billion—a figure I find astonishing, but Ken would tell me that's just my stone-age brain playing tricks. He clearly has a method that's been able to consistently beat the market. What more could you possibly ask for? If you're reading this book, you're trying to make money. You might think you want to be a really cool, successful day-trader. You might think that, but you'd be wrong. What you want is more money, more money than you could make by owning an index fund, or sitting in cash and bonds.

There's a particular kind of investor out there who hurts only himself, but he doesn't care. I like to think of this type of guy as the stock hobbyist. If you're a hobbyist, you don't really mind if you lose a lot of money in the market. You don't mind if the indices clobber you over the head. You're really caught up in practicing whatever it is you think you're doing when you buy and sell stocks. And hey, if you lose money, well, it's a hobby. You lose money on model airplanes, too, or Eagles tickets.

If you're a hobbyist, if you want to invest for the fun of it, you can still get something out of this book. But I hope it will convert you from being a hobbyist to being a successful capitalist in one fell swoop. It's not really about enjoying yourself: It's about making money. Trust me, over the long term; it's more fun to be rich than to play games with your dough. It might not feel that way short term, but that's why we've got people like Ken Fisher, who can humorously tell us why we're wrong and what we need to do better if we want to actually make some money.

By now I've taken up too much of your time. If you're not afraid to let your long-held beliefs about investing come under attack, if you're courageous enough to be adaptable, and if you genuinely want to make a lot of money, without taking on a lot of risk—the best way to make money, as far as I'm concerned—you'll want to keep reading. Ken Fisher has something in here for everyone, and if you only believe half, or even a third of what he says, you will be a better investor. If you follow all of his advice, I know you can beat the market, but even if you just listen to some of it, you'll be a lot better off.

And this is coming from a guy who's just had his whole strategy refuted and demythologized by Ken Fisher in a few short hours. Take it from me, *The Only Three Questions That Count* really are the only three questions that count.

JAMES J. CRAMER
Columnist for TheStreet.com
Columnist for *New York* magazine
Host of CNBC's *Mad Money*
Host of CBS' Real Money Radio

PREFACE

Who Am I to Tell You Something That Counts?

Who am I to tell you anything, much less anything that counts? Or that there are only three questions that count and I know what they are? Why should you bother reading any of this? Why listen to me at all?

Well, for starters, I've been in the investment industry for more than a third of a century and seen lots of water spill over the dam—and I'm not exactly a fan of my industry. I was raised in this industry. My father was in it before me—starting in 1932. He made a pretty big name for himself. I learned lots from him and went on. I founded and am CEO of a money management firm running more than $30 billion with an audited long-term history beating the market in a multiplicity of investing styles. It serves more than 16,000 high net worth individuals and an impressive roster of institutions—major corporate and public pension plans and endowments and foundations—spanning America, Britain, and Canada. I've written *Forbes'* "Portfolio Strategy" column for 22 years making me the fifth longest running columnist in *Forbes'* 89-year history. I've done another column in *Bloomberg Money* in Britain for seven years—and have written three prior books and have been published in numerous scholarly and professional journals. I am, from decades back, the father of the Price-to-Sales Ratio, now a standard part of today's financial curriculum. Without meaning to sound too darned pompous I'm on the *Forbes* 400 list of richest Americans, a self-made richie. I've done lots of things.

And I'm here to tell you the prime cumulative lesson of my long career is when it comes to investing there are only three questions that count. In the following pages, I'll share them with you and discuss how they translate into a way of thinking you can use over and over again as the basis for your investment decisions. That's what this book is about.

Okay, that's not exactly true. There really is only one question that counts. Or at least, only one question that *really* counts. But I don't know how to express that one question in a way you can easily use for everyday investing decisions. If broken down into three subparts I know how. Hence, the book title.

And what is that only question that counts? Finance theory is quite clear the only rational basis for placing a market bet is if you believe somehow, some way, you know something others don't know. Effectively, it's an unfair advantage; but if done correctly is fully legal, ethical, moral, and even nonfattening. The only question that counts is: What do you know that others don't?

Most people don't know anything others don't. Most folks don't think they're supposed to know something others don't. We'll see why. But saying you must know something others don't—it just isn't at all novel. Pretty much everyone who took a basic college investment class was told this, although most people conveniently forget this truism.

Without answering the question—what do you know that others don't—investing with an aim to do as well or better than the market is futile. I'll say that another way. Markets are pretty "efficient" at pricing all currently known information into today's prices. There is nothing new about that statement. It's an established pillar of finance theory and has been repeatedly verified over the decades. If you make market decisions based on the same information others have (or have access to) you will overall fail relative to what the markets would have rendered you on their own without any decision making on your part. Savvy? If you try to outguess where the market will go or what sectors will lead and lag or what stock to buy based on what you read in newspapers or chatter about with your friends and peers—it doesn't matter how smart or well-trained you are—you will sometimes be right or lucky or both, but more often wrong or unlucky or both, and overall do worse than if you didn't make such bets at all.

I bet you hate hearing that. But I already told you I didn't know how to express that truism as a single question in a way useful to you. What I can do is show you how to know things other people don't know.

Before taking you down the path to knowing things others don't, a path you can control yourself and explore in your own unique ways, let me take a little longer to express the pointlessness of not knowing something others don't. It'll be fun, I promise.

Polling for Perfect Truth

Financial markets are "discounters" of widely known information. In other words, whatever information we commonly have access to has already been reflected in today's prices before we can articulate our knowledge of it. People bet to the extent they can on all such information as soon as they see it exists. They bet as fast as the information is widely disseminated. See it this way—compare markets to political elections that aren't discounters of known information.

You know professional pollsters can build a sample of about 1,000 people sufficiently representative of America's voters to foresee the immediate outcome of a national election within a predictable few percentage points. That technology is mature and time tested. You're quite used to it. When a professional poll is done the night before the election, we know within maybe three to five percentage points how the election will end. It's all based on picking the participants in the poll to be representative of total votes.

Envision if someone could build a similar sample of all the world's investors. It would include every imaginable type in just the right proportions. Institutional and retail! Growth groupies and value vamps! Small and big cap fans! Foreign and domestic! Tall and short! Whatever imaginable! Suppose the pollsters polled the sample and suppose the consensus view was the market would rise next month—big time. Could it? No, because if everyone tended to agree the market would rise next month, anyone with any buying power would buy before then. The market might rise before next month but only a fool would wait for next month to buy. Hence, next month there would be no subsequent buying power to drive the market higher. It could fall. It could stay flat. But it couldn't rise. This is an oversimplification but it's a useful illustration of how whatever we agree on has already been priced into the markets by the time we can articulate it, and therefore, it can't occur. Since investors tend to be avid information seekers, the information they have access to has already been priced into the bets they've made.

Instead, it's surprise that moves markets. It's what happens next that few previously fathomed. Another piece of news consistent with what people previously expected can't move markets much further since investors already bet that way (to the extent they were able).

Said differently: You may be smarter, wiser, or better trained than the next investor, but finance theory says that isn't enough. No matter how wise you think you are, you're a fool if you think being smarter or better trained is enough to beat others based on commonly available news and information. Later in the book I'll give you many examples of this, but the only basis for beating markets is knowing something others don't. This book shows you how to do that, but first I'll give you a framework for accepting the Three Questions and then introduce you to them. In the first three chapters, I take you through each question in detail; in the remaining chapters, I go into more depth on how to use the questions in your own ways. As the author of three prior books, that seems like a lot to accomplish and leave with you. But conquer these Three Questions, and you will have a strategy for beating the markets—that seems like a worthwhile undertaking.

Investing by Knowing What Others Don't

Let's back up for a second. Suppose, for argument's sake, you accept my basic premise there is only one question that counts and it can be broken down into three subquestions. You know simply reading the questions isn't the key to endless riches. You must know what the questions really mean and how to use them. And then you must actually put them to use diligently. Over and over again! The Three Questions don't constitute a craft or a simple "Three Steps to Riches" list. It isn't some *Investing Made Easy* to-do list for beating the market. If there were such a thing, I wouldn't be writing this book and you wouldn't be reading it. Instead, I'd put it in a single *Forbes* column and you would glean all you needed to know from it. From there, you would go off and promptly become unimaginably wealthy. No, it isn't *Investing Made Easy*. Instead, it's *Investing by Knowing What Others Don't*. In fact, that's why it's my subtitle.

If you can learn how to use the Three Questions, you will have a lifelong basis for beating markets. You should have an edge over your fellow investors.

Let's think about them. Your fellow investors.

Idiots and Professionals: Oh, but I Repeat Myself

You know some folks are idiots. You don't fear competing with them. But how will you compete with serious professionals who've had serious training, are seriously smart, and have scads of experience? The good news is, in my observation, most investors—amateur or professional—conduct themselves as idiots. How so? Because, despite many of them taking that class where they learn they must know something others don't, they forget or ignore it. Inside the typical investor's mind is the false premise investing is a craft, like carpentry or doctoring. They don't treat investing like a scientific query session, which is what I'll teach you to do. Instead, consider how they approach it. Start with amateurs. They typically have favorite information sources—whether it's cable news, print media, Internet web sites, or a newsletter from their guru du jour. Maybe they have software tracking price patterns. They may have specific rules they adhere to—momentum investing, buy the dips, buy on bad news. They look for clues or signals to buy or sell. They may wait for the S&P 500 and Nasdaq to correspondingly reach certain levels and then they buy or sell or just generally panic. They clock 90-day moving averages and monitor the VIX (the S&P 500 volatility index) or some other supposed predictive market indicator. (The VIX is a statistically provable worthless forecaster, by the way—but many people use it every day, applying a wasteful mythology losing more money than it makes.) They believe investing is a craft-like skill they can learn with enough diligence and effort. Those who acquire the best craft skills must be the better investors.

Investors categorize themselves and develop craft skills accordingly. The wanna-be value investor develops a slightly different toolkit than the wanna-be growth investor. Ditto for small cap fans versus big cap. Or foreign versus domestic. This works perfectly in carpentry. Anyone can learn basic carpentry, though some people are more naturally gifted than others. It works well for doctoring, if you're smart enough. It works for most sports, which are craft-based. Again, some folks are naturally better at some sports than others. Accounting, dentistry, lawyering, engineering, and much more—all learnable crafts, though requiring a varying degree of time commitment and physical or mental prowess.

We know learning a craft is possible because there are countless people who perform craft-based functions after adequate training and apprenticeship (necessary to craft) in high quantities within acceptable and predictable bandwidths. The ability to train an accountant to do an audit in an acceptable manner is a perfect reflection of craftsmanship. But few folks beat the market, amateur or professional. Darned few! You've read it over and over for years and years—and it's true. Precious few professionals beat the market in the long term, so learning a craft obviously isn't enough to do it. Craftsmanship isn't sufficient to the task of beating markets.

Finance theory says it shouldn't be—craft won't help you—because you're supposed to know something others don't. That may excuse an amateur from failing to beat the market, but what about the pros? At a minimum, there are educational licensing requirements professionals must pass to legally advise clients. All stockbrokers must pass a test to receive a Series 7 designation.

Investment advisors have various SEC mandated tests, too. Some in the industry persevere to become Chartered Financial Analysts (CFAs) or Certified Financial Planners (CFPs). Others become Certified Investment Management Analysts (CIMA). None of these be-lettered folks beat the market with any greater frequency than amateurs.

University students and doctoral candidates in investment finance spend years studying markets. They learn to analyze corporate balance sheets. They learn to calculate risk and fancy-dancy but widely known analytical tools like Sharpe ratios and R-squared and CAPM. Some learn market history and how markets responded to a variety of monetary, economic, and political conditions once-upon-a-time way back when. And with all of this, they still can't beat the market any more often than those without a PhD.

Quite wisely, after years of study, some young wanna-be professionals commit to apprenticeship by laboring under another established investor. At the knee of their chosen master, they generally learn a craft the same way a blacksmith apprenticed years ago. Some became generalists and others were specialists who made only weapons like swords and spears, while others made livery gear and plow shears. You name the investing style, there are adherents, apostolic in their allegiance to the modality under which they apprenticed.

Armed with degrees, certifications, and apprenticeships, professional investors embark into the world, dispensing advice and so-called wisdom, all while overwhelmingly they lag markets. Some become media pundits, recapping the day's market movements on network or cable news in gripping fashion. Here the market is never just down. It nosedived or spiraled out of control! Or it exploded! It's all terrifying and thrilling and keeps viewers as tuned in as the next White House scandal or Hollywood megastar's divorce rumor. Listen carefully, and most of what you hear is postgame analysis. Only rarely will a pundit really stick his or her neck out to predict what happens next. And if they do, they aren't tracked far. And if they are, they don't last long. Here is a dirty little secret of why. If they could do it over the long-term, they would go into money management instead of punditry because there is infinitely more money in succeeding in money management. For example, as of 2005, 39 of the *Forbes* 400 were from the broad world of money managing—nearly 10 percent of the total.[1] How about media personalities? Only Oprah got there that way. No financial pundits. Not one. (Actually, I may be the closest thing because of my *Forbes* column—but I'm not one—I'm a money manager and certainly no celebrity.)

If you follow the money, it's in money management, not punditry, newsletters, stockbrokerage, or any other part of the investing world. The most successful new media personality in finance is my friend Jim Cramer, who wrote the Foreword to this book. But Jim is an extreme exception—he was a successful money manager before he retired to start TheStreet.com and had television successes culminating in his *Mad Money* show. No one would have expected Jim to be so successful at it—including him. Or, at least, that's what he maintains. Jim is very much the exception proving the rule. In Jim's case, his decision to move from money management to media was a decision of lifestyle preferences over anything else. But most people can't do the things Jim can. If Jim wanted to be a sculptor or painter, I'm sure he would've excelled at it. Still, if you asked Jim where the money is in this world of players, he would have you follow it back to money management, not media.

So, most investment professionals don't aspire to be media personalities; they aspire to money management. They most commonly start where entry is easiest, the way I did decades ago, rendering advice to individuals. These are your stockbrokers, financial planners, and insurance and annuity salespeople. Some provide forecasts and prescriptions of their own, but those working for the big name firms generally must kowtow to the firm forecasts. This makes sense for the firm since it's the only way these larger institutions can maintain a semblance of control over their huge employee bases. Big firms hire a few folks with extremely prestigious schooling and extensive professional training who look and sound good—for a role like *Chief Economist* or *Chief Market Strategist* or some such title—whose main responsibility is forecasting. Industry analysts then forecast in their own individual realms of experience and training. Clients of said illustrious firms, both private and institutional, get the benefit of not only their individual broker's schooling and experience, but also that of the learned, tenured bigwigs who think bigger and wig-out well when needed.

So why, with all the knowledge, expertise, and battle scars out there, do vastly more professional investors lag markets than beat them? It's a long-term proven fact. Proven over and over again. Few professionals beat the market—depending on your time frame and how you define the market, it varies from maybe 10 percent of them to 30 percent, but no higher. Why? Why are the talking heads and professional forecasters no more successful than dilettantes? Why are so many more dead wrong much more often than a few are right with any regularity (while still being wrong often—the very best are still wrong a lot—being wrong is okay). How are we to understand why so few of even the biggest Wall Street names can beat markets even half their careers?

These are smart people. A lot of them are very smart. Smarter than me for sure. You're probably pretty smart, too. Aren't you? You might be much smarter than me too. But that won't make any difference on whether you can do better than me as an investor. Smarts and training are good—nothing wrong with them. A PhD is good. But they aren't enough. And they aren't necessary. You must know something others don't and then—with that extra something—you can beat the market and do better than people who are smarter than you are.

So, what about you? Maybe you subscribe to quality publications like *Forbes* (or, heaven forbid, mediocre and macabre magazines like *Fortune* or *Business Week*—only having fun now, seriously. Without a little humor, a life living with markets can get a little long in the tooth.). You read whichever of the endless list of financial publications you choose. You watch 24-hour financial news channels. You have a high-speed Internet connection for speedy trade execution and access to even more information sources. You scan sources like Morningstar. You easily download research and quarterly SEC reports for stocks you follow. Maybe you splurged on technical analysis software. Why can't you beat the market, when you have so much information and power at your fingertips? Information and power your grandfather never dreamed of!

Because Mr. Crafty, It's Not a Craft

The answer isn't in perfecting a craft but in knowing something others don't. Investors don't try to do it because they're all so preoccupied with craft. It's as if they think they could learn the craft, get their union papers, do their craft pretty much like everyone else does, and then be qualified somehow to beat the market.

More academic study won't do it. The most learned finance PhD knows free markets are at least pretty efficient (although they do disagree about exactly how efficient). Passing tests like the Series 6, 7, 65—or the CFA or a CIMA certification won't do it. They contain no information not known by millions of other folks and parroted in a distilled form throughout the media. More magazine subscriptions and migraines from pondering pontificating pundits won't do it. They're talking about what is known and therefore priced. And if they knew something everyone else didn't and told you via the media, instantly everyone else would know it and the new information probably would be priced almost instantly. Now, hereto, worthless! (I'll show you how to measure an exception to this later.)

You can study technical investing and buy software identifying price movement patterns. Won't do it! You can buy *Investor's Business Daily's* carefully chosen top-rated momentum stocks. Won't do it! You can study fundamental investing and vow only to buy when P/Es are at a certain level and sell at yet another level. Won't do it! You can hire someone to do it for you who has the most designation letters after his or her name. But you won't beat the market over the long-term if you treat investing like a craft. Well, that's not quite true. If enough people try all this stuff, some very few will get there simply by dumb luck. In the same way, if enough folks line up to flip coins, you will find someone who gets 50 heads in a row; but who that is remains a fluke of luck. It likely isn't you. It isn't the basis for investing or beating markets. And you can count on that.

If investing were a craft, some type of craft (or even some combination of crafts) would have demonstrated market superiority. Someone somewhere would have figured out the right combination to keep beating markets. The right formula, no matter how complicated!

Some say Warren Buffet is the greatest money manager of all time. I don't think he is a money manager at all, a point most observers miss. He is the CEO of a very successful insurance company owning a few stocks and often takes companies private when he wants (something you almost certainly can't do and most money managers don't and shouldn't do). While he is a great man and a great success, he isn't a portfolio manager and has no correctly calculated performance record over the past 35 years as a portfolio or money manager. While folks often call him a money manager he isn't in the sense Peter Lynch was, or Bill Miller or Bill Gross are. Those three are big names and very successful and there are thousands and thousands of real money managers (as stated earlier, most of them lag the market over the long term).

Someone can be an investor without being a money manager. Buy an apartment building and you're an investor. In the long term, regardless of all other things, Mr. Buffett's fame and reputation rest on the results of Berkshire Hathaway stock and what it does—plain and simple. Note, when Berkshire takes over a company, lock, stock, and barrel, it's impossible to know what the return is on that investment after that point because it's simply internalized into Berkshire. Therefore, you can't tell individually if it was a good investment or not. All you can see is how Berkshire Hathaway stock does which is largely driven by its insurance operations. For decades, Berkshire was a terrific stock and made tremendous money for lots of folks in the same way Microsoft or AIG did (or a lot of other great single stocks did). Many investors came to confuse Berkshire the stock with a portfolio, which it isn't. It's a single stock. There is virtually a religion around Berkshire stock and Mr. Buffett. But it's still just a single stock. In that regard, it hasn't done well recently. In the past decade, its returns would have placed it in the 51st percentile relative to the stocks in the S&P 500[2] (if it were included—it doesn't meet the liquidity requirements for inclusion in that index). In 2005, for example, the S&P 500 was up 4.9 percent[3] and Berkshire Hathaway had a return of exactly 0.8 percent,[4] basically no change. It lagged the S&P 500 in 2004 and 2003 as well. And no one seems to notice much. While spectacular in prior decades, Berkshire Hathaway now rests largely on the laurels of its prior glory and somehow avoids being seen as mediocre currently, maybe because there is such a religion around the man and the stock.

But here is my point. Suppose I'm wrong about all that. Suppose Mr. Buffett isn't the CEO of an insurance company but instead the manager of a portfolio in the same way Bill Miller or Bill Gross is. And suppose he is the greatest money manager the world has ever known. He certainly has talked about investing a lot over the years—talked about things like asset allocation and stock selection and many of the things money managers talk about daily. And he has countless disciples devouring his tea leaves to figure out what they should do. And he has been famous for over a third of a century. Yet precious few of his disciples have been able to beat the market over the long term. If what Mr. Buffett did and does were a viable craft, he would have been able to teach his disciples how. But you don't see the top investors (or even some huge percentage of them) all being Buffett-philes. It remains true the person many consider the greatest money manager of all time hasn't been able to pass this along to others in a way that is repeatable with any consistency. Sure, some will stand up and scream, "I'm great at it and I do it that way," but in the competitive world of verifiable performance records, these people are nowhere to be seen.

If it were a craft in the very long term, there would be a clear sense Mr. Buffett's way had generated an army of disciples who did better over the very long-term than conflicting approaches. But such evidence doesn't exist. Mr. Buffett's approach is often seen as a subset of value investing. Yet, long-term, value and growth investors as discrete groups have done essentially the same in alternating waves over the decades as each approach cycles in and out of favor. Despite both value and growth investors claiming their style to be vastly superior to the other, neither style has rendered a preponderance of the top market-beating investors. Within value investing itself, there is no dominant approach broadly accepted as yielding inherently better results through an army of practitioners who have beaten their peers.

If investing were a craft, the decades wouldn't have sired thousands of investment books teaching largely contradicting craft—with gurus, pundits, and seminars touting conflicting strategies. There would be a few differing strategies at most. There would be repeatability and consistency. Investing would be learnable like woodworking, masonry, or medicine. Others could teach you. You could pass the skill on with efficacy. There wouldn't be so much failure. And you wouldn't have bought this book because anything I could say would be passé.

It's All Latin to Me—Starting to Think like a Scientist

When I was a kid, if you wanted to be a scientist they made you take Latin or Greek. I was a good student generally and took Latin not because I wanted to be a scientist—I didn't—but because I couldn't figure out the benefit of my other options, Spanish or French. Since no one speaks Latin, I forgot almost everything immediately thereafter, except the life lessons in which Latin abounds—like Caesar distinguishing himself by leading from the front of his troops, not the rear as most generals did (and do). It's maybe the most important single lesson of leadership.

Another lesson: The word *science* derives from the Latin *scio*—to know, understand, to know how to do. Any scientist will tell you science isn't a craft; rather, it's a never-ending query session aimed at knowing. Scientists didn't wake up one day and decide to create an equation demonstrating the force exerted on all earthly objects. Instead, Newton first asked a simple question like, "I wonder what the heck makes stuff fall down?" Galileo wasn't excommunicated and immortalized for agreeing with Aristotle. He asked, "What if stars don't work like everyone says? Wouldn't that be nuts?" Most of us would see the best scientists of all time, if we could meet them face-to-face, as maybe nuts. My friend Stephen Sillett, today's leading redwood scientist, changed the way scientists think about old growth redwoods and trees in general by shooting arrows with fishing lines tied to them over the tops of 350-foot-tall giants, tying on a firmer line, and free-climbing to the tops. He found life forms and structures up there no one ever knew existed. Dangling off those ropes 350 feet from terra firma is nuts. Nuts! But he asked the questions: What if there is stuff in the very tops of standing trees that isn't there when you cut them down? And if there is, would it tell you anything about the trees? In the process, he discovered much no one had ever known existed. Why am I telling you this?

Because most of what there is to know about investing doesn't exist yet and is subject to scientific inquiry and discovery. It isn't in a book and isn't finite. We just don't know it yet. We know more about how capital markets work than we did 50 years ago, but little compared to what we can know in 10, 30, and 50 years. Contrary to what the pundits and professionals will have you believe, the study of capital markets is both an art and a science—one in which theories and formulas continually evolve and are added and adjusted. We are at the beginning of a process of inquiry and discovery, not the end. Its scientific aspect is very much in its infancy.

Scientific inquiry offers opportunities ahead as we steadily learn more about how markets work than we ever imagined we could know previously. What's more, anyone can learn things now that no one knows but in a few decades will be general knowledge. Building new knowledge of how capital markets work is everyone's job, whether you accept that or not. You're part of it, whether you know it or not. By knowingly embracing it you can know things others don't—things finance professors don't know yet. You needn't be a finance professor or have any kind of background in finance to do it. To know things others don't, you just need to think like a scientist—think freshly and be curious and open.

As a scientist, you should approach investing not with a rule set, but with an open, inquisitive mind. Like any good scientist, you must learn to ask questions. Your questions will help you develop hypotheses you can test for efficacy. In the course of your scientific inquiry, if you don't get good answers to your questions, it's better to be passive than make an actionable mistake. But merely asking questions won't, by itself, help you beat the markets. The questions must be the right ones leading to an action on which a bet can be made correctly.

So, what are the right questions?

The Only Three Questions That Count

First we need a question helping us where we see wrongly. Then we need one helping us where we don't see at all. Third, we need one helping us sense reality when our eyes aren't at all appropriate as tools.

For our first question, we must identify those things we believe that are actually false. The question, simply stated, is: What do I believe that is actually false? Note what you believe is probably believed by most people. In the next chapter, I'll cover this question in detail. But, if you and I think something is true then probably most people do. If most people do, we can predict how they will bet and we can learn to bet against these beliefs because the market will discount them and their false truth. Suppose you believe factor X causes result Y. Probably most people do and we can verify most people believe it. Then when you see X happen, you know people will bet on Y happening next. But suppose you can prove in reality X doesn't cause Y at all. Now you know you can bet against Y happening while everyone else is betting it will happen. You can bet successfully against the crowd because you know something others don't. I'll show you how to do this.

Second question: What can I fathom that others find unfathomable? Here we need a process of inquiry allowing us to contemplate that which most people assume simply can't be contemplated at all. It's the essence of so-called *out-of-the-box* thinking. It's what made Edison and Einstein so successful but weird. They could think about how to think about the unthinkable. Think how unthinkable that is. Almost heretical! It's amazingly easier to do than most people assume, and it's a trainable skill. I'll show you how to do that in Chapter 2. Intuitively you know if no one knows what causes a particular result— let's call it result Q—and we can prove factor Z causes Q, then every time we see Z happen we can safely bet on Q happening because we know something others don't. This is what Chapter 2 is about.

Finally, our third question: What the heck is my brain doing to mislead and misguide me now? To blindside me? Another way to ask this is, "How can I out-think my brain which normally doesn't let me think too well about markets?" This is the realm of behavioral psychology. One thing you can come to know no one else can is how your individual brain works—what it does well in relation to markets and what it does badly and how to re-program yourself to not use your brain in the ways it works worst for markets. Few investors have spent any material time trying to understand how their own brains work. Most focus on craft, not internal deficiency. (*Note:* A craftsman wouldn't think about that at all.) You can learn how your investor's brain works to hurt you and when you do you will know something almost unique since your brain is partly like other people's and partly yours uniquely. Chapter 3 covers this topic in very simple you-can-do-it lessons.

From there on, the rest of the book is simply about putting the Three Questions to work in various ways. We look at how to use the Three Questions to think about the overall market, different parts of the market, and even individual stocks. We'll apply it to interest rates and currencies. We look at lots of things I've figured out over the years using the Three Questions. We also address areas I haven't figured out because there is still a lot of potential figuring to do and you may be the person that figures these things out in the years ahead. We won't be able to cover everything, everywhere—nor is there a need for that.

I will make a lot of statements of fact you won't have heard before, or think sound simply wrong, nuts, and crazy. I've come to those conclusions using the Three Questions and I'll show you how in each case. You can still disagree with me. That's okay. But if you learn how to use the Three

Questions and you want to explore any area, including these, and have the time, you can do it on your own later. Forever! You can use the Three Questions to show me where I was wrong and messed up. I'd be delighted and you should feel free to write me to show me evidence, using the Three Questions, where I'm wrong.

There are endless opportunities to discover new things in terms of what we don't know in 2007. You don't need to know everything. You need to know some things others don't know. If you learn to apply the Three Questions yourself, you'll be empowered to know things others don't for the rest of your life. So, with that said, let's get on with it.

K. L. F.

Woodside, California

1 QUESTION ONE: WHAT DO YOU BELIEVE THAT IS ACTUALLY FALSE?

If You Knew It Was Wrong, You Wouldn't Believe It

It's safe to assume if you knew something was wrong, you wouldn't believe it was real and true in the first place. But in a world where so much of industry applied craft has morphed into long-held mythologies, much of what everyone believes is false. This isn't any different from long ago when humanity believed the world was flat. You needn't beat yourself up if you fall prey to false mythologies. Pretty much everyone has and does. Once you know and accept that, you can begin gaming everyone else.

If sorting false mythology from fact were trivial, there wouldn't be so many false truths. While this isn't trivial, it isn't impossible either. One inherent difficulty is this approach requires being skeptical about all your prior beliefs, something most humans dislike. In fact, most humans hate self-questioning and prefer spending time convincing themselves and others their beliefs are right. Effectively you can't trust any conclusion you thought you knew.

To think through false mythologies, we must first ask: Why do so many people believe things that are false? And why do false truths persist—getting passed down the decades as if they were fact? It comes back to the same point: People persist in believing things that are wrong because, individually, people rarely investigate their own beliefs, particularly when what they believe makes sense intuitively—even more so when those around them agree with them.

As a society, we are often encouraged to challenge someone else's views, as in, "I know those @&%$#! (insert either Republicans or Democrats as you choose) are full of phony views!" But we aren't trained to challenge ourselves or to question the basic nature of the universe the way an Einstein, Edison, or Newton would. Our instinct is to accept wisdom passed to us by former generations, or smarter people, or both. These beliefs don't require investigation because we believe certain truths are beyond our ability to challenge. Often in life, that is right. I mean if "they" can't figure it out, how could I?

Medicine is a good example. We are correctly conditioned to go to the doctor, describe symptoms, hear prognosis, and accept a prescription. Generally that is good conditioning because medicine is an example of science and craft operating largely in parallel harmony—not perfectly because there are certainly plenty of myths among doctors—but generally because over time science modifies the craft and the craft improves. Because there are so many life examples where our conditioning serves us well, we are blind to the few areas, like capital markets, where it doesn't.

There are myriad beliefs you're likely to share with your fellow investors. These beliefs have been built into decades of literature and are among the first things people learn when they start investing and have been accepted by the biggest names around us. Who are *you* to question and challenge them?

Exactly the right person!

For example, take the notion high price-to-earnings (P/E) stock markets are riskier than low P/E stock markets. (For those few of you who are newcomers to investing and not familiar with P/E, it's the *price per share* divided by the *earnings per share*, and is perhaps the most basic and famous valuation metric for stocks. The same calculation can be aggregated for all stocks of a type or the whole market to create a notion, for example, of the entire stock market's P/E.)

Investors categorically believe when the stock market has a high P/E, it's riskier and has less upside than when it has a low P/E. Think about it casually, and it probably makes sense. A high P/E means a stock (or even the whole market) price is high—way high—compared to earnings. Get too far out on that scale, and it would seem a high P/E means a stock is vastly overpriced and likely to start falling. This belief is so widely held by so many people, seems so logical, and has been a basic tenet of investing for so long that if you start proposing to your friends it's false, you will meet with overwhelming rejection, ridicule, and perhaps suggestions you're morally deficient somehow.

Yet, I proved statistically more than 10 years ago the P/E, no matter its level, by itself tells you nothing about market risk or return. Statistics aside, if you delve heavily into theory (as we do later), you will also learn the P/E shouldn't tell you anything about risk or return anyway. But tell that to people, including the overwhelming bulk of people who have been trained and should know better, and they will think you're crazy—a real whack-job. The cool part comes after we accept the truth that P/Es tell you nothing about future return by themselves—when people are freaking out, fearfully fretting over the market P/E being too high, we can bet against the market falling. While that won't always work because something else can come along and knock the market down (we cover how to see that later), it will work much more often than not. In the same way, if the market's P/E is low and we can sense people are optimistic because of it, we can bet against them also. The key is understanding the truth instead of the mythology. This is basic to the scientific approach.

Many false mythologies—just like the P/E one—are accepted widely by the best and brightest minds and passed to the investing public through all forms of media. They don't inspire questioning from you, me, or anyone. We have faith in them, like Catholics do in the Trinity and Environmentalists in Global Warming, and they require no further proof. Holy! Sacred! No one questions these beliefs. No one offers dissenting analysis. And if you do, you're a heathen. Because there is no dissenting opinion, society feels no need to see proof of these alleged investing truisms with statistically valid data. And mythology continues.

How can it be, with over half of Americans having some sort of investment account as of 2005,[1] almost no one demands hard evidence to support generally accepted investing wisdom? Why do investment decisions not get the scrutiny that car mechanics do? We should be at least as skeptical, if not more so, of the financial industry's pronouncements than we are of a Volvo dealer's. To change the success (or lack thereof) you've had so far with investing, be skeptical. Be a cynic. Be the one to point out the emperor wears no clothes. Look around and assess what you and your fellow investors are accepting as truth. But the most important person to be skeptical of is yourself.

Long ago as I read or listened to media, I'd note things I believed were false and run off to do independent checking to prove I was right. (People love to prove they're right.) I'd gather data and do statistical analysis to prove they were wrong and I was right; and I could prove I was right to my satisfaction pretty often. (It's amazing how often people can prove they're right to their own satisfaction—the plaintiff, judge, jury, and executioner all in one.) But later I realized I was doing the wrong thing. What I should have been doing is looking in the media for assertions I believed were true and then checking to see if they weren't really false. Why?

If I believe the assertion is true, then probably so do many others, if not the overwhelming bulk of investors. Maybe everyone. And if we're all wrong, there is real power there. If I can prove I'm wrong and most everyone else is also wrong, then I've got some useful information. I can bet against everyone knowingly. I've got one provable form of knowing something others don't.

Suppose I believe factor-X causes result-Y. If I believe it, probably most other folks do too. But if I'm wrong, everyone else is wrong. When X happens, people will move to bet on Y happening. Suppose I can learn X doesn't cause Y. That means something else is causing Y. That means after X happens, Y happens sometimes, but it's purely random to X's existence. Now when X happens, people will still move to bet on Y happening, but I can bet against Y happening and I'll be right much more often than I'm wrong. (If I can figure out what actually causes Y, I can take a big step further, but we don't cover that step until Chapter 2 and Question Two.)

With our P/E notion, we can see one such perfect example. Say the market's P/E goes up—a lot. Normal investors notice and conclude risk has risen and future return is lower and bet against the market doing well. Sometimes stocks won't do well, but more often than not stocks will be just peachy because the P/E by itself tells you nothing about market risk and direction. When I see a high P/E market and fear of it, I can bet against the market falling. Sometimes, like 2000, it won't work. But more often, like 1996, 1997, 1998, 1999, and 2003, I'll be right. I don't expect you to believe the P/E thing right now. Right now I expect you to believe the traditional mythology about P/Es and not even be very interested in challenging it. (We get to that later in detail.) For now I just want you to accept in your bones if you can learn an accepted mythology is actually false you can bet against it and win more often than you lose.

Using Question One

A good way to think about successful investing is it's two-thirds not making mistakes and one-third doing something right. Hippocrates is frequently credited with the phrase, "First, do no harm," and it's a good investment principle.

To first do no harm, you must think about what you believe and ask yourself whether it's correct and factually accurate. Go crazy. Question everything you think you know. Most people hate doing this, which gives you a real advantage over them. As stated in this chapter's title, this is the first question: What do you believe that is actually false? If you want, you can change "false" to "wrong."

Asking Question One only helps if you can be honest with yourself. Many people, particularly in investing, are constitutionally incapable of contemplating they're ever wrong. They will tell you they do well and likely hoodwink themselves into believing it—but they don't. And they never subject themselves to reliable independent analysis. You must accept that you and the pundits and professionals from whom you glean information can be and probably are wrong about many basic beliefs. Me too!

Have you ever presented such a question to yourself about capital markets? Asking yourself if what you believe is actually wrong requires introspection. As humans, we're hardwired to be overconfident. This is hardly a new development. Behavioralists will tell you our Stone Age ancestors had to be overconfident to hunt giant beasts each day armed merely with stone-tipped sticks. If they practiced introspection and came to the rational conclusion that tossing a flint-tipped branch at a buffalo was utter lunacy, they, their families, and their communities would have starved. In fact, overconfidence—the belief you can do something successfully for which rationality would argue otherwise—is basic to human success in most fields and necessary to our successful evolution as a species. However, it hurts tremendously when it comes to capital markets as we see in Chapter 3.

Just so, investors are loathe to question generally accepted knowledge. If we started doing so, we might soon realize the market exists solely to humiliate us as much as it can for as long as it can for as many dollars as it can. I refer to the market by its proper name, "The Great Humiliator" (TGH for short). I've come to accept my goal is to interact with TGH without getting humiliated too much. TGH is an equal opportunity humiliator. It doesn't care if you're rich or poor, black or white, tall or fat, male or female, crippled or an Olympian. It wants to humiliate everyone. It wants to humiliate me and you, too. To be frank, I think it wants to humiliate me more than it does you. You're fun to humiliate, but if you're fun, I'm more fun. I have my *Forbes* and *Bloomberg Money* audiences laughing at me and over $30 billion worth of clients fussing at me when I screw up. Think how much TGH would love to humiliate Warren Buffett. The bigger you are, the more TGH wants you. But in reality, TGH wants to get everyone and does a pretty good job at getting them all. Can't be sated!

How do you, personally, give TGH the most fun? By making the most bets you can based on the same information everyone else has. How do you spoil the fun for TGH? By restricting bets you make to things you think you actually know that others don't.

Practice using Question One the same way I should have—by scanning the media for things asserted you believe. Make a list of them. They can be about single stocks, whole markets, currencies, or anything. Try looking at a stock, regardless of whether you own it or not, and asking yourself, "What would make me buy or sell this particular stock? What information is providing the impetus for a change?" Make a list of anything influencing your decisions.

Make note of decisions you've made not supported by data or any other information. Underneath there somewhere is something you believe—might be right or might be wrong. Be particularly wary of making a decision simply because of something you know others agree with. Highlight, underline, and asterisk decisions prompted or based on common investor catechism. Ask, what evidence did you figure out for yourself supporting these beliefs? Is there any? For most investors, there isn't much.

Common Myths You Believe In Too

For example, you may hold a stock with a high P/E ratio. You believe a high P/E signals an overvalued stock so you decide to dump the stock and buy one with a lower P/E. It's a fairly rational decision you may have made countless times before, and one many people would agree is rational.

But are high P/Es bad for single stocks or the market? Have you personally checked the data? If you have asked the question, where did you find the answer? Did you look at the numbers, or did you rest easy because conventional wisdom or some big-name guru endorsed your belief?

Take another scenario. You hold a stock that does well in rising markets but badly in falling ones, a typical highly volatile stock. However, you know the U.S. federal government is running a growing budget deficit—not only a deficit, but a historically high deficit and one that "can't go on forever." You know federal budget deficits left unchecked are "bad for the economy," and in turn "bad for the stock market." All that debt caused by the deficit must be paid back by future generations, and the market will reflect that sooner or later, right? The burden of the deficit has long-term rippling implications, holding down growth and earnings. The deficit has grown to such a size you know a bear market looms eventually. In that environment, your highly volatile stock would do badly and so you sell.

But how do you know budget deficit peaks are followed by poor stock performance? Is it true? Most folks won't ask the question or check history. If they did, they would be sanguine about stocks rather than fearful. Historically, big budget deficits in America and around the world have been followed by materially above-average stock market returns. Don't fear deficits—it is big budget surpluses that have been soon followed by bad markets, like President's Clinton's surpluses in 1999 and 2000.

That doesn't make intuitive sense to you. Deficits must be bad and surpluses good, right? After all, the word *deficit* has the same Latin root as *deficient*—and that must be bad. Most folks won't challenge their own beliefs on these kinds of subjects. The notion that big deficits are bad is overwhelming.

Few beliefs have as much broad acceptance from professionals, nonprofessionals, and folks from both ends of the political spectrum alike. A good way to get the proletariat on your side at a political rally is to vow to lower budget deficits. It's a crowd pleaser.

Here's a baker's dozen of some general beliefs you probably hold, or at least most people do. We've already covered two:

1. High P/E markets are riskier than low P/E markets.
2. Big government budget deficits are bad.

Let's think about some more:

3. A weak U.S. dollar is bad for stocks.
4. Rising interest rates are bad for stocks. Falling rates are good.
5. A tax cut causes more debt, which is bad for stocks.
6. Higher oil prices are bad for stocks and the economy.
7. Stocks do well when the economy does well.
8. Stock markets do better in countries with faster growing economies than slower ones.
9. Small stocks do better than big ones.
10. Stocks of firms that grow more do better than those that don't.
11. Cheaper stocks do better than less cheap stocks.
12. Current account and trade deficits are bad for stock markets.
13. America has way too much debt.

They're all familiar to you. This is just a short list—a subset of a much bigger list—of views most folks believe that are partly or wholly false. For example, the notion America is way too heavily in debt is backwards. America needs more debt. As I say that, you may be shriekingly dismissive or maybe the statement makes you mad. It challenges your belief set. If the statement makes you either dismissive or mad, you really need the rest of this book. The most standard reaction to someone stating your belief is wrong is to be dismissive and, if further confronted, to get mad. Anger is a very good warning sign because anger is always, always about fear. Angry people usually don't know they're fearful. But anger is always and everywhere simply a reflection of fear. If you're dismissive or angry, you must question yourself to see how and why you concluded your belief was right in the first place. Was it mythology? Was it basic bias? Are you right or not? Sometimes the items in this list and others beyond it are part true and part false, depending on surrounding circumstances. (We look at all of these and more later on.) But the most obvious question is why would you believe any of these statements?

I'd say you believe myths mostly because of two facts: (1) They make common sense, and you aren't typically prone to challenge your own common sense. (2) People around you tend to agree these things are true, and you aren't prone to challenge widely held views.

Let's Prove You're Either Right or Wrong (or Really, Really Wrong)

As you attempt to debunk investor mythology using Question One, you will find three basic results. Either you were right all along (which you will find happening far less frequently than you might have hoped), or you were wrong, or you were really, really wrong. Any of these outcomes is okay because it tells you how to bet better, later.

Let's examine more closely the instances when you're wrong. You and most of your fellow investors (amateur and professional) often believe something is causal—X happens because of Y—but in reality there is no correlation at all. By now you're willing to embrace that can happen, or you would have stopped reading this book. The example we debunk is the aforementioned commonly held belief high P/E stock markets are risky with subsequent below-average returns. As previously mentioned, it turns out high P/E markets aren't predictive of poor returns—not even remotely. In fact, historically, they've led to some pretty good returns. What's more, low P/E markets aren't predictive of good returns either.

The Mythological Correlation

Forgetting for now why the P/E myth is so easy to buy into, we know people overwhelmingly do believe high P/E markets predict below-average returns and above-average risk.

But if it were true, you could show some form of high statistical correlation between the claimed cause and result. A statistician will say you can have high correlation between two things out of quirky luck with no causation. But the same statistician will tell you that you can't have causation without high correlation (unless you run into scientific nonlinearity, which doesn't happen in capital markets to my knowledge—but you could check on your own with the Three Questions when you're finished with this book). When a myth is widely accepted, you will find low correlations coupled with a great societal effort to demonstrate, accept, and have faith in correlations that don't really exist.

Investors will root out evidence supporting their favorite myths and create justifications for their belief—factor-X causes result-Y—while ignoring a mountain of evidence that X doesn't cause Y at all. Now let's suppose everyone is of good intent. Still, with the best of intentions it's easy for people to latch onto evidence confirming their prior biases and ignore evidence contradicting their views. Looking for evidence to support your pet theory is human. Accepting evidence to the contrary is no fun at all. This is done in varying ways. One way is to look at a particular time period verifying the false belief and ignore other periods. Another is to redefine either X or Y in a bizarre way so the statistics seemingly prove the point and then generalize afterward about X and Y without the bizarre definitions. Discoveries of data supporting popular myths become popular discoveries.

Why High P/Es Tell You Nothing at All

A great example of this is the now famous study by John Y. Campbell of Harvard and Robert J. Shiller of Yale.[2] Their paper didn't introduce a new idea because fear of high P/Es had been around forever. Their study merely introduced a new delivery of data confirming the view high P/E periods are followed by below-average returns, an already widely held belief. This was actually a better re-do of a study they presented in 1996. But this 1998 publication got very popular, very fast, because it supported what everyone already believed with new statistical documentation. Campbell and Shiller were and are noted academics. Inspired by the prior study, in 1996 Alan Greenspan first uttered the phrase "Irrational Exuberance," relative to the stock market, which reverberated around the world almost overnight and entered our lexicon permanently.

My friend and sometimes collaborator Meir Statman, the Glenn Klimek professor of finance at the Leavey School of Business at Santa Clara University, co-authored with me a paper not refuting their statistics but reframing their approach more correctly with the same data—and you will see P/E levels aren't predictive at all. We basically asked Question One from beginning to end. Much of what follows stems from our paper, "Cognitive Biases in Market Forecasts."[3]

Campbell and Shiller, in simple English, found high P/Es acted as people always thought they did, leading to risky and below-average returns 10 years later. First, they noted the P/E at the outset of each year and subsequent annual market returns going back to 1872, which is about as far back as we have half-tolerably reliable data. Prior to the inception of the S&P 500 in 1926, they used Cowles data,[4] which is an imperfect but generally accepted proxy for pre-S&P 500 years. (All old databases are imperfect. Whenever you're looking

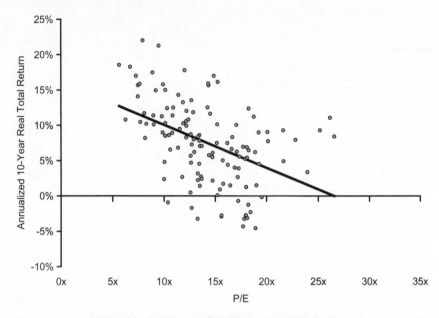

Figure 1.1   Relationship between P/E Ratios at the Beginning of a Year and Stock Returns over the Following Year (1872 to 2005).
Source: **Robert J. Shiller, Ibbotson Analyst, Global Financial Data, Standard & Poor's, Federal Reserve, and Thomson Financial Datastream.**

at old data, there is apt to be lots wrong with it, but the Cowles data is the best we have.) Then they graphed the data points on a scatter plot and found a slightly negative trend line.

We can largely recreate their hypothesis for you in Figure 1.1, showing P/Es from 1872 until 2005—again using S&P 500 and Cowles data.

I've included the years since their paper to ensure our findings are relevant today. But you'd get the same basic effect if we hadn't. The period from 2000 to 2002 happens to support their "high P/E is bad" thesis, so we're being fair to them by including it. The negatively sloping trend line shouldn't influence you. You plainly see the scatter points aren't particularly well-grouped around it. The scatter plot is, well, scattered—sort of like a shotgun blast in a mild wind.

It's Hard to Figure Out

Campbell and Shiller based their work on a bizarre definition of P/E—not one you intuitively leap to. They created a "price-smoothed-earnings-ratio."[5] The newly defined P/E divided the price-per-share by the average of "real" earnings over the prior 10 years.[6] *Real* means adjusted for inflation. Fair enough, but that isn't what you think of when you think P/E, right? But, if so, what definition of inflation would you use? I bet you would use something like the Consumer Price Index (CPI). (The CPI comes up as one of your first few results when you Google "inflation!") Ironically, they chose an esoteric wholesale price index. Again, not what you might default to. So instead of what you think of as P/E, they used a 10-year rolling-average based on inflation adjustments based on an inflation index you wouldn't think of. Got it?

With a normally defined P/E, as you would think of it, there isn't much of a statistical fit at all. Campbell and Shiller's bizarrely engineered P/E gave a result consistent with what society always believed—that high P/E means low returns, high risk. And the world loved it.

In statistics, a calculation is done called an *R-squared* which shows the relative *relatedness* of two variables—how much of one variable's movement is caused by the other. (It sounds complicated but it's not—I show you how to find a correlation coefficient and an R-squared in the box.) For their study, Campbell and Shiller's regression analysis gave them an R-squared of 0.40.[7] An R-squared of 0.40 implies 40 percent of subsequent stock returns are related to the factor being compared, in this case, their reengineered P/E. Statistically, not a bad finding (although not an overwhelming one). Though not a whopping endorsement of their theory, this finding still supports their hypothesis.

CAUSAL CORRELATIONS AND THE CORRELATION COEFFICIENT

When asking the Three Questions, you need some very basic statistical capability you can learn right here—nothing fancy. You can do wonders with a *correlation coefficient* and an *R-squared*. With these two analytical tools, you can credibly disprove, in many instances, that two events have any connection to each other. It's easy. All you need is an Internet connection and Excel (or paper and pen if you're particularly statistically astute, but it's easier on a computer).

To start, let's get some data to compare. For an easy exercise, we can see how much one stock is correlated to the market over 10 days. (Ten days isn't enough to tell you anything about anything, but will give us short columns of data to work with.)

Step 1

Using Yahoo! Finance as a data source, go to http://finance.yahoo.com. (If you're Internet savvy, feel free to use whatever source you're comfortable

(continued)

with. Just be sure you know how to download or copy and paste into Excel.)

- Click on the link to the S&P 500 which is featured prominently—usually on the left hand side of the page. (If you're reasonably Internet literate, this will be a snap for you. If you're not, get a buddy to help you the first time.)
- Click on the link for "Historical Prices"—again on the left hand side of the page.
- Select "Daily" prices, select a short time frame (Use any time frame you like, just choose the same time period during Step 2. I used January 1, 2006, through January 10, 2006.), and click "Get Prices." Now select "Download to Spreadsheet."
- An Excel spreadsheet will pop up with index data for the dates in question.
- Copy and paste the "Date" and the "Adjusted Close" columns into a new Excel spreadsheet page. You don't need the rest of the data for right now. Note—you'll have missing dates because of weekends and holidays. (You want the "Adjusted Close" because it's adjusted for stock splits and dividends.)

Step 2

Now go back to Yahoo! Finance and get a quote for any stock. I used General Electric (GE) because it's pretty basic. When the stock page pops up, click on the price chart and follow the same steps to get historical prices for your stock. Copy the data into the same spreadsheet, next to your S&P data. Your spreadsheet should look something like this:

	J8	fx		
	A	B	C	D
1				
2	Date	Adj. Close	Adj. Close	
3		**S&P 500**	**GE**	
4	10-Jan-06	1289.69	34.67	
5	9-Jan-06	1290.15	34.86	
6	6-Jan-06	1285.45	34.94	
7	5-Jan-06	1273.48	34.71	
8	4-Jan-06	1273.46	34.80	
9	3-Jan-06	1268.80	34.85	
10				

Not too hard, right?

Step 3

Now, don't retch when you see this—you won't need it—I'm just showing you this for laughs—but technically this is how you calculate a correlation coefficient:

$$P_{xy} = \frac{\text{Cov}\left(r_x, r_y\right)}{\sigma_x \sigma_y}$$

Don't bother figuring that out if it's been more than six months since you've taken a statistics class. Go to your Excel spreadsheet and click in any empty box. Go to your "Insert" menu and select "Function." Select the "Statistical" category. Scroll down and select "CORREL." Excel will launch a wizard to calculate the correlation coefficient for you. (Thanks, Excel!)

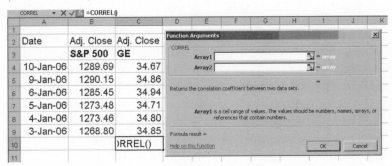

The wizard asks for two "Arrays." The arrays are just your columns of data. Clicking in each array box allows you to click, drag, and highlight each column of data. You might have to try this a few times to get the hang of it.

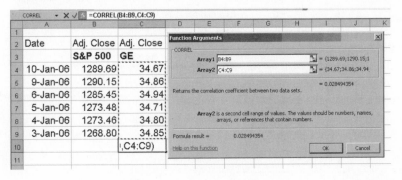

(continued)

Once you have your array data entered, click "okay" and, TA-DA! Correlation coefficient. And without having to do any fancy math or decipher the formula:

	A	B	C	D
	C10 ▾	*fx* =CORREL(B4:B9,C4:C9)		
1				
2	Date	Adj. Close	Adj. Close	
3		**S&P 500**	**GE**	
4	10-Jan-06	1289.69	34.67	
5	9-Jan-06	1290.15	34.86	
6	6-Jan-06	1285.45	34.94	
7	5-Jan-06	1273.48	34.71	
8	4-Jan-06	1273.46	34.80	
9	3-Jan-06	1268.80	34.85	
10			0.028494	

The correlation coefficient tells you how similarly GE behaved relative to the index over the time frame you selected (which was probably pretty small). A number close to 1.0 indicates a positive correlation (you zig, I zig). A number close to –1.0 indicates a negative correlation (you zig, I zag). A number closer to zero means there is little correlation either way (you zig, I Cleveland). Remember, when looking at short time periods, you don't have a basis for making an assumption at all.

Step 4

You aren't quite done. Now you must do something that sounds tough but isn't. To understand the relative *relatedness* of two variables, you must do a *regression analysis* and calculate the R-squared. It's way easier than it sounds. Simply square the correlation coefficient. That's why they call it "R-squared." If your correlation coefficient is 0.5, your R-squared is 0.25 (0.5 × 0.5 = 0.25). If the correlation coefficient is 0.85, the R-squared is 0.7225.

The R-squared tells you what percent of one variable's movement you can relate to (or maybe blame on) the other variable. An R-squared of 0.7225 means 72.25 percent of one variable's movement is caused by another (which would be an impressive find!).

You're now ready to find correlation coefficients and debunk causalities that don't exist, and uncover more of what you can know that others don't.

Note: Campbell and Shiller's study, tepid support or not, became wildly popular because it supported the view society had long held. If you present data violating society's myths, those data won't be met with great popularity. That's nice because when you discover the truth, the world won't be trying to take it away from you in a hurry.

By using the same basic data and traditional notions of P/Es at the start of each year from 1872 to 2005 and actual 10-year subsequent returns, we found an R-squared of 0.20.[8] The P/E only potentially explains 20 percent of 10-year returns—statistically pretty random. Something else entirely, or some group of other variables, explains the other 80 percent of price returns. I wouldn't make a bet on an R-squared of 0.20 and neither should you. Said another way, Campbell and Shiller's R-squared was 0.40 and ours was 0.20—so half of their result was based on how they defined P/E differently.

This myth wasn't hard to debunk. You can arrive at the same general conclusion with Yahoo! Finance and an Excel spreadsheet. When it isn't a myth and it's real, you will find you need no fancy statistical reengineering and no fancy math in your analysis.

But even if it were valid, who cares about views of subsequent 10-year returns? Investors want to know how to get positioned for this year and next, the now and the soon, not for 10 years from now. Would you really have cared what the next 10-year return was in 1996, when the next four years rose massively only to be followed by the biggest bear market since 1929 to 1932? Would you have wanted to miss the big up years in a row, and would you have been content to hold on through the big down years? Starting in 2007, if I could tell you with certainty the next 10 years will have a very high return overall but the next two will have a big negative return—would you invest now? Not likely! When you look at simple P/Es on a shorter-term basis, the high-P/E-is-risky thesis falls apart completely as we shall see.

What's more, forecasting long-term stock returns is a near impossibility because stock prices in the long term are the result primarily of shifts in far distant levels of the supply of equities, which in today's state of knowledge (or ignorance) no one knows how to address. Some of my academic friends get angry when I bring this up. But remember, when anyone gets angry, they are afraid and just can't quite put their finger on their fear. In this case, I think it's because very little real scientific work has been done analyzing shifts in supply and demand for securities. Yet, by definition, shifts in supply and demand are what determine pricing. There are great future advances to be made here but so far the progress is minimal despite supply and demand being basic to economics. (We get to supply and demand for securities in Chapter 7.)

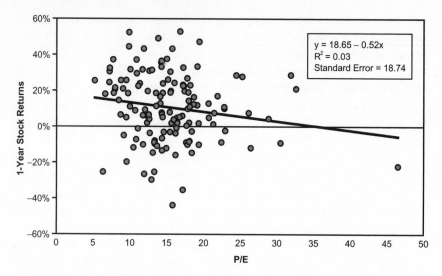

Figure 1.2   Relationship between Annualized (Overlapping) One-Year Returns and P/E Ratios (1872 to 2005).
Source: **Robert J. Shiller, Ibbotson Analyst, Global Financial Data, Standard & Poor's, Federal Reserve, and Thomson Financial Datastream.**

For now, let's take a look at our scatter plot again, this time using normal, nonengineered P/Es and subsequent one-year returns from 1872 until 2005 (see Figure 1.2). Note we have a much shallower negative trend line and the scatter points are even less cooperative. This is our same shotgun blast with a few stray pellets. Does this indicate any sort of correlation at all? With an R-squared of 0.03, the answer is no. If an R-squared of 0.20 is as good as random, an R-squared of 0.03 is randomness itself—pure, perfect randomness.

Finding a correlation where simply none exists is pretty creative; and simply none exists here. To begin debunking myths on your own, you don't need a super-computer and a Stephen Hawking doppelganger (that's probably illegal anyway). If you need ultra-complicated math to support the existence of a market myth, your hypothesis is probably wrong. The more jerry-rigging and qualification your analysis needs, the more likely you're forcing your results to support your hypothesis. Forced results are bad science.

If Not Bad, Can They Be Good?

We have shown there is no correlation between high P/Es and poor stock results (or good ones). Even in light of such damning evidence, some may be reluctant to let go of the "high-P/E-equals-bad-stocks" doctrine. Consider this another way. It may further shock and appall you to learn years with higher P/Es had some excellent returns. Moreover, the one-year returns following the dozen highest P/E ratios weren't too shabby—some negative years, but also some big positive years. This isn't statistical but should give you pause.

Need more evidence? No complicated engineering necessary here either. Figure 1.3 shows a basic bell graph depicting P/Es and subsequent annual market returns.

Here is how I arrived at the bell curve illustration on page 18. We noted the broad market's P/E each January 1 going back to 1872 and ranked each year from low P/E to high P/E. Then, I grouped them into intervals creating the familiar bell curve-like shape—with otherwise unrelated years falling into intervals according to their P/Es. The "normal" P/Es fall in the fat part of the bell curve, while the "high" and "low" P/Es fall on the edges. Again, you don't need an advanced degree in statistics for this. Based on this bell curve graph, anything above a P/E of 20 would be "high." In later years, if you do this for yourself, those numbers might move around a bit, but it would take a number of really high or low P/E years to skew the bell curve much.

When you note the P/E ratios for the past 134 years along with the subsequent market return, some empirical truths emerge. Most startling? Most double-digit calendar-year stock market declines—the monster drops everyone fears—occurred when P/Es were below 20, not when they were very high. Most were actually when the P/E was below average. In the past 134 years, there were 19 times the market's total return was negative more than 10 percent. Thirteen times—68 percent of those most negative years—were on the middle to low end of the P/E range, 16.5 being the middle of the bell curve. Only twice, in 2001 and 2002, did a big drop coincide with a P/E above 20. Read the prior four sentences again. Hardly fodder for a myth. Anyone can get these data off the Internet. Anyone can array them. It doesn't take fancy math. It just takes a little effort—it boggles the mind the myth still exists.

So big double-digit drops don't automatically follow high P/E markets. But the myth is so widely and rigidly believed, there must be some kernel of truth to it. For example, high P/E markets must fall more often than those with low P/Es, even if they aren't the monster drops. Right? Well, no! P/Es were below 20 in 117 of those years and the market finished in negative territory 35 times (29.9 percent). Of those 17 years when P/Es were 20 or higher—the historically high end of the P/E range—the market ended down five times (29.4 percent). You needn't be a statistician to see that neither high nor low P/E markets did materially worse. Moreover, in three of the five negative high P/E years, the market's decline was fairly benign: −9.1 percent

Figure 1.3   134 Years of Historical P/E Ratios and Stock Market Returns.
Source: Global Financial Data.

P/E   5.6x   8.4x   11.3x   14.1x   17.0x   20.0x   22.7x   25.5x   28.4x   31.2x   34.0x   >

P/E Ratio Range

P/E 5.6x band

Year	Return
1918	-4.05%
1917	-2.42%
1949	18.06%
1980	32.50%
1950	30.58%
1951	24.55%
1942	21.07%
1975	37.23%
1979	18.61%
1919	22.20%
1982	21.55%
Average Return	19.99%

P/E 8.4x band

Year	Return
1978	6.57%
1921	-7.55%
1924	11.47%
1981	-4.92%
1948	5.10%
1920	-2.98%
1943	25.76%
1875	3.88%
1952	18.50%
1938	33.20%
1941	-11.77%
1985	31.73%
1926	11.14%
1874	2.10%
1954	52.40%
1908	4.16%
1916	19.58%
1927	37.13%
1878	12.76%
1977	-7.16%
1953	-1.10%
1983	22.56%
Average Return	11.94%

P/E 11.3x band

Year	Return
1976	23.93%
1925	28.39%
1879	26.59%
1989	31.69%
1984	6.27%
1873	1.97%
1974	-26.47%
1872	12.95%
1956	6.63%
1958	43.34%
1876	-1.74%
1907	-13.29%
1904	1.96%
1944	19.69%
1881	24.80%
1877	-16.88%
1911	3.74%
1900	2.27%
1955	31.43%
1923	7.84%
1884	-9.50%
1910	1.13%
1914	-0.04%
1913	-5.33%
1957	-10.85%
1903	-9.72%
1880	31.24%
1882	-0.42%
1930	-25.26%
1883	1.11%
1932	-8.85%
1940	-10.08%
1885	2.14%
Average Return	5.17%

P/E 14.1x band

Year	Return
1988	16.61%
1947	5.24%
1915	7.83%
1986	18.67%
1945	36.46%
1901	31.33%
1906	11.19%
1888	-1.79%
1995	37.58%
1893	-8.84%
1967	23.94%
1990	-3.10%
1912	7.99%
1991	30.46%
1909	29.12%
1898	17.20%
1928	43.31%
1970	3.94%
1892	14.50%
1902	11.11%
1931	-43.86%
1894	-3.54%
1891	-0.27%
1987	5.25%
1887	7.41%
Average Return	11.91%

P/E 17.0x band

Year	Return
1896	-2.47%
1960	0.48%
1905	31.05%
1937	-35.26%
1933	52.88%
1899	27.76%
1963	22.69%
1968	11.00%
1972	18.99%
1890	3.07%
1971	14.30%
1966	-10.10%
1929	-8.91%
1969	-8.47%
1936	32.80%
1996	22.96%
1961	26.81%
1973	-14.69%
1946	-8.18%
1935	47.22%
1965	12.36%
1964	16.36%
1997	33.36%
1959	11.90%
1886	20.37%
1939	-0.91%
Average Return	12.21%

P/E 20.0x band

Year	Return
1897	9.10%
1889	6.19%
2005	4.91%
1994	1.32%
1962	-8.78%
Average Return	2.55%

P/E 22.7x band

Year	Return
2004	10.88%
1993	10.08%
1934	-2.34%
1998	28.58%
1922	28.39%
Average Return	15.12%

P/E 25.5x band

Year	Return
1992	7.62%
2001	-11.89%
1895	7.16%
2000	-9.10%
Average Return	-1.55%

P/E 28.4x band

Year	Return
2003	28.68%
1999	21.04%
Average Return	24.86%

P/E 34.0x band

Year	Return
2002	-22.10%
Average Return	-22.10%

in 2000, −8.8 percent in 1962, −2.3 percent in 1934. Advantage—high P/E markets. Not enough of an advantage to believe in or bet on, but plenty enough to bet high P/E markets aren't the monster mythology has always cowed us into believing.

You've seen the data. You're henceforth unshackled from this investing old wives tale.

Here is a simple test you can use repeatedly. Someone tells you X causes Y in America's markets—like the P/E example—and even has data to demonstrate it's true. If it's really true in America, then it must also be true in most foreign developed markets. If it isn't similarly true in most other developed Western markets, it isn't really true about capitalism and capital markets and hence isn't really true about America—just a chance outcome. I'll not belabor you with the data here—this book already has too many visuals—but if you take the same bell curve approach we used for America's stock market and apply it to foreign markets, the only country where low P/E markets seemed materially better is Britain—and that is based on a few, relatively big years. Elsewhere you get the same randomness as in America.[9] Whenever anyone tells you something works a certain way in America, a good cross-check is to see if it also works outside America. Because if it doesn't, it doesn't really work robustly in America either!

Some will say, "You must see the high P/E problem in the right way." (*Warning:* a precursor to a reengineering attempt to support a myth and it won't hold.) For example, they may agree it isn't just that a high P/E is worse than a low P/E, but when you get over a certain P/E level, the risk skyrockets and when you get under a certain P/E, it plummets.

For example, they may assert market P/Es over 22 are bad and P/Es under 15 good and everything in between is what confuses everyone—throwing the averages off, leading you to not see things the way they would have you see them. Fair enough! That's easy to test. You take all the times when the market had a P/E over 22 and envision we sold and then bought back at some level—you pick it, I don't care what it is as long as you apply it consistently. It ends up historically, regardless of the level picked, none really beat a long term buy-and-hold in America. The same is true overseas (except, again, in Britain where you can make a weak case a low P/E has had a variety of approaches seeming to work—but only in Britain, which is probably just coincidence—and if you throw out a very few, very big years in Britain from a very long time ago, it falls apart there, too).

Suppose you sell when the market's P/E hits 22 and buy when it falls to 15. That approach lags a simple buy-and-hold. Suppose you change the 22 to 23? Still lags! How about dropping the 15 to 13 or raising it to 17? Still lags. What's more, there isn't a buy-and-sell approach that works overseas. You may disbe-lieve all this. Great. Prove I'm wrong. To prove it, you must find a buy-and-sell rule based on simple P/E beating the market with one-, two-, or three-year re-turns. It must work basically the same way in a handful of foreign developed markets and if you start or end your game on different dates. Try to find it. Maybe you're better than I am, but I looked and looked and can't find it in any way anyone would believe.

Every time a high P/E market leads to very bad returns like in 2000, 2001, and 2002, you will find a comparable number of examples where it does well like 1997, 1998, 1999, and 2003. There is simply no basis for this myth.

Always Look at It Differently

Investors fall prey to myth because they are used to seeing investing truisms in accepted and normal ways—as they were taught. Once you start thinking even a bit differently—not in a complicated way, just differently, like graphing a bell curve or looking for the same phenomenon overseas—myths tend to fall apart. Whenever you're confirming an investing belief, try it from a fresh angle. Go crazy. Be creative. Flip things on their heads, back-wards, and inside out. Hack them up and go over their guts. Instead of try-ing to be intuitive, think counter-intuitively—which may turn out to be way more intuitive.

For fun, let's look at why, intuitively, high P/Es don't spell disaster for stocks. Most investors look at stocks with high P/Es and assume their prices are too high relative to the companies' earnings. If a price is proportionately much greater than earnings (so goes the thinking), the stock must be over-priced; what goes up must come down. What investors forget is the P isn't the only moving variable in the P/E.

In years following high P/E markets, earnings often rose faster than share prices. And often after low P/E years, we ran into unexpected rough economies where earnings vanished. In fact, in 1929, the most famous mar-ket peak of all time, P/Es were low, not high, because the soon-to-disappear earnings were too high in 1929, making the P/E low.

When we buy stocks, we're buying future earnings. At some times we're willing to pay more than at others. In high P/E markets, earnings often exceed expectations (as in 2003) and the market prices in higher earnings before we can see them coming. Just by considering what is happening with the denom-inator side of the P/E—looking at it differently—you can reason for yourself why the myth is wrong.

The myth that high P/E markets are dangerous and low P/E markets are safe persists. But anyone with a dial-up modem and a pencil can see high P/E years are, of themselves, not any worse than lower P/E periods. Why does this myth persist? Because fundamentally TGH is perverse and counterintuitive. It can be painful to accept whatever is fueling your water-cooler debates is wrong or already priced into markets. It's humbling, but true.

How Would Your Grandparents Think about It?

Now, I'll steal a page from Chapter 3 and focus on how our brains blindside us on the P/E issue. There is a genetic reason people fear high P/E markets. I can't prove this, but I believe it's true. And you can't disprove it. It's a pretty different way to see this dilemma. You inherited your genes and the information processor that is your brain from your parents, as did they from theirs. Your far-distant ancestors had brains adept at processing certain types of information—that which related to problems they encountered dealing with passing on their genes successfully. Were that not true you and I wouldn't be here. The folks back then who didn't process information well relative to those problems don't have descendents walking the earth now.

Your brain wasn't really set up to deal with the stock market. It was set up to deal with those problems of basic human survival. One problem your ancestors learned to process was heights. If they fell from greater heights, the risk of death or crippling (pretty much the same thing) was exponential. Higher heights increased risk. Falling from two feet is just a stumble. Falling from 10 feet isn't all that tough for a 10-year-old jumping off a roof, but bone breaking for older people. Falling from 40 feet kills usually and a 400-foot height always. Folks learned well when confronted with problems appearing in a framework of heights—more height meant more risk. Greater heights meant you could fall further—exactly how people think of P/Es. They envision higher P/Es as further potential falls and lower P/Es as less distance to smack into the floor, so there is less smacking risk. Any time I present information to you in a form appearing as a heights framework, more height scares you and less height seems safer. If I can present the same information in a way not involving heights, your fear fades instantly. (We do that in a few moments.)

A Quick Preview of Question Three

When the market's P/E is higher than normal, most investors know it. Even those who don't know what P/E stands for can tell you "these days" the market is frighteningly overvalued. Their resulting fear of heights and concern over possibly sustaining a loss can be explained by a behavioral finance truism: People hate losses much more than they like gains.[10]

People talk about investors being risk averse, but that isn't quite right. Investors are provably loss-averse. Two pioneers in the field of behavioral finance, Daniel Kahneman and the late Amos Tversky, demonstrated and proved normal Americans (yes, you're probably pretty normal) hate losses about two and half times as much as they like gains.[11] Investors feel the sting of a monetary loss much more intensely than they enjoy the pleasure of a gain. In your heart, you probably already knew that was true for you. And because loss is more agonizingly painful than gain is pleasant, investors will do more to avoid losses than to achieve gains.

Investors will actually adopt additional risk if they believe it can help them avoid a loss they would otherwise incur. Kahneman and Tversky described this phenomenon in what they called "prospect theory." They discovered normal investors (again, you) confuse actual risk with the *perception* of risk, all in the effort to avoid the possibility of a loss.[12] The perception (or one could say, misconception) of possible losses long mis-associated with high P/E markets is what keeps investors fearful in what would otherwise be a relatively low-risk market environment. The same powers are at work at the bottom of a bear market. Investors are typically most fearful at the end of bear markets when risk is diminished and upside potential considerable. Investors' perceptions are just off.

Investors, particularly many who consider themselves "value investors," have had violent and near-religious reactions to this notion. Instead of practicing introspection and asking themselves Question One—what do I believe that is wrong—they grab at any straw to disavow they're influenced by a very natural bias. In rebuttal, they claim the phenomenon occurs because ultra-high P/Es come from suppressed earnings posted at the end of a recession. Not quite. This sometimes happens, but it's far from universal. It certainly wasn't true in 1996, 1997, 1998, and 1999. To excuse that, investors say the markets are just irrational. Investors' vehemence that ultra-high P/Es must have a high risk is another aspect of the perverseness of TGH.

Upside Down and Backwards If You Can

We've demonstrated how to use Question One with a well-entrenched misconception. As you strike out on your own, testing your own mythology, make sure you're thorough. A good scientist doesn't stop once he gets the answer to a question; he looks at it repeatedly from different angles.

First, be realistic about your findings. Don't jump to conclusions too fast. One might consider the previous data and create a new myth—high P/Es are predictive of above-average returns. Don't fall for that trick. The evidence here is enough to utterly decimate any wrongheaded belief about high P/Es being bad for stocks. Anything more is inconclusive. It isn't enough. It isn't overwhelming. It won't let you bet and win much more often than you lose. Ultimately, you should take away P/Es aren't, by themselves, a predictor of future results.

Furthermore, if you get just one result supporting your hypothesis, no matter how remarkable, it's happenstance, not a pattern. This is true for anything you encounter or study. You don't want to make a bet based on happenstance. For example, you might be tempted to conclude ultra-high P/E markets tend to be low risk and high reward. Yes, it is true ultra-high P/Es have led to some great stock returns. But there haven't been enough occurrences to make this anything more than an interesting observation and probably coincidence. As you create and test, you must test as many occurrences as you find.

We now know P/Es have no predictive power, so is the P/E good for anything? To find out, we need to steal a page again from Chapter 2 and Question Two. What can we fathom about P/Es that is hard for others to fathom? A standard trick to help you see better and see things others don't is to look at it from a different perspective. One powerful way to test your belief and results is to flip your myth on its head and see what you see then.

So take the P/E and flip it on its head to find out. By putting the Earnings over the Price in this equation, you have the exact same information in a different framework—the earnings-to-price ratio, better called the *earnings yield*. This is simply the inverse of the P/E—the E/P. Investors are used to seeing expected returns of bonds and cash quoted in yields; whereas most investors are accustomed to valuing stocks by their P/Es. By inverting the P/E and looking at the earnings yield, you can compare apples-to-apples. What's more, you also escape the heights framework just discussed. Table 1.1 shows how to take a P/E and arrive at an earnings yield—a P/E of 20 is really a price of $20

Table 1.1   What Is an Earnings Yield?

P/E	E/P	=	EY%
33	1/33		3%
25	1/25		4%
20	1/20		5%
15	1/15		6%
10	1/10		10%
7	1/7		14%
5	1/5		20%

divided by $1 of earnings. So the E/P for this is 1 divided by 20 or 5 percent. When you think of the relationship as an earnings yield, it compares to interest rates (as we see later, it should) and the heights framework scaring us about P/E disappears instantly. The P/E of 20 scares you, but the earnings yield of 5 percent doesn't. It's pretty easy math—again, no Stephen Hawking automaton necessary.

This comparison is more rational and straightforward than determining if a stock is cheap or expensive based on P/E. Since stocks and bonds compete for investor dollars, the comparison of bond yields and stock earnings yields gives you something concrete for comparison. For example, if you have a market with a P/E of 20, most folks would say that seems "high." How do you think about a 5 percent earnings yield? If bond interest rates are 8 percent, the 5 percent earnings yield might not be attractive, but if bonds are 3 percent it could be. Compare that with going bond yields now.

Before you think a stock market (or single stock) with a 5 percent earnings yield is inferior to, say, a 6 percent U.S. Treasury bond, remember the tax treatment. The earnings yield is effectively a company's after-tax annualized cost of raising expansion capital by selling stock. What does that mean? Well, since the P/E is an after-tax number, you know the E/P is an after-tax number too. A company can get expansion capital by selling stock or issuing a corporate bond. But if it issues a corporate bond, the interest paid on that bond is deductible for tax purposes against revenue. The corporate bond rate is a pre-tax number. The E/P is an after-tax number.

Suppose the stock has a P/E of 20 and it's an average grade corporation, meaning a BBB corporate bond rating. In mid-2006, it could borrow 10-year money through a bond at about 6 percent.[13] Assuming a 33 percent tax rate, the 6 percent cost is really 4 percent after tax. (To get the tax-adjusted equivalent, multiply the 6 percent rate by 1 minus the 33 percent tax rate—or 0.67.) The stock's E/P is 5 percent, already after-tax. So it's cheaper to raise expansion capital by issuing a bond at 4 percent than selling stock at 5 percent. Corporate bond rates would have to rise above 7.5 percent to make it cheaper for that P/E 20 company to get expansion capital by selling stock. That is the firm's viewpoint.

From your viewpoint, it's somewhat different. The earnings yield needn't be above the tax-adjusted bond yield to make stocks more attractive than bonds. When you buy stocks, you do so assuming future earnings will be somewhat higher due to subsequent future growth. Stocks as a group tend to generate earnings growth over time, sometimes more, other times less. But a bond coupon is fixed. You know it has no chance of rising. If you hold it to maturity, you will get that interest rate. When you buy stocks, you're actually buying the future average earnings yield, which is likely somewhat higher than the current earnings yield. When you buy bonds, the future average bond yield is the current yield. For this reason, the current earnings yield needn't be higher than the bond yield to make stocks attractive relatively.

Has the earnings yield for the stock market ever been higher than the bond yield? Yes, but only for a few and far between years, and that is true all around the world—and these times often were outstanding times to own stocks. When the earnings yield is above the bond yield, stocks are extremely undervalued relative to bonds. *Translation:* Stocks are relatively cheap.

Corporate bond yields bounce up and down based on what happens to government bond yields. Fluctuations in the much bigger government bond market drive shifts in corporate bond rates. Figure 1.4 plots the market's earnings yield versus the government bond yield. You can see times when the earnings yield approached or even surpassed the bond yield, great years in the stock market followed.

Have you ever seen a graph plotting earnings yield against the bond yield? Probably not! They exist but are rare. I think my firm has probably published more of them than all others put together cumulatively. Comparing the earnings yield to the bond yield is a powerful scaling metric you can use over

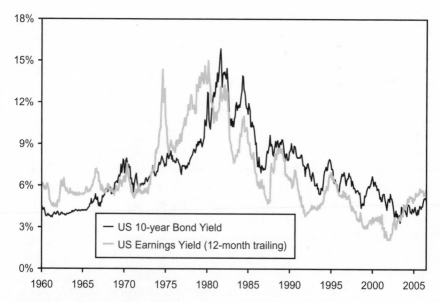

Figure 1.4   U.S. 10-Year Bond Yield versus Earnings Yield.
Source: **Global Financial Data.**

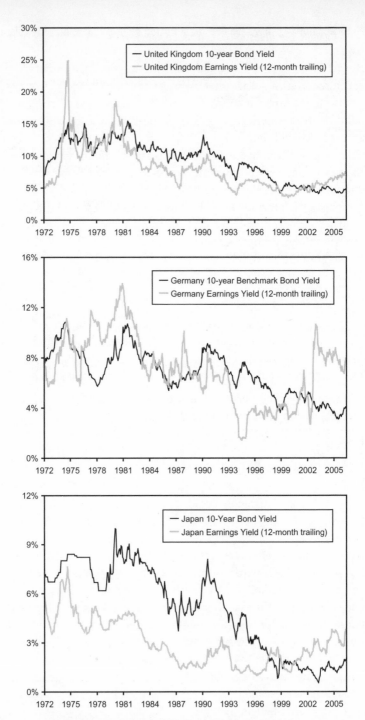

Figure 1.5   Ten-Year Bond Yield versus Earnings Yield.
Source: **Global Financial Data.**

and over to sense relative value and historical norms. Coincidentally, one of the best times to own stocks is when you know they're cheap but everyone else thinks they're expensive. Since 2002, the earnings yield has been higher than bond yields in America, so stocks have been historically very cheap—just when most folks said they weren't cheap but high because P/Es were above historic averages. If you had let high P/Es scare you out of stocks, you would have missed a 75 percent positive move in global markets since the bear market bottomed in October 2002 until June of 2006 (as I write this).[14] Recall what happened the previous time the earnings yield exceeded the bond yield in the early 1980s—uninterrupted years of above-average stock market returns, most of them strong double-digit returns.[15]

But we aren't done yet. Remember, if something is true here, it should be true in most foreign developed countries. We can see all around the world earnings yields exceed bond yields, and by more than in America—and that too is uncommon. Stocks are cheaper globally in recent years compared to long-term interest rates than they've been in a quarter century (see Figure 1.5).

In the United Kingdom and Germany, stock returns were above average following times when the earnings yield was above the bond yield. Just recently, the earnings yield has been above the bond yield in Japan, and Japanese markets have been experiencing strong stock returns.

When You Are Really, Really Wrong

We've talked about those myths perpetuated by investors inventing or imagining causal correlations where none exist. What about those myths so wrong the inverse is actually true? Sometimes, when you ask Question One, you discover you have been not only wrong, but really, really wrong. Don't fret. Discovering you have been wrong and uncovering a reverse truth gives you yet another basis for a market bet. A powerful one, because you know for certain everyone is betting on the exact opposite of what you know will happen.

It may be hard for you to imagine something you and your fellow investors can get so completely wrong. But there are some myths in the misguided investor doctrine held so dearly, questioning them is almost sacrilegious. Suggesting such a belief be scrutinized, if only to confirm its veracity, would bring outrage, scandal, and possible excommunication. These myths, the most sacrosanct beliefs in the investor and social catechism, those no one dares question, are sometimes ones we find to be so wrong the exact opposite holds true.

The Holiest of Holies—the Federal Budget Deficit Myth

You believe a high federal budget deficit is bad. Everybody knows budget deficits are bad. How do we know? We know because everyone knows. Duh! Pundits, politicians, patriots, perverts, poker partners, your parents, your pet parakeet, and worst of all, Sean Penn, Brad Pitt, and Dolly Parton. Everyone! More important, everyone *believes* it. There is absolutely no reason to question this belief. I mean how do you question Sean Penn and Brad Pitt? Which makes this sacredly held myth a great candidate for Question One. What do you believe that is wrong? Better yet, reframe and flip it on its head and ask yourself the reverse.

Is a high federal budget deficit good—and good for stocks?

Ask that question too loudly and someone may come after you with a butterfly net and commit you to a nice, safe, padded cell. Believing a budget deficit is bad is part of our collective Western-world wisdom and culture—nay, our civic duty. As stated earlier, deficit has the same Latin root as deficient. Why question something believed for thousands of years? Because it's wrong! We are taught as children to regard debt as bad, more debt as worse, and a lot of debt as downright immoral. Right after we finished making paper turkeys for Thanksgiving, we got a cookie, some apple juice, a lecture on the immorality of debt, and then naptime.

As a society, we're morally opposed to debt. We haven't evolved too far from our Puritan forefathers in this regard. And deficits make more debt. Abhorring a budget deficit isn't just an American sentiment. Other inhabitants of Western developed nations fret as we do over deficits. In many places, more so! Come to think of if, they fret over ours, too—more than theirs. Nosy foreigners! Maybe if they spent less time thinking about American debt and more time understanding capitalism they wouldn't have such laggard economies. But I digress.

Is any of this anxiety deserved? Looking at the past 15 years, America has run a federal budget surplus in just four years. During the budget surplus of the late 1990s, the stock market peaked, leading to a bear market and the start of a recession. That recession was fairly short-lived and shallow, but the bear market persisted three years and was huge. Clearly, the budget surplus didn't lead to outstanding stock returns. If there is no empirical evidence supporting the hypothesis (yes, Virginia, it's just a hypothesis) that budget deficits are bad for stocks, could the opposite be true?

It appears so. Figure 1.6 shows the federal budget balance going back to 1947 as a percent of annual gross domestic product (GDP). Anything above the horizontal line is a budget surplus and below is a deficit. We've noted rel-

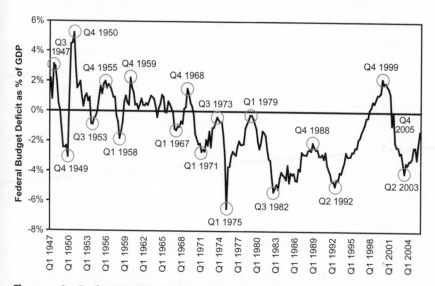

Figure 1.6 Budget Deficits Are Good for Stocks.
Source: White House, Bureau of Economic Analysis.

ative peaks and troughs. The counterintuitive truth is stock market returns following periodic deficit extremes have been much higher than surplus peaks or even decreasing deficits.

Table 1.2 shows subsequent price returns after surpluses and deficits. Look at the 12-month subsequent returns after budget surpluses and compare with the returns after the deficits. Which world do you want to be living in? The one with the average return of 22 percent, or the one with the average return of 0.8 percent? Now look out over 36-month returns. Those appalling deficits get you an average cumulative return of 36 percent compared with 9.2 percent from the surpluses. Oh, the horror! The plain truth is, since 1947, if an investor had purchased stocks at federal budget deficit extremes, he or she would have seen one-, two-, and three-year returns much higher than average and much higher than if purchased at high budget surplus periods. Buying in the aftermath of budget surpluses would have rendered materially below-average returns.

If you're beginning to think perhaps budget surpluses aren't the best thing to happen to stocks, you're getting it. If you suspect the wry hand of TGH, you're also getting it. Budget surpluses aren't a panacea. They lead to bad markets. Don't wish for them.

Table 1.2 Stock Returns Following Budget Balance Extremes

High Points

Date		Subsequent S&P 500 Price Return		
		12 mo	24 mo	36 mo
Q3 1947	Annualized	2.6%	1.6%	8.8%
	Cumulative	2.6%	3.2%	28.8%
Q4 1950	Annualized	16.5%	14.1%	6.7%
	Cumulative	16.5%	30.2%	21.6%
Q4 1955	Annualized	26.4%	13.9%	3.6%
	Cumulative	26.4%	29.7%	11.1%
Q4 1959	Annualized	-3.0%	9.3%	1.8%
	Cumulative	-3.0%	19.5%	5.4%
Q4 1968	Annualized	-11.4%	-5.8%	-0.6%
	Cumulative	-11.4%	-11.3%	-1.7%
Q3 1973	Annualized	-41.4%	-12.1%	-1.0%
	Cumulative	-41.4%	-22.7%	-2.9%
Q1 1979	Annualized	0.5%	15.7%	3.3%
	Cumulative	0.5%	33.9%	10.2%
Q4 1988	Annualized	27.3%	9.0%	14.5%
	Cumulative	27.3%	18.9%	50.2%
Q4 1999	Annualized	-10.1%	-11.6%	-15.7%
	Cumulative	-10.1%	-21.9%	-40.1%
Average	Annualized	0.8%	3.8%	2.4%
Average	Cumulative	3.5%	8.8%	9.2%

Low Points

Date		Subsequent S&P 500 Price Return		
		12 mo	24 mo	36 mo
Q4 1949	Annualized	21.8%	19.1%	16.6%
	Cumulative	21.8%	41.8%	58.6%
Q4 1953	Annualized	45.0%	35.4%	23.4%
	Cumulative	45.0%	83.3%	88.1%
Q1 1958	Annualized	31.7%	14.7%	15.6%
	Cumulative	31.7%	31.4%	54.5%
Q1 1967	Annualized	0.0%	6.1%	-0.2%
	Cumulative	0.0%	12.5%	-0.6%
Q1 1971	Annualized	6.9%	5.4%	-2.1%
	Cumulative	6.9%	11.2%	-6.3%
Q1 1975	Annualized	23.3%	8.7%	2.3%
	Cumulative	23.3%	18.1%	7.0%
Q3 1982	Annualized	37.9%	17.4%	14.8%
	Cumulative	37.9%	37.9%	51.2%
Q2 1992	Annualized	10.4%	4.3%	10.1%
	Cumulative	10.4%	8.9%	33.5%
Q2 2003	Annualized	19.1%	6.3%	26.6%
	Cumulative	19.1%	8.6%	37.6%
Average	Annualized	21.8%	13.0%	11.9%
Average	Cumulative	21.8%	28.2%	35.9%

This may not make sense at first blush. Conventional wisdom depicts a deficit as some sort of gigantic anchor, holding down the economy and ramming debt down its over-indebted throat. As consumers, we're careful to not overdraw our checking accounts and believe the government should do the same. Many politicians will have you believe deficits must be reduced, and now. There are no politicians saying more debt is good (although there are often politicians advocating tax cuts which can cause a similar effect).

Let's Kill the Blood Suckers

If you don't know the origin of the word *politics,* let me enlighten you. The word politics comes from the Greek *poli* meaning "many" and *tics* meaning "small blood-sucking creatures." Unless a poli-tic stands up and announces, "I routinely lie, cheat, and steal to help my career and care nothing about you, whoever you are," you should take anything he says with a grain of salt. (Presume you can tell when they are lying because it's when their mouths move.) You may be affronted. Maybe you married a poli-tic. That's not a big problem. Get a divorce! Maybe you're one yourself. I'm sorry—there is nothing we can do for you. You're permanently mentally ill and need a different book.

People have some difficulty with this. You know you dislike any scumbag poli-tic saying things ideologically you dislike. And you know he is dishonest, a slime-ball, and someone if whom your daughter planned to marry you would instead seek a cult deprogrammer to protect her. What you have difficulty accepting is when another poli-tic says things you like and believe in, that he or she is simply lying. (Again, when their mouths move.) Of course, that's just my view. Suppose I'm wrong.

Poli-tics, overwhelmingly, aren't students of capital markets. More than anything else they tend to be lawyers (some exceptions—like Presidents Eisenhower, Carter, Reagan, or Bush. Or even Arnold Schwarzenegger). Don't look to them to be experts in finance or economics. They may be honest enough until they become Beltway blowhards, but still aren't experts on markets and economics and will never use the Three Questions. Poli-tics never think about when they're wrong, how to fathom what others can't fathom, and how to see when their brains are misguiding them. Poli-tics couldn't use the Three Questions if they had to. (Perhaps I've been bombastic for comedy's sake in the past few paragraphs, but you'll be a better investor and sleep better at night if you tune out approximately 97 percent of what poli-tics say.)

That budget deficits are good for stocks isn't a lucky fluke. Economically, it makes sense if you can get yourself to think about debt and deficits correctly. (We cover that in Chapter 6.) For now, suppose budget deficits really are good for stocks in America and surpluses really are bad. If that is true, we ought to be able to see it happening close to the same way in other developed Western nations. That trick is a really nifty one most folks never use. And we do see it overseas.

In other developed nations (as I demonstrate for you in Chapter 6), budget deficits have preceded good stock market returns, and surpluses have preceded gloomier times. This isn't a socioeconomic-political statement. All we are doing is looking at cold hard facts and encouraging you to do the same. Folks who are hamstrung by bias are plagued with misconception and can't see the truth even when it's right there in front of them. Instead, always ask if what you believe is actually false.

What about Those Other Deficits?

The federal budget deficit isn't the only deficit boogeyman getting investors' knickers knotted. The dreaded "triple deficits" never fail to make panic-inducing headlines. As soon as I tell you the budget deficit isn't bad for stocks, your reaction may be dismissal, anger, and then a framework shift—that other deficits, like the trade and current account deficits, must be bad. You've heard it so often. You've also heard they're bad for the dollar.

We look at such assertions in both Chapters 6 and 7, but I'm telling here and now if you read those chapters, you will become permanently convinced these two forms of deficits aren't bad for stocks or the dollar. I mention this here as another version of something everyone believes that is false. Note you've heard it, accepted it, believed it was true, winced every time a new record trade deficit number was announced but never stopped to ask, "I know I believe it's bad; but is it really and how would I check?" Because you know in your heart, if everyone is wrong, and trade and current account deficits aren't bad for the stock market and the dollar, it would be tremendously bullish because that would be one less thing to fret that to most folks is a huge burden. As Forrest Gump would say, "One less thing!" And that is something you can know others don't.

It's All Relatively Relative

Part of the reason investors freak out about deficits—budget, trade, and otherwise—is they forget to think relatively (a cognitive error). They hear as of

2006 we have an estimated $423 billion dollar budget deficit.[16] "Holy Cow! That's a lot of moo-laa!" they think. "Four hundred billion??? I don't have four hundred billion. Not even Bill Gates has that much." News editors and talking heads lambaste whomever they think is responsible, using words like "record-breaking," "staggering," and "irresponsible" to describe the deficit's size. Well, duh. Of course it sounds high. But is it? Are our perceptions right?

To see this correctly, the first thing we always have to do is scale. We must look at our budget deficit as a percentage of our overall economy. If you think $423 billion is a lot, what do you think about $13 trillion? That is the size of America's GDP as of July 2006.[17] As a percentage of our national income, the budget deficit is a mere 3.25 percent. What's more, as a historical average, it's nothing to sweat about either. The media won't mention the budget deficit as a percentage of GDP, however, because they assume you're rational and won't get exercised over a budget deficit that is 3.25 percent of our overall income.

This doesn't work just with deficits. Anytime the media tries to scare you with huge numbers, think about it relatively—think scale. Another frequent boogeyman is the cost of the Iraq war, which, at $80 billion per year (including our effort in Afghanistan),[18] will cripple our economy, stall growth for years, and usher in another era of stagflation and presumably sideburns, polyester, and more bad disco music. Eek! The media wanted you, the consumer, to choke on your corn nuts and cry out, "Eighty billion dollars! I'm writing my senator. It's just not worth it." Surprisingly, starting at a relative low point in the market in 2003 just before the onset of the Iraq war, the U.S. market shot up 41 percent, to finish the year a net positive 29 percent.[19] The global market was even rosier at a total return in 2003 of 33 percent.[20]

I'm not here to comment on the validity, or lack thereof, of the war in Iraq or the War on Terror. Not my turf. Smart or stupid as foreign policy, the market knew something the media and most poli-tics didn't want you to figure— $80 billion, or $100 billion, or even $200 billion (if it ends up costing that much) per year just isn't that much compared to the size of the American economic juggernaut. We also must remember, America is just a small part of a much bigger world with a global GDP tending to go the same direction at the same time as America. Later we'll come to think globally, but doing so makes the numbers get bigger still. When faced with large numbers that our brains always want to think are scary, we must scale—we must think relatively. Smart or stupid, the cost of the Iraq war just doesn't matter much economically because it's a tiny percent of American GDP and an even tinier, microscopic percent of global GDP.

Question Everything You Know

Success in investing requires you to question everything you think you know; particularly those things you think you really, really know. Using Question One properly gives you discipline to prevent some basic errors. The ability to just avoid mistakes is key to successful investing. As you examine mythology and begin discovering faulty logic, don't simply correct it once and forget about it. Investing is an applied science, not a craft. If you get a validated answer to a hypothesis, don't assume you can apply the results always and everywhere and get the same result. TGH is an ever-changing opponent requiring constant retesting of hypotheses.

Knowing big federal budget deficits signal good times ahead for stocks is fairly shocking, though undeniably true. Some day, in some future universe, the investing public may relinquish this myth and realize the whole world has been wrong on this point. Should that occur, you will have lost your edge. Then you will no longer know something others don't. When everyone knows federal budget deficits are to be cheered not jeered, the market will efficiently price it in. By using Question One and constantly retesting your investing doctrine, you won't fall prey to such an event, implausible though it is.

You may say (and it's a great thing to say), "But if you tell me in this book the market's P/E has nothing to do with future returns and big budget deficits are bullish not bearish, won't the whole world know? And then won't it stop working?" If the world embraces these truths, then because the market is a discounter of all widely known information, these truths would become priced into markets and knowing them wouldn't help you beat markets. They wouldn't work because you wouldn't know anything others don't widely know. But I'll bet that doesn't happen in 2007. I'll bet most folks who read Chapter 1 will think the notions expressed about P/Es and deficits are so screwy they ignore them completely and fall back on the mythologies. That would be comfortable and easy. Most investors will never see this book, and of those buying it, half won't read it. Of those that do, many won't get past this chapter in disgust. They will reject the truth, prefer mythology, and see me as silly. I hope they do because when I see them see me as silly and wrong, I know I will be able to use these truisms for a long time. If they adopt most of these truisms, I'll need to come up with new ones to know something others don't.

Just as the Campbell-Shiller paper was rapidly embraced and quickly became globally famous and popular because it supported the standard mythology—evidence contradicting market mythologies fortunately tends to be about as noticed as a rock thrown into a lake, a minor ripple followed by near-instant absence from societal memory. This isn't the first time I've written about the high P/E myth. I first started 10 years ago. I'll bet it is as prevalent 5 and 10 years from now as it is today, and you can still make gameable bets on it. But, of course, I could be wrong and then you move onto the next myth. That's life.

The real benefit of Question One is it allows you to know something others don't know by knowing where you otherwise would have been wrong but thought you were right. Once you master the skill of doing this, you will be able to improve yourself forever with it. You can keep learning things others don't know while reducing your own propensity to make mistakes.

Discovering new investing truths is a coincidental result of asking Question One—a lucky accident. If you're purposefully seeking what no one else knows, you must also learn to use and apply Question Two: What can you fathom that others find unfathomable? Even contemplating such a thing seems pretty unfathomable to most people, but that is exactly what we start doing if you simply turn the page and continue to Chapter 2.

2

QUESTION TWO: WHAT CAN YOU FATHOM THAT OTHERS FIND UNFATHOMABLE?

Fathoming the Unfathomable

Fathoming the unfathomable by definition seems unfathomable, so most folks don't try. However, like Question One, it doesn't require any additional scholarship, genetic superiority, or magical superhero powers. All you need is Question Two: What can I see that others can't? The more you ask, the more you see. Since the only basis for a market bet is knowing something others don't, this question provides the second basis for a bet. Go ahead and ask yourself: What do I know that others don't? At this point, your answer may be, "Well . . . nothing." It's most people's immediate reaction.

Don't be discouraged. You won't be bombarded with Question Twos like you are with Question Ones. We get bombarded with investing nonsense daily. Discovering something others don't know isn't a "Eureka!" moment. It's not the apple falling on Newton's head. It's what happened afterward when Newton asked, "I wonder what the heck made that happen?" and contemplated what forces, natural or sinister, could be at play. It's the reflection in a quiet room away from the incessant market and media noise when you wonder if factor Q could possibly cause result Y when everyone else is yammering on about X causing Y.

The world is busy insisting high P/Es cause poor stock prices (wrong—usually), debt is bad for stocks (wrong—always in Western nations), you shouldn't fight the Fed (wrong about half), and high trade deficits cause a weak dollar (wrong, wrong, wrong). But to know something others don't, you tune out the noise and wonder—if everything everyone insists moves currencies doesn't, I wonder what actually does? (We go there in Chapter 7.) And if I shouldn't fight the Fed, is it possible the yield curve can tell me anything at all about stocks? Or, must I just look at it differently somehow? I wonder? Wondering is wonderful.

Wondering Is Wonderful

Suppose no one has a clue what causes result-Y. If everyone knows no one knows what causes Y, then probably almost no one is willing to think about what causes Y because they will believe it a waste of time. In our contemporary world, in America and more so elsewhere, if something is seen as unfathomable, normal people will treat it as a complete untouchable. These areas are especially ripe for inquiry because they are so virginal.

Misapplication of Question Two can lead you to waste time plowing through common media sources for clues. Clients often e-mail me a news item they feel might be significant to our investment strategy. While I appreciate the concern, through the miracle of mass production and electronics, pretty much all media is everywhere and all around us. Whether through mainstream sources like the *Wall Street Journal*, the *New York Times*, *Barron's*, the *Economist*, the *Washington Post*, the *Miami Herald*, or lesser sources like the *Ontario Onionpeeler*, or *Invest Romania*, and whether directly or through a consolidator like the *Drudge Report* or *Little Brother's Blog*, it's pretty much force-fed to us from *everywhere*. Your investment edge won't present itself in a ready-to-use format in a front-page news story in any such publication, or in an evening news program, or blog, or e-mail newsletter. No matter how buried a news item or how insignificant a blog, we live in a fast-moving world. Your "news" edge almost certainly will be snatched from you before you've found it. Don't despair; you can still use all that widespread noise to help you find something no one else knows. All it requires is you fight eons of behavioral conditioning. Here is how.

Ignore the Rock in the Bushes

Thousands of years ago, our ancestors grouped together for security against other tribes and giant fanged beasts. When darkness fell, they gathered around campfires for warmth, protection, and the occasional grilled mammoth burger. Glowing by the campfire, they regaled each other with stories of the hunt and mythological tales, carrying their culture to younger generations. On a nice night, warm and mammoth-gorged, they could feel a real sense of security, well-being, and envision a beckoning future. Suddenly, in the dark, a loud and unexplained mammalian noise slices through their sense of security. Instantly, instinctually they all look toward the source of that noise—in the bushes—and prepare for what could be threatening and ugly. An attacking rival tribe, perhaps, or a lion or a stampeding wildebeest herd. Every ear and eye correctly focused on the noise to maximize the human power that can identify and, if possible, overcome the threat.

If you were from another tribe and led a warring group wanting to attack this camp, what would you do? To be clever, you might throw a stone or create some other ruckus that distracts the camp—then attack from a different direction. Of course, a stampeding herd wouldn't do that. But for the camp, in case of a planned attack from clever marauders, a more evolved military-like response would be to have some folks look away from the noise, into the darkness elsewhere, to spot any surprise marauder threat. The problem? Unless well organized, no group of people behaves that way. You hear a noise in the darkness and you turn toward it. Go camping sometime and see. Your instinctual reaction isn't to turn away from the noise but toward it. In Stone Age days, that instinct protected lives from the most common natural forces. From tens of thousands of years of evolution, we are mentally hardwired to turn toward the noise, face it as a group, and instinctually presume our ability to immediately unite our tribal eyes and ears and react.

I suspect some male readers may be tempted to pound their chests and say, "Me evolved. Me sophisticated. Me modern. Me would look in other direction from noise, save women and children, be crowned king of tribe, have many wives, eat many mammoth." I expect many female readers may be tempted to put their hands over their mouths and say, "Me look to child to pull close to save. Me not look to noise." Both groups would be wrong. The next time you hear an unexpected noise, check what your instinctual reaction is. I guarantee you'll look to the noise. If you don't, you're really, really weird. The person who most thinks he won't is most certainly the person turning to the noise fastest. The rare bird that doesn't face the noise doesn't think about it. To know what your fellow investors don't know, you must look anywhere but where everyone else is looking. You must train yourself to stop looking toward the noise. Instead note whenever everyone is looking one direction, whether you hear a noise or not, you should look away—where they're not.

Discounting the Media Machine and Advanced Fad Avoidance

You may be tempted to ignore the media altogether since what you hear or read is either wrong or has already been discounted into current prices. There is some rationality to that view, but it's wrong. By all means, don't avoid mass media—it's your friend and ally on your quest to invest by knowing what others don't. The media is a discounting machine—you must read (watch, listen to) the media to know what everyone else is focused on so you know exactly what you can ignore and look away from and focus elsewhere. Whatever they're fretting, you needn't because they're doing it for you—a service—and you don't even have to pay them for it. They do it for free for you. Such a simple concept is very hard for tribal-oriented humans to get. But anyone can train themselves to do it.

For example, I've already told you the collective histrionics regarding the so-called triple deficits are so much hooey. You may not believe it but I've told you. You also know pretty much everyone misinterprets high P/Es. (We debunk more ubiquitous myths in later chapters, but you get the idea.) Paying attention to what the media covers and consequently discarding what is irrelevant will prevent you from being trampled by herd mentality and let you begin fathoming new paths.

Avoiding being trampled by the herd sounds easy enough—look where they are stampeding and get the heck out of the way. However, if it were easy, it wouldn't be called "herd mentality." It would be called "calm, noncompelling, no pressure here, join us as we run over this cliff if you please, if not, no problem" mentality. Remember when your mom asked if you'd jump off a bridge just because cool-kid Jimmy did it? Of course you wouldn't jump, but you might buy small-cap stocks at the wrong time if your poker group pokes enough fun at you for not having done it when they did. They keep bragging about what a killing they're making—with you sitting there feeling like a schmuck with your lousy balanced portfolio.

My March 1995 *Forbes* column, "Advanced Fad Avoidance,"[1] described how best to avoid getting swept away with the herd. It's still good advice, so I'll repeat the four steps to fad avoidance here:

1. "If most folks you know agree with you on a price move or some event's impact, don't take this as confirmation you are right. It is a warning; **you are wrong.** Being right requires aloneness, and willingness to let others see you as maybe nuts."

   Still very true. And lots of people think I'm nuts. It's okay if people think you're nuts. It doesn't hurt. With the evolution of the Internet and blogs, I've become used to people reading my articles and columns and writing scathing criticisms of my very best things. (Of course, sometimes they're right and that would be when I'm wrong, but either way what they think of me isn't any of my business.) I've trained myself to ignore what anyone who I don't already know very well thinks about me or my work. If my wife is upset at me, I take it seriously. She knows me, my strengths and weaknesses and desires my well-being. Family, friends, associates! Other than that, if you're upset at me and don't like something I've said, feel free to criticize, but know you will run into an emotional desert. You can train yourself to have that same emotional desert too. What most people think about you is none of your business; and if they think you're nuts, it might be good.

2. "If you read or hear about some investment idea or significant event more than once in the media, it won't work. By the time several commentators have thought and written about it, even new news is too old."

Even more true today. The Internet has multiplied the venues and speed by which news travels. Now everything moves faster and gets discounted into pricing faster. Compounding the discounting speed, which has been increasing for decades, traders trade 24 hours a day, fully five and half days a week around the globe. It used to be evening news didn't sneak up on you until morning. Now, not only does news move across the Internet at night, but someone somewhere is trading extensively while you snooze.

3. "The older an argument is, the less power it has. So, for example, inflation fears may have moved markets in 1994, but sometime early in 1995 that view will run out of steam."

Every year's hot fear is obsolete the next year. It's the new thing no one expected that has the herd stampeding around your village, not last year's noise. To think better about this—take any issue and consider when you first heard about it. The older it is, the more certain it won't affect you. The older it is, the more certain everyone has had multiple opportunities to discount the price fully. Here is the best single example I can remember. Recall people expected all computers to break down on January 1, 2000 (01/01/00—GASP!) because of a supposed widespread glitch in everyone's software. The *Y2K* scare was ubiquitous, and in the fall of 1999, it scared lots of folks out of stocks. I devoted my October 18, 1999, *Forbes* column, entitled "*Greater Fools*," to why Y2K wouldn't hurt stocks. Quoting from that column: "Y2K is the most widely hyped 'disaster' in modern history. It is well documented: The only folks who aren't familiar with it are in the upper Amazon basins, rapidly fleeing the rest of humanity. I need not define Y2K for you to know exactly what I'm referencing. My July 6, 1998, column detailed why Y2K could not hurt the stock market." Because it was an old argument and well-discounted, the S&P 500 in 1999 had a back-end rise during the supposed crisis with a total return for the year of 21 percent.[2] Using this simple rule, anyone could have known Y2K wouldn't bite. Fear of Y2K was bullish. But few knew because they couldn't get themselves to embrace the rule. How can you use this rule today, here in 2007? Think Bird Flu. It's too old a story to bite stocks. If we see a future big fear of Bird Flu, that would be a very bullish thing. I discuss bird flu at length in Chapter 5 and how to see it correctly. (If you care to read my two "Y2K" columns, they follow.)

4. "Any category of security that was hot in the last five years won't be in the next five years, and vice versa."

Still true. Always true. And yet investors still fall prey to this one. Energy in 1980. Tech in 2000. Small value stocks in 2007. You can play this game endlessly. That they were hot in the last five doesn't mean they will be the coldest in the next five, or even necessarily cold at all, but no category stays hot for 10 years. And if one did one day, it would be a double warning to seek safer and higher future returning turf elsewhere.

News You Can't Use

READER NEIL BELL E-mails that he is "puzzled by your lack of attention to the year 2000 problem." I write back saying I covered it in my Mar. 13, 1995 column. Reader Bell responded that I ought to look at several of the detailed Web sites showing just how serious this Y2K thing really is.

So I did and have come to the conclusion that Y2K faddists to the contrary, this thing won't seriously hurt the stock market or cause you any other major inconvenience.

My view on such things is very simple: One should be aware of all the buzz in the media, if for no other reason than to go contrary to it. If any subject has more than one Web site devoted to it, it is either wrong or already fully discounted in the marketplace. The most basic of all market notions is that the market (The Great Humiliator) is a discounter of all known information. It succeeds by making sure that whatever we all know is either wrong or is already priced into securities. Yes, listen to the buzz but never try to make money except by acting against it.

Y2K is heavily covered. Even the SEC has pronounced its fear of Y2K. So ignore it. The Great Humiliator does this stuff effortlessly. It is just like everyone's massive fear of high P/Es. In markets it's what you don't see or know that gets you, because the only thing that moves markets is surprise: There's not much surprise in anything that's all over the World Wide Web. And the most likely surprise in a high-p/e stock is from bad news, not good news, which is already in the price. In my 26-year career, now in my 15th year of doing this column, I have never ever known this rule to let me down: The obvious never moves markets; surprises almost always do.

In 1995 I wrote this: "If you read or hear about some investment idea or significant event more than once in the media, it won't work. By the time several commentators have thought and written about it, even new news is too old."

In that spirit I say: Forget Y2K.

> If you read about some investment idea more than once, it won't work as an investment.

I have been taking quite a beating from readers over my recommendation of *Nissan* (6, NSANY, www.nissan.co.jp). I suggested the laggard Japanese carmaker (*May 19, 1997*) at 12. It is now at half that level.

If you are sitting with a loss, my advice is hang on: If Daimler-Benz buys Chrysler, you don't need much imagination to flash forward a few years and see one of the big five buying Nissan. With $54 billion in revenue and 135,000 employees, it's just about the same size as Chrysler—but cheaper—selling at just 60% of book value and 15% of annual revenue. At $7 billion in market cap, it could be bid up 50% and still be bought for less than a probably understated book value.

Two other future auto buyouts that neatly fit a bigger, more global firm's product line are *Fiat* (22, FIA, www.fiat.com) and *Volvo* (28, VOLVY, www.volvo.se). Fiat has too much fat—too many employees—but it dominates the Italian regional market. Selling at a p/e of 18, at just 30% of annual revenue and 1 times book value, its lessor quality is more than discounted. Volvo is a high-image product line and yet is still reasonably priced at a p/e of 8 and 55% of revenue.

Readers also ask about AXA-UOP (54, AXA, www.axa.com). I recommended it on Dec. 15 at 36. Has it gone too far, too fast? I don't think so. I'm content holding it. It is the world's second-largest insurer and second-largest money management firm, and is only starting to be known in the U.S. At 50% of revenue and 18 times rapidly rising earnings, it could possibly be at 100 by 2001. That's 28% per year.

Matsushita Electric (157, MC, www.panasonic.co.jp) was another of my 1997 picks, recommended June 16, 1997 at 185 and again at 163 on Dec. 1. Despite the troubles in the Pacific Rim, this Japanese stock has held up fairly well. It is Panasonic and other great brand names. I still think it could see 350 by the year 2000. Hold on.

Greater Fools

WHAT CAN WE learn about this year-end from 1942? First: that Y2K won't hurt the stock market. It may even drive a nice rally.

What does 1942 have to do with Y2K? Well, 1942 shows how the market works, which isn't in a way that now allows a disaster from Y2K. Those who still fret Y2K's market impact don't fathom the markets, and you simply should be dismissive of them all.

There are two principles here. First, markets don't wait for known events; they move ahead of them. Second, folks who wait for events to drive prices often get trapped and trampled by stampedes.

Which was a bigger risk: Y2K in 1999 or Adolf Hitler in 1942? Yet, in 1942, long before anyone could possibly know with any certainty that we would win the war, the S&P 500 rose 20%. In 1943 it rose 26% more—in 1944, 20% more; in 1945, another 36%, before peaking early in 1946. That last year was largely driven by folks who held back cash waiting for certainty—and then threw in their money, very kindly bidding up prices for those who had bought earlier.

How did the market know to rally in 1942 and 1943, long before definitive news? It's what markets do. They decline before a war or recession or something else ugly starts. Usually, they move with a long lead. They rise long before events improve. Hence the age-old adage, "The market knows." The market is also a "discounter" of all known information. That means whatever we all know, fret, read, and cluck about is well priced into markets.

> Y2K, the most widely hyped "disaster" in history, will probably help the stock market.

It is what we don't all know, fret, read, and talk about that moves markets. It isn't that those things can never be discerned. Often they can. But overwhelmingly folks are blind and ignorant about real market movers.

For example, few can see the huge, unaccounted-for flows of foreign money pouring into America that I first told you about in 1997—that have largely driven our bull market since 1996. They just don't know it is happening. (See my columns of Oct. 20, 1997 and Mar. 22, 1999).

Y2K is the most widely hyped "disaster" in modern history. It is well documented: The only folks who aren't familiar with it are in the upper Amazon basin, rapidly fleeing the rest of humanity. I need not even define Y2K for you to know exactly what I'm referencing.

My July 6, 1998 column detailed why Y2K could not hurt the stock market. But now, with Dec. 31 so close, I'll go a step further and say that the market likely will rise as another Y2K force takes over.

There are just enough investors who do understand how markets work to potentially create a pre-year-end buying stampede. They will sense in coming weeks that a Y2K bust ran out of time and that with year-end the rigid Y2K nuts lose their reason for caution. Those sages may play the Y2Kers for great fools by getting their own money into stocks before year-end. I am never sure where the market will go in the very short term, but there is more likelihood of a big pre-year-end up move than any other possibility.

So, remain 100% in equities, with 67% of that in America's 25 largest stocks. The other 33% should be in big continental European and Japanese stocks. Consider these:

Three telecom stocks to own as a package are *Telecom Italia* (93, TI, www.telecomitalia.it), *France Telecom* (84, FTE, www.francetelecom.fr), and *Teledanmark* (29, TLD, www.teledanmark.dk). As a group they have diversity, a relatively low correlation with other stocks in the telecom sector and good growth potential. And they are a good complement to telecom exposure in the 25 largest U.S. stocks.

Similarly, a great three-stock core bank group is the Netherlands' ABN *Amro* (23, ABN, www.abnamro.com), Spain's *Argentaria* (44, AGR, www.argentaria.es), and Australia's *Westpac Banking* (32, WBK, www.westpac.com.au). I recommended ABN on Apr. 19, at $21. It went nowhere. But be patient. It's cheap at 14 times trailing earnings with a 3% dividend yield. With 1,900 branch banks in 70 nations, it will either grow nicely, be bought or both.

Argentaria offers exposure in Spain and Latin America with great regional growth potential. I recommended it on Nov. 4, 1996 at $21 and said to sell it on June 1, 1998 at $43. The stock has since declined with other European banks. It's time to buy again. Westpac Banking offers Asian exposure without much risk. Its price/earnings ratio is 14 and its dividend yield, 4.8%.

Forbes, October 18, 1999. Reprinted by permission of *Forbes* magazine. © Forbes, 2006.

Follow these four steps whenever you are presented with an investment decision, and you'll be better armed to ignore the noise and see what others find unseeable.

Investment Professionals—Professional Discounters

Another great source of discounted information are investment professionals—stock brokers, financial planners, CPAs, CFAs, and so on. Precious few have access to any information their peers or even a client with a cable modem doesn't have. Brokerage firms across the globe subscribe to the same handful of news and research sources. What's more, they analyze and interpret the same information using similar methods. Whatever they focus on, you shouldn't waste time on. If they're writing about it, ignore it. Focus elsewhere.

Universities teach largely the same curriculum to their students in finance and economics. Harvard, Stanford, Michigan, Boston College, USC, UNLV—it doesn't matter. They're teaching pretty much from the same playbook. They're supposed to. The textbooks, methodologies, and theories taught are widely available; they contain little many tens of thousands of others can't read, learn, and thereby discount into markets. Decades of students have learned all this and been trained to think in these ways with the curriculum as their guide. It is basic to the craft. Every bit of what is taught is known by so many people that the curriculum, while fine, offers nothing others don't know. It offers nothing as a way to process information that isn't already in prices by the actions of the very large number of market participants who use the curriculum as the glasses through which they see the world. It's the way they were taught to see the world. Hence it's in pricing. One very hard fact for craftsman to accept is the curriculum itself is widely known and hence discounted into pricing.

There is nothing wrong with learning it, but it doesn't teach you something others don't know. If professionals as a group have the same education, look at the same information, and interpret it largely the same way, where is their edge? What unique information do they think they have? The answer is most often: none. This is why, along with the media, professionals are useful in figuring out what information is priced and can be safely ignored and discarded.

Friends Don't Let Friends Be Contrarians

The media is generally wrong. Professionals are generally wrong or out to make a buck at your expense or both—and are at least fully discounted into pricing. Following the herd is fraught with peril. Does this mean you should do the exact opposite of what you hear from pundits and professionals? Should you become a classic contrarian?

Absolutely not. No, no, and no!

I am frequently called a contrarian. But I'm not—not as that term is generally used. Of course, I've been called far worse and will be, but the contrarian label happens to be wrong. Contrarianism has become increasingly popular in recent decades, rendering it priced by the market just as much as the consensus view. We are all contrarians now and none of us are. Being contrarian will get you about as far in the long term as being wholly influenced in your investment decisions by the *New York Times* and the nightly news.

The word *contrarian* implies going against the crowd—if folks are bullish, a classic contrarian becomes bearish and vice versa. If everyone thinks electing a given politician as good for stocks, the contrarian sees it as bad. If everyone thinks bird flu will make stocks fall, the contrarian sees higher prices ahead. Technically a contrarian correctly knows what everyone assumes will happen won't, but *wrongly* assumes the exact reverse will happen.

Let's wade further into this. The market is a pretty efficient discounter of all known information so, as we stated multiple times, if people tend to agree something will happen to markets it won't—something else will happen instead. But that doesn't mean the something else that happens is the exact reverse. Suppose most folks agree the market will go up. That doesn't mean it will go down. It might, but it might also go nowhere, which would also make everyone wrong. Or it might go up, but a lot more than anyone expects. That too would make everyone wrong. Over history, all those things have happened and in about equal proportions.

If you're a classic contrarian and correctly see most folks agree the market will go up, so you bet it will go down, and then it goes up but much more than most folks expected, you end up the most wrong guy in town. Being a contrarian is better than betting with the crowd, but not much, and will still have you being right something on the shy side of one time in three. Think of this like a 360 degree circle—like a compass. The consensus thinks the market will go North. Contrarians think it will go South. But it could just as well go East or West, making the crowd wrong and the contrarians wrong and the discounting mechanism work. Because those two other outcomes are less expected than the contrarian position, they actually happen more often.

The key is to remember—something else happens than what the consensus expects, but not necessarily the reverse. True contrarians these days aren't much more right than consensus followers. It is surprise that shifts demand, which drives prices. The problem is the surprise could come from any direction.

Patterns, Patterns Everywhere

To know something others don't, you must focus away from the noise. Ask what you can come to know that others can't. But how can you know about a thing you don't know?

There are patterns to be discovered everywhere. Granted, many are simply meaningless. But there is so much out there we haven't discovered yet, people will make new capital markets discoveries for many decades to come. There is no reason you shouldn't find your share. If you seek them out, there are many patterns you can discover on your own before the rest of the investing world becomes aware. And there is your edge—your basis for a market bet.

Essentially, you seek one of two things when asking Question Two. First, you want a pattern—some sort of correlation—between two or more variables people generally think are wholly unrelated. Second, you're looking for a pattern many people see but disregard, deride, or misinterpret. We show you two such examples here and more in later chapters.

The Shocking Truth about Yield Curves

You can't turn on MSNBC without hearing about interest rates. Switch on the telly and you'll find analysis on interest rates with all the gravitas and excitement of a Monday Night Football play-by-play, riveting bulls and bears alike.

> Rates rose until 11:14 A.M. before plummeting and then rocketing upward! What will the Fed do next to kill off inflation? Will homeowners be killed or thrilled? Tune in tomorrow for more inanity on the show everyone loves—*Raving About Interest Rates!*

Despite all the attention interest rates garner, investors are seeing something horribly wrong and missing a remarkable pattern and life lesson.

Before we delve into remarkable patterns and causal correlation, let's clear the air regarding interest rates. Interest rates are important. They determine the rate at which we can borrow, either short term or long term. They also determine the yield investors can get in return for locking up their liquid assets for a predetermined time period.

How often have you either heard or read, "Interest rates are falling," or "The Fed is raising interest rates," or some such news regarding interest rates (rates—plural)?

What the heck are these interest rates people keep talking about? The short rate (rate—singular) in America or elsewhere is controlled by that country's central bank—in America, the Federal Reserve, a.k.a. the "Fed." A central bank has monopolistic power over setting its country's short rate. If America's Fed feels it should reduce or increase the money supply, it raises or lowers the short rate target respectively. The Federal Open Market Committee (FOMC) meets eight times yearly to discuss if they should raise, lower, or stay the federal funds rate (also sometimes referred to as the *overnight rate* or the *short rate*) and how much the rate should move, if at all. The short rate is that at which banks lend to each other, and drives the interest rate banks pay you for deposits (savings accounts and certificates of deposit [CDs]). This is the rate (singular) investors mean to imply when they talk about the Fed monkeying around with rates. Not rates. Rate. One rate. The short rate. The fed funds rate. Singular rate.

The 10-year Treasury rate, traditionally referred to as the *long rate* isn't set by the Fed, the government, the president, or an evil conspiracy of rich, white Texans. The long rate is set by global market forces. In our contemporary global economy, traders reach across country lines to trade bonds in a global, free, and open market. The market is what sets the long rates, including not just the 10-year Treasury bond, but government bonds of other maturities—3-months, 6-months, 5-years, or 30-years, all of them. Make no mistake—though investors blather about "rates falling" and "rates rising" and "the Fed raising rates"—the short rate and long rates move independently of each other, sometimes in the same direction and other times in opposing directions. Let's say that again differently. Sometimes when the Fed raises the short rate (rate—singular), long rates rise too. Other times long rates fall. Sometimes long rates go nowhere. That is true in America and everywhere else. Shock and awe! I always tell investors to never again say, "Interest rates are going up," or "Interest rates are going down." Always in your speech and thereby your mind separate short rate movements from long rates.

The difference between the shortest-term Treasury bill (which is a very short-term rate, not the short rate) and varying longer-rate maturities can be plotted visually on a graph resulting in the infamous *yield curve*. The vertical axis plots interest rates from zero at the bottom to higher rates up top. The horizontal axis plots time from now at the left to longer-term securities stretching out to the right with the far right being 10 or 30 years into the future. A typical yield curve can look something like the hypothetical one in Figure 2.1.

Shorter-term rates usually tend to be lower than longer-term rates while longer-term rates tend to be higher in return for taking the additional risk of locking money away for longer periods. On our graph, the rates form a curve. It usually slopes upward to the right—which is a positively sloped yield curve. Positive yield curves are characterized as either *normal* or *steep*, depending on the spread between the short-term and long-term rates. Sometimes, rarely, shorter-term rates are actually higher than long-term rates. When this happens our graph slopes downward to the right and is called *inverted*. Still rare but less so than an inverted yield curve is when rates are all at about the same level—this is referred to as *flat*.

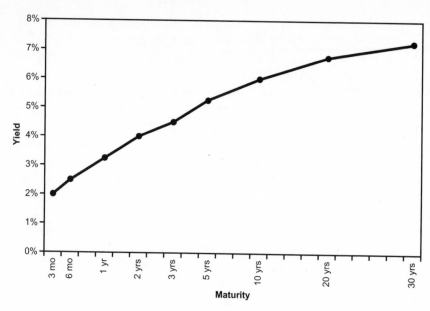

Figure 2.1 Hypothetical Yield Curve.

The Interest Rate Brouhaha

Investors have all manner of theories about fluctuations in the short rate and long rates and what it all means for the stock market. You may have heard an age-old mythology phrased as, "don't fight the Fed," which is meant to prompt you to sell stocks when the Fed raises the short rate. Nonsense—on average, stocks have done perfectly fine when the Fed raised the short rate—although not always. But nothing is "always" one way or the other. Figure 2.2 shows periods of a rising fed funds rate since 1980, and the resulting return on the S&P 500.

What you can see is the S&P 500 and a rising fed funds rate correlate pretty closely at times. I wouldn't take that to mean anything—the stock market is generally more positive than negative, so there is no surprise here. And sometimes the market was more positive than at others. But because positive markets have followed a rising short rate, "don't fight the Fed" is rendered one of those Question One myths you should ignore. This isn't to say a rising short rate is any kind of a bull or bear market indicator—but neither is a dropping short rate. There is no credible link between the short rate moving any direction and bull or bear markets. None.

For example, from 2001 to 2003, the Fed steadily cut the short rate and those who would argue you shouldn't "fight the Fed" would have owned stocks the whole time and gotten killed as the global stock market was in a sustained

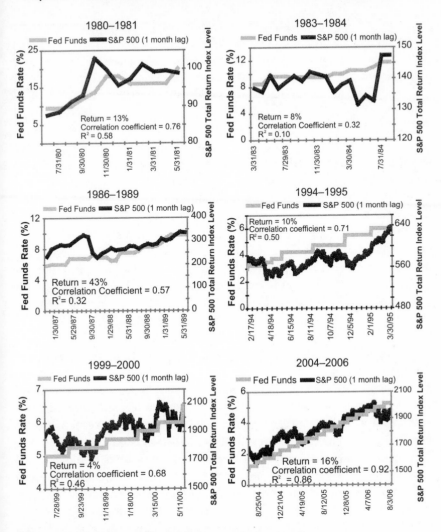

Figure 2.2 Fed Funds and the S&P 500 (1980–2006).
Source: **Global Financial Data, Bloomberg.**

bear market. In 2004 and 2005, the Fed raised the short rate steadily and the Fed-fighting fans would have avoided stocks and been on the wrong side of the market again.[3] What are they missing?

The first step in asking a successful Question Two is setting aside any unproductive fretting about concerns that don't matter. As far as the short rate moving in any one direction—it's priced, so you can set it aside. Anyone can Google the FOMC or go to the web site (http://www.federalreserve.gov/fomc/#calendars) and see when they're meeting. What's more, as the years passed after Mr. Greenspan took the helm, the FOMC became ever more transparent about when it planned to lower or raise the fed funds rate and by nearly exactly how much. By the end of Mr. Greenspan's term, market expectations for what the Fed would do and when were rarely wrong. Mr. Bernanke seemingly started out with a little verbal diarrhea and an inability to know, as Mr. Greenspan did, when to say nothing or simply mumble incoherently. (Greenspan was the all-time master of well-delivered incoherent mumbling—no one ever did it more professionally.) But Mr. Bernanke will likely learn the act before long. Nonetheless, the Fed raising the rate a quarter of a point, or even a half a point, is hardly a market-moving event when the Fed has been talking about the planned pace of rate raises for months.

Instead of focusing on short rate movements, focus on the yield curve (if you can figure out the right one to use—we'll get to that soon). Most investors will tell you a positive yield curve is good and an inverted one is bad. That's more or less true. The yield curve is normally positively sloped. A truly inverted yield curve is rare and has a reputation for being bearish.

But right now you're thinking about yield curves incorrectly, and it can hurt you. Before we can discover something new, let's check if what we believe about yield curves is correct with Question One. Is it true an inverted yield curve is a harbinger of doom? The answer is—it depends on what you mean by "yield curve," or more specifically, where. One problem behind the yield curve—I won't call it a myth so much as a misunderstanding—is folks tend to lump recessions and bear markets together. They're not the same things. You can have a bear market without a recession and vice versa, though they do tend to come together because the stock market will price in dour sentiment caused by a recession. But it doesn't always (for instance, if the recession is long feared and well priced).

A moment for two definitions: A *bear market* is a prolonged stock market downturn exceeding 20 percent. (The difference between a bear market and a correction is magnitude and duration—a correction being much shorter lived, only months, and a drop smaller than 20 percent.) By contrast, a *recession* is generally defined as two consecutive quarters of negative GDP growth, but it's tough to know if you're in a recession while it's happening since GDP numbers get heavily restated afterwards.

Two mildly negative quarters of GDP can be difficult to feel as they occur. Recessions usually aren't labeled recessions until long after they've started— sometimes not until after they're over. For example, the 1973 to 1974 bear market was followed immediately by a recession that was steep and pervasive throughout 1974, extending into 1975. It was one of the biggest of the post-World War II era yet wasn't recognized as having happened until 1975. Meanwhile, in September 1974, President Ford and his economic advisors were still calling for tax hikes to slow the economy and fight inflation. That's because no one knew we were in a recession.

While I was pretty darned young at the time, I remember the period very well. For me it was a strange time. What I remember was all the people I talked to in 1974 thought the economy was strong when later we'd learn it had been declining all year. In many ways, I wasn't very sensitive or plugged in that year. My wife and I had just lost our young daughter. I was pretty well shattered and capable of only working part-time for about six months. I didn't trust myself to have a good view of what was happening with the economy, so I spent a lot of time asking others what they thought was going on. Without intending to, I did a pretty good job of polling a big cross-section of investors and business people. Pretty much no one knew in 1974 we were already long in recession. I don't think much of anyone saw it as a recession until 1975 and by then it was mostly over—and that was a huge one. It was heavily masked by the high level of inflation then—for many firms, revenues remained strong as unit volume shrank. Still, if few saw it, note how few would see a mild economic decline.

A better measure of recession comes from the National Bureau of Economic Research (NBER; www.nber.com). Their definition of a recession captures more data, though one prominent data point is GDP, and more accurately characterizes an economic contraction. The NBER characterizes a recession thusly:

> The NBER does not define a recession in terms of two consecutive quarters of decline in real GDP. Rather, a recession is a significant decline in economic activity spread across the economy, lasting more than a few months, normally visible in real GDP, real income, employment, industrial production, and wholesale-retail sales.[4]

Historically, a steep yield curve suggests an environment in which financial institutions can lend profitably, and lending is an important driver of future economic activity. Whereas, an inverted yield curve creates a disincentive for banks to lend, thereby reducing liquidity (remember this for later in this chapter), and it's a fairly reliable predictor of recessions.

But whether an inverted yield curve causes a bear market or not depends on whether the related bad news is priced into the market. For example, in

1998 we had a flattening yield curve here in America that had people in a collective tizzy. Fear of an upcoming inverted yield curve ran rampant. That, along with the Russian ruble crisis and the supposed Long-Term Capital Management crisis was widely expected to drive stocks down, long, and hard. We had a big midyear correction but no bear market—the S&P 500 finished 1998 up 29 percent.[5] Fear of a flattening yield curve was so prevalent it lost its power to create a major decline.

Fast forward to 2000 when the yield curve actually did invert. This time, nobody paid heed. Instead, folks were lauding the "new economy" and saying, "Earnings don't matter," and "It's different this time," as they rushed off to parties celebrating the launch of SweetLobster.com and other dot-com stocks. Among other things, the recent memory of 1998 convinced them inverted yield curves didn't matter. In 2000, the yield curve, because it wasn't noted and feared—the tribe was looking elsewhere—was a harbinger of economic weakness and peaking tech stock prices that led to a three-year bear market. If everyone is talking about it, dreading it, and stocking up on canned goods because of it, then the inverted yield curve has lost its power, like anything else. If everyone skips about singing, "Tra-la-la! It's different this time," as in early 2000, then an inverted yield curve can devastate stocks.

Even with that clarified, people still see yield curves incorrectly. It's important we see them correctly because of the economic conditions an inverted yield curve implies. You think about interest rates here in America and the yield curve they engender. Why wouldn't you think about U.S. interest rates? What other interest rates would you consider? The Question Two I'm about to share can be recast over and over again into other problem-solving contexts where it works just as well. So here goes.

Question Two: I wonder if there is a yield curve more important than America's? You've probably never thought to ask yourself that question. Why on earth would you? What could possibly be more important than America? Particularly to Americans!

After all, when we look at U.S. yield curves from 30, 50, and 100 years ago, we can see some pretty compelling long-standing evidence they're predictive. Everyone knows that (or at least, plenty of folks believe it—including most reporters which means pretty much everyone). It's widely accepted that America's yield curve matters and is a somewhat reliable indicator of good and bad times ahead. Whenever the short rate has been above long-term rates, banks became disinterested to lend as aggressively. And bad things came after. Thirty years ago when America's yield curve inverted, the only way for a bank to make money lending was to lend to a worse credit risk at a higher rate than the bank's borrowing costs. This was and is risky and banks dislike doing it. In fact, the riskier the customer they need to profitably lend, the less they like it and don't want to do it. In the days of yore, America's yield curve and its camber mattered. A lot! Of course, in those days most folks didn't know the yield curve mattered.

Think Globally, Think Better

Fast forward to now—we have not just national banks but fully global banks, a wide array of derivatives and financial futures for hedging, and electronics allowing instant access to precise accounting and trade information globally. Now money flows fairly freely across borders. A global bank can borrow in one country and lend in another and hedge its currency risk all as fast as you can read this sentence. I can borrow money from an investment bank that got it from a syndicate of insurance firms in Europe who crossed the money through global banks, and I may never know the source was overseas. To me, as the borrower, it's just money. Decades back—in a world of national banks, minimal high-volume electronics for accounting and trading, no material hedging instruments, and fixed instead of flexible currency prices—it was the national yield curve that mattered. Never again! Global tendencies prevail over local ones in every country, including America, the greatest country in the world. Foreign interest rates and yield curves provide or deny liquidity heavily impacting our own. They also determine the cost effectiveness of using leverage as a means to snap up both domestic and foreign assets.

The analysis of any country's yield curve—even a country as massive as America—has become less meaningful. The right way to think about this now, something I fathomed no one had ever written about before I first did, is the GDP-weighted global yield curve. The global yield curve is representative of worldwide lending conditions. In today's world, if the global yield curve says one thing and America's says another, go with the global. America's or any other single stock market will subordinate to the global curve.

Figure 2.3 shows the global yield curve as of June 2006. The reason it's important? If a bank can borrow more cheaply in one country and lend more profitably in another, it will. Everybody, including banks and their customers, likes cheap money. Note this illustration is based on the global yield curve being GDP weighted. It makes sense intuitively that a country with a larger GDP would have greater impact on the global yield curve. It's not hard to arrive at, but a fast Internet connection helps.

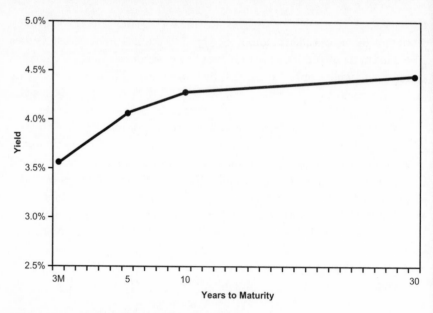

Figure 2.3   Global Yield Curve, June 2006.
Source: **International Monetary Fund, Global Financial Data, and Bloomberg.** *Disclaimer:* **If a 30-year rate was unavailable, the 10-year rate was used.**

As Global as You Can Get

In measuring global markets, the best indexes we have currently are those built by Morgan Stanley Capital International (MSCI). All MSCI indices are properly constructed, in other words, market-capitalization and float weighted, but the two we focus on most are the MSCI World Index and MSCI All Country World Index (the World Index and ACWI for brevity's sake).

The World Index represents 23 developed nations including America, Britain, Australia, Germany, and Japan. I frequently refer to the World Index when discussing market history because it provides ample historical data—and having data to measure helps decipher history. More important, it is comprehensive (representing 85 percent of money value of the world market) and each constituent is weighted by its "float"—its market liquidity. That is, a stock has little market effect if it's not trading actively. One example is Berkshire Hathaway, which isn't included in the World Index or the S&P 500 because it's so seldom traded relative to other stocks.

As a proxy for the *total* global market, another good choice is the ACWI as it also includes emerging nations. Currently 48 countries make the cut—the stocks in the World Index plus Mexico, Brazil, China, India, and so on. Because there is limited history and little data for the emerging markets, it's less useful than the World Index for measuring performance history. But it's a well-constructed index and an excellent proxy for the global market.

To find more information on these indexes and track historical performance, go to www.mscibarra.com.

In constructing the GDP-weighted yield curve, first I made a list of the countries included in the MSCI World Index—all 23. I didn't use the full list of ACWI countries because the developed nations' GDPs dwarf those of the emerging nations, so their interest rates would barely register—and accurate data on emerging nations is devilishly tough to come by. Then, I input the latest GDP for each of the countries. The GDP for all of these countries can be found at the web site for the International Monetary Fund (IMF; www.imf.org). My list looked something like this:

Country	GDP ($ in Billions)	GDP Weight (%)
Country A	50	14.3
Country B	50	14.3
Country C	250	71.4
Total	**350**	

Clearly, that is all hypothetical information, but you get the idea. To get each country's appropriate GDP weight, sum for the total world GDP and divide for each country.

Next, input the short-term and long-term interest rates. (Here I show the 3-month and the 10-year rates.) I have access to some great data sources letting me compile interest rates quickly, but anyone can find this information for free at a little place called Yahoo! Finance (http://finance.yahoo.com/international).

Country	GDP ($ in Billions)	GDP Weight (%)	Rate 3-Month	Rate 10-Year
Country A	50	14.3	3.25	6.5
Country B	50	14.3	2.5	7.2
Country C	250	71.4	4.5	4.25
Total	350			

That part is just data entry. Now, I subtract the 3-month rate from the 10-year rate to get the spread. A positive spread means a positive yield curve and a negative spread means an inverted curve.

Country	GDP ($ in Billions)	GDP Weight (%)	Rate 3-Month	Rate 10-Year	Spread
Country A	50	14.3	3.25	6.5	3.25
Country B	50	14.3	2.5	7.2	4.70
Country C	250	71.4	4.5	4.25	−0.25
Total	350				

Note Country C actually has a negative spread, meaning the yield curve has inverted slightly in that country. And Country C has a massive relative GDP. Does this spell doom for Country C? We aren't done yet. Next, multiply each country's spread by the appropriate GDP weight, and sum up the column for the global yield curve spread, as shown here:

Country	GDP ($ in Billions)	GDP Weight (%)	Rate 3-Month	Rate 10-Year	Spread	GDP-Weighted Spread
Country A	50	14.3	3.25	6.5	3.25	0.46
Country B	50	14.3	2.5	7.2	4.70	0.67
Country C	250	71.4	4.5	4.25	−0.25	−0.18
Total	350					0.95

Though Country C has a negative yield curve, the global yield curve is still positively sloped—the 10-year is above the 3-month. The global yield curve spread is 0.95—signifying a positive global yield curve—a spread from low to high of almost exactly 1 percent. You can imagine Country C, with a much bigger GDP than its friends on this imaginary index, is a country like the United States. The other countries' yield curves matter too, even to a country as big as Country C. If credit conditions are suboptimal for Country C's banks and institutions, they will borrow in other countries without feeling much of a slow-down, if at all, which is not what they would have done decades ago. (You can use the same methodology to calculate the global short-term and long-term rates if you want to create an actual global yield curve. Just multiply each country's interest rate by their GDP weighting, then sum up for the global rate. In our example, the global 3-month rate is 4.04 and the 10-year is 4.99. Subtracting the shorter-term rate, you still arrive at the same yield curve spread of 0.95.)

Therefore, an inverted U.S. yield curve by itself is no basis for immediate panic. Rather, you must look at what global rates and the global curve are doing. Figure 2.4 shows the spread between *global* short-term rates and *global* long-term rates over the past 25 years—another way of depicting the relative steepness of the global yield curve. Anything above the 0 percent line is a positive yield curve and anything below is inverted. The higher the line, the greater the spread between short-term and long-term rates, and hence the steeper the curve.

Note the global yield curve inverted in 1989, signaling the oncoming recession (a global recession—by the way). Now consider 2000. The global yield curve gets pretty flat—which is negative—but not much flatter than 1998 when the economy and stock market returns were robust. The U.S. yield curve inverted but because the global yield curve remained flattish, the U.S.

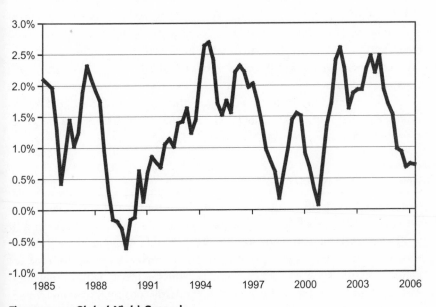

Figure 2.4 Global Yield Spread.
Source: **MSCI World Monetary Zones.**

Table 2.1 Quarterly GDP Growth

Year, Quarter	GDP Growth
2000q1	1.15%
2000q2	2.01%
2000q3	0.40%
2000q4	0.93%
2001q1	0.68%
2001q2	1.07%
2001q3	0.06%
2001q4	0.90%
2002q1	1.05%
2002q2	0.90%
2002q3	0.97%
2002q4	0.61%

Source: Bureau of Economic Analysis.

recession starting in March of 2001 was extremely short-lived, as measured by the NBER.[6]

Those of you preferring the GDP measurement of a recession may be shocked to learn during 2000, 2001, and 2002, we never—not ever—had two consecutive quarters with negative GDP growth. Heck, we didn't have one quarter of negative growth. Keep in mind, when the media runs a story they rarely go back and update you when they're wrong. Table 2.1 shows quarterly GDP growth for 2000 through 2002. The third quarter of 2001 growth was pretty darn flat, but positive nonetheless. Other than that, nary a negative-growth quarter.

Inverted, Schminverted

Starting in December 2005 and continuing through mid-2006, bears bolstered their bearish beliefs based on the flat or mildly inverted U.S. yield curve 2006 ushered in. Fair enough. We were warned repeatedly by pundits throughout 2006 to expect a recession. No recession materialized. And the global stock market was positive. The U.S economy could slow, maybe, but it wasn't about to decline. I'm amused by the CNN.com Quick Vote poll (you can find it each day on CNN.com's homepage) asking readers' opinions on whether we are in a recession. A recession isn't a matter of opinion. We are either in one or not and how CNN.com readers feel about it is simply that—how they feel. Nonetheless, whenever I check, it seems 50 percent or so of the respondents answer yes, they think we are in a recession. A better question would be, "Do you know what a recession is and how it is measured?" Leave the polls about feelings to Oprah.

America's 2006 "inverted" yield curve didn't matter much because the media made sure it was duly priced—and the global yield curve, which no one talks about, remained healthily positive. If one country's yield curve inverts while the global yield curve remains positive, there are still opportunities for businesses, institutions, private clients, and so on to continue doing business globally. Banks borrow in one country and lend in another all day long and over night with myriad risk controls never before thought of in the form of derivatives and other securities, allowing them to lay off risk. They also diversify their risk by investing in bonds in a variety of foreign countries. This is another reason the short and shallow recession of 2001 came and went without any major bank or brokerage firm imploding as happened in most earlier recessions. Banks managed their risk so they better weathered the storm.

You might still be sputtering that I stated the 2001 recession was short or shallow. It's currently fashionable to think the economy went to hell in a hand basket on or around November of 2000 coinciding with the election (or appointment, depending on your view) of George W. Bush. According to many, our economy didn't just go to hell in said hand basket, in ensuing years it hasn't much revived. Why shouldn't the recession have been deep, terrible, and lingering? After all, we experienced a huge three-year bear market.

Because the data show otherwise. Praise or vilify your president all you like over dinner with like-minded individuals, but if you're making investment decisions based on your political affiliations, you're utterly wrongheaded and will miss out on opportunities. The U.S. and global bear market of 2000 to 2003 was one of the more severe on record, but the economy survived it fairly well due largely to a positively sloping global yield curve, smart monetary policy steered by Mr. Greenspan and his peers overseas, and the tax cuts (hooray for supply side economics!). Since then, the U.S. economy has been growing at a healthy clip with GDP growing 3.4 percent in 2002, 4.7 percent in 2003, 6.9 percent in 2004, and 6.3 percent in 2005[7] (2006 hasn't quite ended as this goes to print, but growth will be positive). The global stock market returned a whopping 33 percent in 2003[8] to kick-start a new bull market. Grumpy pundits scramble for other indicators confirming their sour outlook (more of that in Chapter 3), searching for something, anything supporting their preformed biases, but try as they might, they can't counter reality.

So, an inverted U.S. yield curve doesn't signal bad times ahead if the global yield curve is positive. At worst, this condition is an argument for lightening up your U.S. holdings relative to foreign stocks but is no reason to get bearish overall. The global yield curve is a more useful leading indicator for stocks and the global economy than any single country's curve.

A recent practical example of this is Britain in 2005. As 2005 started, the United Kingdom had a yield curve at almost exactly the same level and slope as America's when 2006 started—shown in Figure 2.5. Exactly the same—flatter than a pancake!

Yet Britain experienced neither a bear market nor a recession in 2005. Its economy remained strong. Its market rose—lagging the world—but rose nonetheless. A flat or inverted single-country curve in an overall positive yield curve world is an argument for underweighting that country. Nothing worse! (That is another simple, fathomable feature that has been unfathomable to almost everyone. You can put it to use immediately in your own portfolio.)

To my knowledge, until I did it, no one ever constructed a GDP-weighted global yield curve to summarize global credit conditions. This is a simple and perfect example of a Question Two—fathoming what is unfathomable to most people: The global, not national, yield curve is causal today. And yet fathom-

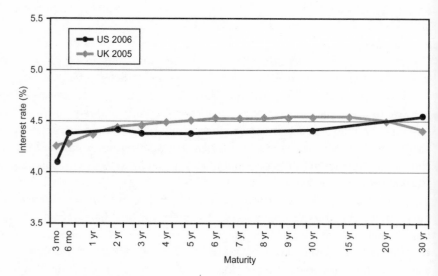

Figure 2.5   2005 U.K. Yield Curve versus 2006 U.S. Yield Curve.
Source: **Bloomberg.**

ing what is unfathomable to most people isn't complicated, prohibitively theoretical, or hard to grasp. It's actually pretty darned basic and simple.

One really neat point mentioned earlier is you can extend this principle to many other phenomena. It's the global budget deficit that matters (or doesn't) to global GDP and markets. It's the global level of inflation that will drive inflation in America and elsewhere. You can use the same methodology I just described to create a GDP-weighted global money supply and watch its growth. Why? Because it's global money creation that will drive global inflation, not what any single country does. You know you worry about trade deficits and current account deficits. By definition, these simply disappear on a global level, but we cover how to think about that later. You can apply global thinking to so many things that the age-old but seldom applied notion of "Think global, act local" is a truly valuable saw—one way ahead of its time.

What the Yield Curve Is Trying to Tell You

Now you're thinking about yield curves correctly and can begin looking for other remarkable patterns and another basis for a market bet. Another Question Two: What is it the yield curve can tell you about stocks that no one else knows? By now you know (or you should know if you don't) all investment styles cycle in and out of favor. We talk more about why in later chapters, but you've probably seen something akin to Table 2.2, which shows changes in leadership among equity sizes and styles.

What Table 2.2 shows is no one size or style leads for all time. More noticeably, no predictable pattern exists to indicate which size or style will lead next. Or is there? Can you know if and when growth will give leadership over to value and cycle back again? And if so, wouldn't that be a Question Two unfathomable? Who wouldn't want to know that? If you could predict which style would lead next and when the change would take place, you would know something others don't—giving you a basis for a big and beautiful bet. And you'd know it in time to buy low and sell high.

Look at Table 2.2 again. If you buy the previous year's winner, you very often end up with this year's loser—except for an unusual lengthy period of leadership in the late 1990s for large cap U.S stocks. Or course, you were then rewarded for your heat chasing with a long period of miserable performance starting in 2000 (as I said, styles pretty much are never hot for 10 years). If a pattern existed indicating when to change equity categories, how could all the smart people who've been investing through all these years have missed it?

Table 2.2   No Style Is Best for All Time

1986	1987	1988	1989	1990	1991	1992	1993	1994	1995
EAFE Growth 71%	EAFE Value 31%	EAFE Value 31%	US Large Growth 36%	US Long Bond 6%	US Small Growth 51%	US Small Value 29%	EAFE Value 40%	EAFE Value 11%	US Large Growth 38%
EAFE Value 69%	EAFE Growth 71%	US Small Value 29%	US Large Cap 32%	US Large Growth 0%	US Small Value 42%	US Large Value 11%	EAFE Growth 71%	EAFE Growth 71%	US Large Cap 38%
US Long Bond 25%	US Large Growth 6%	EAFE Growth 71%	US Large Value 26%	US Large Cap -3%	US Large Growth 38%	US Long Bond 8%	US Small Value 24%	US Large Growth 3%	US Large Value 37%
US Large Value 22%	US Large Cap 5%	US Large Value 22%	US Small Growth 20%	US Large Value -7%	US Large Cap 30%	US Small Growth 8%	US Large Value 19%	US Large Cap 1%	US Long Bond 32%
US Large Cap 19%	US Large Value 4%	US Small Growth 20%	US Long Bond 18%	US Small Growth -17%	US Large Value 23%	US Large Cap 8%	US Long Bond 18%	US Large Value -1%	US Small Growth 31%
US Large Growth 14%	US Long Bond -3%	US Large Cap 17%	EAFE Value 15%	EAFE Value -21%	US Long Bond 19%	US Large Growth 5%	US Small Growth 13%	US Small Value -2%	US Small Value 26%
US Small Value 7%	US Small Value -7%	US Large Growth 12%	US Small Value 12%	US Small Value -22%	EAFE Growth 71%	EAFE Value -11%	US Large Cap 10%	US Small Growth -2%	EAFE Value 12%
US Small Growth 4%	US Small Growth -10%	US Long Bond 10%	EAFE Growth 71%	EAFE Growth 71%	EAFE Value 11%	EAFE Growth 71%	US Large Growth 2%	US Long Bond -8%	EAFE Growth 71%

Source: Thomson Financial Datastream, Ibbotson Analyst.

Pretty easily.

We've already shown you an illustration similar to Figure 2.6 on page 67—demonstrating not the global yield curve but its spread between the short-term and long-term rates. But Figure 2.6 adds on top relative performance of value versus growth stocks. For example, in 1987 after the yield curve steepened significantly to nearly two and a half percentage points of spread—value stocks assumed leadership and out-performed growth for the rest of the decade by an impressive 28 percent. Then the yield curve flattened and inverted, and growth took over leadership until the yield curve steepened again. The pattern just repeats itself—sometimes with longer periods of leadership and even more decisive out-performance—55 percent and 76 percent! Investors who fret over not fighting the Fed or worry about interest rates being too high or too low miss this remarkable pattern.

Figure 2.6 demonstrates that after the global yield curve steepens significantly, value stocks outperform growth stocks. After the curve flattens, growth takes over leadership from value. It's uncanny how the two shift. The change in the yield curve tends to happen abruptly, as does the change in style leadership. The difference in performance between the styles is significant—we're

1996	1997	1998	1999	2000	2001	2002	2003	2004	2005
S Large Growth 24%	US Large Growth 37%	US Large Growth 42%	US Small Growth 43%	US Small Value 23%	US Small Value 14%	US Long Bond 18%	US Small Growth 49%	EAFE Value 25%	EAFE Value 14%
S Large Cap 23%	US Large Cap 33%	US Large Cap 29%	EAFE Growth 71%	US Long Bond 21%	US Long Bond 4%	US Small Value -11%	US Small Value 46%	US Small Value 22%	EAFE Growth 71%
S Large Value 22%	US Small Value 32%	EAFE Growth 71%	US Large Growth 28%	US Large Value 6%	US Small Growth -9%	EAFE Value -16%	EAFE Value 46%	EAFE Growth 71%	US Long Bond 8%
S Small Value 21%	US Small Value 30%	EAFE Value 18%	EAFE Value 25%	US Large Value -3%	US Large Value -12%	EAFE Growth 71%	EAFE Growth 71%	US Large Value 16%	US Large Value 6%
S Small Growth 11%	US Long Bond 16%	US Large Value 15%	US Large Cap 21%	US Large Cap -9%	US Large Cap -12%	US Large Value -21%	US Large Value 32%	US Small Growth 14%	US Large Cap 5%
EAFE Value 9%	US Small Growth 13%	US Long Bond 13%	US Large Value 13%	US Large Growth -22%	US Large Growth -13%	US Large Cap -22%	US Large Cap 29%	US Large Cap 11%	US Small Value 5%
EAFE Growth 71%	EAFE Growth 71%	US Small Growth 1%	US Small Value -1%	US Small Growth -22%	EAFE Value -18%	US Large Growth -24%	US Large Growth 26%	US Long Bond 9%	US Small Growth 4%
S Long Bond -1%	EAFE Value 2%	US Small Value -6%	US Long Bond -9%	EAFE Growth 71%	EAFE Growth 71%	US Small Growth -30%	US Long Bond 1%	US Large Growth 6%	US Large Growth 3%

not talking about a few percentage points. If you can get the change in leadership right, you see serious out-performance based on one of the most basic market differentiators, namely which half of the market based on growth versus value will lead. Simply put, the global yield curve tells you when to switch from value to growth and back. After it has gone completely flat, you head into a period of growth stock dominance. After it gets very steep, you switch into value stock dominance. After it flattens again, it's time to tilt to growth again.

GROWTH AND VALUE—WHAT'S THE DIFFERENCE?

What's growth? What's value? How do you know?

Check the definition of "growth stock" and "value stock" in an investment dictionary or any number of online sources and you'll find various descriptions peppered with incorrect assumptions. Example—growth stocks may be described as having "better returns" but "higher beta," or in other words, more risk. Value stocks may be described as "less risky,"

(continued)

giving you "lower returns" but "greater stability." Nonsense. Neither growth nor value as a category is better or has much different risk characteristics over ultra-long periods. But they cycle in and out of favor. At times, growth steadily beats value, like 1994 through 2000. At other times, value steadily beats growth, like 2000 through 2006.[9] So you need to know how to identify a stock as growth or value.

Pretty much everyone agrees growth stocks have higher P/Es and value stocks lower. But higher or lower than what? Some professionals pick an arbitrary level and stick with it. It's better to be guided by your benchmark (the index you compare yourself to). Here's how.

Find the P/E of your benchmark—let's use the S&P 500 to start. You can find the current P/E for the S&P 500 on any web site you use to find financial data. Just be sure to use the "Forward P/E," not the historical, since we care what happens going forward, not what just got done happening—capiche? For reference's sake, the Forward P/E for the S&P 500 in June of 2006 was 13.6.[10]

Now you can count stocks with a P/E higher than 13.6 as "growth" and those lower as "value." Stocks close to the benchmark P/E are basically, for you, style neutral. Keep that in mind because your benchmark's average P/E will bounce around a bit. The more of a growth bias you want, the higher you need your portfolio's average P/E to be relative to your benchmark's P/E. Same for value but in reverse. Also, there may very well be times when you want to be essentially style neutral. It's also important to remember some companies may temporarily have no earnings and no P/E—then the P/E doesn't tell you if they are growth or value stocks. For these, you need some other metric like the price-to-book ratio or the price-to-sales ratio. You can use the same methodology with either of these ratios and find similar results.

As you do your own analysis, good proxies for measuring U.S. style performance are the Russell and Wilshire indexes. Both have growth and value specific indexes, each in a variety of sizes (small, mid, and large cap), so you can compare apples to apples. Information and historical performance for both of these index families are at www.russell.com/us/indexes and www.wilshire.com/indexes. The people at MSCI produce international growth and value indexes as well. Find those indexes by going to www.mscibarra.com, and selecting either Value or Growth from the Style drop-down box. Now you can compare historical data for these indexes against your own benchmark to see when growth or value has led or lagged.

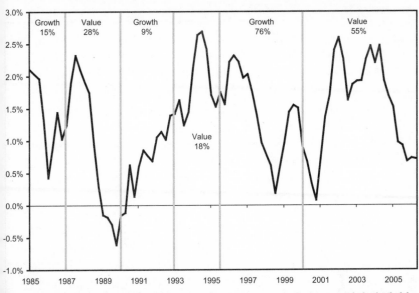

Figure 2.6   Global Growth and Value Performance Relative to Global Yield Curve Position.
Source: **Bloomberg, Global Financial Data, IMF, Thomson Financial Datastream.**

Unless you've been to a seminar given by me or my firm, you've probably never seen yield curve spread and performance of value and growth stocks overlaid this way. Nobody sees this pattern, and yet, the relationship is remarkable. And for good reason.

You see the correlation between the yield curve flattening and growth taking over leadership, and vice versa—but so what? As said before, there are many existing patterns that don't necessarily mean anything. Before you go half-cocked and make serious portfolio changes based on a chart with correlation, you must check your pattern for causality. Without a *causal* correlation, you have no basis for a bet. If something is causal—if something happens *because* of something else—then they're always correlated. But two correlated variables won't always be causal. When you took statistics in school, they told you high correlation doesn't necessarily mean causality but causality does mean high correlation. The essence of a Question Two is looking first for high correlations and then seeing if you can justify causality tied to simple economics.

Two events can show correlation by accident or coincidence (by definition, the same thing). This is the gambler's fallacy in reverse—every time you flip a coin, you have a 50/50 chance of getting heads, no matter if the previous 100 flips resulted in heads. Just because you have evidence of Y happening with some regularity after you observe Q a number of times, you can't bet it will happen again, no more than you have better odds on the 101st flip being tails.

If Y happens to follow Q often, but you can't sort out good economics behind the correlation, go back to the drawing board. There might be something else happening when you observe Q that is really causing Y, and you must figure out what the mystery variable is (X, perhaps?) before you start placing bets. Or you might simply have found a statistical freak. Statistics can be freaky. If you have correlation without causality, you have nothing. Your discoveries must make basic, economic sense before they are useful.

What if you measure Q seeming to cause Y and, what's more, it makes sense? But you observe Q leading to Y only 70 percent or 80 percent of the time. Should you abandon this tool? No way! In investing, 100 percent correlation never happens. There are so many market pressures, so many moving maybes—if you wait for 100 percent correlation, you will never make a market bet. If something is correlated 70 percent of the time, that's a biggie. You can worry about the other 30 percent later. Often in life, Y is caused 70 percent by Q and 30 percent by X or X+L and is simply multifactorial. Still a 70 percent correlation with good causality is heck-a-profitable. If you could bet steadily winning 70 percent of the time, you would blow away all professional investors in no time. All! If you can show Q causes Y with some regularity and it makes economic sense, when no one else has a clue what causes Y—you have found the Holy Grail.

So, does the change in yield curve spread correlating to whether value or growth leads the market link to any basic economics? Absolutely! It stems from how corporations raise capital and how much incentive banks have to lend that capital.

The core business of banking is and has always been borrowing short-term money as the basis upon which they make long-term loans. In the industry vernacular, it has always been phrased, "Borrowing short and lending long." The difference between the short rate and the long rates is the bank's gross operating profit margin on the next loan it makes. The steeper the curve, the greater the profit banks reap on lending. As the curve flattens, banks make less of a profit on the next loan. If the curve goes inverted, banks don't feel much incentive to lend at all, which is why an inverted curve can be so bearish. Recall, banks must seek riskier loans to make a profit in this environment, and banks don't like writing loans likely to default. The yield curve spread determines banking system propensity or eagerness to lend.

If you are a bank CEO and faced with a steep yield curve, and have any sense at all, you are doing all you can to encourage your loan officers to lend. When the curve gets very steep, they get very eager. When it gets very flat, they get less eager. It isn't any more complicated than that in figuring out their eagerness to lend.

Value companies raise capital, by and large, through the use of debt. They leverage themselves to acquire other companies, build a plant, expand their product line, increase their marketing reach, or what-have-you. When the yield curve is steep and banks have an additional incentive to lend, they are more prone to lend to value companies (we see why in a moment), and value companies and their stockholders benefit.

On the flip side, growth companies raise capital, by and large, through the issuance of new stock. They can borrow money too, and do, but they can also issue stock and it's usually cheaper for them to issue stock (again, we see why soon). When the yield curve flattens, banks have less of an incentive to lend because their profit margin gets skinnier on the next loan—or disappears entirely; but investment bankers still have a terrific incentive to help growth companies issue new stock because initial public offerings (IPOs) and new stock issuances are supremely profitable undertakings for them. Consequently, in this environment, value companies begin to fall out of favor and growth takes over leadership. The growth companies now have ample opportunities to raise capital to fuel higher earnings just when the value companies can't raise capital easily.

On the Flip Side, Let's Flip It

Again, when you can't fathom something, reframing or flipping it around so you see it differently often helps. Let's flip P/Es to see this right. You know growth stocks typically have higher P/Es than value stocks, by definition. And they have loftier public images as great firms. Suppose some growth stock has a P/E of 50 and some value stock has a P/E of 5. You know the 50 is really $50 of price divided by $1 of earnings and the P/E of 5 is $5 of price divided by $1 of earnings. Now flip them into an E/P and you have the *earnings yield* we discussed in Chapter 1. The 50 flipped becomes 1 divided by 50 or 2 percent. If the company's accounting is accurate, and its earnings are stable, that 2 percent is effectively its after-tax cost (remember the P/E was after tax so the E/P is too) of raising expansion capital by selling stock—a very low cost compared to borrowing long-term debt at corporate bond rates. The company with the P/E of 5 is an E/P of 1 divided by 5, or 20 percent—a very high after-tax cost of raising expansion capital compared to borrowing long-term debt through bonds.

When companies borrow, the rate they pay is a pretax rate too, so the company with the P/E of 50 (E/P of 2 percent) can make its own earnings-per-share rise by simply selling stock at 2 percent and buying a 5 percent Treasury note and picking up the after-tax spread as profit. The firm with a P/E of 5 (E/P of 20 percent) can make its earnings-per-share rise by simply borrowing 10-year money at 7 percent (if that is what the going rate is) and buying back its own stock with a 20 percent after-tax return. It picks up the after-tax spread as free money. The growth company will be prone, whenever it can, to raise expansion capital cheaply by selling stock. The value company won't; it will want to get expansion capital by borrowing money to the extent it can.

Let's flip and reframe again. Instead of being a corporate borrower or stock issuer, you are a bank loan officer. You've got four loan customers:

1. Microsoft, a famous big-cap growth company,
2. Ford, a famous big-cap value company,
3. Geewhizatronics, a not-famous small-cap growth company, and
4. Local County Cement, a not-famous small-cap value stock.

These four are your only customers, and each one has borrowed the same amount from you. Pretend these loans were issued so you could call them back in, forcing the borrower to pay them off whenever you want. One day your bank president comes in and tells you something goofy has happened with the credit markets and it's no longer profitable for the bank to have so many loans. He tells you to pull in 25 percent of your loan base by cutting off one of your customers—your choice. Who do you cut off?

Well you don't cut off Microsoft, generally regarded as one of the world's greatest companies. If you did, all the good old boys at the Loan Officers Club-and-Pub would laugh you under the bar. You don't much want to cut off Ford either. It isn't quite up to Microsoft's image for quality but it's a pretty big name—although you've heard Ford isn't doing so well recently and Toyota has overtaken them in sales—still you don't want to cut them off. Cut off Geewhizatronics? I don't think so. Some local folks have a rumor it could become the very next Microsoft. If you cut them off, again, the good old boys will be laughing you under the bar when (if?) Geewhiz actually whizzes. Nope! The one you cut off is small-cap value Local County Cement. Doggy, stodgy, been-there-forever—but if construction dries up their profits do too. No seeming growth potential. This decision is easy. You keep Microsoft, Ford, and Geewhizatronics, and cut off Local County Cement. The good old boys won't laugh at you for that. They never think about Local County Cement other than when laughing at them. They won't even let the CEO of Local County Cement into their Club-and-Pub.

In effect, what have we done? We've deprived capital from the value side, primarily smaller value though you were tempted to ding the big boy—Ford (and maybe you will next time)—but not growth. Local County Cement had been planning to expand, but now must scrap those plans and hence its stock tanks. Looking forward it can be nothing but defensive and must live mainly from cash flow without access to any expansion capital other than what it produces through profits. Meanwhile, growth stocks can get expansion capital by selling stock since they have high P/Es—low E/Ps. They keep growing and looking good to investors. In fact, the high P/E firm can grow right then and there, if it wants, by selling some cheap stock and launching the expansion into cement that Local County Cement previously intended, eating its lunch.

Flip It Again

Fast forward three years. You've been living happily with your three loan customers, but one day your boss walks in and says something goofy happened in the credit markets and now he (I say "he" because historically big bank presidents are male—something genetic in the industry I'm sure) needs you to expand your loan portfolio. He tells you the yield curve, whatever that is, is really steep and the bank will make fat gross operating profit margins on the next loan you make. "So go out there and make a loan, Johnson," he orders you. "My name isn't Johnson," you mutter to yourself, but nonetheless you call Microsoft. They don't want to borrow any more money because they just floated some stock. Ford has already borrowed beyond what a drunken sailor on leave could consume and is figuratively lying unconscious on the factory floor. Geewhizatronics just laughs at you because they are planning an upcoming stock offering at 1200 times future earnings and don't want to be seen talking to a banker for fear it could hurt their offering.

And suddenly you get this weird idea. There was that local cement company: Local County Cement. You call them and offer to lend them money. The CEO falls out of his chair because no one has spoken to him in years. He calls downstairs to the basement asking for Ed and says, "Ed! Remember those expansion plans we put on the back shelf a few years ago? Find 'em, dust 'em off, and get 'em up here. There's some crazy banker wants to lend us money and suddenly we can grow just like we're Geewhizatronics."

Actually, Local County Cement can't grow like Geewhizatronics might, but it can become more growth-like with financing than without it. Hence, the swing in the yield curve determines when the bank lends to Local County Cement and when it won't, and when the stock will be priced more like a growth company or more like dead meat—or old, cold concrete.

This anecdote shows the simple economics behind why shifts in the global yield curve, which reflect banking system propensity to lend, define when growth stocks and value stocks alternate in leading and lagging the market. Pretty simple.

Now you have a correlation pattern supported by economics—very funda
mental. What's more, your fellow investors aren't thinking about how the
yield curve impacts corporations in their quest for capital and how that, in
turn, impacts market returns. They're probably not even thinking about the
yield curve correctly to begin with.

The answer to this Question Two gives you a rational basis for a market
bet—understanding when growth and value will cycle in and out of favor
How does this impact you and the decisions you make? Easy! Look at the
yield curve in America and interest rates around the globe. We've gone from
a pretty steep yield curve to a much flatter yield curve in a short time. Value
stocks have led globally all while the yield curve was steep and as it flat
tened—which we know is normal. As I write, America's yield curve is slightly
inverted, though the global curve is slightly positive. Keep an eye on global
rates. They will let you know when growth should take over leadership. It
could be very soon. Might not! When that global curve is completely flat, start
jettisoning value stocks in favor of growth to capitalize on what you know
that others don't.

The Presidential Term Cycle

How changes in yield curve spread impact the growth versus value trade off is
easy to see with data and makes sense. No advanced degree in finance or statistics required—just publicly available data and an Excel spreadsheet, or even
some graph paper. As we learned in Chapter 1, if you need fancy engineered
equations, your hypothesis is probably wrong.

But what if you discover a pattern that is tough to prove with data
though it makes tremendous sense? And what if the pattern is fairly predictable? Here is an example. Table 2.3 shows presidents going back to 1925
and the subsequent annual return on the S&P 500 (which goes back to
1926). By splitting the first two years of the presidential term from the last
two years, you can see, for the most part, the last two years of the presidential cycle tend to be positive.

Take a pencil and put a line through 1929 through 1932. You will remember these years as the beginning of the Great Depression, a period unlikely to
be repeated any time soon due to extensive banking and market reform and
much knowledge we didn't have back then about how economies and central
banking work. Otherwise, you get only three other negative years in the back
halves of presidents' terms. Negative a scant 0.9 percent, 1939 was not such a
bad year.[11] Even 1940 was negative just 10 percent.[12] Those years being nega-

Table 2.3 The Presidential Term Anomaly

President	1st Year		2nd Year		3rd Year		4th Year	
Coolidge	1925	n.a.	1926	11.6%	1927	37.5%	1928	43.6%
Hoover	1929	-8.4%	1930	-24.9%	1931	-43.3%	1932	-8.2%
FDR - 1st	1933	54.0%	1934	-1.4%	1935	47.7%	1936	33.9%
FDR - 2nd	1937	-35.0%	1938	31.1%	1939	-0.4%	1940	-9.8%
FDR - 3rd	1941	-11.6%	1942	20.3%	1943	25.9%	1944	19.8%
FDR / Truman	1945	36.4%	1946	-8.1%	1947	5.7%	1948	5.5%
Truman	1949	18.8%	1950	31.7%	1951	24.0%	1952	18.4%
Ike - 1st	1953	-1.0%	1954	52.6%	1955	31.6%	1956	6.6%
Ike - 2nd	1957	-10.8%	1958	43.4%	1959	12.0%	1960	0.5%
Kennedy / Johnson	1961	26.9%	1962	-8.7%	1963	22.8%	1964	16.5%
Johnson	1965	12.5%	1966	-10.1%	1967	24.0%	1968	11.1%
Nixon	1969	-8.5%	1970	4.0%	1971	14.3%	1972	19.0%
Nixon / Ford	1973	-14.7%	1974	-26.5%	1975	37.2%	1976	23.8%
Carter	1977	-7.2%	1978	6.6%	1979	18.4%	1980	32.4%
Reagan - 1st	1981	-4.9%	1982	21.4%	1983	22.5%	1984	6.3%
Reagan - 2nd	1985	32.2%	1986	18.5%	1987	5.2%	1988	16.8%
Bush	1989	31.5%	1990	-3.2%	1991	30.6%	1992	7.6%
Clinton - 1st	1993	10.0%	1994	1.3%	1995	37.5%	1996	22.9%
Clinton - 2nd	1997	33.3%	1998	28.6%	1999	21.0%	2000	-9.1%
Bush, G.W.	2001	-11.9%	2002	-22.1%	2003	28.7%	2004	10.9%
Bush, G.W.	2005	4.9%	2006	?				
Median		2.0%		5.3%		23.4%		13.8%
Number of Positive Years		10		12		18		17
Number of Negative Years		10		8		2		3
Average		7.3%		8.3%		20.1%		13.4%

Source: Global Financial Data.

tive ought not shock you since the market was discounting the beginning of World War II. The year 2000 was pretty odd as well and in many ways is the exception that proves the rule. After the terrific bull run of the 1990s, we experienced the tech bubble bursting—plus late in the year a near constitutional crisis surrounding the presidential election. It was the first time in modern times we had a president who hadn't won a majority of the popular vote.

Actually, that is widely stated but untrue. We often have a president elected without a majority of the popular vote. Al Gore, despite media commentary to the contrary, didn't win a majority of the popular vote (48 percent) in 2000.[13] Bill Clinton never did because of minority candidates like Ross Perot and later Ralph Nader.[14] Abraham Lincoln didn't win a majority of the 1860 popular vote—he only got 39.8 percent.[15] But he did in 1864 with 55 percent.[16] What people mean is Al Gore got more votes than George Bush. Neither won a majority of the popular vote in 2000, and they are in good company with John Kennedy in 1960 and Richard Nixon in 1968.[17]

What they mean—what was different in 2000—wasn't the lack of a winner by majority vote, but that Gore, who won the most popular votes, didn't win the Electoral College—which is the end game. That launched us into uncharted territory to determine the election's outcome as Gore challenged the Florida vote in court for its precious electoral votes. The challenge created uncertainty and increased the weirdness of year-end 2000. Markets hate uncertainty. To show you the effect of that year-end, on September 1, 2000, the S&P 500 was up 4.3 percent for the year.[18] The negative year is from the election uncertainty in the last quarter—leading 2000 to be one of the very few fourth years of any president's term that has ever been negative.

What we can say is, barring events of epic proportions, the back halves of presidential terms are periods when the stock market hasn't wanted to have negative returns. It's also obvious, as you look at these data, the third year of a president's term has been the best—most uniformly positive with the highest average returns.

All else being equal, the back halves of presidents' terms have been quite positive. Knowing this can alleviate some anxiety as you attempt to forecast. You should be otherwise slightly biased toward bullish in the last two years in an election cycle. This is widely disregarded (and therefore, powerful) information you can put to use immediately as this book first appears in 2007—the third year of Bush's last term.

By contrast, market risk tends to concentrate in the first two years of a president's term, where yet another pattern emerges. When you do get a negative year in the first half, you usually (although not always) tend to get only one. If the first year is negative, the second year is usually not, and vice versa. While you do occasionally get two positive years in the first half, two negatives in a row are rare. Again, ignore 1929 and 1930 as Great Depression years and

---

THE GREAT DEPRESSION

It's important to note that our Great Depression was part of a global great depression and most historians miss that point endlessly. What you normally hear is the Great Depression was punishment rained on the United States for the Fed's banking missteps, individual and corporate greedy excesses, and Hoover's commitment to a laissez faire government. While a great many mistakes were made in America, economic historians tend to paint our Great Depression as if it weren't part of a bigger and therefore largely unavoidable global phenomenon.

For a whole series of discussions on the Great Depression as global phenomena, see my second book, the *Wall Street Waltz*.

therefore an anomaly. You also get a second negative year during Nixon's trun-cated second term, but that was a pretty darned weird time too.

You might find this bit of forecasting technology an assault on your intelli-gence. "Why, it's patently absurd and overtly simplistic," you might say. It is simple, and that's why it's so great. This pattern isn't hidden away, cloaked in mystery. It's right out there, in the open, plain and easy to see. You've probably already heard of the presidential term cycle—it is a term that is well-known and censured as voodoo (although no one uses it like I'm prescribing). If everyone thought it a nifty tool, it would have become priced into the market and lost all its power. As long as folks continue to sneer at it, you know you have an edge.

Nobody Can Predict What a Genuine Phony Will Do

Strong trends not commonly observed or accepted are powerful. Even so, this one is a little hard to prove with raw data statistically—calendar years don't work that way. But it makes tremendous economic sense. The market dislikes nothing so much as uncertainty; and a new president, even a newly reelected president, presents the market with tremendous uncertainty. Among poli-tics, the president is the big tic—the one who ultimately knows how to tic off the fewest people while getting elected and tic off the most afterwards. If a poli-tic is a phony, one capable of winning a presidential election is a genuine and most capable phony. Nobody can predict what a genuine phony will do next.

George W. Bush thoughtfully violated a basic rule in 2002 all presidents have known—their party almost always loses some relative power to the opposi-tion party in Congress during the mid-term elections. Bush was the first Repub-lican president in more than 100 years to have his party gain seats in the mid-terms.[19] A president knows his party is likely to lose relative power to the opposition in the mid-terms, so whatever is the most onerous legislation he would hope to pass, the hardest to get through Congress, the landmark of his presidency, he must try to get it passed in the first two years. If he can't get it leg-islated then, he certainly wouldn't be able to do so in the back half of his term.

The biggest and ugliest attempts at redistribution of wealth, property rights, and regulatory status (which is property rights) almost always have oc-curred in the first half of presidents' terms. Fundamental to capitalism itself and capital markets stability is faith in the stability of property rights. We often take property rights for granted because America has the best, most perfected, and most stable system of property rights in the world's history. It is a key part, going back to George Mason's fundamental force on the founding fathers, lead-ing to America being so great a nation. Anything threatening the sanctity of property rights raises risk aversion and scares the heck out of capital markets.

In the first year of his term, a president is in his honeymoon, eager to spend the political capital he earned during the campaign. Rosy-cheeked, with a sparkle in his eye and his shiny family at his side, the new guy usually shoots out the gate trying to get his toughest stuff passed—this being the infamous first 100 days of a president's term when he lays out his agenda. The threat of those shifts in property rights or wealth re-distribution lead to higher risk aversion and the first halves of presidents' terms being perfect loam for bear markets to propagate in. Hence, the first half of a president's term is generally marked with a busy legislative calendar and a disproportionate amount of our bear markets. This doesn't mean the president's proposed legislation succeeds, mind you, but that he makes a go at it. And there is the risk he gets his agenda passed and the markets don't like that risk.

Remember after Bill Clinton's 1992 election, he raised taxes in 1993 though he had promised in his campaign to cut taxes, and then in 1994, he threatened to nationalize health care (a shift in property rights). All typical first-half politico-tomfoolery of a genuine phony. Other times, as with President Bush, there was never a material legislative agenda proposed at all—not for either term. When there is, it's the grist of a disproportionate amount of our bear markets.

Any new proposed legislation implies potential change and a reapportionment of your money and property rights. No matter what the government decides to do, no matter how wonderful the new programs may sound, no matter how incontrovertible the benefit is—new legislation means money and rights get shifted around. Low cost prescriptions for the poor and elderly! Who could see that as bad? Stiffer penalties for society's worst offenders—pedophiles, rapists, and puppy stranglers? Sign me up! Free ponies for all children? You'd have to be a monster to oppose that! Whatever it is, Uncle Sam takes money or rights from one group, fusses around with it, and passes whatever is left to yet another group. We already know we hate losses more than we like gains. The group on the losing end of the transfer hates losing much more than those on the winning end of the transfer like it. Those not party to the transfer watch it transpire and think they've just seen a mugging. Markets view redistribution of wealth or property rights like witnessing a mugging. It causes fear beyond the size of the action itself because it makes all witnesses realize they could be mugged next. Consequently, the market can be weak somewhere in the first two years because the market doesn't like politically forced change.

By the third and fourth years, we know our president. He may be a poli-tic, and we may dislike him, but he is our time-proven bloodsucker. There's not much left to surprise—we think we know what he is up to, what his agenda is, and how capable he is of getting anything done (or not, and sometimes *not* is a pretty good thing in a world that doesn't like forced political change). Moreover, presidents tend to avoid any potentially controversial legislation in the back half of their terms because they are either trying to get reelected themselves or they're just tired and hanging on, which is often true in a president's seventh and eighth year.

A particularly good poli-tic will hang back in his third year, get little done, and at election time blame his administration's ineffectiveness on poli-tics from the opposing party. "I could have gotten you the free ponies I promised," he might intone, "had it not been for those uncooperative Senators from that other damned party who opposed me! So get rid of those losers, and vote for these other guys who support me, and next time I'll get you your free ponies." Quiet legislative years lead to happier markets. (They almost never lead to free ponies.)

We're not done with presidential terms yet. Ask yourself, what else is going on no one notices or lends any credence? We know the first two years are where most of the market risk will likely be. Is there anything particularly remarkable about the first half of a second term for a reelected president? Ignoring all the first and the single presidential terms, see what patterns you can find in Table 2.4.

Table 2.4 Incumbents Uninhibited

Won Re-Election			1st Year of Second Term S&P 500	2nd Year of Second Term S&P 500
Election Year	Party	President		
1900	R	McKinley	19.8%	4.9%
1904	R	Roosevelt, T.	19.7%	6.8%
1916	D	Wilson	-25.3%	25.6%
1924	R	Coolidge	29.5%	11.6%
1936	D	Roosevelt, F.	-35.0%	31.1%
1948	D	Truman	18.8%	31.7%
1956	R	Eisenhower	-10.8%	43.4%
1964	D	Johnson	12.5%	-10.1%
1972	R	Nixon / Ford	-14.7%	-26.5%
1984	R	Reagan	32.2%	18.5%
1996	D	Clinton	33.3%	28.6%
2004	R	Bush	4.9%	

Source: Global Financial Data.

Again, you tend not to get two negatives in a row, except for that screwy Nixon. But when you don't get a negative year, you tend to get a big positive year. Positive years in the first half of a reelected president's term have averaged 21 percent and 23 percent respectively[20]—big booming positive years. These years typically are either negative or up super big—extreme one way or the other—sort of barbell-like returns. Being on the right side of the market is more important and most keen in its impact during these years. This is a good example of looking beyond averages into what makes up the averages. The historic averages of first and second years of presidents' terms are below average. But within those averages, you get a very wide spread between nasty years and pretty great years. Averages can be very deceiving. And in this regard, your most recently and therefore most emotionally felt experience from 2005 causes you to otherwise not notice the pattern. The small positive return in 2005 is out of character for the first year of a president's reelected term when they tend to be negative or very big. In 2009, I'd bet on negative or huge.

(Technically, Teddy Roosevelt wasn't really reelected in 1904 since he wasn't elected in the first place—same for Truman in 1948 and Johnson in 1964. But I'm not really sure that matters to the phenomenon.)

Should you abandon all other forecasting efforts and let your political calendar be your one determining factor in your allocation of stocks, bonds, and cash? No! That would be beyond super silly! While the presidential term cycle is a trend and makes absolute socioeconomic sense, keep in mind there are many other market forces at work, including all the ones that are outside of America. For example, the U.S. markets correlate to foreign markets in our increasingly globalized economy. Foreign forces can and will impact America. Never assume you have found the one silver bullet.

To summarize, market risk trends higher in the first half of presidents' terms. The back half tends to be positive with the third year most positive. In the front half when it isn't negative, it tends to be up big and particularly so in second terms (even though that didn't happen in 2005 and 2006, making it more likely in 2009 and 2010). What's more, the tendency for nonnegative years to be up big makes sense. Apprehension about political risk fading away can lead to elation causing big positive years. As this book comes out in 2007, I'd see its being a third year as a definite mild market positive. Would I bet the house on it? No way. If lots of people start talking about the third year being positive and getting excited about it, I'd know this phenomenon was discounted into pricing already and I wouldn't count on it at all. That would be bearish. If it were mentioned a lot but only to be demeaned as ridiculous then I'd believe it might have legs and 2007 could be nicely positive. And I'd already remember forces outside America are as powerful as those in America.

Something like this is a simple example of fathoming something others can't or won't fathom. But then, if for whatever reason others start widely fathoming it, it won't work because it will be discounted into pricing.

Reversing the Trend

I'm waiting to see if a president can turn the presidential cycle on its head. Most presidents push through their most controversial agenda in their first two years when their congressional power is greatest and they have political capital to spend. A truly smart genuine phony—a really big, blood-sucking poli-tic—would fool the populace into thinking he's going to follow suit, but instead focus his first two years on gathering still more political capital as opposed to spending it. This would lead to less legislation and happier markets, all the while bolstering the presidential term cycle naysayers's argument that this forecasting tool is bunko. Then, he would parlay his political capital into a mid-term victory with more of his congressional brethren earning seats. Then he could legislate more easily during the back half of his term. Effectively, he would have reversed the trend by saving all the legislation, risk aversion, and negative market-moving change for the back half of his term. Someday someone will pull that off. It will be a thrill to see. So far we haven't had tics skilled enough to do it. But someday, maybe.

Test and Test Again

You may be surprised I'm sharing with you, in this chapter and others, any of what I've come to believe I know that others don't. Why give it away if I think I know something giving me an edge? Now lots of people will know what I know, meaning it will soon be priced into markets and therefore not work anymore, right?

Maybe, maybe not. I've been talking and writing about presidential term cycles for a long time and every time I do, someone looks for a giant butterfly net to haul me away. Just like my views on high P/Es. People think I'm a kook for believing this works, which is how I know this little bit of technology still is powerful. The same is true for most other examples I share in this book. Once I've found something that works, I continually test it to make sure it hasn't become priced. Once I believe I've fathomed something new, I look to see if others can or will fathom it. The way I test it is by giving it away. The more people think it's nuts, the more they don't fathom what I find fathomable and the more I know it will still work. If they start embracing it, thinking it's good and not nuts, then it won't work. It becomes obsolete. When an unfathomable becomes widely fathomable, it's time to abandon it and fathom new unfathomable truths.

The goal with Question Two is to know something now that might be common knowledge in 3 or 30 years. Once everyone knows your new piece of reality it will no longer be useful to you. So test it. Ask your friends and colleagues if they were aware shifts in the yield curve signal a change in style leadership. Ask if there is any truth to the presidential term cycle. As long as the response is a blank look, a "What?" or, "That's crazy!" or an even better, "You're crazy!" you still have a basis for a bet.

I give away some—not all—of the findings I've had over the years so I know what I can safely continue using and what has outlived its usefulness. Far too many of my peers stick to repeating what they learned at the knee of their mentors and wonder why they can't beat the market. Winning at investing requires constant innovation and constant testing.

Now you can use Question One to free yourself from blindness and Question Two to fathom the unfathomable. However, none of this will keep you from persisting in your old investing errors if you can't control your brain. Investing is inherently counter-intuitive. You can remind yourself of that all you like but your cranial command center rebels. In a fight between you and your brain, your unruly brain will always win—unless you learn how to ask Question Three. Next chapter!

3   QUESTION THREE: WHAT THE HECK IS MY BRAIN DOING TO BLINDSIDE ME NOW?

It's Not Your Fault—Blame Evolution

One of the first things we learn about finance is "Buy low, sell high." In the movie *Trading Places,* when Eddie Murphy and Dan Aykroyd prepare to corner the orange juice market (illegally and implausibly, but comically), you can tell the script writer was casting about for something finance-sounding to say. So Dan tells Eddie, "Buy low, sell high." What more advice do you need, really?

We all know the goal, but more often than not we end up doing the opposite. How hard can this be? Buy when stuff is priced low; sell when it's priced high. It's not rocket science. And yet, this problem is ageless and endless. Investors routinely buy and sell precisely backwards. For evidence, look at Figure 3.1 showing fund flows—the amount of money going into and out of equity mutual funds each month.

Inflows for stock mutual funds were highest during February 2000.[1] That was about the best time in recent history to get out of stocks—at the peak of an ensuing three-year bear market. Fast forward to 2002, and the reverse is true. Everyone bailed from funds in July[2]—a fantastic time for stocks—just before a new bull market. Here is incontrovertible evidence of investors buying high and selling low en masse. These weren't a few deranged ignoramuses engaging in this behavior. This shows a widespread group-think—a frenzied mob of loser lemmings lumbering in and out of the market precisely backwards.

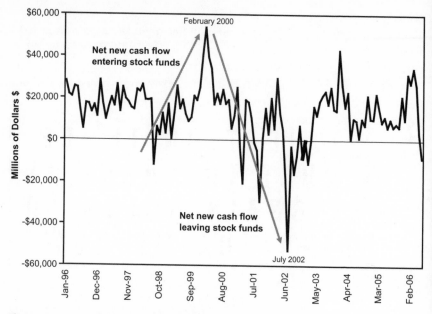

Figure 3.1   Net New Cash Flow in Stock Mutual Funds.
Source: **Investment Company Institute.**

No investor intends to buy high and sell low. That would be stupid. So why do so many of us end up doing the stupid? There are many convenient scapegoats. Recently, following 2002, Enron, MCI, and the like, a popular way to skirt responsibility for poor investing decisions was demonizing crooked CEOs. Your stock portfolio would have done fine were it not for every American CEO being a thief and a liar, right? Jeffrey Skilling, Ken Lay, and the rest—all convicted, right? Or, it's the war in Iraq (Iran, North Korea, Berkeley—whatever socialist or communist or neo-fascist regime we oppose at the time). Or it's outsourcing. Illegal aliens. Inflation. The savings rate. Natural disasters. Hurricanes! Packs of rabid wild dogs roaming free! Killer bees infected with bird flu! It doesn't matter.

Stop pointing your finger at everyone else. If you want to know what causes your investments to fare poorly, look in the mirror. Better yet, get a CAT scan done. Your biggest investing enemy is your brain. Even more precisely, your biggest enemy is the cerebral evolution that formed your brain to be largely focused on keeping you alive in the face of starvation, treachery, and wooly fanged beasts.

To survive as a species, our brains evolved with specific goals in mind—primarily bodily survival in a primitive world. The easy ability to buy good food at the local supermarket or bistro and live relatively free from fear of instant death or dismemberment at the claws of predatory beasts is relatively new to human development—an advancement still in its infancy. Humans spent most of their evolution as hunter-gatherers, traveling in nomadic bands, hunting wild animals, foraging for often spoiled foods, finding mates to perpetuate the species (which is a lot more enticing than investing in stocks), avoiding predators, and seeking shelter. These are the tasks our brains evolved for—to keep us fed, warm, dry, and safe from saber-toothed tigers and brown recluse spiders.

Think of our Stone Age ancestors and how their survival struggle impacts how we behave now. Our ancestors' friends were their tribesmen (and women)—people they could trust. Their enemies were other tribes, rampaging beasts, and the dark things they couldn't understand. As such, they banded together for protection and lit fires to keep the dark (and the dark things) away. Recall our example of the noise outside the campfire—the same cognitive processes kept our ancestors alive and served them well for tens of thousands of years. We've only had a short time when they've caused us to make errors and then only in limited realms, largely offset by other more common life realms where they don't hurt us to this day.

Even with technology and the complexity of modern society, most of this preordained wiring remains intact. Prewiring as a concept is somewhat controversial among psychologists. Evolutionary psychology is sometimes equated with pop-culture thinking by critics. I'll not attempt to retread the literature on evolutionary psychology here. For an introduction to this area, try *How the Mind Works* by Steven Pinker of Harvard (Norton, 1997). It covers a lot of turf fast. But I'm firmly convinced most of our shortcomings in seeing markets correctly stem from cranial hardwiring derived from many eons of evolution and are so fixed in our brains we can't escape them. Because we can't get people from 25,000 years ago to appear for scrutiny now, we can never prove or disprove much of this. But based on studying what has and hasn't been proved and what is reasonable to me, I believe if you simply restrict your thinking about psychology to how we think about markets, you will see evolutionary psychology and hardwiring are very basic.

Our brains are so structured that when information comes in a form our brains are hardwired to receive well, we process it correctly, easily, and quickly. When information comes to our brains in a form or framework our brain isn't hardwired to process well, we are often simply blind to it. And that's because our brains are hardwired by evolution to take certain types of inputs down defined paths and not elsewhere. You have already seen some of that with the P/E and E/P trade off. But you see it throughout this book, recurring in phenomenon after phenomenon. While behavioral finance is not based on evolutionary psychology, many discoveries paralleling evolutionary psychology have been uncovered in the past 30 years in behavioral finance.

Behavioral Finance

Behavioral finance is a recent field of study intersecting the fields of finance and human behavioral psychology. Advocates strive to expand our existing knowledge of how markets work, but more important, how our minds work in relation to risk and markets. Until recently, the study of finance focused primarily on tools of investing including statistics, history, theory, and market mechanics. Does category X typically generate higher or lower returns than category Y? How should a portfolio theoretically be constructed? What is the right way to think of diversification? How do indexes like this compare to indexes like that? What is the best measure of volatility? For mean variance optimization schemes, should we use variance or covariance? These are great but basically all issues of mechanics, history, statistics, and theory in one form or another.

Scholarly finance textbooks written in the 1990s don't differ much from those written in the 1970s. They address new technology, regulations, and products, sure, but they are mainly about the tools of investing. Traditional finance notions derive from traditional notions of economics—that humans in aggregate act rationally, markets are efficient or at least semi-efficient, and individuals acting irrationally can be ignored. The nut-job in the straight jacket has been identified and locked away and doesn't impact markets—in the traditional view.

By contrast, behavioral finance assumes quirky behavior—or that person standard finance might view as a nut-job—is pretty common. Irrationality is assumed to be potential behavior. Investors are presumed to behave in ways that sometimes seem irrational. Behaviorialists try to discover the "why."

I think this is always easiest seen when you accept evolutionary notions that we're still influenced by our Stone Age ancestors. It's true—our modernized skulls contain Stone Age brains. Investors aren't rational automatons; they are humans and regularly behave in crazy ways when making financial decisions. And that is because our brains weren't set up to do this stuff. Our brains were set up to do survival stuff from a long time ago.

I hear people asking, "Where is the smart money going?" By smart money, they mean some category like *institutional*—the huge pools of pension, endowment, or corporate money managed by purportedly cool and collected professionals. Hogwash. There is no such thing as categorical "smart money." There may be such a thing as stupid money and stupider money, but not smart money. There is always someone right and someone wrong on each side of a trade. Some institutions get it right while others don't. Some professionals get it right while others don't. There is no category of market participant who is inherently or consistently more on the right side of the market than any other. The guy on the right side of the trade can be stupid too—just lucky and right. All investment decisions, whether it's regarding someone's individual retirement account (IRA) contribution this year or the latest billion added to a huge university's endowment, are made by people. People who are held captive by eons of Stone Age hardwiring—hardwiring set up to deal with different kinds of problems than those we confront with investing.

If we can understand why people behave as they do, we can understand how markets work and bet better based on what we know about human behavior. If you can understand your brain better, you can understand how to better control yourself so you can begin avoiding many of the typical mistakes investors make and begin lowering your error rate. For this, you need Question Three. Before you take any market action, you must stop and ask, "What the heck is my brain doing to mess me up? To make me blind now? To make me see and feel the situation exactly wrong and backwards?" After all, the market is nothing more than millions of people behaving like, well, cavemen in Mercedes with BlackBerries. If you can unravel this code and understand your own decision making process better, you can conquer your caveman brain and deal with TGH without being humiliated—that is the goal.

It's not your fault your brain suffers cavemanisms. Our minds are conditioned to biases making you do dumb things that seem really smart at the time. Questions One and Two are intended to give you a framework for finding gameable bets. But those two questions are nothing if your brain runs ruinous. Hence, you need Question Three.

At one level, you're very, very smart. Your brain is an amazing pattern recognizer if information is fed to it even partly correctly. If information is fed to it incorrectly, you can't see a pattern at all. Here is an example from a goofy e-mail I got:

fi yuo cna raed tihs, yuo hvae a sgtrane mnid too. Cna yuo raed tihs?

i cdnuolt blveiee taht I cluod aulaclty uesdnatnrd waht I was rdanieg. The phaonmneal pweor of the hmuan mnid! It dseno't mtaetr in waht oerdr the ltteres in a wrod are, the olny iproamtnt tihng is taht the frsit and lsat ltteer be in the rghit pclae. The rset can be a taotl mses and you can sitll raed it whotuit a pboerlm. Azanmig huh? yaeh and I awlyas tghuhot slpeling was ipmorantt!

Kind of makes you wonder why you went to school, right? And kind of makes you wonder why we have editors. But it's a perfect "eaxpmle" of your brain being able to receive information well if delivered well. In this case you don't even need it to be all that well delivered to be able to get it pretty easily. But often, if correct information is delivered exactly wrong, you can't see it at all. Our earlier P/E examples are perfect in this regard. Maybe you've struggled with P/Es forever without them making much sense to you. But by turning the P/E into an E/P like an interest rate—your after-tax return on owning the whole business— it makes sense. A P/E of 8 is a 12.5 percent return, which beats the heck out of a 6 percent pre-tax bond. Your brain gets that easily. The issue is knowing when your brain sees well and when it's actually hurting your ability to see reality.

The Great Humiliator

It all goes back to TGH—how else can you explain why investors mobbed the stock market in February of 2000 and bailed out in lockstep in time for the bottom in 2002? TGH tricked them, that's how, just by letting them all have the same information.

TGH has endless ways to humiliate us. Bull market tops are marked by intense and comforting euphoria. Investors are never so enthusiastic about stocks as when pretty much every single person who might ever buy a stock has already done so and there is basically no place left for stocks to go but down. Even worse, market tops roll and churn. They don't announce themselves with a sudden drop, like a correction. Everyone looks for some announcement-like effect showing a bull market is over but that almost never happens. There is an age-old but almost universally true statement nearly no one can accept: "Bull markets die with a whimper, not with a bang." There isn't a dramatic spike top to bull markets if the historic measure is calculated correctly. Instead, they roll over slowly for many months, just like the market did in 2000. For more than 10 months around the top, the MSCI World Index never got outside of an 8.5 percent bandwidth, slowly churning sideways,[3] innocently dropping a few percentage points here and rallying there. In September 2000, the S&P 500 was still 4 percent positive for the year. At such times, TGH has professionals screaming, "Buy the dips! It's not too late! This bull has legs!" In 1999 and 2000, "day trading" became widely popular and tens of thousands gave up their day jobs—all over the world—to day trade because it was fun and easy (for a short while). People in droves then classified themselves as "aggressive" investors. Civilian investors suddenly became options-trading pros. Maybe your mother was speculating in penny stocks. Yes, TGH, the sick pervert, wants your mother, too.

Bear market bottoms are different only in form. TGH just confuses us differently. Bottoms are often violent and sharp, freaking everyone out so enough fools finally dump their stocks. Just when folks who first got into stocks at the peak abandon them from fatigue, stocks take off sharply, leaving the messes and the masses in the dust. "It's just a bear market correction," pundits murmur. "Don't be fooled," they rasp, cough, and add, "Stocks are done for a long, long time." And then global stocks soar 33 percent like they did in 2003.[4] It's humiliating. TGH wins. Most people lose and even many of the winners feel like losers.

There is so much more to this (we cover much more in Chapter 8). There is always a small universe of pundits who is bearish at the top (and probably consistently for the three previous years) and receive accolades for it, and then remain bearish at the bottom. No one notices that for years as people keep listening to them, fighting the last war. The potential for TGH to suck you in, chew you up, and spit you out is nearly infinite.

Don't think TGH rests on its laurels in between peaks and troughs. During the normal course of a bull or bear market, the market can correct multiple times—that is, go briefly opposite to its longer term trend by 10 percent to 20 percent. During the 1998 correction, mentioned in Chapter 2, the U.S. market spiked downward nearly 20 percent over only six weeks from July 17 to August 31.[5] That can terrify. And though corrections that size are fairly normal in bull markets, few remember or recognize it when next it happens. Corrections have investors witlessly dumping stock just in time for the market to recover and move to new higher prices. Again, take 1998. The market's year-to-date return was only at break-even late in the fall.[6] Yet by year-end, it was up 28.6 percent.[7] The correction disappeared as fast as it came. TGH is fast.

The market needn't move nearly enough to qualify as a true correction to have seemingly rational, intelligent human beings crying for Mommy. It's such a normal thing, even for those trained to know better. My clients and readers, fairly normal people on average—except perhaps richer than average—and trained over time to turn a tough shoulder toward normal market volatility, will still regularly ask if a drop of a few percentage points over a few weeks augurs a bear market, recession, the Apocalypse, or even Paris Hilton being nominated to the Federal Reserve Board of Governors. No, a drop of a few percentage points is what TGH calls Tuesday.

Cracking the Stone Age Code—Pride and Regret

Admitting you have a problem is the first step to recovery. But you won't know you have a problem unless you ask Question Three: What the heck is my brain doing to blindside me now? You can and will get multiple answers when you ask how your brain affects you. Some fall in the realm of your spouse, mother, or psychologist. The only ones concerning us here involve market behavior. Most investing errors result from cognitive errors, the most common of which we cover here.

Look! Me Kill Huge Beast! Me Very Skilled!

As mentioned in Chapter 1, behavioralists have shown normal Americans (we'll assume you're normal) hate losses about two and a half times as much as they like gains.[8] A 25 percent gain feels as good as a 10 percent loss feels bad. Said otherwise, if you gain 10 percent over here and lose 10 percent over there, you feel like you're behind. You feel more chilled by a 10 percent loss than thrilled by a 10 percent gain. Therefore, people exert more effort to avoid pain than achieve gain. This is commonly known as loss aversion, sometimes referred to as *myopic loss aversion,* intimating shortsightedness and an overactive reaction to short-term movements. It explains many investing errors. At root, myopic loss aversion and the mistakes it leads to are about two things—*pride* and *regret.*

Our Stone Age information processors learned to do what is called "accumulating pride" and "shunning regret" as matters of survival. Imagine two hunters returning to camp at dusk. One has a gazelle draped over each shoulder. The other has nothing but some broken spears that missed their mark.

The hunter with the gazelles thrills the camp with his entrance. Before he approaches, he knows he will be regaling the story of his hunt around the campfire that night. He knows his mother will be proud—very proud and elevated among her peers. He envisions the young girls staring at him with doe eyes and even hopes the tribal chieftain may soon think about linking him up with his royal daughter, pulling him into the ruling family. Heady stuff! That night he tells the tribe the story about how he, skillfully and masterfully, hunted and brought down the mighty beasts. He talks about his deftness in forming the spear and how his spears are particularly deadly. He talks about the signs he interpreted leading him to the grazing gazelles. He details his physical prowess in accurately launching his spear into the gazelle with deadly finality. He accumulates *pride.* It feels good and motivates him to eagerly go out to hunt, again and again, so he can continue to experience that prideful high. And that is good for the tribe because they need this young man to kill high-powered animal-based protein that went a long way in those days in separating those whose genes passed on from those whose didn't.

Meanwhile, back at the outskirts of camp the other young hunter, the one with no gazelles, has a different story to tell. It wasn't his fault he didn't bag a gazelle. He has skill in spear making and experience in tracking beasts, too. But on this particular day, a freak bolt of lightening scattered the gazelles south moments before he could aim. Or maybe someone borrowed his spears so they weren't sharp enough. Or maybe there were lions roaming in his hunting ground. Or the wind was wrong. He fabricates seemingly plausible excuses so he can rise the next morning and try again. He shuns *regret*. In so doing his campmates let him hunt the next day as well; their belief in his story motivates him to try, try again. His tribe needs him to hunt too. Maybe he really was just unlucky that day. Even if he is a terrible hunter, he may stumble across an injured animal. Maybe tomorrow he will come across a gazelle just after it has been killed by a wild dog. Either way it's worth it if protein accumulation is possible.

Accumulating pride when successful and shunning regret when failing motivate both hunters to keep trying their hand. Both of these tendencies are good for the tribe. Their tribe's very survival depends on their willingness to make repeated forays. The successful hunter hunts again and again. The unsuccessful hunter hunts again too.

Many sources say investors are motivated by greed and fear. Behavioralists would disagree and suggest investors, and through them markets, aren't driven by greed and fear but by humanity's drive to accumulate pride and shun regret. It just comes out as greed and fear.

Pride is a mental process associating success with skill and repeatability—the hunter who bagged a gazelle believed he wasn't lucky. He believed himself masterful. More important, he believed he could repeat it. By writing this book, I too am displaying pride accumulated over a career span where I don't want to believe it was all just luck—that I was the guy flipping way too many heads for way too long. Who wants to believe that? The natural tendency of humans is to want to think success was because of skill and repeatability—not luck.

Think about your own behavior after buying a stock that went up. Maybe it went up a lot. Maybe you bought Apple in 2002 after your 12-year-old begged for an iPod. Did you pump your fist in the air? Did you congratulate yourself? Did you brag about it to your colleagues, spouse, and father-in-law? More important, did your success make you feel like you could do it again? "I bought it. It went up. I'm smart. Want to see me do it again?" Just like the hunter.

Regret is a process denying responsibility for failure—attributing it not to lack of skill but usually to bad luck or victimization. The gazelle-less hunter isn't a bad hunter. He is just the hapless victim of poor circumstances. He'll kill a gazelle next time. "I bought it. It went down. The broker sold it to me. He's the problem." Or, "I bought it. It went down. The CEO was a crook." There are many ways to do bad luck and victimization. "I wouldn't have bought it if my wife hadn't been ragging on me that morning." The mind-set isn't, "I bought it, it went down, I don't know how to do this so I better not do it again." Or, "I better get some lessons so I know how to do this better."

If the hunters didn't accumulate pride and shun regret, they would have become despondent over failure. They would have given up hunting giant beasts as a fool's errand. Their brains had to function this way to forage enough food to pass their genes. It is a motivational tool. If a hunter became beset by regret and ultimately depressed, those benefiting from his future potentially lucky hunting would have starved and died, and that isn't such a good way to perpetuate the species. Accumulating pride and shunning regret were basic to our ancestors' survival. That was necessary then, and we still do it—motivating ourselves to keep trying.

But in modern times, these behaviors cause investing mistakes. Suppose Bill owns a stock that rises 40 percent. Bill was smart to have chosen such a stock. He is a savvy stock picker, and he believes he can do it again—he accumulates pride.

Then his stock drops 10 percent. He feels the loss about two and a half times as much as the gain, and disregards the fact that overall he is still up 26 percent. The sudden drop causes pain he wants to avoid, so he shuns regret. He believes he was just unlucky on this 10 percent drop because previous pride accumulation convinces him he can and will succeed overall. He considers selling while he can. He concludes the stock will fall further and loses sight of his long-term goals, focusing only on the short-term and acts to minimize potential short-term pain. He sells the stock and protects his ego for another day of hunting. But the stock bounces back and goes to new highs. He chooses to ignore that because acknowledging it would cause too much pain and ignoring it shuns regret nicely.

Regret causes Bill to avoid pain by taking action—selling at a temporary relative low point. Pride prevents him from analyzing his behavior accurately so he is doomed to repeat this vicious cycle. Loss aversion causes investors to buy high and sell low—which is a pretty stupid strategy.

Throwing Spears—Overconfidence

While we are on the topic of hunting, another Stone Age behavior leading to investing errors is *overconfidence*. One behavioral lesson learned in recent decades is the average investor is markedly overconfident. He believes he has greater skill than he really possesses. This is parallel to the notion that 75 percent of drivers believe they are above average drivers. Overconfidence stems directly from accumulating pride and shunning regret over time. That is how we get overconfident. If Stone Age hunters weren't nearly crazed with overconfidence, they would never attempt felling massive beasts with sticks tipped with a stone. They needed to fell those beasts or they would starve. Or be vegetarians—which was effectively the same thing.

For ancient hunter-gatherers, life was short and food was scarce. Consider recent findings regarding Kennewick man—a chap who lived roughly 9,000 years ago in what is now Washington state. (I always have sympathy for anyone named Ken and this guy needed sympathy.) Scientists discovered a spear head embedded in his hip. It wasn't a death blow; this was a healed wound. He also apparently had multiple healed broken bones and other wounds.[9] Life was tough for Kennewick man and his cohorts in 7,000 B.C. But it paid to take big risks—one big kill could mean a month's protein for the tribe. Our ingrained survival instincts urge us to take risks—we frequently choose "fight" over "flight" when facing insurmountable odds. Think how many people persist in paying the stupid-tax, I mean, playing the lottery no matter how long the odds.

Investors by definition are overconfident when assuming they know more than they do—or when overestimating their skill level. Reading the *Wall Street Journal* and a handful of blogs and newsletters every day doesn't make anyone an investing expert. Yet scores of otherwise intelligent people feel their ability to subscribe to and absorb common media makes them sufficient to bet and win. Investing is tough. There is an overabundance of highly educated and experienced professionals who invest as stupidly as rank amateurs. That doesn't make getting in over your head any less dangerous.

Don't mistake me. I'm neither advocating you dedicate your life to scholarly pursuit of investment knowledge nor hire a worthy professional. Quite the opposite! (Remember, all you need to succeed in investing is knowing something others don't, and for that you need only the Three Questions.) Rather, you should beware overconfidence because it leads to very serious errors—the same errors everyone else makes.

For example, overconfidence leads investors to invest in an "Initial Public Offering" (IPO; for the neophyte, IPO alternately means "It's Probably Overpriced"—more on that later) of stock, micro-caps, hedge funds, and other volatile or illiquid interests while ignoring or downplaying the associated risk. Think about how often you've heard pundits, friends, or your broker describe an opportunity as the "next Microsoft." The odds are stacked against you—precious few new businesses survive, much less blossom into a hot stock.

Overconfidence may lead you to hang onto a stock, hoping it will someday bounce back, even when mountains of evidence contradict it. If you bought Level 3 at $130, and insisted to your sobbing wife when it fell to a buck and a half that it's a great firm and will bounce back one day—you were shunning regret and displaying overconfidence.

Behavioralists note one common investor tendency is holding onto a stock hoping it gets back to "breakeven"—refusing to sell until then. Everyone in money management and every stockbroker knows many clients who rush to sell a stock they've been holding onto with a loss as soon as it gets back to breakeven. By refusing to sell until then, the breakeven investor mentally refuses to acknowledge the loss and therefore postpones having to absorb full regret. It's human nature to think you haven't made a mistake and refuse to cut losses. No doubt, selling a stock just because it drops in price is a loser's strategy. But sometimes you must admit you've erred and your money is better placed elsewhere.

Figure 3.2 shows the lagging performance of some very fine companies in the energy sector following the energy-led bear market of 1980. As of this writing, energy has been high on everyone's list of talking points—either because the sector has been on a tear in recent years and investors are thrilled with their returns, or because evil energy CEOs are conspiring to impoverish us all by intentionally manipulating what Saudi Arabia, Iran, Mexico, Canada, Nigeria, and Venezuela charge us for crude oil (because those countries have a long history of doing whatever we desire).

Yet considering the performance of individual stocks in a formerly hot sector, as energy was in the 1980s, you see it took years, more than a decade in some cases, for prices to breakeven. The opportunity cost of hanging onto those stocks after 1980 was great. As shown in Figure 3.3 on page 94, the S&P 500 greatly outpaced the beleaguered energy companies over the subsequent five and, in most cases, 10 years. Try doing this with some big tech names from the recent tech bubble, and you'll see the same phenomenon. Stocks don't obey some arbitrary time line for growth—nor should you expect them to.

When thinking of the breakeven investor—one way we know he is doing it to avoid absorbing full regret is watching the exception proving the rule. The time he wants to rush to sell and take a loss is when he gets to year-end and can shun regret via tax loss selling. In a taxable account at year-end, an investor can sell stocks that are way down and carry forward a tax loss to offset other gains and reduce future taxes. In taking that loss instead of absorbing regret, the investor can accumulate pride. He tells himself he has done something smart, not stupid. His stock is down but by selling it he has pulled a rabbit out of the hat and done something smart, and he turns his back on regret and instead accumulates pride (which is what everyone is always trying to do).

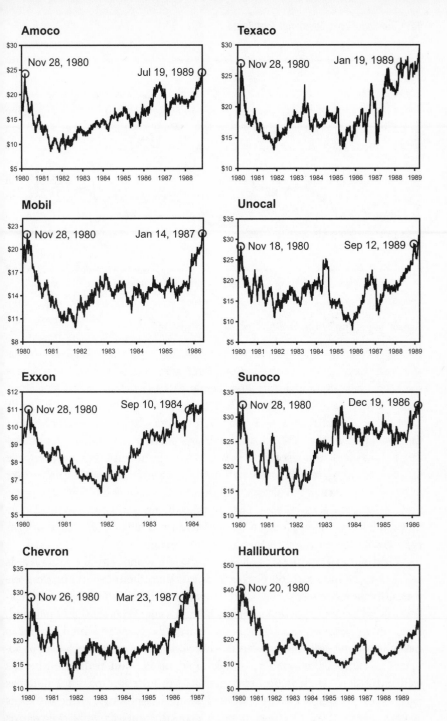

Figure 3.2 Don't Hold Your Breath.
Source: Bloomberg.

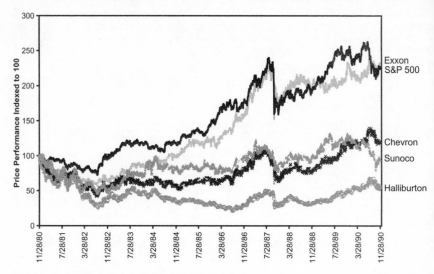

Figure 3.3   The Opportunity Cost of Holding On.
Source: **Bloomberg.**

In measuring this activity among large numbers of investors, we know less than 5 percent of investors who take tax losses ever look back and analyze if they would have been better off not doing so—which tells you they don't want to know. Said alternately, if you poll investors who take tax losses and ask them what happened to the stock after they sold, they almost never know. Because if they look and discover they would have been better off not taking the tax loss—if they knew the stock bounced up big after they sold—they would have even more regret to absorb, and they would have to give back the pride they had recently accumulated. That would be just way too much to handle, so they don't look. The brain is a tricky self-deluder and TGH is waiting around every corner to entice you further into self-delusion.

Overconfident individuals often own too few stocks—maybe just a handful. You might have a 401(k) plan or a company stock purchase plan in which you buy your employer's stock. Many investors do. But is your overall allocation to your company stock (or any stock for that matter) more than 5 percent? If so, you're being overconfident unless you really do know something material others don't. Most folks who do this don't know anything others don't know. No company, no matter how seemingly robust and healthy, is guaranteed not to lose stock value. Investors load up on company stock because they've heard examples where it worked because some single stock was spectacularly successful. They forget about the backfires. Investors say things like,

"But I'm comfortable holding this stock because I *know* the company." You may be an astoundingly productive accountant, but as fabulous as you are, your presence doesn't grant immunity from market depreciation to your employer.

The Tragedy of Enron

Remember a little Houston company called Enron? In case you have been needlessly living in a Cold War bunker, cut off from humanity and all modes of media, Enron went bankrupt after a number of accounting abuses emerged. En route the stock plummeted, all but a handful of employees found themselves suddenly and violently unemployed, and Enron became the poster child of corporate malfeasance. Suddenly CEOs everywhere, regardless of history and ethical makeup, were regarded as greedy scoundrels like the Enron executives.

The biggest story engendered by Enron's gory, self-inflicted demise was the army of employees who found their life-savings wiped out because their 401(k)s were all in Enron. Night after night, the news covered tragic stories about lifelong loyal Enron employees who had responsibly and religiously socked away hundreds of thousands or even a few million in Enron stock to fund their retirement. Nice upstanding folks who worked hard and penny-pinched and saved and were good decent Texans and thought, "I know the company." Nearly overnight, these unfortunate souls found the value of their retirement savings decimated. They were desolate, having to sell their homes, put off retirement for many years, or find second or third jobs. Being poor when you're young is no big deal, but impoverishment at 69 can be annoying.

The real Enron tragedy isn't that so many lost almost everything. The tragedy was it was utterly preventable. Whatever evil may have lurked in the hearts of Ken Lay, Andrew Fastow, and Jeff Skilling, it wasn't their fault their employees plowed everything they owned, or much of it, into one stock. Having too much of a portfolio in any one stock is potentially catastrophic, as many Houstonians learned first hand.

If they followed my rule of thumb of having no more than 5 percent of your portfolio in any single stock, the Enron disaster would have downgraded from apocalyptic to minor bummer. Yes, employees would have become unemployed. Yes, they would have been simultaneously seeking work in a worse work world, competing with their former friends, all sporting relatively similar resumes. Yes, they would have lost money. Vacations would have been vacated, part-time work at the local Applebee's commenced, second cars sold. None of this is fun or ego-flattering. But working at the local Gap to pay the bills is less humiliating if one has a 401(k) and net worth still intact—decreased by one small stock's implosion instead of one huge one.

Enron did match employee 401(k) cash contributions with Enron stock[10]—a sleazy maneuver to be sure—but even more reason for employees to never buy another nickel's worth of Enron. Overconfidence is to blame. Not Ken Lay. Not Jeff Skilling. Yes, for other things, but not for that. After five years and a lengthy trial (that's how it works in America—slowly—if you don't like it, I hear Pyongyang has lovely patriotic dance recitals, interesting cuisine, and decisively speedy trials), those gentlemen were deemed guilty by a jury of their peers. Whether or not the punishment fits the crime will be fodder for discussion for years to come. Not my turf.

Let's pause to clarify what they did do, and what they absolutely didn't do. I hear sloppy journalists and pundits claiming the Lay-Skilling-Fastow triumvirate "stole" money from their employees 401(k)s and "raided" the pensions. They did nothing of the sort. Think about your own 401(k). How easy is it for someone to just "take" money out of it? Come to think of it, how easy is it for you to take money out of it? You fill out a barrage of paperwork and provide all kinds of written assurances you're who you say you are. No—they didn't "steal" money out of 401(k)s. Lay and Skilling were found guilty (and Fastow pleaded guilty so as to avoid a trial) of essentially monkeying with Enron's balance sheet, attributing losses to other entities so Enron looked more robustly healthy than it was, when in fact it was teetering on financial ruin. When the truth came out, the stock plummeted, which is why their employees lost so much value in their 401(k)s. And then Enron went bankrupt, making it nearly impossible for stockholders to glean even pennies on the dollar.

But no matter the degree and severity of their crime, they didn't hold a gun to anyone's head and force them not to diversify their retirement savings. The overconfidence of the Enron employees themselves, those who invested their entire liquid net worth in one stock, is to blame for the total (or near total) loss of value of their retirement and other savings accounts. That may seem harsh, but sometimes the truth hurts. They need to absorb their regret.

You needn't hold stock in a firm infamous enough to warrant a few Trivial Pursuit questions to experience an implosion. GE is generally regarded as among the world's best-run firms—a view I share. Investors who had most, if not all, their net worth in GE stock are probably still smarting from a blistering

62 percent drop in return from its high in August, 2000 to its low in October 2002.[11] The stock has rebounded but, as of this writing (mid-2006), is still 37 percent off its highs.[12] Imagine thinking you're ready to retire in comfort and then scrambling for a way to live on one-third less years later. It needn't happen to you, if you aren't overconfident.

See! I Told You So—Confirmation Bias

As investors, we intentionally seek those fragments of evidence supporting our pet theories and preexisting notions. We tend to ignore those contradicting our biases. With differing biases, two investors can consider the same data yet espouse two completely opposing conclusions—both swearing the data supports him and not the other fellow. I've seen this all my life. What's more, almost never will either investor set out to use simple statistical techniques to demonstrate being right. They have a bias and they're overconfident so they don't have to check and validate. Correlation coefficients? That's for the other guy.

Another easy technique to support a preset notion is seeking a big name who says the same things you believe and relying on him as an authority for why you should do what you already want to do. Whatever nutty thing you believe, I promise there are plenty of seemingly credible authorities to support you in that lunacy.

How did we get this way? Think about the Stone Age hunters again. Each hunter may be predisposed to liking a particular hunting ground. Maybe the first gazelle one hunter caught was in Gazelle Gulch to the north. He envisions Gazelle Gulch as perfect for hunting. His feeling is bolstered each time he kills a gazelle there. "Yep," he thinks, "this is where it's at." And, because he feels better in the Gulch he probably hunts better there. He justifies times he doesn't catch a gazelle by telling himself he cannot catch one every time. Over many hunting sessions, he reassures himself, there will be times he must come home empty-handed. But on average, when looking at three or four months worth of hunting expeditions, Gazelle Gulch is tops. And if he doesn't go to other hunting grounds, he will never disprove his bias.

His hunting buddy is equally convinced Kangaroo Canyon to the south is best. Both hunters hunt every day. They observe the number of times they each kill gazelles and kangaroos. They both run hot and cold streaks in which they each go for days bagging nothing or they have back-to-back successes. And they each remain firmly convinced of their favorite area's superiority though neither one can statistically demonstrate long-term superiority. (Stone

Age folks didn't do statistics—which is why you don't naturally.) Neither hunter will have his thesis tested and therefore rejected as wrong. Doing so would be painful.

We have evolved less than you might hope. Recall the Chapter 1 example regarding the myth of high P/E ratios spelling doom for stocks. Utter unsupported nonsense—yet a near universal belief! This is a great example of what behavioralists call *confirmation bias*—the instinct to seek out information confirming our preset notions and rejecting or overlooking contradictory evidence. Believers of the high P/E myth are quick to point out data supporting their theory, but they tend to reject contradictory evidence.

Confirmation bias is comfortably consistent with religious views throughout humanity, starting with early paganistic days up until the neo-paganism of popular contemporary Environmentalism in which folks hold warm and fuzzy but deeply seated views about what is good for the environment that isn't supported by science. (By this I'm not arguing against the environment or that environmentalists don't have many points supported by science. I'm saying many of them see the arguments supporting their view and ignore perfectly valid factors contradicting them—because they believe. Nature worship is, of course, one of our oldest religions.)

Many myths are thus propped up by confirmation bias. It's an overwhelming part of being human. It's natural. But in markets, being natural hurts us. Confirmation bias makes us feel good—it reaffirms our conviction we are clever (overconfidence, yet again). And we like thinking we're clever. But as any doctor will tell you, things that feel good aren't necessarily good for you.

Confirmation bias perfectly explains the resilience of the "So goes January, goes the year" myth. As each year starts, particularly if the start of the year is negative, pundits pound their "so-goes" drums. Some particularly zealous adherents go further, claiming, "so goes the first week, goes January, goes the year." This puts the world on notice should January happen to be a negative month. It's a great story and has that freak-out effect TV news producers love.

Years when both January and annual returns are negative provide the confirmation adherents require. The same goes for positive results, but the "so-goes" crowd seems to prefer bearish results. For example, during January 2006, which was rousingly positive, you'd be hard-pressed to find a mention of this dubious effect in the media. However, a Google search turns up plenty of mentions of the dreaded effect for January 2005, which was a negative January. By the way, overall 2005 was positive 9.5 percent as measured by the MSCI World Index.[13] The "so-goes" adherents somehow ignore that.

How many pundits who claim "so-goes" in January come back in December to issue a mea culpa when wrong? None—they don't have to. Years like 2005, when the year didn't go the way January did, cause investors to *reframe*. Suddenly, you can't expect it to work every year. Rather, you must look at longer time periods, like 5, 7, 10, or 23 years. Or after the pundit retires. Here the "so-goes" crowd rejects contradictory evidence, clings to the bias, and reframes the issue by giving some arbitrary time frame.

Reframing is an important by-product of confirmation bias. They go hand-in-hand. Behavioralists see framing as fundamental to our ability to see information correctly or incorrectly. When something is framed in ways we see well, then we can see it—jsut liek ew ddi wtih hte mssieplled praagarph eraleir. When it's framed in ways we see badly, we're blind. You shouldn't find that surprising. Few people would ever stop to ask, "How about instead of starting the 'so-goes' game in January, try playing it starting June or any other month? While we're at it, instead of thinking about the U.S. market, let's think about some other country that moves in parallel to the United States, like Britain." I assure you, only weird people think like that and when they do, they find no more reality within the data than the notion that January predicts annual stock returns for America.

Though year after year we're regaled with "so-goes" warnings, this myth remains wholly unsubstantiated. Any fifth grader with an Internet connection and a functioning knowledge of Excel can figure this one out. Table 3.1 shows the power of January as an indicator for overall annual results.

Table 3.1 shows every year going back to 1926, ranking the year by the worst first 10 days of January to the best. We also show first quarter, mid-year, and year-end results. Any year ending with a return greater than 20 percent—undeniably a great positive year—is shaded. You can see the shaded years are peppered haphazardly throughout the chart, regardless of how the year kicked off. In many instances, the market declined at first only to rally magnificently for a positive finish. The only analysis you can derive from this illustration is a short time period—such as the first 10 trading days of the year—has little predictive power.

Here's another way to look at this myth. Figure 3.4 shows three years when the first 10 days were negative. Had you bought into the catechism, you would have missed big years—huge years even. Flipping this on its head—if you expect a positive year based on a positive start, you can easily be disappointed as well.

Believing in this investing myth is a good symptom of a brain paralyzed with confirmation bias.

Table 3.1 The January Ineffect

Year	First 10 Days	First Quarter	First Half	Annual
1939	-6.67%	-16.87%	-17.83%	-5.43%
1978	-5.96%	-6.19%	0.45%	1.06%
1982	-5.08%	-8.64%	-10.56%	14.76%
1991	-4.99%	13.63%	12.40%	26.31%
1990	-4.64%	-3.81%	1.31%	-6.56%
1935	-3.71%	-10.87%	8.36%	41.51%
1974	-3.40%	-3.66%	-11.84%	-29.72%
1947	-3.29%	-0.82%	-0.58%	0.00%
1977	-3.21%	-8.41%	-6.50%	-11.50%
1957	-3.18%	-5.50%	1.49%	-14.32%
1956	-2.94%	6.62%	3.30%	2.63%
1940	-2.92%	-1.92%	-20.06%	-15.32%
1962	-2.91%	-2.80%	-23.48%	-11.81%
1996	-2.62%	4.80%	8.88%	20.26%
1960	-2.52%	-7.60%	-4.96%	-2.97%
1948	-2.30%	-1.48%	9.46%	-0.66%
1969	-2.16%	-2.26%	-5.92%	-11.36%
1998	-2.03%	13.53%	16.84%	26.67%
2005	-2.26%	-2.59%	-1.70%	3.00%
1955	-1.96%	1.68%	14.01%	26.38%
1953	-1.66%	-4.83%	-9.15%	-6.64%
1986	-1.43%	13.07%	18.72%	14.62%
1981	-1.13%	0.18%	-3.35%	-9.73%
1950	-0.54%	3.16%	5.55%	21.78%
1928	-0.45%	8.32%	8.66%	37.88%
1970	-0.41%	-2.64%	-21.01%	0.10%
2000	-0.28%	2.00%	-1.00%	-10.14%
1934	-0.25%	6.48%	-2.87%	-5.99%
2002	-0.16%	-0.06%	-13.78%	-23.37%
1968	-0.05%	-6.50%	3.22%	7.66%
1973	0.33%	-5.53%	-11.68%	-17.37%
1993	0.33%	3.66%	3.40%	7.06%
1930	0.34%	17.20%	-4.59%	-28.48%
2001	0.48%	-12.11%	-7.26%	-13.04%
1929	0.49%	4.85%	13.43%	-11.91%
1992	0.88%	-3.21%	-2.15%	4.46%
1971	0.95%	8.86%	8.19%	10.79%
1959	1.12%	0.42%	5.90%	8.48%
1999	1.14%	4.65%	11.67%	19.53%

Table 3.1 (continued)

Year	First 10 Days	First Quarter	First Half	Annual
1966	1.16%	-3.46%	-8.32%	-13.09%
1944	1.20%	3.00%	11.23%	13.80%
1952	1.22%	2.54%	5.01%	11.81%
1972	1.27%	5.01%	4.95%	15.63%
1949	1.33%	-0.91%	-6.88%	10.25%
1984	1.36%	-3.49%	-7.12%	1.40%
1965	1.72%	1.66%	-0.74%	9.06%
2004	1.81%	1.29%	2.60%	8.99%
1994	1.81%	-4.43%	-4.76%	-1.54%
1943	1.84%	18.53%	26.41%	19.45%
1988	2.01%	4.78%	10.69%	12.40%
1931	2.05%	8.79%	-3.28%	-47.04%
1985	2.13%	8.02%	14.72%	26.33%
1936	2.16%	11.06%	10.40%	27.83%
1964	2.16%	5.28%	8.89%	12.97%
1995	2.20%	9.02%	18.61%	34.11%
1941	2.26%	-5.83%	-6.90%	-17.86%
1989	2.31%	6.18%	14.50%	27.25%
1954	2.49%	8.58%	17.77%	45.03%
1958	2.50%	5.28%	13.13%	38.06%
1961	2.53%	11.96%	11.25%	23.13%
1937	2.57%	4.33%	-10.34%	-38.64%
1945	2.71%	2.71%	12.65%	30.72%
2006	2.77%			
1980	2.96%	-5.42%	5.84%	25.77%
1963	3.19%	5.50%	9.94%	18.89%
1951	3.43%	4.85%	2.69%	16.46%
1997	3.57%	2.21%	19.49%	31.01%
1942	3.80%	-7.83%	-4.49%	12.43%
1946	4.03%	4.15%	6.16%	-11.85%
1983	4.27%	8.76%	19.53%	17.27%
2003	4.36%	-3.60%	10.76%	26.38%
1979	4.77%	5.70%	7.08%	12.31%
1933	4.94%	-15.17%	58.50%	46.62%
1967	4.95%	12.29%	12.83%	20.09%
1975	5.22%	21.59%	38.84%	31.55%
1976	7.12%	13.95%	15.62%	19.15%
1932	8.37%	-9.92%	-45.43%	-15.19%
1987	9.63%	20.45%	25.53%	2.03%
1938	10.75%	-19.35%	9.68%	25.33%

Source: Global Financial Data.

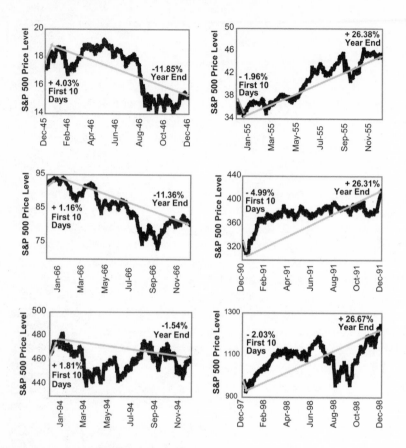

Figure 3.4   The January Ineffect (1946–1998).
Source: Global Financial Data.

Following a Trail—Pattern Recognition and Repetition

Our ancestors—those wily hunters and gatherers and their tribesmen (and tribeswomen)—learned to recognize repeating rewards. They noted what led to their own and their neighbors' successes so they could repeat them and have yet more success. For example, they might have said to themselves, "This weapon is good for hunting, so I'll always use it," or, "I never get lost when I follow this trail, so I'll keep on it," or, "These berries didn't kill my neighbor, so I'll eat them." Pattern recognition and repetition was a safe, rational thing to do. Who wants to be adventurous with poisonous berries? No one knowingly picks the bad berries.

Like our Stone Age ancestors, investors still create control rules and follow them instead of assessing each individual situation. This leads to the popularity of "charting"—poring over graphs looking for predictable patterns. A cottage industry exists around "momentum investing" and "technical analysis," which claim certain formations—cup-and-handle, saucer-bottom, head-and-shoulders, deer-in-headlights (ok, I made that one up)—are predictive of a stock's future movement. Pick up the *Investor's Business Daily* (IBD) and you'll find the "IBD 100" list—100 stocks with strong price performance *from the previous week.*

What is the purpose of this list? To mock us? These are the top 100 stocks you should buy if you can figure out how to build a time machine and successfully travel back in time? If they really want to be helpful, why don't they print the stocks that will be hot next week? That is what we want. But they don't because they can't. And they can't because despite what someone may have told you, no amount of charting tells you anything about what a stock will do next other than the random occasion of serendipitous luck. Ever. End of story. Stocks are what a statistician would call, "not serially correlated," which means when a stock is heading in a particular direction, the odds are 50/50 the stock continues in that direction or reverses course. For every chart you show me indicating a pattern leading to an expected result, I can show you many more where the exact same pattern leads to nothing at all. Stock price patterns by themselves are well measured to have no predictive power. Yet folks still use them.

We practice finance as a craft, using stodgy technology and iffy indicators, rather than reinventing it for modern use or creating new capital markets technology. We cling to outmoded and useless craftery because we love patterns. They feel safe, reassuring, and nonpoisonous. Investors place reverence in the predictive power of a plethora of patterns—yield curves, high P/Es, moving averages, CPI, budget deficits—the list goes on. We rarely stop to ask, "What is my brain doing now to make me see something completely bassackwards and hence act bassackwardsly?" If an indicator (or a group of indicators) existed that could reliably predict the market, everyone would know about it (or them) and we'd all use it (or them) and we'd all be unimaginably wealthy. Since that isn't the case, and since it's only the unknown that has the power to move the market, we must get over our bias for following the known path.

20/20 Hindsight Bias and Order Preference

Hindsight bias, one result of our desire to follow a trail, is our tendency to exaggerate the quality of our foresight while conveniently forgetting our initial errors. What behavioralists call hindsight bias leaves no room for luck. Investors deceive themselves into believing they have some sort of special ability or knowledge that led to a good outcome. In hindsight, everything is 20/20 vision.

Hindsight bias is hard at work in an investor who claims he knew Altria would be a great stock when he bought it in January of 2000 (up 352 percent over the next six years).[14] His stock skyrocketed as the global stock market imploded and then couldn't fully recover. He's a genius, of course, and credits that decision to his sheer mental acuity. What this investor forgets to mention is he bought Yahoo! at $108 and sold it when it was trading at about $4 two years later. Excess pride accumulation and regret shunning go hand-in-hand with hindsight bias. All these biases work together and none of them lead you to make smart decisions.

Hindsight bias also leads us to presume prior patterns persist—the stock that did well will continue to be a star, and the doggy stock is a continual canine. And where there has been no action? There won't ever be. The simplest form of hindsight bias is to project the past into the future. It's so easy and rarely will folks argue with you when you do it.

Order preference is a manifestation of our instinct to predict and collect. For example, investors want each piece of their portfolio to perform well. If they are benchmarking (you should be—managing your portfolio against the S&P 500 or MSCI World and then regularly comparing your portfolio to it), they expect each and every stock they own to do as well or better than the benchmark. This is a natural instinct but impossible. Note in any benchmark, whatever it is, there are stocks with a very wide array of returns. This is not like the berries that were either ripe, not ripe yet, or past ripe—and otherwise all the same. To think you should have stocks without a wide array of returns means your portfolio doesn't have anything like the benchmark's diversification. And then, even if your stocks do uniformly well, it's only because you took a huge bet against the benchmark and got very lucky, very temporarily.

Simply said, order preference motivates so that if an investor owns, say, 60 stocks (not necessarily a bad number to own if you are investing globally), he wants each of the 60 stocks to be up as well as the entire portfolio. He forgets all that matters in finance is how the whole portfolio does. That's what impacts your net worth.

Investors suffer from order preference when they brag about the stock they bought that is up 800 percent but don't bother to look at how the portfolio as a whole is performing. When assessing performance, the whole is more important than the parts. This is a nearly impossible concept for most investors to get in their bones.

Imagine a portfolio containing only two $10,000 stocks. One rises by 25 percent and the other declines by 15 percent. The antiquated parts of our brain will tell us to regret the stock that declined. Standard finance tells us not to regret the parts—the totality did fine. Standard finance is right. The movements by themselves don't really tell us anything about the future, and we shouldn't act based on them anyway.

Think about it another way—imagine you owned an S&P index fund in a year it did great, like 1997 when it was up 33 percent.[15] You feel good, right? Now, imagine instead of the index, you owned 500 individual stocks. Five hundred stocks is far too many to own, by the way, but for the sake of this argument let's pretend you did.

Among those five hundred stocks you have some down 40 percent, 50 percent, and 60 percent.[16] Now how do you feel about your portfolio? You should feel equally as good as you did about the index fund, because the 500 stocks you own are the ones comprising the index, appropriately weighted. It doesn't matter you had a few down 50 percent anymore than it matters you had a few up over 150 percent.[17] In total, you were up 33 percent, which is what matters. Order preference causes you to focus on the individual parts and makes you lose sight of what is important.

The Great Humiliator's Favorite Tricks

If we were more evolved as investors, perhaps TGH would be reclassified as The Mild Humiliator (TMH) or even The Softer, Gentler, and Kinder Trickster (TSGKT). Our preconditioning keeps us repeatedly humiliated by the market through psychological tendencies we fall for over and over again. Unfortunately, our biases don't work alone—they work in concert with each other, making completely nonsensical investment decisions seem rational even while we commit them. Your brain won't tell you when you're making a stupid mistake because it doesn't think the cognitive errors you make are stupid. Rather, your brain tells you the investments "just didn't work out." And then you look for something to blame it on—regret shunning.

Your only weapon is Question Three—with every decision you make, ask, "What the heck is my brain doing to lead me astray this time?" The more sane and rational a decision may seem, the more important it is to ask. I've given you some examples already of your brain working against you, and I give you more later in this book. I teach you how to use them. You can make a list of them and keep it by your desk or bed stand. But you must keep asking yourself the question with every decision: "What is my brain doing to blindside me now?"

Remember, your brain is designed with bodily survival in mind, not financial survival. What may be a great instinct for avoiding ambush by a fanged beast can be very dangerous—completely harmful—when analyzing capital markets. Asking Question Three and recognizing the symptoms of a financial brain gone haywire is your best defense against yourself.

Consider the following all-too-real scenario involving a hypothetical investor we'll call Jim. See if you've ever made similar decisions. Let's say Jim's overall portfolio has risen 50 percent over the past three years. That's a pretty believable result after a few bull market years. Then, a market correction hits and the portfolio drops 18 percent over several months. Corrections are perfectly normal in a bull market—expect one every year or two. They happen in history more years than not. Jim knows this and realizes the markets are volatile and knows markets can correct 10 percent to 20 percent in a jiffy and still move onto higher prices. He knows he has a long time horizon, and short-term moves don't matter. Even so, when it happens to him, it feels terrible. Just terrible!

First—*myopic loss aversion.* That 18 percent loss feels more like 45 percent. He's about as miserable about his short-term 18 percent loss as he is happy about the gains of recent years. (The more recent and the short-term are the myopic part of myopic loss aversion. We tend to weigh the short-term more than the long-term despite the fact that eventually it's the long-term we end up with.) Jim starts thinking about doing something to stop this (myopic) pain. If Jim asked himself Question Three, maybe he could have stopped the downward spiral of the rest of this scenario. He would have recognized myopic loss aversion was making him consider selling at a terrible time—in midst a correction. Unfortunately, Jim didn't buy this book and his Stone Age brain took over.

Next—*order preference.* He notices some of his stocks are down—way down. He overlooks that overall, even in the midst of this correction, his whole portfolio is still up over 20 percent. He fixates on a few of his stocks that are down over 40 percent. He has one, XYZ, that is down 65 percent. He thinks his life would be so much better if he hadn't bought XYZ. Poker buddies tell him it's probably going lower. It eats at him. He has a few stocks still up 80 percent or more. Those stocks are so much better. Why did he ever buy that turkey XYZ—down 65 percent? Why didn't he buy more of the ones up 80 percent?

Then—*regret shunning.* He should never have delegated these decisions to a broker since he could have done a better job if he had been paying attention.

Then—*confirmation bias* and more *regret shunning.* The last stock he picked himself immediately rose 50 percent. At least this XYZ isn't his fault. He wouldn't have allowed a stock to be down 65 percent if the decision was his alone. This is the idiot broker's fault. Jim is a smart cookie.

Followed closely by—*hindsight bias.* He *knew* XYZ was no good when the broker pitched it. He was going to pass on it and buy one currently up 140 percent and knew that was what he should have done. He just wasn't paying attention. He should follow his instincts more often, since he tends to be right about this stuff. But then why does he feel so bad?

More *loss aversion*. If he doesn't do something soon, his wife may mistakenly think Jim is the idiot instead of the broker. (Hey, Jim, I don't know if you know this or not but your spouse probably already knew in her heart you were an idiot. She is banking on it.)

Next up—*overconfidence*. Forget that idiot broker. Though Jim has no background in finance or capital markets he knows he can do it better. He was smart enough to get through medical school, after all. What's the difference? If you're smart, you're smart. And Jim is really, really, really smart.

Jim has had it. He can't take the pain of being down 18 percent, or the greater indignity of having that XYZ dog down 65 percent, so he sells every stock down over some arbitrary time period or maybe just every stock down more than some arbitrary amount. Two weeks later, the entire market and the stocks Jim sold finish correcting and are trading higher than before. And Jim is sitting with about 40 percent of his liquid net worth in cash. He tries to think about medical things and doctoring and his upcoming vacation and anything but the market.

Jim would currently be a wealthier man had he (1) asked Question Three or (2) made no decisions at all, and (3) recognized his brain was trying to protect him from attack by a saber-toothed tiger, not guide him toward rational investing decisions. Meanwhile our smart doctor, in other realms a scientist, learns nothing from his cognitive mistakes as he shuns regret. "At least I didn't lose more," he tells himself. And he lives to repeat these errors and more another day.

Get Your Head Out of the Cave

Jim may not be beyond all hope. Neither are you. We suffer these behaviors, to be sure, but we aren't doomed. The way to overcome Stone Age thinking is regular and rigorous application of Question Three. After you've asked if what you believe is correct, and after you ask what you can fathom that others can't, it's imperative you pull your head out of your cave and ask whether your brain is sending you bad messages.

There are some practical things you can begin doing, right now, to help combat the more common cognitive errors. Once you learn to repeatedly ask Question Three and are suspicious you're on the brink of making a cognitive error, you can apply some of the following practices to keep yourself on this side of the millennium.

Another Flip—Accumulate Regret, Shun Pride

The Bible tells us pride goes before a fall. In capital markets, pride goes before myopic loss aversion as well as overconfidence, hindsight bias, and just about everything else that is evil, including selling at the bottom. You must reverse your natural inclinations permanently. You must shun pride and accumulate regret. It's the simplest, most basic trick I know to becoming a better investor. If you have a stock up a lot, assume you aren't a genius. Assume you're lucky, and luck can run out. If you have a stock down a lot, don't run from your regret. Accumulate regret with every loss. Live with it. Love it. Assume you weren't victimized by Enron management, your stockbroker, or your spouse (although I can't help you much with that). Assume you and only you were wrong about every down stock and your job is to learn a lesson about why you were wrong that teaches you how to do the same thing correctly the next time. If you can embrace your regret, you will be less inclined to sell at relative low points. Remember, the idea is not to buy low and sell whenever stock prices have you freaking out.

Accumulating regret and shunning pride have many benefits. First, you can learn from your mistakes. Second, instead of becoming more overconfident you become less confident and start seeing markets closer to the way they really are. Studies show less overconfident investors do better than more overconfident ones and you can make yourself less overconfident over time by accumulating regret and shunning pride.

Have you ever sold a stock because it was down, bought something else, and never looked back? You were glad to be rid of a dog and that was that? Maybe you didn't sell a stock—you sold the whole kitty and bought some quote-unquote safe bonds because the market as a whole scared you. Many investors do that—act emotionally and never check afterwards to see if their decision made them better or worse off. And they never evolve.

Embrace your regret. Know you can and will be wrong and your decisions have consequences. This is a game in which if you're right 70 percent of the time, in the long-run you're a super monster success. That means being wrong often, too. Being wrong is okay. The more you embrace your wrongness and see it as an opportunity for learning, the less wrongness you will have long-term. Don't be so busy patting yourself on the back that you "didn't lose more" to realize you have made a colossal error in selling out of the market or buying the wrong thing. Maybe that stock you sold wasn't a dog. Maybe the one you bought in its place was. Maybe the one you sold turned out to be the best performing stock for years afterwards and you pulled the trigger because you suffered from loss aversion, hindsight bias, or some other simple cognitive error. Maybe the market wasn't headed for a downward spiral. Maybe it ended the year up 25 percent or so, and you are a chump with your cash-like return of 3 percent, lagging the market, and putting a serious damper on your chances of reaching your long-term goals. Know you will be wrong again (and again and again) and take steps so when it happens you do your best to learn from your mistakes. Look for lessons to be learned from your mistakes so you make less of them in the future.

Question Three will prevent you from committing many crazy, irrational acts. More important, you need an all-encompassing and overriding strategy guiding every decision, and you absolutely must have a benchmark. (We discuss benchmarking and why it is vital to survival in Chapter 4.) But for now, know a benchmark can be any well-constructed index and is your road map in portfolio construction. If your benchmark is 50 percent U.S. stocks, you only want to vary from 50 percent U.S. stocks if you think you know something others don't about why U.S. stocks should do better or worse than foreign stocks. If your benchmark is 10 percent energy stocks, you should be 10 percent energy stocks unless you used the Three Questions to know something others don't, causing you to overweight or underweight energy. Otherwise you should just be passive to your benchmark. The goal is to perform similarly to your benchmark and better if you know something unique. Over time, the benchmark will get you where you need to go. Major deviations from your benchmark caused by your brain blindsiding you, such as myopic loss aversion, will seriously impact your ability to get to your long-term goals.

Here's an example. In March of 2000, I nailed the tech cycle pretty well, one of my better calls of the past 20 years. (I tell you how I did it in a later chapter.) My firm cut our clients' weight from slightly overweight (when tech was a third of the U.S. market and 25 percent of the world) to half the sector's weight. Clients were annoyed later that we hadn't cut it more, but I always know I could be wrong. Most particularly when I think I know something others don't, which I did then, I still know my brain is working to blindside me, so I try not to get too carried away—I don't make my bets too big. You should do that too—always seek to know what others don't but also always know you could be wrong. If you're wrong, and were bearish on tech when it turned out to be the best performing sector, you've still participated in it to some extent and won't lag the market too darned badly. If you're right, then you've participated less in a poor performing area and done better than the market—which is the game over time.

Accumulate regret. Shun pride. Focus on your benchmark. Only veer from it when the Three Questions lead you to believe you know things others don't. That is how to beat myopic loss aversion and overconfidence. It's how to engage TGH without getting humiliated.

Curb Your Overconfidence

A benchmark often helps offset many cognitive ills your brain will commit. But that doesn't mean you can't get a few (or many) market bets wrong. Here, and in other places, I share with you some bets that, despite best efforts, didn't go my way.

After successfully turning bearish on tech and then the whole market for 2000 through May 2002, my firm got back into the market in full force too early, including a slight technology overweight. Ouch! That smarted as stocks fell. Then things improved for a bit. The tech overweight did fine in 2003 when tech returned 49 percent[18] compared to the MSCI World at 33 percent.[19]

Wrongly, we maintained that tech overweight for two more years, believing tech would lead other sectors. Using the Three Questions, we identified several reasons tech should outperform. First, sentiment overall remained dismally bearish—so we knew the most important decision was to remain in the market. Second, the dismal sentiment specifically surrounding tech pointed to a psychological rebound. Using tools you will see later in this book, we could measure that sentiment was too low. Third, we could see things others couldn't pointing to a stronger and more resurgent U.S. GDP than commonly expected—leading to healthy U.S. corporate earnings as a nice surprise likely making the United States lead the world out of the global recession and bear market. Because overwhelmingly the big tech names are U.S. firms, it was natural to envision tech, driven by U.S. returns, as a good performer reversing the prior few years.

Lastly, overall we expected upside volatility. Partly we expected volatility because the first and second years of presidential terms historically are the most volatile times in the market as we saw in Chapter 2. (People tend to think of downside volatility as bad and upside volatility as not volatility at all. Not so. Volatility is volatility, regardless of whether it's positive or negative.) When the market is volatile to the upside, high beta stocks outperform, and tech is a perfect example of a high-beta sector. Expecting an "up-a-lot" and volatile year in 2004 and 2005, we positioned to do well in those conditions. That meant a relative overweight to tech.

As it turned out, tech was one of the worst performing sectors in 2004 and 2005, returning just 12 percent cumulatively over those two years[20] compared to the World's cumulative 26 percent.[21] Here's what went wrong.

By and large, despite sentiment on tech being low, my firm underestimated its inability to improve. After a volatile (positive, but still volatile) 2003 with tech doing well, in 2004 tech stocks absorbed fear of heights. We hadn't anticipated this because tech stocks were still so much lower than in 2000 or 2001. But investors re-anchored their frame of reference on tech to the lows of 2002 to 2003 and the subsequent rise caused investors to see tech as very high—too high, meaning they could fall very far. We didn't notice they had re-anchored their reference point forward. In retrospect, they were looking to replay the decline of 2000 to 2002. Fear of heights coupled with myopic loss aversion caused investors to fear tech falling two and a half times as much as any benefit they could envision if tech kept rising. Sentiment on tech was very low; yet it kept falling. We simply saw it wrong.

While thinking the market would rise nicely in 2004 and 2005, we were particularly caught off guard by how relatively nonvolatile those years were—and with middling returns. We got the direction right—that was good—but were wrong on magnitude. Those two years were the least volatile 24 months in 40 years, and just when we'd expected volatility in an up-a-lot market. Without that volatility, there was no way the tech bet would work.

Why was the market so nonvolatile? I don't know. It's something beyond any explanation I now know. I've tried to figure it out. I've tried to learn from the mistake. I did accumulate that regret. And I know the tech bet not working was not someone else's fault. There is no regret to shun. It wasn't my wife's fault. It wasn't the fault of Jeff Silk or Andrew Teufel who share with me the burden of investing decisions at my firm. We all saw it the same way. It wasn't anyone else's fault. It was simply a matter that at this point, we know we don't have the basis for predicting volatility. We don't know enough others don't know to be able to do it.

Once we saw we were wrong and knew we didn't know how to predict volatility, we unwound the bet—but our clients suffered two years of underperformance before we did that.

(continued)

Ironically, we were right about many other bets in those years. Materials, financials, and energy did fine as anticipated—but not tech! At this point, I'm still trying to learn what went wrong in our foreseeing volatility where it never occurred. Sometimes it takes time to study your mistakes. Looking back, I see parallels after the 1980 energy bubble—energy stocks lagged for quite some time and were volatile on the way down then not on the way up. That might have helped had I studied it better earlier. (We're certainly still studying that now. You can see charts of some of those energy stocks from that comparable period in Figure 3.2.) Also, small-cap stocks led for a considerable period. Small stocks are the reverse of tech stocks, which are largely big-caps on a dollar-weighted basis. I should have been able to figure that out. That was simply not putting together two things we knew. We won't miss that one again.

The good news in all this? First, every time we make a mistake we can be better prepared next time. Second, as mentioned earlier, we only had a slight overweight to tech and America. Overconfidence here would have been disastrous, since tech and America lagged relatively. What saved me in those years was adhering to the benchmark—limiting the overweight on tech and America meant the mistake wasn't carried to crippling extremes. Despite believing we had the basis for a bet, we didn't bet the house on it. Even when I'm certain I know things others don't—I always know I could be wrong; it happens. That principle permeates everything I do.

I prefer being right. Everyone does. But I know there will be times when I am mostly wrong. And that's okay. It's a big opportunity to accumulate regret and learn—and to be better in the future. It happens and will happen again, and it's never fun. But because I always manage against the benchmark, and because I work hard not to be overconfident, I can be wrong without suffering too badly or too long. And then I can learn. Use the Three Questions and a benchmark, and you can be more right on average, and not irreparably harmed when wrong. And, you can avoid the perils of overconfidence.

Less Can Be More

When combating *overconfidence*, women have a distinct advantage over men. A wonderful academic study was done to see who are better investors—men or women. It was no surprise to me they found women to be much better investors with better long-term results.[22] Why? While the men were hunting boar and gazelles, women were gathering berries and grains. Picking berries doesn't require as much overconfidence as flinging stone-tipped twigs at charging beasts. Because women weren't hardwired from eons of hunter evolution to be as overconfident as men, they tend to trade less and make fewer changes to their portfolios. Both women and men tended to be wrong more than right and in the same proportions. But because men are more overconfident, they trade more often without knowing anything unique. Those extra senseless trades work against them relative to the fewer senseless trades made by women. Fewer changes result in better performance—unless you actually do know something others don't to justify the extra trades. Maybe that's why the fairer sex lives longer. They have more money to support themselves. (I always thought it was because they presumed we men were stupid and overconfident, so they got us to do all the dangerous stuff; but I'm not really sure about that.) Of course, that is something for the gentlemen to ponder.

Something for the ladies to consider? Throughout history, essentially all of the very top, most famous, and richest investors have been men. The only big-time exception was Hetty Green from the nineteenth century (see my book, 100 *Minds That Made the Market,* for a cameo biography of Hetty Green). Women have almost never made it to the ranks of the very most successful investors. Why? Many women will tell you historical (or current) social bias didn't allow it or even dissuaded women from trying. Of course, TGH doesn't care who you are. It's an equal opportunity humiliator and is delighted to humiliate a woman as much as a man. That Hetty Green did it more than 125 years ago proves it could be done then, and many women have been in the industry these past 35 years. I'd guess, without really knowing for sure, few women have been historically among the very best investors because of the following: Women are proven less overconfident than men (as in the earlier cited research) and better investors on average than men (a point provable but still not widely accepted). Still it's always a mistake to confuse a single incidence with an average. Because women are less overconfident than men, they probably don't fare as well as the very few supremely overconfident males on the far end of the bell curve that end up being the few who are right or lucky or both. Those few men just pushed further.

Still, less overconfidence means less unwarranted trades and here women have an undisputed advantage. If fewer trades mean fewer bets without knowing something others don't—which means better performance—then toss any day-trading plans. There isn't a single good reason why someone would day-trade unless they suffered a God-complex or are admittedly and hopelessly masochistic. To rise from bed each day, a day-trader must be a consummate pride-accumulating regret shunner—basing heavy action on not knowing anything others don't. And you know how bad that is. Day-traders will gladly boast of the returns they got on one stock or another. But ask about their overall return and they become strangely silent. Do they not know? Or is it just too painful to admit? Or will they lie? Probably depends. Day-trading requires some order preference to go along with regret-shunning overconfidence.

Any time you get ready to make a trade, use your other two Questions to make sure you aren't trading on false myths and your action is based on an advantage over other investors. If you aren't sure your reason to trade is correct or you're in possession of unique—or uniquely framed—information, then you're overconfident. Sometimes being passive is the most active and appropriate thing to do. Don't trade just to trade. Practice humility.

Genius? Or Lucky and Forgetful?

You're most likely to suffer *hindsight bias* after a run of luck with an individual stock, sector, or even a broad market call you've made. Luck being the operative word.

A little pride shunning and regret accumulation goes far toward helping combat this bias. When you're right about a bet, your reaction shouldn't be, "I knew I was right about that." Rather, it should be, "I knew I could have been wrong and I was probably at least partly lucky. Where was I lucky? How could I have been wrong?" Every decision you make should come with the assumption you can be wrong. If you think this way, you will take steps to ensure you're not injured too badly by bad assumptions.

Thinking about building an all energy portfolio? (If you're benchmarking, that would never happen, but let's pretend.) Maybe you were thinking about it somewhere in 2005 or 2006, after you saw your Exxon and ConocoPhillips and Chevron stocks appreciate in value for several years. What a genius you were for picking those stocks! You *knew* a global economic expansion following the recession, including labor reforms and a boom in China and India, would lead to increased global oil demand and hence higher oil stock prices. And you knew fears about higher gas prices impacting the industry and causing inflation were overblown and priced into markets anyway. In fact, you're pretty sure you told your tennis group the net of that back in 2003. They don't remember this alleged conversation, but you sure do.

Stop. Ask yourself, what if you were wrong? What if your success wasn't due to your adroit analysis of global oil consumption, but rather some dumb luck? Would you want to take that big a gamble? Just because you were right once (or twice) doesn't mean you will be again. Many investors were heavily invested in tech in 1998 and 1999—some with 100 percent of their assets there. Being grossly overallocated in a hot sector makes you a terrific dart-thrower but a risky money manager. It definitely doesn't make you a market genius. If you were one of those people heavily invested in tech, you might have been patting your back in 1999 just as some are patting their backs over energy in 2006. But if you turned out to be wrong about tech in 1999 or 2000 (or energy today, or the next hot sector whenever it rolls around), you would have lost your shirt (and your money and your home and your clients and . . . and . . . and . . .). Being *lucky* and right is no way to manage your assets. Being cautious and right more often than you're wrong is how to beat the market. When I see investors vocalize what hot dogs they've been, I always note hot dogs are dogs. They are dogs waiting to be bit by TGH.

If you're tempted to brag you *knew* Altria would be a superstar, or you *knew* Apple would go on a tear, ask yourself if you *knew* about any of the stocks that turned out to be losers. You didn't, otherwise you wouldn't have bought them. Shun that pride, accumulate regret, honor your benchmark, and avoid hindsight bias.

The Whole Versus the Sum of Its Parts

On *order preference*, remember all that matters is the overall result. Nobody cares if you have a stock up 800 percent and you shouldn't care if you have one that is down 80 percent. Your individual stocks will gyrate wildly and perform, by and large, the way most of the stocks in their respective categories do (e.g., tech, health care, large cap, value, Japan). Say to yourself, "I have a stock that is up 800 percent. So what? I guess I got lucky somehow. I wonder how?" Look at the progression of the portfolio as a whole. Learn to calculate the performance of your overall portfolio, and ignore (for the most part) what the individual stocks are doing (we cover the other part later).

I'm not saying you shouldn't consider how each stock does relative to its category. You should, just not pathologically too often. Watching individual stocks too often and too intently leads to serious loss aversion as well as other cognitive errors. When you look at your individual stocks, it shouldn't be to check whether they are "up or down." It shouldn't even be to check how they are doing relative to your overall portfolio. If your overall portfolio is up 25 percent for the year and you have some stocks that are up less than that or even down, it doesn't mean they're bad stocks. If a stock is performing similarly to others in its category, then it's doing its job.

A little out- or under-performance over a month or two is nothing to even think about. But if a stock performs significantly worse or even significantly better than its peers over a longer time period, then you can start asking what makes it behave differently.

If you select stocks that are good representations of the categories in your benchmark, then you have no need to obsess about how each one is doing. The only basis for any bet, including one stock versus its category, is rationally thinking you know something others don't while also knowing you could be wrong. That implies not being obsessive. If your portfolio in totality is performing similarly (again, not over a week or a month or a quarter—think longer term) or a little better than your benchmark, you're doing fine.

Bunnies or Elephants? Always Think in Terms of Scalability!

Yet another way to combat a whole slew of cognitive errors is relative thinking. Every investing concern, every finance issue, every news item has scalability. Remember our example of the Iraq war from Chapter 1? Reporters love to solemnly report the per-year or even the cumulative cost of a war. They know when they say, "The cost of the Iraq war has been $320 billion so far,"[23] your Stone Age brain is hearing, "Blah blah blah, cost is 320 million gazillion bajillions," so much money you can't wrap your brain around it. But when you think about it relatively, as an annual percent of our nation's income (GDP), it's a lesser deal economically. That still isn't an argument for whether a war is smart or stupid, but it's a way for you to rationally consider a news item that the media intends to be panic-inducing.

Our Stone Age brethren knew a bunny rabbit was small and an elephant was big. They also knew the elephant was scary and hard to kill and it might stomp on them, and the fuzzy bunny was cute and cuddly and easy to catch and soft and delicious. Big was scary, small was tasty (and not scary). But ask the same Stone Ager if the H1 Alpha Hummer is bigger or smaller than the elephant and he has no basis for comparison. Are we talking height? Weight? Cubic inches? Elephant power? Coming at you or going away? Of course, Hummers didn't exist back then. (I believe Fred Flintstone drove an early model Sand Rover.)

Modern man can learn to always scale and think relatively. Still, investors rarely think in terms of scaling and relativity on investment decisions. Inability to scale is a cognitive error our caveman brains want to commit when we see big numbers. Big numbers seem scary, like a crazed, stampeding elephant. However, scalability can make us see big numbers correctly—debt, deficit, GDP, jobs, wars, sick chickens in Turkey, whatever. Practice scaling when you read the news. Sure, the perky blonde on your ABC affiliate delivers the latest dread news on the trade deficit being many, many billions (Egads! Hundreds of gazillion bajillions!), but does she really help you with perspective? You can do it easily by thinking what is the percentage of this big number versus GDP? Better yet, global GDP? Usually it's nothing to worry about once you start thinking relatively (we look at that in more detail later).

A pattern should be emerging here. Many cognitive errors can be avoided—once you recognize a brain gone haywire by using Question Three—if you shun pride, accumulate regret, use a benchmark, have a strategy, think relatively and focus on your long-term goal.

Questions One and Two will give you a gameable bet, an edge your fellow investors don't have. But without Question Three, you will be adrift, subject to the powerful suggestion of a brain intent on saving you from long extinct dangers. In Chapter 9, I show you how to pull your Three Questions together and create a strategy to keep your brain disciplined, even when it most wants to stray. But first, in Chapter 4, let's talk about how the Three Questions can be used together to build ahead-of-their-time, beyond-state-of-the-art technology to beat the market. Thanks for reading on.

4 CAPITAL MARKETS TECHNOLOGY

Building and Putting Capital Markets Technology into Practice

By now you know the Three Questions work together, helping you identify what you can know that others don't. While this book demonstrates how to debunk some common myths and uncover some surprising truths via the Three Questions—don't stop with the few examples the limited space these pages allow. The point isn't to garner a few useful investing tidbits, but to use the questions always with every decision. Stop and ask, "Why am I buying or selling this stock, sector, fund, whatever? Why do I think this is a good idea? What do I know that others don't? What do I believe that is false here? What can I fathom?" Simply asking the questions puts you ahead of most investors. Then ask, "Is my brain just messing with me?" This isn't a static how-to book. It gives you a dynamic process and a tool set to keep you three steps ahead of the investing populace for your investing life.

The answers to the Three Questions, either one-by-one or together, provide you with a new way of approaching markets—one amounting to a technology you can repeatedly test and apply. Your goal in repeatedly asking the Three Questions is to build, over time, a dynamic arsenal of capital markets technology.

We don't know much today about how capital markets work compared to what we will know in 10, 20, or 50 years. One way to know something others don't is to build capital markets technology of the future now. If you can know something now others won't know for 5, 10, or 20 years, you have a long lead. Capital markets technology will help explain parts of the investing world never before understood and, like any other piece of technology, give you a dependable, usable tool. The technology you create allows you to make more accurate forecasts and bets on freely traded markets, sectors, and categories or even analyze individual stocks. What's more, technology allows you to discover and create even more unique technology.

History as a Research Lab

If approaching investing correctly (like a scientist—not a blacksmith), you must test your capital markets technology. And there is no better laboratory for testing new technology than history. Far too many of our investing myths, the ones comprising the documented and accepted ways of thinking, are based on ideology, theoretical whim, political inclination, or worse, cognitive bias. When tested against historical data, they simply fall apart—just like the myth about high P/Es and the misplaced fear about federal budget deficits. Proving something is true takes more rigor than proving something isn't true. To prove something isn't true, you just need to show consistently lousy correlation. History can teach us if something is beyond reasonable to expect.

If throughout history, X wasn't tightly linked to Y, and in fact X is linked to a bunch of stuff other than Y, you have no basis to bet X will suddenly start causing Y. Stubbornly clinging to a popular causal theory without supporting evidence is how myths become firmly entrenched in our culture. But it takes a long time and the longer the myth runs, the less people are prone to verify its validity.

The good news is you needn't own a Bloomberg terminal to have access to data. Vast quantities of neatly organized data in varying levels of granularity are available for free on any number of web sites. A sampling of web sites that might be useful can be found on page 121.

If you can't figure out how to download or analyze the data using Excel, see the example in Chapter 1 or find a high school student to show you how. By 2007, I assume most readers are at least generally comfortable on the Internet.

That said, the data in your proof can be either quantitative or qualitative. The high P/E myth was debunked with quantitative data. You saw how easy it was to disprove a very widely held theory using standard data simply by doing simple tests based on asking the question.

But what if the data is either hard to come by or measure? Can your capital markets technology be qualitative in nature? Sure, as long as you have plenty of examples to analyze and it makes economic sense. A great example is the presidential term cycle we previously examined. The cycle is difficult to measure numerically but thus far is still powerful. In terms of data, you can examine all the election cycles going back to 1926. It's not exactly quantitative, but there is a clear pattern with underlying fundamentals. And, of course, an important reason it works is the fundamentals aren't well understood, the pattern is not well accepted, and most often when articulated, it's ridiculed.

Authority	Website	Data Includes:
Bloomberg	www.bloomberg.com	Global stock market news and quotes, calculators, other media
Bureau of Economic Analysis	www.bea.gov	GDP, current account balance, import/export
Bureau of Labor Statistics	www.bls.gov	CPI, unemployment, productivity, inflation
Centers for Disease Control and Prevention (CDC)	www.cdc.gov	Statistics: births, deaths, health trends and statistics, demographics, etc.
Department of Commerce	www.commerce.gov	Trade conditions
Energy Information Administration	www.eia.doe.gov	Energy source statistics, historical data
Forbes Magazine	www.forbes.com	Business and market news, personal finance
International Monetary Fund	www.imf.org	International economic and financial statistics
Lexis Nexis	www.lexisnexis.com	Comprehensive search engine of news, public records, information sources
Morgan Stanley Capital International	www.mscibarra.com	MSCI indexes, data, characteristics, performance
National Bureau of Economic Research	www.nber.org	Business cycles (recession timing)
New York Stock Exchange	www.nyse.com	New York stock exchange
Organisation for Economic Co-operation and Development	www.oecd.org	International economic and trade statistics
Real Clear Politics	www.realclearpolitics.com	Essential political news, headlines, blogs, polls, etc.
Russell index service	www.russell.com	Russell index data, characteristics, valuations
Standard & Poor's index service	www.standardandpoors.com	S&P indexes, data, characteristics, constituents
The Economist	www.economist.com	World financial and economic news, current events weekly
The Financial Times (UK)	www.ft.com	International stock market, business, and world news
Thomas/US Library of Congress	www.loc.gov	Legislative information
U.S. Census Bureau	www.census.gov	Statistics by region
U.S. Congress	www.house.gov	Representative sites, bills, laws, roll call
U.S. Department of Defense	www.defenselink.mil	Official news, reports
U.S. Federal Reserve	www.federalreserve.gov	Bank balance sheet, credit statistics, money stock, flow of funds
U.S. Government Official Web Portal	www.firstgov.gov	Links to all government branches, departments, areas
U.S. House of Representatives Office of the Clerk	clerk.house.gov/	Legislative branch details, history, election statistics
U.S. Office of Management and Budget	www.whitehouse.gov/omb	U.S. Budget
U.S. Treasury	www.ustreas.gov	Taxes, interest rates, social security, medicare
Wall Street Journal (US)	www.wsj.com	International stock market, business, and world news
Wilshire index service	www.wilshire.com	Wilshire stock indexes, valuations
World Health Organization (WHO)	www.who.int	Global health & burden of disease statistics, mortality, news, alerts

But your proof must make basic economic sense. If you find a reliable pattern but don't have a good causal explanation for it, don't bet on it. Did you know every year ending in a 5 since 1926 has been positive?[1] Every year. You might feel thus justified betting the farm (or whatever you have to bet) on the next 5 year. Don't! Simple numerology! There is no known economic reason why every 10th year should always be positive. For that matter, years ending in 5 since 1955 have seen more fierce land falling hurricanes as evidenced by the number of hurricane names retired.[2] So what? I doubt the NOAA is relying on the "year 5" theory in any way whatsoever in its forecasting. And you sure as heck can't argue heavy hurricane incidence causes years ending in 5 to have good stock markets. What we have here is a statistical anomaly—a freak of nature. The lucky guy flipping 50 heads in a row. They happen, so be cautious. Again, correlation without causation is no basis for a bet.

Then again, maybe you can uncover a sound economic reason why 5 years are always positive and that can be your personal capital markets technology. Good for you. Then you've done a Question Two and fathomed what is otherwise unfathomable to the rest of us. Fair game—if you can do it you have the basis for a bet.

Once you have tested and put a new piece of capital markets technology to good use, don't become overconfident and assume you have a sure winner every time you make the same bet. Nothing is perfect or works all the time. Suppose X causes Y 70 percent of the time. That's pretty good. It's worth betting on. Every time. And yet some other thing or things cause Y 30 percent of the time. So while it's worth betting on X to cause Y, you will still be wrong 30 percent of the time. No one thing is perfect.

It's Good while It Lasts

The price-to-sales ratio (PSR; sometimes P/S) is a good example of ground-breaking capital markets technology I pioneered that was powerful in its day, yet isn't so much now. I had uncovered a way no one had yet used to tell if a stock might be over- or undervalued, and I wrote a book about it in 1984 called *Super Stocks*. While Ben Graham made passing mention of the relationship between price and sales being potentially interesting, the first published work anywhere on the relationship was mine. I'm very proud of that—just like I am of my third grade school report on Guatemala. But otherwise neither is noteworthy today. Just memories. But 25 years ago, if you could simply screen for low PSR stocks, which wasn't easy, you could beat the market. After my book and subsequent exposure, the PSR became widely used and even, off and on, part of the required curriculum for the

CFA exam. Most analytical web sites include the PSR today. But as capital markets technology and a forecasting tool, the PSR has become largely priced into the market, and the rest is history. Even a great discovery becomes obsolete with popularity and time.

For the uninitiated, you no longer must calculate the PSR yourself. You can find it at common web sites, like www.morningstar.com, close to the stock's P/E, market capitalization, and the earnings-per-share. The PSR tells you, in the event the name didn't give it away, a stock's price relative to its per-share sales. It's just like a P/E but uses annual revenue or sales where the P/E uses earnings. A stock selling for $25 with $25 in sales per share has a PSR of 1. Pretty straight-forward. This may not sound revolutionary now—like trying to imagine a time before someone said, "Hey, what would happen if we divided a stock's price by its earnings?" But when I first started writing about it, no one had done it. Now they use it all the time, so it's less useful. I only bring this up to show you can't hang on to discoveries. If they become popular, they lose their power. It's always time to be working on the next discovery.

For the purposes of this book, there is no need for an in-depth rehash of PSRs or my first book, *Super Stocks*, which was largely about them. After all, the book is almost a quarter-century old. But there are a couple of points I should make. First, about the book! Reading old investment books is useful and a great way to learn the canvas of what developed in terms of capital market technology—when, how, and by whom. Whether my old books or anyone else's, if you want them, you needn't buy them new. And often they're hard to find or out of print, but you can always get a used copy cheap. As a general rule for those of you who like to buy books but would prefer them used, inexpensive, and delivered to your door instead of going to a store—by far the best used book search engine in recent years is www.ABEbooks.com, the successor to the former American Book Exchange. Check it out. It spans the online used booksellers' world and lets you search by author, title, price, and more. It covers far more booksellers than any other single source. And it gives you a wide array of choices. As of this writing, you could find used copies of *Super Stocks* ranging from $4.80 all the way up to over $200. On the pricier end of the scale, the $200-plus book was not valuable because of me but because of who once owned it and his autograph. And maybe you like to collect autographs. But as a general rule, my first stop in looking for an old book is ABEbooks.com. If you haven't tried it, you will be impressed.

Finding Earnings When There Were None

Anyway—anyone who plans on making money in stocks knows you want to buy a stock before it becomes "in favor." The requisite flip side is you must buy the stock when it seems *out* of favor. The trick is knowing which stock will be in favor soon while currently seeming doggy. How can you know that? Well, that was how I got interested in PSRs initially. My early PSR evolution translates directly into how to think about developing capital markets technology.

Investors have long used P/Es looking for cheap stocks. One hundred years ago—plus! But some emerging companies may not have any earnings to report. Even established companies may be profitless during cyclical downturns and times of individual corporate crises, and those can be interesting times to consider a stock—when it's out of favor. You can't get a P/E in those scenarios because you can't divide something by zero. Sometimes a company has a P/E of 1,000 because its earnings have almost completely disappeared. Sometimes a company has a P/E of 5 because of temporarily high profit margins that can't be sustained.

But even if a firm doesn't have earnings, it still has sales (or at least it should or is in big trouble). This is where Question Two came into play for me decades ago—what could I fathom others could not? It made sense any stock with a low price relative to its previous 12-month sales would rise—if its future earnings might become large enough to make the current PSR translate into a low future P/E ratio (or in other words, a high future earnings yield). What today people don't like, tomorrow they would. How tough is that? People would eventually discover this undervalued stock was posting super revenue, fat future profit margins, and was cheap, and they'd come around and drive the price up. Hence, if you were rational, you'd want to buy a stock when its price relative to the company's sales is low and yet it didn't appear cheap based on P/E. Low relative to the market, but more important, low relative to its category and low relative to its future earnings. When I wrote *Super Stocks*, I defined low PSR stocks as generally ones where the company's total market value was less than 75 percent of the company's total annual revenue. I defined high PSR stocks as ones where the market value of the company was more than three times its annual revenue.

There was the theory, but that's all it was. At the time, there were no sources citing PSRs like there are now. There were no databases. Bloomberg .com and Morningstar.com didn't exist to neatly calculate a PSR for me for every stock like they and many other sources do now. I extrapolated data from publicly available information and built my own data to arrive at my ratio. Back then, there was actually money to be made by compiling data because data was still scarce and expensive. Today, data is essentially free. If you're younger, you may have difficulty realizing just how hard data was to get. In 1981, I paid Goldman Sachs $20,000 for a simple one-time screen of the New York Stock Exchange (NYSE) based on current PSRs. It was that expensive for something anyone can get now for free. Historical data had to be built by hand, which was effectively prohibitive unless you knew exactly what you wanted to do.

When I back-tested historical PSRs against subsequent stock market returns, my theory held up. I built data against several stock universes ranging from a 1970s tech universe compiled by the former investment banking firm, Hambrecht & Quist, to general 1930s stocks based on Moody's data retrieved by hand. Stocks with lower PSRs did far and away better than those with higher ratios. Not every single time with every single stock, but enough to provide me with a reliable indicator for forecasting and a good basis for a market bet. In other words, stocks with low PSRs were superior stocks, which ultimately led to my book title.

Before I wrote *Super Stocks* I used this nifty new technology with a fair amount of success. Effectively, my usage of PSRs got my career propelled in many ways. You may again wonder why I would advertise something giving me a competitive edge in a mass-produced book. You may think I should have kept what I knew about the PSR a secret so I could have maintained my advantage. Not so! Wrong way to think.

Any advantage you have is likely temporary. Behind you there is someone else looking for what you just found. I knew I had discovered something neat, but I hadn't done anything magical or prohibitively mathematically complicated or both. I hadn't done anything anyone else couldn't do. All I did was look at available data (hard to get data, but available data nonetheless) in a new way and do a little back-testing and a little linkage to fundamental theory. Other people were bound to see what I saw sooner or later. Probably sooner! So I kept putting the idea out there to see if anyone else was biting. For a while, no one was.

After I published the book, people bit but it took a long time. For about 10 more years, I had the PSR pretty much to myself. For example, in 1997 James O'Shaughnessy wrote a best-selling book titled *What Works on Wall Street*[3] in which he analyzed all the common ratios to see which might lead to higher subsequent returns. He labeled the PSR as, "The King of the Value Factors," and he claimed his analysis showed PSRs generated higher subsequent returns than any other single ratio. Jim's handwritten inscription in the copy he gave me reads, "Boy did you ever come up with a good ratio! Think how horrible us poor money managers would feel if instead of market cap, S&P had based their index on low PSR stocks." O'Shaughnessey's book propelled PSRs further into prominence, and soon the PSR lost most of its power. It got priced.

Was I upset my innovation became widely used and therefore thoroughly priced? Not at all! I was thrilled. First, if it really was good, it was inevitable—at least this way it happened on my terms and I was ready for it. There was no way the dot-com era would arrive with all its free data without someone stumbling on the PSR and popularizing it. I got a good run from that technology and was able to see when it was time to move on. By then, I was off on other new things I'd never dreamed of when I first did the PSR. I wasn't so overconfident (a cognitive error) in the 1970s and early-1980s to assume I had out-thought all investors for all time. If the PSR was clever in the early-1980s in a world of CP/M based PCs with 5-1/4 inch floppy discs and no hard drives, the guys who created the Commodore 64 were pretty clever too. The subsequent wave of 1980s and 1990s electronics would wipe out the world of expensive data. It would make the PSR visible to everyone. Markets evolve and so must we.

If the PSR no longer works much, why am I wasting ink telling you about it? First of all, because some people are still convinced this antiquated piece of technology still works like it did. A gentleman named Jack Hough marveled at his ability to forecast stock returns with the PSR in a 2006 *Wall Street Journal* article.[4] With any ratio like this, once popularized, sometimes it works and sometimes it doesn't—just enough to keep people interested—same with the P/E, dividend yield, price-to-book, you name it. You can even take the most nonsensical ratios and find times when they appear to generate excess returns. Just looking at the companies with the highest cash per share will sometimes give you market-beating stocks. Looking at companies with the lowest cash per share will sometimes beat the market. But neither has anything to do with being able to beat the market in the long term.

Over the past 15 years or so, low PSR stocks have been a bit less volatile than both low P/E stocks and the market and have no long-term, risk adjusted, excess return—now. They're priced. However, when value stocks have outperformed growth, low PSR stocks have generally beaten both the market and value and been more volatile than the market overall. When growth stocks beat value stocks, low PSR stocks have lagged the market and value.

Now pause for a minute. What did I just tell you? What can you do with this knowledge right now—the way you've learned to think in Chapters 1 through 3? How can you use what I've told you to make rational, workable bets here and now—at least until making those bets becomes well-known and popular? Let's do a Question Two. What can you fathom that no one else fathoms about this? We saw in Chapter 2 how to know when growth stocks will best value stocks and vice versa. I just told you when value stocks lead the market PSRs still have some extra oomph relative to value but not when growth stocks lead. So, I just told you when you can and can't expect to get some temporary excess return by using PSRs as a screening device. Your goal is to figure out when value stocks will lead the market and then incorporate low PSR stocks into your stock selection—but not when growth stocks lead the market. When growth leads the market, you want your stocks to be high PSR stocks. Today the PSR isn't a uniform tool for all seasons, but a tool to use temporarily when incorporated with other successful capital markets technology. Figure out when value will do better than growth, include low PSR stocks in your portfolio then, and you will have a tool to help you beat the market. During those times, low PSR stocks have not only temporary market-beating returns, but also, because they are more "oomphy" than low P/Es and other value measures, the ability to temporarily beat other value-based tools. Of course, you must use the same technology from Chapter 2 to know when to reverse course and discontinue using low PSR stocks in your portfolio. Then you want higher PSR stocks.

The Stock Market Is Not a Ballpeen Hammer—But It Can Hit You Hard

Consider this another way briefly. Some category of stock outperforms the market for five years. A preponderance of investors jump on its band wagon, doing whatever it was that was so successful in those years. But those things stop working for the next five years or so, leading investors to think they will never work again. Because investors think they won't work anymore, it's very possible for them to start working again. They are no longer discounted into pricing but simply ignored because of cognitive error. This is what happens to low PSR, low P/E, dividend yield, and others. They come through long periods where they haven't worked, so they are ignored for another long period. Then, when value comes back into favor they can and do work temporarily. Traditional craftsmen hate this kind of very real market phenomena because they want their tools to work the same way all the time.

This further illustrates the importance of continued testing and ongoing innovation. I repeatedly tested my PSR technology before deploying it so I wouldn't be guilelessly relying on it when it became priced and useless. I gave up on it long ago as a primary tool and have since developed many other capital market technologies because developing the next new thing is what the game is all about. But it is still a secondary tool that can be used at times.

Sure, you can use the Three Questions a few times and stumble on a thing or two others don't know. But if you don't make the Three Questions a part of your way of thinking, you will eventually lose any advantage you might have stumbled on. There is a term for investors who discover one gimmick and never innovate again—a one-trick pony. The history of investing is full of them. Bookstore shelves and MSNBC are fraught with one-trick ponies who leveraged their 15 minutes into an inexplicable lifetime of dated and ineffectual advice.

Let's take another sidestep on Warren Buffett. He doesn't or hasn't thought at all like I do, and my guess is he would say much of what I say is silly. Again, what other people think of me isn't my business. But I've spent a lot of time thinking about him for many obvious reasons. Among other things, I wrote the introduction to the second edition of *The Warren Buffett Way* by Robert Hagstrom (published by John Wiley, 2005)—the bestselling biography of the man. A quality standing out about Mr. Buffett is his ability to morph. If you read his materials from the 1960s, he said very different things than in the 1970s and early-1980s. Early on he was buying dirt-cheap stocks by simple statistical standards and typically smaller stocks—which would today be referred to as small-cap value (although that term didn't exist until the late 1980s). Later he bought what he called "franchises." Then he entered a period of buying great managements of big companies and being a long-term holder—otherwise thought of as big-cap growth today—that many ascribed to the influence of my father coupled with Charlie Munger. When Mr. Buffett was buying Coke and Gillette, you couldn't quite reconcile those activities with the kinds of things he owned two decades earlier. Then, amazingly, seven years ago, at just the right time, he was buying smaller things dirt cheap again just as value came back into play as the twenty-first century began. I have other comments about Mr. Buffett throughout this book but I'd like you to see, while he never lost the core of what he was doing or what he was looking for, he tactically morphed steadily over the decades. Trying to freeze his tactics from any decade and replicate them in the next few would never have led you to his actual actions. There is nothing wrong with that. It's as it should be. That he doesn't develop capital markets technology is just his way because—I think—he is mainly intuitive and in that regard very rare. But whether developing capital markets technology or being instinctual like Mr. Buffett, morphing, adapting, and changing are fundamental to success. Stagnancy is failure long term. Since I don't know how to be instinctual, I rely on the Three Questions and building capital markets technology.

Forecast with Accuracy, Not Like a Professional

Occasionally there is a capital markets technology priced into the market in its initial application but still proving useful elsewhere. Just because the masses adopt a new technology doesn't mean they use it correctly or even everywhere they could—or maybe it can be used with something else they haven't considered. One example is something I call sentiment-based bell curve forecasting. It's something I created and used for a number of years. Like PSRs, this technology as I first introduced it in the 1990s is today largely priced into the market—in some applications and in some places. But in other applications and places, it still works (we get to that in a bit).

How did I get to sentiment-based bell curve forecasting? We all now know if everyone agrees some market move will occur, it can't. But let's consider why for another moment to lead us in a circuitous path to some valuable technology. Remember our analogy from the Preface about creating a representative sample of investors for a poll? You know polling technology is sufficient because it can discern within a predictable level of error the outcome of the election of a president, governor, or senator just beforehand. You hear polls prognosticating things like, Joe beats Blow 52 to 48 within a margin of error of 5 percent—and you can't quite tell who will win. But another time, you hear Jane beats Joe 60 percent to 40 percent with a 5 percent margin of error and you do know who wins. This technology is mature. The pollsters start by building a representative sample of the actual voter world. If the sample isn't built correctly, the polls don't work; but if the sample is representative, it needn't be huge. You can forecast a big state election with a sample of just 500 people if they're picked right.

So we took our imaginary sample of investors (value vamps, growth groupies, and the rest) and polled them about what they thought the market would do next month, let's call it March. And they overwhelmingly concluded the market would soar in March. So we knew it couldn't. Because if they were overwhelming in their view it would go way up, and if they were reflective of all investors as a group, then whatever buying they had to do would be completed before March began—or before it went on for long—and there would be no subsequent buying to drive stocks up. Their belief priced it in, and it couldn't occur.

Sadly, we don't have technology today letting us correctly build a sample of all investors. There are sentiment universes existing that claim to be useful this way, but they aren't. One commonly used is the so-called Investors' Intelligence data, based on newsletter writers. Another is a regular poll of members of the American Association of Individual Investors. Meir Statman and I looked at these in some detail and demonstrated they aren't predictive despite often being used by many investors as if they were. (For this study in detail, see "Investor Sentiment and Stock Returns.")[5] These tools don't stand up to statistical analysis and are grossly lacking.

There are many reasons we don't know how to build a correct sample today. To start, individual investors have little incentive to be vocal with a pollster about their money views. Why should I tell you about my money life any more than I would tell you about my sex life? In addition, different investors use the same words for different meanings, leading to conflicting conclusions when you poll—they don't really speak a common language. Consider the fact that we have a glossary in the back of this book—for just that reason—because not all of you may use the terms similarly. This becomes very clear and fascinating when you run a focus group. Focus groups are usually the province of marketing people at consumer firms—like Procter & Gamble. They pay maybe 10 people, supposedly carefully picked to be representative of some category, to meet with a moderator who explains that interested observers are behind a one-way mirror listening and watching. The moderator leads the 10 through a discussion about whatever—maybe new toothpaste—and the marketing mavens behind the mirror glean information useful to improving the product or its marketing or both. In the heat of the discussion, participants often forget the people behind the one-way mirror and the discussion gets more intimate than you might imagine. My firm is one of the few in money management running regular focus groups with investors of all types, and they generate interesting information outside of marketing, bearing directly on human behavior in markets. But when you do this with normal high net worth individual investors, you find the same words often have multiple and conflicting meanings leading to a complete inability to really poll them well.

Also, individual investors are actually hesitant or incapable of being open to pollsters about who they are. There is nothing new about this. This problem was well-known and documented before 1954 when Darrell Huff wrote his classic, *How to Lie with Statistics*,[6] which is one of the best, brief, easy reads ever written and I encourage everyone to read it. If you get nothing else out of my book except to go to ABEbooks.com and get a copy of Huff's book, my book will have been well worth your time.

Wronger, Stronger, and Longer

Something can fill the gap until we figure out how to build that elusive sample. Professional investors are avid seekers of information. As a group, they have access to all the same information as other investors. But luckily, professionals are a smaller sample size, more manageable statistically, and easier to categorize and sort. They are also very vocal about their views—indeed they have incentive to vocalize. Professional investors speak in a commonly trained language, so output from them is relatively consistent, unlike individual investors. And best of all, professionals' views are more heartfelt. Because they believe in their training, they tend to hang on to their views longer. When they price something into the market, they tend to be wronger, stronger, and longer. When they agree something will happen, it won't for a good long time. If you can determine what professionals believe will occur, you don't know what will happen, but you do know what won't happen—what they agree on—and that is an important first step in figuring out what may happen. Here's how.

Unless you're in the upper Amazon basin fleeing humanity, you can't miss the professional finance world's compulsion to make annual forecasts as each and every year starts. The January forecast barrage is a result of order preference (in this case insisting on certain things in a certain order for no purpose other than societal convention) and another symptom of our brains gone haywire. Good or bad, right or wrong, every year most investment institutions engage in this ritual. The wire houses have in-house economists making predictions. Fund managers have theirs. Professional money managers responsible for smaller pools might throw their hats in the ring via quarterly reports to clients. A great many big-name gurus will tell you forecasting is impossible and then proceed to tell you what they think will happen. You can't pay a blogger not to tell you what he thinks. Blogger pollution is ubiquitous! Everyone's got an opinion. There is nothing wrong with that. Over the years, an increasing flow of characters make public prognostications such that now we have a huge menu of forecasters.

But most are usually wrong. And you already knew that.

At any point in time, a few will be right—some few because they know something and some few more because they're lucky, just like the lucky coin tosser and his 50 consecutive heads. But you don't see most of them being right. The factors driving their forecasts are either broadly known or flat-out wrong and already priced into the market. Because they are avid seekers of information and collectively have access to all widely available information, what they agree on is what has already been priced into the market and therefore can't occur. By the time Mr. Muckety Muck at brokerage firm ABC tells you he thinks the market will return XY.Z percent in 2008, ABC has already gotten their clients to act on it to the extent they're able. Ditto for money management firms, mutual funds, hedge funds, and the rest. By the time we can build the survey, their views have been priced and whatever they agree on, we know won't happen.

In the early-1990s, I wanted to see how much forecasters differed from one another. I found all the published annual forecasts I could going back as far as possible from as many sources as possible. Then, I plotted the forecasts for each phenomenon and the actual subsequent return on a graph. One thing I found was the forecasts usually fell into a seemingly natural bell curve. The masses grouped in agreement in the fat part of the bell with decreasing numbers of forecasters having more extreme bullish and bearish views out to either side of the curve. In each year, there were a few outliers but most ended up somewhere bunched around a consensus range.

Figure 4.1 shows the consensus bell curves from 1996 to 2003 and respective returns for each year (more on why we don't show through 2006 in a bit). Each number represents one professional forecaster's forecast. The middle of the bell curve is what they agree on. You can see in every year the actual return fell not within the consensus but either outside the bandwidth or in a hole somewhere. In several years, one or two maybe lucky kooks got it right, but they're not the same kooks each year. Some years, people were bullish and the market did poorly. Some years, they were bullish and the market did much better than they forecast. In other years, the market did something weird and different than what they could agree on. This is a perfect example of why being a classic contrarian, as discussed in Chapter 2, doesn't work. The market does something different, not necessarily the reverse of what people expect.

Figure 4.1 demonstrates where the forecasts were wrong and the outcomes themselves were already priced. The consensus agreed on a range of outcomes—the range was what most folks believed would happen, so it couldn't. From this I concluded a consensus was therefore somewhat gameable. (If you want to build a bell curve for yourself it won't be as comprehensive as the ones I build in terms of modeling the universe, but the last issue of *BusinessWeek* each year has a long list of professional forecasts for the S&P 500—each and every year.)

With this technology, forecasting became a matter of exclusion. I knew the consensus couldn't happen so I considered both extremes and any potential holes within the consensus range. I also know the market does only one of four things each year—it can be up a lot, up a little, down a little, or down a lot. Just those four things (more on that in Chapter 8). So I ruled out scenarios I thought were unlikely, and my forecast was whatever market scenario seemed likeliest where there weren't other forecasters. That logic is consistent with the market being a discounter of all known information, consistent with history, and an example of Question Two—fathoming something the forecasters couldn't fathom—they, themselves, are part of the market and can be gamed collectively.

Another way to say this is you don't want to make your forecast until after year-end when everyone else has and then you want to make sure, at a minimum, you aren't forecasting what everyone else is.

For example, in 1999, the consensus was wary of Y2K and ready to capitulate after a wondrously positive decade. The consensus was indifferently bullish—most forecasters couldn't see any reasons why the market should break double digits, so I knew it could—might not, but could. A fair few were bearish with a hole on the "down-a-lot" side of the bell curve. There were plenty of bearish concerns being rehashed daily on the evening news, but I couldn't see anything bad on the horizon not already priced into the market, so I ruled out "down-a-lot." There was another hole between about 15 percent and 23 percent. I could see a number of things largely disregarded or ignored by the masses that could drive stocks up. As previously discussed in Chapter 2, I knew Y2K must be a nonevent, which would be a pleasant surprise to those stockpiling canned goods and fashioning tin foil hats. People also ignored the election cycle—1999 was the third year in Clinton's second term. You'll recall from Chapter 2—third years are rarely negative and often smashingly positive. Folks were dour on the prospects for U.S. businesses, but I

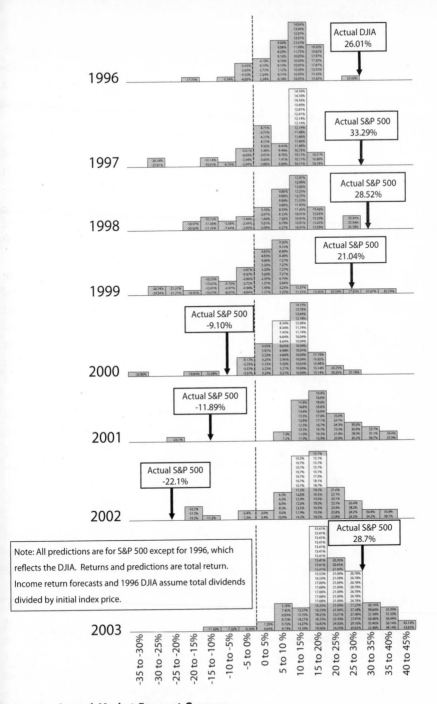

Note: All predictions are for S&P 500 except for 1996, which reflects the DJIA. Returns and predictions are total return. Income return forecasts and 1996 DJIA assume total dividends divided by initial index price.

Figure 4.1 Annual Market Forecast Surveys.
Source: BusinessWeek, Fisher Investments.

thought corporate earnings would continue to surprise to the upside. I thought it was pretty likely America's stock market would be up a lot, possibly over 20 percent in 1999. Hence my *Forbes* forecast, in my December 28, 1998 column entitled *Bullish for '99*, was for the S&P 500 to be up 20 percent. And it was—the S&P 500 finished 1999 just over 21 percent.[7] I was beyond lucky my 20 percent forecast was so close to the actual outcome—that was pure luck—but the bell curve technology I'd perfected in the mid-1990s let me see how to be on the right side of the market.

Did I pat myself on the back for getting it almost spot on in 1999? Well, of course I did, over alcohol and good cheer on New Year's Eve at the same New Year's Eve party I go to most years with local friends. And that 20 percent number was worth a couple of extra drinks that night just for the heck of it. And it was a heck of a night for obvious Y2K reasons too. But, no, after that, no; that would be hindsight bias and overconfidence. My goal in forecasting isn't to get the actual number right. I don't much care about forecasting an actual return at all (but the editor of *Forbes* wants me to). It's far more important to use the Three Questions to get the market direction right. Direction is far more important than magnitude. If I get the direction right and number wrong, I'm as happy as if the number is closer (more on that in Chapter 8).

Just one example for one year, but you get the idea. This technology kept me on the right side of the market throughout the late 1990s and into the early part of the next decade, helping me beat the market as it went down in 2000 and 2001. My annual *Forbes* forecasts were based on this technology year after year, and I was right and very lucky throughout those years. I waited to make my forecasts until everyone else had made theirs—I let them go first—so I could game them. Sounds great, right? Like a silver bullet. And it was, for a while. But here's the dirty little secret. Just like the PSR, it doesn't work anymore. At least, not like it used to.

It worked beautifully for years and you can see clearly it stood up to back-testing. When I described it in *Forbes* at first or wrote about it in *Research* magazine,[8] it was derided as voodoo. Starting around 2000, the voodoo epithet stopped being used, and I was nervous. By then, others were adopting the technology or similar ones. I felt reassured when the bell curves were initially being used incorrectly as a contrarian tool. If the consensus was bullish, the early adopters were automatically bearish and vice versa. They looked at 2001 and 2002 when the consensus was gleefully bullish but the actual results were quite bearish. That further bolstered misuse by contrarians. They were using it wrong but getting lucky, which fueled them on.

But wrong and lucky is still wrong. If you used them correctly, you might have been bullish too when the consensus was. Take 1996, 1997, 1998, 1999, and even 2003. In every one of those years, the consensus was mildly bullish, falling far shy of the much more bullish results. If you had used the bell curves to arrive at a bearish conclusion in those years, you would have missed out on terrific returns.

Eventually, people began getting it right. I knew I was in trouble when Richard Bernstein was promoted to Chief Wangateur at Merrill Lynch. Bernstein had built a very good parallel technology that had worked well looking backwards at the 1990s. Meir Statman and I had also covered his data in the previously mentioned "Investor Sentiment" paper.[9] Bernstein's model demonstrated useful predictive powers historically. His becoming a bigwig foretold the impending demise of my bell curve technology working as it had before. It worked a few years more and, lo and behold, by 2004, it stopped working altogether. By then you could read on the Internet multiple sources mimicking or paralleling my original bell curves—still can now. Some folks actually use my old technology directly. Just like the PSR, what had once been novel became popular enough to be priced into the market and therefore obsolete.

Granted, 2004 might have been a one-time fluke. But as more professional forecasters raced to adopt this technology, I knew it was doomed to not work. By 2005, it didn't.

Now, every year some material subset of forecasters all gamefully watch each other as they forecast and then revise their forecasts. When they make their initial forecast, it doesn't have the gravitas and permanent intent forecasts had only a few years ago. Everyone is gaming everyone now, so we must move on to a new game. This technology has become priced and effectively the power to predict with it is lost.

For U.S. stocks, that is.

Once I'd built this technology, I discovered it worked on any freely traded market where there were sufficient forecasters making public prognostications. We used it regularly to triangulate Nasdaq, for which there were a plethora of forecasts in the 1990s, to the S&P 500. In fact, this technology partially influenced my decision to go bearish on the tech sector in February, 2000. (You can read my tech market bubble call from my March 6, 2000, *Forbes* column titled, *1980 Revisited*[10]—recreated for you in Chapter 7.) Once I saw you couldn't use this capital markets technology for the major U.S. indexes anymore, we set our sights on determining if folks in other parts of the world thought to use this technology there.

You probably can't use this technology for the Croatian stock market in 2007 as you'd be hard-pressed to find enough published forecasts to create a bell curve. But no one (other than my German associate, Thomas Grüner) is using it to forecast Germany's DAX despite plenty of published year-end forecasts. Recall if something works in the United States, it should work most other places. And it does—as the illustration in Figure 4.2 demonstrates. If

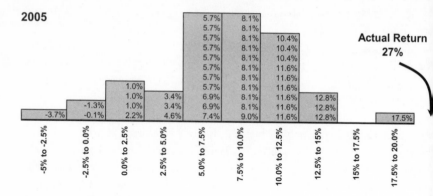

Figure 4.2   DAX Bell Curves.
Source: Thomas Grüner, Fisher Investments.

you're a global investor, this remains a powerful tool for foreign equity markets. You can use it for any market outside of America having a large number of local forecasts. The two main ones I can usually count on are Germany and Britain. Other countries come and go. Sometimes there are enough forecasts and other times very few forecasts.

In Figure 4.2, you can see in Germany, the consensus is still gameable. The example from 2005 shows the return falling outside the consensus. What's more, *any freely traded market* doesn't mean stocks only. This technology, while no longer working for the S&P 500, has continued to work for long-term interest rates inside and outside America as well as for the biggest major currencies. Figure 4.3 shows the bell curves for the U.S. 10-year Treasury from 2002 to 2005 and their outcome.

Year after year, the consensus keeps getting the long bond wrong and never learns from past mistakes. Good news for you, because for now you can keep using this technology. Building the bell curve is easily done—the *Wall Street Journal* publishes professional forecasts on a variety of economic indicators, including both short-term and long-term interest rates in the first two weeks of the year. (*Business Week* publishes forecasts too, but the interest rate forecasts are more comprehensive in the *Journal*.) Again, it won't be as comprehensive as the representative sampling I would do, but it will give you a significant advantage over your peers.

Remember, this technology doesn't guarantee you will be on the right side of the market. Or that it will work every single year—sometimes weird things

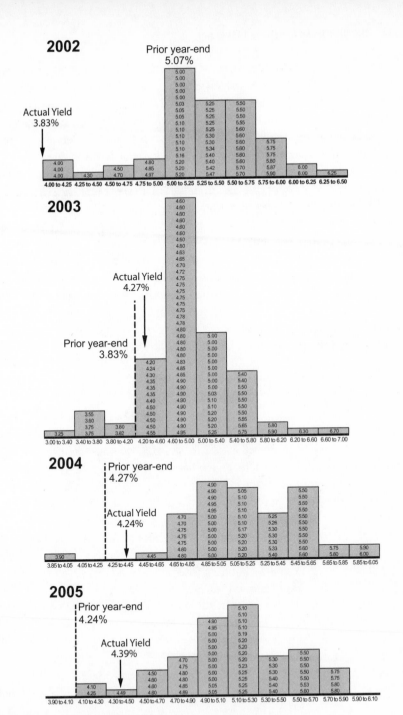

Figure 4.3 Ten-Year Treasury Bond Forecast Bell Curves.
Source: Wall Street Journal, Fisher Investments.

can and will happen. What it does is define what won't happen most years and crystallize for you what the other possibilities are, minimizing the options to just a few—putting the odds on your side and allowing you to avoid making the same mistake most people are making. If you know what won't happen, you can block out a big part of the possibility spectrum and then define a few other alternatives that may. It's still up to you to pick correctly among those few.

Though this technology currently works for the long bond, you certainly can't expect it to work on the fed funds rate. The short rate isn't free market-set like long rates. Plenty of people make prognostications on where they think the short rate will go. You can even bet on it at www.tradesports.com. (I wouldn't recommend it, but you can—and Tradesports.com is a very interesting site for seeing what people think about all kinds of things.) The fed funds rate is set by our monopolistic central banking system—making it impossible to game any consensus. Whether the consensus ends up right on the short rate or not isn't a market event, but the planned activity of a single monopoly provider putting the rate anywhere it decides. This bell curve technology only works on free-market-set prices, including currencies.

Why Tell You Any of This?

Again, you may wonder why I open my proverbial big mouth. Won't remaining silent let me use these longer? Maybe. Maybe not. I might have gotten a few more years out of my bell curves for the U.S. markets had I not vocalized them. But Richard Bernstein and others were coming along anyway and would have created the same effect regardless. The U.S. makes up about 50 percent of the world's publicly traded markets (give or take a little, depending on when you check), so losing this forecasting tool for the U.S. markets is a big deal—right? The answer for this is the same as for the PSR. I knew this advantage would go away one day. Did I speed the adoption of this technology by publicizing it? Possibly. Graphing forecasts into a bell curve format in the mid-1990s is the sort of unique research we do at my firm you don't readily see from most places. It's derivative of always asking the Three Questions. So why give the results and discoveries away? Two reasons! First, because I'm not fearful of losing one piece of technology when we're constantly innovating and know we must. Second, because if the world continually ridicules what I know to be good technology—like they do with the presidential term cycle material or my P/E work from a long time ago—then I learn it has legs. I know my technology will last a long, long time, and I can count on the world's cognitive bias to keep it from seeing reality and thus the tool remains useful. Then I can focus my efforts to innovate in other areas knowing this area still has legs. It is worthy to open it up and give it away to see if you must innovate faster or can rely on the tool for a good, long time if it is widely rejected. And you never know until you give it away.

If bell curve forecasting were my only arrow, maybe I would have jealously guarded that secret. But if you use the Three Questions and keep building capital markets technology, you will constantly be seeking the next thing and won't fear losing the old thing. Without the Three Questions, if I lost a tool or two, I might be forced to retire to my wife, redwoods, and cats. But with the Three Questions the next thrill is always on the tip of the next question. Constant innovation invites me to do the most fun part of asset management. And if I'm not innovating in this day and age, I don't deserve to be managing over $30 billion for other people.

Staying competitive in this game takes constant innovation and most people dislike that or don't even get it. The big name brokerage firms predominantly don't get it. When I think about a corporate role model for my firm, I don't look to them or other Wall Street firms. My corporate role models are Intel from the early-1970s, Sam Walton and Wal-Mart from the same era, Procter & Gamble for marketing, and GE in terms of management. These were visionary innovators from my young adulthood. I look to Bob Noyce, co-inventor of the integrated circuit, co-founder of Intel, and long-time partner of Gordon Moore. Back in a simpler world, I got to meet and know Bob Noyce, and he blew me away. Noyce knew he and Moore could never stop moving at a time I didn't know it was necessary. While not tall (actually quite short), he was such a towering intellectual presence most folks presumed there would be no Intel of materiality after him. Here they missed the power of the combined spirit of Bob Noyce and Gordon Moore, and how each knew what they knew then about making semiconductors would be dwarfed by what innovators would soon know. Their goal was to move along Gordon Moore's learning curve faster than the next guys. What was really proprietary was their faith in the learning curve and innovation.

That role model has been ever present in my thinking since, which is why my focus is now, always has been, and always will be on constant innovation. I don't want my firm to be like Merrill Lynch. I want it to be like the Intel of Noyce and Moore circa 1975. So no, when I've developed something I think is really neat, I don't mind if it gets accepted and priced into markets and subsequently rendered useless. I assume it will. That's called progress.

So publishing my innovations may help them become priced. The best ones, the ones readers assume are ridiculous won't be—at least not anytime soon. After my first book, it took about 10 years for the PSR to get fully priced into the market. The ideas in this book will take time to be priced too, if they ever are. Some faster, some slower! It could happen faster if more investors bought this book. But think about that. If this book sells 100,000 copies it would be a monster success in the world of investment books. By contrast,

Forbes' pass-on readership is about 15 times that level, and I've been talking about many of these things in *Forbes* for a long time. And *Forbes* only addresses a small percentage of the global world of investors of all forms. It would be fine if the piddling percentage of total global investors who do read this book believe what I say, but most won't. I've been working with investors long enough to know our Stone Age hardwiring is difficult to overcome and most readers will be resistant. Plenty of investors will pick up this book and yell, "This is nonsense! Only a dangerously deranged moron could think budget deficits aren't bad, and worse, that they might be good!" Or maybe another investor might say, "That Fisher guy is a moron. What does he know about P/Es? I know all about them because I am smart and I read the *Investor's Business Daily* every day and have a CFA and work in the industry and have done so for 20 years, and I will only buy low P/E stocks."

My strongest naysayers are missing the whole point of the Three Questions. I'm pretty sure they would have survived swimmingly in our tribal existence 5,000 years ago. But you needn't rely on just those examples presented here—my conclusions—which you can agree with or disagree with because I don't care which you do—you will still have learned a methodology to develop your own capital markets technology for the rest of your life.

Better Living through Global Benchmarking

One mature capital markets technology alive and well in my firm, to which I've already alluded, is global benchmarking. This isn't new, and I didn't invent it! We spoke about benchmarking as a cure to many Stone Age ills in Chapter 3. You may scoff at this idea of picking an index to follow and manage against and measure yourself against as being technology. It's too simplistic and not a new concept—maybe too widely dispersed already. And anyone can do it! Yes, it is simplistic, and anyone can do it—but mostly they don't, and if they do, they usually do it wrong. If they did, they would have more success and make fewer massive errors. This is why it's great. You measure yourself against your benchmark, but more important, you manage yourself against it.

Your inclination, like many U.S. investors, may be to shy away from global investing, preferring to focus on the S&P 500 and U.S. stocks and mutual funds. After all, you know America is better and are more comfortable with it. Cincinnati doesn't scare you but maybe Tampico does. Still, it remains true global thinking helps you think better about everything, including understanding America better. One prime purpose of global benchmarking is to think better.

For example, many wrongly claim they don't need to think globally or own foreign stocks because they can get the equivalent of global exposure through

U.S. firms that have heavy sales exposure overseas—through U.S. multinationals. This is a widely held view and easily proven false. I've taught you how to prove it false in Chapter 1. Now you just have to do it on your own. If U.S multinationals give you foreign exposure, then they should correlate tightly with foreign stocks, right? If not, you're not getting the exposure you want. But if you get a bunch of U.S., Japanese, German, and Dutch multinationals, you will find they correlate much closer with their own countries than they do with each other. That is to say Exxon, Coke, and Ford correlate much closer to each other and the S&P 500 than they do with Sony, Toyota, Hitachi, and the Morgan Stanley Topix. The correlations teach you that U.S. multinational stocks act like U.S. stocks and don't give you foreign exposure. The reason, of course, is each country has cultural effects impacting its stocks beyond where the company generates its revenue. A Japanese firm has Japanese employees primarily, is centered on Japanese laws more than non-Japanese laws, and primarily gets more financing from within Japan than outside Japan. But the answer remains in the correlations. This example also teaches you that until you start thinking globally, you can't really understand that about the U.S. multinationals—which is my basic point. To understand America better today, whether through global yield curves or relations between U.S. stocks and how they perform, you must think globally.

Xenophobes don't know and have a hard time accepting that the index you pick as your benchmark doesn't much matter if you have a very long investing horizon. Believe it or not, all correctly calculated major equity benchmarks end up in about the same place if you give them 30 years or so—they just get there via very different paths (as I detail later). But a rational person would select a benchmark getting to that long-term equity return with the least volatility—for a smoother ride. Additionally, a rational person would pick the benchmark that provides the most opportunities to make market bets and win and has the most to teach using the Three Questions—and that must be the whole world, leading us back to global.

A benchmark is absolutely vital because it's your road map for your portfolio. Investing without a benchmark is like getting on an unfamiliar road in an unfamiliar state in an unfamiliar car even, meandering without a map or directions and wondering why you're getting no closer to your destination. But you aren't really sure what your destination is except you might recognize it when you see it. The benchmark, as your road map, instructs you on what to include in your portfolio, in what percentage, and when.

Your Benchmark Is a Road Map for Your Long Journey

On the morning of September 11, 2001, I happened to be on a train with a group of my East Coast staff on the way from Washington, DC, to Philadelphia.

The day before we had done seminars for our Washington, DC, clients and we were on our way to do the same in Philadelphia when the terrorist attacks shattered normality. From Philly, staff dispersed toward homes and families posthaste in all different directions—from New Hampshire to Florida. Unable to fly, two colleagues and I rented a van and drove west toward California. We broke the speed limit whenever possible—most of the time. There are two main routes to take. We took the longer southern route through St. Louis for fear if there were more bombings, Chicago and the northern route was a more logical target—hence we picked the road less traveled. We dropped off one fellow in St. Louis who planned to take a midnight train south to his home in Dallas. We drove on in three hour shifts (the passenger calmed down for 45 minutes, slept for 90 minutes, woke for 45 minutes) and then we stopped at a convenience station for gas, food, and to switch for the next three hour shift, repeating the process. We made it across America, amazingly, in 32 hours. If you really set your mind to it, nonstop, that is how long it takes.

We never could have done it without a road map. It helped us see the southern route wasn't much longer and maybe faster and certainly less traveled. It told us where to go, with detours how to get back on track, which way to drive around Denver. From Denver, whether to take the northern route through Salt Lake City and the Donner Pass or the southern route through the Mojave Desert (this time we went northern). It helped us manage and plan our trip. It let us control our risk. A good stock market benchmark provides the same benefits.

The benchmark also serves as a measuring stick for performance. When you look at your portfolio each year, do you check if you were up or down and by how much? If you do, how do you know if you had a good year or a bad year? If you were up 20 percent, is that good? Is it still good if you find out the broad market was up 35 percent? If you were down 5 percent is that bad? What if you were down just 5 percent while market was down 25 percent? As you drive from Philly to San Francisco there are simply stretches where you can beat the speed limit and stretches where you can't be anything but patient. Markets are like that. I'm not a patient person, but I know how to be and can be when necessary.

Many investors claim their goal is to beat "the market," but fail to identify which market they mean and how they will go about beating it. The market could refer to the U.S. equity markets, the world equity markets, even the bond markets. For a few years, myriad investors wanted to beat the Nasdaq. You cannot rationally aim to beat the market unless you choose a specific one to beat. The market you select will be your benchmark and drive every conscious portfolio decision you make. Once you've selected your benchmark, you can choose to beat it by plowing everything into one narrow stock subcategory, but the risk if you're wrong is huge. The benchmark helps you define your risk profile—how concentrated or diverse you are compared to the road map you're managing against.

Broad equity indexes like the S&P 500, the MSCI World, and the MSCI ACWI make good proxies for market performance and, hence, a benchmark against which to manage and measure results. But your benchmark can be any well-constructed index—the Russell 2000 if you like small caps. Most British investors use the FTSE and Germans the DAX. Or the Nasdaq if you're a technophile. Whatever the index, you must be specific about what you compare and measure your portfolio and investing activities against.

Pick an Index, Any Index (but Don't Believe More Volatility Gets You Higher Returns)

Maybe the fresh memory of the tech bubble bursting makes you fear the Nasdaq. The Nasdaq tanked in 2000, 2001, and 2002 and led the global market into an unusually long bear market. Is it therefore bad and to be avoided? The Nasdaq isn't a bad index per se; in fact, it's a perfectly fine, well-constructed index. It's just very narrowly focused and hence volatile. The narrower the index, the more volatile you can expect it to be—which is a fairly intuitive investing truth. It has very little that zigs when something else zags to reduce total volatility. Tech-heavy Nasdaq will gyrate wildly with the fortune of tech and tech alone, as we saw in recent history. Fear not, there is no reason to suffer such an intense roller-coaster ride since over long periods (like your 20- or 30-year investment time horizon) all well-constructed indexes should, near the end, yield very similar returns though traveling wildly different paths to get there. Maybe you don't believe that. I hope to convince you.

But you can accept that if all well-constructed major equity benchmarks eventually get you to about the same place, one prime concern should be how smooth the ride will be. Figure 4.4 shows a variety of indexes or benchmarks converging over time but taking different paths en route. These aren't real indexes, but rather a representation of different types.

Index 4 is a volatile benchmark that vastly outperforms other major indexes at its peaks, but vastly underperforms at its troughs. Think of this as a narrower index such as the Nasdaq. Index 3 lagged a bit early on, but outperformed in later years, somewhat like the U.S. market over the past 30 years. Index 2 might be a foreign index, which did better early on, but trailed off a bit in the past 15 years. A rational investor would prefer the index with the lowest volatility as represented by Index 1, which arrives with the smoothest ride. The smoothest ride will be the broadest benchmark. Currently, the broadest indexes are the globally oriented MSCI World Index, which reflects developed nations and has a long

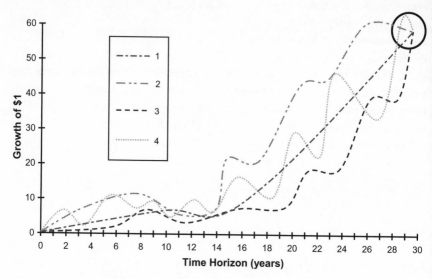

Figure 4.4   Benchmark and Time Horizon.

history, and the ACWI, which includes emerging markets (which I still prefer to call "less developed nations"—after all, some of them emerge and some of them submerge). The ACWI has a shorter history and is less useful in measuring historical data, but is darned acceptable as a benchmark.

Risk versus Return?

How can it be the volatile Nasdaq will get you to about the same place over time as the S&P 500 or even the über-broad ACWI? If the Nasdaq is more volatile, you should get more return, right?

Many who have studied finance believe this common myth which is widely taught. It is conventional wisdom—wrong—and propagated commonly by infinitely educated people who should be able to see right through it but somehow can't. The notion is that to get higher return you must take more risk as measured by volatility so you should have a volatile portfolio if you want to beat the market. That works for stocks versus bonds versus cash—which is historically where the concept originated. But within equity types, it's measurably wrong in history. This is one reason history is so beautiful as a way to test if commonly accepted wisdom is right. If it were true, tech would have higher long-term returns than less volatile indexes but it doesn't.

Volatility has to do with how much the components inside an index are negatively correlated to each other in the short-term—how much short-term zigging and zagging goes on within the index. In essence, volatility measures how narrow the index is—how much all the parts move the same way in the short-term. You can create a narrow, volatile index by taking almost any pure category of stocks that all move the same way in the short-term. You get volatility that way but it has nothing to do with long-term returns (as we cover extensively in Chapter 7 when we discuss supply shifts determining long-term pricing). Were that not true, all the subsectors that make up a broad index, all being more volatile individually than the total index, would have higher returns than the index itself—but that can't be—the returns of the parts can't be different than the parts of the returns. This is a very fathomable Question Two that most people can't get themselves to contemplate at all. Within equities, short-term volatility has nothing to do with long-term returns. All correctly calculated equity indexes get you to about the same return—the equity return—if you give them 30 years or so. And the ones that come out ahead don't come out ahead by much and only by serendipity, likely soon reversed.

Mind you, lots of readers will have been taught that what I'm telling you here is wrong. But this is a provably false assumption. History says, "It ain't so." History is beautiful.

Figure 4.5 shows the trade-off in return spread between the "risky" Nasdaq and broader categories. Figure 4.5a shows the Nasdaq and the British FTSE (starting in 1972—Nasdaq's first full year). When the line is above 0 percent, Nasdaq led, and when the line is below 0 percent, FTSE led. You can see big peaks in performance variability as the categories trade leadership at varying irregular intervals. The spread in performance is significant in any given year—40 percent, 80 percent, even 120 percent at one point in the mid-1970s. For a number of years in the 1980s, the FTSE seemed to repeatedly best the Nasdaq, but in the late 1990s, performance swung decisively the other way. Yet, with all that variability, over this long period, you don't get much excess return. Intuitively you can see there is about as much grey shading above the line as below the line. Simply, from 1972 until 2005, the FTSE returned 11.7 percent annualized (in local currency) and the "risky" Nasdaq 12.5 percent. I'd say those returns are pretty darned close to identical. Maybe you disagree. Maybe you think that out-performance by Nasdaq is a premium for its higher volatility. Think again.

You can see the same thing in Figure 4.5b and 4.5c with two broader indexes, the MSCI Europe, Australia, Far East Index (EAFE) and the S&P 500. EAFE is more volatile than the S&P. And there are huge performance spreads over the years between each and the Nasdaq, and sometimes prolonged periods of out-performance and under-performance. Still, you don't get any excess return for your "risk." Again you see visually the same amount of gray above and below the line. Over this same time period, EAFE returned 12.8 percent annualized, and the S&P 500 12.7 percent—amazingly just like Nasdaq's 12.5 percent. Where is the excess return for Nasdaq's higher volatility?

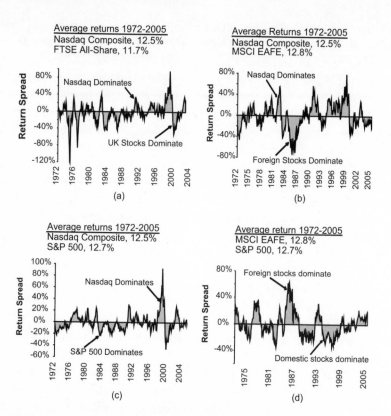

Figure 4.5   Twelve-Month Rolling Performance Spread.
Source: **Thomson Financial Datastream.**

You cannot expect a more volatile category to provide excess return in the long-term because all well-constructed equity indexes will converge over time, properly accounted. Look within EAFE and S&P 500 returns (Figure 4.5d). You already know their long-term average returns were identical, but look at how variable their performance is year-to-year. One will lead and the other lag—sometimes for years—but that performance variability doesn't matter in the long term. You will get to the same place eventually.

This Question One myth persists because we don't question our assumptions and don't use history to verify if theory is real. Investors are biased toward their favorite category and confirmation bias props up their preset notions. Many investors incorrectly assume their pet category—small-cap growth, energy, tech, large value, emerging markets, whatever it is—is inherently superior. It's so provably wrong, yet precious few bother to check, which is why this is a great myth to debunk. There is absolutely no evidence any one category is permanently better. A fan of a category can show you a cut from time period A to L where that category beat the market. Pick a different start-ing and ending date and its dominance fades. Take a slightly different cut of the same noun and adjective and their meanings fade, too.

A data mine is when someone, intentionally or unintentionally, picks data conveniently seeming to prove their point, but if you used slightly different data or alter the time frame the whole thing falls apart. Take the long-held myth small-cap stocks do better than big-cap stocks. Historically, there is some valid-ity to this because since 1926 small stocks on average have done better than big-cap stocks. Most observers confuse averages with (1) what happens most often and (2) reality. We know it's a myth because if you take the data series used to prove the point, and then took the homogenous periods coming off the bottom of the four biggest bear markets (times when small caps have always done well)—1932 to 1935, 1942 to 1945, 1974 to 1976, and 2002 to 2004—and looked at the rest of history, you would see in the remaining time periods big-cap stocks did better than small-cap stocks by more than 2 percent per year. All the excess small-cap return comes from those few periods. But if you could identify the bottom of the four biggest bear markets correctly you wouldn't need small-cap stocks to figure out how to beat the market. (Or if you took the very small-est, least liquid small caps out of the study, the whole thing falls apart again.)

My point is the supposed long-term small-cap effect touted by so many is worse than a data mine. It's a confusion pit for most observers (courtesy of TGH). Otherwise there is simply no validity to it. Some long times, like the period since 2000 to date, small stocks do lead and markedly. Other times, they lag for a long time.

Said another way, if you were 35 in 1945, just back from World War II and starting to invest, and thought you knew small-cap stocks did better on aver-age than big-cap, you would have gotten all the way to retirement age at 65 in 1975 and seen big-cap beating small-cap on average during that overall period. That's just a little too long to count on something working that gets most of its payoff rarely in history. Or say you got back from Vietnam at 25 in 1973, went through psychological counseling for five years, cut your hair, and started in-vesting in 1978 at age 30—for the next more than 20 years big-cap stocks did better on average than small-cap (although for the first few years, you would have done well and absorbed some confirmation bias). A quarter century is a long, long time to wait for averages to revert.

Pick your time period carefully and you can seem to prove a lot of things. But despite most investors having longer time horizons than they think they have, darned few can afford to be wrong for a full quarter of a century.

If one category was better than all the others, we'd all know it and invest our money in it; all other equity categories would go away. We're all subject to capitalism. Stock prices are determined by supply and demand. And no one index, size, style, or category is best forever. None. And you don't have 25 years to wait for the next time category X leads the market.

Global Thinking Equals Better Thinking

It should make sense the more you spread out your exposure globally, the more you spread your risk. No country leads consistently, and no one knows with certainty who the next leader will be. Table 4.1 on page 151, illustrates the changing leadership of country performance from year to year. The opportunity cost of not diversifying across geographic lines can be huge. Instead of fearing the unfamiliar, you should fear missing large opportunities to be had abroad. And you should fear your own country of origin may be where the roughest risk resides next.

If you aren't comfortable picking individual foreign stocks, you can easily get global exposure through a low-cost index fund or an exchange-traded fund (ETF). The MSCI EAFE, reflecting the developed foreign markets, has been widely available as an inexpensive index fund for years. Using such an investment vehicle spreads out your risk, getting you needed foreign exposure while being completely otherwise passive. *Note:* I'm generally not a fan of mutual funds or index funds (as I wrote in a *Forbes* column that follows). They are usually far too expensive and eliminate too many tax benefits for high net worth investors. But if you have a smaller kitty to work with, they can help you get the diversification you need. And, if you don't know anything others don't, passiveness is always appropriate.

I Hate Funds

THIS ISSUE, the mutual fund guide, is a great one in which to tell you this: I hate funds. So should most of you. The average *Forbes* subscriber (net worth at last count, $2.1 million) is too wealthy for funds. Funds were never meant for you. They were meant for folks with a small pool of money in search of diversification. But at a price. A big one.

For years I've urged a global approach. I won't retread that now (see, for example, my Nov. 27, 2000 column). But foreign and global funds are expensive.

The average global no-load fund has a 1.8% annual expense ratio—for portfolio management and overhead costs. On top of that are the soft-dollar fees, which are trading commissions, over and above competitive rates, funneled to brokerages for research help they give the fund. Average soft-dollar cost to fund customers: 0.3% of assets annually. It's a fee that rips you off but is legal. The fund should pay for research from its own revenue.

Then people go haywire and hire a person or service to tell them what funds to own, because there are so many, and sorting through them is confusing. The normal fee here is 1% annually. Add these three fees and you could be spending 3% a year to own a global stock portfolio. At that you need real genius to come out ahead. If stocks do 10% in the long term, and if inflation averages 3%, your real return is 7%. A 3% annual fee eats up almost half of that. You wind up with bondlike returns while taking stocklike risks. That's a sucker's game.

Then comes performance. Everyone knows the average mutual fund hasn't kept pace with the market. What they don't understand is why. It isn't about stock picking. It's structural. Here's why.

Funds tend to be overweighted in small companies, underweighted in large ones. There could be a lot of reasons for this, but a big one is probably just that it's hard for the portfolio manager to justify a fat money-management fee if he owns only big, obvious stocks like General Electric and ExxonMobil. So during an era like the past decade, when big outperformed small, it was inevitable that funds would underperform the large-cap S&P 500 Index.

They lag market indexes, nick you with fees and run up unnecessary tax bills.

You can quantify this disparity. A portfolio has what's called a weighted average market capitalization. A fund 80% invested in a $10 billion market-cap stock and 20% in a $100 billion market cap would have a weighted average market cap of $28 billion. For an index fund tracking the S&P 500, this calculation results in a $110 billion figure. For the average U.S. equity fund, it's only $24 billion.

It is very restrictive for an actively managed fund to get its weighted average market cap up near $110 billion. There are, at the moment, only 15 companies with market caps above that figure. Funds own many more stocks than that.

And when small stocks beat big? Funds lose again, at least if they trade actively. Small stocks (that is, stocks of companies with market capitalizations below $5 billion) tend to have low share prices and high big/ask spreads. If a fund goes in and out of a stock quoted at $20 bid, $20.50 offer, it will lose 2.5% to transaction costs. This is as bad as 3% fees.

So I don't like funds. The actively traded ones will cost you a bundle. The passive index funds are a lot cheaper, and of course an S&P 500 fund will track

(continued)

that index pretty well. But I don't like those, either. Why? Taxes. There are no tax advantages to funds, only disadvantages.

Fans of funds, including the editors of this magazine, make much of the fact that index funds are tax-efficient. That is, they have not had the habit of forcing out taxable capital gain distributions onto helpless shareholders. But they have been successful at this game in large part because they have been taking in new money over the past decade. Come a time of massive redemptions and the index funds might have to sell some of their low-cost-basis shares of stock, making taxable distributions inevitable. Also note that even a tax-efficient fund can't pass capital *losses* through to shareholders. If you can use capital losses on your tax return, own shares directly.

Anyone with more than about $350,000, which is most *Forbes* readers, can do better than a fund by buying stocks. Let me put in a plug for following this column's advice. It is global. As measured by *Forbes* annually and after adjusting for phantom 1% brokerage costs, it has beaten the MSCI World, EAFE and S&P 500 for years. It costs you almost nothing. This year? I've been cashlike all year. When I turn bullish, I will be recommending stocks. Not funds.

Forbes, August 20, 2001. Reprinted by permission of *Forbes* magazine. © Forbes, 2006.

If you do go the mutual fund route, be sure to buy a sufficiently broad fund or a collection of funds. Also, remember to check the expense ratios. Most funds are much too expensive. Diversifying your portfolio globally is smart, but not if fees eat all the benefit.

Truly, you need not fear foreign investing. Many foreign stocks can be purchased easily with U.S. dollars in the form of American Depository Receipts (ADRs). What's more, you need only check your fridge, medicine cabinet, closet, workbench, or garage (or heck, your employer) to find plenty of familiar names from foreign lands.

Never Say Dow

I keep saying your benchmark should be a "well-constructed" index, but I haven't mentioned what a "poorly constructed" index is. Say hello to the Dow Jones Industrial Average, a very poorly constructed index indeed. Many investors live and die by the Dow Jones Industrial Average, frequently referred to reverently as "The Dow." People associate up moves on the Dow with healthy markets, a strong economy, sunny days, bumper farm crops, and who knows what else. Investors assume the Dow is a reliable market indicator but in reality, the Dow is poorly constructed, tells little, and should never be used as a benchmark. I haven't paid any attention to the Dow in decades and can't

Table 4.1   Leadership Keeps Shifting

	1	2	3	4	5
1990	UK 10.3%	HONG KONG 9.2%	AUSTRIA 6.3%	NORWAY 0.6%	DENMARK -0.9%
1991	HONG KONG 49.5%	AUSTRALIA 33.6%	USA 30.1%	SINGAPORE 25.0%	NEW ZEALAND 18.3%
1992	HONG KONG 32.3%	SWITZERLAND 17.2%	USA 6.4%	SINGAPORE 6.3%	FRANCE 2.8%
1993	HONG KONG 116.7%	FINLAND 82.7%	SINGAPORE 68.0%	NEW ZEALAND 67.7%	SWITZERLAND 45.8%
1994	FINLAND 52.2%	NORWAY 23.6%	JAPAN 21.4%	SWEDEN 18.3%	IRELAND 14.5%
1995	SWITZERLAND 44.1%	USA 37.1%	SWEDEN 33.4%	SPAIN 29.8%	NETHERLANDS 27.7%
1996	SPAIN 40.1%	SWEDEN 37.2%	PORTUGAL 35.7%	FINLAND 33.9%	HONG KONG 33.1%
1997	PORTUGAL 46.7%	SWITZERLAND 44.2%	ITALY 35.5%	DENMARK 34.5%	USA 33.4%
1998	FINLAND 121.6%	BELGIUM 67.7%	ITALY 52.5%	SPAIN 49.9%	FRANCE 41.5%
1999	FINLAND 152.6%	SINGAPORE 99.4%	SWEDEN 79.7%	JAPAN 61.5%	HONG KONG 59.5%
2000	SWITZERLAND 5.9%	CANADA 5.3%	DENMARK 3.4%	NORWAY -0.9%	ITALY -1.3%
2001	NEW ZEALAND 8.4%	AUSTRALIA 1.7%	IRELAND -2.8%	AUSTRIA -5.6%	BELGIUM -10.9%
2002	NEW ZEALAND 24.2%	AUSTRIA 16.5%	AUSTRALIA -1.3%	NORWAY -7.3%	ITALY -7.3%
2003	GREECE 69.5%	SWEDEN 64.5%	GERMANY 63.8%	SPAIN 58.5%	AUSTRIA 57.0%
2004	AUSTRIA 71.5%	NORWAY 53.3%	GREECE 46.1%	BELGIUM 43.5%	IRELAND 43.1%
2005	CANADA 28.3%	JAPAN 25.5%	AUSTRIA 24.6%	DENMARK 24.5%	NORWAY 24.3%

Source: Thomson Financial Datastream.

even tell you its absolute level because I trained myself, as titled in my November 19, 1999, *Forbes* column, to "Never Say Dow."[11] My advice to you is you will see markets better if you train yourself to ignore the Dow for the rest of your life as well. The only time to ever say Dow is when you're referring to a publishing company, a chemical company, or an Asian philosophy (spelled Tao). But never use the Dow Jones Industrial Average.

First, but not most important, The Dow is comprised of only 30 big stocks and represents less than a quarter of the $16-trillion plus market value of all U.S. stocks[12] (hardly a fair and total representation of U.S. markets). Those few Dow stocks are picked arbitrarily. Some get taken over and drop out. Others are dropped out and replaced by the Dow committee doing the picking. It has maintained its stature in the popular press mainly for sentimental and cultural reasons—the same type of reasons allowing market myths to persist for multiple decades. (That its sponsor also owns the *Wall Street Journal* and *Barron's* doesn't hurt either.) But its biggest deficiency is it's a *price-weighted index*. Never pay attention to price-weighted indexes—any, ever. Let me say that again for emphasis. Never pay attention to any price-weighted index.

Consider, as of mid-2006, 3M had more potential impact on the Dow's outcome than any other stock even though then, it was only the 80th largest U.S. stock.[13] Why would the 80th largest U.S. stock have more impact than, say, the first largest stock? Welcome to price-weighting. And how about this— even though IBM is the 16th largest U.S. stock, and a bigger company than 3M, it has the least potential impact on the Dow.

The higher the price-per-share of a stock in a "price-weighted" index like the Dow (and the NIKKEI—by the way, don't use it either—another very misleading price-weighted index), the more impact it has relative to other stocks in the index. In a price-weighted index, a $100 stock has 10 times the future impact on the index as a $10 stock, even though the $10 stock can from a firm worth vastly more and much bigger by any standard. Madness.

Price-weighted indexes are inherently problematic because if a stock splits, its weight in the index is also split. The overall level of the index hasn't been affected but the split reduced the impact of that stock relative to index's other stocks. You don't want to believe that—most people don't—but it's true. The reverse is also true—if a stock does a reverse split as rarely happens (meaning you get one share for every two you owned previously, as an example), the stock's weight in the index doubles. Stock splits and reverse splits are purely cosmetic and don't impact a company's market capitalization, dividends, investors' net worth, or any other form of real economics—not at all. However, stock splits absolutely affect which stocks have impact and power within a price-weighted index. Unless you can predict stock splits, and there has never yet been a technology capable of it, you don't have a rational basis for predicting a price-weighted index for even a year or two at a crack—even if you could perfectly predict the price performance of every single stock in the index. That's a fact. In some years, the Dow would have done 10 percent better or worse than it actually did depending on which stocks in the index could have ended up splitting or not. I don't mean 11 percent instead of 10 percent. I mean 20 percent instead of 10 percent.

The Dow's structure is skewed away from economic reality with every stock split (which happens pretty frequently). Mathematically, year-by-year, the Dow's value is quite technically purely random depending on which stocks split and when.

In any year, if the split stocks do worse than the stocks that don't split, the index does better than the average stock. If the stocks that split do better than the stocks that didn't split, the index does worse than the average return of the stocks.

Which stocks split really do affect the Dow. Crazy, hey? Said alternately, if the high-priced-per-share stocks beat the low-priced-per-share stocks, then the Dow does better than economic returns of its stocks. Conversely, if the low-priced-per-share stocks do better than the high-priced-per-share stocks, then the Dow does worse than its stocks.

You don't believe that's true. You've heard the Dow has a thing called the "divisor" to adjust for splits. Let's truly alter your sense of reality. When a stock in the Dow splits, Dow Jones and Company does adjust the "divisor"—just like with any price-weighted index. This divisor keeps the level of the overall Dow constant from before the change to afterwards so it's cosmetically seamless. That is, changing the divisor makes the split not effect the overall level of the Dow as the split occurs. The divisor is continually adjusted. As of this writing, the divisor was down to 0.125, which is why you won't see Berkshire Hathaway (recent price, over $90,000 per share) among the Dow 30 anytime soon. There isn't anything wrong with Berkshire Hathaway, but with a share price of $90,000, if it were included it would distort the index by overpowering the other stocks completely in the computation of the average. If the Dow added Berkshire Hathaway, the index's future moves would depend almost completely on what happened to Berkshire and almost not at all on anything else. There would be 90,000 reasons for Berkshire to matter and only a few thousand reasons for the other 29 stocks to matter—all together. That hardly seems fair.

The Two-Stock Index

Here is an easy demonstration why price-weighted indexes are to be shunned and you should wholly disregard the Dow. We're creating a price-weighted index made up of just two stocks—ABC and XYZ—each initially worth $100 per share. Our index works exactly like the Dow but it only has two stocks, making it easier to see how it works. For simplicity, they both have the same overall market value and every other quantitative feature about them is identical. The only difference is name: ABC and XYZ. To get the initial index value we simply add the prices of ABC and XYZ together, divide by the total number of stocks (two), and get $100. So our Two-Index starts out at 100. Straight forward! You didn't even need a calculator for that.

On Monday, ABC is up 10 percent to $110 and XYZ is down 10 percent to $90. Add 110 to 90 and you get 200, divide by two (our initial divisor), and you still get $100, which makes sense because the 10 percent move in each perfectly offsets the other. Again, easy math! Nothing weird—yet. Later Monday, they reverse and are now both $100 again and the index remains at 100. But wait!

On Tuesday, both stocks trade at $100 initially, but ABC announces a 100-for-1 stock split. Mind you, most splits are usually on the order of 2-for-1 or 3-for-1, but for the sake of example, clarity, and insanity (since price-weighted indexes are insane) it's easier to use extreme numbers. ABC now trades at $1 per share though the overall value of the company remains unchanged. Nothing changes for shareholders either. If a shareholder earlier had 100 shares of ABC at $100 a pop, now he has 10,000 shares each worth $1—and in both cases owns $10,000 of ABC. ABC sells for $1. XYC is still $100. Add the two together and you get $101. Divide by two and now you get $50.50. But wait, that isn't right. That won't work.

We know the index must remain at 100 because nothing has changed but the split. Time for a divisor adjustment! Just what the Dow would do. Instead of dividing by two like we did initially, now we ask, "What number, divided into 101, gives us 100?" Simple algebra—you learned that one in the seventh grade—the answer is 1.01. Common sense. So we set the new divisor at 1.01, just about half of what it was before the split, and our index remains at 100 and we're fat, dumb, and happy. This is the same way the Dow would do this. If nothing else has changed except the cosmetics of the split, then the value of the index should remain the same, right? And the way to do that is by adjusting the divisor exactly as we did.

On Wednesday, ABC rises 10 percent again and XYZ falls 10 percent. But now instead of the index remaining unchanged as it should and as it did before the split, now it will change markedly. ABC is now $1.10. XYZ is now $90. Add them together and you get $91.10. Divide by our new divisor of 1.01 and you get an index value of $90.20. What the . . . ? The index fell nearly 10 percent for no reason other than the two stocks in the index had identical but reverse percentage moves. How can that be? Welcome to the dirty little secret reality of price-weighted indexes. While the economic returns of the companies haven't changed one iota since the creation of the index, the index itself has—markedly. If the companies are worth the same, they should have identical impacts on the index, but this is impossible with any price-weighted index—even the most holy Dow Jones Industrials.

Said again, now that I have your attention: In any year, if the split stocks do worse than the stocks that don't split, the index does better than the average stock. If the stocks that split do better than the stocks that didn't split, the index does worse than the average return of the stocks.

I'm always amazed, with most professionals focused on craftsmanship, how few of them in their training ever took a course in index construction—which are always craft-like. Almost none! Hard to figure why! For those of you who would like a further, easy to self-learn tutorial on index construction, I'd recommend chapter 5 of Frank Reilly's, *Investment Analysis and Portfolio Management* (Dryden Press, 1996). It's one of my favorite investment textbooks. And Frank is one of my favorite academics and a very nice guy. As of this writing, there were 191 copies of Frank's text available on ABEBooks.com, starting at the lofty price of $1.00—just the price of ABC.

A well-constructed index is market capitalization weighted, which means companies worth more actually weigh more heavily in the index. Exxon, with its behemoth market capitalization of over $370 billion[14] has much more impact on the S&P 500 and the ACWI than 3M with its market cap of around $60 billion.[15] As it should. Few would argue a bigger stock shouldn't be more impactful on the index.

Never Maximize Return

So, benchmarking should be based on market capitalization-weighted indexes. This specific capital markets technology—global benchmarking—is intended not to forecast returns, but to keep you on your path and to force you to think globally. It is the essence of conquering your Stone Age brain and gaining self-control to help you master Question Three.

Even after selecting an appropriate benchmark, many investors end up hurting themselves by trying to maximize return. They want to see big positive returns each and every year—hit home runs—and forget to check what the benchmark is doing as a way to control risk. Tied to order preference, they disregard the importance of *relative return* versus *absolute return* in a preference for absolute return. And in doing so they forget about risk completely.

Relative return is the return realized relative to your chosen benchmark. For instance, if your portfolio returns 5 percent in a year, you may think it's a rather poor showing. But if your benchmark was down 15 percent over the same time period, you've beaten the market by 20 percent—huge in anyone's book (though undoubtedly you took on huge risk to get there). Likewise, you might feel pretty good if your portfolio returns 15 percent in a year. But if the benchmark did 30 percent that year, you've lagged by a very big 15 percent. Seen this way, if the market is up 5 percent and you lag by 15 percent, you would be down 10 percent and hurting.

Usually, your focus should be on relative return—how you did versus your benchmark—rather than absolute return. Why? Because we already know if you can do a little better than the market over the long-term, you do better than almost all investors—it's that simple. More important, you should aim to be benchmark-like. If your benchmark is up 20 percent over a year, you had a great year if you beat it by a little bit with returns of 23 percent or 25 percent. If it's up 20 percent and you're up 40 percent, you may be elated and think you're a genius. (Beware pride accumulation, overconfidence, and hindsight bias!) However, if you take a bet big enough to beat your benchmark by 20 percent—if you were wrong with that same bet you would lag it by 20 percent. If the benchmark was up 20 percent and you were flat for the year, you wouldn't feel so smart anymore. Remember—don't try to beat your benchmark by much more than you are comfortable lagging it. We talked about this in Chapter 3, but it's central to managing portfolio risk, so it's worth repeating several times. Never try to beat the benchmark by more than you're comfortable lagging it if you're wrong with your bets.

If you don't want to lag your benchmark by much more than 5 percent and you do beat it by 30 percent you can do a joy dance to the luck gods, but don't try to repeat it. You're taking on too much risk for your result and should figure out how and why or next time you may be on the negative end of the spread. Those who swing for the fences regularly strike out much more than average. Try to maximize return, and you may end up maximizing losses. Nobody likes that.

This means, usually, if your benchmark is down, you will be down too (we look at the one exception a bit later). If your benchmark is down 10 percent in a year and you're down 5 percent, you didn't have a bad year. Your benchmark was slightly negative, it happens, get over it. You actually had a good year and beat your benchmark quite nicely. If you can beat the market on average by two percentage points annually by knowing something others don't—just a few percent—compounded over the long term you beat essentially 95 percent of everyone. That's plenty good. For now start thinking about relative return and not absolute return. Do a good job managing risk and you'll get good results. Portfolio management is all about controlling risks, not about hitting home runs. Do a poor job by taking on too much or too little risk, and in one year you'll blow your chances of achieving your goal. One really bad year compared to your benchmark can scar you for a very long time in getting to your objective.

The Greatest Risk of All

In the long run, the greatest risk you take as an investor is benchmark risk. *Benchmark risk* is how much you differ from your benchmark, for good or bad. If you have an all-equity benchmark because you need long-term market-like returns to reach your goal, but think you're being safe and conservative by holding large allocations of cash and bonds most of the time, you are taking on enormous risk. It just isn't the volatility risk you're thinking about. You're betting that in the long term, stocks do worse than cash and bonds, which is a very long-shot prediction and historically backwards. Permanent allocations of cash and bonds for someone who needs more than bond-like returns is a huge risk and out-right silly.

Consider the risk of needing to average 8 percent a year (over a long time period, of course) to get the growth needed to support your desired retirement lifestyle, and getting only a measly 4 percent or 5 percent instead because you held too much in cash and bonds. If you have a long time horizon, you can handle short-term volatility—it's perfectly natural and normal. But you probably won't be able to handle cutting your lifestyle in half in 20 or 30 years because you're taking on too much benchmark risk now and your long-term returns are too low. Really great investors, almost to a person, have hardened themselves to not feel normal volatility at all for just this reason.

Investors who have long time horizons wrongly assume cash and bonds are "safe" and don't realize they're taking the greatest risk they can assume. If you need equity-like returns, you can't be too different from your equity benchmark. Whether an all-equity benchmark is right for you is something we tackle in Chapter 9.

Benchmark risk doesn't apply only to stocks versus bonds. You take on benchmark risk by becoming too heavily weighted in any category relative to the benchmark. Think of the investors who got killed in the recent tech bubble crash—maybe you were among them. If your benchmark was 30 percent technology in 1999[16] (about the S&P 500's weight then) and you were one of many who let their tech allocation creep up to 50 percent or 60 percent (or 80 percent or 90 percent) of your overall holdings, you adopted tremendous benchmark risk. With such a big relative overweight, your portfolio had to crumble relative to the market as tech imploded. This happened to many, many folks without them ever knowing what hit them. What hit them? A lack of risk control by failing to control benchmark risk! When you focus on benchmark risk, the risk of something like tech going crazy on you is ever present in your foresight. Must be!

Investors blamed anyone they could for tech's implosion. Greedy CEOs like Bernie Ebbers. Crooked auditors like Arthur Young. Misbehaving investment bankers—take your pick. The Bush-Cheney-Halliburton axis of evil. (Mind you—Bush wasn't in office in 2000, but he still gets blamed for it—and why not? He is so easy to pick on. He's a poli-tic.) Evil foreigners buying our debt. (Eek! The Chinese!) The proliferation of SUVs and suburban sprawl. But the real culprit was overconfidence leading far too many investors to take on too much benchmark risk and blindly concentrate in what they thought was a hot area that couldn't fail but did.

Overconfidence can cause benchmark risk in the other direction too. Heavy underweighting or divesting entirely of a benchmark sector can hurt you just as much as being a crazed over-investor. This would be all the folks who said in 1995 they would never own tech because they didn't understand it. It isn't so hard to understand. And from there over the next five years, tech did great and not owning it at all seriously hurt. Making that decision—saying I won't own something that is a huge part of the world and one easily learned with a little effort—is a little like saying, "I don't understand women, so I won't ever associate with any." Tough choice! Stupid choice! A lot of benchmark risk. A lot of lifelong opportunity cost.

On the other hand, with certain hindsight bias, many investors who had been overweight to tech were fatigued and feeling whipsawed by it at year-end 2002 and wanted nothing to do with it ever again. Many again took excessive benchmark risk, just as they did when they were zealously overloaded on tech, by purging their portfolios of the pesky sector. Paralyzed by Luddism, these investors missed a whopping 49 percent tech move in 2003[17] and probably lagged their benchmark significantly once again.

Investors who either tremendously overweight or underweight any sector aren't asking Question Three. They're suffering from overconfidence (among other errors) and can't see they might be wrong about the bets they make. That was what guided me when I maintained a small position in tech in 2000 even though I was certain I knew something others didn't about what would cause a tech implosion. I was ready to act on my bet, but I didn't want to make it too extreme knowing I could be wrong. If you make a big bet against your benchmark and are wrong, you won't get the performance your benchmark would have given you without the bet. Investors overweighted in tech in 2000 were wrong and paid the price. Investors hiding under a rock in 2003 were wrong about tech and the rest of the market to boot. Because they took big bets away from their benchmark and were wrong, they lagged. Benchmark lag can be very hard to make up. The remedy is simple—if you don't believe you know something others don't, just be like your benchmark. If you believe you know something others don't, bet on it but don't be too darned extreme—because you still may be wrong. And will be sometimes.

There is one, and only one, instance when it's appropriate to adopt huge benchmark risk and seriously deviate from your benchmark; but we're not ready for that—not quite. Get the Three Questions under your belt and we'll talk about how to recognize and avoid a true bear market in Chapter 8.

You may wonder how to be like your benchmark, and how to know what a benchmark looks like. All major equity indexes have web sites (www .standardandpoors.com and www.mscibarra.com for example) where the indexes are conveniently broken down into sectors and even percentage weightings. Usually, you can even find the P/E for your index, helping you decide if you want to be more value or growth oriented. Let those percentages guide you, not your overconfident Stone Age brain. Start from those weightings and make departures from there based only on what you know but others don't. Bet where you can. Where you can't, be passive and benchmark-like. The benchmarks are good road maps toward long-term equity returns.

You Too Can Beat the Market

Beating the market shouldn't be an occasional lucky accident. There are those among professionals and academics who want you to believe the market is so darned efficient, if you do beat it—it was unrepeatable serendipity. They would have you believe Bill Miller, Bill Gross, and Peter Lynch were simply lucky. Nonsense! What did they have in common? They knew things others didn't. You can begin beating the market today if you know something others don't by using the Three Questions. How? Take measured amounts of benchmark risk. The idea is to outperform the market if you're right with your bets and not get hurt too badly if you're wrong. You needn't be right with every bet. You just must be more right than wrong on average—as long as you don't try to be too extreme with any bets.

Remember what you learned in Chapter 3—if you're really bullish on a sector and the sector is about 10 percent of your benchmark, consider making a small bet by increasing your holdings to 13 percent or maybe 15 percent of your overall assets. Heck—double the weight and make it 20 percent if the Three Questions have you convinced you have found something really unique. If you're right, you participate even more in a hot sector. If you're wrong, you aren't hurt too badly. Same on the flip side—if you think a sector is for the birds and it's 10 percent of your benchmark, don't axe your entire holding. Instead, drop it back to 5 percent or 7 percent or 8 percent. If you're right, you have participated less in a lousy sector. If you're wrong about the sector and it's the best performing one this year, you won't feel like a chump for having none.

You have plenty of potential decisions every year—each with a chance to make a bet. More foreign or U.S.? More value or growth? Small-cap bias or large? Health care or tech? Energy, materials, telecom, utilities? The list goes on. Decide where and when and how much to make a relative over- or under-weight on each part of your benchmark (always limiting yourself to what you think you know others don't). You don't need an educated opinion about each and every category. Don't know how to analyze the telecom sector? If you can't make a bet based on knowing something others don't for a category, just be benchmark-like. Telecom is 8 percent of your benchmark? Then hold 8 percent in telecom—maybe hold 2 percent to 3 percent in a few different telecom stocks to be diversified. Or buy a telecom ETF. That's easy.

Get more bets right than wrong on average over your long time horizon, and you will find yourself beating the market. As Warren Buffet used to say, this is a game where you can wait for a great pitch—the ball coming at you that you know something uniquely about.

If you use your benchmark, beating the market is easier than most people would have you believe—not each and every year and not even for two, three, or four years in a row, but more often than not, over the long term. I've had multiple periods where I lagged the market for several years because I got my bets wrong, but by controlling benchmark risk I didn't lag by a lot and you can make that up later—particularly when a bear market finally hits. The reason so many have failed—including most investing professionals—is (1) they don't restrict themselves to making investing decisions based on something others don't or can't know, and (2) they don't use a benchmark to control risk and their risky bets go haywire on them.

Some folks claim they use a benchmark and do actually check how the S&P 500 does each year. But mostly those people are more focused on maximizing return than on maximizing the odds of beating the benchmark. They aren't managing benchmark risk on an ongoing, forward-looking basis. They just use the benchmark return to tell them how well or badly they did—after the fact. Even investors who focus on relative return often use their benchmark incorrectly. Compare their portfolios with their benchmark's sector weightings and you will find them far too heavy in their favorite sectors and light to nil in those sectors they "don't understand" or "don't like." That is why proper global benchmarking is a wonderful Question Three capital markets technology you can use right away, and it won't fade away from you no matter how many others adopt it.

Emerging Markets and the GDP Myth

One last word on global investing since emerging markets engendered a mountain of press in recent years. Mention "emerging markets" and you'll be greeted by two responses. Investors are either paralyzed with fear of the unknown or believe emerging markets hold the key to endless riches. There is a bunch of regret shunning and pride accumulating going on with emerging markets. You may remember China being a darling of many investors after having been up 136 percent in 2000 and 92 percent in 2001. Of course it did dreadfully after that—down 34 percent in 2002, down 8 percent in 2003, down 28 percent in 2004, and down yet again, 18 percent in 2005.[18] In 2005, Zimbabwe was hot with a 38 percent return.[19] (Quick—name two Zimbabwean stocks. How about one?)

Emerging markets may seem risky to you—all that upside must come with lots of risk. But you're using a benchmark now. If you're interested in investing in emerging markets, go ahead and do it, but keep an eye on the benchmark. At this writing, emerging markets make up about 8 percent of the overall world markets. Table 4.2 lists all countries and weightings in the ACWI.

The weights of the smallest countries on their own are tiny and have very little impact on the world overall. People may tell you investing in China, India, Poland, and the like is outrageously risky. Those people are wrong. Just as you shouldn't own 60 percent in technology stocks if the benchmark is 20 percent, you shouldn't become drastically overweighted in any one country, including both developed and emerging markets. Frankly, it's less risky owning a few percent of emerging markets in your portfolio than none at all because a small allocation puts you closer to the weight of the whole world. If you really like China, limit yourself to a small position. China makes up less than one percent of the weight of the world's stock market so a 2 percent weight in your portfolio is reasonable—one that won't kill you. For that matter, even if you're ridiculously bullish on the United Kingdom, you shouldn't become too overweighted there either. Emerging markets are not risky; benchmark risk is risky.

What if you aren't using a global benchmark and you still want some emerging market exposure? I assure you, Brazil is nowhere to be found in the

Table 4.2   MSCI ACWI Country Weights

Country	Weight	Country	Weight
USA	46.67%	DENMARK	0.32%
JAPAN	10.81%	GREECE	0.29%
UK	10.65%	AUSTRIA	0.24%
FRANCE	4.34%	ISRAEL	0.20%
CANADA	3.57%	PORTUGAL	0.14%
GERMANY	3.07%	POLAND	0.12%
SWITZERLAND	3.01%	CHILE	0.12%
AUSTRALIA	2.33%	TURKEY	0.11%
SPAIN	1.68%	HUNGARY	0.08%
ITALY	1.67%	NEW ZEALAND	0.06%
NETHERLANDS	1.45%	CZECH REPUBLIC	0.06%
KOREA	1.32%	ARGENTINA	0.06%
SWEDEN	1.04%	EGYPT	0.05%
TAIWAN	1.01%	PERU	0.03%
HONG KONG	0.73%	COLOMBIA	0.02%
CHINA	0.69%	MOROCCO	0.02%
SOUTH AFRICA	0.66%	PAKISTAN	0.02%
FINLAND	0.65%	JORDAN	0.01%
RUSSIA	0.64%	VENEZUELA	0.01%
BELGIUM	0.51%	BRAZIL	0.00%
INDIA	0.45%	INDONESIA	0.00%
NORWAY	0.38%	MALAYSIA	0.00%
SINGAPORE	0.37%	MEXICO	0.00%
IRELAND	0.35%	THAILAND	0.00%

Source: Morgan Stanley Capital International, as of June 30, 2006.

S&P 500. You can still take small amounts of benchmark risk and hold small positions in something not even a component of your benchmark. That goes for country exposure and sectors as well. For example, you would be hard-pressed to find a real estate investment trust (REIT) sector in many equity indexes. You can hold a moderate amount, just be sure to rein in your overconfidence and not overdo it. Hereto, staying focused on your benchmark helps you see where risk is and isn't. You picked your benchmark for a reason—supposedly it was appropriate for you. (We analyze how to pick a benchmark that is right for you in Chapter 9.) When you step outside your benchmark, you're adopting benchmark risk.

A major error investors make in foreign investing—developed countries as well as emerging markets—is assuming a country with a growing GDP must have good stock returns. By the same logic, a flat or negative GDP is often assumed to lead to poor stock returns. This easily debunked Question One myth has been a major cause for investor interest in China over the past few years. China's economy has been growing by leaps and bounds—their GDP growing 11.5 percent in 2003, 17 percent in 2004, and 33 percent in 2005.[20] You already know China's stock market performance was utterly demoralizing in 2002 through 2005—and did much worse than the world overall and lost money. Great growth sometimes leads to great markets and sometimes it doesn't. (Also, beware governmental data produced by despotic countries without a free press. The data aren't reliable.) Prices are determined by shifts in supply and demand, which may or may not parallel whether GDP growth is strong, weak, or nonexistent.

GDP growth isn't always a determining factor in the growth of a country's capital markets (as we discuss in Chapter 7). So China's GDP has been growing—so what? Germany's GDP growth in 2003, 2004, and 2005 was 0.9 percent, 2.4 percent, and 1.4 percent,[21] respectively. Pretty flat, all things considered, and certainly lagging America's robust growth. Yet German stocks returned 38 percent, 8 percent, and 28 percent in those years, also respectively.[22] How about Japan? Japan's GDP growth was 1.3 percent in 2005.[23] Positively flat compared with China's cracking economy, but Japan had a gangbuster 2005 with stock returns of 45 percent.[24]

Now that you know the Three Questions and can use the results to develop tools to create forecasts and remain disciplined, you're ready for some more applications of the Three Questions and ways to know something your fellow investors don't or can't. In other words, you are ready to start beating the market. Onward!

5   WHEN THERE'S NO THERE, THERE!

Johns Hopkins, My Grampa, Life Lessons, and Pulling a Gertrude

This chapter expands on examples of how Question One helps uncover false myths "everyone" knows even though no one bothered to fact check. But first, pardon me as I digress while getting personal before we start on these examples. Like many of you, my paternal grandfather was very important in my youth. My mother's father passed away before I was born. But my father's father—I idolized him from before I can remember. I was his favorite. We were playful pals until he passed on when I was eight. I still keep pictures of him all around wherever I sit. He was my hero. I wanted to be a doctor, just like him. For no other reason than I idolized him. I didn't learn until later I didn't like any of the parts of doctoring—particularly blood. Yes, I appreciate we need doctoring; I just don't want to be the one doing it.

But Grampa did a superbly cool thing. Arthur L. Fisher was in the third graduating class of Johns Hopkins School of Medicine, graduating and becoming Arthur L. Fisher, MD in 1900. By definition, he started at Hopkins before they had graduated their first full class and well before they built their reputation. He was a pioneer, doing something before others knew how to do it—on a very different scale, a similar leap of faith Bill Gates would make starting Microsoft. After all, there were computers and software before Bill Gates. He just changed everything with a pioneering vision. In medicine, Johns Hopkins changed everything.

Hopkins, by any real standard, was the first modern American medical school, accomplishing myriad firsts from the get-go that eventually became included in the standard mix. For example, it required what we today would call a premed technical education—pretty much something other medical schools didn't do then. (My Grampa's undergraduate degree was in chemistry from U.C. Berkeley.) Hopkins was also first to emphasize early on what we now call interning—working with real patients overseen and mentored in the craft by journeymen doctors—real practical supervised experience. Back then, overwhelmingly most doctors were licensed with no patient experience at all.

Also, Hopkins admitted women from the very first class, in every class—beyond unusual then. In the coming decades, Hopkins defined modern medicine for America. Before Hopkins, an American who wanted to be a really good doctor went to Europe to study. Even after Hopkins, this was standard practice for a while and my grandfather did European post-doctoral work to gain his specialty in orthopedics (again, specialties didn't really exist then). But Hopkins was the early U.S. model for how a school would combine creating state-of-the-art medical science with the disciplined craft of medicine.

Even what didn't come from Hopkins often came from Hopkins. For example, Rockefeller University, which has had a huge imprint on medicine, started in 1901 as Rockefeller Institute for Medical Research. It was conceived by John Rockefeller's vision and philanthropy, but the legendary William Welch at Hopkins guided its origination from Baltimore. Rockefeller knew, and was advised by others, there was simply none other than Welch for that job. My grandfather was there, in Baltimore, at Hopkins, doing preinstitute post-doctoral research under Welch between 1900 and 1902, funded by John Rockefeller as Welch was starting the Rockefeller Institute. My Grampa, funded by John Rockefeller. I have that in handwritten letters from Welch that are treasures. Grampa may have been the first person to receive a scholarship in medicine funded by Rockefeller. Hopkins actually has in its archives some of my grandfather's original handwritten research from those years. Hopkins was the very yeast in which grew the explosion of America's early-twentieth century medical successes. While idolizing my grandfather in the 1950s, I had no clue he had been at the epicenter of an amazing and early American example of transformational evolution. In that regard, as I've evolved through a more recent transformation of capital markets science and technology, I've held Hopkins in my mind as one long-term model of how science and technology were built correctly in America and wedded to craft, in a world when few thought about such a possibility.

By now you're wondering where I'm going with all this. Well, one of those very first women in that early Hopkins world, going to school with my

Grampa, was a woman who dropped out and later became an international literary figure, Gertrude Stein. Toying with science from her youth, like my grandfather she came from German Jewish origins. (My family's paternal origins come from Buttenheim, Germany, the same town Levi Strauss came from. In fact, my great-grandfather, Philip I. Fisher, was Strauss's chief accountant until he retired in 1906.) Like Grampa, Stein was born in America. She was raised in Oakland, California. German American Jews were pretty cliquish back then. One year behind Grampa at Hopkins, both from the Bay Area, in a world of tiny classes and few women, they naturally knew each other and associated.

There are several lessons we can learn from Gertrude Stein. When I first heard about Ms. Stein, I had no idea my grandfather knew and went to school with her. What I heard was her infamous line about Oakland, California, on the east side of the Bay from where I was raised—"There is no there, there." Disparaging line! Maybe her most famous! Cuts to the bone! From 1902 on, she did everything she could to separate herself from her youth in pedestrian Oakland. Of course, there is a there, there. Still, her point "there isn't" is a famous literary reminder of Question One. She was asking the right question even if she got the wrong answer. Is there or is there not a there, there. You can ask that about everything and remembering your Gertrude Stein will help keep that in mind. That is my Gertrude Stein corollary of investing.

One fact few know about Gertrude is she had a wealthy father. Her time at Hopkins and, in fact, her later literary career were all funded with income provided by daddy's estate. But daddies die, and she had no interest in worldly realities. Fortunately, she had a caring brother, Michael, who was a great investor and very good to her and took care of her money all her life so she could live life in an otherwise artsy and economically nonproductive way until late in her life when her works finally started to catch on and make money—primarily her most famous work, *The Autobiography of Alice B. Toklas*. I wanted to give you the top 10 investment lessons from Gertrude Stein's life but at best could only fathom six. Sorry Grampa!

The Six Investment Life Lessons of Gertrude Stein

The Number Six Most Important Gertrude Stein Life Lesson

A rich daddy and a fat inheritance is a great career if you can land it early enough. Stein made a life of it. Or marrying into it is ok, too. If you've got that, maybe you don't need this book.

The Number Five Most Important Gertrude Stein Life Lesson

If you've got a great investor for a sibling like Stein's brother, Michael—one you really trust—who will take care of your money for the rest of your life, no matter what silly and embarrassing things you do, you needn't read this book. You've wasted your time so far. Go to France and fritter if you want. No one can stop you.

The Number Four Most Important Gertrude Stein Life Lesson

Gertrude could have benefited from Question Three. Don't let your mind blindside you into doing something stupid. She dropped out of Hopkins in the midst of a world-changing transformation and seemingly never, ever knew it or saw it around her. What in the dickens was her brain doing to blindside her? The people creating the Hopkins reality were way cooler than her early 1900s Parisian artisto pals. Somehow Stein saw life backwards. But then again, so do so many investors because they can't use Question Three. The Hopkins folks saved lives and changed modern medicine and modern life forever (we get to that soon when we talk bird flu), which is way cooler than anything Gertrude's friends did. (Except maybe her buddy Ernest Hemingway. I'll admit he was pretty cool—for a while. Finally, as an alcoholic, he killed himself and that isn't too cool.)

The Number Three Most Important Gertrude Stein Life Lesson

If you start something, finish it. Why not? Don't drop out when you've still got lessons ahead. Only Bill Gates and Michael Dell can pull off stuff like that—dropping out—and you're not them or you wouldn't be reading this book. Had Stein stayed in Hopkins and graduated she would have known a reality that changed the world in ways her fictional, artistic world couldn't fathom. It takes a long time to learn capital markets and build capital markets science and technology. Don't drop out as a freshman or sophomore because you don't know enough yet. Right now you're halfway through this book. Finish it. If you want to drop it, you can always do that later just like she could have.

The Number Two Most Important Gertrude Stein Life Lesson

When thinking stock market, remember what Ms. Stein didn't get—science is vastly more important than art, hands down. Folks say things like, "Markets are part science and part art." Think capital markets science. Markets are really part science and part making mistakes. Learn something never known before. Imagine you're at Hopkins in 1900 and your goal is to help learn what's never been known before. It's what others don't know that you profit from, not fictional works you create. If you want to do art, go to Paris and be an artist. If you want to do markets, be a scientist of capital markets.

The Number One—All Time Most Important Gertrude Stein Life Lesson

Is there, or is there not, a there, there? This is basically a restate of Question One. And who would think Gertrude Stein would, in a different phraseology, make Question One a world-famous statement I knew long before I ever thought about being a money manager?

Skip Oakland—Think Bird Flu

I'm no expert on social or cultural issues, or art. So I don't really get Gertrude Stein's dissing Oakland as a place where there was no there, there. It's a real place with many of the same qualities permeating America. And America is the coolest place ever. If you don't get that you don't quite fathom the full beneficence, grandeur, and tolerance of capitalism which through creative destruction has offered unparalleled contributions to humanity during decades of American growth. No place has ever done capitalism as well as America on a sustained basis; so, if Oakland is representative of the great unwashed of America, more power to Oakland. Of course, as I said, I'm no expert on this social stuff. So, maybe I'm wrong.

But I am an expert on asking Question One and all the rest is for the birds. For example, many folks these days are anxious about bird flu. Some for health reasons and others for stock market type reasons—both fair concerns. A standard fear is a huge Avian Flu pandemic will cause stocks to implode. In speaking to clients, both in groups and individually, I can't tell you how many times the bird flu question has popped up in 2005 and 2006. Way too many. All the time.

My normal response in a group format like that is to presume pretty much everyone in the room has heard of Avian Flu and ask them to raise their hands if they have. Usually almost all hands go up (well, actually only one hand per person—so technically almost half the hands go up). Then I describe how anything that is widely discussed you needn't worry about relative to markets because markets are discounters of all known information and anything so widely known must be fully discounted. Then I ask if they've known about Avian Flu for some long time, like a year or so, and they nod affirmatively. And per Chapter 2, I remind them old arguments don't have power over markets the way new ones do because older ones are more fully discounted.

Then someone disagrees saying that would be fine if it were financial, but something big from the nonfinancial real world, like a huge chunk of people dying causing survivors to become paralyzed with fear—then maybe the discounting effect wouldn't work.

So, I offer two examples. The first they envision easily: What happens if Avian Flu never becomes a pandemic? They can easily see that wouldn't be something to fear—and actually something to embrace. Just like when Y2K had been widely and long feared and priced into markets, its ultimate nonevent status led to markets doing great afterwards. So many being afraid of it beforehand means when folks finally see it as a nonevent, sentiment (and therefore demand) improves, helping stocks. Few fight me there.

Then I give the second example—I go Gertrude on them. Recall, Ms. Stein was, in fact, trained at America's top medical school. Ask her what happens if Avian Flu goes pandemic? How would she know what might happen? This is so simple, few can go there but Gertrude, my Grampa, Hopkins folks, me, a few others in finance, and now, I hope, you. You've read enough of this book to see me coming at you. Suppose it was a pandemic. Have we ever had a huge pandemic before? If so, where, when, and what happened to markets then? And after? Gertrude was trained to be a scientist. She would know how to do this. It's such a simple, straightforward, "Is there a there, there" question most people can't go there. But you can.

The best example is the 1918 global flu. If you don't know the background of this tragic pandemic, the biggest single killer in history, I suggest a great and easy read on the topic, *The Great Influenza* by John M. Barry (Penguin Books, 2004). (As of this writing, there were 133 copies available used on AbeBooks.com, starting from $2.47.) It even has some added commentary on Avian Flu. Great book! I'll not recount the 1918 flu in any detail—and if you don't want to read the book, you can get a lot of quick information via a Google or Yahoo! Internet search. But, simply said, in a much smaller global population than today, it wiped out about 100 million people in less than 24 months—devastating the Western world! It seemingly started in the heartland of America at the height of World War I, when the world wasn't well able to organize against anything. If you read Barry's book, you will also witness the wall of force that was Hopkins Med's impact on this pandemic. It details how the fight against disease in those days could only come from the minds created at Hopkins. You can read about William Welch, a host of others, and John Rockefeller, but you won't read about Gertrude Stein.

To get a Gertrude, just ask yourself, "Was there a there, there?" relative to the stock market. What happened? In Appendixes A and B, we have the generally accepted returns of the U.S. market going back to 1830. You can get other versions other places and I encourage you to do so. But simply said, throughout 1918, with the exception of a few small corrections, the stock market was gangbusters. It had a small correction late in 1918—but that's it. And all through 1919 as the flu progressed, the market went through the roof. A stock market bust during or after a massive flu pandemic? Didn't happen! There was no there, there. The market did great in the midst of the biggest pandemic of all time.

Admittedly, the market took a pretty good whack in 1917 stemming from war news, so some air had been deflated from the market before the pandemic arrived. Still, the pandemic could disrupt life but not the market, even without having a long time to discount fully into pricing such as we have with today's Avian Flu fears.

As I said, I'm no medical expert, but my gut reaction (which could well be wrong) is the current Avian Flu likely will never morph and become human-to-human transmittable. After all, this strain has had a long time to try, and it hasn't morphed sufficiently. It certainly still could; but if it doesn't, you must accept my first Y2K-like example applies and no one will experience an Avian Flu pandemic and that's bullish. If it does morph, the 1918 example is a perfect parallel phenomenon for asking if there is a there, there from which we can learn. As with Y2K, you will hear many more "responsible experts" telling you this is likely a disaster, so we should throw a wall of money at them now, than you will hear anyone telling you not to worry. But when it comes to markets I'm telling you not to worry. There is no there, there. Now let's look at a slicker version of pulling a Gertrude.

In the Center Ring—Oil versus Stocks

As investors, we seem compelled to assign causality where none exists, creating the basis for false investing "truisms." As our Stone Age brains try to establish order in a disorderly world, we data mine, look for data confirming our biases, ignore contradictory evidence, and commit other cognitive errors. Unfortunately, this trend of taking two otherwise unrelated events and creating hysteria by purporting causality shows no sign of stopping. Hence the need for Question One.

Recall, your goal in asking Question One is to prove or debunk the factors behind your decisions. When you discover a baseless myth with

Question One, you haven't just avoided another investing mistake. You usually have a basis for a market bet. If everyone is fretting over something they believe will surely cause stocks to drop or rise, and you can disprove the connection, you can bet against the consensus and win. You have found something where the outcome they expect simply won't happen. An excellent example, and currently a popular cause for panic, is the high price of oil. Investors presume oil's high price is a negative for stocks. If oil's price keeps rising, stocks must suffer. Few disagree. You hear it in the media consistently by an unending barrage of TV wags—so this is a great Question One candidate.

Oil as a cause for hysteria isn't new. It cycles in and out every few years or so. In the 1970s, we had disco, Jimmy Carter, and oil embargos. In the 1980s, we had power suits, Charlie Sheen in *Wall Street,* and an oil crash. In the early 1990s and again more recently, we had a few wars with what some would say was the sole intention of stealing all the oil from a benignly quirky Mesopotamian despot. Apparently, 450,000 soldiers[1] did such a bad job stealing oil the first time around, we had to send 250,000 back in 2003.[2] Sheesh! How hard can this stealing stuff be? Let's get that oil stolen and those boys home and put to better use. Like invading Canada! After all, we get way more oil from Canada and Mexico than from Iraq or Saudi Arabia.[3] And the transportation costs are lower here in North America. If we really wanted to steal oil the right way, we'd have boots on the ground in Ottawa, Calgary, and Tampico.

America's miserable record at stealing oil aside; oil is regularly high on investors' freak-out list. A primary worry is our reliance on so finite a commodity. Reading a wide swath of nonsense media, you hear that our future includes running out of oil. To the chagrin of the entire population of Berkeley, California (Gertrude's hometown neighbor!), that won't happen. Oil is indeed finite. But we keep finding more of that elusive sludge. A fact few people appreciate: We're aware of materially more oil reserves now than we were in the 1970s.[4] Yes, we were supposed to run out of oil a long, long time ago. That oil didn't magically regenerate—the oil companies invested in technology and better ways of finding and getting to newly discovered oil fields. Will we find more reserves? Yes! Will we run out of oil one day? No. Not in your life!

We Just Don't Know

You don't believe me, but we have no way of knowing what the total supply is now or any time—and never did. Oil firms haven't explored unendingly because once they get a big enough stock-pile of reserves, more exploration isn't cost effective. And besides them, no one else will do the searching. Waves of exploration come and go over the decades and will continue. Every generation thinks not much more can be found, and every generation finds more. Once the price gets high enough and reserves low enough, they start searching and find more. And they will in the future. And no one believes it until it happens. How much? Who knows? We can all speculate on how much. But that is all it is—speculation. And it doesn't matter all that much.

One big supply side problem isn't oil in the ground but refineries, or the lack thereof. The NIMBYs in Congress have made certain no new refinery has been built on U.S. soil since 1976.[5] Our refinery capacity can't pace our demand, even if oil were infinitely available. When something unexpected happens, like a natural disaster in the Gulf Coast temporarily knocking out a significant chunk of refining capability, gas prices will rise. With more domestic refineries, we could better and more flexibly deal with national disasters, wars, senatorial idiocy (sorry for being redundant), and other supply disruptions.

Those predicting doomsday insist no matter how efficient we get, we cannot escape oil's depletion. At a price, they're certainly wrong. In the short term, that can't be proved. In the long term, it will be. Meanwhile, many fear prices will run so high Joe Sixpack won't be able to fuel his pickup truck, he'll be out of a job, the economy will falter, the moon will turn to blood, and toads will fall from the sky. (I made up those last parts.) Maybe these folks skipped Econ 101 the day supply and demand were taught. Oil is a freely traded open-market commodity. The only two things in this entire universe determining oil's price are supply and demand. Not George Bush. Not Halliburton. Not Osama bin Ladin. Not oil executives. Supply . . . and demand.

Our elected officials think we're a bunch of drooling idiots who need their expert coddling and advice. They don't seem to believe in supply and demand, so they occasionally decide to "cure us" of our "oil addiction" by proposing to artificially raise oil's price through taxes. Only a poli-tic can cook up such a stupid idea. You needn't visit Washington for this. In New York, the gasoline tax is 43.9 cents per gallon. In California, it is 44.7 cents—whereas in Alabama, it's only 20.3 cents.[6] Political stupidity is in infinite supply most everywhere.

Most experts agree we've got five decades worth left of supply[7]—assuming we don't discover more and we don't get any more efficient (we will on both counts). Quite naturally, as supply dwindles and demand continues unabated, oil's price will rise. We don't need taxes or regulations or anything else for that. And it's not because oil companies are evil or greedy—it's because that is how a free market works. In the long term, if the poli-tics don't inten-sify their meddling, the market will price in any dwindling supply. Oil prices will rise to where either a replacement energy source will alleviate the supply pressure or demand will start to drop or some combination of the two. What definitely won't happen is one day you go to the pump and—surprise, sur-prise—no more oil! While oil is becoming prohibitively expensive, a replace-ment will come along to power our vehicles and laptops. What that is I don't know. But it will happen. Maybe hydrogen, solar, or nuclear power. No, cars won't run on Skittles or Juicy Fruits. But the early steam engine innovators certainly didn't envision Volvos running on gasoline anymore than you fore-see a Skittle engine.

You may think I'm flippant, but necessity is often the mother of invention. Seriously! We will never get to the last barrel of oil and say, "Oh, well, it was fun while it lasted," and as a society don potato sacks and wander into the wilderness to spontaneously take up subsistence living with resurrected Whole Earth catalogs. In 2110, the gas-powered SUV will seem as quaint to our great-great-grandchildren as the steam locomotive seems to us.

Lurking behind these oil histrionics is the ripple effect people think a high oil price has on the economy and stock market—right here and now. This concern is misplaced and easy to disprove; higher oil prices don't dampen the economy or markets—a growing economy creates increased de-mand and therefore higher prices. Investors get cause and effect backwards.

The headlines are relentless:

Oil Hits New Highs!
Oil Hits New Highs Again!
Just Kidding About Yesterday, Today Oil *Really* Hits Record-Breaking Highs!

That your paper rarely mentions the magical phrase "inflation-adjusted" is one clue. Throughout 2005 and 2006, oil hitting new highs was a perennial lead-off story. But on an inflation-adjusted basis, the story was much more mundane. We've seen higher real inflation-adjusted prices 27 years ago and Western society marched forward just fine and we're in much better shape now (as we see soon).

Folks also mistakenly think higher oil prices cause inflation, economic stagnation, and worse. Led by eco-warriors whose last coherent thoughts were circa 1979, this seems rational. It isn't. You recall in 1979 we were in the midst of a staring contest with the new Iranian regime led by fervent religious fun-damentalists. Enraged at slights—real or imagined, but probably imagined—from "The Great Satan," Iranian students took 66 American hostages, 52 of whom were held for 444 days. That capped off a decade of sanctions and OPEC embargoes that helped drive gasoline prices up and created long lines at the pump, even rationing. Before you think you're dizzy with déjà vu seeing today's Iranian problems, recall during most of the 1970s we had a frightfully horrendous inflationary monetary policy to go with our bell bottoms. Driven by endless money creation in and outside America, runaway inflation did its best to dampen an already lackluster economy which in turn led to high prices of all types including oil, long-term interest rates, and everything else—as well as an ugly unemployment rate of 9 percent here in America.[8] Times weren't so rosy, economically speaking, mostly due to poor governance.

Colorado, Canada, and China Have it in Common—Not "C"

We don't have a supply problem. We have a pricing concern. Following the 1973 Oil Embargo, President Ford introduced the Energy Policy and Conservation Act, which established the Strategic Petroleum Reserve (SPR). At almost 700 million barrels,[9] the SPR is the world's largest supply of emergency crude oil—giving us a huge new stockpile of oil. Its initial accumulation at our instigation pushed oil prices higher in the late 1970s than they would have been otherwise, a point few Americans know or appreciate. The only two emergency draw-downs were ordered during the 1991 Gulf War when only 17 million barrels were sold[10] and just after Hurricane Katrina when 11 million barrels were sold.[11] Ordered to be kept filled to capacity by George W. Bush in 2001, those purchases of 28 million additional barrels have contributed to oil's rising price in recent years. If we ever used this oil in a big way in an emergency, it would make prices markedly lower than they would be otherwise. That's what it's there for.

But is a high oil price so bad? Ask Question One. First, at some price, we will seek alternatives for economic reasons. Beyond oil is the shale rock under Colorado, Utah, and Wyoming estimated to be 2 trillion barrels[12]—eight times more than the known oil reserves in all of Saudi Arabia.[13] And don't forget the tar sands in Canada exceeding all known mid-Eastern reserves[14] many times over. Developing all this is just a matter of price. We can debate exactly what price it takes but not that it's just a matter of price. That's simply fact. In my view, and I could be wrong, but double the price of oil from here, and it's a done deal. Of course, that's just opinion, not fact. But as it happens, the threat of oil embargoes won't have nearly the potency we've feared. After a certain price, shale will be developed, meaning we will never run out of oil because as the price of oil rises, shale will substitute for it. This is simple economics, and yet I'm amazed at how few folks in the world accept it.

You have a choice. Do you want oil's price up or down? Outside a few temporary supply disturbances like Gulf Coast hurricanes, the price has been driven largely by demand growth from an expanding economy—not just in America but around the world, including India and China. Higher oil prices are a symptom of a healthy, growing global economy, not an unhealthy one. Yet people cower at the impact China's future growth may have on energy demand and prices and how that may hurt us. China has more energy under it in the form of coal than the total of all its energy needs until many decades from now. As with the shale in North America, it's simply a matter of price when coal substitutes for oil there. In fact, it's on coal, not oil, that China bases its future energy needs—for what should be obvious reasons.

Pray for High Oil Prices—Not Low Ones

Unless we discover a massive new oil field or radical new technology, if oil prices dropped a lot it would be because demand dropped because our economy soured. You won't like that, I promise you. Pray for high oil prices. You think I jest. No!

Oil's price won't hurt us if it is high. First, despite what you may have heard, we're less dependent on oil today than ever. If that shocks you—causing you to spill your chai tea latte into your iPod whilst driving your SUV and listening to this book on CD, I apologize. But it's fact. We're far less dependent on energy than 25 years ago. In 1980, U.S. energy intensity, or total primary energy consumption per dollar of GDP, was 15,000 Btu per dollar.[15]

Now it's below 10,000 Btu per dollar, as energy intensity has steadily dropped. Our GDP's composition has greatly changed. Two of the fastest growing sectors—information technology and the financial sector[16]—are much less energy intensive than manufacturing and agriculture, both of which have dwindled in relative size. All this means we've gotten much more efficient and less dependent on oil since the groovy 1970s. If prices remain high and get higher, we will get still more efficient (see Figure 5.1)

Even if oil's price skyrockets, the fact is it will have minimal impact on our economy overall. Here's an easy way to think about it: Today oil and petroleum-related products are responsible for driving only 2.5 percent of our total GDP.[17] Hard to imagine, hey? But true. Oil's overall impact on our national income today is slight. What's more, our nominal (preinflation adjusted) GDP grew an average of 6 percent[18] annually since 1980. Future growth will make oil even less important because we're growing most in nonenergy intensive industries.

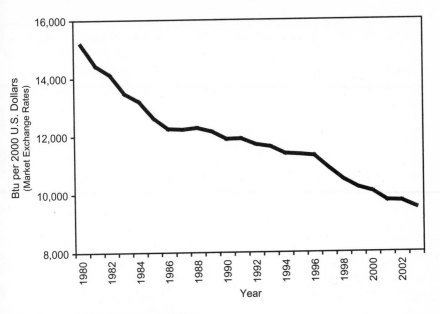

Figure 5.1 U.S. Energy Intensity.
Source: Energy Information Administration.

Believe the Stock Market—Not Me—Stocks and Oil Prices Don't Correlate

If you won't believe me, believe the stock market. A primary investor concern is oil and stocks have an inverse relationship. People believe when oil prices rise, stocks fall, and vice versa. Oil being up is seen as bad—and bad gets reflected in stock prices. Investors worry about oil wars, dwindling supply, environmental devastation, and their neighbors negligently driving Hummers. They're sure all this will drive up oil's price and drive down stocks. Nobody wants that. There is plenty of support for this view. On any given day, you can log onto your favorite web site and see "[Stocks] Skidding on Oil,"[19] and "Stocks Fall as Oil Rises,"[20] and "Oil Falls as Saudis Up Output, Stocks Rise,"[21] and "Stocks Rise as Oil Falls."[22] This is a mere sampling. Try a Google search to see how often articles claim an inverse relationship between oil and stocks.

It seems commonsensical. Higher oil prices lead to higher gas prices, which means folks have less money to spend on other things—like groceries and plane tickets and tube socks. Firms making and distributing groceries, plane tickets, and tube socks must suffer because Joe Sixpack is stubbornly wearing holey socks and refusing to fly to resort destinations so revenues fall, scaring stockholders. Soon Joe changes his last name to Fivepack. Oil rises, stocks fall—end of story. Everyone knows. Not Gertrude. She would ask if there is a there, there. Is it true oil and stocks have an inverse relationship—do rising oil prices drive stock prices down? Both prices exist all the time. If there is a there, there, we can measure it.

We supply the data for you in Figure 5.2, but if you want to test it on your own you can download historical S&P 500 data from Yahoo! finance. Historic oil prices can be found at the Energy Information Administration's (EIA) web site.[23] If you don't know how to use Excel to analyze data, flip back to Chapter 1 for a brief primer. In Figure 5.2 we graph historic oil prices against the S&P 500 from 1982 to 2006. You can see overall there isn't much of a there, there, other than they both seem to rise over time. That shouldn't be too shocking, given most prices tend to rise over time with inflation.

Unscientifically, the chart doesn't look too convincing—like Chapter 1's high P/E scatter plot. For a more conclusive answer, we need the correlation coefficient. (Again—flip back to Chapter 1 or find a teenager.) If the variables both rise and fall at the same time and by the same amount, then the correlation coefficient is 1, meaning a 1-to-1 relationship. If they're strongly *negatively* correlated—one zigs when the other zags, like we think oil and stocks do—the

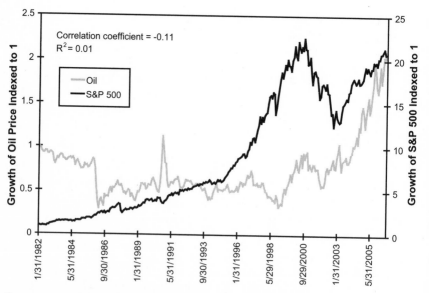

Figure 5.2   High Oil Prices Hurt Stocks. Do They Really?
Source: Global Financial Data.

coefficient will be close to –1. The closer the coefficient is to 0, the less the variables correlate at all.

The 1 Percent Solution

Fact: Oil and stocks have a correlation coefficient of –0.11—a negligible correlation—smaller than anyone wants to think. To know how much the two variables may impact each other, you create the R-squared from Chapter 1. (Remember, R-squared shows the relative *relatedness* of two variables.) Here, the R-squared is 0.01. That means you can blame only 1 percent of stocks' jumping around on oil price movements. One percent only! Focus your thinking on the other 99 percent.

Here is another way to see this since the prices of oil and stocks move around so much and sometimes, over short spurts, one may impact the other. Figure 5.3 shows a one-year monthly rolling correlation between oil and the S&P 500.

Figure 5.3 clearly shows peaks and valleys of correlation. You see a big positive spike in 1980 culminating with the oil bubble bursting. You also see troughs of negative correlation in the early 1990s following the 1990 to 1991

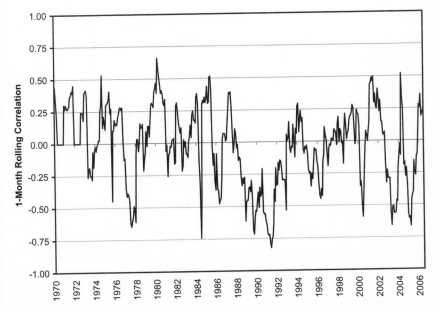

Figure 5.3   Oil versus S&P 500: 1-Year Monthly Rolling Correlation.
Source: **Global Financial Data.**

recession. They were all short lived and all rotated around a mean of nonexistent correlation. Yet another way to see this is the rolling R-squared showing how much impact the variables may have on one another (as in Figure 5.4).

From late 1992 to early 1994, over 20 percent of the movement in stock prices could be attributed to oil, and that was an unusual high point—and right then no one noticed. You didn't notice. There was a bit of a there, there, briefly, and we all pretty much missed it. Before that and ever since, oil hasn't had much power to move stocks. Hasn't been a there, there. Not up, and not down. Not at all. Still people think there is. Isn't that cool! And you, me, and Gertrude know.

You may be pretty satisfied now in knowing oil's price movements don't impact stocks much. But remember if something is true in America, it must be true in most places or it isn't really true. Whenever possible, test your conclusions in foreign markets for verification. If something only works here, then it might be something unique to some domestic situation (like the election cycles), or a fluke. Even Gertrude thought outside of America, even if she didn't get that America was better. Figure 5.5 is an illustration of the relationship between oil and stock prices in Britain.

In Britain, you get very similar results. The correlation coefficient is −0.09, and the R-squared is 0.01. Pretty much no correlation and yet the

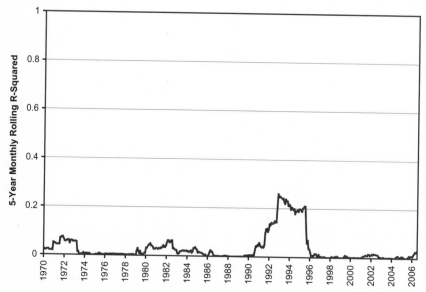

Figure 5.4   Oil TO S&P 500: 5-Year Monthly Rolling R-Squared.
Source: **Global Financial Data.**

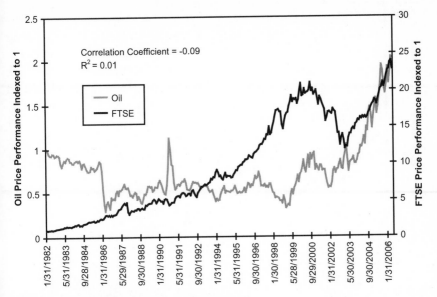

Figure 5.5 Oil Prices and the FTSE All-Share.
Source: **Global Financial Data.**

Brits panic about high oil prices driving stocks down just like Americans. In fact, my gut says they worry more (and I spend lots of time studying Britain). Comparing oil prices to an all-foreign stock index shows globally, oil doesn't much impact stock prices either. In Figure 5.6, the correlation coefficient is 0.05 with R-squared of 0.00. No impact—none! Yet your fellow investors can't or won't see there is no correlation—positive or negative—no there, there.

I Can Confirm It's Confirmation Bias

This is compelling evidence against a particularly pervasive myth. So why does it have such sticking power? Enter Question Three. The way your brain is messing you up is *confirmation bias* and *illusion of validity*. Our brains cling to instances confirming our prior biases and "common sense" and ignore instances contradicting them. Gertrude suffered confirmation bias her whole life. That's how she saw Parisians as better than boring Americans whether in Oakland or at Johns Hopkins in Baltimore. She saw confirmation of what she wanted to see. Most folks do. Recall those earlier headlines. Headlines like that are common—but when was the last time you saw a headline reading, "Oil was up, pushing up stocks!" Never, because that isn't a good news story! When oil is up, the chance of stocks being down is measurably and provably

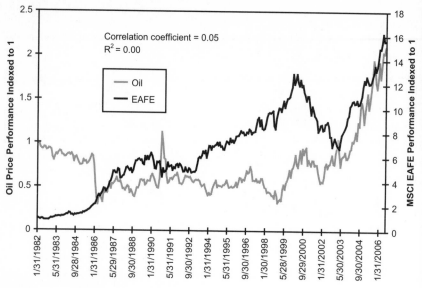

Figure 5.6   Oil Prices and MCSI EAFE.
Source: **Global Financial Data.**

pretty much a coin flip. But that isn't how our brains remember it. And that certainly isn't how our newspapers want us to see it. They and we remember instances confirming our biases—focusing only on the days when oil and stocks move in opposite directions. My writing this book and teaching you or reporters how to do simple correlations won't change our human confirmation bias.

When the opposite is true, and oil and stocks rise or fall together, investors excuse this by *reframing*. Instead of the daily prices of oil and stocks, they insist some other arbitrary time frame matters. They reframe the issue claiming you can't look at just one day—it takes longer periods—like one week, three months, or a year—or particularly extreme examples. (Of course, then they don't prove it.) Still the daily moves obeying their bias confirm the myth in their minds, while contradictory evidence necessitates a longer or different observation period or scale not actually accounted for. Apples and oranges.

Some claim oil being up doesn't drive stocks down that same day; instead, you must allow for a time-lag—another reframe. They say this but they don't check it out. I've looked. I've yet to see a time-lag providing for any material correlation. I don't believe it exists (must work overseas too). When testing for any number of time-lags—three days, one week, 2.5 weeks, seven months, 7.82 months—the results were similar. No matter what arbitrary lag you pick, oil and stock price movements don't correlate enough for any sane soul to bet on. Insisting on a "time-lag" is just another way of data-mining, reframing, and submitting to your confirmation bias. It shows what a good Stone-Age-cognitive-error generator humans are. Data-mine all you want, but you won't find a credible link between oil and stock prices. Or, maybe I'm wrong and you will—more power to you—you're better than I am and I accept that. Let me know when you find it. But I'll bet you don't. I'll bet there are many more readers of this book (not you—those other readers) who will simply presume I'm wrong and never lift a finger to run correlations on their own.

This is a great example of a myth debunked without expensive tools or complicated equations. Recall, if your analysis must be convoluted or compli-cated to prove your hypothesis, it's probably false. Let me give you some more gas on this one.

The Gas-Pump Quiz

My suggestion for mitigating oil price hysteria is requiring every consumer to pass a little quiz before filling their tanks. Anyone who fails is too stupid to vote. You must get three of the following five correct to qualify to vote:

1. Crude oil, the primary component of the gasoline powering most cars, is a:
   a. Tool of the devil
   b. Conspiracy cooked up in Texas
   c. Commodity
   d. Primary cause of global warming
2. Oil prices are determined by:
   a. George W. Bush
   b. Halliburton
   c. Supply and demand
   d. a & b
3. The U.S. Government could *immediately* lower gas prices by:
   a. Reducing regulation
   b. Reducing taxes
   c. Sending Dick Cheney bird hunting—with Shell's CEO
   d. a & b
4. The number one exporter of oil to the United States is:
   a. Iraq, but don't tell them because we steal it
   b. Saudi Arabia

    c. Halliburton
    d. Canada
5. The War on Terror is primarily:
    a. Yet another War for Oil (which is terror-able)
    b. A conspiracy cooked up in Texas (which is terror-able)
    c. A primary cause of global warming (which is terror-able)
    d. None of these

Never fear, my test won't be instituted. Poli-tics will see to that. But meanwhile you have another gameable bet. Whenever most folks freak out, predicting stock prices will drop because of rising oil prices, you know that won't happen. First, because the concern is priced, and second because it's flat-out wrong. I'm guessing as you read this book in 2007, high oil prices will still be a cause for concern. Ignore it. The price of oil can go as high as it wants without issue.

Anything the French Can Do We Can Do Better

Before leaving oil behind, let's take a few more swipes at Gertrude, the funny French, President Bush, Texas oil men in general, and China. First, were I seeking a seventh Gertrude Stein life lesson I'd suggest, "A life spent in America is better than in France." A politically incorrect parallel statement is, "Anything the French can do, Americans can do better." I say that being Californian and partial to California wine. You want to see 20 buck barrels of oil again? It's easy. It's certain. Technically, it's trivial. Just remember the French get half their energy needs right now from nuclear power and have for a long time. George Bush can't quite get the word "nuclear" out of his mouth for two sentences in a row. In his 2006 State of the Union address, he advocated alternative energy but didn't drop the N-word even once. Obviously, he isn't all that interested in weaning America from fossil fuel with a nuclear alternative.

If America, Britain, Japan, and China all somehow announced a cooperative treaty to build their nuclear capacity over 10 years such that these big four energy consumers got as much of their energy from nuclear as the funny French do right now, the price of Texas Crude would implode toward $20 faster than you can say, "Remember the Alamo." It's a no-brainer. Berkeleyites wouldn't fantasize about punishing fat, rich, white Texan oil men because it would have just happened already.

We haven't built a nuclear power plant in America in more than 30 years.[24] Been scared of nuclear! Those political and social decisions are long-standing and hard to shake, but certainly are political decisions nonetheless. Even as I say "Nuclear" I can see many now grey-haired, 1970s eco-combatants cringing in their Birkenstocks at the thought of allowing America to do what the French have done all along. Remember your Gertrude. Is there a there, there? The French have been living safely with nuclear in abundance for decades. And if the French can do it, we can do it better. And if we did, with a little help from our friends, instead of five decades of proven oil reserves we would have hundreds of years. I don't know about Gertrude on this, but my Grampa would like that—he loved his touring car for exploring the Sierras.

Sell in May because the January Effect Will Dampen Your Santa Claus Rally Unless There Is a Witching Effect

Another popular myth—or set of myths—are what I'll lump together under the category "Sell in May." Sell in May comes from the old saw, "Sell in May, go away"—which is supposed to mean summers have lackluster returns. These kinds of myths include all the month-of-the-year, day-of-the-week, holiday myths and so on. Santa Claus rallies. The October effect. Monday effect. Friday effect. The summer rally. Triple Witching. The month-end effect. The third-Thursday-during-a-waxing-moon effect. The second-Tuesday-each-month-of-baseball-season effect. Okay, you got me again. I made those last two up, but they don't sound much sillier than the others.

Investors usually don't believe all these all at once. They believe some and not others. But they don't check to verify validity. "Who would believe in a Friday effect? That's silly," one investor may say while preparing for the Santa Claus rally. You may instinctually know these are so much hogwash. Yet the media loves reminding us of them and telling us the market did thus-and-such on Friday, so we know this, that, and the other should happen on Monday. There are a fair number of published studies—some in scholarly journals that should know better and others described in popular media—showing from time X to Y if you bought on day A and sold on day C you would beat the market. Invariably, if you vary the beginning and end dates—or look overseas—the effect vanishes completely showing the signs of a planned or unintentional data mine.

Perhaps the most popular recent myth is "Sell in May, go away" because it's been on a roll, like someone flipping four out of five heads. It's been around for decades and its popularity comes and goes with its luck. At one point, it may even have made some seeming economic sense. Eons ago, summers were marked by a slight slowdown in U.S. business tied to farming cycles and later vacation cycles. Even now much of Europe basically checks out during warmer months. But does it hold true now, if it ever did? It was never a real stock market cycle. It's silly and demonstrably false. In an age of instant, wireless, 24/7 communication, is it possible there is a routine arbitrage lethargy during summer months? Many perfectly respectable investors believe whole-heartedly summer months are bad for stocks. This is another easy one to test with Question One. Table 5.1 shows market returns for June through August, along with the total return for each year, starting in 1926.

In Table 5.1, the average total return for the June to August period is 4.7 percent—making the returns positive on average and beating cash or bonds. Of course, the market itself is generally positive more often than negative. *Note:* There have been plenty of times when summer months were very strong. That it's markedly more positive than negative tells you the "Sell in May, go away" strategy is a money loser. Some investors instead will say "Sell in May" really means the summer *half* of the year is inferior to the winter half—May to October yields lesser returns than November to April. Sheesh—how much of a data mine do you want? Examine the data. Yes, May to October on average has yielded 4.4 percent versus 7.4 percent for the winter half. What does that tell you? You want to sit in cash and yield much less? There is no economic reason why one set of six months should be better than another. Why May to October? Why not "Sell in July, so you won't cry"? Some years seem to confirm the illusion. The steep May 2006 sell-off surely motivated people to believe the strategy. This again is confirmation bias and illusion of validity. The same folks would be impressed by three head flips in a row.

This isn't like the oil versus stocks myth where there is a 50/50 chance of the two variables confirming an investor's previously formed bias (though believers in this myth are certainly guilty of both illusion of validity and confirmation bias, too). If a given summer is positive, a "Sell in May" fan will simply say you should use longer observation periods (or shorter specific ones). What they miss is the cold hard truth the market is obviously positive more often than negative during the summer months. No fancy analysis to figure that out. Of course, by definition, you will have negative summers. That is true for every season and every month.

What about other seasonal myths—ones cautioning us about certain days, months, holidays, and so on? Is there any truth to any of them? No. They all fall apart under statistical analysis. Remember, based on Question Two, if something seems to have correlation, you must show it working

Table 5.1 Sell In May and Go Away?

Year	Summer Return (June-August)	Whole Year Return (January-December)	Year	Summer Return (June-August)	Whole Year Return (January-December)
1925	5.7%	0.0%	1966	-9.7%	-10.1%
1926	12.3%	11.1%	1967	5.9%	23.9%
1927	11.5%	37.1%	1968	0.9%	11.0%
1928	5.4%	43.3%	1969	-6.9%	-8.5%
1929	28.7%	-8.9%	1970	7.6%	3.9%
1930	-11.8%	-25.3%	1971	0.2%	14.3%
1931	7.9%	-43.9%	1972	2.2%	19.0%
1932	91.4%	-8.9%	1973	0.1%	-14.7%
1933	15.9%	52.9%	1974	-16.4%	-26.5%
1934	-3.9%	-2.3%	1975	-3.7%	37.2%
1935	19.3%	47.2%	1976	3.7%	23.9%
1936	12.1%	32.8%	1977	1.9%	-7.2%
1937	-0.1%	-35.3%	1978	7.5%	6.6%
1938	31.9%	33.2%	1979	11.8%	18.6%
1939	-2.4%	-0.9%	1980	11.5%	32.5%
1940	15.7%	-10.1%	1981	-6.2%	-4.9%
1941	12.2%	-11.8%	1982	8.5%	21.6%
1942	7.8%	21.1%	1983	2.3%	22.6%
1943	-1.3%	25.8%	1984	12.0%	6.3%
1944	5.1%	19.7%	1985	0.6%	31.7%
1945	4.5%	36.5%	1986	3.1%	18.7%
1946	-12.3%	-8.2%	1987	14.5%	5.3%
1947	7.7%	5.2%	1988	0.6%	16.6%
1948	-3.0%	5.1%	1989	10.5%	31.7%
1949	9.2%	18.1%	1990	-9.9%	-3.1%
1950	-0.1%	30.6%	1991	2.2%	30.5%
1951	10.0%	24.6%	1992	0.4%	7.6%
1952	6.5%	18.5%	1993	3.7%	10.1%
1953	-3.6%	-1.1%	1994	4.9%	1.3%
1954	3.5%	52.4%	1995	6.0%	37.6%
1955	15.0%	31.4%	1996	-2.0%	23.0%
1956	6.1%	6.6%	1997	6.5%	33.4%
1957	-3.8%	-10.9%	1998	-11.9%	28.6%
1958	9.3%	43.3%	1999	1.8%	21.0%
1959	2.4%	11.9%	2000	7.1%	-9.1%
1960	2.9%	0.5%	2001	-9.4%	-11.9%
1961	3.0%	26.8%	2002	-13.8%	-22.1%
1962	0.0%	-8.8%	2003	5.1%	28.7%
1963	3.2%	22.7%	2004	-1.0%	10.9%
1964	2.6%	16.4%	2005	2.9%	4.9%
1965	-0.7%	12.4%	**Average**	**4.7%**	**12.2%**

Source: Global Financial Data, S&P 500 Total Returns.

overseas as well and be able to demonstrate the fundamental underlying economics of why it should work. You can't do that with any of these seasonal myths.

Let's say the Monday effect, to pick on just one, is real. In a way it is. The Monday effect tells us Monday will continue Friday's trend. If Friday is positive, Monday will be too; if Friday is negative, expect a down Monday. This obviously contradicts another popular myth—the "weekend effect," which purports stock prices fall over the weekend. But never mind. For now, just consider the Monday effect actually works. It does if you account for it wrong. On years when the market is up, Friday and Monday and every other day are more likely to be positive than negative. So in those years, a Friday, any Friday—positive or negative—tends to lead to a positive Monday. And since there are more positive than negative Fridays in bull market years, the scheme works. In bear market years, Fridays and Mondays and every other day tend to be more negative than positive. Any Friday in a bear market year is more likely followed by a down Monday than an up Monday—and the same is true for every other day of the week. So it works.

But this is just seeing what you want to see because in a bull market year, betting a down Friday leads to a down Monday loses money heavily. In bear markets, betting an up Friday leads to an up Monday also loses money. The fact the market is up about two-thirds of the time on average makes any day followed by any day more likely to be up than down and make the basic principle work—if you account for it wrong—but still be a misleading and money-losing strategy.

There is no good statistical evidence to support any of these myths. Table 5.2 illustrates the average monthly total returns for the S&P 500 since 1926.

All the average returns are positive save a modestly negative (on average) September because—say it with me—the market is positive more often than negative. Were there any truth to seasonally related myths, some month (or months) would blow away the others. Some months look, on average, marginally better than others—but remember this is an average and takes into account the market's volatile nature and the random nature of luck. Obviously, you can't expect a 1.50 percent return each April and a 1.17 percent return each November. Averaging this in the past tells you nothing about what may happen in the future because those numbers include past random luck, which may be different than future random luck. This demonstrates there is no credence to any of the sentimental myths regarding days, months, seasons, and so forth. All any month in a year can tell you is when to change your clocks or plant your corn.

Table 5.2   S&P 500 Average Monthly Returns

1926-2005	Monthly Average Returns
January	1.69%
February	0.26%
March	0.62%
April	1.50%
May	0.30%
June	1.37%
July	1.87%
August	1.25%
September	-0.80%
October	0.62%
November	1.17%
December	1.78%

Source: Global Financial Data.

Many of these myths were propagated by someone, once upon a time, wanting to make some money off commissions by getting investors to trade too often—making a good living off transaction fees. I'm sure some advisors advocate these things out of well-intentioned but wrong-headed analysis. If you're solicited to make a stock transaction because of an alleged impending seasonally related move, simply ask for supporting documentation. You may find someone who will send you a "research report" from his firm or elsewhere "detailing" the seasonally related move. It won't include the raw data. It will be based on averages over a set time period confirming the bias and isn't adjusted for the market's normal tendency to be up more than down. But you can get the raw data. You've got the monthly returns in Appendix B, or you can get them off the Internet. You've got your Excel spreadsheet. And you can run Question One to see if there is a there, there, and answer it for yourself without him. The fact is, when you do, there is no there, there.

ANNUALIZED VERSUS AVERAGE

We often mention "annualized" returns and "annualized" averages. So what is an annualized average? And is there a difference from a plain old average? Heck yes.

A plain old average, or what your statistics professor would call the arithmetic average (or arithmetic mean), is different from an annualized average (called the geometric average or mean). Both types have appropriate analytical uses. But when talking about returns, always use the annualized average. Why? Because arithmetic averages don't reflect reality.

For illustration's sake, use a pretend index with crazily extreme returns. In Year 1, our index rises 75 percent. In Year 2, it falls 40 percent. In Year 3, it rises again—60 percent. You know how to calculate the arithmetic average: add 75 percent +(−40) percent + 60 percent and divide by 3—an average 31.7 percent return.

But for the annualized average (and bear with me, because it sounds ludicrous and actually isn't hard), you must multiply 1 plus each year's return to the power of the *n*th root—where n is the number of years, in this case 3. Once you've got that, subtract 1—giving you an annualized average of 18.88 percent. You can do it easily in Excel—it should look like the formula below:

Arial		▼ 10 ▼	**B** *I* U	≡ ≡ ≡ ⊞	$
B2	▼		*fx* =(1.75*0.6*1.6)^(1/3)-1		
	A	B	C	D	E	F
1						
2		0.188784				
3						
4						
5						

I multiplied 1 plus each year's return (75 percent becomes 1.75, −40 percent become 0.6, and so on), raised it with the caret to 1 over *n* (3 in this case), then subtracted 1.

We've got two very different averages—how can that be? The arithmetic mean of 31.7 percent and the annualized average of 18.88 percent. They are both technically correct, but the annualized is vastly more useful and real than the arithmetic mean.

If you invested $10,000 in the index at the start of Year 1, at the end of Year 3 you'd have $16,800—there is no disputing that. But if someone told you the index averaged 31.7 percent a year over three years, you would expect $22,843.22. What happened to the other six grand? You aren't missing any money. The 18.88 percent annualized average better represents what happened to your assets. Try calculating it now—an 18.88 percent return on $10,000 compounded over three years gives you $16,800.

Why care? You must be able to calculate portfolio performance correctly. Say someone is selling you a mutual fund. He may say the fund averaged 19 percent returns over a decade, beating the benchmark average of 10 percent. He's not lying and he is—he may be giving you a skewed arithmetic average fund return and an annualized benchmark return—so as to make a sale. The fund's higher arithmetic mean may have resulted from one or two wild years skewing the average and the annualized return may be much lower. Always think about and ask for annualized averages.

Time for Some Homework

Now that you've seen a few examples and can calculate a correlation coefficient and an R-squared, you can begin testing myths on your own. Getting started is easy—just ask Question One about something. Anything! Start with those things you are most confident need no testing, No one will think you're crazy. Even if they do, it won't hurt. You know what else doesn't hurt? Making fewer mistakes and more money. Tell that to your poker group if they laugh at you.

Here are a few investing beliefs for you to practice Question One on— right now! You may believe some, all, or none of these, but in general they are widely believed and easy to check and therefore debunk:

> Plenty of investors believe a high unemployment number is bad for stocks, low unemployment better. Is it true? I'd tell you there's no correlation either way, but it's easy to check for yourself (find unemployment numbers at the Bureau of Labor Statistics, www.bls.gov).
>
> While you're at it, you can check if unemployment numbers—high or low—impact GDP growth. Most investors will tell you high unemployment spells doom for GDP. I'd tell you growth begets jobs, not the other way around. But check it and see!

The VIX (the Chicago Board Options Exchange CBOE Volatility Index) is a popular negative indicator for the S&P 500. As they say, "When the VIX is high, it's time to buy!" Really? Run some correlations, and I bet you'll find the VIX is statistically worthless.

High dividend yields have long been thought to be predictive of good stock returns, and low dividend yields of poor returns. Find historic dividend yields on the Internet to see if you should bet on this myth. (*Hint:* You shouldn't.)

Pundits and professionals wail over low consumer confidence numbers and their impact on GDP and the stock market. Is it warranted? I'd tell you there's no there here, there, or anywhere with consumer confidence numbers. Check two consumer confidence indexes published by the Conference Board (http://www.conference-board.org/economics/consumerconfidence.cfm) and the University of Michigan (http://www.sca.isr.umich.edu/) to see if you can prove me wrong.

Particularly timely right now, investors worry disagreements with Iran and North Korea will culminate in another war. Me too! But will it impact the stock market? Not likely—it's priced. Check how the markets behaved after the onset of other wars America participated in, and you'll see war—even a global one—can't whack the stock market.

You'll be a pro at doing Question Ones in no time. But the real fun of using Question One is when you can discover a myth so widely, passionately, and irrevocably held, no one dares breathe even a whisper of dissent. That is where you can find investor beliefs so wrong, the complete reverse is true. Let's find some now.

6 NO, IT'S JUST THE OPPOSITE

When You Are Wrong—Really, Really, Really Wrong

This chapter may seem whacky to you. But it isn't. Chapter 5 expanded on how Question One helps uncover false myths "everyone" knows even though no one bothered to fact check. A curious mind is the best weapon you have—in investing but also in life. The Questions aren't just for investing. You can use them for many life decisions. For example, suppose you're embroiled in divorce. Nobody wants that. Yet it abounds. It's bankrupting—financially and emotionally. Had you used the Three Questions when deciding to marry maybe you wouldn't be so embroiled. Things may have turned out differently had you done some scientific inquiry into the person whose life and bank accounts you came to share. Let's see how that goes: What do I believe that is really false? What can I fathom others find unfathomable? What the heck is my brain doing to blindside me now? Am I suffering confirmation bias? How about illusion of validity? Am I overconfident? All the same stuff. But once you get to marriage on the rocks of divorce, you know you were really, really, really, really wrong. But I digress.

Using Question One, you discover ever more myths. More exciting, you'll find myths so broadly, irreversibly, and passionately held the exact reverse ends up being true. Where mythology is so really, really, really, really wrong—it's actually backwards—like our example of federal budget deficits leading to great stock market returns instead of disaster. You link a Question One to a Question Two and learn the exact reverse of common mythology is a bet-able truth. How cool is that? Just start with anything people are intensely righteous about. You may be labeled a heretic by acquaintances, but so what? (It's not your business what people think about you, remember?)

One reason so many investors fail is they fear asking questions that make them seem like a crackpot. Don't fear being seen as a crackpot—fear making bets based on fabrications.

When Debt Is Good!

Let's begin by exploring a topic sure to unite just about everyone in an appalled uproar—from the Kansas farmer on his tractor listening to Rush Limbaugh to the tie-dyed San Francisco vegan carrying a "Bush lied!" placard.

Debt.

In Chapter 1, I showed you how the universally deplored federal budget deficit doesn't lead to poor stock returns, rather to good ones. I showed you the data—the what—but not the how and why. For that, you must understand debt and deficits better—know something others don't and see how they're used, abused, and misconstrued.

From infancy, we're taught debt is bad, more debt is worse, and loads of debt is downright immoral. It's almost biblical, our aversion to debt. For many centuries, collecting interest on a loan was considered a sin throughout Christianity—leaving money lending to seemingly shadowy social fringes. Never accused of being the life of the party, Cato the Elder equated usury with murder. Early Christianity, Judaism, and Islam all prohibited lending with interest. (Jews weren't permitted to charge interest to other Jews, while Sharia law prohibits charging interest to this day.) Modern society (well, at least, Western modern society) struggles with the portrayal of Shakespeare's Shylock. Elizabethan audiences were less fastidious—they presumed the moneylender was the bad guy.

Investors perceive our debt and budget deficit to be a massive economic drain because eventually someone will pay it back—creating a presumed stranglehold on our children, our children's children, their children, their pets, the future aliens who colonize those great-great-great grandchildren, and the cockroaches who overthrow them all—living, debt-laden, in a *Mad Max* post-World War III style world where there is no Kevin Costner or Mel Gibson to save us. (Oops, maybe Mel doesn't like moneylenders either.) All because of debt!

Everyone knows we're over-indebted. You read it everywhere—multiple times in multiple places—a never challenged fact. Even if our federal debt doesn't last long enough to see the deep freeze of the next Ice Age, everyone agrees someone must pay back all that moola. And when that happens, it will be heinous. Stocks can't rise into that, right? Let's ask Question One and see. Is it true debt is bad for the economy and stock market? Are we really over-indebted to the point of difficulty?

For this question, you must know how much debt we really have, properly, in scale. Then you must ask a question so basic no one ever asks it—but you will, very soon. But, first, if you hear that talking head on the evening news say the U.S. federal government has almost $5 trillion in debt,[1] you'd probably do a spit-take. Five trillion is a lot of anything in absolute terms.

For perspective, just one trillion is 1,000 billions. And just one billion is hard for our Stone Age information processors to conceive. For example, a billion hours ago, our ancestors were in the literal Stone Age. A billion minutes ago, Jesus lived. So five trillion buckaroos must be overwhelming, right? But is it bad? Most people think so. But remember the bunnies and Hummers in Chapter 3? You must think relatively and consider scale whenever you see big numbers. For that, you need an accurate picture of the U.S. hard asset balance sheet (see Table 6.1).

Unless you're a client of my firm, you have probably never seen a balance sheet for America presented as shown in Table 6.1. (This balance sheet isn't cloaked in mystery. All these data are publicly available.) It's built just like a business balance sheet totaling all U.S. assets and liabilities. It includes public and private debts of all forms and our assets. Adding up the left side—the asset line items gives the United States approximately $111 trillion in total assets. ($5 trillion immediately feels smaller, doesn't it? Scalability!) Moving to the right side (the liabilities side), we have $50 trillion in total debt outstanding. As with any balance sheet, subtract the liabilities from the assets and you get America's net worth of $61 trillion. (*Note:* Our balance sheet doesn't address assets and liabilities that are contractual one-for-one offsets, like life insurance policies and reserves, and pension obligations and benefits. They perfectly offset each other and therefore don't impact our analysis—nor do off-balance sheet obligations like Medicare and social security—ones easily later politically eliminated by a mere vote of poli-tics.)

Of course, $50 trillion still seems like a lot of debt, but $111 trillion in assets seems big, too. One good way to look at debt is to think of a debt-to-equity ratio—like you would for a corporation. To understand our debt and begin to understand if it's "bad," divide debt by equity to arrive at our current debt-to-equity level of 83 percent. Now we know what we're dealing with and we can ask if 83 percent debt-to-equity is bad or not (we find out later).

The Killer Question—What Is the Right Amount of Debt for a Society to Have?

But a better question—the real killer question—a Question Two—is what is the right amount of debt for society to have? And how would you know it was the right amount? This is a question I've never heard asked in public or

Table 6.1 Aggregate Hard Asset Balance Sheet of the United States

Assets	(billions)	Liabilities	(billions)
Cash & equivalents	$10,224	Home mortgages	$8,683
Public stocks*	15,542	Credit cards & auto loans	2,178
Other corporate stock	6,617	Non-corporate business debt	2,763
Non-corporate businesses	9,305	Non-financial corporate debt	5,350
Fixed income	34,625	Financial sector debt	12,880
Total Financial Assets	**76,313**	Savings/checking accounts	11,918
		Federal government debt	4,702
Residential real estate	21,648	State & local government debt	1,851
Other real estate	13,091	**Total Debt**	**50,325**
Real estate**	**34,738**		
		Net Worth	60,727
Total Assets	**$111,051**	**Total Liabilities & Net Worth**	**$111,051**
U.S. Income (GDP)	12,766		

* Market value as of December 31, 2005.
** Excludes government-owned real estate.

Sources: Standard & Poors and Federal Reserve Flow of Funds Accounts (FYE 2005). *Note:* Other assets and liabilities considered one-for-one off-sets excluded. Examples of such items are life insurance policies and reserves, consumer durables like a sofa or dishwasher, and pension obligations and benefits.

commented on—ever. It's a Newtonian-like question because at its roots are heretofore unthinkable fundamentals. What is the right amount of debt of all types for a society to have? Most folks presume less debt is better and the best amount is none. But we know that must be silly. Look at corporations. They use debt to finance their activities prudently—do it all the time. They do it to maximize their net worth over time by achieving a higher return on assets than their borrowing costs. Having no debt isn't optimal, so what is optimal? How would you figure it out? It would be an amount where having more debt would be bad but having less debt would also be bad, that is, just the right amount. No one ever thinks to ask what that level is because their confirmation bias leads them to presume less debt is always better. Maybe you do too, but you can benefit by asking Question One to see if you could be wrong. Because if you've been wrong about this, you're in vast company.

To find out what level of debt is correct (and what level of debt is incorrect or "bad"), we must revisit basic economics and finance theory where we learned debt by itself isn't bad, immoral, or a sign of character weakness. Debt is obviously a right and necessary tool of capitalism. And we've already defined capitalism as inherently good. An early lesson of corporate finance is how to calculate an optimal capital structure for a firm, or the right mix of debt and equity to maintain on a corporate balance sheet. If you're a CFO, you calculate the optimal capital structure for your company to capture maximum return on investment. Though this is different for different firms, and even varies sector to sector, the right debt level is almost never zero. Most firms can't maximize profit without leverage. Therefore, having no debt isn't optimal for a society. So, again, how much?

Borrowing—whether you're a CEO running a $100 billion behemoth or a mom running a 5-person household—is good if the cost of borrowing (the interest rate), after tax, is sufficiently lower than the conservatively estimated expected rate of return on a contemplated investment. I don't think you'll fight me there. The spread between the two, quite simply, is profit. An optimal ratio of debt to equity is achieved when the incremental borrowing cost just equals the incremental return on investment from those funds. The "just equals" part makes you nervous. But if I told you our widget firm had a 15 percent return on investment from widgetry, and a borrowing cost of 6 percent pretax (say, 4 percent after tax), you wouldn't be upset if we borrowed money and added on to our widget plant. You know we would make money on the spread and you'd like that. But still—"just equals" is scary.

Did you take microeconomics in school? If you didn't, it's okay. Just bear with me for a few sentences because the next few lines are for those who did. If you did, you recall in economic theory, profit maximization occurs when marginal costs equal marginal revenue (sales). You can get that from any introductory microeconomics text. I'm not saying anything racy here. One marginal cost may be interest costs from borrowing. Via what they taught you in school, when the marginal cost of borrowing just barely exceeded the marginal return generated from the activity in which the borrowed funds were used, optimization did occur. Because we would have borrowed all we could use to profit by—being maximally efficient—and no more!

I'm Saying It—Right Here—In the Next Sentence

The right amount of debt for society to have is that amount where marginal borrowing costs of all kinds equal marginal return on assets of all kinds. This is very simple, purely rational, and straight from economic theory. So extend that. If a society's return on assets is very high compared to its borrowing costs, it should borrow more money, invest it, and get the return on assets to make its citizenry richer. For those of you still hung up on morality and debt, richer citizenry is moral. Poorer citizenry is immoral. Got that?

When it comes right down to it—whether more debt is good or bad, or less debt is better or worse—it's all about the return on assets. If return is high relative to borrowing costs, more debt is good, less debt is bad. If the reverse is true—if return on assets is lower than marginal borrowing costs, less debt is in order. So how do we know if the United States has the right level of debt? Simple—by looking at our return on assets relative to borrowing costs. How do you do that?

To figure our borrowing costs, take a look-see at the liabilities side of our balance sheet again. You know approximately what the interest rates are on the various types of debt. The interest on home mortgages for the most part is tax deductible, so that cost is lower than you think, but it hovers around 6.8 percent right now for 30-year money,[2] but after tax, is maybe half that, and plenty of folks have a lower rate for a shorter term. Credit cards have sky-high interest rates—17 percent and 19 percent and 23 percent on balances held past the first month, but there isn't much of that! (Credit card debt as a percent of overall debt is much lower than you think—actually tiny.) When you average in auto loans, which are basically interest-free, total consumer debt isn't so high as a rate. We've discussed corporate borrowing rates in this book as well as federal debt. And intuitively, you know state and municipal debt, being tax-free, are lower rates still. Looking at all of the debt together, it's safe to assume our average interest rate for all our debts is about 5 percent to 6 percent. Give or take. And after tax it is lower, maybe 4 percent. Something like that. You will see the exact number isn't necessary for our example and lesson.

Surprise!

What is really important is the U.S. return on assets, but how do we figure that? It's so easy no one thinks about how easy it is to do. Just like a corporation does! Take our total income (GDP) and divide by our total assets. The most recent data shows our GDP to be about $13 trillion.[3] GDP is the right number to use because it's our national income and someone receives and benefits from every bit of it. Our income is our "return." It's no different than the income a family or corporation gets—which is how they calculate their return. When we have more income, people are better off. That, of course, is the goal. More income for more people—that's more moral. And while you don't think about it this way, GDP is an after-tax number too because taxes wash out as your income tax is still included in GDP—it's just the part our government gets. So dividing our GDP by our total assets gives us a return on assets of 12 percent.

Huh?

Allow me to relieve the suspense and point out that our return on assets is nicely higher than our after-tax borrowing cost of about 4 percent. Our return on assets is about three times higher than our borrowing costs. Hence by definition we're not over-indebted, we're under-indebted. What the . . . ? Who the . . . ? How the . . . ? I know. It should be freaking you out. And if our guess as to the average borrowing rate is off a bit, or GDP or total assets is a little off because government accounting is inherently sketchy—it doesn't really matter much because however wrong we are, our borrowing rate is still tiny compared to our return on assets.

First, a 12 percent return on assets is impressive—very! Second, to optimize, we need to borrow and invest somehow, someway, until we've driven our borrowing costs up or our return on assets down to where they begin to get close to each other. Until then, we need more debt. We're under-indebted. Say it after me, "We're not over-indebted and wallowing in a morass of debt; we're under-indebted and need more debt." Ouch! That hurt some of you.

We've never had enough debt. From where we are, more debt would be good, less debt would be bad. We aren't taking enough risk with debt. If we borrow a lot more, you can see how that would put pressure on interest rates, driving them up, right? And if we buy enough more assets, we will engage in ever more marginal activities and our return on assets must eventually fall. Doing the two together is exactly how you move to optimization in economic theory. We maximize profit and wealth for our citizenry when we do, and until we do we're under-indebted, suboptimal, and morally corrupt in letting down our citizenry. And you just won't believe it because it goes against everything you've ever been taught. But hang in there with me. Why? Well first, because in my head, I envision the words in this paragraph trailing off—like a Doppler effect—as you toss this book out the window of a moving car and accelerate. And second, if you haven't chucked the book yet, hang on for some fun.

Fun Times—Here and Now

First and fastest, can you see if we aren't over-indebted but under-indebted, that thought alone would be fun? We don't have to worry about that dismal *Mad Max* future for our descendants—and that's a relieving and fun thought by itself. *Note:* No one has bothered to ask if we have too little debt. And they don't because consensus mythology is so overwhelmingly pro-debt reduction. It's like some kind of sociological religion where questioning the mythology makes you a heretic. But flipping Question One on its head is about the most fun you can have in finance. Let's get really perverse: Is more federal debt actually good for our economy and stock market? How about this question: If we're under-indebted, how much more debt should we have and what could we do with it? That is the Question Two kicker part that, when answered, lets you fathom something others can't fathom. To see this, we start thinking from a corporate view and then move through individuals to government debt.

The average firm in the S&P 500 has a debt-to-equity level of 172 percent,[4] which is fully twice—more than two times higher—than America's 83 percent.[5] Some consider GE the world's best run major corporation, or for that matter, institution of any kind—or at least pretty good. As of this writing, it's the world's second largest stock. And its debt-to-equity ratio is 339 percent.[6] If GE isn't at its optimal debt-to-equity level, it's probably pretty darn close. GE and other firms, as discussed earlier, simply use debt rationally to optimize their capital structure to maximize profit.

You may say, "I'm okay with corporate debt in theory. And I have no problem if GE borrows to build a plant to make money, or corporations in general do—they're rational about their usage of it—but not for idiotic consumers or, worse by far, the idiotic government."

What you aren't okay with is a heroin addict ringing up credit card debt to finance more heroin and the purchase of Pink Floyd songs on Apple iTunes—squandering meager borrowed funds on foolery and drugs. What an idiot! Still, many of you are more okay with the heroin addict's iPod debt than our federal government's debt—because you envision the heroin addict as basically smarter, more disciplined, and a better spender than the federal government. As far as total governmental debt goes, you hate your local municipality's debt, but see them as less stupid than your state and your state is less stupid than the federal government. (Unless you live in California—then you see the state as more stupid.) Now, if you don't think heroin addicts and your government spend money stupidly, you needn't read the next few paragraphs. But I do think they're stupid and that's why I wrote these paragraphs.

To see the government's and heroin addict's debt better, let's start with corporate debt again. Suppose you're CEO of an average quality corporation with a medium grade Standard & Poor's credit rating of BBB. In mid-2006, your company could borrow 10-year money for just over 6 percent.[7] To afford this debt while generating additional income, you need a return on assets better than your net after-tax borrowing cost. Suppose you have a 33 percent corporate tax rate. Then your 6 percent borrowing cost is 4 percent after-tax. If you don't believe you can beat 4 percent a year over the long-term, you shouldn't be CEO in the first place and your board should fire you. So, if you can build a plant or launch a product or otherwise do anything yielding maybe a 12 percent return—but anything markedly higher than 4 percent—you absolutely have a moral obligation to your shareholders (and your customers and employees, in other words, everyone including the general citizenry) to borrow more and invest to create wealth. Borrowing then is good for everyone and moral and right.

Here's a good example of debt and corporate morality. Assume you're CEO and your stock has a P/E of 16, which is an earnings yield (E/P, the reverse of the P/E) of 6.25 percent. Recall, that's after-tax because the P/E was after-tax. (I hope you already see where I'm going here.) If you can borrow at 4 percent after-tax and buy back your own stock, reducing available supply, you boost your earnings per share, capturing the 2.25 percent spread as profit—getting free money for your shareholders. It's a no-lose trade as long as your earnings aren't about to fall otherwise. And if you're the CEO, who would know that better than you? Again, you should be fired if you can't do that. It's the moral thing to do. Not doing so is the immoral thing to do. But maybe not! Maybe you have higher uses for borrowed money because you can build a plant making widgets yielding 15 percent. More power to you. Do it—instead of buying back your stock. Or do both. You should keep borrowing more as long as you have abundant opportunities to make ready profit at high returns materially exceeding your borrowing costs. I'm sure this seems rational to you and somehow doesn't have the mental sting normally associated with debt in our society.

Using debt in these ways provides capital for research, development, and making acquisitions; increases shareholder value; and improves long-term prospects for the firm—we all understand that. The company in turn provides better goods and services for a more competitive price, which benefits the consumer. And let's not forget the employees who receive better salaries, health care, and other benefits because of the growth involved. It's beautiful!

Multiplier Effects and the Heroin-Addicted Apple iPod Borrower

Let's shift to the heroin-addicted Apple iPod borrower and the similarly stupid government. For those of you who took a college economics class, you may recall when a bank makes a loan, it increases the quantity of money. It doesn't matter to whom the loan is made. The quantity of money rises by the amount of the loan. When a bank makes a loan, it's effectively just like printing money from thin air. I'll not detail that for you here, but ask you to take it as fact. (If you want more on that, you can again check any introductory macroeconomics textbook.) Simply said, every loan has a "multiplier" effect. In America, money newly created through a new loan gets spent—changes hands—on average about six times in the first 12 months of its existence. How fast existing money changes hands is known in economics as the "velocity" of money. Again, if you took an economics class, you may remember that. But here we're talking about the turnover of newly created money—created by a bank loan.

So there is this banker who is stupid enough to lend money to a known heroin addict who is tired of his old Apple iPod and wants to borrow to buy more heroin and upgrade to an Apple iPod Nano. How dumb is that? The banker lends to him. The addict buys some heroin from his drug dealer and the Nano from his Nano dealer. The money has changed hands stupidly. Now, the Nano dealer is rational and normal. He got some of that addict's money and spends some on sales tax, some replenishing his inventory from Apple—which is pretty normal and Apple likes it—and some feeding his family in normal ways, not stupidly at all. You're used to that and that is the second spend out of six spends happening after the money was created. The money is spent four more times before the first year is out, and every time after that first stupid spend by the addict, it's spent pretty darned normally—boringly so by normal, rational people and corporations. After the stupid first spend, the next five spends end up being very average.

That money the heroin addict borrowed which didn't go to the Nano dealer went to the drug dealer. Here there is no sales tax for obvious reasons. This dealer isn't so terribly stupid or he would already be in jail. After all, the biggest single chunk of American inmates got there by being stupid drug dealers. The ones that stay out on the street are the ones smart enough to avoid getting caught. So, this smarter-than-your-average drug dealer spends some of his new money doing what the Nano dealer did—replenishing inventory (which never shows up in GDP accounting for, again, obvious reasons) and the rest supporting his family in normal ways. For example, he buys clothes at the clothes store, but then the clothes store spends it again in normal ways. And he perhaps buys some produce from the local hippie organic farmers, who spend it in fairly normal ways—maybe at the tie-dye T-shirt store. Maybe the drug dealer even has some druggie employees, so he pays for employee salaries and health insurance premiums. And this all gets re-spent afterwards pretty normally—about four more times in the first year.

When a loan is made to a person, even a heroin-addicted Apple iPod borrower, the multiplier effect assures the money gets passed on and is spent pretty normally after the first stupid spend. When someone (or some corporation—or anyone!) spends money, they can only pass it onto a few different types of recipients: a corporation/business entity, another person, a government, or a charity. That's it. Of course, people don't normally borrow money to give to charities, but it happens. The government does it all the time! But the charity then takes the money and spends it on baby formula, light bulbs, liability insurance, job training, or something. And still it ends up being spent pretty normally after the first spend.

So when the heroin-addicted Apple iPod borrower borrows and spends, it isn't as good as when GE does. But after the first spend, the rest of the spends are pretty much the same—identical in their normality. If you and I borrow personally and spend, it's only slightly smarter on average than the six spends by the heroin-addicted apple iPod borrower (maybe a part of one-sixth smarter) and only slightly stupider than when GE borrows to put in a plant for profit—the only thing different is the first spend, or maybe just part of it. Only the first spend! Ditto when the idiotic government borrows.

Just my opinion, but I do think our various governments are inherently stupid spenders on average. That doesn't make the outcome of their stupid spending necessarily bad in and of itself. Not as good as if GE were doing the spending—to be sure—but still not bad because of the next five normal spends. Mind you, if the government could be a smarter spender that would be better than being a stupider spender. But I assert, even with the government being a stupider spender, it's good, not bad, because just one out of six spends is stupid and the rest are average. The initial stupid spend by the government generates only a little less economic activity and income than when the first spend is optimally smart and efficient.

Yep! Whether they spend it on $500 hammers, bridges, dams and roads, or hard liquor for heroin-addicted Apple iPod borrowers who would much prefer heroin—no matter how stupid—still it can only be spent a few ways. It's either spent on government employees (people), vendors which are typically corporations but sometimes are people, or in transfer payments to people, corporations, charities, or another government entity. Think about that.

The only other thing they can do is spend it overseas—which isn't very different in effect than when you take a foreign vacation and spend there. That may negatively take money out of America, but if you're thinking globally like you should, you know it contributes to the global economy. Even when they blow it up in bombs in Iraq, the next five spends are normal. And when they spend it on another government entity, like when the federal government gives money to your state who gives money to your county, the same thing happens. All the county can do is the same thing—spend on people, business entities, charities, or other stupid governments. There are no other choices. Then the recipients re-spend the money five times normally and averagely.

So, if a society is under-indebted, meaning it has a very high return on assets compared to its borrowing costs as we do here in America, then society will be better off if borrowing occurs, even if the first spend is more stupid than normal—even very stupid—even completely stupid. Why? Because the next five spends will be average and the economy will benefit from those five spends that wouldn't have happened had the borrowing and stupid spending never occurred. More money being spent, exchanged, invested, churned, whatever it is, no matter how smart or how stupid the first spend is, eventually ends up being spent, exchanged, and invested in a way leading to an expanded economy, providing more wealth for more people and above-average stock market returns.

I showed you this in Chapter 1—flip back and look at Figure 1.8 again. You'll recall years following budget deficit peaks were decidedly rosier for markets than years following surpluses. In years when we run a deficit, we're adding debt while being under-indebted—getting closer to our optimal debt level. Hence, future income and wealth will be higher and the market knows that and prices it in. In years when we run a surplus, we're reducing debt when we're under-indebted and moving farther away from optimality—going backwards. The market knows that too and prices it in and the market acts badly. The market knows we are under-indebted, not over-indebted, and its response to more or less government debt—the stupid kind—is to react extremely rationally—much more rationally than your friends do. It knows more debt is good for everyone, even when it's stupid old government debt.

If you're still not convinced, let's take another look at actual stock market returns here in America following peaks in budget deficits versus surpluses by flipping back to Chapter 1 again and Table 1.2.

These facts are pretty clear. Following deficit peaks—shown as relative troughs on Figure 1.8—markets averaged 22 percent after 12 months and 36 percent cumulatively 36 months later. Surpluses and even peaks where we've gotten close to a balanced budget have had much worse results—less than 1 percent after 12 months and a mere 9 percent after 36 months. You should prefer the higher returns. But maybe not. Maybe you're French! Or addicted to heroin. Or both! At least I spared you from considering a French heroin-addicted Apple iPod borrower.

Remember always, if it's true federal budget deficit peaks signal good times for U.S. stocks, then it must be true in most other Western developed capitalistic places. And it is. High budget deficits have led to good stock returns and surpluses to poor returns in other developed economies, as you can see in Figure 6.1, which shows the same phenomenon in developed economies the world over. Deficits bring them closer to their optimal capital structure, and surpluses take them farther away.

Not the Dow Again! EEK!

Let's have some fun considering this yet another way and return to our original question—is debt bad? Our federal debt is the cumulative result of running budget deficits. Our state and municipal debt is similar if accounted for similarly. Let's start with the stupidest, biggest, and dumbest government, Uncle Sam, and why intuitively its deficits and, hence, debt lead to good stock returns and its surpluses are onerous. Simply think of Uncle Sam as a corporation using leverage to spur growth. No one opposes the CEO using leverage to grow. People don't picket in the streets, holding placards reading, "Our grandchildren will pay for GE's profligate debt."

Figure 6.2 shows total federal government debt outstanding (including that held by the Social Security system) divided by GDP going back in time. Today, such debt accounts for 65 percent of GDP.

Consistent with our theory, periods following debt levels similar to today, such as 1942, 1956, and 1992, were all followed by perfectly fine stock markets and economies, so you know our current debt level as a percent of GDP isn't indicative of past problems. If we could do it then, we can do it now. In fact, our debt is a mere half of what it was in the midst of World War II, and we came out okay after that.

Flip that on its head to see that we're under-indebted, not over-indebted. Have you ever heard people talk about the famous 17 years when the stock market did so terribly from 1965 through 1981? It's very common to hear supposedly knowledgeable people claim the market was flat overall from 1965

United Kingdom

UK Budget Deficit as % of GDP (1955–2003)

Germany

Germany Budget Deficit as % of GDP (1955–2006)

Japan

Japan Budget Deficit as % of GDP (1960–2006)

FTSE All-Share (United Kingdom)

High Points

Date		Subsequent FTSE All-Share Return 12 mo	24 mo	36 mo
Q3 1970	Annualized	30.7%	19.8%	9.4%
	Cumulative	30.7%	43.5%	30.8%
Q4 1989	Annualized	-14.3%	-0.7%	4.2%
	Cumulative	-14.3%	-1.4%	13.2%
Q3 2000	Annualized	-22.7%	-22.9%	-12.5%
	Cumulative	-22.7%	-40.5%	-33.1%
Average Annualized		-2.1%	-1.3%	0.4%
Average Cumulative		-2.1%	0.5%	3.6%

Low Points

Date		Subsequent FTSE All-Share Return 12 mo	24 mo	36 mo
Q3 1981	Annualized	29.9%	26.5%	24.4%
	Cumulative	29.9%	60.0%	92.4%
Q1 1994	Annualized	-1.5%	8.6%	10.4%
	Cumulative	-1.5%	18.0%	34.4%
Average Annualized		14.2%	17.6%	17.4%
Average Cumulative		14.2%	39.0%	63.4%

DAX (Germany)

High Points

Date		Subsequent DAX Returns 12 mo	24 mo	36 mo
1969	Annualized	19.1%	-21.5%	9.3%
	Cumulative	19.1%	-6.5%	2.2%
1977	Annualized	13.1%	10.3%	-8.4%
	Cumulative	13.1%	24.7%	14.1%
1989	Annualized	37.1%	-14.7%	4.7%
	Cumulative	37.1%	17.0%	22.5%
2000	Annualized	-9.9%	-17.9%	-39.9%
	Cumulative	-9.9%	-26.0%	-55.6%
Average Annualized		14.8%	-11.0%	-8.6%
Average Cumulative		14.8%	2.3%	-4.2%

Low Points

Date		Subsequent DAX Returns 12 mo	24 mo	36 mo
1967	Annualized	38.0%	16.1%	19.1%
	Cumulative	38.0%	60.2%	90.7%
1975	Annualized	35.6%	-4.6%	13.1%
	Cumulative	35.6%	29.3%	46.2%
1981	Annualized	3.5%	20.6%	39.3%
	Cumulative	3.5%	24.8%	73.9%
1996	Annualized	22.1%	40.8%	15.5%
	Cumulative	22.1%	72.0%	98.7%
2003	Annualized	37.6%	8.5%	28.2%
	Cumulative	37.6%	49.2%	91.3%
Average Annualized		27.4%	16.3%	23.0%
Average Cumulative		27.4%	47.1%	80.2%

Topix (Japan)

High Points

Date		Subsequent Topix Returns 12 mo	24 mo	36 mo
1961	Annualized	-3.7%	4.2%	-2.2%
	Cumulative	-3.7%	0.4%	-1.9%
1971	Annualized	35.5%	117.1%	-25.9%
	Cumulative	35.5%	194.0%	118.0%
1990	Annualized	-39.4%	-0.4%	-23.0%
	Cumulative	-39.4%	-39.7%	-53.6%
Average Annualized		-2.5%	40.3%	-17.0%
Average Cumulative		-2.5%	51.6%	20.9%

Low Points

Date		Subsequent Topix Returns 12 mo	24 mo	36 mo
1966	Annualized	10.9%	-4.7%	36.8%
	Cumulative	10.9%	5.7%	44.5%
1978	Annualized	24.3%	8.6%	10.7%
	Cumulative	24.3%	34.9%	49.4%
2002	Annualized	-17.5%	25.2%	11.3%
	Cumulative	-17.5%	3.3%	15.0%
Average Annualized		5.9%	9.7%	19.6%
Average Cumulative		5.9%	14.6%	36.3%

Data for UK is quarterly; Germany and Japan are represented yearly.

Figure 6.1 Budget Deficits Are Good for Stocks.

Source: Thomson Financial Datastream, Office of National Statist...

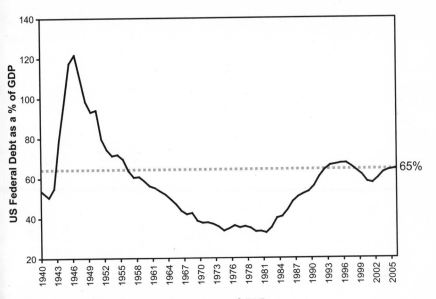

Figure 6.2   Federal Debt as Percentage of GDP.
Source: **White House.**

through 1981. But that is because they're ignorant enough to use the Dow Jones Industrials Average (which we covered in Chapter 4 as a completely misleading index in terms of economic reality) to measure returns. If you use the S&P 500 as a reasonable proxy for America, it had a 7.7 percent average annual total return over those years[8]—below average for sure, but still positive and less below-average than you might have thought. Even so, for most investors it was a long—almost-two-decades-long—period of grindingly below-average returns. Partly that was because more of the return came from dividends than appreciation and it sure felt like the market went nowhere. Well, those grindingly below-average returns are exactly when we completed the process of getting our debt as a percent of GDP down to its lowest levels of your life. Reducing debt relative to the size of the economy isn't a good thing to do because under-indebtedness is bad and the market knows it and prices it correctly.

Has America ever had no government debt at all? You may think debt is a twentieth century creation. Many people do. But, no, we've always had debt except once, in the mid-1830s, when Andrew Jackson paid it off with gold garnered from Western land sales. For a chronicling of that mishap, I refer you to my 1987 book *The Wall Street Waltz*.[9] Jackson's pay-down was disastrous, leading to the infamous Panic of 1837 and the Depression of 1837 to 1843—one of the three biggest, longest, and worst Depressions and stock market crashes in U.S. history (the others being those starting 1873 and 1929). The history of paying down debt isn't stock market or economy friendly because it goes the wrong way when we're under-indebted.

Look back at Table 1.2 again (in Chapter 1) at what happened when President Clinton began paying down our federal debt. We smacked into a fierce three-year bear market—the fourth biggest in U.S. history. Ironically, we weren't the only ones doing this. Similar debt reduction was happening all over Europe then. Again, foreign activities confirmed U.S. ones, leading to the second biggest global bear market in a century and even bigger outside America than inside.

Does President Bush bother me? Of course! He's a president. He is a politic. In fact, the president is always the head tic, the one that really knows how to tic you off. So, of course he bothers me. They always do. But do his deficits frighten me? No—because I know we're under-indebted. I don't know if he knows that or not, but to markets it doesn't matter.

Does Someone Need to Pay Back This Debt? No

Still, some detractors, brain-deadened by decades of debt dread, shake their heads and worry we are greedily enriching ourselves now at the detriment of future generations who, they fear, must pay it all down one day.

Ask another Question One here—Is it true we must pay down the debt? Look at what happened before when we have. Not good! If we can afford our debt (we can) and we get a good return on assets (we do), there is no need to ever waste cash flow on reducing debt service. We simply roll over the old debt, and as we grow bigger we add more. As said earlier, being under-indebted, we should increase debt to increase net worth overall. We trust firms to do it. And even though we know our governments spend money stupidly, the multiplier effect means other far less stupid entities will do most of the spending—averaging to be not too stupid at all. The answers to our Questions here are—debt isn't bad for the stock market or the economy. In fact, it's just the opposite. Debt is good, right, and important, and we have yet to reach our optimal debt level. Federal debt in America shouldn't be feared, demonized, or intentionally reduced.

Now, don't get me wrong. I'm all for smaller government—and I don't like government spending at all. I'd like to see government spending as a percent of GDP shrink markedly. I already told you I think governments are pretty stupid spenders. I'm actually pretty anti-government at basically every turn, but decidedly not because it would reduce our debt! I'm anti-government because

I see government as largely anti-capitalistic in most things it does and to me all good things come from capitalism ultimately. So reducing government activity reduces anti-capitalistic activity and that's good. But you didn't buy this book to get my social views.

So, if we're under-indebted instead of over-indebted, how much more debt in dollars should we have? I have no clue, only wild guesses. The answer to how much more debt we should have is that amount where our borrowing costs rise and our return on assets falls and they begin to get close to each other. But in absolute dollars how much is that? Going back to our balance sheet and noting we currently have $50 trillion of debt—I would guess we could easily handle twice the total debt we have now if its proportional make-up was the same. Twice the government debt. Twice the corporate debt. Twice the personal debt. That might move our borrowing costs and return on assets both to approach about 8 percent. But I could be way off and the right amount might be tens of trillions higher or lower. It's just a wild guess.

Still, pretend it is the right amount for a moment. Imagine what we could do if we could buy $50 trillion more assets. Now that would be fun, indeed. I won't even begin to burden you with my ideas on this—but instead refer you to the best advice I have on it. Consult Question Two and keep at it. It's tremendous fun.

The Dwindling Savings Rate and the Decline of Humanity

Another popular myth the news media loves is the "profligate consumer." The profligate consumer image is intended to paint a picture of the typical American as fat, lazy, self-indulgently over-indebted, carelessly drowning in credit card debt, obstinately refusing to save, and constantly tottering on the verge of bankruptcy. Shame on him! This is exactly how the French see Americans. Do you and I deserve such censure? Let's use Question One to see.

Rampant credit card debt concerns should be a snap for you to debunk by now. Flip back and take a look at our U.S. balance sheet again. As a nation, we have $2 trillion in personal debt. But that line item is broken out into both car loans and credit card debt. People need cars to get to work so they can buy groceries and tube socks. And car loans are currently essentially interest-free; let's not fret about those. As always, when faced with large numbers, we must scale and think relatively. Personal debt is a mere 4 percent of overall U.S. debt. The rest is corporate debt, mortgage debt, and other forms of debt not impacting your personal budget. What's more, all personal debt is just 3.6 percent of the U.S. overall net worth. I'd hardly call that "drowning." I'm not urging you to make for your closest Neiman Marcus and max out your credit card, but you can set aside concerns credit card debt will slow our economy as just plain wrong.

But the charge that we slovenly Americans just don't save is more serious. Without savings, how can we spend, invest, and drive the economy and the market forward? The official personal saving rate, the number released by the Commerce Department, has been dwindling over the last 20 years,[10] it's true. These days—and I'm sure you've heard this as a potential sign of impending doom—the savings rate has actually turned negative, implying Americans aren't saving but dis-saving. We are *unsaving!* A low or negative savings rate combined with a high level of debt (in many misguided minds) eventually pushes us over the edge. And if we're not saving but dis-saving, the stock market must eventually plummet, right? If no one is saving, no one can be investing. Right? No! This is all wrong—way, way, way wrong.

Here's another chance for Question One: Is it true a low personal saving rate negatively impacts the stock market? Here's a follow-on Question Two: Is the government-calculated saving rate even important or indicative of anything at all? What's more, is it possible a low or even negative saving rate, the way it's measured, actually isn't bad but just the opposite? (By now, I hope you're seeing each Question engenders more Questions, each one giving you further basis for a market bet.)

To begin assessing the saving rate issue, use one of our favorite tricks. Think globally. While the United States has seen "saving" evaporate over the past two decades during an economic growth boom for both corporations and personal net worth, Japan experienced huge personal saving rates, but a long stagnant economy and stock market. One might conclude, just from that simple observation, something is wrong correlating saving rates with progress. Japan saves and flounders. We dis-save and prosper. What gives?

First, the personal saving data are broken and don't reflect a darned real thing. You shouldn't place much stock in government data. Mostly, governmental macroeconomic data aren't very accurate to begin with (GDP, CPI, PPI, unemployment numbers, all of them). The collection methodology and index construction techniques leave much to be desired, being primitive but including vast assumptions, gross generalizations, and accounting techniques making corporate accounting look pinpoint precise by comparison (and corporate accounting is pretty gross and inaccurate itself). They are nothing better than a blurry snapshot of reality that isn't very precise (and isn't really supposed to be), coming as announced numbers that will be revised many times and materially before being finalized—and still the numbers won't be very precise then. Reading the tea leaves of governmental economic data as they are announced isn't useful. It's harmful.

Case in point: The official saving rate is a whacko "residual" calculation—the difference between what the government deems "personal disposable income" (after-tax) and "personal consumption expenditures." Let's take a look at how this figure is derived and why it's to be derided.

Too Weird and Whacky—Weird, Weird-II, Weird-III, Weird-IV

First, *personal income* includes employer contributions for employee pension and insurance funds, but excludes benefits paid out by such funds. Retirees receive income from pensions, but the U.S. government doesn't feel like including it in their income measure. There's no rationale why this big chunk of income doesn't get included in the official saving rate—it just . . . doesn't. When you pay in, it reduces saving. When you get the money back, it isn't income. It's just the way they do the accounting. Weird!

Second, *personal consumption expenditures* include outlays for "owner-occupied nonfarm dwellings space rent." Translated into English, this is a guestimation of what homeowners *would* pay themselves as landlords to rent their homes. What? It's a purely fictitious account, but, for example, it "reduced" savings by $963 billion in 2005[11]—many times the cost of the Iraq war if that exercises you any. By comparison, rent paid by actual tenants across America only totaled $257 billion.[12] Since homeowners generally don't spend their incomes paying themselves rent to live in a home they own and occupy, there must certainly be more cash saving available somewhere than measured by the personal saving rate. Weird-II!

Then, most amazingly, official saving doesn't include capital gains. In America, this is how people save. As personal saving steadily declined to zero, total household net worth continued climbing to record highs. This is mainly a result of securities and real estate values increasing, making households wealthier even as government data says little or no current income is being saved. Figure 6.3 shows the saving rate decline overlapped with the growth in per capita net worth. Clearly, Americans' net worth isn't being negatively impacted by a low (or negative) saving rate. Weird-III!

Consider this another more basic way. The main way Americans "save" is through capital gains. Our largest individual saver, Bill Gates, is purported the world's richest guy—worth more than $50 billion and number one on the 2006 *Forbes* 400 and *Forbes* list of global billionaires. Basically all his worth was created by starting Microsoft, which we all know was worth nothing once upon a time and is now very valuable. According to the saving rate data, Bill Gates never saved much of anything his whole life. The only thing he may have saved, according to saving rate data, is part of the dividends Microsoft

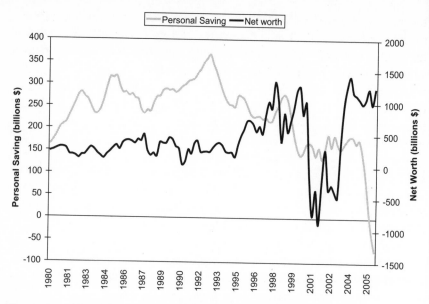

Figure 6.3   The Personal Saving Rate and Households' Net Worth.
Source: Federal Reserve, Bureau of Economic Analysis.

paid out and part of his (relatively) puny $600,000 a year salary.[13] The bulk of his $50 billion he never saved. It just happened. When he spends on charity, he is spending money he never officially saved. He got to be the richest guy in the world by not ever "saving." What he did was start a firm and plow back profits and cash flow into future growth (which most folks think of as saving), but because the firm did it, and he didn't, even though he controlled the firm, there was no official saving.

I'm a poor working slob compared to Mr. Gates, worth only a bit over one 50th of what he is. But hereto, the saving rate data says I never saved either—because I took a small salary (smaller than Bill's) and plowed everything back into growing my firm. Again, most folks would consider "plowing back" saving. The government doesn't.

When someone buys a house in California in 1956 for $10,000 and holds it until 2006 when it's worth $1.5 million, officially they never saved anything. America actually saves a lot and may have the world's highest real saving rate, but because it's almost all aimed at capital gains, it never shows up in the government's whacky official saving rate. The media will never explain this to you because it doesn't make a good, bad story. Weird-IV!

We may soon see a long-term sustained negative personal saving rate as the baby boomer generation retires. This shouldn't cause alarm, nor does it mean you must earn more to make up for them. All it means is the personal saving rate doesn't actually measure what you want it to measure and it serves no purpose beyond creating the level of panic editorial boards so love. In fact, a low personal saving rate, as Uncle Sam currently measures it, seems to signal a responsible citizenry saving via capital gains. The next time you see fear of the saving rate, the fear alone should make you a bit more bullish because fear of a false myth is always bullish.

Let's Trade This Deficit for That One

So, maybe the debt and budget deficit are okay. Maybe we even need more debt. And maybe people really are saving. But there are other headline-making, panic-inducing deficits giving investors frights—principally the trade and current account deficits. The current account deficit consists mainly of the trade deficit, so let's focus on the trade deficit first. The trade deficit was $717 billion[14] in 2005 (EGAD! Infinite gazillion bajillions!). Freaks folks out—particularly those fearful of a weak dollar. Disapproval of the trade deficit and a desire to reverse it is exceptionally widely and passionately held. You don't read anywhere that you shouldn't worry about it at all. Suggest that in public and you will be widely ridiculed. That is always a great time for a Question One. Is it true trade deficits are bad for our economy, stock market, and dollar? While we're at it, throw in a Question Two: Is it possible the trade deficit might be something good rather than bad? If so, how?

Again, here is an investing concern bred seemingly from common sense analysis, confirmation bias, and an inability to scale (all errors combatable via Question Three). A trade deficit seems to signal we spend more on imports than we garner on exports, and are bleeding money. Folks in a tizzy over the trade deficit see it like a gigantic zero sum game—if you have more minuses than pluses you lose. By that logic, a trade deficit is bad for the economy because it's unsustainable and bankrupting. If America were a gigantic hardware store, a sustained trade deficit could be bad. If everyone acts nuts, the money bolts out the door (nyuk, nyuk). You want your hardware store to sell more stuff (nuts, bolts, drill bits) than it buys (computers, employee time, Cheetos for the employee break room), else the hardware store would bolt to bankrupt.

Nonetheless, folks who think this way make several cognitive errors. First, as a general remedy, think globally. If you do, you realize trade deficit concerns are global nonsense. *Note:* No one worries whether Montana runs a trade deficit with the rest of America. Or California or New York for that matter. It's obviously impossible for the whole world to run a trade deficit or surplus—it balances. Among developed nations, trade deficits and surpluses aren't materially more important to the overall level of global stocks than the trade balance between Montana and New York. That's a bit hard to accept, but we'll get you there.

One key point in seeing this clearly is U.S. and developed foreign markets with whom we have deficits behave similarly. They tend to rise and fall together. Sometimes America does better. Sometimes other countries do. And that is true of countries with similar deficits and ones with surpluses. We have a big trade deficit, current account deficit, budget deficit, and debt. Some countries have none of those. Some run huge surpluses. If deficits are bad, the U.S. stock market and varying foreign markets should be zig-zagging all over the map. The United States should be down big when foreign is flat or up big. But it's not so.

Consider this—since 1926, there have been 47 years the U.S. market has been up and the foreign market has been up too. How many years has the U.S. market been down big—over 10 percent—and the foreign market positive? Not many—3 times. And in the past 25 years, when we've had our big trade and current account deficits? Never! Many decades ago the markets weren't as correlated but, in recent decades, while these deficits have increased massively, the markets have treated these different countries more similarly. When it comes to market direction, countries do a whole lot more of going the same way than not, which we can see in Figure 6.4.

Figure 6.4 clearly shows the U.S. and foreign markets moving—not identically—but certainly in the same direction and sometimes the same darned magnitude.

Let's think of the logic of this for a second. Once you get in your bones the U.S. market may lead or lag the rest of the world but doesn't go a markedly different direction, you know trade balances don't matter to the global stock market. They just can't. If the deficits mattered, and we have a big deficit to the rest of the world, then why are our stock markets more correlated than not? If a U.S. trade deficit is bad for America and American stocks, then by default, a surplus should be good for America and American stocks. Fair enough? If a trade surplus is good for America and American stocks, then a trade surplus in another Western nation should be good for that country and its stocks. That means an American trade deficit, implying a foreign trade surplus, should be good for foreign stocks and the two would offset each other perfectly with no overall effect on global stocks. (Remember the U.S. market is almost exactly half the world stock market in total money value.) Make

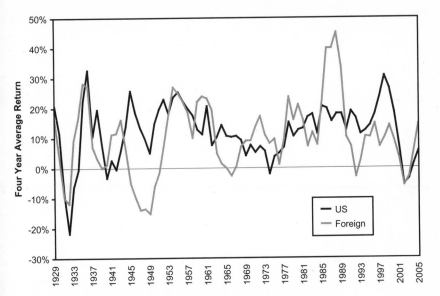

Figure 6.4   U.S. and Foreign Market Stock Market Movement.
Source: Global Financial Data.

sense? People talk as if that's so. But if it were, U.S. and non-U.S. stocks would be negatively correlated, not positively.

That still assumes a trade deficit is bad for U.S. stocks, a point I'm unwilling to concede. I'm still on Question One. The logic falls apart as soon as you get to global markets. We can all agree globally, trade balances. To argue cogently a U.S. trade deficit causes the global market to fall, you must argue trade deficits are more negative than trade surpluses are positive. To date, no one has ever expressed such a notion publicly, must less the theoretical economic justification for such a notion. No one even thinks that far. They simply stop at "the sky is falling" before getting to the notion the world can't have a trade surplus or deficit.

Consider our massive trade deficit and how it impacts life here. Is our trade deficit, in fact, bad for U.S. stocks and our economy? Here's where investors make another cognitive error in forgetting to scale a big number. Our trade deficit is big, but we have a massive economy too—the world's biggest. In Figure 6.5, we show the U.S. trade balance back to 1980 as a percent of GDP which is the right way to think about it. The United States has run a trade deficit the entire time—continuing irregularly to get both bigger and bigger as a percent of GDP.

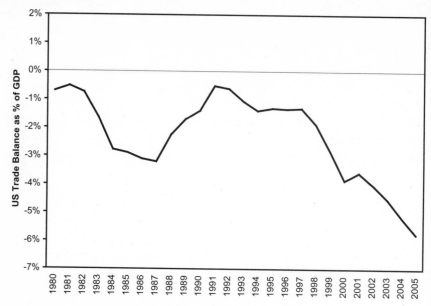

Figure 6.5   U.S. Trade Balance as Percentage of GDP.
Source: **U.S. Census Bureau.**

It currently is about 5.8 percent.[15] Now, a better question: Is that trade deficit too big and bad for our economy and stock market? Or, seeking a Question Two: Is a big trade deficit a symptom of a healthy economy and a sound financial system and not an indicator of future financial ruin?

Yes, our trade deficit has gotten remarkably wider since 1980. Over the past 25 years, the United States also had one of the world's healthiest economies, growing nearly the entire time. In fact, over those years our economy grew faster than almost all the developed world. Since we've been running a trade deficit consistently starting in 1980, we've enjoyed average annualized real GDP growth of 3 percent[16] and annualized market total returns of 13 percent.[17] If our trade deficit were bad, per se, our market returns should have been worse than average and our GDP growth shouldn't have been among the world's best. As such, we have an economy that is the very harsh envy of the developed world. Maybe not of privileged French students protesting in the streets for their inalienable rights to a lifelong, lackluster governmental career, but the French don't get Capitalism as evidenced by their slower, more lackluster economy over the past quarter century.

So maybe the trade deficit is something that happens as we do well. Can that be? Critics make several arguments. First, they say it hasn't hurt us *yet* but things haven't yet come home to roost and will, all at once, in a future big-bang financial crisis coming straight to your backyard soon. Well, fine, but at what level of trade deficit or cumulative trade deficit does that occur? To date, I've never heard such a trigger point articulated—nor, even more important, articulated with an underlying fundamental argument as to why that is where a trigger point should be. Second, some may concede the trade deficit hasn't done enough damage to make our growth negative or nonexistent—but they ask, how do we know what our growth *would have been* without the trade deficit? We might have had even *more* growth were it not for this damaging deficit.

For example, consider Britain. Their markets have done well. Their currency has been stronger than ours. In fact, arguably the pound sterling has been the world's strongest major developed currency in recent decades. Surely this is the proof in the pudding (the Brits love their pudding) that our trade deficits have hurt us relative to them.

This is very wrong. The U.K. is actually a litmus test for many of our own economic conditions because the U.K. has been in almost exactly the same economic situation in the same proportions in terms of deficits, trade balance—everything. They ran a trade deficit since the early 1980s in almost exactly the same size relative to their economy—which you see in Figure 6.6. Their current trade deficit (accounted for the same way as ours) is about 5.5 percent of their GDP[18]—a tiny fraction of a percent smaller than ours. And their economy and markets have been strong just like ours. The British stock market has averaged the same annualized 13 percent return since they started running a trade deficit in 1984.[19] Coincidentally, their economy has also been healthy, annualizing 2.7 percent GDP growth per year over that time period— just a whisker lower than ours (see Figure 6.6).

Other British deficits as a percent of GDP are similar but their currency is stronger. What gives? What does that tell you about trade deficits? It tells you they don't impact currencies. If pound sterling has been strong, and trade deficits impact currencies, how can their trade deficit, which is comparable to ours, be good for the pound sterling but ours be bad for the dollar? Critics may say, "That's just this year's deficit." Look at the charts again. You see the progression is similar. What you can't eyeball is if you take America's cumulative trade deficit over all these years, you get $5.096 trillion. Divide it by our $13 trillion economy and you get 39.2 percent. Do the same for Britain relative to its economy and you get 38.8 percent—statistically identical. You simply can't argue the size of our trade deficit relative to our economy is too big causing the buck to fall here while arguing their almost exact same size trade deficit relative to their economy now and cumulatively over time has

Figure 6.6 U.K. Trade Balance as Percentage of GDP.
Source: **Thomson Financial Datastream.**

somehow allowed the pound to be strong. Only a fool would go there. Is something else causing the relative strength or weakness of our currencies? Sure—but that is for Chapter 7. This litmus test is never contemplated by grumpy trade deficit bears.

Let's Play the "Which Country Do You Want to Be?" Game

Think about this yet another way. If a trade deficit is bad and a trade surplus is good, we can settle the question just by looking at examples of developed countries with big deficits and big surpluses. Without analyzing anything further than which country you'd rather be, look at Figures 6.5 and 6.6 again, both showing countries running "big" and growing trade deficits. Would you rather be the U.S. and U.K. with big and growing trade deficits but robust GDP and strong market returns over the past quarter century? Or, would you rather be a country with a steady surplus? How about those clever Germans—responsible for driving machines *par excellence* and punctual trains. They have run a trade surplus for the past 25 years (see Figure 6.7).

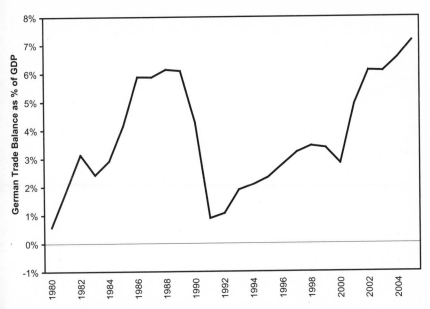

Figure 6.7 Germany Trade Balance as Percentage of GDP.
Source: **Thomson Financial Datastream.**

Unfortunately, their vaunted trade surplus has been paralleled by a notoriously sluggish economy and a stock market that has slightly lagged the world's average. And poor Japan! Their big trade surplus over the past 25 years hasn't helped at all in getting their economy or their market to do as well as global averages (see Figure 6.8).

So, who do you want to be? Would you rather be the countries with the trade deficits and the zipping economies and above-average market returns? Or do you want to boast a trade surplus and desolate growth rates? All but the irrational would opt for the deficit and growth. Again, our trade deficit is a symptom of our economic vigor and rapid growth, not a political problem to be tackled. Those who think otherwise are ignorant.

Circle back to the current account deficit, which as we said earlier, includes and is largely comprised by the trade deficit. If you can't worry about the trade deficit driving stocks and the economy down, you really can't worry about the current account deficit either. But people will.

Most of the logic we used for trade deficits applies equally—there can be no global current account deficit. What's more, by definition, the current

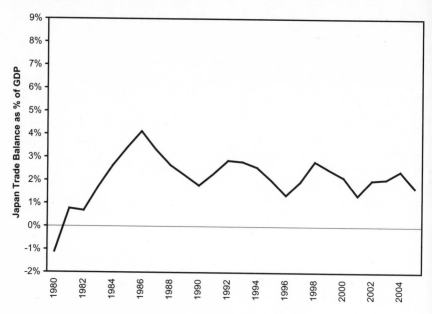

Figure 6.8 Japan Trade Balance as Percentage of GDP.
Source: **Thomson Financial Datastream.**

account deficit is self-financing. The current account deficit is the complement of the capital account surplus. Much of the confusion over the current
account deficit is because the cause and effect of balance of payments are
often wrongly reversed. The current account doesn't drive the capital account. America doesn't "import" capital to "fund" the trade deficit. Rather,
foreigners voluntarily (yes, voluntarily) choose to invest in U.S. securities and
other forms of direct investment (because of our above-average growth and
abundant opportunities compared to most of the rest of the developed
world). This capital inflow invested in America and American securities,
caused by foreigners, on balance perceiving better investment opportunities
here than abroad, caused America to spend on overseas goods and services,
adding to the trade deficit and creating the other side of the current account
deficit. This allows you, me, and Joe Sixpack to buy more foreign products—
creating the offsetting current account deficit. It balances, and there is nothing alarming to worry about here. The scary part is how few can see the
simple beauty in this.

Mercantilists Are Darned Near as Bad as Commies— And I Hate Commies!

Note the real problem: the trade surpluses in Germany and Japan and many European nations. Why do they have them and why is it a problem? It must be a problem because the countries with trade surpluses have had markedly slower growing economies than the countries with trade deficits. Why? Before capitalism evolved in America and Britain as a dominant means of the creation of goods and services, mercantilism preceded it. People forget about mercantilism. Find a basic economic history text and read about it. My personal favorite fast read on all this is Douglas C. North's, *Growth and Welfare in America's Past* (Prentice Hall, 1966), but from his references you can find many other sources. Real capitalism first reared its head just as America was birthing. Recall Adam Smith's legendary *The Wealth of Nations,* the very most seminal book on capitalism, was published in the year of our nation's birth.

Mercantilism operated then to a more extreme extent but much as Japan and Germany do now. They deploy government-based economic throttles to purposefully create trade surpluses on the theory surpluses should help their economy. They think just like those who think our trade deficits are bad. They think trade surpluses help and deficits hurt, so they purposefully manufacture trade surpluses by constricting consumption governmentally and pushing exports. But forcing policy through an economy to create anything at the expense of freer markets and purer capitalism leads to sub-optimization and slower growth. Always! Why? To maximize growth, you must let capitalism run wild. Positively amok! That is the basic economic lesson of the past 200 years. Deficit bears are too clever by half with their views of good and bad and can't get the beneficence of Adam Smith's invisible hand. They want to interfere—with a policy hand that gets in the way and simply stifles growth. Bet on capitalism and growth, not on mercantilism and trade surpluses. Our growth creates the capital flows sustaining our trade deficits; as long as we continue to grow rapidly, our current account and trade deficits will remain high and we will remain happy. If our growth slows or ends, our twin deficits will too. That is all there is to it.

Summing up, in using Question One with a Question Two follow-up, we've learned debt and the triple deficits—the budget, trade, and current account—aren't the negatives most people would have you believe. There is no actual evidence, other than mythological babble based on wrong-headed thinking, to support assertions deficits and debt will impale our world. In fact, nowhere will you hear or read a good trigger-based explanation of what the various deficits and debt are too high in relation to. When you hear drumbeats warning of market decline and worse because of a "too large" or "unsustainable" deficit or debt or both, know that fear of a falsehood is bullish—always. You can bet against it driving the market down. Keep that in mind, because deficits and debt frequently recycle as reasons for bearishness.

You should fear any effort to force a reversal in these deficits a la mercantilism—usually from senators. And you should fear surpluses. Repeat after me, "I would prefer not to see budget, current account, and trade surpluses in America. I would prefer to see rapid growth and deficits." Say that at your next cocktail party, and someone may throw a drink in your face. First, that reaction tells you this truth still has power and legs. Second, hey, free drink!

The New Gold Standard

For another Question One myth and reverse truth, consider William Jennings Bryan. Remember him? The Populist with the booming voice and his famous "Cross of Gold" speech and his indifferently supported campaign to move to a silver standard as 1900 approached?

America abandoned the gold standard in 1971, but a new standard has arisen—the widespread belief gold is the ultimate portfolio hedge. In 2006, you heard endlessly that gold is up when stocks are down, and vice versa. Common advice urged holding some gold in your portfolio as a good hedge against downside volatility. A long-held derivative is gold will protect you when capitalism inevitably fails. Something like that!

Hand-in-hand with that myth is the view gold's price is a reliable inflation indicator. Rising gold prices should signal bad news all around for stock investors because stock prices will drop and rising inflation will stagnate growth. But is it true? The love affair with gold comes and goes, but naturally intensifies if gold prices do well for a while. If gold prices rise fast, like in 2005 and 2006 (to 25-year highs!), inflation concerns reach a fevered pitch and investors fear for stocks.

Gold, like any freely traded security, has its own heat chasers. As an ounce of gold rose to $500 then to $600 then to—gasp—$700, suddenly folks who didn't even think about it when it was under $300 needed in. Gold-investing products naturally followed, as did Las Vegas-based gold investing seminars and gold coin TV advertisements. Own a piece of history! Protect your loved ones with real gold coins stamped with scenes from the Wizard of Oz! (Did you know our friend William Jennings Bryan was immortalized in that beloved movie? Check out my following commentary on the Wizard of Oz.) You needn't even buy the commodity itself to cash in on gold fever. You could buy gold mining shares, limited partnerships in mining-related REITs, or open a dental franchise doing vanity work on rap stars. If you're a newsletter subscriber, you probably receive direct mail admonitions to load up on gold because most of them sell their subscriber lists to each other, including all the gold newsletters.

THE WIZARD OF OZ AND AN OZ OF GOLD

Did you know when L. Frank Baum put pen to paper to write *The Wonderful World of Oz* (published in 1900 and later immortalized in the film starring, among others, Judy Garland, Ray Bolger, and Bert Lahr), he didn't intend to write a magical children's story? No. He meant it as sharp political satire and monetary allegory, involving the economic debates and political players of the 1890s.

Don't scour the movie for hidden meaning. The 1939 film was indeed intended as light-hearted fare during dark times. Instead, go back to the original text, where no one in 1900 could miss the meaning behind Dorothy's *silver* shoes. (Red looked better in Technicolor.) It should grab you instantly that "Oz" is an ounce of gold. Here is the story as Baum meant it.

In the 1890s and into the early part of the twentieth century, debate raged between those who supported the gold standard for our currency and those who would abandon it in favor of a bimetallic or even silver standard. After America returned to the gold standard in 1879, a period of ravaging deflation followed—prices and wages fell nationwide. A variety of policy mishaps, domestic and foreign, culminated in the Panic of 1893 and a subsequent global depression. This wasn't one of our very biggest depressions, but it wasn't insignificant either. Gloomy times all around. Though we now know there wasn't a single culprit, and American economic woes were part of a larger global trend, in America, the gold standard got its share of the blame.

Fervent support to lift the restriction on minting silver gained sudden popularity. William Jennings Bryan and his booming voice played front and center in the "free silver" movement. Critics saw this as inherently

(continued)

grossly inflationary. Supporters felt some inflation was in order. In popular press, the struggle was frequently framed as a struggle between the "people" (who would benefit from a silver standard and increased inflation) and Eastern banking interests with the politicians in their pockets (who would benefit from a status quo). This is a gross simplification but paints the general picture. Incidentally, the "common man" versus "big business" is a story that still plays today. Funny how some things never change.

Against this backdrop Baum crafted his tale, showing his support for the silver movement and Populist disgust for Grover Cleveland, William McKinley, and their gold-standard buddies. All the characters he created would have been familiar to his turn-of-the-century audience.

Dorothy, an impoverished yet dauntless farm girl from barren Kansas (where the Populist movement began) serves as our Everyman. She is plucky and represents the center of America—innocent, good of heart, young, energetic, and hopeful. Oz is a barely disguised reference to an ounce of gold—and the City of Oz signifies America itself, particularly the East and specifically Manhattan—a land blinded by and wedded to gold and the gold standard. And, of course, the Yellow Brick Road! What are those yellow bricks? Gold, of course!

The Witch of the East was pro-gold former Democratic President, Grover Cleveland, an apt villain in the Populist view because he was elected president in 1892 (the second time—remember he was also president from 1885 to 1888, then lost to Harrison in 1888) and was in office when the Panic of 1893 unfurled. He was also a villain because he was a Democrat supporting the gold standard, abandoning the Populists, when in the Populist view a Democrat should oppose the Republicans who supported the gold standard. Just as Cleveland got politically wiped out, the twister (the silver movement) drops Dorothy's house on top of the Witch of the East leaving only the treasured silver shoes behind. Naturally, the Munchkins, living in mindless deference in an Eastern suburb of Oz, didn't understand the power of the silver shoes. The Munchkins couldn't even find Kansas on a map, provincial Easterners they were, so they sent Dorothy to see the Wizard.

She is joined first by the Scarecrow—the underestimated Western farmer who in reality is quite astute. He is kept in blissful ignorance about the silver debate because the folks from Oz think he is too simple to understand such a complex topic—that is, until Dorothy and her silver shoes liberate him. Next up is the Tin Woodsman. Cruel Eastern interests have mechanized the common workingman and stolen his craft, and therefore his heart. Like so many in the 1890s, this once hearty and hale laborer is unemployed (rusted and unable to lift his axe). Finally, the Cowardly Lion joins the movement. The Lion is none other than William Jennings Bryan himself, the Democratic presidential candidate in 1896 and 1900—losing both times to William McKinley. Bryan indeed had a commanding roar, but ultimately he was a loser and didn't have a lion's capability or courage. As the economy improved in the later 1890s, his supporters splintered. Some felt he should focus on other pressing political concerns of the day. Others preferred he continue to be the standard-bearer of the silver fight, and anything less was cowing to Eastern interests. He lost courage. He didn't have a lion's heart.

The Emerald Palace, where the Wizard resides, is of course, the White House—filled with acquiescing bureaucrats. The Wizard seems friendly and wants to help, yet he sends the four friends into the very den of the Witch of the West and is no friend to their cause. The Wizard, himself, is in reality Marcus Alonzo Hanna, whom many saw as the "man behind the curtain" of McKinley's presidency. Hanna, from Ohio, was the ultimate backroom political boss of American history. He very much controlled Republican politics and, to a large extent, McKinley in the 1890s. The role of the Wizard having no real power but illusion is allegorical to politics being all about illusion.

The Wicked Witch of the West is President William McKinley, also from Ohio. How can someone from Ohio be the Wicked Witch of the West? Easy, if you're writing from Baum's view that everything was controlled by wicked New York City-based banking interests—then anything west of New York's Hudson River is "West." In those days, it was very common to refer to Minnesota and Wisconsin as part of the "Northwest." This is still why "Northwest Airlines" is based in Minnesota— same evolution of the word. We still refer to Ohio today as the Midwest. By contrast in the vernacular, the "mid-east" doesn't exist in America.

McKinley was staunchly pro-gold, pro-tariff (poli-tic!), and worse than Cleveland in the Populist view. (His annexation of Puerto Rico, Guam, the Philippines, and Hawaii did little to endear him to his foes who saw him as a greedy imperialist.) This Witch is anxious to get the

(continued)

silver shoes from Dorothy before she learns their true power, and tries to kill her (and the silver movement) off through a series of trials (the aforementioned annexations and Spanish-American War) meant to separate the four friends and the power they have as a united group. Glinda, the Good Witch of the South, waves her wand and resolves the foursome's problems, just as support from the South bolstered the Populist movement, before it ultimately died out, and Dorothy returned to Kansas, without her silver shoes.

The story is filled with more political and monetary allegory. The flying monkeys, the enslaved Winkies (nowhere to be found in MGM's version), the poppy field (golden), even the gifts the Wizard bestows on our heroes (a little liquid "courage" for the tee-totaling lion—Bryan was a well-known Prohibitionist) didn't escape Baum's audience—they knew the meanings.

Don't believe me? There is a wonderful 1990 paper by Hugh Rockoff, "The 'Wizard of Oz' as a Monetary Allegory,"[20] which is available online or in your local library. Rockoff delves into more detail about the economic, monetary, and political climate, along with the characters and narrative itself. Read that, and then re-read Baum's classic. It will be eye-opening for you. Sometimes even your favorite childhood stories aren't what they seem to be. Question One. Question Two. Question Three.

The Golden Hedge

The gold hedge belief, like many entrenched investor beliefs, appeals to our common sense. Gold is a commodity—it has weight and heft and you can see, feel, and take possession of it. Stocks are slips of paper—nowadays barely even that—you get an e-mail confirming you own a piece of a firm changing in value constantly. It seemingly makes sense two such different asset classes might behave differently. And because of prior long history of the government pegging currency value to gold, both here and globally, there is sentimental value in owning gold.

But is it right? The more I hear old, long-held governmental policies paralleling our faith in gold, the more skeptical I get—particularly when I remember gold standards started during mercantilism's reign.

Use Question One. Is it true gold makes a good hedge? If gold is a great hedge, it should be negatively correlated to stocks. Think short and long term. As these words are committed to paper in mid-2006, we just had what is probably a pretty normal global stock market correction. I say "probably" a correction because the drop, starting May 9, 2006, was sudden and sharp, unlike a rolling, grinding bull market top. But regardless, the global market fell 10 percent—and as that happened, if gold were a proper hedge, it should have continued to rise as stock prices dropped—or at worst, remained flat. Figure 6.9 shows the price of gold and the S&P 500 from the beginning of the year to mid-2006.

Clearly, gold isn't doing what hedgers expect. Over this time period, gold is correlating strongly with the stock market, not the reverse. The market is declining sharply, and so is gold. If you hoped to protect yourself against downside volatility with gold, you're instead getting it double. It moves with the market and is just about as volatile as the market. Plus, if you're buying an asset near historic highs when nearly everyone you know is uniformly enthusiastic about it, you're likely committing a whole host of cognitive errors.

If gold doesn't make sense as a security hedge, could it make sense as a long-term investment? Even though gold is at 25-year highs, on an inflation-adjusted basis, the returns have been miserable. Stocks clearly have been a better investment over the past 25 years. The story is the same going back to 1926. Investing in gold beats stashing greenbacks in your mattress, but can't

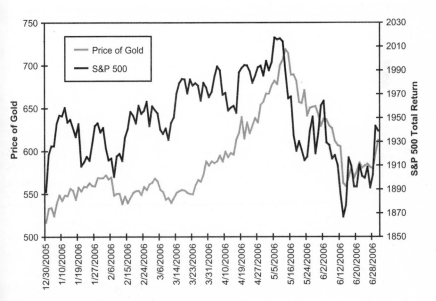

Figure 6.9   Price of Gold and the S&P 500.
Source: **Global Financial Data.**

compare to stocks or even bonds. That is really hard for a gold bug to swallow. Even some cash equivalents do better over the long term. The current gold hype is nothing more than some run-of-the-mill heat chasing brought on by a Stone Age mentality. Gold may continue to climb, it may not, but the odds are you aren't well served using gold as a hedge or as a long-term investment if any kind of growth is your goal. To do well with gold, you must be good at in-and-outing. If that is your plan, you should ask yourself, if you're not good at in-and-outing stocks, why will you be with gold? The answer, as with all other things, comes down to the question: Do you know something others don't about gold.

Gold, Inflation, and 206 Years of the Long Bond

Gold could serve a useful purpose if its price can tell us something about where inflation is headed. Look at Figure 6.10, which shows gold and S&P 500 prices since 1926. Gold has been practically flat, adjusting for inflation. If gold appreciates basically at the rate of inflation, maybe it's predictive of inflation—it's plausible. Voices abound saying it is so and that runaway inflation is ahead because gold is up.

Except Question One shows us this is a myth, too. Inflation is a monetary phenomenon relating to how tight or loose monetary policy is—caused and

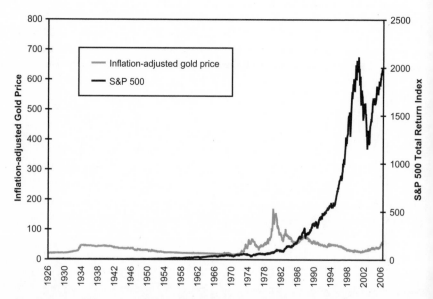

Figure 6.10   Price of Inflation-Adjusted Gold and the S&P 500 (1926–2006).
Source: **Global Financial Data.**

controlled by central bank actions. Inflation occurs when central banks create more money than society creates goods and services. Inflation isn't necessarily bad. Few fear very low inflation rates and everyone fears high ones.

Runaway inflation, such as in the 1970s, is a problem, which no one disputes. It's easiest to think about runaway inflation on the extreme end. Recall Germany's Weimar years in the early 1920s. The central bank was so loose, printing so much money—money became worthless. Germans burnt money as fuel because crates of their valueless cash couldn't buy coal or even wood. And before too long the Nazis took over, so you know hyperinflation isn't so good. But low inflation levels aren't scary. Which would you prefer, modest inflation or modest deflation? Probably inflation, though statistically they are two edges of the same sword. Deflation, made by creating less new money than new goods or services, causes prices to drop and can lead to problems, including massive unemployment and depression. No fun!

So what does all this have to do with gold? Nothing. Gold is a commodity and is traded on a free and open market. Inflation is a monetary phenomenon, as Milton Friedman once famously said, "Always and everywhere." Just because gold has appreciated at roughly the rate of inflation, you shouldn't conclude gold can tell you where inflation will go. It should tell you over long time periods gold investors get pretty darned low returns—which is what you should intuitively expect from most commodities. Easy as that!

But the perception remains a rising gold price is indicative of increasing inflation. Look back at Figure 6.9. Gold (and the S&P 500, too, but never mind that for now) climbed as did the histrionics regarding inflation. Then, the price of gold dropped. If it's true rising gold signals increased inflation, then dropping gold must signal disinflation (the slowing of the rate at which prices rise).

Officially inflation was perfectly unremarkable in 2003, 2004, 2005, and 2006. So for years, gold has been up and official inflation moderate. Some will tell you official inflation figures don't correctly reflect inflation and we come back to that. Most gold fans will tell you big inflation must be right around the corner—gold's rise tells you so. Will runaway inflation become a reality going forward? Maybe, maybe not, but gold won't tell you either way. We're certainly less likely to see monetary policy errors on the magnitude of the 1970s and prior periods due to advances in theory, accumulated experience, and technology. But that doesn't mean inflation can't and won't occasionally reach disruptively high levels. But how can you know if that might happen? Having cleared up the gold myth, you can us Question Two to figure out what is a better indicator for inflation. This one is really simple.

What Is It? What Isn't It?

This Question Two requires a Question Three reminder to think globally. But first, let's think about what inflation is and isn't quite literally. It isn't what is happening to your cost of living, which people often confuse with inflation. Inflation is an averaging of prices of all types of newly produced goods and services whether you buy them or not. It isn't about the price of gold or any other commodity. It isn't about the price of art collections although they may or may not move speculatively with inflation. It isn't about the cost of used cars although used car prices may be impacted by inflation. It isn't reflective of wages although wages are part of what it's about. It is an averaging of all goods and services produced and, in that regard, is simply a reflection of the change in the value of money to buy the average item.

Maybe some prices are going up a lot and some a little—some down a little, and maybe some down a lot. Gasoline up a lot. Health care up a lot. Electronic gadgets down a lot. Brokerage commissions down a little (a service). Shoe prices down a little! In a perfect world of zero percent inflation (correctly calculated), it isn't true all prices would remain flat and unchanged. No, in such a world it would be true half the prices would be rising, half the prices falling and some doing both more than others.

Older Americans who pay for lots of health care and their grandchildren's private school and college educations often presume inflation is rampant and our inflation indexes are massively off and understate inflation. I hear that from individual clients all the time. They confuse what they buy with inflation. I'll not defend the inflation indexes because as said earlier, pretty much all government economic indicators are very inaccurate. I'll teach you a better way to see inflation. But whether the Consumer Price Index reflects inflation correctly or not has nothing to do with whether the items you buy are reflective of the average items produced and therefore reflective of inflation. They aren't. Few people experience an average experience. Consumer buying habits are very diverse. It would be bizarre for a very young person to buy a similar basket of goods as an elderly couple—and again different from a middle-aged one.

Take this further. In 1900, most of what you might buy was made in America. In today's more global world, much of it comes from here, there, or anywhere. Much of what is made in America is only partly made in America. Today, higher prices on one type of good from one country may be wholly or partly offset by lower prices on another type from another country. Today inflation takes on global aspects. During the past 15 years, we saw American inflation while Japan and much of Asia felt deflation because they created more goods than they created money, and the type of goods they created were often prone to falling prices. But still, within their deflation, some prices would rise, others would fall and others would go down even more. Inflation as a concept is always an averaging. Japanese deflation then, including the prices of goods created there and sold into America, helped keep American inflation down to lower levels than they would have been otherwise via substitution. At one level, we partly exported inflation to them and they partly exported deflation to us and both partially offset the other.

So if what you buy isn't necessarily reflective of inflation, then what America averages isn't necessarily totally reflective of inflation. One way to think better about inflation is to try to see it globally. Thinking globally, you worry less because globalization can reduce country-specific inflation effects. Global competition leads to ever-increased specialization of labor and technology, and short-term excess production capacity in one country offsets shortages elsewhere. American prices for many goods and services subject to foreign competition are actually falling. Everyday items from tube socks to toys to cars to sundries are cheaper today than just a few years ago, adjusted for inflation. This is a lost story because rising oil prices make for better television. The media had consumers so focused on the higher price of crude and steel they didn't notice the cars they were fueling up were actually cheaper. A cheaper car is as much a good thing as higher gas prices an annoying thing.

But is there something that can signal if inflation is rising? Well, it can't be your buying habits. It can't be Montana's buying habits. It really shouldn't even be America's buying habits. What it should be is something measuring the value of money spanning the whole wide global world because that is what inflation is all about. Use Question Two to ponder, what is a good measure of the value of money? What is the price of money today? What is its price tomorrow?

Well, we know for a fact we can borrow money today so we can have it tomorrow. We know what the rent is for that borrowing. In the long term, the price of renting money is what we otherwise call long-term interest rates. The 10-year Treasury bond rate, for example, is one way to measure the cost of renting long-term money in America.

From a lender's view, money rental is very vulnerable to the ravages of accelerating inflation. Lenders want to be paid for higher inflation and higher inflation risk by getting a higher interest rate. America may not exactly be experiencing the world's buying habits, but global long-term rates react to global long-term inflation fears. Therefore, global long-term rates are most sensitive to changing inflation expectations. For this, I refer you back to Chapter 2 where we introduced to you the concept of global short- and long-term interest rates. The global long-term rate we showed you (which can be constructed on your own with GDP numbers and interest rates from Bloomberg.com or Yahoo! Finance) is a perfect way to see if global inflation is rearing its ugly head or not. As of this writing, it quite clearly isn't. If inflation is rising as a problem, global long-term interest rates must rise. If it is falling as a problem, global rates will reflect that. Remember, the global interest rate is the price of renting money. Figure 6.11 shows the global free market measuring precisely the problem of concern—the total global or country-based value of money. That global long-term rates have been benign in recent years tells you inflation hasn't begun to rear its head in a materially increasing way. That U.S. rates are up a little over the past few years tells you it's a little problem here but much of that is offset overseas. You just fathomed something most can't fathom. More important, we can see historically the long bond has been sensitive to inflation concerns and is a good measure.

Beginning in the 1980s, Figure 6.11 shows central banks steadily gained the upper hand against the 1970s war on inflation with help from free trade and globalization. This in turn caused global long rates to fall from historically elevated levels. In 2005, the 10-year Treasury yield was just returning to historical averages after a multidecade inflation shock.

Maybe you don't remember it that way. Figure 6.11 certainly makes it look like all the 10-year rate has done over the long term is fall—with a little wiggle en route. How could that be predictive about inflation at all? What's more, in

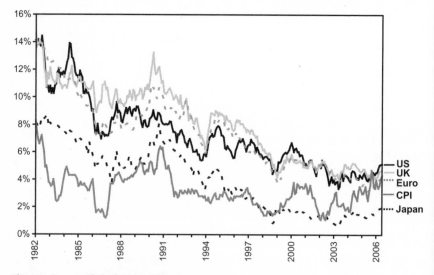

Figure 6.11   Global Long Bonds.
Source: **Global Financial Data.**

recent years, professional forecasters have tended to believe this 25-year downward trend will reverse. Except, flipping back to Chapter 4, you know the professionals keep getting their long-term bond forecasts wrong as well. What we have been experiencing hasn't been an unusual falling period, but a return to historical normalcy. Figure 6.12 shows long-term U.S. interest rates going back—way back—to 1800.

Figure 6.12 puts long-term rates into perspective. First, investors tend to talk about today's 10-year Treasury rate as "historically low." No! The long bond rate during the 1970s was "freakishly high." Investors may be frustrated they can no longer buy Treasury bonds with a 13 percent coupon as they did when they were young in the 1970s, but they fail to remember stock market returns were dreadful then, the economy was stagnating, and inflation wiped out even super-high coupon payments. Save your 1970s nostalgia for the Bee Gees. Okay, I take that back.

Second, the long-term interest rate spike clearly correlates with the onset and recovery from horrid monetary mismanagement and resulting 1970s hyperinflation. Why? Because the long bond is traded on a free and open market and accurately represents the market's true inflation expectation. Don't focus on short rates—remember, they are monopoly set by the central bank. Long bond interest rates aren't controlled at all; instead they are perfectly free

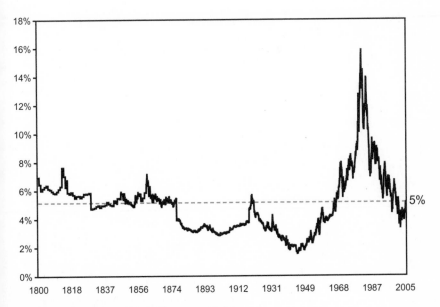

Figure 6.12   U.S. 10-Year Treasury Yield.
Source: **Global Financial Data.**

market set. And that reflects the market's expectation for the quality of the job central banks are doing, and is a great indicator, at least for right now, of where the market is pricing future inflation risk.

Now that you're getting the hang of asking Question One and debunking myths, you can move on to finding new or ignored patterns that will give you a basis for market bets using Question Two. More examples in Chapter 7.

7

SHOCKING
BUT TRUE

Supply and Demand . . . and That's It

This book is partly about how to know something others don't—by processing information others find unfathomable and creating capital markets technology to do that. If information can't be processed well by our brains one way, reframe it in another more useful way like our P/E to E/P flip. Cut it in half and look at it anew. What does it correlate to?

The news is full of useful information if you can use Question Two to connect the dots. Just be creative and ask, "I wonder if that could mean anything? Wouldn't that be nuts?" One recent phenomenon, starting in 2002, is increased merger and acquisition activity. It's normal for merger and acquisition activity to increase in an expansion. Firms with improved balance sheets awash with cash look to acquire additional valuable market share, parallel product lines, vertical integration, new core competencies, new product categories, or just simply to diversify. In one way, this is unremarkable and mundane.

But can it mean anything for the stock market? Conventionally, market lore says merger manias lead to poor stock market results. Partly that is because mergers happen after the economy has been improving for a while— and after that, at some time, comes another recession. So, it's easy to see why folks see merger manias leading to bad times. Look at the late-1990s mergers coinciding with the tech IPO craze. After a wave of deals like the Time Warner takeover of AOL, we were rewarded with a severe bear market and recession.

It makes sense takeovers should backfire often. After all, sellers, knowing the business inside out, usually know more about what they sell than buyers, being outsiders, know about what they buy. So shouldn't it be true buyers fare less well than sellers—arguing for lower prices later when reality sets in and the buyer and its shareholders realize they've been fleeced?

I made this point in my second book, *The Wall Street Waltz*. And I was wrong. Historically, there is some validity to the argument, but I put too much emphasis on some time periods and not enough on others. My conclusions were too dependent on takeovers of the 1920s and late-1960s. There was a lot of unintentional data-mining and confirmation bias in what I said then. Now I'd say I was wrong then, and the whole thing is very 50/50. It depends on the nature of the deals involved and half are this way and half that way—and it varies with time.

Cash, Stock, or Hybrid?

There was a crucial difference in how most of those 1990s mergers as well as the late-1960s and 1920s deals were structured compared to the post-2002 deals. The bulk of corporate mergers taking place in 2003, 2004, 2005, and 2006 were mostly transacted in cash, whereas those done in those three earlier periods were transacted mainly in stock. In the one, an acquirer pays earnest money for the shares of the acquiree; in the other, the acquirer simply issues newly created shares to fund the takeover. Question Two: Is there a difference between the two and their potential impact on the stock market? What can you see differently about this situation others don't see? What can you fathom that is unfathomable to most?

When Company A buys Company B for cash, it exchanges the cash for Company B's shares and then simply destroys those shares. After the deal, there are the same number of Company A's shares as before the deal and no shares for Company B. Company A now has its earnings and Company B's earnings so Company A's earnings per share rise. Very simple! This assumes on an annual basis Company B is profitable and its earnings exceed the interest payments Company A pays to borrow the money to buy Company B. But otherwise, the acquisition is immediately *accretive* to earnings—shares are destroyed and, all else being equal, the acquirer's earnings per share rise immediately. The supply of equity outstanding in this case is reduced as the acquired company's stock is destroyed. Let me say that again. Cash-based acquisitions reduce the supply of equity outstanding. If demand remains constant and supply shrinks, prices will rise. Cash-based acquisitions tend to be bullish.

Takeovers transacted wholly in stock are different. Afterwards, usually the acquirer's earnings per share fall because more shares are dumped on the market, diluting value. See it this way. Firm A is worth X. Firm B is worth Y. To acquire Firm B, Firm A must bid up B's price. Perhaps Firm A bids Firm B up by 25 percent to 1.25Y. That extra 25 percent is paid for by increasing the supply of stock of Firm A—newly created, never before existing shares. Firm A issues enough new shares to cover all of the prior value of Firm B plus enough newly created shares to cover the 25 percent markup. So, there are more real share equivalents after the deal than before. Now, if Firm B has a higher P/E than Firm A at 1.25Y, Firm A's earnings per share fall when the deal is done. This is most of the deals in the 1920s, late-1960s, and 1990s. It is the AOL Times Warner deal. These increase supply of equity, are dilutive, and make earnings per share fall.

There is a third type of deal—Firm A buys Firm B partly for cash and partly for newly created shares. Hybrids deals are common, having some of the qualities of both but usually are more cash-like than a pure equity deal. Why? In these deals, usually the acquirer can't borrow enough cash to take over all of Company B, so it borrows what it can and issues shares to make up the difference. Usually, these are bigger deals.

Suppose Firm A is worth $10 billion and B is worth $20 billion. A buys B. The smaller A swallowing the bigger B may frighten lenders. Maybe lenders will only lend Firm A $14 billion to buy B—exactly why doesn't matter for this example. Before the deal there were $30 billion of equities outstanding representing A and B together ($10 + $20 = $30). To buy Firm B, Firm A bids B up 20 percent to be worth $24 billion. It uses the $14 billion it borrowed and issues another $10 billion of its own newly created shares to total the $24 billion it needs. At the end of the deal, there are $20 billion of equities—down from $30 billion before the deal. The supply of equity shrank by $10 billion—not by as much as if they'd financed the whole thing with debt—but the equity supply shrank nonetheless. Almost always a stock and cash deal reduces the supply of equity and is accretive to earnings—just not as much as pure cash deals.

These aren't radically new ideas. Anyone who took accounting or perhaps Economics 101 in college (meaning lots of folks) should know the difference between accretive and dilutive. What's more, you can easily monitor which firms are doing takeovers and which ones are dilutive or accretive. In our über-regulated business world, we get plenty of notice when a company launches a merger, acquisition, IPO, new stock issue, a global plot to steal oil—you name it. We know when the mergers are taking place, for how much, and in what form.

Merger manias financed by newly created shares increase the supply of equity and are bearish. Merger manias transacted for cash destroy stock supply; reduced supply means prices should rise, which means time periods following increased cash merger activity, other things being equal, should see perfectly fine stock returns. But few people see the difference.

What Really Makes Stock Prices Move

Before tackling what you can know about the impact of cash mergers on the stock market, we must delve into what really drives stock prices. This combines Question One and Question Two. There are countless myths regarding what people think cause price movements you can debunk with Question One. But Question Two—what can you fathom about what causes stock prices to move that others cannot fathom—is easy. Way too easy for humans to want to fathom.

There are just two factors in this whole, wide, wonderful, and whacky world driving stock prices. Always and everywhere, stock prices are derived singularly by shifts in supply and demand. I've said so throughout the book, but sometimes the easiest concepts are the toughest for human minds to accept. Supply and demand are commonly known concepts, but few investors make the cognitive leap to securities pricing. Most folks who took college economics forgot about supply and demand as fast as possible after finishing finals, and never thought about securities prices in terms of supply and demand. Folks with PhDs in economics were trained but usually not in securities prices, and decades later don't think in terms of supply and demand for securities.

Myriad brokerage firm "research" reports tell you where they see the market going but almost never based on analysis of supply and demand shifts. Your news anchor, poli-tic, stockbroker, or tennis partner wants you to believe it's any number of economic or technical indicators, pop-culture concerns, political conspiracies, or self-fulfilling prophecies driving stock prices. Go to your favorite finance web site and you'll see:

Interest Rates Buoy Stocks
Jobless Report Drives Stocks Down
Oil Scares Spook Stocks

You never hear a talking head say, "Supply of stocks remained stable today, but demand increased for reasons we can only guess about, causing stock prices to rise." It's boring. Supply and demand of stocks as a storyline doesn't sell advertising or influence you to a particular side in a political, social, or economic feud. There is no reason why media would be so understated. These two dueling pressures set prices of all we buy. Seeming pressures, such as increased regulation or an alien space invasion, are just more forces on supply and demand—an alien invasion likely decreases demand for equities and increased securities regulation likely decreases supply of equities.

Supply and demand shifts explain why people eagerly pay extraordinary amounts for an original Beatles vinyl, an original Le Corbusier chair, or for a limited edition Star Wars poster—if those things float your boat. However, no one pays up for plain old paper clips. First, there are billions of paper clips floating neglected in office desk trays everywhere. Second, if you run short and don't feel like a run to your local Office Depot, you can use a binder clip or even a rubber band in a pinch. That's called substitution. Things with easy substitutes never command premium pricing like those that can't be replaced. Third, paperclips are easy to make. Unless Andy Warhol bent a particular paperclip into a reasonable rendering of Marilyn Monroe, a paperclip won't fetch much of a premium.

In college economics, your professor should have told you supply and demand are both about eagerness. Eagerness is emotional. Demand describes how emotionally eager consumers are to buy something at varying prices. Typically, but not always, at higher prices, consumers want less of something than at lower prices. Makes sense! Alternately, supply is a concept depicting how eager suppliers are to generate output of some good or service at varying prices. Generally, but not always, suppliers want to produce more of something at higher prices than at lower prices. If the price is low enough, they won't want to produce at all.

It starts getting interesting when either producers or consumers become more eager to supply or consume at the same prices. If producers become more eager to supply—meaning supply increased—but consumers aren't any more eager to consume, the market floods with supply and prices drop. You say, "Why would suppliers ever do that?" Maybe new technology cuts their costs and prods their eagerness—sort of like Moore's Law pushed the semiconductor learning curve to lower prices for decades, making electronics firms ever more eager to make more at lower prices. On the flip side, if consumers become more eager—meaning demand rose—but producers don't step up supply to match increased demand, prices rise. Straight-forward.

Eagerness to buy or eagerness to supply can shift for psychological reasons deriving from any number of factors. After all, eagerness is an emotion and emotion is psychological. And markets are psychological. All I've said on this is pretty much a simplification and summary of what you would hear in any economics class—nothing remotely controversial.

But supply and demand are a little different when it comes to securities in several ways. Unless you did very unusual work in graduate school, you never saw any college study of supply and demand for equities. Demand for equities is about the eagerness to own or not own existing securities. Do we want to own GE stock more than we want to own a bond or an Andy Warhol Marilyn Monroe paperclip? Has that changed for some reason? How do we feel about owning GE stock versus Pfizer? The aggregate emotion of demand for equities can shift within the bandwidth of our human emotion very quickly and freely in just the same way tempers can flair or a movie can suddenly make you cry or laugh. Witness this by watching the volume of daily shares traded. In our super-connected world, people can become worked up and decide to buy or sell, and within moments complete a transaction. If their eagerness waxes or wanes, they can nearly instantaneously act in massive volume. They can completely reverse course hours, days, or months later if they are so inclined—emotionally.

Demand can shift fast, but only as far as people can become emotionally eager or un-eager. See it like this—you can only be as angry as you get or as happy as you get and you can quickly swing from one extreme to the other in the right circumstances, but at the extreme only as far as you go personally. Someone else might get a lot angrier than you do or a lot more giddy. Maybe you suffer depression. Some people do. Others don't—ever. Maybe you're manic depressive, heaven help you. Maybe you're very steady rolling—maybe too much so and your spouse complains about that. We vary a lot individually but overall as a group we're average. For people as a whole, total demand only shifts within the average bandwidth of our aggregate emotion, although it can do that quickly—nearly instantaneously. Think how much emotion shifted in the hours after 9/11. Hence, demand has a tremendously powerful effect on pricing in the short-term because it can shift so fast. It has less power in the long term because it can only shift within our emotional bandwidth and not further. It can only go so far.

Think of this differently. It's hard for you to keep your emotions at extreme levels for long. This is why most folks can't stay extremely angry or giddy very long. It's just like that super party when you were 23 on a warm summer night where you had a few drinks and the right friends and circumstances—it was just perfect—and you felt perfect. But the next day you felt tired. Things scar some of us sometimes and as individuals we never get over them. As we live life, those things have changed us. But newly changed—for good or bad—we only get so high or low. Altogether, when we get very angry or very ecstatic, we tend not to stay that way too long because there is too much energy exerted in staying away from our emotional norm. Shifts in demand tend to be forceful, fast, not too far, and then revert to the mean with time. This is part of why demand shifts impact short-term pricing so much more than long-term pricing.

Shifts in supply are different. In the short run, the actual supply of securities is almost completely fixed as it takes time and effort and a cooperative multiplicity of players to create new shares or destroy existing ones. Think about how long IPOs or mergers—or even just a debt offering—need to evolve, and the amount of advance notice the companies are required by law to give the public. An increase in supply technically means increased eagerness to supply equities. But initial eagerness is dampened early on because no one is actually sure if the deal can be pulled off. There is no assurance all the necessary pieces will come together for that offering—a process which will take many months if it happens at all. You can't be overly eager about something you know may not happen. Eagerness on a deal grows over the time period in which the deal is successfully pursued.

Take a new stock offering or IPO, which you already know means "initial public offering" or as I call it, "it's probably over-priced." Or a debt offering. When a company decides to issue stock or debt, they first must find an investment banker to manage the process. That alone takes time, particularly if they create a competition between several investment banking firms, which is common. At this point, the potential issuer doesn't know what the deal might look like, if they will go through with it, if they *can* go through with it, or even when it can happen should they be willing and able to do it. The investment banker will require freshly audited financials from a major auditing firm—typically one of the "Big Four"—also taking time. Then, in an equally uncertain process in a debt offering, the investment banker works with the issuer to secure an adequate rating from the three main rating agencies: Moody's, Standard & Poor's, and Fitch. Also in parallel, they start the filing process with regulators who must approve the offering—from the Securities and Exchange Commission (SEC) federally down to the state regulators in every state where the issue is to be sold (or appropriate regulator overseas such as the Financial Services Authority [FSA] in Britain). Then, they market the deal, which takes another few months. It's only toward the end of that process the issuer has any real sense of how eager they can be to offer the securities or not.

Maybe by the time all this is done, the market has faded. Maybe it's fading throughout the marketing process. Maybe a similar competitor got to market two months ahead of you, beating you to the punch and sapping demand in your category of offering. Plenty of deals get pulled at the last minute. Think how depressing that can be.

Under the best of circumstances, when the stars align, this is never a speedy, painless process, allowing you to assume supply is pretty well-fixed in the short-term. Conversely, no matter what anyone would have you believe, no one has any way to predict supply in the far distant future. This is among the reasons why long-term mechanical forecasting notions are usually way, way wide of the mark. No one knows what whacky things may happen to the creation or destruction of supply of equities 5 to 20 years from now. If you hear someone forecasting stocks to be a good or bad investment over the next 10 or 20 years, you're dealing with someone who is telling you more about what they don't know about how capital markets work than what they do know.

Stock prices 10 years out will be determined more by what happens to supply 7, 8, and 9 years from now than anything else. No one in 2007 has any capital markets technology or know-how allowing them to predict such a thing. In general, stocks are more positive than negative. Beyond that generality, no one should make a forecast for more than 12 to 24 months ahead. Said alternatively, shifts in demand are often more powerful in the short-term and shifts in supply are regularly more powerful in the long term. Sometimes you can see shifts in demand others don't see—justifying a 12 to 24 month forecast. But longer than that, you're just peering into fog. In the very long term, demand will bounce from very low to very high many times, but supply, subject to fundamental forces, can be almost infinitely bullish or bearish if the right conditions exist to increase new supply or destroy it.

Because supply of securities is relatively fixed over the short term, all you need do as an investor in most times is measure demand. Figure out the direction of demand and you've figured out how to make a short-term forecast. (Usually—sometimes you must account for supply—we get to that later.) That is something your fellow investors probably aren't seeing clearly, and something you can know they typically don't. And they won't just because I wrote this book. Set aside everything else—what you hear in the media, what you hear from friends, what so-called experts tell you about technical or fundamental investing—and focus on what impacts demand. For this, the Three Questions are handy. There are three broad forces at play impacting investor demand—economic, political, and sentiment.

SUPPLY AND DEMAND CURVES

What I'm going to show you now pretty much no one in the world has seen. It's a fun, activity-filled way you can demonstrate for yourself the power of supply and demand on security prices. The following figure on the left represents supply of equities and the figure on the right represents demand:

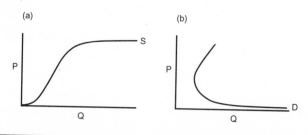

The supply curve is S-shaped, showing an increase in aggregate supply as prices increase. When prices are very low, supply tends to be low. And why not? This is like anything else. When prices (P) are low enough, firms won't want to issue new shares. If you were a CEO, you wouldn't be eager to issue new shares at four times earnings (an E/P of 25 percent) when you could always borrow money much cheaper than that. Conversely, above some break point, the higher the price, the more securities a firm would like to issue. Why? As the price rises, the cost of raising capital gets ever cheaper in direct proportion to the stock price increase. At a certain price level, suppliers would offer virtually infinite quantities of shares—as firms have an endless, infinite desire to issue more shares if their cost of capital is effectively zero. Think of a firm with a real P/E of 1,000 (an E/P of 1/1,000)—an annual cost after tax of 0.1 percent. At that cost of capital, why not issue infinite shares? You do so—buy a Treasury and make your earnings per share (EPS) increase almost infinitely. So, the supply curve flattens as it runs out to infinity along the quantity line (Q).

The demand curve is a backward-bending hyperbole. If you study economics, they never expose you to backward-bending demand curves until graduate school, if then. At one extreme, when the price of a stock is low enough, quantity demanded becomes 100 percent. Think of a corporation already in bankruptcy that you could buy for $20. I don't mean $20 per share—I mean the whole firm for $20. Since a corporation can't pass losses onto to its owners like a general partnership, you have nothing to lose by buying the whole outfit. Anyone in their right mind would buy the whole thing. You can control it if you want, ignore it if you want. If something good comes of it, you make the profit. If nothing good comes of it—no skin off your nose. How about at $25! You would buy that, too, just be out one more beer at the end of the transaction. As the price climbs, you would still take over the whole company, with slightly decreasing eagerness as the price rises. At a certain price, everything gets rational. The higher the price, the less you want, just like they taught you in college. When the price rises 20 percent, you still might like the company and be eager about it but not as eager as you were at the lower price.

Suddenly, above a certain price, weird things start happening. This is where a value company stops being thought of as a value company

(continued)

and starts being thought of as a growth company. Now the higher the price, the more prestige associated with owning the stock. The more the stock goes up, the more eagerness there is for it, and the quantity of stock demanded at any price rises. This is Microsoft throughout the 1990s; Yahoo! in 1999. This represents euphoric demand, something like what we might see at a bubble's peak. Instead of growth stocks, some call these "glamour" stocks—as prices rise, demand also rises because of the glamour. Value investors view this as irrational. For example, from 1995 to 2000, prior to the tech bubble bursting, increasing demand occurred for tech stocks as prices rose. Qualcomm, Amazon, eBay, and all the rest—they were stocks investors felt they just had to own, and the higher the price, the more they felt it. The same is true of Google more recently. It's within this realm a bubble forms—higher prices actually lead to a higher quantity demanded.

Try this exercise. Copy each curve on a separate piece of near transparent paper, making them the same scale. Lay the demand curve over the supply curve, lining up each axis. The intersection of the curves represents current pricing, and you should get something like the figure below:

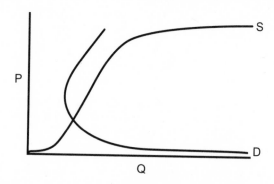

Remember when you were in college and they did those stick drawings of supply and demand? An increase meant the whole curve moved to the right, a decrease to the left. The shifting to the right—an increase in demand—meant that at every price people were eager for more. A decrease in demand meant a shift to the left where at every price people were less eager for the item. An increase in supply meant a shift to the right so that at any price suppliers wanted to supply more (maybe because of new technology or changes in laws). And a decrease in supply meant the whole curve shifted to the left, reflecting suppliers less eager at every price. So play with the curves you've drawn just like that and weird things pop out.

Slide the demand curve just a skosh to the right, representing an increase in aggregate demand in the short run. This leads very logically to higher prices. Move the curve back a bit to the left (decreasing demand) and prices fall. Now move your demand curve far enough to the right so the supply curve passes the inflection point on the demand curve and begins to run up the backward bend of the hyperbole. As this occurs, the supply and demand curves seemingly overlap for an extended series of prices, leading to nonlinear pricing. The price explodes upward. In this overlapping area, momentum investing quickly becomes glamorous ("glamour" stocks) and prices increase dramatically—just as many of those dot-com stocks did in 1999.

If you move the demand curve back, even just a bit to the left, reflecting a slight decrease in demand, or the supply curve to the right, demonstrating an increase in aggregate supply, you can see how quickly a glamour stock can fall out of favor, leading rapidly to lower prices. Just as fast as it went up. Recall again just how quickly the hot dot-com stock prices imploded in 2000. This is exactly what was happening. The increase in supply overtook demand in this same region causing the bubble to burst and then demand fell, driving tech through the floor.

Playing with the graphs in this way shows the naturally occurring decrease or increase in prices for stocks or categories of stocks as a result of shifts in supply and demand. Repeating this simple exercise whenever you see seemingly weird price action will help you understand it. In the short term, demand has the most influence on pricing, while over the long term, pricing is almost completely a function of supply. Play it and see.

The Three Drivers of Stock Demand

Economic Drivers

Phenomena like GDP growth, corporate earnings, technological innovations, budget deficits, monetary conditions, and the like are economic drivers. Except for technology, none of these things actually directly impact the health of companies or the value of stocks themselves. Just because the United States is enjoying a period of strong GDP doesn't mean a given company is any more or less productive or valuable. And a company may experience a normal, cyclical lull in earnings while creating an innovative product and new and better management—making it more valuable. If GDP is growing at a fast clip and corporate earnings are beating expectations, people usually feel more positive about the economic future and more inclined to take on equity risk (unless they think everything is too good so it must get worse—which happens sometimes). If the economy is in recession and CEOs are being perp-walked to the curb, investors will be less keen on the stock market.

Investors get in trouble here because either they or their information source misinterprets economic news. What's more, investors focus on known information. If a surprisingly good unemployment report comes out, it's too late for you to act on it. The market moves ahead of or simultaneously to news—good and bad—but not after it's disseminated.

Political Drivers

Elections, shifts in political control implying new future legislation impacting the tax code, and the like are examples of political drivers. Recall from Chapter 2, the threat of material new legislation, particularly any threatening property rights, may cause widespread loss aversion and fear of political muggings. Politics have more impact on market risk aversion than even their narcissistic little brains can fathom.

Sometimes it has nothing to do with legislation. When Ronald Reagan started his "Morning in America" ad campaign, he may not have appreciated he was advertising America to America. The ads worked marvels, making Americans feel better about our country and boosting sentiment. From there it was a hop, skip, and a jump to Lee Greenwood's 1984 music hit, *God Bless the U.S.A.*, which did the same thing. Sometimes all it takes is a good stump speech to be a political driver.

Generally, capital markets fear change, which is why the presidential term cycle capital markets technology works. The market is never sure if a poli-tic is a zealot, a phony, a genuine phony, or just a moron. Usually the best thing, politically, is gridlock, as we saw in the mid- to late-1990s, because it implies little change. The markets doing so well from the November 1994 election into 2000 with perfect gridlock isn't coincidence. The market wasn't worried about much legislation getting passed by a Republican Congress with a tiny majority and a Democratic president embroiled in multiple scandals and obsessed by polling numbers.

A Question One political myth you already know you can make a market bet on is the belief (by many) that tax cuts lead to budget deficits, which are bad for the economy. The Op-Ed pages and media commentaries are full of otherwise rational people advancing their political agenda by making you believe tax cut-based deficits rob the government of desperately needed capital to run the government correctly, which leads to recession, bear markets, high unemployment, and dashed hopes. Nonsense. Those folks don't understand what we covered in Chapter 6—deficits have generally and measurably resulted in zippier GDP growth and strong stock market returns. Most important, the government doesn't run anything very correctly—regardless of whether you have a Democratic or Republican Congress or administration—or as President Ford once said, "If the government made beer, it would be 50 bucks a six-pack and taste bad."

Investor Sentiment

The third driver, investor sentiment, is pure emotion. Sentiment is constantly moving—weekly, daily, even second to second. It's everything else that impacts investor's feelings. In many ways, it isn't any more complicated than that party we mentioned earlier. It got you feeling great. The next morning you didn't feel great. The day after that you'll likely feel better. It is partly that we can't sustain our emotions at extremes for long, as mentioned earlier. But we can artificially push them there temporarily.

That Wall of Worry

When headlines are most dour and your friends and colleagues are bemoaning how terrible things are, you can be confident they will feel better later and sentiment will improve. Those who were most worried and sold their stocks low with hindsight bias gradually regain confidence and begin buying again. An initial reaction to higher prices is glee. You get pulled back to the middle of your emotional bandwidth by fear of heights. New higher prices scare people. Since they didn't expect stocks to rise as much as they did, they now fear they may fall. Since investors fear losses more than they enjoy prospects of gains, this creates rising anxiety. This is the proverbial "wall of worry" bull markets climb. The higher it goes, the more angst those who didn't predict it feel. Since they didn't see why it should go up, they can't see why it shouldn't go down. Since they hate losses much more than they like gains, the fear of downside dominates.

A good illustration of this is the first-year returns following a bear market. When people assume they face the most market risk, they miss out on a remarkably low-risk period. First-year returns following true bear markets are super above-average, as shown here:

Stock Market Returns Following Bear Markets

Bear Market Bottom	S&P 500 12-Month Returns from Bottom
July 8, 1932	171.2%
March 31, 1938	29.2%
April 28, 1942	53.7%
May 19, 1947	18.9%
June 13, 1949	42.1%
October 22, 1957	31.0%
June 26, 1962	32.7%
October 7, 1966	32.9%
May 26, 1970	43.7%
October 3, 1974	38.0%
August 12, 1982	58.3%
December 4, 1987	21.4%
October 11, 1990	29.1%
October 9, 2002	33.7%
Average	45.4%

Source: Global Financial Data.

The reason the bell curves I showed you in Chapter 4 worked for equities is they're a good measure of sentiment. The bell curves showed where sentiment was at a point in time, not where it was going. If you know and accept that, you can game the future direction. For example, in the late 1990s, the forecasting consensus wasn't bullish enough. Markets came in high because demand was too low and had to move higher. The bell curves were a good capital markets technology innovation for measuring investor sentiment.

Supply: How It Works

Supply is like an unending accordion that can be expanded or contracted continuously. Other than what the market can bear, there is no limit to how many shares may be issued in IPOs or re-issues or how much debt can be raised if underlying economics justify it. Or how many shares can be bought back and destroyed through stock buy-backs or cash-based takeovers.

When there is sufficient incentive to flood the market with new supply, prices will eventually drop, overpowering any demand. This is how it works. Take a hot sector, like tech in the late-1990s. As prices appreciate rapidly, everyone wants in on the action. Suppose Firm A makes a novel product and has a total private market value of $1 billion. It floats a hot offering at a high price raising lots of money while giving up very little control of the company—they raise $250 million but only give up 20 percent of the company in newly created shares to do so. The prior existing 80 percent of the shares remain as previously held. Effectively that values Firm A before the money at $1 billion. With the money the deal is completed at $1.25 billion. The founders and other shareholders who initially had private stock of questionable liquidity now have a public security with a daily price making them multimillionaires. They're happy. The investment bankers are thrilled with their 7 percent of the $250 million—$17.5 million in fees!

Eager observers watch the postoffering price rise and hope the market can handle an offering from another similar outfit. So they find an entrepreneur and venture capital and create privately held Firm B, which is a Firm A lookalike. They get their investment banker to take Firm B public to get in on the cheap money. Maybe they have just a plan and no revenue, like many of the 1990s dot-coms. If B's offering goes well, someone else will attempt it with Firms C, D, E, and even F. This can go all the way to A-2, B-2, C-2, and on.

Firm A now realizes, as the high-quality, granddaddy of this product line, it can raise more capital with more newly created shares. It senses it can garner premium valuations over the group of inexperienced newbies and wannabe outfits. This time it raises another $350 million, but only gives up 17.5 percent of Firm A in newly created shares. Now Firm A is valued at $2 billion.

Now Company X, a mature, boring firm worth $100 billion, decides it can't take the risk of not being in on the hot new product category. They initiate a hostile takeover bid to acquire Company A for $3 billion, paid for with new Company X stock. Company A shares disappear and are replaced with new Company X shares worth $1 billion more than the $2 billion Company A previously had been selling for. Again, Company A shareholders get rewarded but, suddenly, there are a lot more newly created shares. Earnings are the same as before. This, like most stock mergers, was dilutive to earnings. It's the same amount of earnings but many more shares. All the IPOs and new issues start flooding the market with shares in the hot category. Eventually, supply drowns demand and prices roll over. If demand drops, prices implode.

Just as they did when the tech market crashed close on the heels of the tech-IPO craze in March, 2000.[1] Demand fell all the way to the market's ultimate global double bottom in 2002 and 2003.[2] The scapegoats were many for the tech bubble. People blamed tech companies for being overvalued. I'm not sure what that means—companies are worth what people pay for them at a point in time. If investors pay a high price for a dopey outfit with no discernable business strategy, that's the investor's fault, not the company's. Greedy CEOs got their share of blame, too. Corporate accounting rules were deemed too lax or not expansive enough.

The reality was the tech bubble burst because the market was inundated with supply and demand couldn't keep pace and then fell. That is the only explanation. Some would blame investment bankers, but that isn't fair or appropriate—no matter how you feel about them. Investment bankers simply respond to investor eagerness for more supply (demand). The real culprits (say it with me) were investors' overconfident brains, letting them run rampant and overallocate to a sector. Investors were too eager—demand was too high. Absent their demand, investment bankers and issuers can't flood the market with supply.

You should pretty much always be wary about excessive euphoria regarding IPOs in the latest "hot sector." Every time we see a hot sector—throughout the entire history of investing—investors claim, "It's different this time." It's never really different this time—just the niggly details. There is never anything different about an inundation of supply surpassing demand and causing prices to drop. (For more evidence on how it's never different this time, see the following reprint of my March 6, 2000, *Forbes* column "1980 Revisited," calling the top of the tech bubble due to parallels to the 1980 energy bubble.)

1980 Revisited

TECH STOCKS ARE in a late-stage bubble. It should break later this year. I usually dislike "bubble," a word bandied about too often by extremists. But I watched a bubble like this one 19 years ago, and I have seen how it ends. Right now technology stocks are just where oil stocks were in early 1981.

Recall how unstoppable energy appeared in 1980. That was a time of high and rising inflation, booming commodity prices, OPEC's success as a cartel and the Iran-Iraq war. By late 1980 oil was $33 a barrel, with consensus forecasts of $100 four years out. No one envisioned oil's falling.

It's happening all over again. This time around it isn't oil's price that is supposed to triple in four years but rather the population of Internet users.

Here are some other disturbing similarities. Tech's share of the S&P 500 has grown from just 6% in 1992 to 19% in 1998 and 30% in 1999. Energy's S&P weight climbed from 7% in 1972 to 22% in 1979 to 28% at year-end 1980.

You know about technology's great returns: rising 44% in 1998 and 130% in 1999. In 1979 energy stocks were up 68%, and in 1980, 83%.

Then the bubble popped. The energy sector's weight fell to 23% by the end of 1981, mostly in the second half of the year. Energy stocks lost 21%. The S&P 500 lost 4.5%. In 1982 energy stocks fell another 19%, while the S&P rose 21%. Since 1980 the energy sector has returned 9% per year. It has lagged three points a year below the next-worst-performing S&P 500 sector. Yet energy consumption has grown steadily.

The parallels between energy stocks in 1980 and tech stocks today are eerie.

Check out America's 30 largest stocks. They represent 36% of the U.S. market's entire value. Exactly half are tech stocks. At year-end 1980 exactly half the 30 largest stocks were energy stocks. Of course, if you believe in the demand for and future of technology, today's weights may make sense. But if you believe in the increasing supply of the stocks, it doesn't.

Here's another eerie similarity: Back then energy stocks sold at twice the S&P's average price-to-book ratio. Today tech sells at 2.5 times the market's price-to-book.

Look at initial public offerings in 1980 and now. That year was a busy one, with energy making up 20% of the offerings. That boosted the overall number of U.S. stocks by 2%. In 1999 tech comprised 21% of the offerings and, again, increased total stocks by 2%. While that may not sound big, it is. Newly public companies are where the bubble breaks, when they run out of cash.

Most energy initial public offerings were formed to develop some esoteric energy technology or to drill for oil in bizarre places. They were hardly the vertically integrated giants, like Exxon, which extract, refine, and sell oil. And they weren't huge: None of 1980's 50 largest energy stocks was a 1979 or 1980 initial public offering. Eventually most went bust. But now 11 of our 50 largest tech stocks are 1998 or 1999 initial offerings, which means the damage will be greater if any fail.

Most new techies are as shallow in their areas as 1980's offerings were in energy. Who has the most Internet sales? Amazon? No. Intel, selling chips to its customers, did more online business in 1999 than all the dot.commies put together. Federal Express had more business on the Web than America Online and 17 times more business than Yahoo.

Most Internet stocks are merely marketing firms with no clearly defined or provable strategy. Most Net vendors have no real gross margin on sales, and that lack is a disaster waiting to happen—later this year.

(continued)

As with 1980's energy initial offerings, these new tech companies burn feverishly through cash, hoping to catch on with the public. Later this year, just as happened two decades ago, dozens will run out of cash—there are 140 now with less than 12 months' cash supply. Folks will then worry about who will run out of cash next, causing many more sound stocks to fall. Selling will run rampant in tech from small to large, even hurting the most solid tech stocks.

I have no clue which ones will implode first. Some will float more stock and lengthen their lease on life. But the large group of them without a viable business model are top candidates to go down hard. I don't see this immediately ahead; but instead in the second half of 2000.

Last month I forecast a flat S&P 500 in 2000, with tech stocks down 15%. I stand by that forecast. As 2000 progresses, you should lighten your holdings in technology, keeping the biggest and most solid companies. This is a year for moving forward with foreign equities while lowering U.S. expectations.

Forbes, March 6, 2000. Reprinted by permission of *Forbes* magazine. © Forbes, 2006.

Merger Mania

Supply of stock can increase infinitely (which wouldn't be so good for stock prices in the long term) but may also be reduced when a company, thinking its stock is too cheap, uses cash to repurchase its own shares. Through stock buy-backs, as discussed in Chapter 6, and cash-based takeovers as discussed earlier, supply can be destroyed nearly infinitely. Using Question Two, we know cash-based merger manias should be followed by good stock market returns. If demand remains the same (or even greater) but supply is reduced, prices must rise. What does this mean for you right now in 2007? Because stock destruction has been occurring on a large and sustained scale, this should be bullish as you position for 2007 and possibly 2008 if supply doesn't start growing again. Whereas cash takeovers were less than a $1 billion a year in America in 2002, by 2006 they were running at more than a $50 billion a year. Outside America it was bigger still. All else being equal, massive reduction in supply should help drive demand and stock prices up. Naturally, it won't be your only bullish factor—but it might be a major counter to any bearish concerns.

Suppose you didn't buy this book in its first printing—how does knowing this Question Two truth help you? Simply keep in mind the difference between equity-based (dilutive) and cash (accretive) mergers. Are there a lot of IPOs hitting the market, and on average more equity-based mergers taking place? That's a potentially bearish concern. Conversely, lots of cash mergers probably present a little-noticed bullish surprise—news most investors don't process correctly because they don't know how.

Knowing increased cash-takeover activity leads to better stock markets helps you forecast the broad market's direction. But does that provide additional insight into which sectors you should overweight, and which individual stocks you may want to buy? Abso-positive-alutely! Look at the sectors where the mergers are occurring and work your way, top-down, to a good buy-out target. If you're right on a few of your buy-out targets, you get a nice price bump if (and when) the merger is announced. It's easy, free money. (If you're not sure how to do that, the following gives you ways to identify buy-out targets and a few examples.)

RIDING THE M&A WAVE

When firms have earnings yields (the E/P—inverse of P/E) higher than their after-tax borrowing costs, they have great incentive to borrow money cheaply and spend it buying back their own stock or acquiring competitors. Using cheap borrowed money to acquire competitors, firms effectively incorporate the acquired company's earnings and make their own earnings per share rise. Buying back their stock accomplishes the same thing. It's free money!

Finding Takeover Targets

You can ride the M&A wave by finding stocks ripe to be taken over. Acquisition premiums paid to shareholders of buy-outs often yield large increases in share prices. Good buy-out targets are likely to have some or all of the following characteristics:

Low valuations
High free cash flow
Strong balance sheets
Quality brand names
Regional strength
High relative market share

(continued)

Smaller in size
Strong distribution networks
No concentrated controlling shareholders

The good news is you can check for those attributes by reading shareholder reports—available for free on corporate web sites. Here are two examples of stocks I identified as buy-out targets in *Forbes* that generated good returns when the takeovers were announced.

MBNA (KRB)

I wrote about MBNA in my May 9, 2005, *Forbes* column.[3] MBNA was the world's largest credit card company, issuing familiar cards like Visa, MasterCard, and American Express, with a successful strategy of focusing on affinity groups like associations and financial institutions. If you had one of those cards (who didn't?), it was probably issued to you by MBNA, whether you knew it or not. Besides credit cards, they had strong business in consumer and home equity loans. They had all the qualities of a perfect takeover target—strong brand name, healthy balance sheets—plus, valued at 12 times trailing earnings, they looked darned cheap. Bank of America thought so too. They announced their intention to buy MBNA on June 30, 2005, and MBNA ended the day up 24 percent.[4] Had you bought on the day I recommended it, you would have been up a very nice 30 percent.[5]

CP Ships (TEU)

Far too many American investors avoid foreign investing to their detriment. CP Ships was a great takeover candidate I wrote about in my April 18, 2005, *Forbes* column.[6] Though this container shipper was domiciled in Britain (the Brits are way more American than they are European anyhow), 80 percent of its business activity focused on North America. With a fleet of 80 ships, it was the leader in most of its routes. In 2005, this little British stock was overlooked as shipping is a cyclical business. But it's also a growth business, and this stock looked cheap at 13 times 2005 earnings and $3.7 billion in very real revenue. The Germans at TUI AG, a massive, well-diversified tourism and shipping company, expanded their shipping business quickly and cheaply by announcing a merger with CP Ships on August 22, 2005. CP Ships shareholders got a nice 8 percent[7] boost that day. However, had you bought when I recommended it, you would have been up 56 percent.[8]

Categorically, you know the bulk of cash-based deals will occur with stocks that are cheap in terms of having a high earnings yield compared to the acquirer's pretax cost of long-term borrowing. Suppose the average company borrowing rate (the BBB 10-year bond rate) is 6 percent and the average corporate tax rate is 33 percent. The after-tax average cost of borrowing is therefore 4 percent. Takeover targets will tend to have earnings yields greater than 4 percent after they've been marked up with a maybe 25 percent pricing premium. Hence, most takeover targets will have an earnings yield above 5 percent before the deal is announced, translating to a P/E below 20. To get the acquirer's earnings per share to rise the most from the deal, the higher the earnings yield the better. Most cash-based takeovers will tend to be value stocks with low P/Es (high earnings yields). Seek those kinds of stocks to capitalize on cash-merger mania.

No One Stock Style Is Always Better—Period!

Supply and demand being the only determinants of stock pricing—and the potential to create or destroy new shares being nearly infinite—is why no correctly calculated index, size, style, country, or category is better for all time. (Remember our graphs in Chapter 4?) While collectors of a particular category type (small-cap value, large-cap growth, Japan, bio-tech) believe the category they like is permanently better, it isn't and can't be.

But when an equity category collector tells you his or her category is permanently better—and they do all the time—you're being told what the teller doesn't understand about markets. Supply creation is infinitely elastic if given enough time in the right circumstances. And demand bounces constantly in the short to intermediate term. There is no evidence supply of any equity category is capped, can't be bought back and destroyed, or is in anyway predictable in the long term. Consider this—if there is a demand for a category, the investment bankers will meet it—they don't care about investor perception about a particular category needing to be superior over time.

Since 2000, small-cap value has been hot. I'll give you a simple tip. Whenever big-cap growth does lousy, small-cap value does well—they are polar style opposites. Saying one does well is the same as saying the other does badly. Nowadays, there are many investors saying small-cap value is permanently better. I started doing small-cap value stocks three decades ago, long before the word small-cap value existed. My first book *Super Stocks* (published in 1984) was about PSRs—but specifically how to use PSRs to find small-cap value stocks others couldn't find. Even then the term *small-cap value* didn't exist. The term evolved in the mid-1980s off the heels of that earlier period as small-cap value stocks did well. A period much like the past six years.

In 1989, when Callan Associates, a major consulting firm to institutions (primarily defined benefit pension plans), introduced the very first small-cap value peer group for institutional investors to use in calibrating how well or badly a given manager did, there were only 12 of us included in that initial group. They couldn't find any other pure-play small-cap value managers. That was how primitive this category was not quite 20 years ago.

Today my firm still manages well over a billion dollars in the category for large defined benefit pension plans, endowments, and foundations. It's a perfectly valid part of the market to include in a much broader portfolio (which all these institutional investors have). But the category has times when it shines, and times it's a real dog. Folks forget that—many who should know better.

One of America's top scholarly minds, a novo-unabashed small-cap value fan, penned an opinion article for the editorial page of the *Wall Street Journal* published June 14, 2006. He stated emphatically small-cap value is better for all time based on long-term history. Wrong! Small value's supposed long-term superiority is somewhat of a data mine. It's in the data, but isn't harvestable in a real sense, as I showed you in Chapter 4. You can go through periods long enough to lose your mind where small-cap value is the worst performing part of the market—decades. If you must wait two decades for superiority, there isn't really superiority.

Despite the period from 1928 (which is as far back as small-cap value has been measured) demonstrating small-cap value stocks doing better than large stocks or the whole market,[9] most of that small-cap return came from terribly tiny stocks—ones too small to own without having a very illiquid and risky portfolio. No one ever mentions that. Also, these companies had much higher bid-ask spreads in early history. Back in the 1930s and 1940s, the bid-ask spreads of these tiny stocks were often 20 percent to 30 percent of the purchase price and those spreads aren't adjusted for in the calculation. Doing an in-and-out ate up most of the return just in the give-up between the bid and ask—all unaccounted for transaction costs.

I'm not arguing against owning small-cap value, or for owning big-cap, or the market as a whole. I'm saying there are painfully long stretches when things seeming to work in the very long-term don't actually work. And these times are too long to not drive everyone, including you, nuts. For periods of 5, 10, or 20 years, it will be shifts in supply determining most of the return of the market and of the subsets of the market. In the very long term, and lots of subsets thereof, all major categories, correctly calculated will have very similar returns. Falling in perpetual perma-love with some category won't get you superior perma-future return.

Weak Dollar, Strong Dollar—What Does It Matter?

Can what you know about supply and demand be applied largely to any freely traded security category? Sure. We can apply it to the dollar and discover still more unnoticed Question Two investing truths (while dispelling more myths).

The poor U.S. dollar has been much maligned in recent years. It has been weak, so goes prevailing wisdom, and will lead to our economic undoing. Views down this line are near-religious in their conviction. Investors forget: In the late-1990s, we were all concerned a too-strong dollar would keep foreigners from wanting to trade with us, leading to our economic undoing. Following that logic, what doesn't lead to our economic undoing? Maybe there is an optimal exchange rate with every other world currency we should aspire to achieve. I don't know what that exchange rate would be or how we'd endeavor to maintain it in a free market. And I'll take a free market over a government jigger any day of the week or year of my life. But investors must think such a state of jiggering perfection exists because they love to complain about the dollar and its direction leading us to hell.

Warren Buffet is well-known for betting against the dollar. Unfortunately, his dollar timing hasn't been terrific on average. Mr. Buffett is a super smart guy, but forecasting the overall market, interest rates, commodity prices (yes, make no mistake, currencies are commodities)—none of these are his greatest strengths, nor does he have any special training in them, nor has he done very well forecasting them. In a *Fortune* magazine article on November 10, 2003, Mr. Buffett warned our trade deficit would cause the U.S. dollar to weaken (forever) and wreak irreparable harm to our economy.[10] Clearly, he was wrong for the intermediate term. As we covered in Chapter 6, our trade deficit is growing, not shrinking, yet we've enjoyed impressive average annual real GDP growth of 3 percent since he made his doomsday proclamation and have had positive market returns since the latest recovery began way back in 2002. And while the dollar was weak in 2004 and 2006, it was as strong in 2005 as it was weak in 2004 and 2006 put together. From January 2004 through June 30, 2006, the trade-weighted dollar is down exactly 1.96 percent,[11] hardly enough to get excited about or trade on in any regard. It just hasn't done what Buffett divined.

By now you know from Chapter 6 that big trade deficits are symptoms of strong economies and don't cause weak ones—so, they don't have much to do with making the dollar strong or weak. Here's a Question Two: Does a weak or strong dollar even matter? Pretty hard to fathom that one, huh? Though the dollar is a monetary indicator, it qualifies as an economic driver of demand. Knowing where the dollar is headed and how it can impact the stock market can be valuable if you fathom it while your fellow investors can't. That would be another good Question Two: What is it you can understand about where the dollar is heading? But first we have to hit Question One—what do you believe about what causes currency prices to move that is wrong? Let's hit on some popular myths.

Five Myths and More Supply and Demand

Myth Number One—The Dollar Is Still Falling

As of this writing in 2006, investors tend to think the dollar has been falling far and forever. Misconception of the relative strength of the dollar is widespread. Ask a friend (colleague, family member, or golf partner) where they think the dollar is, and they usually feel the dollar has continued to do whatever it did the past few years or so up until the past few months. Many professionals based their 2005 and 2006 forecasts on the assumption the dollar would continue to weaken badly. What they miss is the dollar is by no means unidirectional. After being weak in 2004, it strengthened tremendously in 2005. By mid-2006, it had reversed, falling flat relative to 2004.[12] Mind you— during all this time there were ups and downs. Currencies are like any other security traded on an open market—they experience volatility. And yet, the belief remains the dollar is generally weak and always falling.

This is an easy Question One: Is it true the dollar is always weakening (or strengthening)? Let's take a look at some data in Table 7.1 and see.

Table 7.1 breaks down the dollar, euro, and pound sterling against major Western currencies. Years when the dollar was weakening are shaded, and years when the dollar was strengthening aren't. Paying attention to just the shading and not the numbers, you see the dollar clearly doesn't always move in one direction. No Western developed nation's currency does.

It's very clear when looking at currency price moves in this format, major Western currencies typically experience strengthening and weakening cycles against other major Western currencies for no more than two to four years at a crack—rarely as long as four—before reversing. Longer is rare. I call this the Three Year Rule. There are a few places where the Three Year Rule falls apart. First, from 1993 through 1996, the dollar weakened versus the New Zealand dollar for four straight years. However, it might be a stretch to call the kiwi dollar a major currency since New Zealand is about as populous as Colorado. When looking at the yen versus the euro and pound sterling, you get several four- and five-year cycles. But the yen is an Asian currency, not a fully Western currency.

Table 7.1 Currency's Rule of Three

Currencies	1990	1991	1992	1993	1994	1995	1996	1997	1998	1999	2000	2001	2002	2003	2004	2005
USD/EUR	(12.2%)	1.7%	10.7%	8.5%	(9.3%)	(6.4%)	4.9%	13.5%	(5.4%)	16.4%	6.8%	5.4%	(15.2%)	(16.8%)	(7.2%)	14.6%
USD/GBP	(16.4%)	3.2%	23.4%	2.4%	(5.5%)	0.8%	(9.3%)	3.7%	(0.5%)	2.7%	8.0%	2.8%	(9.6%)	(9.9%)	(6.9%)	11.4%
USD/JPY	(5.5%)	(8.1%)	0.0%	(10.6%)	(10.8%)	3.8%	12.0%	12.7%	(13.1%)	(10.0%)	12.0%	14.5%	(9.3%)	(9.7%)	(4.3%)	14.9%
USD/Australia	2.3%	1.6%	10.5%	1.3%	(12.4%)	4.3%	(6.4%)	22.2%	6.2%	(6.7%)	17.4%	9.1%	(8.8%)	(25.5%)	(3.5%)	6.6%
USD/Canada	0.2%	(0.4%)	10.0%	4.1%	6.0%	(2.7%)	0.4%	4.4%	7.0%	(5.6%)	3.8%	6.5%	(1.5%)	(17.7%)	(7.1%)	(3.3%)
USD/New Zealand	1.0%	8.9%	5.0%	(8.1%)	(12.6%)	(2.0%)	(7.6%)	21.3%	10.4%	1.0%	17.8%	6.5%	(20.6%)	(20.1%)	(8.7%)	5.2%
USD/Switzerland	(17.3%)	6.4%	8.0%	1.3%	(11.9%)	(11.8%)	16.1%	9.1%	(6.1%)	16.0%	1.3%	3.0%	(16.7%)	(10.4%)	(8.0%)	15.4%
EUR/JPY	7.2%	(9.3%)	(10.1%)	(17.3%)	(1.8%)	8.2%	9.1%	(0.6%)	(7.5%)	(22.4%)	4.6%	8.9%	6.3%	8.3%	2.9%	(1.5%)
EUR/GBP	(5.0%)	1.9%	11.0%	(5.5%)	3.9%	5.4%	(11.9%)	(8.3%)	6.3%	(12.2%)	1.2%	(2.8%)	6.4%	8.2%	0.3%	(2.8%)
EUR/Australia	15.9%	(1.4%)	(2.2%)	(8.8%)	(3.5%)	11.9%	(10.6%)	4.6%	14.4%	(20.0%)	10.3%	2.9%	7.1%	(10.2%)	3.6%	(7.3%)
GBP/JPY	12.9%	(10.7%)	(19.1%)	(12.6%)	(5.5%)	2.6%	24.0%	7.7%	(12.3%)	(12.1%)	3.4%	11.8%	0.2%	0.4%	2.5%	3.0%
GBP/Australia	22.5%	(1.5%)	(10.5%)	(1.1%)	(7.5%)	3.5%	3.2%	17.2%	7.4%	(9.2%)	9.1%	5.8%	0.6%	(16.9%)	3.1%	(4.4%)
GBP/Canada	19.9%	(3.5%)	(10.6%)	1.3%	12.0%	(3.5%)	10.8%	0.4%	8.5%	(8.5%)	(4.1%)	3.5%	9.5%	(9.0%)	(0.6%)	(12.8%)
GBP/Switzerland	1.1%	(3.0%)	14.3%	0.9%	7.3%	14.6%	(22.3%)	(4.3%)	5.0%	(11.4%)	6.6%	0.2%	8.6%	0.5%	1.4%	(351.0%)

Source: Thomson Financial Datastream.

By and large, this rule stands up when comparing Western currencies. They don't seem to want to move in one direction for more than about three years. Hence the name: Three Year Rule. During the tail end of 2004 and throughout 2005, most forecasters foresaw weak stock market returns due in part to an imploding dollar leading to the devil and dismay. Without knowing anything else, I knew to look for a turning point someplace before too long because of the Three Year Rule. I also knew global and domestic markets were likely to be positive in 2005 (as I forecast in my January 31, 2005, *Forbes* column) due, not primarily, but in some small part because of the positive surprise of a stronger dollar and the lack of a dollar disaster. Note there is no reason by itself a stronger dollar should contribute to stronger markets, except if people have a big fear of a weaker dollar that fails to materialize, they will end up being pleasantly surprised and their sentiment should improve, boosting demand for stocks with it. (It all comes back to supply and demand for stocks.) In 2005, a stronger dollar and the lack of demise therewith was a bullish surprise not priced in—simple as that.

Myth Number Two—The Budget Deficit Will Cause the U.S. Dollar to Fall

You're a pro on deficits by now, so you already know this is ridiculous. Yet, budget deficits are another favorite patsy for a weak dollar. (Yet again—the assumption that a weak dollar is bad and a strong dollar is good.) But this lunacy runs something like this—foreigners fear our inability to put our fiscal house in order, thus creating less dollar demand.

First, as covered in Chapter 6, a federal budget deficit in the United States isn't bad for the economy or the stock market. Rather, it's a good thing as it increases velocity of money, increases debt (which you know is a good thing, not a bad thing), and puts more money in the hands of the private sector (you, me, and even our heroin-addicted Apple iPod borrower). Historically, as we showed in Chapter 1, time periods following peaks in the federal budget deficit were followed by lush economic times and positive stock markets, whereas budget surpluses were followed by less rosy conditions.

Second, exchange rates are monetary phenomena while budget deficits are fiscal. They are wholly unrelated. One doesn't beget the other. At all! There is no connective mechanism. Yes, if the central bank monetized the debt created by the deficit, it would create new money that might weaken the dollar. But why not just focus directly on the money creation because it's the money creation that does the do? Money creation can weaken the dollar whether there is a deficit or not.

Third, the United States ran huge budget deficits (some even bigger than today as a percentage of GDP) throughout the 1980s and early 1990s. During many of these periods, such as 1992 through 1993, the dollar soared. Today, the British, Germans, and Japanese are running budget deficits, as illustrated in Chapter 6. If a budget deficit is bad for the U.S. dollar, why isn't it bad for the sterling, the euro, and the yen? If the dollar is weak, it will be weak against the aforementioned currencies. If those countries' budget deficits are all causing their currencies to be weak too, against what are they weakening? The Malaysian ringgit? The truth is, no major Western country's budget deficit or surplus has any relationship to the relative strength of its currency.

Myth Number Three—The Current Account Deficit Causes the Dollar to Fall

By now, you have this one cold too. I won't waste much time on it. From Chapter 6, you know this myth is wrong for the same reasons the trade deficit myth is wrong. All the same logic applies. Only two points. The United States has run current account deficits ceaselessly since 1981; yet we've had periods of both a strong and weak dollar. If you run a correlation coefficient against this deficit as a percent of GDP versus the dollar's price, you get basically zero correlation over these 25 years regardless of whether using daily, weekly, monthly, or quarterly data.[13]

The New Zealand and Australian dollars and pound sterling all strengthened relative to the U.S. dollar in 2002, 2003, and 2004, yet those nations were also running big current account deficits then. No one has offered an explanation why our current account deficit is bad for our currency while their deficits are good for their currencies. Probably because there is absolutely no demonstrable relationship. And maybe because people pay no attention when New Zealand and Australia run current account deficits! I bet you never do!

Myth Number Four—Currencies Are Determined by Trade Balances, Foreign Policy, International Popularity, and So On

Hereto, trade deficits were largely covered in Chapter 6. You can't argue our trade deficits are bad for the dollar but Britain's, Australia's, and New Zealand's are good for their strong currencies. Trade deficits are never "paid back." Per Chapter 6, this is a mercantilist view and about 250 years behind the times. We have lots of perma-mercantilists and, I guess because they can't catch up, they'll always be around. But you needn't be one of them. We live in world where Apple imports memory chips and other components manufactured dirt cheap overseas, creating a trade deficit. But Apple turns around and sells the latest iPod creation (to heroin addicts and normal people) at a hefty 50 percent profit margin (according to market researcher iSuppli),[14] increasing their earnings per share, which in turn increases shareholder value. The mercantilists' heads would explode if they tried to contemplate a world where trade deficits co-exist with increased wealth for everyone. But that is our world and it's beautiful.

Tied to both this and the current account deficit is the myth that foreigners are "propping up" our dollar. This is often referred to as, "being dependant on the kindness of foreigners." I simply have no evidence of foreigners being kind. Certainly Americans are kinder. Not only does America proportionately engage in vastly more foreign aid than other countries put together, we give away more private charity by far than all the rest of the world combined. And I don't know that many kind Americans. But kind foreigners? What foreigners do you know who act like that? Or a better question is: Why would a foreigner act any differently than you? When you're investing, do you place your money where you think it's likeliest to make money, or do you invest where you think it will do the most good for the world? Where the world needs the most propping? Foreigners aren't propping up anything in America. Mercantilists think foreigners "prop 'til they drop." Those who think correctly know they "invest where they think best." They invest here because they think they will get a better return for their money than other alternatives. If they didn't think this was the case, they would invest elsewhere. No other rational explanation

Finally, Myth Number Five—A Weak Dollar Is Bad for Stocks

If you're holding foreign securities during a time when the dollar falls, your foreign securities may seem to net a higher return. The reverse is true as well—stocks domiciled in a country with a relatively weaker currency may seem to perform not as well at exchange time. Don't forget, to invest globally, you needn't trade your dollars for euros, yen, or ringgit. Buying foreign ordinaries (stocks in foreign countries in the local currency) can be an ordeal for individual investors—you may have to establish a custodian account in that country. Skip the hassle. If you're an American, trade in American Depository Receipts (ADRs)—foreign stocks traded in gringo dollars.

Over the long run, because currencies are so cyclical, the currency effect nets out to be close to zero anyway. Since 1970, investing globally using local currencies decreased an American investor's return by a total compounded 27 percent, while the MSCI World has risen a cumulative 2000 percent plus.

Over 36 years, a difference of 27 percent compounded isn't much—the currency impact equals 0.7 percent per year—hardly worth hedging, particularly when transaction costs are considered. You were mildly better off leaving your global investments in U.S. dollars. Yes—leaving them in U.S. dollars—but not enough to be doing a little joy dance. Over 36 years, your excess return might have paid for a couple of speeding tickets.

Fine, so the impact is nil, but what can the dollar tell us about where the stock market is going? It can make some sense that a strong U.S. dollar might help U.S. stocks—and vice versa. We can check to see if the facts support this theory. If the dollar is weak, then stock returns would similarly be weak. But we can see in Figure 7.1, stock returns can be strong—very strong—even as the dollar is weakening.

And that is something true in the United States and around the globe. Currencies don't dictate the direction of the stock market, or vice versa (see Figure 7.2).

There is no basis for thinking a strong dollar leads to good stock returns or vice versa. The dollar isn't predictive of U.S. stock performance, global stock performance, Polish stock performance—none of them. Weak or strong, by itself, you shouldn't fret currencies.

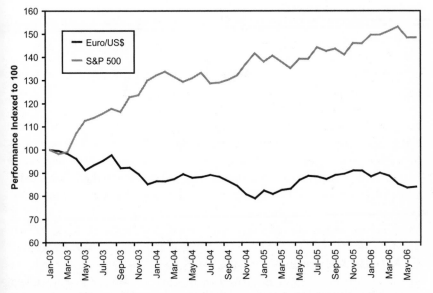

Figure 7.1   A Weak Currency Doesn't Mean a Weak Stock Market Return: United States.
Source: **Thomson Financial Datastream.**

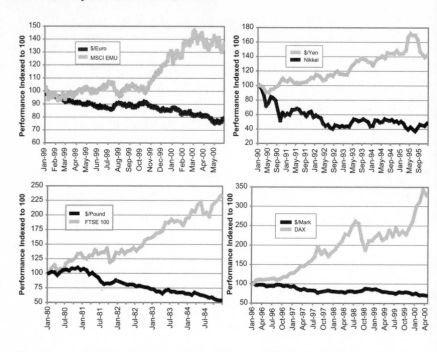

Figure 7.2 A Weak Currency Doesn't Mean a Weak Stock Market Return.
Source: **Thomson Financial Datastream.**

Let's bring in Question Three and think about the dollar the way we thought about the U.S. current account deficit and our stock market versus the rest of the world. When the global stock market explodes upward you know the U.S. market probably will too, right? They're positively correlated. If the global stock market implodes, you know the U.S. will probably be down, too. Sometimes America goes up more than the world, and other times it falls more. But they tend to go the same direction when there is any material direction. And the U.S. is about half the world stock market. So, if the falling dollar is supposedly bad for U.S. stocks, shouldn't the rising non-dollar currencies be good for non-U.S. stocks? They are an equal offset. But there can't be a global falling currency, only global inflation. Likewise there can't be a global trade deficit or current account deficit, yet people act as if the negative is more powerful than the positive though they never explicitly state this. (Although despite them never saying this, there is some behavioralist basis for it—in the concept of myopic loss aversion.) Yuk! Mercantilists!

Said another way, the United States is about 38 percent of global GDP, making the rest of the world about 62 percent. If a falling dollar is bad for the U.S. economy, shouldn't a rising non-dollar be good for the other 62 percent and more than offset the deteriorating U.S. economy with improvements to the non-U.S. economy? Alas, no one thinks globally much so they can't quite get themselves to see it this way. These mercantilists aren't stuck in the 1960s; they're stuck in the 1690s.

In Case You Forgot, Supply and Demand Determine Currency Prices

Different currencies are simply flavors of money identified by their issuers (central banks), and their banking systems. Because they're commodities traded on free and open markets, they derive their relative value in the same way as other assets, by supply and demand.

An exchange rate reflects the value of one currency quoted in another currency's terms. It's entirely relative and has no absolute meaning otherwise. Each particular exchange rate is driven by a complex combination of the supply and demand characteristics of each of the two currencies. Relative increases in demand or decreases in supply will drive one currency's exchange rate up versus another, and vice versa.

Currency Supply

The base supply of a currency is determined solely by the issuing central bank, expedited by banks operating under it. It has a monopoly on the creation or destruction of its currency. Central banks desire relatively stable prices with moderate monetary growth, which in turn should yield relatively low inflation rates. If they act responsibly, major currencies should have fairly stable exchange rates in the long run—though volatility is normal over shorter periods.

However, an irresponsible central bank or a government taking control of its country's central bank can undermine its country's position as a major, developed country. Remember Germany's Weimar years? That was arguably a singular example in modern history, as they completely wiped out the German currency in the early-1920s due to excessive money creation, leading to hyperinflation. Developing countries, like Brazil in the early-1990s, often don't have independent central banks and can experience much longer directional currency moves, almost always on the weakening side. But big countries have reasonably disciplined and independent central banks, like our Fed, and won't experience permanent, unidirectional currency moves.

Demand for currency is determined by several factors. Principal among them is the amount of economic activity conducted in that currency (e.g., a grocery store in Dallas uses dollars, not yen). The more economic activity using a particular currency, the more demand for that currency. Another important money demand source is the "store of value." If investors believe assets denominated in a currency will hold or grow in value versus other assets in different currencies, demand for that currency grows.

Over the long-run, just like with stocks, supply determines relative currency strength or weakness. When a central bank allows excessive money creation relative to real economic requirements, the excess supply depresses the currency price and boosts inflation. More money for the same amount of assets decreases the currency's store of value. The reverse is true if the central bank is too restrictive in creating money—but too strong a currency isn't a goal either. There's absolutely nothing investors can do about the monopolistic central banking system, besides hoping it won't make too many mistakes, nor is there any way to predict the long-term direction of supply. Keep in mind, our central bankers have gotten better in recent years. Make no mistake, the Fed was a disaster between 1929 and 1932 as it shrank the quantity of money at the worst possible time by 30 percent, making the Great Depression vastly worse than necessary and arguably causing it. That was its low point, to be sure. Since then the Fed hasn't always been great, but on average, it has been getting better.

Traditionally, former Fed chairmen were derided for their many mistakes at mismanaging the economy. William McChesney Martin Jr., Arthur Burns, G. William Miller—they were all criticized widely and wildly after their time. Before he became chairman, Burns criticized Martin nearly endlessly. Martin ran the Fed from 1951 to 1970, giving Burns plenty of time to attack him. Burns claimed Martin knew better than to make the mistakes he did. Martin later claimed when you became head of the Fed, you took a little pill making you forget everything you ever knew, and the effect lasted just as long as you were head of the Fed. After becoming head of the Fed, and coming under attack himself, Burns claimed he took "Martin's little pill." (To people under 50, this was a play on a famous health aid called "Carter's Little Liver Pill" that had nothing to do with being good for your liver, whose name was changed to "Carter's Little Pill," and is, in fact, a laxative.) They were all criticized. And rightly so, as they all made many mistakes—but fewer as the decades went on and they learned from prior mistakes.

Paul Volcker was the first Fed head not roundly criticized later—although Volcker forced the 1980 and 1982 recessions in the name of breaking inflation's back. Some would say that was too heavy handed, but overall he did a better job than any prior Fed head. Greenspan was next and did better still because he was capable and could learn further and more. Their predecessors were assuredly not idiots (though Miller might have been politically, but he is another story altogether)—they were just doing the best they could, stabbing in the dark based on largely untested theory with, by today's standards, very primitive data-collection capabilities and vastly inferior electronic analytical capability. Only with the onset of improved technology and 24/7 instant information could Fed heads test theories and check for correlations (i.e., do Question Ones) before deploying policy to horrific results. And they could react faster and learn from prior mistakes. As a result, we've seen fewer policy errors in recent decades.

Errors still happen—like when Greenspan created way too much money in 1999 in fear of potential Y2K problems, flaming the economy. Then, he sucked it back out in 2000 after Y2K wasn't problematic—helping make the 1999 and 2000 boom-bust bigger than otherwise. But mistakes are made less routinely and massively than in the pre-Volcker era. Greenspan's worst mistakes were pretty good compared to the best of earlier decades. The same has been going on overseas. My guess is, as central bankers benefit from future improved information flows and accumulated lessons of the past, on average they keep making mistakes but the mistakes are fewer and not as bad. As major developed nations' central bankers tend to make fewer dumb errors, intermediate term currency volatility may decline somewhat from historical levels (increasing the validity and regularity of our currency Three Year Rule).

Currency Demand

Short-term (from minutes to months) effects impacting demand include when a senior government or central bank official *jawbones* (speaks favorably or unfavorably about a currency or interest rates) which can push short-term sentiment and shift demand. This has fairly fleeting impact—sometimes moving currency markets for a few minutes up to perhaps a month. Think about what happened in the markets whenever Greenspan would make one of his famously indecipherable comments: Mumble/jumble/grumble/fumble—and sound humble! The market would think it could understand what he was getting at, and go through a temporary whip-saw. Usually the next day, the markets would be back to business as usual.

Also, discretionary central bank *open market operations*—when a central bank buys one currency in exchange for another—can have a short-term impact. But no one bank has a big enough balance sheet to overwhelm all the other factors impacting the currency market by simply exchanging currency.

Even the frequently demonized speculators can have some small and fleeting impact on demand and the relative prices of currencies, but the speculators have an even smaller impact than central banks because their balance sheets are so much smaller. Decades ago, George Soros did take down the Bank of England—down hard—but only because in that earlier era it had put itself in a position to be taken down. And Soros is widely quoted as saying the same could never happen these days. Further dissipating the impact of speculators is the fact they generally don't act in any organized fashion. Speculators speculate on different currencies going in different directions and, to some extent, they cancel each other's impact.

Like stocks, currency movements are exceedingly fickle in the very short term. You shouldn't care much about what a currency does from day to day or even month to month anyway (unless you're betting on currencies—which has all the same qualities of betting on any other commodity).

What Really Drives Currency Demand

Time for another Question Two: What can you see driving currencies and demand for them others can't? There are a few obvious factors contributing to short-term shifts in supply and demand for currencies. First, nondiscretionary central bank operations. When a country pegs its currency to another currency (the Chinese yuan to the U.S. dollar, for example), the pegging central bank must either buy or sell the other currency to maintain the relationship. Second, when one country's economy grows faster than another, the demand for its currency increases because more transactions take place in that currency. Both of these are easy to fathom—you don't need Question Two for them. But what else could drive currencies? What can you fathom?

Each and every day, speculators make bets on exchange rates through what is called a *carry trade*. A carry trade works thusly: You borrow short-term money in one currency, convert it to another currency, and buy a short-term bond (though you might choose to make a longer-term bet with a longer-term bond) in the new currency. The idea is to borrow at a lower interest rate and buy a bond yielding a higher rate on the presumption the higher yielding rate won't fall enough to reverse the interest rate spread during the period you hold the bond. The difference between the two rates is free money, and everyone likes free money.

The key is to borrow in a currency you think won't appreciate markedly against the higher interest rate currency where you will park the money—a great Question Two. Since you are selling the borrowed currency and buying the currency you lend into, if many people do this all at once, it tends to make the acquired currency appreciate. Then, you get not only the interest rate spread but also the appreciation on the currency. Icing on the cake. Very attractive.

It would be completely irrational to borrow at a higher interest rate and buy a bond with a lower interest rate. That is the reverse of free money. That's un-free money. So, if Country A's short-term rate is lower than Country B's, investors are more likely to borrow at Country A's lower rate and invest at Country B's higher rate, putting downward-selling pressure on A's currency and upward-buying pressure on B's currency. Currency prices then become a bit of a self-fulfilling prophesy, as carry trades take place in huge volumes daily.

In theory, it makes sense, but let's scope some actual scenarios to see if this is correct. Figure 7.3 shows the yield curves for the U.S., the U.K., Euro, and Japan at the beginning of 2004. At the short end of the curve, the U.S. curve is well below the U.K. and Euro, yet still above Japan. It so happens the dollar was weak that entire year. Investors were borrowing in America and investing in short-term instruments abroad, contributing further to a weak relative dollar. If you borrowed in America at a 1 percent six-month rate and lent into Euroland at above a 2 percent rate, you picked up the 1 percent spread as free and easy money as long as the Euro didn't fall in value. Since lots of people did it all at once, they sold dollars and bought Euros, pushing the dollar

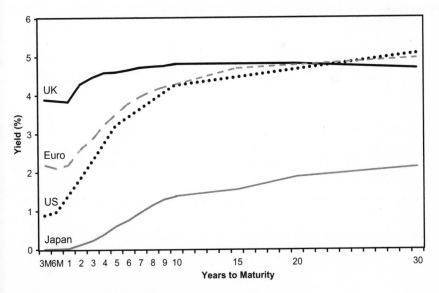

Figure 7.3   Global Yield Curves January 1, 2004.
Source: **Bloomberg.**

down and Euro up. The opportunity was even more extreme if you lent in Britain, which is the reason pound sterling was so strong.

In 2005, after multiple Fed fund rate raises, the short end of the U.S. yield curve had risen above Germany and Japan, and was closing a lot of the gap with the United Kingdom. The dollar strengthened considerably during 2005 against pretty much every major world currency, as the carry trades started going in the other direction. Effectively, as the Fed raised short rates, it choked off the carry trades that had been holding the dollar down (see Figure 7.4).

The evidence supports this theory, but examine it further. Figure 7.5 shows the spread between U.S. and Euroland short-term rates over the past 20 years, as well as the dollar's relative strength (we substitute a GDP-weighted basket of European currencies prior to the euro's introduction in 1999). When the interest rate spread is increasing (meaning our short-term rate is getting higher than theirs), the dollar is generally strengthening against the euro, and when our short-term rate moves lower, the dollar is generally weakening. Not each and every year, as there are other supply pressures at work here as well, but enough to make this a somewhat reliable indicator.

It typically doesn't work when the market can somehow anticipate in advance the lower rate country will raise rates and hence choke off the currency carry trades. Then the currencies move in advance of the central banks, but

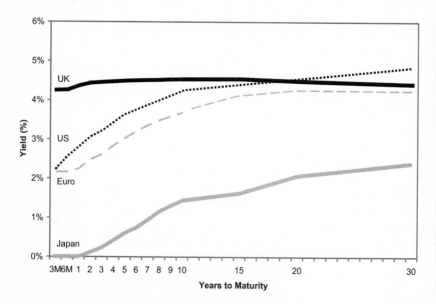

Figure 7.4   Global Yield Curves, January 1, 2005.
Source: **Bloomberg.**

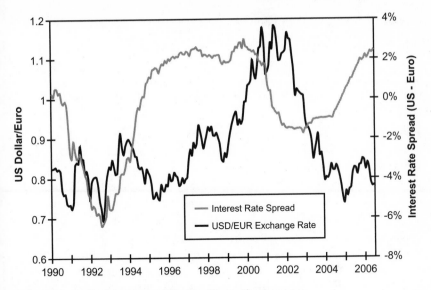

Figure 7.5 **Interest Rates and Dollar Strength: Eurozone.**
Source: **Bloomberg.**

normally, currency movements are overwhelmed by either interest rate spread differentials or speculation based on future interest spread differentials.

With some exceptions within developed Western nations, countries with higher short-term interest rates that keep moving higher tend to have the stronger currencies. Countries with low short-term interest rates that remain unexpectedly low tend to have weaker currencies. This pattern is compelling, and makes sound economic sense due to carry trade activity. Another way to say that is: Demand for a currency increases and the price with it when appropriately moving yield curve differentials between countries pay people to be more eager to own a given currency. This is why British pound sterling has been so strong, so long—they've kept their interest rates higher than everyone else's. Pretty simple! As the Fed paid up in 2005, people stopped borrowing in U.S. dollars, selling, and investing overseas, and instead started doing the reverse—borrowing overseas and buying dollars—then the dollar strengthened. Demand for currency, more than not, increases when central banks pay people to demand more of their currency—which relates to them adjusting their supply. What I'm telling you isn't unknown, but few notice it, and fewer still believe it, which is why it will have legs for some years. You can use this information to discount strong currency sentiment based on myths we debunked earlier in this chapter. And, you can use it for a rational basis for a market bet.

Fear of a False Fact Is Bullish

What if you can see the dollar's direction over the next year or so? First, you could trade the currency directly, like any other commodity. If you know what others don't, you have the basis for a bet. Second, what can you fathom clearly about the stock market if you can understand the dollar's direction? That would be a great Question Two. You now know the dollar's relative strength isn't predictive of stock prices. But the dollar's strength does matter when professionals base their forecasts on the dollar's direction as they did in 2005. When forecasters predict stock market doom and gloom tied to a dollar implosion, you've got something you can bet against. You have an advantage because fear of a false factor is bullish. In fact, if most folks fear a weak dollar will cause weak stock prices, but you can fathom the dollar won't weaken much, that is a bullish surprise helping sentiment and hence demand for stocks—despite no fundamental mechanistic connection—just like in 2005.

Investors talk about supply and demand, and know intuitively supply and demand drive prices, but just aren't applying these concepts to the securities, bonds, and commodities they buy. And if they do, they typically aren't thinking about supply or demand correctly. Now that you know securities pricing is always and everywhere a result of supply and demand, you can focus your energy on what counts and start to make more reliable 12-month forecasts. And that is something you can know that others don't. But how can you make a forecast? And how can you know what the market is more likely to do? For that, we move to Chapter 8.

8

THE GREAT HUMILIATOR AND YOUR STONE-AGE BRAIN

That Predictable Market

Presume at every turn the market is actually out to get you. I'm not being paranoid—it's true. I don't call the market The Great Humiliator (TGH) for nothing. Think of it as a dangerous predatory living instinctual beast doing anything and everything to abjectly humiliate you out of every last penny possible. Just knowing and accepting that is the first step to getting the whip hand of TGH. Your goal is to engage TGH without ending up too humiliated. In the next chapter we talk about how to create a strategy to beat the market, but first, let's talk about exactly how to use the Questions to see clearly how the market operates so you can cease being humiliated.

TGH headfakes you by moving in disorderly patterns. We know the market historically has averaged about 10 percent yearly over long time periods.[1] Many investors say all they want is a 10 percent absolute return each and every year, but that's tough to do with TGH. Since 1926, there have been relatively few years the stock market has actually returned about 10 percent to 12 percent—only five times—in 1926, 1959, 1968, 1993, and 2004.[2] Other than that, normal market years are anything but average. This is an easy Question One truth you can see demonstrated in Table 8.1.

Not only are returns wildly variable, but it's a global truth. Think globally and check elsewhere. This is how markets behave. In the United Kingdom,

Table 8.1　Average Returns Aren't Normal. Normal Returns Are Extreme (U.S.)

S&P 500 Annual Return Range			Occurrences Since 1926	Frequency	
	>	40%	5	6.25%	⎫ Big Returns
30%	to	40%	13	16.25%	⎬ 38.75%
20%	to	30%	13	16.25%	⎭ of the time
10%	to	20%	14	17.50%	⎫ Average Returns
0%	to	10%	12	15.00%	⎬ 32.50%
-10%	to	0%	13	16.25%	⎭ of the time
-20%	to	-10%	5	6.25%	⎫
-30%	to	-20%	3	3.75%	⎬ Negative Returns
-40%	to	-30%	1	1.25%	28.75%
	<	-40%	1	1.25%	⎭ of the time
Total Occurrences			80		
Simple Average				10.0%	
Annualized Average				9.8%	

Source: Ibbotson Analyst.

TGH goes by Ye Olde Humiliatour (YOH) as shown in Table 8.2. (In Germany, TGH is Der Grosse Demuetiger—DGD.) Returns should continue to be wildly variable year-to-year.

From this disorder, your brain doesn't neatly notice the market doing one of only four things in any given year. Those four market scenarios are:

1. The market can be up-a-lot,
2. The market can be up-a-little.
3. The market can be down-a-little or,
4. The market can be down-a-lot.

Investors will sputter, "But the market has pullbacks, rallies, goes sideways, has perverse reversions, and does inverted triple-dipple flips!" The market does all (or most) of those things often in a seemingly disordered way. But it really does just one of the four things. I defy you to find a year where the market did anything but one of those four. These four conditions simply simplify possible outcomes and help you see more clearly and make more disciplined decisions. They also provide a way for you to assert self-control over your behavior—note, I said behavior, not skill—and is the essence of asking yourself Question Three.

Table 8.2 Average Returns Aren't Normal. Normal Returns Are Extreme (U.K.)

UK FTSE All-Share Annual Return Range			Occurrences Since 1926	Frequency	
	>	40%	7	8.75%	Big Returns
30%	to	40%	5	6.25%	35%
20%	to	30%	16	20.00%	of the time
10%	to	20%	18	22.50%	Average Returns
0%	to	10%	14	17.50%	40%
-10%	to	0%	12	15.00%	of the time
-20%	to	-10%	5	6.25%	Negative Returns
-30%	to	-20%	2	2.50%	25%
-40%	to	-30%	0	0.00%	of the time
	<	-40%	1	1.25%	
	Total Occurrences		80		
	Simple Average			10.0%	
	Annualized Average			9.7%	

Source: Global Financial Data.

Your brain, working with TGH, tries to persuade you the market will do any number of things. But all you must focus on is whether the market will end up-a-lot, up-a-little, down-a-little, or down-a-lot—looking out about a year. Everything in between is TGH distracting you. Four things! Is it nudging up or down-a-little or is it a melt-down or melt-up? (Investors almost never think about a melt-up but it's as important as a melt-down.)

Direction, Not Magnitude

Focusing on these four market conditions helps you make the key decisions having the most impact on your portfolio—the asset allocation decisions. The four conditions are a framework for guiding your *behavior* and keeping your brain from leading you astray. What's most important about your forecast is getting market direction right, not magnitude. (That's really hard for most investors to get.) Why? Because getting the market scenario right keeps you on the right side of the market. Note: If I forecast up-a-lot, up-a-little, or yes, even down-a-little, I'm going to be 100 percent in equities. It doesn't matter if you think the market will return 8 percent or 88 percent. Either way your asset allocation decision is equities. Yes, your sector weights might be impacted by an up-a-lot versus an up-a-little forecast, but even if you get all of that wrong, and still make the right decision to be in the market, you will enjoy the return you get from getting the asset allocation right. This is all about getting the horse before the cart and not vice versa.

You may rebel at remaining fully exposed to stocks in expectation of a down-a-little year. Should you try to avoid downside by shifting to cash? Only if you're really confident (and not overconfident) you know things others don't. Otherwise you're too likely wrong for what is only a little benefit. Trying to avoid a down-a-little year is the perfect example of a brain overcome by overconfidence. Even if you expect down-a-little, you should focus on relative return. Beating the market is beating the market, even if your absolute return is negative. If you think the market will be down-a-little, ask Question Three. First, you're suffering from myopic loss aversion and you should accumulate some regret. Second, recall you may be wrong and the market might be up-a-little or a lot instead. The difference between up 5 percent and down 5 percent in a year can be just a psychological wiggle toward year-end based on serendipity. But even if you're right, and the market is down-a-little, the transaction fees you incur selling your stocks or funds, ensuing tax bills on your gains, and inherent timing errors outing and inning can seriously reduce any benefit you might gain by skipping a negative 5 percent move.

Then ask, if you get out, will you know when to get back in? Will you time it right? Probably not and certainly not perfectly! If you're really looking for market-like returns, remember the long-term market average includes negative years, and your long-term return isn't much harmed by small negative years. If the market is down 7 percent and your portfolio is down 5 percent there is nothing terrible about that, and in the long run won't keep you from your goals. Renew your faith in Capitalism. Grit your teeth and know better times are ahead.

Investors think they would like a portfolio that's up when the market is down, but a portfolio like that likely lags when the market is up—a more important and higher percentage of the time. If the market is positive more often than negative (which it is), and you have a portfolio running counter to the market, or cutting off the downside at the expense of upside, you won't average out to be happy.

Recall always—when you go to cash you adopt massive benchmark risk. You become completely unlike your benchmark. And just think what happens if you're really, really wrong and there is a "melt-up." You incurred transaction costs, paid taxes, and lost maybe 25 percent relatively or more which comes to about 1 percent a year over the next 25 years—very hard to make up. This is exactly what people do at the bottom of major bear markets when they choose to remain out so they can wait, "for things to become clearer." In exchange for avoiding a down-a-little possibility, they forsake an up-a-lot market.

Look Out Below!

As for the fourth scenario, the down-a-lot scenario, it's the only time—the ONLY TIME—to take on massive benchmark risk by going to cash or another defensive posture. Your goal here is to combine defensiveness with wang dang doodling TGH by a lot. It's the only time you should ever try to beat the market by a lot. Then, and only then, should you focus more on absolute return instead of relative return—but if you're right you get relative return too, at no extra cost. If you think the market will be down big time, 20 percent or more—maybe 35 percent, 40 percent, or even 50 percent—then you want to get safe single-digit cash or bond-like returns. Getting a 5 percent cash return doesn't sound like much, but if the market is down-a-lot, you have blown the market away on a relative basis.

This should be rare and only prompted by something you know that most others don't. It shouldn't be done by gut feel, by fear, or by your neighbor's opinion. The Three Questions should do it. And the benefits can be huge. If for 30 years, you simply invested in a passive index fund, but once in those years you sidestepped a 25 percent drop while getting a 5 percent cash return—over the 30 years, you would do 1 percent per year better than the market. In the process, you would have beaten more than 90 percent of all professional investors based on only one correct bet. Getting defensive successfully, even if you don't do it perfectly, can provide you with a major and lasting performance boost.

At a bull market peak, there is endless advice saying you should never turn bearish and you should never "time the market," and that people who do are destined to miss the big returns of bull markets. In 2000, this advice was rampant. The financial services industry marketed heavily that any professional who turned bearish was a quack or a charlatan. That advice is simply TGH sucking you into the bear market as it moves disorderly down a path few will fathom. Make no mistake; the rewards from occasionally seeing a bear market correctly are big enough to justify building your bear market muscle—knowing you use it exceptionally rarely.

After bear markets, the heroes are those who did "time the market" and turned bearish. Many of them will have been bearish way too early—often for years before the bull market peak—having been a "perma bear" (stopped clocks with miserable returns, but short-term media heroes nonetheless).

Alternately villainizing then making heroes of those who went defensive is TGH at his finest as he teases investors' brains to keep looking backward instead of forward.

At the end of every bear market, the media canonizes those who were bearish as it began. At the end of every bear market, timing services become more popular—just when you won't need them for years. This happens *every* time. The key is to keep the bear market timing skill for long periods of time when it's never used—dry powder for the rare day you need it.

I've only turned defensive three times—mid-1987, mid-1990, and late 2000. I was very lucky each time. The next time I'll probably screw it up. (Reminding myself of that is one way of reducing overconfidence.) Avoiding a big slice of those bear markets is a huge piece of what built my career. When you avoid a slice of a full-fledged bear market you simply buy years of excess return. If you went into the bull market peak slightly lagging the market, one successful by-pass of a bear market catches you up and moves you ahead. It's hard keeping a skill set honed and available you use only a few times in your investing life. Most folks won't, which is why you should. They want to hone the skills they use daily, not once a decade.

Many get all this very wrong. It's 2000! My firm and I turn bearish and generate cash and cash equivalents for clients. The market falls. It's going exceedingly well. Every year we take on new clients. Making that call well pulls clients in droves. Some clients join my firm in the year before we re-enter the market. They're sitting in cash. Some clients join just weeks before we re-enter the market. They're sitting in cash. As mentioned earlier, we re-entered the market too early in 2002 and portfolios fell with the market. Some of these clients stayed on. Some terminated our services. Those terminating our services thought we lost them money. Think it through. Neither my firm nor I ever claimed to have perfect market timing capability. If we did, we would own the world fast. If you were a client when we turned bearish, we put some distance on the market as just discussed, doing so without perfect market timing, yet helping get to the long-term goal. If you became a client just before we re-entered the market too early, we still didn't keep you from your long-term goal: to get equity-like returns and try over some long period to do a little better than the market. But those terminating at that point thinking, "You lost us money," shifted their benchmark to a myopic focus on the short-term that doesn't serve them in the long-term. They missed 2003—a whopping big year, erasing losses and more as 2004 and 2005 continued with positive returns. Those folks inning-and-outing in 2002 simply missed all that. This is TGH at its finest—getting people to get out at the worst time and never really

IT'S TIME IN THE MARKET, NOT TIMING THE MARKET, THAT'S IMPORTANT.

S&P 500 Daily Returns
January 1, 1982 - December 31, 2005

Average Annual Return = 10.6%

What if you missed the BEST days?

If you missed the BEST:	Your average annualized return DROPPED to:
10 of the 6261 trading days (.16%)	8.1%
20 of the 6261 trading days (.32%)	6.2%
30 of the 6261 trading days (.48%)	4.6%
40 of the 6261 trading days (.64%)	3.1%
50 of the 6261 trading days (.80%)	1.8%

Source: Global Financial Data.

understand what happened to them. If they asked Question Three it could have helped them a lot.

Never forget how fast the market moves. Your annual return can come from just a few days of big moves (as you can see illustrated in the table). Do you know which days those will be? I sure don't and I've been managing money professionally for over a third of a century. No one knows what the market will do in the next or any other few days. No one can tell you which 3, 6, or 9 days this year render the bulk of your gain or decline. If you want to get market-like returns, you must hang in there with the market. Look at 2005. Though most major indexes were positive (except that dirty Dow) it was an unimpressive year. The world market, via the MSCI World Index, was up 9.5 percent.[3] The S&P 500 was up less than 5 percent.[4] Not rip-roaring! At the end of 2005 the media was predictably glum. Many investors decided they'd had it with this go-nowhere market. So, the world market rose 4 percent the first two weeks of January 2006.[5] In just two weeks, the market did half of what it did the entire prior year! Investors who were fatigued from a flat year and bailed on the market missed what they had waited for. TGH was lying in wait for them, and their Stone-Age brains played right into it. Stopping to ask Question Three can alleviate many cognitive errors induced by market fatigue.

How to Build a Defensive Portfolio

You've used your Three Questions and are confident the most likely market scenario over the next year (or so) is down-a-lot—a true bear market. But what do you do? What should a defensive portfolio look like? It depends. You hate hearing that, I know, but it's true. Different bears are different. In some bear markets, some sectors survive swimmingly, but you won't know which until it is on you and maybe not then.

In bear markets, you're safest in a mostly cash portfolio. Liquidity is key—markets move fast as bull markets begin so you need to be prepared to get back in. If you're illiquid or you ease your way back into the market, you're likely to miss the big bang off the bottom. Use money markets and short-term government bills. You don't want to buy anything with a long maturity unless it can be sold instantly. You don't want bank CDs that hold you hostage for a specified period because when the time comes to get back in, you don't want to be held back. Be defensive but liquid.

Market Neutral

During the 2000 to 2002 bear market, I wanted a portfolio that acted cash-like but with better than cash returns. I wanted to be immunized against downside volatility and to be very liquid, so I could quickly get back into the market when needed. I wanted tax efficiency. And I wanted to take advantage of knowing something others didn't by overweighting certain sectors and underweighting others. Since I expected tech to be weak and had dedicated significant resources to that call, I wanted to get some juice from it. To do that I had to be market neutral—own equities with sector exposure but no net exposure to owning equities. What does that mean?

I created what I called a "synthetic cash" portfolio encompassing all those goals. My asset allocation during that time added up to 130 percent of my real portfolio. Here's how:

- First, I had 30 percent in huge, blue-chip, defensive European and U.S. stocks—big drugs, banks, and consumer staples. Anything that was considered "defensive," so cyclicals were out. I wanted companies with inelastic demand for their products, not elastic, since during bear markets folks tend to dial back their spending. A lot of these were super-cap stocks bought in the late 1990s with capital gains I didn't have to realize because I didn't have to sell them. Effectively, you can think of it this way. When the time comes to create synthetic cash, sell what you can that doesn't involve a capital gain, and then do the index-shorting (mentioned shortly) to ensure you don't lose capital from the bear market decline.

- Next, I had about 38 percent in liquid U.S. Government Bonds (not too risky).
- I had 2 percent in index puts against the S&P 500. I bought puts expiring about a year out. Index puts are a classic dream—they're relatively cheap insurance with relatively low premiums at the right time (market tops), and very expensive insurance at the wrong times (market bottoms). Index puts are just like casualty insurance where the casualty is the index dropping big. The puts would pay off handsomely if that happened and simply expire worthless if it didn't. I had little to lose with such a small position. A two percent loss, if they didn't pay off, would largely be covered by my bond income. But the portfolio would get considerable juice if the bet paid off. Every time the stocks sagged the puts soared in value.
- Then with 30 percent I sold short the Nasdaq 100 and the Russell 2000 (20 percent and 10 percent respectively), took the proceeds and held it in cash—another 30 percent. (30 percent + 38 percent + 2 percent + 30 percent + 30 percent = 130 percent. That's how I reached 130 percent.) Those of you who are individual investors probably don't have enough leverage versus your broker for them to give you the cash when you sell short and there is nothing I can do to help you overcome that. My bet was the combination of the Nasdaq and Russell would drop more than the stocks I held. So I borrowed the indexes and sold them short with the hope when they dropped, I could buy them back at a lower price and the difference was all profit—and bigger than the losses I had on my stocks that fell. Instead of reinvesting the proceeds from shorting the indexes, I held the cash in the event I was wrong. But even the cash earned income.

(continued)

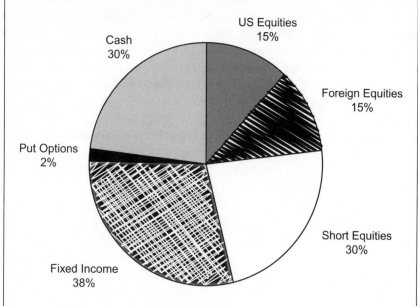

Hypothetical Defensive Portfolio Allocation

Cash 30%

US Equities 15%

Foreign Equities 15%

Put Options 2%

Short Equities 30%

Fixed Income 38%

This time I wasn't wrong, and the market fell a lot during those bear market years. This portfolio fared very well in those conditions. The Nasdaq 100 short did a lot better than the Russell 2000 but together they worked just fine, rising in value as the stocks I held fell. I don't know how I'll construct my next bear market portfolio, but next time, based on the conditions then, we'll try to create contemporary synthetic cash that is nonvolatile, liquid, tax-efficient, and still allows for some stock and sector picking.

Anatomy of a Bubble

As mentioned previously, I did fine foreseeing the past three bear markets—in 1987, 1990, and 2000—and you don't want to hear this but it's the absolute truth, I have no idea what will cause the next one. If I'm skilled and lucky I'll know it when I see it and hopefully you will too if you use the Three Questions and aren't blinded by myth.

I'll share what I've learned about spotting bears and show how to know when it's not a bear. But first, what led me to forecast the tech-sector-led bear

market in March of 2000 were worrisome realities I saw others missed. Seeing something dreadful others miss is the basis of a successful bear hunt.

Pros were too bearish, expecting negative or single digit returns, in 1996,
1997, 1998, and 1999 as TGH exceeded 20 percent each and every year. The
consensus finally turned bullish in 2000, as measured by my sentiment-based
bell curves (which, you recall, still worked then), agreeing the market would
break the 10 percent mark. The 2000 bell curve is shown again in Figure 8.1.

I knew I could rule out anything under the consensus bell—from flat to
up 20 percent. I was left with the possibility of an up-a-lot year, and two holes
on the bearish side, either down-a-little or a lot. I wouldn't turn bearish just to
be a contrarian. But I was concerned about an inverting yield curve because
no one talked about it. As you know, inverted yield curves are fairly reliable
predictors of bear markets and recessions (if few notice them)—and it was
happening globally. But no one was talking about it so there was no fear of it.
By contrast, in 1998, the financial press couldn't stop clamoring about an inverted U.S. yield curve even when the yield curve didn't get past flat. But in
2000, no. (They talked about it in 2005, probably because no one talked about
it as it happened in 2000.) Then, too, in the United States, Britain, and many
other countries, budget surpluses had popped up recently, a bearish sign.
Bond yields were very high compared to earnings yields (see Figure 1.5 in
Chapter 1). There had been a lot of equity-based takeovers. The only really
bullish feature was it was the fourth year of the president's term.

And there certainly wasn't fear, period. *BusinessWeek*'s January 2000
cover story lauded "The New Economy."[6] Hindsight makes the article a
laugh riot from start to finish now—you can find it on their web site. (Find
what *BusinessWeek* has said about me. It's a laugh riot, too.) The author
couldn't cram enough affectionate adjectives in to describe the state of the
U.S. and global economy. But *BusinessWeek* wasn't the only offender. Few
harbored heavy bearish feelings except the cadre of perma-bears. Just a year
earlier, Y2K was supposed to be the end of all life as we knew it. Two years
earlier, the Russian ruble crisis and the bankruptcy of a second-tier hedge
fund was supposed to cripple the world. Having made it through all that,
folks opted to optimism. Based on sentiment alone, it was reasonable to contemplate the possibility of a defensive posture. But that is a long step from
actually turning bearish.

There was something worse that no one saw. After years of tech IPOs,
supply threatened to drown demand. The late-1990s tech boom was measurably almost identical structurally to the 1980 supply-demand imbalance
in energy stocks. I wrote about it in my March 6, 2000 *Forbes* column entitled "1980 Revisited" (which is reprinted in Chapter 7). That the article

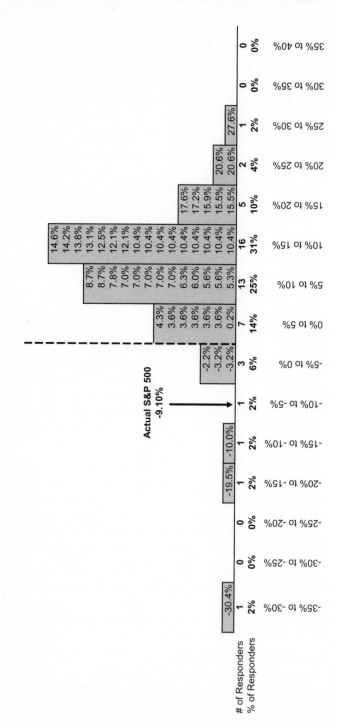

Figure 8.1 The Sentiment Bell Curve Shifts to the Right (S&P 500 Forecast 2000).
Source: BusinessWeek.

was published mere days before the tech and U.S. market top was pure luck—I had no idea this particular market call would be so timely. I had cut my own clients' tech holdings to a mere half of their benchmark weight as 2000 started—and by March I was lagging because tech had risen steeply the first two months of 2000. We got a steep increase in client terminations as we cut tech's weight. The fact many clients were upset at being pulled out of what seemed to be the new perma-hot-sector further bolstered my belief the time was ripe to exit tech—even if too early.

Bubble Trouble? What Bubble?—It's Always a New Paradigm

As that column said, I'm hesitant to use the word "bubble" since it's bandied about so much by so many who understand bubbles so little. As I write this in 2006, the world has anticipated a residential real estate bubble bursting for four years. Not only all over America, but they anxiously await it in London, Paris, and much of the Continent. For four years! Why won't it burst, darn it? Manhattan-based journalists renting overpriced railroad flats are waiting in gleeful anticipation to dance and chant, "I told you so! I told you so!" Stopped clocks! At any rate, real bubbles are few and far between. Applying the word "bubble" should never be done lightly.

A little noted point about the supposed residential real estate bubble: In the history of the world, there has never—not ever—been a bubble widely called a bubble before it burst. Before they burst, real bubbles are widely seen as a new paradigm, a new era, fundamentally different from the past, where the old rules no longer apply, where you get great returns with little or no risk because it's different now. Before Japan's bubble started bursting in 1990, they were seen as superior businessmen with whom the West couldn't compete. When tech was a bubble it was, "The New Economy, Stupid." But when something is called a bubble that hasn't actually burst yet, it means the price has gone up a lot, as happened with residential real estate, and a lot of people fear it will go back down. (This is our heights framework again.) That fear is already in the market and taken a lot of risk by its mere presence.

When something is really a bubble, it isn't called a bubble and people don't fear it. In the years 1997, 1998, and 1999, there was no national press coverage of tech as a bubble. Tony Perkins wrote a book late in 1999 describing Internet stocks as a bubble but it didn't sell well. My *Forbes* column calling tech a bubble was one of the first appearances of that word in national print associated with tech. If everyone recognizes something as a likely bubble, it isn't one. But what I saw in early 2000 was eerily similar to what I had witnessed and later measured without having actually forecasted it in the energy sector in 1980—a real bubble with the potential to start a rippling, fierce, sector-led bear market.

Think back to 1980 and how unstoppable the energy sector seemed. Thanks to 1970s global central bank gross monetary mismanagement, inflation was soaring and commodities booming. OPEC was powerful while the Iran-Iraq War was raging. Oil was $33 a barrel and the consensus was forecasting $100 a barrel in four years. No one was calling for oil prices to fall. Just so, in early 2000, the consensus foresaw Internet users tripling globally in four years, and most folks, not just the dingbats at *Business Week*, were heralding "The New Economy." Earnings don't matter. It's a new paradigm. Its clicks, not bricks! You remember.

There were abundant energy to tech parallels—in the rapid growth of the sector, the number of IPOs being foisted on the market as a percent of all stocks, swelling supply, and the shallowness of the business models coming to market. In March 2000, the 30 largest U.S. companies represented 49 percent[7] of the U.S. stock market's value—and half of those were tech stocks. Rewind to 1980, and the 30 largest U.S. stocks made up a third of the U.S. market's value and half of those were energy stocks. Effectively, the equity supply-demand picture for tech looked almost identical to what had happened in 1980 so I could fathom an outcome not dissimilar to 1980's. The relative valuation multiples compared to the whole market for energy in 1980 were similar to those for tech in 2000. Too many parallels—all unnoticed seemingly by anyone. In the box, I detail two such parallels we tracked closely that contributed tremendously to the decision to bail on tech.

THE MAKING OF TWO BUBBLES

The 1999 and early 2000 tech IPO explosion reminded me eerily of the 1980 energy bubble that led the whole market into a bear market. I fathomed tech could do the same. Via Question Two, I tried to see how many parallels I could find between the two sectors that no one was commenting on.

Because I know stock prices are determined—always and everywhere—by supply and demand, I started with the notion that a flood of supply might topple prices. The following table demonstrates the rapid increase of stock supply in both of these sectors through respective IPO booms in the late 1970s and late 1990s. In 1980, nearly half of the increase in value of all new and existing U.S. companies came from the energy sector. In 1999, nearly all of the increase came from the technology sector.

The Making of Two Bubbles

US Energy stocks	12/31/79	12/31/80	Change	US Technology stocks	12/31/98	12/29/99	Change
# of Energy Companies	229	301	72	# of Companies	1460	1652	192
Value of Energy Companies (000's)	$189,795	$324,629	$134,833	Value (000's)	$2,307,384	$4,930,559	$2,623,175

All US Stocks	12/31/79	12/31/80	Change	All US Stocks	12/31/98	12/29/99	Change
# of Companies	4291	4417	126	# of Companies	8656	8785	129
Value (000's)	$1,024,832	$1,325,489	$300,656	Value (000's)	$12,881,072	$15,748,729	$2,867,657

		New Technology Companies as a % of Total New Companies	21.2%
New Energy Companies as a % of Total New Companies	20.3%	New Technology Companies as a % of Total New Companies	21.2%
New Energy Companies as a % of Total Companies	1.7%	New Technology Companies as a % of Total Companies	2.2%
Increase in Energy Value Relative to Total Market Value	44.8%	Increase in Technology Value Relative to Total Market Value	91.5%
Price/Book of Energy Stocks	2.6x	Price/Book of Technology Stocks	13.9x
Price/Book of S&P 500	1.3x	Price/Book of S&P 500	5.6x
Energy/S&P 500 P/B Ratio	2:1	Energy/S&P 500 P/B Ratio	2.5:1

Source: Standard & Poor's Research Insight.

Also, note the similarities between the percentages of new tech stocks relative to all new stocks and all U.S. stocks in 1999 to those of 1980's energy bubble. Note also the price-to-book value of each sector relative to the market. Each was trading at roughly twice the market multiple. Who would remember today that in 1980 energy stocks were priced like growth stocks? Scary times. The key is no one saw it or mentioned it.

Now look at the relative weights of these two sectors in the following table. The top three tables show energy relative to the S&P 500 during the bubble and after the crash in 1979, 1980, and 1981, the bottom three show tech during 1998, 1999, and 2000.

(continued)

A Brief History of Sector Bubbles S&P 500 Economic Sector Weights

December 1979		December 1980		December 1981	
Basic Materials	9.64%	Basic Materials	8.88%	Basic Materials	8.58%
Capital Goods	10.28%	Capital Goods	10.82%	Capital Goods	10.03%
Communication Service	6.05%	Communication Service	4.62%	Communication Service	6.53%
Consumer Staples	10.90%	Consumer Staples	9.23%	Consumer Staples	10.58%
Consumer-Cyclicals	9.86%	Consumer-Cyclicals	8.00%	Consumer-Cyclicals	8.84%
Energy	22.34%	Energy	27.93%	Energy	22.80%
Financials	5.79%	Financials	5.34%	Financials	6.01%
Health Care	6.42%	Health Care	6.54%	Health Care	7.42%
Technology	10.86%	Technology	10.69%	Technology	10.33%
Transportation	2.17%	Transportation	2.89%	Transportation	2.95%
Utilities	5.70%	Utilities	5.07%	Utilities	5.92%
	100.00%		100.00%		100.00%

December 1998		December 1999		December 2000	
Basic Materials	3.11%	Basic Materials	2.99%	Basic Materials	2.41%
Capital Goods	8.07%	Capital Goods	8.40%	Capital Goods	9.01%
Communication Service	8.33%	Communication Service	7.93%	Communication Service	5.47%
Consumer Staples	14.89%	Consumer Staples	10.88%	Consumer Staples	11.35%
Consumer-Cyclicals	9.13%	Consumer-Cyclicals	9.14%	Consumer-Cyclicals	7.56%
Energy	6.22%	Energy	5.43%	Energy	6.45%
Financials	15.59%	Financials	13.20%	Financials	17.22%
Health Care	12.07%	Health Care	9.05%	Health Care	14.10%
Technology	18.54%	Technology	30.02%	Technology	21.85%
Transportation	0.93%	Transportation	0.70%	Transportation	0.67%
Utilities	3.11%	Utilities	2.28%	Utilities	3.91%
	100.00%		100.00%		100.00%

Source: Standard & Poor's Research Insight, Thomson Financial Datastream.

Note the similarities between the relative weights of energy and tech. At its 1980 peak, energy was 28 percent of the U.S. market. But tech's explosion was more remarkable—growing from 5 percent in 1992 to just over 30 percent in 1999. The way I saw it, tech had further to fall. But it didn't need to fall much further to create the same major bear market energy created between 1980 and summer of 1982. (Today, tech makes up 15 percent of the U.S. market as measured by the S&P 500.)[8] Both of these observations weighed heavily in my decision to call a peak in the tech market in 2000.

In some ways, I could fathom tech being worse than the oil bubble. In 1980, none of the 50 largest energy stocks were an IPO of just a few years before, say 1978 or 1979. The 1978 to 1980 IPOs, though many, were smaller. In 2000, 11 of the 50 largest stocks were IPOs in 1998 and 1999. That increased risk. Most unsettling was no one noticed the parallels between the tech fervor and the last sector bubble 20 years earlier. I wasn't the only financial practitioner to have witnessed the energy crash—by any means. I wasn't the world's only person with access to the data for comparison. There were lots of folks who should have seen this before me. But I couldn't see them seeing it anywhere, which was scary. Around the campfire, they were peering a different direction.

Was I certain tech would implode and the market drop? No, but it was logical. First, all the ugly parallels to 1980 were invisible to everyone. Second, you had to wonder who was left to buy who hadn't done so? Who was left as fresh fodder for TGH? Based on sentiment, the yield curve, the budget surpluses, equity-based takeovers, and oil parallels I was content to eliminate possibilities of an up-a-lot or up-a-little scenario. Then again, down-a-lot seemed unlikely too. As I knew from looking at 1981, it took a long time for the oil meltdown to ripple out through other sectors. A sector bubble bursting doesn't ripple to other sectors fast. So my presumption was tech would start down and be down-a-lot. But it would take time to drag down the rest of the market. So, for a major market meltdown we would be waiting longer. Finally, I knew bull markets die with a whimper, not with a bang. Basic rule! Normally bull markets don't have a dramatic spiking top, but roll over slowly. Around the 2000 peak there was over a 10-month period where the world stock market never got out of a 9 percent bandwidth (see Figure 8.2).

As 2000 faded, with the Nasdaq down 39 percent and the S&P 500 down 9 percent for the year[9] and investors and professional forecasters still bullish,

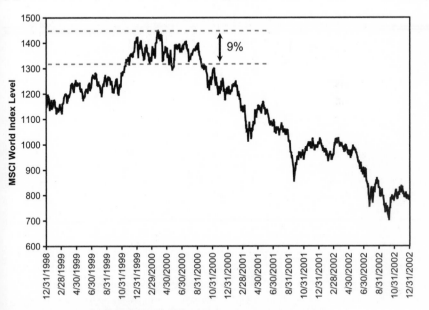

Figure 8.2   Bull Markets Die with a Whimper, Not a Bang.
Source: **Thomson Financial Datastream.**

I finally concluded the time was nigh to turn fully bearish. Not just bearish to tech but overall bearish. By then the tech bubble bursting was in process. Additionally, I could see new tech companies were burning feverishly through their cash, just as new energy companies had in 1980—almost identically the same proportions (as I detail in the following box). We could measure how many would run out of cash if they didn't get back to the public market to raise more money—implying either company implosion or yet more new stock supply—either had to be bad looking forward.

INTERNET BURN RATE

In September of 2000, after the Nasdaq was 16% off its peak and the S&P 500 was at 4% for the year, investors remained generally bullish, though we now know we were headed into a prolonged downturn. An easy way to check sentiment and combat hindsight bias is to review old magazine covers and articles. Sentiment remained widely euphoric.

I had already made my tech bubble market call and my firm had been defensive against tech for nine months. We were considering getting bearish as a whole. Adding to this was research we did on the flood of new companies entering the market during tech's IPO boom.

Many of the new tech stocks relied on capital markets to keep the lights on and computers running. They didn't generate cash them-

Internet Burn Rates

	Ticker	Company	Market Cap	Total Debt	Q1 Cash	Q2 Cash	Q4 1999	Net Income Q1 2000	Q2 2000	Burn Rate
1	ONEM	ONEMAIN.COM INC	282.12	30.45	17.06	1.42	-32.73	-39.84	-35.88	0.04
2	FLAS	FLASHNET COMMUNICATIONS INC	52.3	8.61	0.23	-	-11.42	-4.96	-	0.05
3	GENI	GENESISINTERMEDIA.COM INC	86.98	33.15	0.35	0.41	-6.66	-5.13	-7.34	0.06
4	HCOM	HOMECOM COMMUNICATIONS INC	8.14	0.48	0.08	-	-2.3	-1.49	-	0.06
5	3EFAX	EFAX.COM INC	16.07	1.5	1.6	0.18	-10.14	-5.38	-2.56	0.07
6	CLAI	CLAIMSNET.COM INC	23.19	0	2.49	-	-2.39	-1.93	-9.31	0.27
7	NETZ	NETZEE INC	120.52	16.22	1.33	5.41	-18.85	-15.67	-17.77	0.3
8	LUMT	LUMINANT WORLDWIDE CORP	235.83	6.79	9.44	-	-24.47	-29.65	-29.12	0.32
9	3ESYN	ESYNCH CORP	83.41	0.11	0.5	-	-2.14	-1.49	-	0.33
10	RMII	RMI NET INC	66.39	3.78	3.26	-	-12.24	-7.4	-8.41	0.39
11	DGV	DIGITAL LAVA INC	26.88	0.27	2.59	0.68	-2.25	-1.54	-1.74	0.39
12	ECMV	E COM VENTURES INC	22.18	54.42	2.91	-	-0.13	-6.62	-	0.44
13	ZDZ	ZDNET	135.59	0	0.02	1.21	2.05	-1.57	-2.64	0.46
14	MRCH	MARCHFIRST INC	2679.63	20	369.83	176.43	8.36	-117.33	-374.45	0.47
15	GEEK	INTERNET AMERICA INC	48.92	0.73	3.3	1.72	-0.9	-1.58	-3.27	0.53
16	ROWE	ROWECOM INC	51.25	6.96	9.29	10.13	-1.61	-15	-19.16	0.53
17	PRGY	PRODIGY COMMUN CORP -CL A	677.28	109.36	21.13	20.73	-29.76	-34.91	-38.95	0.53
18	WAVO	WAVO CORP	22.19	3.37	10.23	4.77	-14.42	-3.51	-8.91	0.54
19	ELTX	ELTRAX SYS INC	150.96	17.7	14.2	-	-1.66	-5.24	-26.34	0.54
20	KANA	KANA COMMUNICATIONS	5575.49	1.72	35.67	162.84	-	-14.45	-284.94	0.57
21	ATHM	AT HOME CORP	7578.71	873.23	502.28	388.73	-723.01	-676.52	-668.26	0.58
22	PILL	PROXYMED INC	30.88	1.75	7.91	7.38	-	-5.72	-10.48	0.7
23	AHWY	AUDIOHIGHWAY.COM	14.36	0.46	8.34	3.47	-5.86	-4.01	-4.78	0.73
24	BFLY	BLUEFLY INC	10.77	2.87	3.91	3.93	-5.69	-5.67	-5.3	0.74
25	ELIX	ELECTRIC LIGHTWAVE -CL A	941.85	710.4	25.99	-	-35.02	-35.14	-34.96	0.74

Source: Standard & Poor's Research Insight.

selves, so they turned to investment bankers to keep raising capital for them. (Remember, the investment bankers are happy to do it for the big fees!) These firms relentlessly spent, hoping one day to be bigger than a bubble. The problem was, if they couldn't or didn't raise more money, many of these neophyte dot-commers would simply hit the wall with no more cash and implode. The choices were to sell new stock creating new supply or die. One is bearish; the other is deadly.

For a gauge, we calculated the *burn rate* for as many new tech stocks as we could find data. Burn rate measures how fast a firm will run out of cash in the absence of new cash. To measure burn rate, we compared cash and net losses through the second quarter of 2000 (it being September when we last did this). Assuming these firms found no further outside funding, we divided current cash by second quarter net loss to get the burn rate. For example, Wavo Corp (remember them? You don't? Neither do I. They Wavo-ed out of existence), which rung in at number 18, had $4.7 million in cash on June 30, 2000 and a quarterly net loss of $8.9 million. Dividing cash by net income yields a burn rate of 0.54 quarters. This meant wacky Wavo had only one half of one quarter's worth of cash left, assuming they continued to bleed money at the same rate and couldn't pull off an offering of new stock really fast. That's not Wavo. That's Whacko!

In all, we found 223 material publicly traded companies so short on cash that if they didn't pull off a new stock offering very fast they would be a quaint memory. The table shows the 25 worst offenders. In just one quarter, the aggregate market cap of companies fitting this mold jumped from $140 billion to over $312 billion—not from the prices rising, but because so many were increasingly close to hitting the wall and no one was counting. The market was flooding with stock supply from profitless companies. With the IPO market soured, pretty much all these companies were gone 12 months later. The bubble had only just begun to burst.

Putting together this table is pretty straightforward, should you ever want to measure burn rates yourself. All of the information we detailed is publicly available. You just need a fast Internet hook-up and a sector you suspect.

Note that tech started 2000 worth 30 percent of the total S&P 500. If a 30 percent sector is down 39 percent, as Nasdaq was in 2000, and everything else is flat, then the whole market should be down 11.7 percent. But the S&P was only down 9 percent in 2000. So technically the rest of the market—the nontech part—was up a hair. It was true. The sector breakdown hadn't yet rippled out to take down the rest of the market with it.

Nothing had yet changed to alleviate the cash-starved supply flood of tech IPOs and secondaries. I knew supply had finally drowned demand. Dot-com after dot-com quietly ran out of cash. This had to ripple out of being a sector-specific phenomenon—the rest of the global market would price in the supply. If there had been even a little fear in the market about tech or the yield curve or anything, I could have seen the market being down just a little in 2001. When most everyone has no fear is the best time to get really fearful. Repeat after me Mr. Buffett's wonderful mantra: "You should be greedy when others are fearful and fearful when others are greedy." I could fathom at the end of 2000 there simply being no buying pressure in 2001 to keep the market from being down-a-lot.

Sympathy Selling

Often in a bear market, some sector goes bad first. Selling ripples to other sectors in a process I call *sympathy selling*. It works like this. Suppose you were a generic tech mutual fund. You own little dot-coms and big established tech giants. Out of nowhere, as some of your dot-com holdings implode, you get simultaneous redemptions. You must sell something to get the cash to cover redemptions. What do you sell? You can't sell the little dot-coms getting hammered so badly—they aren't that liquid and you hope they'll bounce back—so you sell your Intel, Microsoft, and Oracle because you can. And that selling hits those stocks. But this is also happening to all the other generic tech funds. But then, some growth stock funds own tech, drug stocks, consumer products companies, and whatever else. As Intel, Microsoft, and Oracle get hit, that fund manager must sell something else to cover his redemptions, so he reaches out and sells Merck and Procter & Gamble. This ripples from fund to fund having the most impact where the process started but eventually rippling far enough to hit, not all, but most of the market. From 2000 to 2003, the only parts of the market that escaped were the small, steep discount value stocks—exactly the reverse of where the damage began with high-end growth tech stocks.

So in 2000, I cut my tech holdings and at the end of the year I got completely defensive, holding 100 percent cash or cash equivalents, and stayed that way for 18 months.

Some Basic Bear Rules

Why 18 months, you ask? While bull market durations vary considerably, most bear markets last about a year to 18 months on the outside. Very few in modern history last fully two years or longer. You shouldn't bet on one lasting so long. The longer a bear market runs, the more likely you're waiting too long to get back in. The 2000 to 2002 bear market was unusual, to say the least, and you shouldn't think of it as the norm. Its magnitude and duration we haven't seen on a global basis since the Great Depression.[10] We probably won't see another three-year bear market for a long time, maybe not for decades. Even if we do see one sooner, cutting out an 18-month swath would still put you in a pretty good place anyway. If you remain bearish for longer than that, you may miss out on the rocket-like ride that is almost always the beginning of the next bull run. Missing that can be very costly.

Further, if you get out successfully and time proves your success, your Stone-Age brain would like to keep you out until after that initial next bull market rocket ride. It won't let you get back in without a fight. Staying out is more comfortable—it lets you feel right longer, particularly if you convince yourself the start of the rocket ride isn't real. Your brain wants to accumulate pride for having gotten out successfully. Switching back to bullish means you might be wrong and if you are people will ridicule you. (Believe me, in 2002 I got heavy ridicule for getting in too early—TGH bit me very nicely that time, thank you.)

Bear markets rarely last as long as your brain wants to think they do once you've gotten out successfully. You hear plenty of rhetoric about "cyclical bulls within long-term secular bears" which is supposed to mean positive years are blips in an overall downward super-cycle. What nonsense! These are all people who've been TGH-ed. You've been hearing that steadily since 2002, but starting in 2003 the market has been up every year any way you measure it. People who insist bull market periods are the exception rather than the norm should stop playing Doom, change out of their jammies, and leave their parents' basements where they no doubt have canned goods and water stockpiled in anticipation of the Apocalypse. Now!

Understanding the nature of bear markets makes it clear why it's good to define, in advance, a re-entry time frame. Historically, only a minority, maybe about a third, of bear market losses occur in the first two-thirds of their duration—or what I call my "Two-Thirds, One-Thirds Rule." It's a gross generalization, but about two-thirds of the loss doesn't happen until the back of the bear. The 1973 to 1974 bear market was a good example, as you can see illustrated in Figure 8.3.

You won't time your re-entry perfectly (I sure didn't last time!), so get over that. The back of bear markets being brutal is TGH's way of humiliating you out of the initial rocket-surge of a new bull market.

The flip side of this rule is: The start of bear markets isn't steep. It's later they get steep. For the first 10 percent to 20 percent of the duration after the peak, the market slips slowly. Per Figure 8.2, 2000 was a perfect example. This isn't true for all countries—small countries can have very steep drops off the peak. But for America, the total foreign market, and the world as a whole, it's very true. So, when looking for a major bear market you needn't try to forecast it before it peaks. Wait until the quiet period after the top and scope out what has already occurred rather than trying to see a vision beforehand. It's always easier to see a peak after something has happened than beforehand when nothing has actually happened.

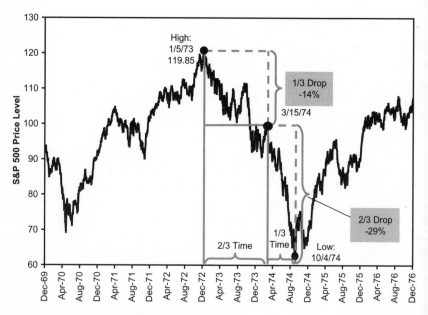

Figure 8.3 The Two-Thirds One-Third Rule.
Source: **Thomson Financial Datastream.**

At market bottoms, the reverse is true. While bull market tops don't spike top, bear market bottoms do V-bottom or sometimes W-bottom. Think about the bottom like a V (or a W—if there is a double bottom)—like Figure 8.4. If you successfully get defensive sometime after the peak, does it matter which side of the V you get back in on? Not really. You still end up in about the same place, no matter whether you get in on the left side of the V or the right (adjusted for a little interest lost from getting in too early).

TGH wants you to wallow in loss aversion and hindsight bias, waiting to get back in until the market has rallied materially. Once you get out successfully, inertia settles in. Exiting at the right time takes guts. Getting back in is equally agonizing. The 18-month rule helps provide needed discipline and self-control. If you want to exceed my 18-month rule, fine. But create your own limit beforehand, whether 20 or 22 months or whatever, and stick to it. One way to combine my rule with yours is to take the 18 months and see where you are. If after 18 months you believe you still know something others don't as to why the market should keep going lower, let it go lower. If it isn't lower a month later, force yourself back in. If it is lower let it keep falling but if it gets back up to where it was after 18 months, then force yourself back in. You're just on the same place on the other side of the V. Either of these approaches

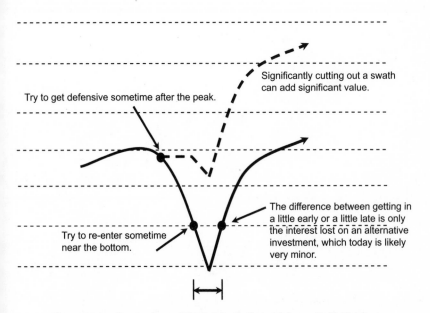

Figure 8.4   Every Bear Market Is Followed by a Bull Market.

will give you very similar results as long as you commit to it and don't let your brain and TGH talk you out of it.

Here's another reason you needn't time the start of a bear perfectly. Every U.S. and global bear market we've looked at, except one, had an average monthly decline, top to bottom, ranging between 1.25 percent and 3 percent, but 2 percent is a fair enough average—1973 to 1974 is a good example again (see Figure 8.5). The exception proving the rule was 1987, which was so short-lived in duration, by the time you bailed out the market had recovered and you were left looking and feeling pretty foolish. (TGH!!!)

If you suspect you're experiencing a bear, be patient and watch. If you see a market decline exceeding the 2 percent average, wait for it to bounce back before getting out. You may simply be experiencing a correction. But, with a typical bear market, you'll soon see a short-lived pullback to higher prices within that 2 percent per month range off the top and have a better chance to get out. Patience is a virtue here.

Joe Goodman was a wise man and the fourth longest running columnist in *Forbes* history (whom I hope to surpass in that capacity in August 2007). To my thinking, he was the best columnist *Forbes* ever had. He advised readers in the 1940s and 1950s to never call a peak too soon. He advocated waiting three months after you suspect a peak has happened before calling a

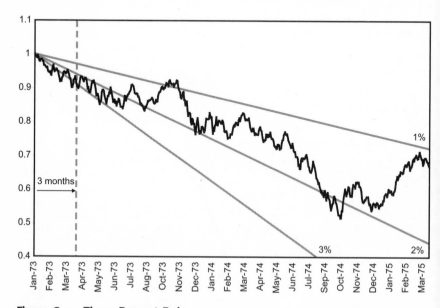

Figure 8.5   The 2 Percent Rule.
Source: **Thomson Financial Datastream.**

bear a bear (as I showed you in the previous illustration). The notion that bull markets die with a whimper, not a bang, the two-thirds one-third rule, the 2 percent rule, and Goodman's three-month rule keep you from pulling the rip-cord too soon on a correction and then watching a bull market soaring still higher. If it's a real bear market, the rolling, grinding, whimpering top gives you plenty of chances to exit with no more than a 6 percent to 10 percent drop off the top. Losing a little is fine if you can cut out and save a slice of a big bear.

Once you are out, there are infinite rationalizations for not re-entering the market. As investors, we misremember past events and our reactions to them (*hindsight bias*) so we think we handled them better than we did. We re-cast ourselves as having been cool cucumbers during past national tragedies and other historic events when we were often over-the-top emotional. We think back to when the market corrected almost 20 percent in July and August of 1998[11] and fool ourselves into "remembering" we "knew" it was only a correction and were cool and levelheaded. We think the 2006 war in Iraq is more devastating than Viet Nam or Korea, or we've never faced an enemy like Al Qaeda, or our nation has "never been so politically divided," or . . . or . . . or.

Look at the list of historic events in Table 8.3 and try to remember—honestly—what you felt during, say, the Cuban Missile Crisis (if you were around). Or when JFK was shot. Or when the American Embassy in Iran was seized. Or Y2K's approach.

The list of epic events isn't supposed to make you feel all is lost for humanity. Rather, this shows how resilient markets are. Don't let hysteria scare you. That is just what TGH wants.

When Bulls Cross-Dress

TGH will try fooling you into thinking every bull market is really a bear market in disguise. TGH conspires so a new bull market comes dressed in all the trappings of a "secular bear" market. Bull markets are unabashed cross-dressers. I've never seen a bull market that didn't come to the party wearing a full-on bear suit. Unfortunately, most investors aren't looking for cross-dressers. All they know is, way late into the party, they've been fooled into thinking they've been sharing a few laughs with a bear, and WHAMMO! They've missed out on the first 50 percent up-leg of a bull market because TGH had their minds warped.

Arm yourself against TGH by knowing how to tell a cross-dresser from the real deal—a correction from a bear market. The major differences between the two are magnitude and duration. A correction is a short-term 10

Table 8.3   Never a Dull Moment

Year	Events	S&P 500
1934	Depression; first margin requirement; Hitler declares himself Fuhrer of Germany	-1.4%
1935	Spanish Civil War; Italy invades northern Africa; Hitler rejects treaty of Versailles	47.7%
1936	Economy struggling; record high P/Es; Hitler occupies Rhineland	33.9%
1937	Capital spending & industrial production decline severely; recession	-35.0%
1938	World War clouds gather; Wall Street scandals uncovered	31.1%
1939	News of war in Europe dominates headlines; Germany & Italy sign 10-year military pact	-0.4%
1940	France falls to Hitler; Battle of Britain; U.S. institutes the draft	-9.8%
1941	Pearl Harbor; Germany invades U.S.S.R.; U.S. declares war on Japan, Italy, & Germany	-11.6%
1942	Wartime price controls; Battle of Midway	20.3%
1943	Meat & Cheese rationed in the U.S.; FDR freezes prices & wages	25.9%
1944	Consumer goods shortages; Allies invade Normandy	19.8%
1945	Post-war recession predicted; Invasion of Iwo Jima; FDR dies; Atom bomb dropped in Japan	36.4%
1946	Employment Act of 1946 passed; Steel & shipyard workers strike	-8.1%
1947	Cold War begins	5.7%
1948	Berlin blockade; U.S. Government seizes railroads to avert strike	5.5%
1949	Russia explodes Atom bomb; Britain devalues the Pound	18.8%
1950	Korean War; McCarthy and the "Red Scare"	31.7%
1951	Excess Profits Tax	24.0%
1952	U.S. seizes steel mills to avert strike	18.4%
1953	Russia explodes H-bomb; Economists predict depression in 1954	-1.0%
1954	Dow tops 300- common belief that market is too high	52.6%
1955	Eisenhower illness	31.6%
1956	Egypt seizes Suez Canal	6.6%
1957	Russia launches Sputnik; Secretary Humphrey warns of depression and President Eisenhower agrees	-10.8%
1958	Recession	43.4%
1959	Castro seizes power in Cuba 1	2.0%
1960	Russia downs U-2 spy plane; Castro seizes U.S. oil refineries	0.5%
1961	Berlin Wall erected; Green Berets sent to Vietnam; Bay of Pigs invasion fails	26.9%
1962	Cuban Missile Crisis-threat of global destruction; JFK cracks down on steel prices, scaring Wall Street	-8.7%
1963	President Kennedy assassinated; South Vietnam government overthrown	22.8%
1964	Gulf of Tonkin; race riots in New York	16.5%
1965	Civil rights marches; Rumor of LBJ heart attack; Treasury warns of gold speculation	12.5%
1966	Vietnam War escalates-U.S. bombs Hanoi; highest price/debt ratio in a decade	-10.1%
1967	Race riots in Newark & Detroit; LBJ signs huge defense spending bill	24.0%
1968	U.S.S. Pueblo seized; Tet Offensive; Martin Luther King & Robert Kennedy assassinated	11.1%
1969	Money tightens-markets fall; Prime rate at record high	-8.5%
1970	U.S. invades Cambodia-Vietnam war spreads; money supply declines; bankruptcy of Penn Central	4.0%
1971	Wage price freeze; U.S. Dollar devalued	14.3%
1972	Largest U.S. trade deficit in history; U.S. mines Vietnamese ports	19.0%
1973	Energy crisis-Arab oil embargo; Watergate scandal; Agnew resigns	-14.7%
1974	Steepest market drop in four decades; Nixon resigns; Yen devalued; Franklin National Bank collapses	-26.5%
1975	New York city bankrupt; clouded economic picture	37.2%
1976	Economic recovery slows; OPEC raises oil prices	23.8%
1977	Steep market slump; Social Security taxes raised	-7.2%
1978	Rising interest rates	6.6%
1979	Oil prices skyrocket; Three Mile Island nuclear disaster; Iran seizes U.S. embassy	18.4%
1980	All-time high interest rates; Health hazards in New York (Love Canal); Carter halts grain exports to Soviet Union	32.4%
1981	Steep recession begins; Reagan shot; energy sector begins collapse; AIDS identified for first time	-4.9%
1982	Worst recession in 40 years-profits plummet, unemployment spikes	21.4%
1983	U.S. invades Grenada; U.S. embassy in Beirut bombed; WPPSS biggest muni bond default in history	22.5%
1984	Record federal deficit; FDIC bailout of Continental Illinois; AT&T declared monopoly-broken up	6.3%
1985	U.S. & Soviet arms race begins; Ohio banks closed to stop run; U.S. becomes largest debtor nation	32.2%
1986	U.S. bombs Libya; Boesky pleads guilty to insider trading; Challenger explodes; Chernobyl	18.5%
1987	Record-setting single day market decline; Iran-Contra investigation blames Reagan	5.2%
1988	First Republic Bank fails; Noriega indicted by U.S.	16.8%
1989	Savings & Loan bailout begins; Tiananmen Square; SF earthquake; U.S. troops deploy in Panama	31.5%
1990	Iraq invades Kuwait-sets stage for Gulf War; consumer confidence plummets; unemployment rises	-3.2%
1991	Recession; U.S. begins air war in Iraq; Unemployment rises to 7%	30.6%
1992	Unemployment continues to rise; economic fears; monetary supply tightened; bitter election contest	7.6%
1993	Tax increase; economic recovery uncertain-fears of double dip recession	10.0%
1994	Attempted nationalized health care	1.3%
1995	Weak dollar panic	37.5%
1996	Fears of inflation	22.9%
1997	Tech "mini crash" in October & "Pacific Rim crisis"	33.3%
1998	Russian Rubble crisis; "Asian Flu"; Long-term Capital Management debacle	28.6%
1999	Y2K paranoia & correction	21.0%
2000	Dot-com Bubble begins to burst	-9.1%
2001	Recession, September 11th terrorist attacks	-11.9%
2002	Corporate accounting scandals, Terrorism fears, Tensions with Iraq	-22.1%
2003	Mutual fund scandals, Conflict in Iraq, SARS	28.7%
2004	Fears of a weak dollar and US "triple deficits"	10.9%

Source: Global Financial Data.

percent to 20 percent scary global downturn. It's short, sharp, and comes from nowhere with a spike top and a fantastic story leading you to believe more downside is ahead. It's over just as fast and rockets higher returning to new highs about as fast as it fell. One to four months down and then back up. Four months later the whacky story that pervaded the downturn sounds silly but at the time it first appears you can't really disprove it.

You may think 20 percent, just like mid-1998, is quite a lot and officially qualifies for a bear market, but the operative words here are "short and sharp"—right off the cliff, defying our 2 percent rule. Corrections are common in bull markets (one every year or two on average) and devilishly tough to time—you shouldn't try because they down-and-up so fast. To time these little suckers successfully you must be right on both ends. Odds are you'll miss either a good exit or re-entry point or both. Don't bother. (No one—and I mean no one—in the history of asset management, with all of the tens of thousands of practitioners, has ever made a successful long-term practice of timing short-term downturns. If it were possible, at least one person would have done it by now. But no one has. Ever. And if you could you wouldn't be reading this book.)

Similar to a down-a-little scenario, any benefit you get by being super lucky and accurately timing a correction can get eaten up by transaction costs and taxes. Just sit tight, know you're probably being entertained by a bull in drag, and you'll get your reward for patience.

When Bears Cross-Dress

But a bear market's beginning feels nothing like a correction. It feels fine. A bull market top won't announce itself with a sudden price drop. There is no announcement effect (except 1987, the exception to the rule). Instead of a bull in a bear suit, you get a bear in a bull suit. As stated earlier, bull markets have grinding, rolling, whimpering tops, and a relative absence of bearish sentiment (other than perma-bears). You won't hear a bang. You won't "feel" like you are about to experience a prolonged downturn. In fact, you might "feel" like your diversified portfolio is boring and you should place big bets on individual stocks or spectacular sectors to boost returns.

Historically, if markets have been positive 71 percent of the time,[12] and some of those negative years were only down-a-little, you're looking at very few years of the truly scary, bearish, down-a-lot type. Since 1980 there have only been four[13] so you shouldn't expect to see them too often. The future shouldn't be too different. Another way to see this is, if you're bearish much more than 3 or 4 times in two decades, you're overdoing it. Recall as human beings, we normally exert more effort to avoid pain than achieve gain. Remember that. If your brain keeps telling you a bear is always impending, your brain is wrong. Successful bearishness requires being virtually alone. You must act alone, without others. But if you have the Three Questions you're never really alone.

WHAT WENT REALLY WRONG

Making a successful bear market call is only half the battle. If you get defensive on the stock market, you still must decide when to get back in. Our Stone-Age brains make deciding when to "re-equitize" more fraught with peril than deciding to get out. Just as you can't rely on a fixed set of indicators to get out, there is no magical way to know when to get back in. As mentioned earlier, had I gotten back in the market in October 2002, I would have timed the global bottom perfectly. I didn't expect to time the bottom perfectly, but it's never fun to get in the market just in time for TGH to throw a precipitous drop at you, which is exactly what happened to me.

The following are key reasons we got back in during May 2002. Despite being wrong and too early, you can see these are rational, disciplined decisions driven by the Three Questions:

- According to my 18-month rule, I was committed to re-equitizing by June of 2002. I was not comfortable with missing equity exposure for longer than that period for clients expecting equity-like return.
- The consensus was bearish for the first time since the bear market started. Therefore, I thought down-a-lot was the least likely condition. As it turns out, 12 months later, the global market was down—but basically down-a-little. It remains impossible, in my view, to ever know with certainty where the market is moving in the next few months. This time, even though I was right the market wouldn't be down-a-lot a year out, it was down-a-lot almost immediately. I stepped into a hole. No one likes negative returns, but I always remain equitized in the expectation of the first three scenarios.
- Bear market investment products were proliferating, such as mutual funds specifically designed to do well in down markets. Bear-

ish newsletters were now wildly popular and their writers considered rational sages.

- Major sources of bad news were widely known and discounted into pricing, their "surprise" power having largely dissipated over the previous 2.5 years, including recession, earnings deterioration and potential bankruptcies, terrorist attacks and the impending war, accounting scandals (Enron, WorldCom), and the rest.
- At the time, it looked as though a double bottom had formed between September 2001 (just following the terror attacks in New York; Washington, DC; and in the skies over Pennsylvania) and May 2002 lows.
- Monetary conditions were generally favorable. Broad money growth was greater than the inflation rate, short-term liquidity was on the rise, and we had a steep U.S. and global yield curve. Most important, few noticed.
- For the first time, foreign markets were acting stronger than America's, signaling a potential shift and possible end to the global bear (although this would fade away again until returning with a vengeance in 2003).
- A capital markets technology we developed, the Run Strength Indicator, showed the market was vastly oversold and ready to move up. Unfortunately, all the data we had built it on were from post–World War II smaller global bear markets, and on its first real-time maiden voyage it didn't adequately reflect reality.

The Run Strength Indicator

The Run Strength Indicator was a measure of sentiment fatigue. It's a great example of capital markets technology my firm developed by using Question Two. It's a way to measure short-term sentiment that is a major driver of stock demand—and a big part of determining stock prices in the short-term. It was a complicated algorithm combining many factors that basically offered hope of knowing when a market move, up or down, was simply too fatigued to continue. Giving it an indexed number of 0 to 100, we had observed when a variety of different equity indexes all fell below 20, a strong rally followed. Conversely, when it rose above 80, an extreme overbought condition existed and prices usually fell. We back-tested this, and it stood up well.

(continued)

In May 2002, the indicator fell to extreme lows, far below 20—seemingly signaling an extremely oversold condition. We witnessed this on most major indexes. This seemingly extreme oversold condition hadn't been seen in decades and might not be seen again for decades. To not use it when we did would mean we probably wouldn't any time soon either. But it had never been used real time before. While we back-tested it extensively, we hadn't been able to test it in relevant, real-time conditions. But time was of the essence. Effectively, the Run Strength Indicator simply wasn't up to measuring something as extreme as that bear market, reflecting instead more normal bear markets. By normal standards, sentiment was extremely low. In hindsight, we can see that sentiment can (and did) get very much worse.

By late June, we knew the indicator clearly hadn't been working right as a timing mechanism. Still, all the other rules applied so we had no reason to turn and get back out. I accumulated regret and learned some good lessons (a small way to get back at TGH).

Creating capital markets technology for infrequent extreme phenomena requires using old, historic data that are comparable. But will those data be clean? I already knew, but better learned through this process, that old data are pretty consistently corrupt in ways hard-to-know. This experience really put through my forehead the need to be sure the old data are good. As a result, we have yet more stringent and exacting ways to confirm old data to make sure we're basing assumptions off as close to reality as we can get. The more extreme and infrequent, the more you must be sure. Clean data are next to Godly data and also next to impossible.

Here's another important lesson I learned. I learned to listen more to my clients—but not how you might think. When we got re-invested in May 2002, we noticed virtually none of our clients fought us. They were eerily complacent about the decision to take their assets from entirely cash and synthetic cash to fully exposed to stocks. When we got out of tech, they fought us tooth and nail. When we got out of the market, they fought us. In both cases, some clients fired us—our termination rate rose temporarily from its normal 5 percent per year up to 10 percent. They were then opting to stay with tech and stay in the market. But in May 2002, when we got back into the market, they didn't fight us at all. In fact, our existing clients overall gave us more money to invest and put into the market. Clearly, in retrospect, optimism wasn't adequately shaken out.

We thought then our client base wasn't representative of the rest of the world. Since we had avoided most of the downside in the bear market, we subsequently thought they had heavy confidence in us and therefore didn't fear stocks. We found out within a month that couldn't have been true as the market fell and clients recoiled.

As a result, we have built redundant technology aimed at measuring the same thing in our client base real-time moving forward. Our client base is big enough to be representative of American high-net-worth investors as a whole—and hence a great laboratory for testing sentiment. If our clients don't feel the fear, it's probably not out there. Today we can measure daily incoming call volume of clients and calibrate it and aggregate the degree to which our client base is fighting us. As future cycles mature, this will be a valuable sentiment tool.

Of course, I missed other things. I didn't see the Sarbanes-Oxley legislation coming at us in July 2002, which was and remains a negative. I underestimated the degree to which society would temporarily adopt the "all CEOs are crooks" mentality late in 2002 that both led to Sarbanes-Oxley and seemingly was also partly fueled by it. For example, by July, rumors were rampant in and out of the media that Jack Welch was a bad guy and GE would be the next Enron. If GE could go bad then everything could go bad. All that was just sentiment but I didn't ever see it coming. But seeing the sentiment twists of the last stages of a bull or bear market is both difficult and often done wrong. And this time I was simply too early and wrong. Getting in too early was a big mistake to make, but as long as you're right more than wrong, even if you are really wrong from time to time, you can still beat the market in the long term which is what the game really is about. When I was back in, I was still moving with the market.

The 70-30 Rule

Throughout 2006, CXO Advisory Group, an independent web site ranking market prognosticators, ranked me as the most accurate long-term public forecaster anywhere based on my *Forbes* columns starting in 2000. (My *Forbes* columns are a good but not perfect proxy for the

(continued)

market strategies my firm deploys for our clients.) You can see the CXO analysis and how others stack up by comparison at www.cxoadvisory.com. My point is, in ranking me most accurate, which by itself is very dubious, they claim I'm accurate 70 percent of the time. By their count, I'm wrong 30 percent of the time. That's great. Being 70 percent is huge. If you're 70 percent right, you're at the very top of the pack. If you can do that long term you become a super-hero—maybe even a legend. That means learning to live comfortably being wrong 30 percent of the time. If I could simply sign a contract to be right in the market 70 percent of the time and wrong 30 percent, I'd sign the contract, put down my money and never bet beyond that again. You might still get some market bets pretty astoundingly wrong, but over time being right more than wrong wins out over pretty much everything.

So, am I upset I got back in the market too early in 2002? You bet. I wish I could go back in time and change that, but I can't, so I must keep looking forward. But if I had my choice between getting in too early and getting in too late—I'd pick too early any day. Bounces off the bottom of bear markets aren't something you want to miss, even if it means taking a bit of a hit in the near term.

What Causes a Bear Market?

There's simply no single answer to the question, "What causes a bear market?" It might be monetary conditions, yield curve, surpluses, a sector implosion, excess demand reverting, or bad legislation impacting property rights. But it won't be what it was last time. Two bear markets in a row rarely start with the same causes because most investors are always fighting the last war and are prepared for what took them down last time. The last bear market was led by a tech implosion. The next one won't be. It may not be led by a sector melt-down at all.

Maybe you suspect a bear market will start because the bull market has run on too long. Question One—is there a "right" time a bull market needs to last? No! There is no "right" length for a bull market. As bull markets get longer than average in duration, there is a steady stream of folks who say it must end because it's too old. That isn't right. They all end for their own reasons and will end eventually—but age isn't among them. People started saying the 1990s bull market was too old in 1994, only about six years too soon.

"Irrational exuberance" was first uttered in 1996, again way too early. Bull markets can die at any age.

Use your Questions to test some of these. Find a few of your favorite indicators and see if they reliably led to bear markets before. You will find there is no fundamental indicator on its own, no technical indicator on its own, no single silver bullet, no nothing on its own perfectly predicting when a bear market will start. Nor can you have a "feeling" indicating when you should get out. I hear from far too many readers, investors, and clients they "have a funny feeling" about the market going one direction or the other that they "can't explain," but they "just know." That's TGH. If it isn't, take an aspirin and an antacid and get over it. Then take Question Three for this one because that's what you really need. If you believe you've been right about a "funny feeling" in the past, you may have been. Luck happens. But you're also suffering hindsight bias and forgetting times you had "funny feelings" that were completely wrong.

Osama Bin Laden, Katrina, and Foghorn Leghorn Walk into a Bar

Some of you may say, "But we live in a different world now. A terrorist attack would break the market, right?" That's a fair question. The tragic attacks on September 11, 2001, came two-thirds of the way through a material preexisting bear market and a recession—possibly stalling off market resurgence (though we have no way to measure if that's true or not). So pull a Question One. Is it true September 11 had a lasting, devastating impact on the market (see Figure 8.6a)?

The U.S. stock market closed that day and stayed closed until September 17 when trading resumed—Wall Street's inhabitants scattered to the winds. The S&P 500 nosedived when the market opened—down 11.6 percent by September 21.[14] But amazingly, in only 19 days the U.S. market was trading above September 10 levels. And it remained above those levels for months. We remember this differently because long before the attack the global economy was in a recession and bear market. Did the attack exacerbate the situation? Maybe! But reread this paragraph and repeat after me: "Back to where it was only 19 days later and then higher for months." Note the higher period included all those fears in the fall of 2001 about anthrax. Remember anthrax? The market moved higher right through it without interruption, lifting to prices steadily higher than on September 10. Let's delve further, think globally (as always), and see how the more recent terrorist attacks on Western nations have impacted the stock market (see Figure 8.6b).

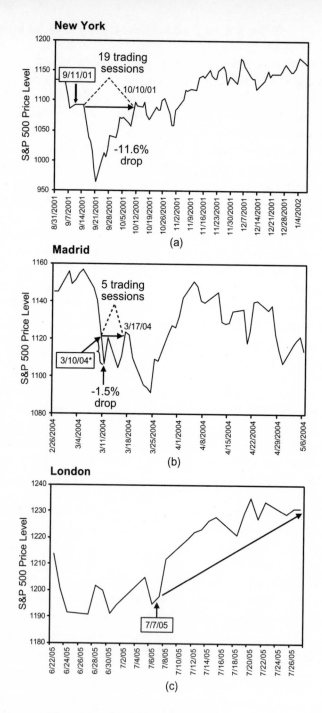

Figure 8.6 Have No Fear: The Market Doesn't.
Source: Thomson Financial Datastream.

On March 10, 2004, more Al Qaeda goons took credit for a massive train bombing in Madrid. The Spanish referred to the event as "Our 9/11." In other words, this "surprise" was a devastating national tragedy. And yet, the S&P 500 dropped 1.5 percent that day and traded at pre-attack levels a scant five trading sessions later.

On July 7, 2005, they bombed the London Underground (see Figure 8.6c), not far from where some of my firm's employees work and live. Yes, we worried until our London counterparts were confirmed safe. But the market was downright callous about their well-being. The S&P 500 was positive that day. The market was indifferent to the attack. Terrorists lost that battle.

Terrorism has since continued, mostly isolated to the Middle East and Africa. Then, on August 10, 2006, well after I'd rough-drafted this book, a group attempted to construct liquid-based bombs for 11 London wide-bodied flights bound for America. They were apprehended. The aftermath was another ratcheting-up of security standards for flights across America and Europe—causing increased flight delays and inconvenience as the new rules for carry-on items were implemented. The market yawned. It dropped a hair the next two days and rallied 3 percent the next week. The market is getting calloused to terrorists.

Whether all future attacks have already been discounted or not is debatable. So far, they haven't been able to pull off a hugely successful attack since 9/11. Recall, these were guys with box cutters in a world where pilots were instructed to take hijackers wherever they wanted to go. But since then, there has been no market panic to terror anywhere. How can investors be so blasé about terrorism? This is a new, terrible, and very real threat to us wherever we live, work, travel, and defend ourselves and our friends. Or is it? We have had previous terror attacks here in the U.S. and on U.S. interests. There was the USS Cole bombing in 2000. And Khobar Towers were bombed in 1996. And that first attack on the Twin Towers in 1993. And the attack on the Marine barracks in Lebanon in 1983. And Pan Am Flight 103. And the entire history of Israel. And the Irish Republican Army in Britain. The British lived with terrorism on their soil seemingly forever and their markets did fine then. World War I was sparked by a terrorist act. There were the Barbary pirates and Tripoli. You get what I am saying. Terrorism isn't new, devastating as it is at a human level. But we are resilient, and so are our markets. Figure 8.7 shows a number of terror attacks in recent history, and the time the markets took to recover.

But would a large terror attack now break the market? First, ask if another terrorist attack would surprise you? You may be more surprised—knock on wood—we've yet to experience another major American attack (as

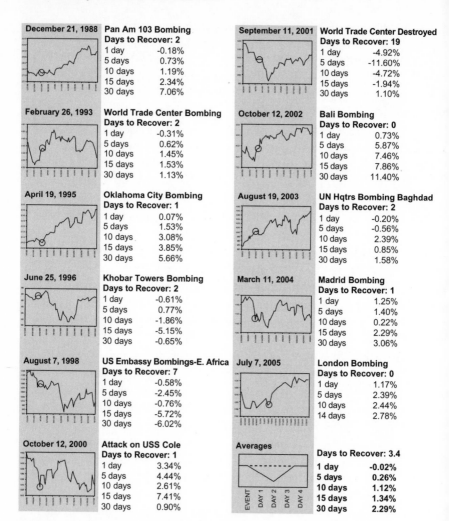

Figure 8.7 Have No Fear: The Market Doesn't—Historical Perspective.
Source: **Thomson Financial Datastream.**

of this writing). Put yourself back to September 10, 2001. If someone told you 19 thugs armed only with knives and box cutters would perpetrate a coordinated attack using planes and their inhabitants as bombs, you would have thought it was the plot for a Bruce Willis movie, not reality. That what happened would happen seems unthinkable.

Today there is nothing they could do that would surprise us. Yes, it would be negative, but whatever it is it would have less market impact than you may fear because we've been psychologically preparing for it for five years.

What If They Destroyed a Major American City?

What if terrorists destroyed a major American City? Well, certainly that would be terrible. But how big would the market impact be? Again, it would be less than you might think and the way you know is partly by looking at the market impact of Katrina on New Orleans.

New Orleans and parts of the Gulf Coast were obliterated by the one-two punch of Hurricanes Katrina and Rita. Much of the Gulf of Mexico's oil refining capability came to a screeching halt. Hundreds of thousands in Texas, Louisiana, and Mississippi were homeless or displaced. Businesses closed; employees jobless. And yet, the market acted wholly apathetic about the plight of those poor folks. The day Katrina hit Louisiana, August 29, 2005, the market rose 0.6 percent.[15] A pretty normal day given flooding and ensuing chaos. And yet, GDP growth for the fourth quarter of 2005 was 1.8 percent,[16] and the S&P 500 was up 2.1 percent.[17] It's not blow-your-socks-off growth, but it wasn't the economic and market dilemma many pundits predicted. Think about it this way—the global market was up 3.1 percent in the fourth quarter of 2005,[18] so the U.S. market, even post-Katrina, was not too far off the world. And the market was up net from September through December and then up still more in the first few weeks of 2006. Of course, maybe it would have gone up even more without Katrina. Who can prove that?

Shouldn't GDP have been hurt hugely based on work stoppage and disruption of refining in the Gulf? New Orleans was decimated. That is a great Question Two to explore. (See how this gets easier to do, once you are on a roll?) Let's flip this one on its head: Why shouldn't GDP and stock returns be healthy following such a major natural disaster? Scale it, like always!

Suppose every person in Louisiana was suddenly unemployed after the two storms. Didn't happen; but suppose the worst case scenario imaginable. There are 4.5 million Louisianans. Louisiana's income per capita is historically only about three-fourths as high as America's average.[19] So think about the population of Louisiana instead as about 1 percent of the United States's 300 million souls. If every single person in the state of Louisiana stopped contributing to GDP as a result of the hurricanes, GDP growth would have been shaved by about one percent, one time. For one year, instead of maybe 4 percent growth, we would have gotten 3 percent and then moved on normally. That's the worst it could have been. I don't mean to say Louisianans aren't productive people and important—but you shouldn't be surprised there was little impact on the overall economy's growth. America is huge. Louisiana is too small to impact America's GDP much. Then remember it's a global market and global economy, and America is only 38 percent of global GDP[20] so the impact on global growth would be smaller still. Simple scaling.

Remember Grampa Fisher?

We also have history to use conveniently. The first thing I did when Katrina struck was pull out my stock charts and history books to remind myself of the natural disaster that devastated my hometown. When the 1906 fire and earthquake leveled San Francisco on April 18, 1906, little was left. Grampa Fisher (see Chapter 5) had to put off his wedding to my grandmother until later that year. They and their families lived with most of the rest of the city in tent camps in Golden Gate Park. My grandfather's medical practice was on hold for months as he devoted himself to pro bono work for those injured by the tragedy. It was a massive tragedy. But the market didn't buckle. The U.S. market dropped-a-hair in April, which might have happened anyway and might have been caused by other things (I don't really know) but was higher again in May and June and didn't implode that year. The major buckle was the next year, 1907, with a New York-based banking panic and the market dropping 49 percent, peak to trough.[21] But San Francisco in 1906 was more important to America than New Orleans in 2005. San Francisco's demise not causing the market to implode in 1906 was a pretty good guideline from history to tell you not to worry about Katrina too much. And to tell you not to worry about markets too much if the terrorists, heaven forbid, ever do succeed at causing real havoc in an American city.

You can use the Questions and this methodology to attack other presumably "bearish" events such as outbreaks of SARS, the bird flu, Ebola, hanta virus, anthrax, chicken pox, or JuJuBees (just joking on that last one—trying to see if you're awake). Just as SARS was a big 2003 health scare, now long forgotten, in 2005 and 2006, concerns about bird flu morphing to human transmittable were rampant. Could it happen? I guess so. Return to Chapter 5 because we covered it there. But after bird flu there will be another scare and another and you can use the Questions each time. Use your Questions to test if any geopolitical event, natural disaster, health crisis, anything we all worry about, plan for, fret about, and hear on the news can move the market. You will find none of these events are a silver bullet for predicting bear markets.

Now that you have Question Three tools for recognizing the likely direction of the market and can understand what a real bear market does (and doesn't) look like, you are ready. Ready to stop being humiliated by TGH. Ready to use the Three Questions. Ready to beat the market. Ready for building a real strategy to serve you your entire life. Read on.

9

PUTTING IT
ALL TOGETHER

Stick with Your Strategy and Stick It to Him

This chapter is largely about the investment advice of managing a portfolio, picking stocks, and avoiding common mistakes. It isn't about knowing something others don't with the Three Questions. By now you've seen the Three Questions at work. I've demonstrated examples of what I've learned over the years with the Questions. Chapters 5 through 8 were largely example after example of looking at the world through the Three Questions. I hope you can start investing by seeing things others don't. I hope you can see things I can't.

But we're not done yet. As Chapter 3 hinted, one tool to stay disciplined with the Three Questions and keep your scurrilous brain in check and not be humiliated by TGH is having a comprehensive strategy driving decisions. Just using the Three Questions is great! But a strategy provides a basis and framework from which you can ask the Three Questions and make small (or big) bets keeping you on path toward your goals.

Maybe you think you already have a pretty good strategy. Fair enough— but many investors who believe they have a strategy actually confuse tactics with strategy. For example, some investors want market-like returns with low fees, so their "strategy" is buying no-load mutual funds. That is a philosophy, not a strategy. Operating that way without a strategy, 10 years later, you won't have paid any load fees but you won't have gotten great returns. A strategy would involve planning what funds and why and how to change them.

Another misguided tactic is static asset allocation. A static asset allocation is the rigid adherence to fixed percentages of stocks, bonds, and cash. Brokers and the media have preached static asset allocation for decades. It's a fine self-control mechanism for people who otherwise lack self-control, just like having someone else prepare all your meals can control your weight if you can't hack it on your own. But static asset allocation ensures you can't take advantage of the Three Questions when opportunity knocks.

Investors also use stop-losses and dollar-cost averaging (both self-control mechanisms and also provably losing strategies which I detail in the box), buy and sell options and covered calls (another losing proposition in another box), short here, go double-long there, all believing they have a strategy that works, not realizing they're just spinning their wheels with tactics. Some, fine. Some, not. But tactics. A gaggle of fancy but ineffectual tactics do not a strategy make. There is nothing wrong with deploying any particular appropriate tactic at a given time. But it's no more a strategy than a carpentry tool like a hammer is a blueprint for a home. What's more, what is the point of using tactics if you don't know something others don't? You only want the hammer when it's the right tactic to accomplish the strategy. You're far better off using the Questions to figure out something others don't know, and using that knowledge to get ahead rather than losing your money in a slow trickle through tricky investment tactics without a strategy.

POPULAR BUT PROBLEMATIC

Many popular tactical myths are problematic and costly yet continue in their popularity because they appeal to our blindsided brains—they feel so right—and we typically don't know how to think them through. Sometimes, like with stop losses, they were promoted by the brokerage industry decades ago because they increased trading and hence transaction fees. Questions One and Three help you here because you can measure if they work and see why your brain finds them appealing. Here are two.

Stop Losses? More Like Stop Gains

The concept of a stop loss—even the name—is so appealing it's easy to see why this maneuver is popular. A stop loss implies setting some arbitrary percent (or dollar) amount of decline. When a stock hits that level you recognize it as a failure, sell, and buy something else that may do better. For example, if you always stop losses at 15 percent, you will never have a stock that is down more than 15 percent. No disasters. No Enrons. Sounds good. If not 15 percent, you can pick any other arbitrary amount like 10 percent, 20 percent, 12.725 percent. Whatever! This is a control mechanism.

But stop losses don't do what investors want them to do. On average they lose money, they don't make money. They feel good but are bad. Why? Because stocks aren't serially correlated. Huh?

Stock prices are what a statistician would call not *serially correlated*—meaning when a stock moves in any given direction, by itself, the odds are 50/50 that it continues in that direction or reverses trend. There is a huge body of scholarly research based on real data proving historical price movement by itself has absolutely no bearing on future stock movement. Being down any given arbitrary amount tells you nothing about what the stock does next. Nothing.

If stocks were serially correlated, you could simply buy stocks that have gone up and not buy stocks that have gone down—follow the rule to cut losers and let winners run as momentum investors do. If stocks were serially correlated in the long term, momentum investors would have markedly above-average histories of performance. But it isn't so.

Even if you were adamant in wanting to use stop-losses, despite my best efforts to discourage you, what level would you choose? People tend to pick round numbers like 10 percent and 20 percent and those who use stop losses tend not to pick numbers bigger than 20 percent because if you believe stop losses will work, why favor 30 percent over 20 percent? In fact, why favor 20 percent over 15 percent? We could do that all the way down to 1 percent. When a stock drops a given amount and hits your stop loss, there is a 50 percent chance it keeps falling and 50 percent it starts rising. You're trading on a coin flip.

What if you put a stop loss on individual stocks at 20 percent, and one drops 22 percent before shooting up 50 percent? You garnered a 20 percent loss, paid a transaction fee, and face the task of replacing it. Can you guarantee what you buy next will only go up? What if the replacement stock drops again? You can keep buying 20 percent losers all the way to zero. History shows no stop-loss level—down 10 percent, 20 percent, 30 percent, 53 percent—leads to market beating returns.

Another scenario. Reframe to see it clearly. Amy buys a stock at $50. It rises to $100. Sue then buys it at $100 and it falls to $80—a 20 percent drop from its high. Should they both sell out at $80? Or just

(continued)

314 The Only Three Questions That Count

Sue with her higher cost basis? There is no right answer as past price movement isn't indicative of future price movement.

Some propose replacing the sold stock with a similar one from the same industry. But why is that better? And if the sector begins to gain, chances are either stock would also rise. The decision to buy or sell shouldn't be driven by arbitrary price movements or targets but on the forward-looking outlook for that stock.

Some propose using stop losses without replacements so you never suffer a bear market. But then, in a normal bull market correction, stop losses tend to force the sale of most stocks at relative low points. Aren't we supposed to buy low and sell high, not the reverse? The outcome tied to an absolute stop loss is purely random. In other words, it doesn't work.

The only stop-loss certainty is increased transaction costs. In an otherwise random process, this alone makes a stop-loss strategy a money loser. Brokers love stop losses and promote them to this day because they know stock prices are volatile and when a stock moves through the stop-loss price, they get two commissions! One as you sell and one as you reinvest.

Dollar Cost Averaging—Higher Fees, Lower Returns

Most investors accept without question that *dollar cost averaging* (DCA)—spreading out investment additions or contributions over time—is a good strategy for reducing risk and possibly increasing return. If you add regularly to your 401(k) or other retirement saving plan, in essence, you're dollar cost averaging.

Regularly adding to your retirement saving plan is absolutely rational. First, many investors don't have the cash flow from their paychecks readily available to fully fund their 401(k)s, 403(b)s, or other plans all at once, preferring to make smaller regular contributions monthly or at other intervals. Second, many companies match contributions to a retirement saving plan, which equates to risk-free growth of your account. I'm always a fan of free money. Third, you should always max out every vehicle available for retirement saving.

Any other form of DCA is costly. DCA is intuitively appealing. Investors are concerned the day they buy could be a relative high point. Spreading it out over time, so goes the thinking, reduces the risk of getting all in on a "bad" day. If you did get in with all your money on a "bad" day, you would have a lot of regret and people hate regret.

DCA is seldom mentioned by the media when returns are robust, like the late 1990s. In boom times, its supposed benefits are lauded only by brokers. DCA is a boon to brokers. Why? The industry typically charges more commissions per dollar traded on small trades than large. When you break your money up into many little pieces, the total commissions on your total assets rises markedly, all to the broker. The broker tells customers it's all in the interest of managing risk, and the customers rarely figure it out.

However, data show DCA hurts a portfolio's risk and return characteristics. Michael Rozeff at University at Buffalo (SUNY) conducted an especially thorough study about 10 years ago, comparing DCA with single lump-sum investments.

Using the S&P 500 as an investment choice, each calendar year from 1926 to 1990 Rozeff compared the results of a single lump-sum purchase to averaging the purchase over 12 months. The results were conclusive: in about two-thirds of the years, the lump-sum method proved more profitable than DCA with less return variability. More importantly, for the entire span, the lump-sum approach yielded 1.1 percent higher average annual returns than DCA. When applied to a portfolio of small stocks, the advantages of the lump-sum approach were even more dramatic, with an average annual return that was 3.9 percent greater than a DCA strategy.[1]

My firm has done our own studies with similar conclusions. Lump-sum investing works better than DCA on average because the market moves higher in the future more often than not. Not always, but enough to make DCA irrational.

Discovering DCA is an inferior strategy doesn't require fancy math or analysis, and the findings are compelling. The reason why this myth persists can be dispelled with Question Three and the concept that people feel the pain of a financial loss more than twice as much as they enjoy a similar-sized gain.[2] Investors are inclined to accept an inferior strategy like DCA because it eliminates any possibility of one big mistake that would cause big regret accumulation and maybe make your spouse see you as an idiot (probably already does). People think DCA reduces risk so they think it's smart. DCA actually increases risk and reduces future returns. No matter what substantial gains they miss out on in the long run, most investors feel giving up profits hurts only about half as much as suffering losses.

(continued)

Simply put: Dollar cost averaging doesn't work and only benefits your broker with higher total fees. You're better off without DCA even though that feels wrong. Your feelings are your enemy here once again—always existing so TGH can use them against you even when you think you're beating him.

COVERED CALLS—COVERING WHAT?

For years, brokerage houses have offered clients covered calls, which combine a long stock position and a written call. Investors like this for two reasons: They can gain instant income (from the premium for writing the option) and they see it as safe because there is limited risk from the option. The general consensus among investors would be that covered calls are safe or "conservative."

But what exactly is a covered call? This is best shown by graphing the potential pay outs at the exercise date. As with all option positions, the range of possible exercise profits and losses are known. The x-axis shows the stock price at the exercise date, and the y-axis shows profit or loss from this position. X indicates the strike price of the option:

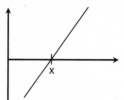
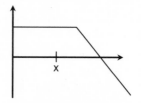
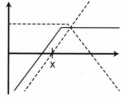

(a) A stock, S, has a value and payout that are always the same. S has unlimited gain potential, and loss potential equal to the purchase prices.

(b) A written call has a gain limited to the premium received, and unlimited loss potential for increasing stock prices.

(c) With the combination of S and the written call, for values greater than X, the gain becomes a fixed positive amount. This combination still has loss potential as S decreases to 0.

So the covered call actually pays out a fixed amount for an increasing stock price (thereby limiting your potential upside), but still has the stock's downside risk, less only the premium received.

This does not sound so appealing anymore. The fact is, this is exactly the same pay out that a naked put would have! There is no difference.

And finance theory tells us that two securities that have identical pay-
outs are, indeed, the same security:

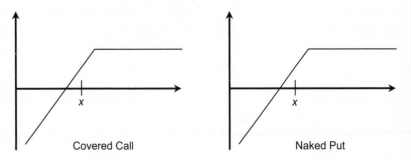

Covered Call   Naked Put

Of course, most investors would frown on the idea of selling a
naked put, but that is really what they do with covered calls.

So the perceived safety in a covered call is just that—perception.
With a naked written put and a covered call being equal, they should be
viewed equally. This is a strong case of investors being confused by the
framework in which identical information is provided. In standard finance theory, investors are rational and never confused by frameworks,
but in reality people blindly do covered calls thinking they're safe when
they would never write the naked put because to them it seems highly
risky—fooled by framework.

So the next time someone wants you to invest in covered calls—you
should just ask them to sell a naked put: It is the exact same thing!

A strategy is a plan guiding your every decision. It keeps you disciplined
when you're tempted to stray. The market simply isn't intuitive—one reason
so many fail at it. Usually what's right feels wrong; and what feels wrong
often is right. This is why you need the Questions and a strategy to keep your
brain in gear.

Before you begin thinking about a strategy, let's establish a few ground
rules about what you can hope to achieve. Ask anyone what their investing
goals are and you'll find a plethora of confounding answers. Think of your
own goals. Can you describe them in four words or less? If it takes 10 pages
with accompanying visuals, you've been swayed by a financial salesperson
who wants you to believe you have unique goals unlike those of millions of
others—ones requiring a stunning array of fancy financial products.

No, it should be fairly straightforward. Investors have long been instructed by the financial services industry to categorize their goals across a broad spectrum of often confusing or conflicting categories. If you've met with a broker or a financial planner, they probably asked you how "risk-tolerant" you are. Most investors don't know and aren't trained to quantify their own risk tolerance. They see it as one thing after a bull market and very differently after a long bear market. Your inquirer may have had you fill out a questionnaire to determine what kind of investor you are—which really reflects how you feel that day. Are you a "growth" investor or even "aggressive growth?" Are you "growth and income?" Maybe they had you pick from a selection of colorful pie graphs or rank yourself on a scale of 1-to-7, or 1-to-10, or 1-to-37.

Here's the dirty secret. These so-called risk rankings don't mean anything—simply reflect no reality. So-called "risk tolerance" for anyone varies when confronted with varying circumstances. The same folks who filled out questionnaires in 1999 saying they were highly risk tolerant and sought 20 percent returns year-after-year, in 2002 and 2003 were saying they were risk averse and merely wanted low, safe, absolute returns. But it gets much more detailed than that. Most people are simply unable to assess how risk tolerant they are any more than most people who've never taken a hard punch to the gut can know how they'll feel emotionally after one—until it happens to them a number of times and various ways—like a boxer. I used to be a boxer and I know from my gut.

I've met few investors who really had a good handle on their risk tolerance. Most simply haven't a clue; they just have a feeling at a point in time. Their sense of their risk tolerance is molded by what they've read recently, what has happened to them recently, who they're talking to, and what they think they're supposed to say in response to such questions. Often it's different if they're with their spouse and offspring or not. It's a lot easier for a guy to fancy a pirate's lifestyle buccaneering the South Seas for adventure and booty when he's alone watching a pirate movie than with his wife. Pretty often you ask a man how risk tolerant he is, and he says he is very risk tolerant and can handle volatility. Later you meet the wife and describe her husband as risk tolerant and she laughs. I kid you not. Happens all the time. Is the husband wrong? The wife? Everyone is wrong because they all treat risk as if it were a uni-dimensional metric. It's not!

As Meir Statman and I demonstrated in a scholarly article titled "The Mean Variance Optimization Puzzle: Security Portfolios and Food Portfolios,"[3] risk is multifaceted and virtually impossible to fully comprehend in any moment for anyone. Your brain deals with investing risk just like it does with food and diet. Eaters and investors want at least six things at once—in both investing and their next meal. The risk they feel at any time is tied to whichever of those things they're not getting without regard for how they would feel if they didn't get the things they *are* getting. Your brain just can't put it all together at once—it fixates on what it isn't getting and to you that's risk.

I won't fully rehash that article here. But investors not only want return, of course, they want to keep up with the Joneses, or not to suffer from excess opportunity cost. This is why the person who envisions he only wants 10 percent a year actually feels angst when the market is up 35 percent and he is only up 20 percent. It's risk. Investors also fear volatility and see it as risk. It is. Finance theory has been excessive in portraying volatility as the risk measure. But it's just one risk and preys more on some than others. Of course, investors want pricing. Different investors want the pricing differently but they feel risk if it becomes inconsistent with their sense of what it should be. They want packaging. Packaging ripples into all the other risks, but includes presentation, ease of use, and part of the sense of confidence implying safety and less risk that is basic to all marketing. They want prestige. Prestige can mean many things including branding (appealing to that sense of uniqueness), a general sense of safety or lack of risk from perceived quality, and a sense of higher social order than others. Another way to think of this is "bragging rights," that is, "I got in on Google's IPO and you didn't." But if you take the prestige away suddenly it feels like risk to them.

Then they want order preference. Few appreciate how important order preference is to everyone but you can see it two ways in diet. One is why people eat breakfast foods in the morning and dinner foods at night—why not switch them around? Same calories and yet people largely obey order even when no one is looking. The second is how people don't experiment with the foods they combine. Why not try putting salad dressing in your coffee and cream on your salad or even your steak to see how it would taste? Might be better! You don't try because it violates order preference. And if you tried that in public at a restaurant, the people with whom you dine won't dine with you again. They would think you were a nut.

My point is, at any moment, the risk you notice and fret it associated with what you're *not* getting. And you can't make your brain realize all the other things that you *are* getting and how you would feel—how you would experience the risk—about not getting some combination of them. Very few folks have any real clue of how they'll feel confronting risk in the future. At this point it has never been measured in a meaningful way domestically or overseas, but I'd guess, and it's only a guess, less than 5 percent of society has a real clue about their risk tolerance and I'm delighted to include myself in that other 95 percent. And I'd bet you're in the other 95 percent too.

Another important point is the questionnaires and the "investor-types" and the colored charts and graphs aren't for you. They're for the salesperson and his firm. For the salesperson, "risk tolerance" translates into, "Number one—what is this sucker likely to buy? Number two—what will cover my tuckus when he tries to sue me later?" It's a sales technique and a legal defense technique—little more. Once they know how you categorize yourself, they know not only what to sell you but how to defend themselves under the "Know Your Client Rule" if you attack them later in court or arbitration. Having engaged in this catechism doesn't mean the things they sold you were appropriate for you. Only that you were inclined toward whatever it was that particular day. Strawberry, please, not chocolate.

Growth—Or Income—Or Both—That's It

You're a unique, wonderful person, I have no doubt; however, you're probably unique just about like everyone else. You're not statistically unique. In a statistical sense, being unique is to be way, way out the end of the bell curve on some set of attributes. If you're really unique, you're technically quite weird. Unique means weird. Most folks like to think of themselves as unique. They don't like to see themselves as weirdos. You probably share extremely similar investing goals with about 98 percent of humanity.

What you have are goals that feel unique to you but almost certainly are very similar to most people. The people who are most certain they're unique are almost always by definition narcissists. Narcissists always think they're unique which by definition means they're not. It's just a cognitive error. But society commonly says everyone is unique. It's touchy-feel-good and politically correct! The financial services industry sells into that with a blister of products supposedly suited uniquely to you. You're not unique unless you're weird. The real and common investing goals people have are quite straightforward, and you don't need a questionnaire or a graph to figure them out. Here's what they are.

Maximize Terminal Value against a Primary Purpose

You're either looking to grow your portfolio to fund retirement, to purchase something now or in the future (a first or second home, a college education, or a boat perhaps), or to pass to loved ones or a favorite charity. You might also think of this goal as "growth." But "maximizing terminal value" isn't necessarily increasing your pot of money. You might be drawing down more cash to spend each year than your investment returns generate—purposefully shrinking your pot of money—yet you still need to stretch your assets further. For example, a common response when asking someone what the primary purpose of his or her money is that it's to take care of him or her and the spouse for the remainder of their lives. That may involve growing their total money or simply stretching it. But it's probably the most common single case among investors everywhere. Very real! Very basic!

Cash Flow

Many investors say the purpose of their money is to provide "income" to cover living expenses. They want some level of income or cash flow now or in the future. In an extreme example, some folks might be very happy if Daddy simply died and left a guaranteed income stream and they had no say in the investments and not necessarily any knowledge of how the assets are invested. Just like Gertrude Stein. Party time!

Of course, the party-time inheritor isn't really concerned with "income" as that term is technically defined. What she wants is predictable and secure cash flow. This is right and as it should be. Finance theory is clear we should be agnostic about our preferences for type of cash flow on a real, tax and risk-adjusted basis. For example, after-tax, we shouldn't care if our cash flow comes from dividends (which may be risky or not) or capital gains (which may be risky or not). Income streams are neither better nor worse for generating total return than capital gains. We should care about total return after adjustment for tax and risk—otherwise how the cash flow comes is unimportant.

Cash flow needs are exceedingly important to investors. Too many investors were raised with no appropriate sense of how to think about this. Hence it's a key part of client education at my firm and should be everywhere—teaching clients how to think about cash flows consistent with their needs because most haven't been taught beforehand.

Terminal value or cash flow—that's it! Typically most investors are either looking for one or the other goal, or for some combination of the two. (Although there is a very wide variety of subsets falling under these headings, such as, "I want to leave as much as I can after I die to the Save the Seals League," which means maximizing terminal value, in this case for the purpose of charity.) Sound fair? For example, an investor who is 50 may see the primary purpose of his money as taking care of him (or her) and a spouse for the rest of their lives—but they have a secondary purpose of leaving a certain amount to their offspring and more to charity. They want to maximize the likelihood of that being done successfully by maximizing their terminal value at the end of their lives. Doing so allows the cash flow they need to support their lifestyle while leaving a present for the kids and the seals. That seals it for them. Most every investor is somewhere on the scale of either needing terminal value, cash flow, or both. You must be off that spectrum to be really unique (or weird).

There is yet a third possible goal—capital preservation. True capital preservation means taking absolutely no risk to preserve the nominal value of your assets. Investors often claim they want capital preservation, but this is almost infinitely more often claimed than true. As a long-term goal it rarely makes sense. True capital preservation in the long-term is only appropriate if you know you already have much more money than you'll ever need—so you have no desire for more and your primary purpose is to minimize your worry or hassle-factor. Then it can make sense, but there are precious few such folks.

On a shorter-term basis, it makes sense if you're young and saving for the down-payment on a home in six months. It makes complete sense to preserve the cash needed for that home in a low-risk instrument such as a CD. But generally, if you bought this book, you're not stashing your cash under the mattress and have some longer-term purpose for your money. Capital preservation is the polar opposite of growth. You often hear investors hankering for—and you certainly hear marketing from firms offering up—"capital preservation and growth." Most folks who desire this would also like to get a fat-free steak. Thinking of it, I'd love one but I know it's impossible. Don't let anyone tell you the two are possible at the same time. They aren't.

Why are growth and capital preservation together a complete and total impossibility? To get growth, you must take some risk. Capital preservation is the absence of risk. The notion of combining the two implies riskless return which is impossible. Now, if your goal is growth, and 20 years from now your account has doubled three times (which isn't unlikely if you benchmark against an equity index), you have effectively grown your account and preserved your initial capital to boot. Sure, during those 20 years your account was up and down with the market, but who cares? You got growth while enduring volatility and other risks. You had a long time frame, and at the end of the day you got your equity-like return. But if your goal is really capital preservation, 20 years from now you'll still have your initial capital and nothing else.

If someone in the finance world offers you "capital preservation and growth," know they either don't know what they're doing or they're deceiving you—blissfully ignorant or ill-intended—either way dangerous. Saying "capital preservation and growth" is like saying "a selfless politician," "a mature child," or "love plus date rape." The two have nothing to do with each other. The industry loves selling capital preservation and growth. It sounds warm, comforting and fuzzy—like a cute and cuddly puppy. Who doesn't want to protect what they have and grow at the same darn time—and who doesn't love puppies? Which is why the suggestion of growth and capital preservation is insidious.

Make no mistake. Most investors need some degree of growth or they wouldn't bother with stocks, bonds, or anything involving risk in the first place. If your goal is to never lose a dime over any period—true capital preservation—you should have saved what you paid for this book and stashed it under your mattress. Of course, even if your goal is avoiding all monetary loss, the mattress stash isn't the best bet because of inflation's long-term effect. Inflation risk is the weak underbelly of those seeking capital preservation. How do you preserve capital without risk if inflation ignites? It really is hard, if not impossible, to avoid all risk.

The Richest Have It Tough!

Consider this at the very rich end. Since 1982, each Fall *Forbes* magazine analyzes and lists the 400 richest Americans—the *Forbes* 400. The individuals change a lot over the years. It isn't easy staying on that list. New people come in from below by doing really well. People on the list suffer bad fates and drop off. The bottom 50 names are in constant flux. Via the 2005 issue the poorest member of the *Forbes* 400 was worth $900 million.[4] There were actually 17 of them tied at that level. But in 1982—not quite two years before my *Forbes* column started—the poorest member, number 400, was worth $75 million.[5] Staying on the list over the ensuing 23 years required that poorest little 1982 rich boy to increase his net worth by at least 11.5 percent per year (after-tax). That's scary. Just to stay on the *Forbes* 400 people had to do about as well as the S&P 500 after-tax, which you know precious few people do. Only about 10 percent of the original members of the 1982 *Forbes* 400 are still there. That is very consistent with few professional investors beating the market. Sure, some dropped off the list by death, but many more simply couldn't achieve enough growth to keep up with their peers. It isn't easy.

How about cash flow as a goal? Since the company pension has been falling out of favor, many investors must rely on savings, whether via a 401(k) or other vehicles, to fund retirement. But how much consumable cash flow can you expect your assets to produce without running the risk of having to return to work at age 85? An imperfect, rough rule of thumb is about 4 percent of your portfolio or less. That is a gross generalization. If you have a shorter time horizon you can safely consume more—with a longer time horizon, less. But if you need $50,000 in today's dollars to maintain your lifestyle and you have a long time horizon, you should retire with at least $1,250,000 (also today's dollars). And even then it might not be enough if future returns are low and inflation is above average. Remember, there are no guarantees. Risk is ever present.

Think you may need more than 4 percent cash flow from your assets? As the percentage increases, so does the likelihood your money runs out before you do. If you don't have heirs or still haven't forgiven your kids for throwing that keg party when you were off to Europe, then depletion is a lesser worry. Let the final check bounce, as they say.

To figure out the probability your nest egg will keep supporting your lifestyle, you can do a simple Monte Carlo simulation. You can find a good Monte Carlo simulator at http://www.moneychimp.com/articles/volatility /montecarlo.htm. In general, you'll find annual distributions of 4 percent or less of your asset size improve your odds and are your best bet. Anything higher and you may find yourself sharpening your job skills in retirement instead of lowering your handicap.

Four Rules That Count

So—terminal value or cash flow or both! But how do you achieve those goals? And how do you stop the failure cycle and start being right more often than wrong? Just as you don't need advanced scholarship or apprenticeship to learn to use the Questions, building a strategy is as easy as following four rules I employ every day in managing money:

Rule Number One: Select an appropriate benchmark.
Rule Number Two: Analyze the benchmark's components and assign expected risk and return.
Rule Number Three: Blend noncorrelated or negatively correlated securities to moderate risk relative to expected return.
Rule Number Four: Always remember you can be wrong, so don't stray from the first three rules.

Let's examine these four rules more closely.

Rule Number One—Select an Appropriate Benchmark

You know the benchmark is vital to success. You know what a benchmark should be (well-constructed) and what it shouldn't be (priced-weighted like the Dow). As important, your benchmark should be appropriate for you. It will dictate your volatility, your return expectation, even to some extent what ends up in your portfolio—it's your road map, your measuring stick. You can't change it soon unless something really radical happens to you changing the primary purpose of your money—like your wife (or husband) and kids all die, heaven help you, also causing you to no longer feel charitable. So it's crucial you select the right benchmark for you.

Your benchmark can be all equity (as we discussed), all fixed income, or a blend of the two. Picking a benchmark—deciding if you need an all-equity, blended, or even an all fixed income benchmark—depends on four things, and only four things. Throw the nonsense "risk tolerance" baloney out the window. The only four factors for figuring which benchmark is appropriate for you are: (1) your time horizon, (2) how much cash flow you need and when, (3) your return expectations, and (4) the off chance that you have weird but strong felt views like you hate the French or don't want to own stocks that produce you-name-it—tofu—I hate that stuff.

The First Determinant—Time Horizon

Your time horizon may be your life expectancy but is likely longer. Unless you hate your spouse, you should consider his or her life expectancy as well. That may extend your time horizon as your spouse may outlive you. If you like your kids and want to leave something behind for them, that also extends your time horizon. Simply put, your time horizon is how long you need your assets to last. Your time horizon is decidedly not how long it is until you retire or start taking distributions. Far too many investors think exactly wrong about time horizon; they aren't using Questions One and Two to see this clearly. The industry even promotes wrongheaded thinking, likely in an effort to sell static asset allocation or other inappropriate but feel-good products.

I couldn't tell you how often I hear someone say, "I'm retiring, so I must become conservative and I can't take risk." Legions of people say that but it's usually wrong. Suppose you're a 65-year-old man and your wife is 60 and she is likely to live to 90 (very common). Then, you have a 30-year time horizon that includes a third of her whole life and you better take risk and have an eq- uity benchmark or she is likely to suffer aged poverty. Now, if you really hate her, then aged poverty is a pretty good idea. It is, after all, more brutal in the long-term than just punching her now. I think you get my point. But I can't tell you how many times I've seen the older husband with the younger wife with a long horizon investing as if he hated his wife without realizing what he was doing because he was managing their money based on his life expectancy rather than hers. From time to time, I ask them if they hate their wives and they always get mad at me. You may have some reasonable date in mind for when you plan to start living off your assets, but the money still needs to work your whole life or beyond, or you or your loved ones will suffer. That whole period is your time horizon.

You might have a shorter time horizon, for some reason—maybe you're a 32-year-old who needs every penny to pay for that first home in three years. But in most cases, investors tend to grossly underestimate their time horizons. Because my father died at 96 and my mother is still alive at 87 and I have been both of their conservators in their agedness, it's darned easy for me to envision long time horizons. It's late in life people need their money because there are so many comforts that benefit the aged that aren't covered by any form of health insurance.

Figure 9.1 helps you think about how your time horizon relates to your benchmark. The longer your time horizon, the more equity is appropriate in your benchmark.

Stocks or Bonds? The 929 Percent Question

If your time horizon is over 15 years—and if you're reading this book it probably is—an all-equity benchmark is probably most appropriate for you. Over long time periods, stocks are by far the best performing liquid asset class

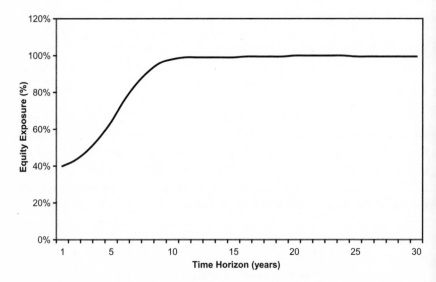

Figure 9.1   Benchmark and Time Horizon.

and the likelihood of stocks outperforming bonds is great. Since 1926, there have been 66 15-year rolling time periods. In 61 of them (92 percent), stocks beat bonds, returning an average of 481 percent while bonds returned 150 percent.[6] That is a 3.2 to 1 out-performance. The five times bonds outperformed stocks, the margin was only 2.3 to 1.

If you have a 20-year time horizon (or more—and you probably do), the odds are stacked even more heavily in your favor if you have an all-equity benchmark. In 60 of the 61 20-year rolling time periods since 1926, stocks have outperformed bonds by still greater proportions.[7] That's over 98 percent of the time. In return for investing in stocks over a 20-year period, folks got an average return of 929 percent compared to 240 percent for bonds. During the one 20-year period (January 1, 1929 through December 31, 1948) when bonds beat stocks, bonds returned 115 percent and stocks 84 percent.[8] Big whoop! That one time period included the global Great Depression and a World War, by the way (not to mention the creation of the SEC, the emergence of Blues, and, of course, Al Capone, Gertrude Stein's one big hit, and Stalin). In the highly unlikely event that bonds outperform stocks over the next 20 years, you probably wouldn't get much more bang for your buck. It's clearly better to take on the odds and get the superior return.

You may feel as though I'm banging an equity drum. Guilty as charged. I am a big fan of stocks because of their superior longer-term returns (and lots of other reasons—recall that I pray at the altar of Capitalism's multitudinous blessings and you can't have Capitalism without stocks). However, there are times when stocks do lousy—in a bear market—and avoiding a down-a-lot world through cash holdings becomes a great tactic. But it's not a strategy.

The Second Determinant—Cash Flow

The other time a 100 percent equity benchmark may be inappropriate has to do with the second determinant of benchmark selection—cash flow. If you need 3 percent or less each year from your assets, you probably don't need a blended benchmark and the all-equity option is probably most appropriate. An all-equity benchmark should get you the inflation-adjusted cash flow you need while still appreciating over time. Suppose you do need 4 percent each year (or even more, though I don't recommend taking that much) but you're more concerned the assets grow as much as possible over your time horizon. If so, you also should use an all-equity benchmark.

Now suppose you're drawing close to retirement or plan on taking money from your portfolio on a regular basis for some other reason. You've saved $1 million in your 401(k) and IRA and some taxable savings combined. You know that starting in three or five years, or maybe even next month, you'll want $40,000 a year to help cover your living expenses. Let's also say you don't care one whit about leaving anything to your kids or grandkids. Couldn't care less—call them "ungrateful degenerates." Your primary focus is ensuring you get your $40,000 per year, adjusted for inflation of course. Then, having some fixed income as part of your benchmark may be appropriate—maybe something like 70 percent equity and 30 percent fixed income.

Actually, I'm a bit goosey about this blended allocation approach due to the well-known "curmudgeon factor." I've seen some pretty big curmudgeons through my decades helping investors. And I doubt you're a bigger curmudgeon than I am. (It's probably obvious—I'm very opinionated and pretty independent.) In observing curmudgeons, as they age, many get a softer heart for their "ungrateful degenerates" and finally wish they had more to leave them and would have been better served had they earlier assumed a longer time horizon and a need for higher returns. Think about it.

Even with a blended benchmark—60 percent equity and 40 percent fixed income or 70 percent/30 percent or whatever—there may come a time when you should boost your cash to 100 percent to be defensive temporarily, and you shouldn't get lulled into a false sense of security with a fixed allocation. Your benchmark is your road map, but not necessarily what you own all the time. In a major bear market you'll still lose money with a rigid fixed allocation. Sometimes you need a detour. Or a dividend!

Homegrown Dividends

Another reason investors hit a panic button at or near retirement and plow all of their hard-earned assets into bonds and high-dividend paying stocks is they think they need the coupon payments and dividends for income. They believe if they kick off a decent percent in income, they can sit back and let the portfolio provide for retirement. As mentioned earlier, this confuses *income* with *cash flow.*

Use Question One for this myth—and it is a myth. Is it true a portfolio stacked with bonds and high-dividend stocks will provide income throughout retirement? Maybe! Maybe you're worth $10 million and want only $50,000 a year. Maybe you don't need the assets to grow so your income remains inflation-adjusted. Maybe it doesn't matter much if you see your assets diminished through reinvestment risk or if the high-dividend paying stocks tank in value.

But most folks can't afford to have their assets stagnate or decrease significantly throughout retirement. What happens when you reinvest a maturing 9 percent bond from 1997, and the only thing you can buy in 2007 that isn't risky yields 5 percent? And how about when that dandy utility stock paying an 8 percent dividend depreciates 40 percent in price? Eight percent of 40 percent less market value is probably not what you were banking on. And what about inflation?

It's simply not true coupon payments and dividends are a "safe" way to garner income from your portfolio. But how else do you get cash? If you have an all-equity benchmark and you need cash flow, you don't want to sell stock to provide cash for yourself. Do you?

I can't tell you how many investors I've heard over the decades say, "The last thing I'll ever do is use any of my principal." Why the heck not? What's it there for? This is a Question Two solution I've come up with for maintaining healthy growth while providing cash flow from portfolios, and I call them home-grown dividends.

Let's say you have a million dollar portfolio, and you take $40,000 a year in even monthly distributions of $3,333 a month—give or take. You should keep about twice that much in cash in your portfolio at all times so you don't rush to sell a nit-picky number of stocks each month. Then, you can be tactical about what you sell and when. But you're always looking to prune back, planning for distributions a month or two out. You can sell down stocks to use as a tax-loss to offset gains you might realize. You can pare back positions that are over-weighted. You'll probably always have some dividend-paying stocks to add some cash, but that is a derivative of picking the right kinds. Homegrown dividends are tax-efficient, cheap to raise, and keep you fully and appropriately invested.

The Third Determinant—Return Expectation

The third factor in selecting an appropriate benchmark is return expectation. If you're 50 and want to retire in five years and need $500 thousand a year to maintain your lifestyle and have $2 million you're in for a caught-with-your-pants-down rude awakening. Your return expectations are gonzo high. Unless you anticipate a windfall on the order of $10 million (or so) sometime in the in-your-dreams future, plan instead on taking $80,000 a year or less and get over it. Or keep working. Start figuring out a way to explain this to your wife (or husband) now.

But imagine an investor, call her Jane, who has a reliable income source lined up for her retirement (a pension, perhaps, with some rental income). She doesn't need her assets to grow to provide for her and her husband. Jane intends to leave her money to her kids but doesn't really care about "maximizing terminal value." Instead she is nervous about volatility and looking for that "sleep-at-night" factor. I'd still recommend an all-equity benchmark and some warm milk.

Why? Because Jane has a long time horizon and needs no income. She may think she is "risk averse"—but remember, how much risk investors can handle has nothing to do with their prior feelings. As stated earlier, few investors envision their future risk orientation correctly. I'll repeat that—it has *nothing to do with feelings*. Many people in the industry try to make you think it does, but it's not true. A few years down the road Jane will get used to volatility.

The Fourth Determinant—Individual Peculiarity

Just because most investors have similar goals and aren't as unique as they think doesn't mean they're not peculiar. This isn't about "being uncomfortable" with foreign investing, health care stocks, tech, emerging markets, or whatever because that is more stubbornness than peculiarity. This is about having strong feelings about a particular company or a narrow sector deriving from personal belief or peculiarity. And it's okay to create a customized benchmark reflecting your own weird idiosyncrasies.

Suppose you really do hate the French so you don't want to own French stocks. Well if you do, were I you, I'd prefer to buy their assets cheaply and sell them back at higher prices later. It's about the cruelest thing you can do to those you dislike—legally with head held high. But you may feel differently about it. Some folks do. You may simply want to never, ever own a French stock. Or the stock of a firm making tobacco products. Or a firm making tofu (ugh!). Whatever! Your idiosyncrasies are up to you. It's fine to have a customized benchmark that is the World ex-France. Or the World ex-France and ex-tofu. Or whatever bizarre (or not so bizarre) moral code you sport. Since all major categories have similar long-term returns, the degree of return variation caused by those slight variances from a vastly bigger and maybe global benchmark won't be enough to count. And they'll make you feel better about what you're doing so you're more likely to keep doing it. There are no investors who have had a bad investing history having otherwise done portfolio management right because they chose to create their own customized benchmark that was the World ex-Iowa (for those of you who divorced someone from there once. Still, were I you, I'd rather get my revenge on the Iowans by buying Iowa stocks too cheap).

Whatever it is, you may have strong enough personal feelings to warrant a particular benchmark free from some offending stock or microsector. But watch if you start having feelings about whole sectors, because that might be driven more by loss aversion and hindsight bias than your own individual freakiness. Plenty of investors decided they had developed a severe allergic reaction to tech post-2002. That is a cognitive error, not a peculiarity.

So, the amount of risk you can handle has to do with (say it with me) (1) time horizon, (2) income needs, (3) return expectation, and (4) extreme individual peculiarities. Jane thinks she is risk averse now, but in 1999 considered herself aggressive and was overweight to tech stocks and now thinks she has learned. She might feel differently again—maybe aggressive about energy. Feelings can change fast—they don't mean much. What does mean much is how long your assets must last and how much cash flow you will take. And, of course, if you're morally opposed to tobacco now, you probably will be in the future too. That won't go up in smoke.

Hey, I'm not saying you must have the all-equity benchmark if it will cause (or exacerbate) ulcers. I'm just saying the cause of the ulcers may be something else. Explore it a bit.

Heat Chasing—To Shift or Not to Shift

Choose your benchmark carefully, because once selected, it's yours for a very long time, maybe the entire life of your assets. Forever and ever, Amen. Superficial benchmark shifting is a recipe for disaster. Let's call benchmark shifting what it really is—heat chasing. When someone shifts their benchmark from the Nasdaq in 1999 to the Russell 2000 Value Index in 2005, you know they were matching their benchmark to what had been hot—simple heat chasing. People chasing heat, trying to get better returns, forget about transaction costs and taxes and invariably in-and-out relatively backward—lagging the market by going into what used to work instead of what will work.

You now know all well-constructed benchmarks will get to about the same place over the very long-term. If you get the urge to switch benchmarks, check yourself and ask Question Three. Benchmark switching is the direct result of regret shunning and pride accumulation, possibly some order preference and overconfidence to boot. Don't give in. If you switch, you usually end up chasing heat and missing returns altogether. Only heartache and harm comes from it.

There are two good exceptions to this rule—only two. One is if something happens to drastically change the primary purposes of your money, including your time horizon. This is the 75 year-old in bad health from a short-lived family with a 70-year-old wife in good health from a long-lived family where the wife dies unexpectedly in a car crash. No kids, no charity, and his time horizon just collapsed. That's a good justification for switching to a benchmark more appropriate for a new shorter and sadder time horizon. Or, the other way around! Maybe late in life you remarry a younger or healthier person, extending your time horizon. It would be okay to switch to a more appropriate benchmark then, too.

The second reason to switch benchmarks, beyond a change in the fundamentals of your life, is if a future benchmark is created reflecting the same universe as your current benchmark—but the new one is somehow better constructed. This is purely tactical. Here is an example: The MSCI World Index is an excellent, broad benchmark but it doesn't include so-called emerging markets, restricting itself to developed markets. Then, MSCI created the ACWI. Same construction but broader. That should be better for the whole world.

Should you use one over the other? In my mind it isn't a big deal one way or the other and I'm prone to not switching—it's hard to argue the one is drastically superior to the other. If you're currently using the MSCI World, the time to switch would be when ACWI was older, after a period when emerging markets had done lousy for years.

The whole World versus ACWI issue is sort of like choosing either the northern 80/90 route or the southern 70/44/40 route to motor across America. Either is an okay benchmark and gets from East to West Coast just fine. But if there were a new world index—improved and drastically more reflective of the whole world stock market—that would justify switching, too. What I want you to see is it takes something pretty material to justify a benchmark switch.

Rule Number Two—Analyze the Benchmark's Components, Assign Expected Risk and Return

The second rule of portfolio management helps determine what exactly belongs in your portfolio, how much, and when. It's a lot less complicated than it sounds. Your benchmark, particularly if you use a broad one, will be made up of different components, as discussed in Chapter 4. The Nasdaq is fairly easy—do you think tech will do well this year or not? But unless you seek an exceedingly bumpy ride, we've already established you're not using Nasdaq as your benchmark.

No matter which benchmark you pick, it's your guide for building your portfolio. If your benchmark is about 60 percent U.S. stocks, your portfolio should be about 60 percent U.S. stocks unless you've used the Questions to know something others don't. (If you have, you might at a point in time own no stocks at all.) If your benchmark is about 10 percent energy, you should be about 10 percent energy if you don't know something others don't through the Questions. (But if you think you know something others don't, you might own no energy, 5 percent energy, or be double weight at 20 percent energy because you have the basis for a bet.) Your aim is to perform similarly to your benchmark if you don't know something others don't and better than the benchmark if you do know something. Of course, the more you know that others don't, the bigger you'll make your bets and the more dissimilar you'll be to your benchmark. (If you can't recall how the heck to tell what "components" are in your benchmark, flip back to Chapter 4.)

Nervous about doing it right? Don't be. If you have less than $200 thousand or so to invest, you will probably and primarily be buying funds anyway. There are plenty of index funds that can get you the exposure you need. For example, if the S&P 500 is your benchmark, you're covered beautifully with an S&P 500 index fund. Using the MSCI World or ACWI as your benchmark? Check www.mscibarra.com for the approximate weight of the United States relative to the world (it's been fluctuating around 50/50). Buy the aforementioned S&P 500 index fund with half your dough, and an MSCI EAFE (Europe, Australia, Far East) index fund. Want to beat the market? It's harder to do if you have fewer choices to make, as you will with funds. This is why a broad benchmark with lots of components gives you more market beating opportunities. You can use your Three Questions to make foreign versus U.S. bets. And you can use other ETFs to make bets on sectors or styles without ever owning individual stocks, which is hard to do with a smaller portfolio.

If you're richer, you can and should buy individual stocks. The more money you have, the higher the proportion that should be in underlying stocks because in large volume stocks are cheaper to own than anything including mutual funds, ETFs, or any other form of equity. One benefit of stocks is they're cheap to buy and pretty much free to hold. But whether ETFs or individual stocks—start paying attention to individual sectors and subsectors now. All this information is also on the index's web page. For example, your components and their weights will look something like Table 9.1, where we have listed the percentage weights of countries and sectors in the MSCI World Index as of June 30, 2006.

You should check back periodically to ensure nothing has gotten out of whack. Don't feel compelled to rebalance if your portfolio or the benchmark has shifted a few percentage points here and there. Don't sweat the small stuff. Think about rebalancing once or twice a year unless there is a major sector or country move or you come upon something in between where suddenly

Table 9.1 MSCI World Weights

SECTOR	WEIGHT
FINANCIALS	25.6%
CONSUMER DISCRETIONARY	11.2%
INDUSTRIALS	10.8%
INFORMATION TECHNOLOGY	10.4%
ENERGY	9.9%
HEALTH CARE	9.6%
CONSUMER STAPLES	8.0%
MATERIALS	6.1%
TELECOMMUNICATION SERVICES	4.2%
UTILITIES	4.1%
GRAND TOTAL	**100.0%**

COUNTRY	WEIGHT
USA	49.5%
JAPAN	11.5%
UNITED KINGDOM	11.3%
FRANCE	4.6%
CANADA	3.8%
GERMANY	3.3%
SWITZERLAND	3.2%
AUSTRALIA	2.5%
SPAIN	1.8%
ITALY	1.8%
NETHERLANDS	1.5%
SWEDEN	1.1%
HONG KONG	0.8%
FINLAND	0.7%
BELGIUM	0.5%
NORWAY	0.4%
SINGAPORE	0.4%
IRELAND	0.4%
DENMARK	0.3%
GREECE	0.3%
AUSTRIA	0.3%
PORTUGAL	0.2%
NEW ZEALAND	0.1%
GRAND TOTAL	**100.0%**

Source: Thomson Financial Datastream, as of June 30, 2006.

you know something others don't. You'll make fewer mistakes and pay fewer fees. Trading too often is a by-product of overconfidence (thinking you have the basis for a bet when you don't).

With benchmark components in hand, move on to assigning expected risk and return. This too is easier than it sounds. Suppose you're using the ACWI. It's made up of 48 countries including America.[9] Which countries should perform well this year, and which should lag? Here's one way to think about it—which countries have a narrower economy prone to greater volatility fits? The United States is a very broad economy, the broadest, and likely to be less volatile than Finland whose economy is heavily impacted by the fate of Nokia, for good or bad.

The same goes for sectors. Look at the sectors and how they respond to market conditions. Here's one example. Some sectors, like technology, consumer discretionary, and financials, tend to do well in periods of economic expansions—they have elastic demand for their products. (That is, of course, a gross generalization—during 2004, 2005, and 2006 the economy expanded and technology lagged markedly. You still must know something others don't.) If times are good, are people more likely to buy flat screen TVs? Sure. Will companies spend on updating computers and other equipment they had put off during the leaner times? Sure. Will anyone rush out and buy twice as much toothpaste or heart medicine? Not unless they sprouted additional teeth or a spare aorta. Sectors with inelastic demand, like health care and consumer staples, usually do better when the economy is slowing—but again, not always. Still, you won't stop brushing your teeth or taking your heart medicine because of the economy. That is why health care is often thought of as a "defensive" sector.

The object is to beat or meet the benchmark fairly consistently while controlling risk relative to the benchmark. For each sector and country comprising the benchmark, assign expected risk and return. It's your assignment. Your call. You decide. Ultimately you're right or wrong but it's up to you to do it and no one else. You don't need some fancy formula for this—use the Three Questions to figure out what you can know others don't, and what you can safely ignore. Using your findings, rank the sectors and countries (if you invest globally) from high to low in terms of how much volatility you think they have and assume volatility is risk. Make a list, and assign a "risk" factor to each category from 1 to 10—10 being riskiest. It needn't be any more complicated than that. Then, rank which category you see doing best. For this, you don't need my staff of researchers. It's your assessment that matters, because later you'll use the rankings to blend your portfolio and lower your overall risk (see Rule 3). Table 9.2 is an example of how your list might look. Don't be

Table 9.2   Rank Your Preferences

Risk	Return	Sector
6	3	Consumer Discretionary
8	10	Consumer Staples
1	1	Energy
5	2	Financials
4	9	Health Care
9	8	Industrials
2	4	Information Technology
10	6	Materials
3	5	Telecom
7	7	Utilities

influenced by our rankings—these are just dummy numbers for now from your friendly dummy book author.

Anticipation of market conditions in specific sectors and countries allows you to weight accordingly in building your portfolio. Do your Three Questions lead you to you see some countries or sectors doing much better than others? Give them a higher return ranking—maybe a 7 or 8—so you know to take modest amounts of benchmark risk by overweighting those. Ditto for those you see doing badly—give them a lower ranking so you know to underweight there. Is there one sector you're sure you know something unique that is bullish? Give it the highest ranking so you overweight it more materially. Maybe it's a 7 percent global weight and you double it to 14 percent because you're just sure you're right, not just overconfident.

What if you can't find something others don't know, and you don't feel comfortable making a particular forecast for a country or sector? What does Yoda say? Benchmark-like, you must be. Give it a middling rank. If you haven't used the Three Questions and you know nothing others don't know, you're better off being just like the benchmark. The idea is to be right more often than wrong, not lucky and right some and unlucky and wrong more.

The purpose of this list isn't to give you a pointless exercise. The list clarifies your analysis and simplifies your decision making. You won't be constantly revisiting the thoughts behind each decision—you'll know how to weight a two versus a five versus an eight versus a ten. And with your list, you're ready for Rule Number Three.

Rule Number Three—Blend Noncorrelated or Negatively Correlated Securities to Moderate Risk Relative to Expected Return

This rule is about managing risk relative to benchmark. Most investors, even new investors, understand intuitively that diversification helps reduce risk. Remember the poor Enron employees with their 401(k)s all in Enron stock? It can be avoided through diversification. Companies go bankrupt for many reasons. Stocks implode for even more reasons. The CEOs may have done nothing wrong—just couldn't compete with fire-breathing competitors. The stock of a perfectly healthy firm can tank for no seeming reason—with no forewarning. This is why no one stock should make up too much of your holdings.

My father was a lifelong advocate of concentrated portfolios. Warren Buffett has always been an advocate of concentrated portfolios. Yet I say to you the only basis for a concentrated portfolio is near infinite faith you know a lot others don't know. That won't allow for overconfidence. You must be certain you're not overconfident. If you don't really know a lot others don't know, concentrating portfolios is simply an exercise in overconfidence and increased risk. Owning less than 5 percent of one stock doesn't mean in just one account. If you have a 401(k), an IRA, and a taxable brokerage account, make sure you keep single stock ownership to less than 5 percent across all of your accounts.

You've heard the saying, "You must concentrate to get wealth, diversify to protect wealth." Those who got rich on one, two, or ten stocks are fortunate fools. Yes, with one stock you can experience thrilling upside. You can also experience crushing downside. Note the fool who gets lucky and wins this way will accumulate pride and assume he is smart. His wife and kids will know better and the more so for his success. (Of course, by this I don't mean owning one stock that is a firm you started and control. That's how Bill Gates, the world's richest man, and any number of other super rich people got their riches—they started and built a firm, nothing else, and along the way got phenomenally rich. I'm talking about being concentrated in one or a few stocks you don't control.)

The Magic of Diversification

As no one equity type outperforms all of the time (which you can test for yourself again using Question One), diversification helps spread risk between countries, industries, and companies. It hedges your bets against crises (such as war or oil shortages), unexpected events (earnings shortfalls, accounting scandals, or natural disasters), and combinations of the two (natural disaster induced oil shortages).

Though there are really many types of risk, standard finance theory defines risk as volatility measured by the standard deviation or variance of returns. Most investors think when the market is up it's good and when it is down it's volatile. But volatility is a dual edge sword and ever present. Your question should be: Is this category or stock more or less volatile than its peers? Diversification reduces the volatility of your overall holdings, and therefore reduces risk. Modern portfolio analysis has shown even a random mix of investments is less volatile than putting everything in a single category.

Make sure your portfolio has elements behaving differently in different market scenarios—which happens naturally if you have a broad enough benchmark and obey it. Each sector or country in your benchmark moves differently than the others. If you follow Rule Number Three and keep those sectors and countries that have low or negative correlation in your portfolio at all times, even if you suspect they won't be your portfolio MVP, you'll reduce overall volatility and improve long-term performance.

Recall our discussion about sectors with elastic versus inelastic demand—technology and health care, respectively. These two sectors are good examples since they usually have a short-term negative correlation—one is up when the other is down. Notice in Figure 9.2 that the performance of the two in 2000 is nearly a mirror image.

Rule Number Three, blending dissimilar elements, is about managing risk relative to return. The standard deviation, which is a risk measure, for each sector during the time period was 3.5 percent for tech and 2.5 percent for health care. But, if you had half your portfolio in each sector (not a good idea, but pretend for illustration's sake), your standard deviation, and therefore your volatility risk, was actually 2.0 percent.[10] You get lower risk simply by holding two differing kinds of stocks, which over this time period, had a negative correlation.

Then again, maybe you used the Three Questions to develop a strong confidence that one will best the other. By all means overweight the one and underweight the other. Your list from Rule Number Two helps you—just be sure to include all your benchmark's components and you should have a well-blended portfolio. Use that list to make decisions about how big, small, or nonexistent you want your relative over- and underweights to be. Be ruled by

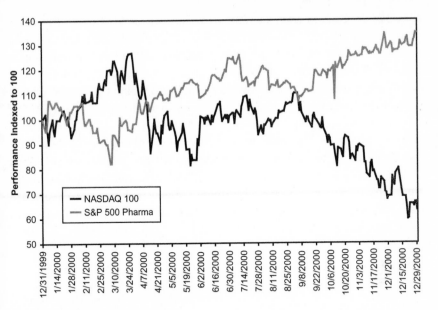

Figure 9.2 Drugs versus Tech.
Source: **Thomson Financial Datastream.**

your rankings, which were driven by what you used the Three Questions to know. But to the degree you're not very confident, leaving the reverse-correlated position in your portfolio is like paying an insurance premium against being wrong. This doesn't just work for components with negative correlations. Any blend of dissimilar categories—whether they have negative, low, or no correlation—improves return over time while lowering risk. (Use Question One to test it out. Take any two, four, or six stocks from different categories and test over long periods.)

Rule Number Four—Always Remember You Can Be Wrong, so Don't Stray from the First Three Rules

Rule Number Four, possibly the most important rule of the four, is about controlling your behavior. It's a way to ensure including Question Three—always. Without this rule, you are carried away by cognitive errors. Rule Four forces you to accumulate regret and shun pride. With Rule Four, you reduce the risk of being overconfident. Anytime you're tempted to disregard the first three rules and make a decision not based on the Three Questions but on some herd-mentality or Stone-Age inclination, Rule Four keeps you in line. With every decision you make—regardless of how confident you are, you can always be wrong. Once you accept that, you're less likely to do something too crippling.

Rule Four forces you to use your benchmark like a leash for a puppy in training. With a short leash, your pup can't get in too much trouble. The same dog on a long leash can dig up a garden, run into a pit bull, get hit by a car, or chase a stray cat across town.

For example, suppose you're confident tech will do well this year. Tech is 15 percent of your benchmark. But you're not satisfied with overweighting it to 20 percent or even 25 percent. You KNOW tech will be tops. Your confidence tempts you to jettison all your health care stocks for an even larger tech allocation because you know health care typically lags when tech is hot. Before changing your portfolio, ask yourself, "What if I am wrong?" Are you prepared for the consequences of such a big bet?

Core versus Counter Strategy

This rule is the primary reason I manage money with a core strategy and a counter strategy. The core strategies are market bets I make—relative benchmark overweights—based on what I believe I know that others don't. For example, if I believe America will outperform foreign, tech will outperform health care, consumer discretionary will outperform consumer staples, I make overweights relative to the benchmark in those areas. Those are my core strategies.

In my underweight sectors, I build my planned counter strategies. These are areas I don't expect to do well. I have them there because—what if I am wrong? Hey—I'm wrong a lot. I've been fortunate to be right more often than wrong in my career, but I know I've been wrong and will definitely be wrong again and plenty of times. Each of the counter strategies are areas I expect to do well in the event one of my core strategies fails and does badly. If I'm wrong about tech, health care will likely be a better performing sector. Either American or foreign stocks will be the lead pony, so I don't want to miss out if I'm wrong about that. I always ask myself, "What will do really well if what I think will do well actually does badly for some reason I can't foresee?" I want some of that too. Most investors never think this way.

Having a counter strategy means you'll always have "down" or "laggard" stocks. If you're really right like you expect, your counter strategy stocks *should* be down or lagging. If counter strategy stocks are down, it means your core strategies are kicking into high gear and you're doing great overall on a port-folio level. Counter strategy stocks being down isn't bad. They keep you from getting killed when you're wrong. That's managing risk which is good. One thing about my career I'm pleased with is when I've been wrong and lagged I haven't lagged by a lot. And I haven't lagged by a lot because I've built in the counter strategies.

Here's a practical example of core and counter strategies, again using tech and health care for consistency. Pretend you're benchmark neutral on every sector but tech and health care. You're new to this Three Questions thing, so you focus on just health care to start. You believe you've uncovered something no one else is seeing which should make health care super hot. Maybe you discovered every member of Congress hit their heads over the weekend (I'd vote for that). You also know the congressmen (and women) have a vote pending Tuesday on drug regula-tion. They want their new pain relief medicine, and fast, so they'll do something contrary to their nature—reduce governmental control. As such, you believe the FDA will begin green-lighting a whole slew of in-sanely efficacious drugs. (I said we were pretending.) No one else sees this. Everyone else thinks congressmen with headaches are bearish because they believe it will make them groggy and stupid. But you know better! You know they were already idiots.

Based on your unique view you decide to overweight health care. When you used Rule Number Two, you assigned health care an expected return ranking of 8, so you decide to increase your health care holdings to 15 percent from a benchmark weight of 10 percent. That is a 50 percent overweight and constitutes your core strategy.

Now, unless you're using margin, your assets must add up to 100 percent, not 105 percent, so you must reduce your holdings elsewhere by 5 percent. Where? Suppose tech is also 12 percent of your benchmark. If drug stocks do badly your full 12 percent tech weight will soften the blow. But if you're very confident about your drug play, you'll take the whole 5 percent out of tech, de-creasing your tech weight from 12 percent to 7 percent and increasing the real size of your bet by minimizing how much counter strategy you have. You still have a 7 percent weight, but it is a smaller counter strategy than if you took the 5 percent haircut from elsewhere.

Thinking it through with the Questions, you discover most folks agree tech is undervalued because tech P/Es are low. Also, the dollar has been strong recently (for argument's sake) and folks expect that to continue and from that they think U.S. stocks will be strong. Everyone remembers the 1990s when America led and so did tech.

But you know low P/Es aren't automatically low-risk, high-return. You know a strong dollar last year doesn't mean a strong dollar this year. You know a strong dollar doesn't make American stocks beat foreign. Noting the near-universal bullishness on tech you conclude you really won't need a full counter strategy and decide to underweight tech by 5 percent—putting your weight at 7 percent. Still you have a counter strategy that helps if your core drug strategy fails. If you're right about health care, you'll probably (but not necessarily) also be right about tech, and you'll have participated more in a hot sector and less in a lame one. You beat the market, just from getting one core and one counter strategy right (in this case by betting big and minimizing your counter strategy).

Now you could have been more extreme. You could have moved your drug weight from 10 percent to 22 percent and your tech weight from 12 percent to 0 percent. And if it worked, you would have won huge. But you didn't. You kept that 7 percent in tech.

Suppose you're wrong about your head injury theory. Congress convenes with nothing more than a few mild head aches. The poli-tics ban all pharmaceuticals except aspirin. No one expected that, so health care tanks, and folks flock to a "hotter" sector, like tech. Two sector bets wrong. You've participated less in the hot sector and more in the lame one. Ugh! You lag benchmark. But not by much, because you didn't go nil in the hot sector and you didn't grossly overweight the laggard. It's never all that bad to lag the benchmark by a few percentage points in a single year—maybe you do 16 percent or 17 percent when the benchmark does 20 percent. After all—this isn't a game where slight differences in one year's performance count all that much. If you lag by a little for a few years you can always make that up (the operative words being "lag by a little"). You have the rest of your life to be more right than wrong.

In a year when more of your core strategies are right, you meet or beat your benchmark. There have been up-years when I've been wrong about most of my core strategies, but because I got the big decision right—the decision to hold stocks instead of cash or bonds—I lagged my benchmark but not too badly and not by an amount I can't make up later. Why? Because I never aim to beat by more than I am comfortable lagging. The counter strategies save you from lagging too much in years you're wrong.

The only time I am ever comfortable beating the benchmark by a lot—taking on massive amounts of benchmark risk—is when I believe down-a-lot is by far the likeliest scenario. Then, I will try beating the benchmark by a lot to avoid the bulk of a bear market. It's the riskiest thing I ever do for clients, but over long time periods, if you beat the benchmark modestly on average, and beat the occasional bear market by a lot, you put serious spread on TGH. It's the only time I want to embrace huge bench-mark risk.

Finally! How to Pick Stocks That Only Win

That heading was there to fool you. I hope it worked! I don't know how to pick stocks that only rise. Many claim to. No one does. I've never seen anyone do it. Your goals in stock selection are two things and only these two. First, find stocks that are good representations of the categories you're trying to capture, and second, stocks you think will most likely do better than those categories. Note I didn't say, "Find stocks that will go up the most." I said, "Most likely do better than the category." Your goal is to get the attributes of the category plus a little, with "most likely" as your goal.

In building your portfolio, make sure you spend most of your time deploying the Three Questions for the most important decisions and don't get distracted by the least important decision—the individual selection of stocks. The stock selection, amazingly, has the least impact on how your portfolio performs. You may find that shocking and downright sacrilegious. Maybe you bought this book hoping to get an edge in picking stocks, and here I have spent several hundred pages talking about anything but how to pick stocks. There are several reasons—first, it just doesn't matter that much. Volumes of scholarly research have been written and there is general consensus among academics that most of your return is driven not by stock selection, but asset allocation—the decision to hold stocks, bonds, or cash in any given year, and what types. Scholars quibble about how much that most translates into. Some studies have shown more than 90 percent of return comes from asset allocations. Others say less. I won't quibble. "Most" is okay.

My research says about 70 percent of return in the long-term comes from asset allocation (stocks, bonds, or cash), and about 20 percent comes from subasset allocation—those decisions regarding types of stocks to own—whether to overweight or underweight (or be benchmark-like) on foreign or domestic, value or growth, size, sectors, and so on. But few finance academics would disagree that stock selection itself generates a small piece of your total portfolio return—it's a secondary or tertiary matter.

Think about it this way—in the late 1990s, if you used a dart to pick 30 large-cap growth stocks, you did pretty well. It didn't matter much whether you picked Merck over GlaxoSmithKline—they were large-cap growth pharmaceutical stocks that behaved similarly. Investors spent time hand-wringing and analyzing Merck's pipeline and Glaxo's earnings and this one's balance sheet and that one's 90-day moving average, but the effort had little additional benefit.

Whether Merck or Glaxo, they did pretty much the same during the 1990s, up 552 percent and 534 percent, respectively. How could you have used the Three Questions to figure out something others didn't know about Merck or Glaxo? Wouldn't it have been easier to figure out something about health care as a whole? Or large-cap stocks? Or growth stocks? Or the United States versus the United Kingdom? Had you done that, heck, you might have decided to hold both these stocks—a perfectly fine outcome (see Figure 9.3).

Fast forward to 2000 through 2002. During these years, the best decision was to be defensive and hold largely cash and bonds. If you couldn't do that, then it was small-cap value stocks. If you did that you did okay. If you did stock picking in any other part of the market you did badly. It was the decision whether to own stocks or even the type that determined return, not stock picking.

People believe in stock picking. Stock pickers are heroes. Any number of mutual fund commercials feature analysts looking thoughtful, wearing hard hats and grasping clipboards whilst inspecting airplanes or telephone poles or some such nonsense. If you wonder what the heck those suits are doing in midst a heavy machinery plant, you're on the right track. Don't get me wrong, stock selection is important. Picking the right stocks definitely adds value over time, otherwise I'd recommend everyone—even if you have vast sums to invest—to suck up the management fees and buy index funds or ETFs. And like all other investing decisions, you needn't pick the best performing stocks of all time, you just need to be right more often then wrong and let the benchmark do its work.

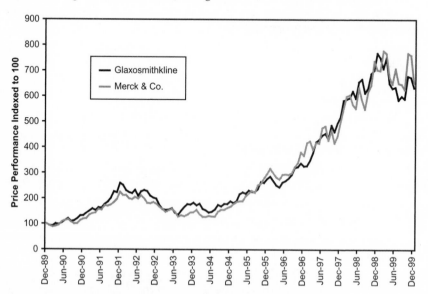

Figure 9.3   Same Sector, Same Performance.
Source: **Thomson Financial Datastream.**

So where do you want to spend the majority of your investment time? On the decision that drives 70 percent or even 90 percent of your return, or on the decision that is responsible for about 10 percent of your return? (That's a rhetorical question.)

Just Tell Me How to Pick Stocks Already!

Okay! I already did that once. It was my first book *Super Stocks*. I don't and wouldn't do it now the way I did it then, but what I did back then wasn't bad. It was fairly state-of-the-art then. Come to think of it, there is pretty much nothing I do now like I did 25 years ago—I'd be pretty embarrassed if there were. I sure hope I know things 10 years from now that cause me to change what I'm doing now. At this point in evolution, change is the name of the game and my goal is to keep developing new things and changing. So how would I do it now?

Here's how. It's a process of elimination.

Imagine the portfolio construction process as a funnel, like the one in Figure 9.4. Into this funnel, you pour the whole world's securities—stocks,

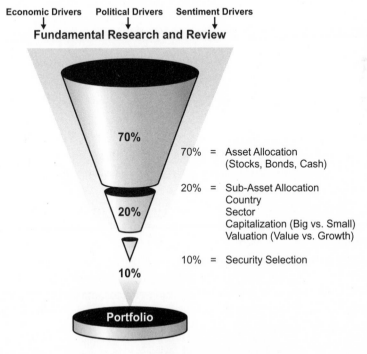

Figure 9.4 Portfolio Engineering Funnel.

bonds, cash, the whole gamut. The only securities that drop to the bottom are those that pass a screen at each level.

Use the Three Questions to determine if you want to hold stocks this year, or get defensive. Examine the three drivers—economic, political, and sentiment—to determine which market condition is most likely. In the highly likely situation you determine the market will be one of the first three scenarios (up-a-lot, up-a-little, or down-a-little), your job is easy—you belong fully exposed to equities as dictated by your benchmark. The entire world's stocks drop through the screen to the next level.

Now you have subasset allocation screens. Use the Three Questions to decide how to relatively weight countries and sectors compared to your benchmark. (Been there done that—earlier in this book.) Here you screen stocks based on your core and counter strategies—what you want to overweight and underweight. In this midsection of the funnel, you determine percentage portfolio weights without thinking of a single stock name. Use some of what we've demonstrated in this book. At the end of your scientific inquiry, you'll have a simple list of countries, sectors, and their appropriate percentages. Stocks drop through the next screen into a bucket based on your subasset allocation decisions, and only then are you ready for individual stock selection.

ACT SMALL, BE BIG—DOLLAR-WEIGHTED AVERAGING

This is a Question Two truth you can't see because of a Question Three problem. Investors don't realize most stocks they think are big-cap act much more like small-cap. Maybe exactly like them. They just don't know how to get the small-cap effect out of these "big" stocks. And that's because they can't fathom size correctly because of natural scaling problems.

Getting a small-cap market call right can give you a big boost, just as getting a big-cap call can. But many investors tactically can't get the big-cap or small-cap effect correctly because they see size wrong. First, some investors shy away from small-cap because of inherent potential problems of smaller companies. If you're looking to capitalize on what you foresee as a period of small-cap dominance, you needn't scrounge for tiny, illiquid, unknown names where you might get trapped if things sour.

An interesting Question Two pattern shows you can get small-cap performance with what you see as big-cap stocks. Fed-Ex and The Gap may not sound like small-cap names, but they behave more like small-cap than you think. Our research shows stocks in the S&P 500 that are smaller than the S&P's dollar-weighted average market cap act more like small-cap indexes than like the S&P 500 itself. "Dollar-weighted average" is a statistical term that may confuse you. It's a different form of average than median or mean average market cap. And it's the average that the market actually acts like. That is to say the market acts like a stock with that market cap.

Small-Cap Performance, Big-Cap Stocks?

No need to panic—here's how to see it. The 10 largest S&P 500 stocks are so big their aggregate market value is nearly as big as the rest of the S&P. The table below shows you the total market value of the 10 largest S&P 500 stocks each year versus how many of the smallest stocks in the S&P 500 it takes to come up with the same total dollar market value. It also shows each group's performance versus the overall S&P 500 and the small-cap Russell 2000 Index:

	Market cap (in billions)		Performance			
	10 Largest stocks	Smallest S&P stocks (# of stocks in group)	10 Largest Stocks	S&P 500	Smallest S&P Stocks	Russell 2000
1992	$595	$ 593 (334)	-1.2%	7.6%	17.8%	18.4%
1993	$579	$ 579 (310)	1.7%	10.1%	16.7%	18.9%
1994	$581	$ 580 (288)	2.2%	1.3%	0.7%	-1.8%
1995	$596	$ 594 (292)	40.2%	37.6%	26.5%	28.4%
1996	$812	$ 813 (293)	29.5%	23.0%	16.9%	16.5%
1997	$1,051	$ 1,052 (306)	35.0%	33.4%	25.0%	22.4%
1998	$1,386	$ 1,387 (304)	40.0%	28.6%	9.2%	2.6%
1999	$2,053	$ 2,050 (304)	34.3%	21.0%	19.2%	21.3%
2000	$3,122	$ 3,112 (403)	-26.9%	-9.1%	12.7%	-3.0%
2001	$2,680	$ 2,688 (370)	-7.6%	-11.9%	5.1%	2.5%
2002	$2,544	$ 2,540 (371)	-24.7%	-22.1%	-16.0%	-20.5%
2003	$1,844	$ 1,839 (362)	14.5%	28.7%	47.1%	38.8%
2004	$2,337	$ 2,331 (347)	-0.2%	10.9%	19.4%	18.3%
2005	$2,397	$ 2,379 (325)	-0.2%	4.9%	2.6%	4.6%

Source: Standard & Poor's Research Insight.

Most years, the smaller S&P 500 stocks as a group act very much like small-cap—because they're small compared to the correct average for the index. The 10 largest stocks have a huge impact on the S&P's

(continued)

return because their aggregate market value is generally as big as 300 or 400 of the "smallest" S&P 500 stocks combined. The biggest stocks have market caps bigger than the correct average of the market and they pull up the smaller stocks to that average.

By looking at the overall S&P 500's return, you simply can't detect that the "smaller" S&P stocks, as a group, get small-cap-like returns. The market acts, size-wise, like its dollar-weighted market cap and anything smaller than that has some smallness in it, even if it feels big to you. But you can't see it in the S&P 500's returns.

Your brain thinks an elephant is big and a bunny rabbit small. And a $10 billion or $20 billion-cap stock you think of as huge. What a party we could throw for $10 billion! But in reality, the dollar-weighted average cap of the market is $86 billion as of mid-2006,[11] and it acts like an $86 billion-sized stock. A $10 billion-cap stock is only 12 percent as big as the market and acts small compared to it.

The good news? You needn't scour the financial pages looking for unknown "small" stocks to give you a small-cap boost. You can get small-cap returns simply by hanging out in the smaller end of the S&P 500 with hundreds of liquid, respectable names to choose from. Names that don't feel strange to you like: Black & Decker, Clorox, Dow Jones & Co., Eastman Kodak, H&R Block, Goodrich, Hershey, Hilton Hotels, Liz Claiborne, Mattel, Radio Shack, Stanley Works, The New York Times, and Whirlpool. Just a few examples!

The bad news? You can't get a big-cap effect from $10 billion, $20 billion, or even $50 billion-cap stocks. For a big-cap effect you need market caps bigger than the market's dollar-weighted average—ones over $86 billion—what you otherwise may think of as super-cap stocks. Sadly, in America as I write, there are only 25 of them.[12] They're easy to buy, yet few to chose from. In reality, it's harder to get a diversified big-cap effect than a small-cap one.

Take each category, one at a time. Attacking stock selection this way is much easier and clearer. Instead of wading through the stock world, you're looking only at stocks falling in each of the specific categories you need. You're not looking at 15,000 stocks, hoping to find a handful of good ones; you're looking through 15 or 20 names per category to pick three or four stocks.

Say your higher level decisions lead you to needing a certain percentage of U.S. small-cap value industrials. You need a few decent ones—as a group likely to do as well or better than the category overall. The idea is to find stocks priced relatively cheaply compared to peers. More importantly, you want to look for a story that, should it catch on, will drive returns. I'm not talking about what you read in the front page of the *Wall Street Journal*, I'm talking about what you can use the Three Questions to unearth.

Here's an example. As 2005 started, I expected U.S. small-cap value industrials to continue doing well. A stock I wrote about in *Forbes* at the beginning of 2005 was Flowserve (FLS).[13]

By the way, I generally don't write in *Forbes* about stocks I select for my client portfolios. I'm not being secretive about my strategy; I just don't want to turn my clients into criminals. And I won't become one myself. If my clients were holding stocks I write about in *Forbes*, they could be accused of front-running, or I could be accused of doing it for them for pay. It would work like this. I buy for my clients, then recommend it in *Forbes* strongly, getting Forbes readers to buy it, pushing it up, and then I sell it for my clients, taking the profit. That would be criminal—a form of insider trading, a felony. I hate felonies. Always have! I've got a lifelong philosophy that says, "No felonies." To keep well out of the gray area and on the spic-and-span side of the law, I write about stocks that—for whatever reason—are perfectly grand but I don't use for client portfolios. Because (as cited earlier herein) stock picking is only a small percentage of portfolio return, I can pick different individual stocks for *Forbes* and my clients and have both places work out just fine, thank you. There are plenty for everyone. More than enough for what we need to do for clients and for *Forbes* without getting the two groups entangled in a potentially sticky way. I'll occasionally remind my readers of that in the interest of full disclosure.

Anyway, back to Flowserve. It manufactures pumps and valves for difficult liquids (corrosive ones, for example) in the chemical, petroleum, and food-processing industries (and how sexy can that be). Exciting right? I mean, don't you get up each day and think about pumps and valves for corrosive liquids? And how to capitalize on companies doing a spiffy job at valving and pumping? (There is a movie in here somewhere.) You don't find stocks like this from looking for a needle in a valve-stack. You find them by winnowing down categories.

Why Flowserve? Why not Kennametal or Idex Corp? Also great U.S. small-cap value industrial machinery stocks. Nothing wrong with them. But this was what I could fathom about Flowserve I felt no one else had. At the onset of 2005, investors were still hypersensitive about accounting "irregularities." In late 2004, Flowserve announced a new CFO, which can be fairly suspicious. A few days later, the Chief Accounting Officer resigned and just a few days after *that* reversed his decision. Next thing you knew, they were delaying their third-quarter SEC 10-Q filing. It was all fishy, and the stock behaved erratically in response. If you were a fundamental investor, this one would have scared you away because their balance sheet wasn't impressive. Even the price, at 26 times trailing earnings, seemed not so cheap.

All reasons most investors would stay away. Everybody knows fishy accounting coupled with an "overpriced" stock spells trouble. But it *was* cheap. The stock sold at 60 percent of annual revenue. There was potential for nice gains if their profit margins improved to a normal manufacturer level. Any positive news about this firm would be pleasant upside surprise. It was priced for no good news. It was priced with the expectation of more bad news and further decline. Therefore, any good news would be bullish and in a category that should do well, it should do well relative to its category—which is the goal.

Using Question Three, I made sure I wasn't being carried away by overconfidence or any other cognitive errors. I asked myself—what if I'm wrong? Suppose the stock failed to deliver? If that were the case, I would expect it to bounce around somewhere with its peers, maybe doing not quite as well. Because I expected the category to do pretty well, I thought I wouldn't be too disappointed by a laggard that everyone expected to be a laggard.

Note I didn't fly out to Flowserve's Texas headquarters and wander around their plant in a hard hat gleaning hat tricks. I never met the CEO. I didn't hire a mole to infiltrate upper management to find out something others didn't know (which is illegal along with being ridiculous—but would make a great Bruce Willis corporate spy movie). I read what was publicly available—the same information you easily find. Then I did what I always do when I'm looking at individual stocks. I ask myself, "What is everyone else worried about?" And I toss that aside. Then I ask myself, "What can I read between the lines? What kooky thing could happen to surprise to the upside or downside? How likely is that kooky thing to happen?" Finally, like Homer Simpson, I say, "All right brain, you don't like me, and I don't like you," and I figure out how my hardwiring, biases, and ego might lead me to make a poor decision about the stock. That's it. That is how you pick stocks that always win. Just kidding. That is how you pick stocks that, more often than not, are better than their peers.

If you had read *Forbes* and bought Flowserve at my recommendation, you would've been pretty happy. In 2005, the stock returned 44 percent[14] compared to 2 percent for its sector,[15] 5 percent for the S&P, and 9 percent for the global broad market.[16] Flowserve was a great stock pick—it did better than its category. Was it the best performing U.S. small-cap industrial machinery stock? No. You might have happened upon JLG Industries Inc. or Joy Global Inc., returning 133 percent and 109 percent, respectively.[17] Either would have made it through the top-down selection process as well. Those two stocks might have fallen out of your funnel instead of Flowserve (or heck, you might have decided to hold all three). But what would have made you select those? You needed to see something others could not which is easier to do when looking at a small pool of stocks at the bottom of your funnel, rather than an ocean at the top. Making the right big decisions first increases the likelihood of picking better stocks like Flowserve, JLG Industries, or Joy Global from the categories you need. If you're spending hours trolling web sites and CNBC to study some German small-cap value utility stock without first considering if you even want to hold stocks or what types this year, you're wasting time and brainpower.

Repeat this process for all your equity categories, and you'll have a good representation of your benchmark. Know you will never pick only the best stocks consistently. Get used to it right now. You will always have a stock or three or five in your portfolio that end up dogs. The best investment managers in the world don't pick stocks that only go up.

Is it possible you manage to make the right decisions regarding subasset allocation—you pick the right size, style, country, sector, everything—but you manage to pick the one stock that misses earnings, has an accounting scandal, gets embroiled in a political melee, or otherwise has peevishly poorer results than its brethren? Sure.

We've already established you should be diversified. If the energy sector is 10 percent of your portfolio, you should be picking three, five, or even seven different stocks there. If you pick one bad one (it will happen), you aren't hurting yourself too badly. (Rule Number Four.) You want three, five, or seven that you see as most likely to beat the category. I didn't pick Flowserve because I thought it would go up so darned much. I picked it because I thought it would likely beat the category. When you do that, some of them, like in this case Flowserve, go up a lot more.

Focusing on diversifying among stocks you think are most likely to beat their category doesn't mean you've given up on stockpicking. You haven't. But it also means you won't put it all on the line in one stock and then learn you picked badly—the stock did terribly while the category did well and didn't inject the category's effect into your portfolio. I always want the effect of the category I need in my portfolio. Stock picking without a top-down approach for most investors snatches defeat from the jaws of victory eventually. Those who don't accept this often have egos bigger than brains.

What about stock picking for a small sector or category? Say you're itching to have 2 percent or 3 percent in an emerging markets allocation. Emerging markets make up a small percentage of your benchmark, but you're making a very measured, controlled relative bet (hey, good for you). You don't want to buy just one stock—that will hardly diversify your emerging markets category. Which one do you pick? A Zimbabwean stock? A Chilean stock? But if you buy enough stocks to diversify that small an allocation, you'll be buying odd lots and definitely paying huge transaction fees. Here, you might simply find a low-cost ETF and call it a day. I'm not a fund fan, but they can serve a purpose. I mean, do you really know something others don't that justifies owning Zimbabwe versus Chile or the single stocks of East Pategonian Pepper versus The Central Cluj Transportation Authority? (That's another rhetorical question.)

When the Heck Do You Sell?

Picking stocks is only half the battle. How can you know when to sell? Just like buying a stock, a sell decision should be attacked top-down. The first and easiest answer for when to sell is if you fathom the likeliest market scenario over the next year is down-a-lot. Then, selling most of your stocks is good—but also rare. What about in between true bear markets? How do you know when to cut and run? Easy—if you have used the Three Questions and discovered something fundamental has changed about why you hold a stock. For example, after a fairly flat yield curve, the yield curve suddenly gets steep. You might decide to pare back your growth stocks in favor of more value stocks.

If you think firms with elastic demand (tech, consumer discretionary) will do better than those with inelastic (health care, consumer staples) you can change your weights—necessitating the sale of some stocks. Or maybe you fathom some other economic, political, or sentiment force impacting a certain sector. For instance, you know Congress will enact yet more accounting restrictions which you (and few others) fathom will harm the financial industry. Or maybe, after a lengthy period of high-dividend stocks outperforming, everyone is deliriously enthusiastic about utilities, so you somehow know it's time to underweight utilities shifting to nondividend paying stocks. Mind you, this doesn't mean the stocks you sell are bad. They just don't fit what you now need as a result of using the Three Questions—you need stocks that represent your asset and subasset allocation decisions.

Lock and Load

What about if a stock has been up-a-lot? Shouldn't you sell and "lock in profits?" Locking in profits is one of the sillier things investors do. Lock in profits how? The gains you take from a stock that is up don't get locked in a vault somewhere. You reinvest those dollars (don't you?) and the stocks you buy with "gains" you've "locked in" aren't guaranteed to only rise. The next stock you buy may fall, erasing profits an investor thinks are "locked in," which means paying taxes on the gain from the first stock and still losing money on the second. There is no such thing as "locking in profits." That is something only crazed cavemen say to their country club partners when they're beset with overconfidence and hindsight bias. Don't sell to "lock in profits." Sell to get out, pare back a weight you need to reduce, or because the stock no longer is more likely to best its category whose effect you need in your portfolio.

And just because a stock is up-a-lot doesn't mean it can't keep rising. It happens all the time. Remember, stocks are not serially correlated—they have a 50/50 chance of continuing in the prior direction or reversing course. Continue to hold a stock that is up if the fundamentals that led you to hold the stock remain intact. Easy as that.

Togas, Puppy Strangling, and Other Profit Killers

What about when a stock is down-a-lot? Shouldn't you cut the dogs, take the loss, offset taxable gains, and go your way? Maybe, maybe not—but probably not.

First of all, why is it down-a-lot? Is it because the entire market is having a correction, and it's just doing what the market is doing? If so, don't cut and run. Relative return is what matters, not absolute return (usually). Is it down because the stock's sector or category is down—either because the sector is correcting (sectors correct too) or because it's out of favor? Is it down because the stock is part of your counter strategy? That stock is behaving as a counter strategy stock should—also no reason to cut. (Focusing on one stock's performance or one sector's performance instead of how the whole portfolio is performing is order preference—a cognitive error you use Question Three to combat.) Is the stock down because some horrendous news surfaced? The CEO cooked the books, they hosted lavish Greek-themed parties on the shareholders' dime, or they have a Bulgarian puppy-strangling factory?

The fact of the matter is, by the time the bad news has come out, the market has already responded and you've likely missed the chance to avoid the big drop. Now, you can sell at the absolute lowest and take your dough and move on, but that is buying high and selling low. And the stock where you reinvest isn't guaranteed to only go up. It might drop too and now you are super wrong but twice. There is still a 50/50 chance the prior direction continues—or reverses.

Look at the company as we did when we were buying. Ignore the hype because that is priced in, and look for what you can fathom that others can't. Is the "bad news" such that the company can recover from it? I point out two examples in the box, but is the company essentially sound? Maybe the puppy-strangling factory is tiny and was established without upper management's knowledge, and the stranglers can be fired and the puppies rescued. Maybe the CEO was discovered with both hands in the puppy purging jar, but it wasn't pervasive, they have a decent succession plan, and the next in line is Jack Welch or, better yet, the next Gordon Moore.

WHEN TO SELL A STOCK

Sometimes you get surprised and an otherwise seemingly good stock tanks. Then you must decide—at the new, lower, and maybe cheaper price, is your stock worth hanging onto, or are you better off selling? I got surprised by two stocks providing a good example of both scenarios. Or rather, I got Spitzer-ed, and so did many investors.

On October 14, 2004, Elliot Spitzer, then Attorney General of New York State (AG NY) and World Crusader (WC), decided Hank Greenberg, then CEO of AIG, was guilty of something.[18] I believe there has never been a male member of the Greenberg family Mr. Spitzer doesn't believe is guilty of something—he's pretty much gone after all of them one way or another.

Meanwhile, one of Greenberg's sons, Jeff, ran another huge public insurance company called Marsh & McLennan (which also owns the Putnam mutual fund family—which Spitzer attacked heavily the year before). Essentially, Spitzer claimed Marsh & McLennan was guilty of bid-rigging for its insurance contracts and named other insurance companies, including AIG, as being complicit. Later, Spitzer very publicly accused AIG and indeed, Hank Greenberg, of being party to the alleged misdeeds. Along the way, Marsh & McLennan's board, under attack from Spitzer, forced out Jeff Greenberg. Then AIG's board, also likely wary of Spitzer's force and power, forced Hank Greenberg out. Eventually the charges against AIG were dropped and Marsh & McLennan settled. Meanwhile, Spitzer and Hank Greenberg had it out in the press, and some of Greenberg's friends got involved, including former CEO of Goldman Sachs, John Whitehead, whom Spitzer may or may not have threatened with both bodily and professional harm—depending on whose version you believe.

Anyway, both stocks tanked big time on the news. Markets hate surprises, particularly surprises involving the AG of NY and WC. Both stocks fell immediately on the news—AIG was down 10 percent[19] on October 14, 2004, and MMC down a big 25 percent.[20] What to do?

Avoiding the drop ahead of time would have been nearly impossible. There was no way to know Spitzer was planning this, not unless you had special and illegal insight into his intent. When such a market event occurs, you especially need Question Three. Sudden drops in stock prices get loss aversion working full throttle. Selling out after a big drop sometimes makes sense, sometimes is epically stupid—and you won't know which is which until later, and you won't get any appropriate cues from the market, the *New York Times*, or your friendly WC (who after all is an elected poli-tic and future governor of New York).

I was bullish on the finance sector, and insurance specifically. Everything about both stocks was right, category-wise. The only reason to sell a stock fitting my bigger portfolio themes was if something was rotten individually about it. Now I'd met Hank Greenberg a couple of times. And while he can be abrasive at times, sort of like me, he was a phenomenal CEO for a very, very long time. Truly phenomenal and I couldn't believe he had actually done anything very wrong because he didn't need to. (Basic rule: The most capable people don't need to break rules and won't.) On the other hand, he was 80 so he couldn't be phenomenal for long.

But I also had no idea Spitzer would later in 2005 quietly excuse Greenberg of any criminal wrongdoing (announced during Thanksgiving week,[21] no less, where news items go to die. If you want to bury a news release, announce it over Thanksgiving, Christmas, the Fourth, or Easter—far fewer folks will ever see it). I knew—everyone knew—AIG was a massive company with well-diversified product lines. I understood the crime of which AIG stood accused, but I couldn't see how it would impact the long-term health of AIG overall—wasn't a big enough crime. If it turned out something was wrong with the business group involved with the alleged bid-rigging, AIG could easily spin-off the

(continued)

group, rout the evil-doers, or otherwise cut out the (alleged) cancer. I couldn't see any reason why the rest of AIG should be infected. Also, there was speculation of Greenberg stepping down, and though Greenberg built AIG into what it was, at 80 his departure couldn't hurt too much. What's more, his leaving could please the market and take heat off the stock. Finally, because there was so much dour sentiment about AIG, any bad news was pretty well priced—so I could fathom any good news, no matter how weak, would be a pleasant, bullish surprise. I opted to hang onto AIG.

The story was different for Marsh & McLennan (MMC). Marsh & McLennan stood accused of flim-flammery in its main business line and core competency. The case seemed stronger. To survive, MMC would have to navigate at least one major lawsuit, with possible copy-cat suits from other states. They would likely do a strategic reboot, cast-off a number of their upper management, and generally be in a major state of disarray for months, if not years. But that was small.

The new CEO they brought in, Michael Cherkasky, a perfectly fine fellow, was the CEO of Kroll, a public company specializing in corporate security work that MMC bought the year before. Cherkasky was picked as CEO not because he was the optimal guy to run a big insurance firm, having extensive background and success in insurance. He didn't have that. He was picked because he had a prior background as a regulator and had worked with Eliot Spitzer before and it was presumed Cherkasky could get along with Spitzer. To me this was all wrong and bad. Cherkasky's prime experience as a CEO was at Kroll—a little firm, smaller than my firm. I know something for sure—I'm certainly not qualified to be CEO of something the size of MMC. Said otherwise, I'm fully as qualified to be CEO of MMC as Cherkasky was because, while I'm no insurance guy at least I'm a financial services guy, and Cherkasky was neither an insurance nor financial services guy and hadn't been CEO of anything nearly the scale necessary to be truly qualified to run MMC's far-flung diversified operations. I knew if I couldn't run it well, he couldn't. So, my firm decided to take our double-digit loss and sell.

My firm's clients thought that an odd decision. Why sell one and not the other? Aren't they cut from the same cloth? Wasn't Spitzer gunning for them both? Shouldn't we cut the dogs and buy some winners? That sounds great in theory, but we all know the stocks you buy to replace your dogs may be woofers themselves. Never sell a stock because it's down. Sell because something fundamental has changed about the reason you hold it. Think about that funnel again and the fundamental reasons, top-down, why you might sell. The fundamental reason could be that you forecast a down-a-lot scenario, and you're shifting largely out of stocks. It could be you're shifting from growth to value, small to large, or the reverse. Your sector outlook may have changed and you need to move from an overweight to an underweight. Maybe you're dangerously overweighted because the stock has appreciated far beyond 2 percent or 3 percent of your total holdings. Or maybe, you wake up to discover the company has done something illegal from which recovery will be either lengthy or impossible.

When Spitzer formally subpoenaed AIG in February of 2005, the stock had another stomach-churning drop—over 31 percent to a relative low in April.[22] Nothing had changed since October of the previous year except increased fear of Spitzer, so we hung on. Based on some larger portfolio themes, we finally sold AIG in January of 2006, after it rallied 42 percent[23] from its low in 2005, for a 19 percent[24] net gain from October 14, 2004 when its woes began. We couldn't guarantee anything else bought with the proceeds from a sale on October 14 would have been up 19 percent—AIG did about as well as the S&P 500[25] over the same time period. When we sold AIG, MMC was still down more than 3 percent from when the news hit and lagging its category big-time. I felt pretty good about that call.

Also, deeply consider if the bad news is correct or credible. Could be just cuckoo. Not to put too fine a point on it, but frequently journalists don't know what in the heck they're talking about. Often what they report is overblown or simply wrong. Most of them don't know that much about business. Most of them were journalism or English majors. Something routine can easily be misinterpreted or blown up to sound ground-shaking. Or a minor infraction not material to the firm's core business may get the misinformed full-court-press. Or, the journalist may be going on the hearsay of a disgruntled employee without doing further fact checking. Happens all the time! It's happened to me a lot. Journalists frequently have and do get their news very wrong.

If the besieged firm is sound despite the hysteria, the stock will probably rebound, giving you a chance to sell at a relatively higher point. What's more, since sentiment will be so poor about a stock that had a sudden and precipitous price drop, any good news, no matter how meager (yes, they were killing puppies, but doing it humanely) can drive it up.

What if you're cool-headed and don't sell just because everyone else has (good for you), and you take a reasonable look at what is true about why the stock dropped suddenly? What if the bad news truly signals something rotten in Denmark, something even a big management shake-up won't help, something rotting the core business? Despite the relative low, that's still a right time to cut your losses, utter a few obloquies, and know you simply can't help it when you get blindsided sometimes. This is why you diversify and never put more than you're willing to lose in any one stock.

If that makes you diabolically depressed, consider this. If you have a well-managed portfolio, you won't have much more than a few percent in any stock. If one stock gets halved tomorrow from sudden bad news, maybe you lose 1 percent. If you think relatively and scale (always!), you can combat order preference and focus on the overall portfolio, not the one, small, imploded position. You lost 1 percent. Oh well. In reality, stocks rarely lose 100 percent of their value fast. You can experience a 10 percent to 20 percent individual stock drop, and then the overall impact is minimal. Even a massive drop in one stock should have minimal impact on a well-managed portfolio. Shake it off, accumulate regret, learn what you can for next time, and move on. If something fundamental didn't occur, continue to hang on for now—but keep an eye on any such change.

Remind yourself you aren't collecting a bunch of high-flying stocks. You aren't a stock collector. Stock collectors are hamstrung by order preference and overconfidence and focus on the two stocks that did well and forget about how their whole portfolio is doing, not to mention risk management. Your aim should absolutely not be to find the next hot stock you can brag about to your poker group (or yoga class, or worse—tofu tasting party). Rather, you're maximizing the likelihood of beating your benchmark. You need stocks that act like the components of your benchmark. That is what this exercise is about.

With that, you have a strategy to keep you disciplined—a strategy requiring constant application of the Three Questions. Garnering market-like return when your Stone-Age brain wants to cave to TGH so very badly and either hit homeruns daily or cower with a few CDs and money market funds is quite an accomplishment. But I want you to aspire to more. I want you to be disciplined with a strategy. I want you to advance the science of capital markets technology and be among those who can move down the learning curve faster. I want you to master the Three Questions and use them always. I want you to stick it to The Great Humiliator. Stick it to him hard.

CONCLUSION

Time to Say Goodbye

In concluding, before saying goodbye and sending you on your way, allow me to get personal and address why I would write this book at all—what some might think of as an introduction. You can blame it on the U.S. Forest Service. I fell in love with forests as a kid. My parents lived in a suburb where their back fence was adjacent to the woods. As a kid, I was over the fence and off— into a live oak forest. From my parents' home, in a world long gone, I could hitchhike up to Kings Mountain, 20 minutes out, and be in the redwoods at 2,000 feet in elevation. That's where I live and have for more than a third of a century. But as a kid I saw myself living and working in the woods always—as a forester. I went to forestry school because I loved trees.

A summer job pulling chain for a U.S Forest Service survey crew convinced me I'd never, ever work for the government under any circumstances. And today, forestry is almost always either working for or with the government in one way or another or against the government. That summer taught me everything about government employment is suppressing. What I knew was that I simply didn't want to have anything to do with the government. I also knew right then, for the same reason, I'd never be a career politician because it too meant working for the government. Might have saved my mortal soul. Somehow I hoped I had something better to do with my life. With no sense of what to do next, I switched majors to economics because I'd been good at it earlier.

Forests still jazz me, redwoods in particular. In fact, I'm very proud that the only endowed academic chair in the whole wide world dedicated to any single tree species bears my name and is devoted to my beloved redwood. I've built and maintained a serious hobby life devoted to redwoods, including locating and excavating more than 30 pre-1920 steam-era redwood lumber mills and collecting and cataloging the artifacts. I've also compiled what I believe is the world's largest noninstitutionally owned forest history library, spanning more than 3,000 volumes. But you could never get me to go to work for the government. Serious hobbies are okay, but it is important to separate what you do career-wise from what you do purely for fun.

Capital markets are fun, but they're also work. I hope the Three Questions will be profitable for you, but along the way, I also hope you liked this book and found it educating. When I first started my *Forbes* column, Jim Michaels, then the Editor of *Forbes* and generally the dean of American business journalists, taught me that a column was supposed to be three things—entertaining, educating, and profitable. Those are pretty good goals for much of life. But as fun as they are, markets are a great deal of work—which you can see in the large amount of data and analysis in this book. The Three Questions are a tool to let you know what you need to know to do well. But you have to apply the effort. No book can do that for you.

The opposite of a governmental employee is a worshiper of free markets and Capitalism. By the time I was finished with school, I was pretty well hooked. So after school, I went to work for my father. I learned what I could from him, including that I'm not a very good employee, and struck out on my own. I was too young to know I was too young at the time to be able to succeed on my own—so I could. Thirty-five years and many good whacks from TGH later, I'm still at it. Why such a long career of flagellation at the hands of TGH? Why keep going to work and dealing with all the real world's dull cares when I could retire and dedicate the rest of my life to redwoods, my cats, and my wife? Why keep making very public prognostications in *Forbes* these decades, verifiable by anyone who wants to prove me wrong or attack me? I could have retired 15 years ago with plenty of money and done any other thing. Why do any of this?

Several reasons. First, I love the thrill of it—the battle with TGH. Some people climb Mount Everest. Others swim the English Channel. I'm not athletic. You won't see me strapping on an oxygen tank and summiting Aconcagua. So I take on TGH. What could be more thrilling than that?

Transformationalism

Second, this is an opportunity to keep discovering and doing new things forever. The most important part of being alive at this point in history, in my view, is the ability to do the new. In Chapters 5 and 9, I spoke about my grandfather at length. When he died in 1958, he had seen amazing evolutions ranging from autos, radio, movies, antibiotics, airplanes, and more. He could sit in his living room and see the president speaking to him real time in a wooden box—right there. When he was five in 1880, if he could have described to his grandfather what he would see by 1958, Isaac Fisher, my great-great grandfather, would have thought my grandfather was nuts. He would have turned to his son, Philip Isaac Fisher, and said, "Philip, what are you doing to let such crazy notions in my grandson's mind?" But Isaac would have been wrong. My grandfather's generation saw more relative change in basic life than any other generation before or since. They were at the inflection point of the explosion—the nonlinear launching point Americans regularly underestimate, which we otherwise refer to as the American Industrial Revolution. The most singularly powerful unleashing of mental force ever. Capitalist force—the most powerful kind! Before his generation, every generation lived life almost identically to their grandparents. They might move. They might war. They might take a different career. But the basics of life changed very, very slowly in the eons before my grandfather's birth.

My father, born in 1907, saw tremendous change too—more absolute change than my grandfather did, but less relative change. He saw jets, integrated circuits, and the beginnings of biotech before he died in 2004. My generation has seen tremendous absolute change and will continue to—but less relative change than my father or grandfather saw. My three sons are 30 to 35. They assume change is normal. Yes, now it is, but it's still very new. To wake daily as a normal person and participate in changing the world in some small part like my grampa did as one of the pioneers at Hopkins Med or my father did in growth stock investing—that's new. That didn't happen centuries ago except for a few weird ones like Isaac Newton. Normal folks didn't do that. Now they do. We live in exceptional times because we can rise every day, if we choose, and participate in developing new things never before known that will be taken largely for granted by those following us.

I call this process *transformation*. Normal people now leave their field changed in their wake because of things they developed. Newton was a transformationalist before they were common. The industrial revolution unleashed transformationalists throughout our world—people whose imaginations knew no bounds and could fathom the unfathomable

It happens mainly among scientists and capitalists. Julius Rosenwald was a transformationalist when he started Sears, Roebuck and Co. changed how people envisioned retailing for 100 years. Carnegie was. Ford was. Adam Smith was when he wrote *The Wealth of Nations*. But most authors aren't—they're usually just incrementalists. Einstein certainly was and there are a great many in science—famous and not so. More recently, Bob Noyce and Gordon Moore, cofounders of Intel, combined scientific backgrounds with business to transform their little part of the world. Bill Gates is. He changed the world in ways that leveled the playing field for small businesses versus big. Chuck Schwab was. The list is long—even endless. But you need not be huge to be a transformationalist. You just have to change your little part of the world permanently so others always see it differently through your new science, knowledge, technology, or vision.

Our lives—the way we live them daily—are fundamentally changed by every transformationalist. Sometimes we don't know it because we don't see it. When I endowed the Kenneth L. Fisher Chair in Redwood Forest Ecology, I did it partly because I love redwoods but also because its initial holder, Steve Sillett, is a transformationalist who is very rapidly changing the way we think about redwoods. He has no limits in his mind as to the questions that can be answered that we've never addressed. He is transforming how we know redwoods and big trees in general. I wouldn't have endowed the chair if I didn't see a transformationalist to support.

In capital markets, there is no limit to what you can do to learn and build capital markets technology that no one has ever understood before. You can be a transformationalist of capital markets. You couldn't do that 200 years ago. Today you can. Today you can wake up and work daily on asking questions simply challenging what we know—opening the vista of what we may know soon. The Three Questions are specifically for that purpose—so you, some of you who read this book, may get it in you to stretch to become a transformationalist yourself.

When I developed the PSR, I was trying to do that. When I did early work on small-cap value (before that word existed) and showed the institutional investing world how it fit in terms of variance and covariance into traditional finance theory's Markowitzian framework of Mean Variance Optimization, I was trying to do that. I'm no Newton, no Bob Noyce. I'm no great genius by any standard. But I can ask questions. And so can you. And you may be a great genius able to fathom things I never could and become a great transformationalist.

I keep doing what I keep doing because at this point in human evolution the most exciting and fun thing we can do is to develop the new that has never been developed before and decimate past mythologies. We will make mistakes to be sure. But we will progress for sure. You can do it as well or better than I can. If you're younger, you can do it far longer than I can. You can make a huge difference. I know most of you won't because you won't want to. But if a few of you get the idea while young or willing to ask the Questions and attempt transforming parts of finance and market theory, you can have a huge impact on the future.

The most important reason I keep pushing ahead is because I can get up every morning and address the new in my little part of the world and maybe in 2007 I'll use the Questions and fathom a Question Two that really creates something new and shattering. Or maybe you will.

Yes, managing money is a valuable service and doing a good job is vital in a world where so many don't. But I hold no illusions that I'm saving lives like the graduates of Hopkins Med 100 years ago. I'm no capitalistic version of Mother Theresa. Yes, my firm's many clients rely on my firm's services for their well-being and that is a pretty important undertaking—one I am honored to provide. But my firm today can do that without me. If I retired, it could carry on just as it does now because we built it with the ability to do that. The reason to get up and do it at this stage in life is for the fun of the new and different and challenging.

And I've done okay. My long-term history managing money puts me in a tiny group of money managers with a documented long history of beating the market. You can view part of that in Appendix K. Had a typical high net worth individual invested with my firm midyear 1995, by midyear 2006 (as this book goes to press), your assets would have appreciated 231 percent net of all fees. Had you merely been passive to the global market, you would have done a respectable 131 percent. That's an annualized difference of 3.6 percent—again—after all fees have been paid. Had you invested in the S&P 500, our management, net of fees, would have beaten your index by 1.7 percent per year. And that's while making a lot of mistakes over the years. I'm pleased with that.

I chose 10 years of history because I have another verifiable 10 year public record you can compare it to—my monthly Forbes stock picks. (I've been writing in Forbes for 22 years, but they only started publishing the accounting of my results 10 years ago.) You can see that history in Appendix L, along with detailed methodology and disclosures. It isn't managed money, rather an arm's length measurement of the success of the stock picks from my column.

Over those years, they have me beating the S&P 500 by an annualized 5 percent, which is too much. While that includes a hypothetical brokerage commission, it doesn't include other real-world transaction costs like bid-ask spreads, friction, or money management fees. Even so, though not everyone has enough liquid assets to be a client of my firm, anyone can buy Forbes or see it for free online (how capitalistic is that). There have been years my Forbes picks have beaten what my firm has done for clients and vice versa. That shouldn't tell you anything—I pick far fewer stocks for Forbes most years than are held in client portfolios, so some performance variability is normal when comparing a smaller, hypothetical portfolio not having the risk controls I build into actual portfolios. But I'm proud of my history—it validates what I've done and it might convince you I know a bit of what I'm talking about—but in investing, what's past is merely prologue. I cannot rest on past laurels if I want to keep doing what I'm doing.

Which gets to the third reason I do what I do! I love Capitalism. In my view, it is thus far the most holy, perfect accomplishment of humanity. Under Capitalism, all are born to opportunity. The poor become rich. The richest were mostly born not rich. Those on the *Forbes* 400 mostly fall off over time. Bill Gates was born simply upper middle class and as a youth became the richest man in the world and created the biggest endowment in history. The world's great innovations and transformations and transformationalists have all come from capitalistic societies and none from elsewhere in the past 200 years. Contemporary elitist intellectuals have wrongly snubbed capitalism since long before I was born, but they are no more right in their vision than Gertrude Stein from Chapter 5.

The stock market is pure capitalism. The stock you buy doesn't know if you're white or black, male or female, old or young, American or French. Prices are dictated by supply and demand and nothing else. It's global, efficient, wildly volatile, always surprising, raw, and beautiful. In many ways, TGH and I have a very intense love-hate relationship.

And by writing this book, I'm bringing the message to you—that Capitalism is good and the stock market is unpredictable but beatable. So what should you do now? I want you to move down that learning curve fast—hopefully faster than others—and advance capital markets science. As I've said repeatedly, you can't make market bets and win long term unless you know something others don't. I didn't share some of what I know to wow you with cute analytical tricks. It was a demonstration of applying a scientific method to the market. To show you how. The advantages I showed you will all fade away one day. Maybe some sooner than later—but all some day. Yet asking the Questions will go on forever. The only thing that will help you or me beat the market going forward is innovation. To my knowledge, while there are many books showing people investing tools—just like my first book showed my innovations like the PSR of 1984—I'm unaware of any investment book before this one, not a single one, showing you how to innovate for yourself.

So here it is. Maybe you think all this is wrong, or maybe just part of it is wrong. That's fine. I'm okay with you seeing me as wrong. But I don't want you to just think I'm wrong. I want you to prove it. If you don't believe what I've shown you then at least use the methodology to prove me wrong. Show me an R-squared, show me a cognitive error, fathom something for me scientifically I haven't fathomed—and write to tell me. But really prove me wrong. And don't be rude when you do it. Science isn't rude. If you just write me to tell me I'm an idiot, I won't pay attention. It's none of my business. Truly, I invite you to be skeptical about everything in this book. I've given you a bunch of Appendix data. You can find much more on your favorite web sites. Get the data, run an analysis, do it over long periods with different starting dates. Check it overseas to make sure you haven't found a flukey factor. Show me the data and stats and then tell me I'm wrong.

What I don't want you to do is think I'm wrong but never prove it. That won't do you any good. It's just a waste of time. If you think I'm wrong and can show it satisfactorily with data, you haven't hurt anyone. In fact—you've just helped yourself because you've established or confirmed reality. And if you've made it to this conclusion, you must, in some small way, believe that what everyone knows and accepts isn't always right. So show me how I'm wrong. I can take it! Show me the data and how you ran your analysis. Maybe you will discover a new way to stick it to TGH, and for that I salute you. But if you prove I'm wrong, you will have proved the methodology works. And in a different way then, I'm still right—isn't that beautiful?

APPENDIX A

U.S. Equity Total Returns 1830 to 1925

Date	% Change		Date	% Change		Date	% Change		Date	% Change
1830	14.29%		1854	-23.68%		1878	11.44%		1902	4.88%
1831	12.50%		1855	6.90%		1879	49.11%		1903	-14.65%
1832	11.11%		1856	9.68%		1880	24.25%		1904	30.95%
1833	0.00%		1857	-26.47%		1881	7.71%		1905	19.66%
1834	20.00%		1858	24.00%		1882	2.01%		1906	6.81%
1835	8.33%		1859	-6.45%		1883	-3.07%		1907	-29.61%
1836	-7.69%		1860	24.14%		1884	-13.35%		1908	44.52%
1837	0.00%		1861	5.56%		1885	26.11%		1909	18.94%
1838	8.33%		1862	68.42%		1886	12.84%		1910	-7.88%
1839	-7.69%		1863	46.88%		1887	-2.75%		1911	5.72%
1840	8.33%		1864	13.83%		1888	1.89%		1912	7.97%
1841	-7.69%		1865	-2.80%		1889	7.59%		1913	-9.60%
1842	-8.33%		1866	10.58%		1890	-10.15%		1914	-3.67%
1843	45.45%		1867	8.70%		1891	22.61%		1915	35.51%
1844	25.00%		1868	17.60%		1892	5.94%		1916	8.94%
1845	15.00%		1869	8.16%		1893	-15.93%		1917	-25.26%
1846	-8.70%		1870	11.95%		1894	2.11%		1918	25.56%
1847	9.52%		1871	13.48%		1895	4.47%		1919	20.67%
1848	4.35%		1872	12.87%		1896	1.81%		1920	-19.69%
1849	4.17%		1873	-6.58%		1897	16.96%		1921	14.59%
1850	28.00%		1874	9.39%		1898	23.20%		1922	27.80%
1851	3.13%		1875	2.15%		1899	9.87%		1923	4.18%
1852	27.27%		1876	-12.18%		1900	18.67%		1924	25.70%
1853	-9.52%		1877	-3.83%		1901	19.78%		1925	29.55%

Source: Global Financial Data. Total returns as calculated by GFD to simulate a backtested S&P 500 index; not official S&P 500 data.

APPENDIX B

S&P 500 Composite Returns

Date	% Change	Date	% Change	Date	% Change	Date	% Change
Jan-26	0.23%	Jan-29	5.99%	Jan-32	-2.31%	Jan-35	-3.78%
Feb-26	-4.02%	Feb-29	-0.31%	Feb-32	5.95%	Feb-35	-3.67%
Mar-26	-5.53%	Mar-29	0.03%	Mar-32	-11.32%	Mar-35	-2.81%
Apr-26	2.45%	Apr-29	1.88%	Apr-32	-19.75%	Apr-35	10.06%
May-26	1.46%	May-29	-4.02%	May-32	-22.75%	May-35	3.59%
Jun-26	4.75%	Jun-29	11.53%	Jun-32	-0.05%	Jun-35	7.70%
Jul-26	2.31%	Jul-29	4.83%	Jul-32	38.51%	Jul-35	8.07%
Aug-26	4.80%	Aug-29	10.07%	Aug-32	38.28%	Aug-35	2.49%
Sep-26	2.71%	Sep-29	-4.66%	Sep-32	-3.21%	Sep-35	2.65%
Oct-26	-2.71%	Oct-29	-19.71%	Oct-32	-13.61%	Oct-35	7.95%
Nov-26	2.67%	Nov-29	-13.06%	Nov-32	-5.34%	Nov-35	4.15%
Dec-26	2.10%	Dec-29	2.90%	Dec-32	5.73%	Dec-35	4.10%
Jan-27	-1.66%	Jan-30	6.65%	Jan-33	1.21%	Jan-36	6.87%
Feb-27	5.21%	Feb-30	2.50%	Feb-33	-18.10%	Feb-36	1.96%
Mar-27	1.06%	Mar-30	8.29%	Mar-33	3.87%	Mar-36	2.80%
Apr-27	2.14%	Apr-30	-0.65%	Apr-33	42.87%	Apr-36	-7.45%
May-27	5.64%	May-30	-1.30%	May-33	16.46%	May-36	4.91%
Jun-27	-0.55%	Jun-30	-16.15%	Jun-33	13.50%	Jun-36	3.38%
Jul-27	6.91%	Jul-30	4.02%	Jul-33	-8.66%	Jul-36	7.22%
Aug-27	4.84%	Aug-30	1.14%	Aug-33	11.82%	Aug-36	1.11%
Sep-27	3.59%	Sep-30	-12.72%	Sep-33	-11.12%	Sep-36	0.48%
Oct-27	-3.96%	Oct-30	-8.50%	Oct-33	-8.71%	Oct-36	7.93%
Nov-27	7.16%	Nov-30	-1.71%	Nov-33	10.72%	Nov-36	0.72%
Dec-27	2.26%	Dec-30	-7.01%	Dec-33	2.47%	Dec-36	-0.24%
Jan-28	-0.16%	Jan-31	5.40%	Jan-34	10.92%	Jan-37	4.17%
Feb-28	-1.41%	Feb-31	11.88%	Feb-34	-3.45%	Feb-37	1.84%
Mar-28	11.21%	Mar-31	-6.58%	Mar-34	0.29%	Mar-37	-0.63%
Apr-28	3.58%	Apr-31	-9.20%	Apr-34	-2.43%	Apr-37	-7.90%
May-28	1.58%	May-31	-13.27%	May-34	-7.89%	May-37	-0.65%
Jun-28	-3.73%	Jun-31	14.46%	Jun-34	2.41%	Jun-37	-4.84%
Jul-28	1.59%	Jul-31	-7.06%	Jul-34	-11.28%	Jul-37	10.63%
Aug-28	7.76%	Aug-31	1.47%	Aug-34	5.73%	Aug-37	-5.11%
Sep-28	2.71%	Sep-31	-29.63%	Sep-34	-0.06%	Sep-37	-13.81%
Oct-28	1.76%	Oct-31	9.08%	Oct-34	-2.98%	Oct-37	-9.67%
Nov-28	12.31%	Nov-31	-9.30%	Nov-34	8.81%	Nov-37	-9.64%
Dec-28	0.58%	Dec-31	-13.90%	Dec-34	-0.19%	Dec-37	-4.50%

Date	% Change	Date	% Change	Date	% Change	Date	% Change
Jan-38	2.05%	Jan-43	7.67%	Jan-48	-3.49%	Jan-53	-0.27%
Feb-38	6.73%	Feb-43	5.54%	Feb-48	-4.23%	Feb-53	-1.37%
Mar-38	-24.51%	Mar-43	5.72%	Mar-48	8.15%	Mar-53	-1.93%
Apr-38	14.79%	Apr-43	0.52%	Apr-48	3.14%	Apr-53	-1.67%
May-38	-3.77%	May-43	4.91%	May-48	8.27%	May-53	-0.33%
Jun-38	25.39%	Jun-43	2.39%	Jun-48	0.80%	Jun-53	-1.16%
Jul-38	7.66%	Jul-43	-5.02%	Jul-48	-4.98%	Jul-53	3.05%
Aug-38	-2.29%	Aug-43	1.46%	Aug-48	1.25%	Aug-53	-5.32%
Sep-38	2.02%	Sep-43	2.79%	Sep-48	-2.54%	Sep-53	0.61%
Oct-38	7.86%	Oct-43	-0.90%	Oct-48	7.25%	Oct-53	5.64%
Nov-38	-2.93%	Nov-43	-7.12%	Nov-48	-10.35%	Nov-53	1.36%
Dec-38	4.09%	Dec-43	6.36%	Dec-48	3.60%	Dec-53	0.69%
Jan-39	-6.54%	Jan-44	1.98%	Jan-49	0.71%	Jan-54	5.62%
Feb-39	3.63%	Feb-44	0.18%	Feb-49	-3.44%	Feb-54	0.76%
Mar-39	-13.24%	Mar-44	2.13%	Mar-49	3.58%	Mar-54	3.46%
Apr-39	-0.17%	Apr-44	-0.81%	Apr-49	-1.53%	Apr-54	5.36%
May-39	6.63%	May-44	4.48%	May-49	-3.18%	May-54	3.73%
Jun-39	-6.02%	Jun-44	5.53%	Jun-49	0.33%	Jun-54	0.50%
Jul-39	11.33%	Jul-44	-1.67%	Jul-49	6.93%	Jul-54	6.11%
Aug-39	-6.72%	Aug-44	1.29%	Aug-49	1.75%	Aug-54	-2.99%
Sep-39	16.85%	Sep-44	0.10%	Sep-49	2.89%	Sep-54	8.72%
Oct-39	-1.05%	Oct-44	0.42%	Oct-49	3.57%	Oct-54	-1.55%
Nov-39	-4.51%	Nov-44	0.81%	Nov-49	0.71%	Nov-54	8.47%
Dec-39	2.80%	Dec-44	3.92%	Dec-49	4.96%	Dec-54	5.45%
Jan-40	-3.11%	Jan-45	1.84%	Jan-50	2.31%	Jan-55	2.15%
Feb-40	1.06%	Feb-45	6.56%	Feb-50	1.57%	Feb-55	0.73%
Mar-40	1.47%	Mar-45	-4.24%	Mar-50	0.97%	Mar-55	-0.13%
Apr-40	-0.08%	Apr-45	9.20%	Apr-50	5.09%	Apr-55	4.10%
May-40	-23.52%	May-45	1.51%	May-50	4.48%	May-55	0.21%
Jun-40	8.33%	Jun-45	0.03%	Jun-50	-5.27%	Jun-55	8.58%
Jul-40	3.58%	Jul-45	-1.64%	Jul-50	1.48%	Jul-55	6.43%
Aug-40	3.12%	Aug-45	6.17%	Aug-50	3.87%	Aug-55	-0.47%
Sep-40	1.60%	Sep-45	4.55%	Sep-50	6.19%	Sep-55	1.45%
Oct-40	4.42%	Oct-45	3.37%	Oct-50	1.04%	Oct-55	-2.74%
Nov-40	-3.70%	Nov-45	3.57%	Nov-50	0.52%	Nov-55	7.82%
Dec-40	0.18%	Dec-45	1.31%	Dec-50	5.24%	Dec-55	0.20%
Jan-41	-4.23%	Jan-46	7.30%	Jan-51	6.75%	Jan-56	-3.31%
Feb-41	-0.94%	Feb-46	-6.64%	Feb-51	1.23%	Feb-56	3.78%
Mar-41	0.95%	Mar-46	4.96%	Mar-51	-1.25%	Mar-56	7.26%
Apr-41	-5.87%	Apr-46	4.07%	Apr-51	5.42%	Apr-56	0.10%
May-41	0.88%	May-46	2.54%	May-51	-3.48%	May-56	-6.28%
Jun-41	6.01%	Jun-46	-3.62%	Jun-51	-2.00%	Jun-56	4.26%
Jul-41	6.09%	Jul-46	-2.24%	Jul-51	7.47%	Jul-56	5.47%
Aug-41	-0.28%	Aug-46	-6.97%	Aug-51	4.49%	Aug-56	-3.51%
Sep-41	-0.42%	Sep-46	-9.79%	Sep-51	0.46%	Sep-56	-4.21%
Oct-41	-6.21%	Oct-46	-0.36%	Oct-51	-0.87%	Oct-56	0.84%
Nov-41	-3.61%	Nov-46	-0.79%	Nov-51	0.25%	Nov-56	-0.79%
Dec-41	-3.91%	Dec-46	4.69%	Dec-51	4.40%	Dec-56	3.84%
Jan-42	2.04%	Jan-47	2.70%	Jan-52	2.08%	Jan-57	-3.87%
Feb-42	-2.53%	Feb-47	-1.05%	Feb-52	-3.16%	Feb-57	-2.95%
Mar-42	-5.42%	Mar-47	-1.25%	Mar-52	5.27%	Mar-57	2.30%
Apr-42	-3.68%	Apr-47	-3.48%	Apr-52	-3.79%	Apr-57	4.02%
May-42	7.11%	May-47	-0.86%	May-52	2.79%	May-57	4.01%
Jun-42	2.51%	Jun-47	6.13%	Jun-52	5.13%	Jun-57	0.18%
Jul-42	3.76%	Jul-47	4.08%	Jul-52	2.27%	Jul-57	1.45%
Aug-42	1.31%	Aug-47	-2.46%	Aug-52	-0.96%	Aug-57	-5.31%
Sep-42	3.26%	Sep-47	-0.97%	Sep-52	-1.48%	Sep-57	-5.87%
Oct-42	7.00%	Oct-47	2.63%	Oct-52	0.37%	Oct-57	-2.85%
Nov-42	-0.86%	Nov-47	-2.40%	Nov-52	5.16%	Nov-57	1.97%
Dec-42	5.69%	Dec-47	2.57%	Dec-52	3.99%	Dec-57	-3.79%

Date	% Change	Date	% Change	Date	% Change	Date	% Change
Jan-58	4.64%	Jan-63	5.20%	Jan-68	-4.13%	Jan-73	-1.49%
Feb-58	-1.71%	Feb-63	-2.61%	Feb-68	-2.24%	Feb-73	-3.53%
Mar-58	3.45%	Mar-63	3.82%	Mar-68	0.57%	Mar-73	0.08%
Apr-58	3.53%	Apr-63	5.13%	Apr-68	8.32%	Apr-73	-3.83%
May-58	1.83%	May-63	1.70%	May-68	1.51%	May-73	-1.63%
Jun-58	2.94%	Jun-63	-1.76%	Jun-68	1.16%	Jun-73	-0.40%
Jul-58	4.63%	Jul-63	-0.08%	Jul-68	-1.59%	Jul-73	4.07%
Aug-58	1.49%	Aug-63	5.14%	Aug-68	1.40%	Aug-73	-3.41%
Sep-58	5.14%	Sep-63	-0.85%	Sep-68	4.11%	Sep-73	4.27%
Oct-58	2.83%	Oct-63	3.49%	Oct-68	0.97%	Oct-73	0.17%
Nov-58	2.52%	Nov-63	-0.80%	Nov-68	5.04%	Nov-73	-11.09%
Dec-58	5.48%	Dec-63	2.70%	Dec-68	-3.93%	Dec-73	1.98%
Jan-59	0.65%	Jan-64	2.95%	Jan-69	-0.57%	Jan-74	-0.72%
Feb-59	0.25%	Feb-64	1.24%	Feb-69	-4.49%	Feb-74	-0.07%
Mar-59	0.32%	Mar-64	1.77%	Mar-69	3.71%	Mar-74	-2.05%
Apr-59	4.15%	Apr-64	0.86%	Apr-69	2.40%	Apr-74	-3.59%
May-59	2.15%	May-64	1.39%	May-69	0.03%	May-74	-3.02%
Jun-59	-0.10%	Jun-64	1.89%	Jun-69	-5.31%	Jun-74	-1.14%
Jul-59	3.75%	Jul-64	2.07%	Jul-69	-5.75%	Jul-74	-7.42%
Aug-59	-1.25%	Aug-64	-1.38%	Aug-69	4.29%	Aug-74	-8.64%
Sep-59	-4.31%	Sep-64	3.12%	Sep-69	-2.23%	Sep-74	-11.52%
Oct-59	1.39%	Oct-64	1.06%	Oct-69	4.58%	Oct-74	16.81%
Nov-59	1.59%	Nov-64	-0.27%	Nov-69	-3.14%	Nov-74	-4.89%
Dec-59	3.02%	Dec-64	0.64%	Dec-69	-1.58%	Dec-74	-1.56%
Jan-60	-6.88%	Jan-65	3.57%	Jan-70	-7.36%	Jan-75	12.72%
Feb-60	1.21%	Feb-65	0.09%	Feb-70	5.57%	Feb-75	6.38%
Mar-60	-1.10%	Mar-65	-1.21%	Mar-70	0.44%	Mar-75	2.54%
Apr-60	-1.46%	Apr-65	3.68%	Apr-70	-8.75%	Apr-75	5.10%
May-60	2.98%	May-65	-0.53%	May-70	-5.78%	May-75	4.76%
Jun-60	2.24%	Jun-65	-4.62%	Jun-70	-4.66%	Jun-75	4.77%
Jul-60	-2.19%	Jul-65	1.61%	Jul-70	7.69%	Jul-75	-6.44%
Aug-60	2.90%	Aug-65	2.51%	Aug-70	4.78%	Aug-75	-1.76%
Sep-60	-5.75%	Sep-65	3.46%	Sep-70	3.62%	Sep-75	-3.12%
Oct-60	0.06%	Oct-65	2.99%	Oct-70	-0.83%	Oct-75	6.53%
Nov-60	4.33%	Nov-65	-0.63%	Nov-70	5.06%	Nov-75	2.82%
Dec-60	4.92%	Dec-65	1.14%	Dec-70	5.98%	Dec-75	-0.81%
Jan-61	6.59%	Jan-66	0.74%	Jan-71	4.32%	Jan-76	12.17%
Feb-61	2.95%	Feb-66	-1.54%	Feb-71	1.17%	Feb-76	-0.84%
Mar-61	2.81%	Mar-66	-1.93%	Mar-71	3.94%	Mar-76	3.37%
Apr-61	0.63%	Apr-66	2.32%	Apr-71	3.89%	Apr-76	-0.78%
May-61	2.16%	May-66	-5.15%	May-71	-3.91%	May-76	-1.11%
Jun-61	-2.63%	Jun-66	-1.34%	Jun-71	0.33%	Jun-76	4.43%
Jul-61	3.52%	Jul-66	-1.06%	Jul-71	-3.87%	Jul-76	-0.48%
Aug-61	2.21%	Aug-66	-7.49%	Aug-71	3.88%	Aug-76	-0.18%
Sep-61	-1.73%	Sep-66	-0.39%	Sep-71	-0.44%	Sep-76	2.58%
Oct-61	3.08%	Oct-66	5.07%	Oct-71	-3.91%	Oct-76	-1.86%
Nov-61	4.18%	Nov-66	0.61%	Nov-71	0.02%	Nov-76	-0.41%
Dec-61	0.56%	Dec-66	0.15%	Dec-71	8.88%	Dec-76	5.61%
Jan-62	-3.55%	Jan-67	8.12%	Jan-72	2.06%	Jan-77	-4.73%
Feb-62	1.87%	Feb-67	0.47%	Feb-72	2.77%	Feb-77	-1.82%
Mar-62	-0.34%	Mar-67	4.22%	Mar-72	0.83%	Mar-77	-1.05%
Apr-62	-5.95%	Apr-67	4.49%	Apr-72	0.68%	Apr-77	0.42%
May-62	-8.34%	May-67	-4.99%	May-72	1.97%	May-77	-1.96%
Jun-62	-7.90%	Jun-67	2.02%	Jun-72	-1.94%	Jun-77	4.94%
Jul-62	6.67%	Jul-67	4.80%	Jul-72	0.48%	Jul-77	-1.54%
Aug-62	1.83%	Aug-67	-0.91%	Aug-72	3.69%	Aug-77	-1.42%
Sep-62	-4.53%	Sep-67	3.54%	Sep-72	-0.25%	Sep-77	0.16%
Oct-62	0.76%	Oct-67	-2.65%	Oct-72	1.19%	Oct-77	-3.90%
Nov-62	10.47%	Nov-67	0.37%	Nov-72	4.81%	Nov-77	3.16%
Dec-62	1.63%	Dec-67	2.89%	Dec-72	1.42%	Dec-77	0.75%

Date	% Change	Date	% Change	Date	% Change	Date	% Change
Jan-78	-5.74%	Jan-83	3.72%	Jan-88	4.21%	Jan-93	0.84%
Feb-78	-2.03%	Feb-83	2.29%	Feb-88	4.66%	Feb-93	1.36%
Mar-78	2.94%	Mar-83	3.69%	Mar-88	-3.09%	Mar-93	2.11%
Apr-78	9.02%	Apr-83	7.88%	Apr-88	1.11%	Apr-93	-2.42%
May-78	0.92%	May-83	-0.87%	May-88	0.87%	May-93	2.68%
Jun-78	-1.38%	Jun-83	3.89%	Jun-88	4.57%	Jun-93	0.29%
Jul-78	5.83%	Jul-83	-2.95%	Jul-88	-0.38%	Jul-93	-0.40%
Aug-78	3.01%	Aug-83	1.50%	Aug-88	-3.40%	Aug-93	3.79%
Sep-78	-0.32%	Sep-83	1.38%	Sep-88	4.25%	Sep-93	-0.77%
Oct-78	-8.72%	Oct-83	-1.16%	Oct-88	2.82%	Oct-93	2.07%
Nov-78	2.15%	Nov-83	2.11%	Nov-88	-1.43%	Nov-93	-0.95%
Dec-78	1.96%	Dec-83	-0.52%	Dec-88	1.74%	Dec-93	1.21%
Jan-79	4.43%	Jan-84	-0.56%	Jan-89	7.31%	Jan-94	3.40%
Feb-79	-3.21%	Feb-84	-3.52%	Feb-89	-2.48%	Feb-94	-2.71%
Mar-79	5.96%	Mar-84	1.73%	Mar-89	2.32%	Mar-94	-4.36%
Apr-79	0.63%	Apr-84	0.95%	Apr-89	5.21%	Apr-94	1.28%
May-79	-2.17%	May-84	-5.54%	May-89	4.05%	May-94	1.64%
Jun-79	4.35%	Jun-84	2.17%	Jun-89	-0.57%	Jun-94	-2.45%
Jul-79	1.34%	Jul-84	-1.24%	Jul-89	9.03%	Jul-94	3.28%
Aug-79	5.77%	Aug-84	11.04%	Aug-89	1.95%	Aug-94	4.10%
Sep-79	0.43%	Sep-84	0.02%	Sep-89	-0.41%	Sep-94	-2.45%
Oct-79	-6.40%	Oct-84	0.39%	Oct-89	-2.32%	Oct-94	2.25%
Nov-79	4.75%	Nov-84	-1.12%	Nov-89	2.04%	Nov-94	-3.64%
Dec-79	2.14%	Dec-84	2.63%	Dec-89	2.40%	Dec-94	1.48%
Jan-80	6.22%	Jan-85	7.79%	Jan-90	-6.71%	Jan-95	2.59%
Feb-80	-0.01%	Feb-85	1.22%	Feb-90	1.30%	Feb-95	3.90%
Mar-80	-9.72%	Mar-85	0.07%	Mar-90	2.64%	Mar-95	2.95%
Apr-80	4.62%	Apr-85	-0.09%	Apr-90	-2.49%	Apr-95	2.94%
May-80	5.15%	May-85	5.78%	May-90	9.75%	May-95	4.00%
Jun-80	3.16%	Jun-85	1.57%	Jun-90	-0.67%	Jun-95	2.32%
Jul-80	6.96%	Jul-85	-0.15%	Jul-90	-0.32%	Jul-95	3.32%
Aug-80	1.01%	Aug-85	-0.85%	Aug-90	-9.04%	Aug-95	0.25%
Sep-80	2.94%	Sep-85	-3.13%	Sep-90	-4.87%	Sep-95	4.22%
Oct-80	2.02%	Oct-85	4.62%	Oct-90	-0.43%	Oct-95	-0.36%
Nov-80	10.65%	Nov-85	6.86%	Nov-90	6.46%	Nov-95	4.39%
Dec-80	-3.02	Dec-85	4.84%	Dec-90	2.79	Dec-95	1.93%
Jan-81	-4.18%	Jan-86	0.56%	Jan-91	4.35%	Jan-96	3.40%
Feb-81	1.74%	Feb-86	7.47%	Feb-91	7.15%	Feb-96	0.93%
Mar-81	4.00%	Mar-86	5.58%	Mar-91	2.42%	Mar-96	0.96%
Apr-81	-1.93%	Apr-86	-1.13%	Apr-91	0.24%	Apr-96	1.47%
May-81	0.26%	May-86	5.32%	May-91	4.31%	May-96	2.58%
Jun-81	-0.63%	Jun-86	1.69%	Jun-91	-4.58%	Jun-96	0.38%
Jul-81	0.21%	Jul-86	-5.59%	Jul-91	4.66%	Jul-96	-4.42%
Aug-81	-5.77%	Aug-86	7.42%	Aug-91	2.37%	Aug-96	2.11%
Sep-81	-4.93%	Sep-86	-8.27%	Sep-91	-1.67%	Sep-96	5.63%
Oct-81	5.40%	Oct-86	5.77%	Oct-91	1.34%	Oct-96	2.76%
Nov-81	4.13%	Nov-86	2.43%	Nov-91	-4.03%	Nov-96	7.56%
Dec-81	-2.56%	Dec-86	-2.55%	Dec-91	11.44%	Dec-96	-1.98%
Jan-82	-1.31%	Jan-87	13.47%	Jan-92	-1.86%	Jan-97	6.25%
Feb-82	-5.59%	Feb-87	3.95%	Feb-92	1.30%	Feb-97	0.78%
Mar-82	-0.52%	Mar-87	2.89%	Mar-92	-1.94%	Mar-97	-4.11%
Apr-82	4.52%	Apr-87	-0.89%	Apr-92	2.94%	Apr-97	5.97%
May-82	-3.41%	May-87	0.87%	May-92	0.49%	May-97	6.09%
Jun-82	-1.50%	Jun-87	5.05%	Jun-92	-1.49%	Jun-97	4.48%
Jul-82	-1.78%	Jul-87	5.07%	Jul-92	4.09%	Jul-97	7.96%
Aug-82	12.14%	Aug-87	3.73%	Aug-92	-2.05%	Aug-97	-5.60%
Sep-82	1.25%	Sep-87	-2.19%	Sep-92	1.18%	Sep-97	5.48%
Oct-82	11.51%	Oct-87	-21.54%	Oct-92	0.35%	Oct-97	-3.34%
Nov-82	4.04%	Nov-87	-8.24%	Nov-92	3.40%	Nov-97	4.63%
Dec-82	1.93%	Dec-87	7.61%	Dec-92	1.23%	Dec-97	1.72%

Date	% Change	Date	% Change	Date	% Change
Jan-98	1.11%	Jan-01	3.55%	Jan-04	1.84%
Feb-98	7.21%	Feb-01	-9.12%	Feb-04	1.39%
Mar-98	5.12%	Mar-01	-6.33%	Mar-04	-1.51%
Apr-98	1.01%	Apr-01	7.77%	Apr-04	-1.57%
May-98	-1.72%	May-01	0.67%	May-04	1.37%
Jun-98	4.06%	Jun-01	-2.43%	Jun-04	1.94%
Jul-98	-1.06%	Jul-01	-0.98%	Jul-04	-3.31%
Aug-98	-14.46%	Aug-01	-6.26%	Aug-04	0.40%
Sep-98	6.41%	Sep-01	-8.08%	Sep-04	1.08%
Oct-98	8.13%	Oct-01	1.91%	Oct-04	1.53%
Nov-98	6.06%	Nov-01	7.67%	Nov-04	4.05%
Dec-98	5.76%	Dec-01	0.88%	Dec-04	3.40%
Jan-99	4.18%	Jan-02	-1.46%	Jan-05	-2.44%
Feb-99	-3.11%	Feb-02	-1.93%	Feb-05	2.10%
Mar-99	4.00%	Mar-02	3.76%	Mar-05	-1.77%
Apr-99	3.87%	Apr-02	-6.06%	Apr-05	-1.90%
May-99	-2.36%	May-02	-0.74%	May-05	3.18%
Jun-99	5.55%	Jun-02	-7.12%	Jun-05	0.14%
Jul-99	-3.12%	Jul-02	-7.79%	Jul-05	3.72%
Aug-99	-0.49%	Aug-02	0.66%	Aug-05	-0.91%
Sep-99	-2.74%	Sep-02	-10.87%	Sep-05	0.81%
Oct-99	6.33%	Oct-02	8.80%	Oct-05	-1.67%
Nov-99	2.03%	Nov-02	5.89%	Nov-05	3.78%
Dec-99	5.89%	Dec-02	-5.87%	Dec-05	0.03%
Jan-00	-5.02%	Jan-03	-2.62%	Jan-06	2.65%
Feb-00	-1.89%	Feb-03	-1.50%	Feb-06	0.27%
Mar-00	9.78%	Mar-03	0.97%	Mar-06	1.24%
Apr-00	-3.01%	Apr-03	8.24%	Apr-06	1.34%
May-00	-2.05%	May-03	5.27%	May-06	-2.88%
Jun-00	2.47%	Jun-03	1.28%	Jun-06	0.14%
Jul-00	-1.56%	Jul-03	1.76%		
Aug-00	6.21%	Aug-03	1.95%		
Sep-00	-5.28%	Sep-03	-1.06%		
Oct-00	-0.42%	Oct-03	5.66%		
Nov-00	-7.88%	Nov-03	0.88%		
Dec-00	0.49%	Dec-03	5.24%		

Source: Global Financial Data.

APPENDIX C

Simulated Technology Returns

Date	% Change	Date	% Change	Date	% Change	Date	% Change
Jan-39	0.32%	Jan-42	6.09%	Jan-45	1.19%	Jan-48	-0.99%
Feb-39	-3.16%	Feb-42	-2.36%	Feb-45	4.86%	Feb-48	-7.61%
Mar-39	0.92%	Mar-42	-4.51%	Mar-45	-1.20%	Mar-48	2.38%
Apr-39	-10.23%	Apr-42	-1.84%	Apr-45	0.36%	Apr-48	7.40%
May-39	4.38%	May-42	-1.41%	May-45	1.84%	May-48	2.94%
Jun-39	5.74%	Jun-42	2.79%	Jun-45	4.15%	Jun-48	0.51%
Jul-39	2.93%	Jul-42	4.28%	Jul-45	-1.39%	Jul-48	-4.45%
Aug-39	-0.95%	Aug-42	0.83%	Aug-45	0.44%	Aug-48	-1.05%
Sep-39	7.67%	Sep-42	0.11%	Sep-45	7.68%	Sep-48	-1.54%
Oct-39	3.07%	Oct-42	3.52%	Oct-45	6.44%	Oct-48	0.80%
Nov-39	1.30%	Nov-42	2.66%	Nov-45	3.90%	Nov-48	-3.14%
Dec-39	-1.04%	Dec-42	-0.93%	Dec-45	1.15%	Dec-48	-4.03%
Jan-40	1.68%	Jan-43	5.12%	Jan-46	1.53%	Jan-49	-0.12%
Feb-40	3.39%	Feb-43	4.12%	Feb-46	-1.35%	Feb-49	-1.61%
Mar-40	1.46%	Mar-43	3.20%	Mar-46	-1.37%	Mar-49	-1.61%
Apr-40	1.12%	Apr-43	3.28%	Apr-46	9.11%	Apr-49	-1.92%
May-40	-16.07%	May-43	3.27%	May-46	1.54%	May-49	-4.04%
Jun-40	1.22%	Jun-43	0.22%	Jun-46	-0.21%	Jun-49	-4.24%
Jul-40	2.77%	Jul-43	3.72%	Jul-46	-4.53%	Jul-49	8.34%
Aug-40	-1.12%	Aug-43	-1.21%	Aug-46	-2.73%	Aug-49	2.25%
Sep-40	5.92%	Sep-43	1.43%	Sep-46	-17.46%	Sep-49	3.28%
Oct-40	5.10%	Oct-43	1.00%	Oct-46	1.42%	Oct-49	3.81%
Nov-40	2.63%	Nov-43	-2.10%	Nov-46	-0.64%	Nov-49	0.12%
Dec-40	-4.37%	Dec-43	-1.56%	Dec-46	5.53%	Dec-49	3.29%
Jan-41	2.07%	Jan-44	5.09%	Jan-47	1.75%	Jan-50	2.53%
Feb-41	-5.12%	Feb-44	0.81%	Feb-47	2.46%	Feb-50	1.41%
Mar-41	1.51%	Mar-44	1.33%	Mar-47	-4.97%	Mar-50	-1.45%
Apr-41	-3.50%	Apr-44	0.44%	Apr-47	-2.15%	Apr-50	1.30%
May-41	-2.53%	May-44	2.34%	May-47	-5.05%	May-50	2.24%
Jun-41	1.73%	Jun-44	2.36%	Jun-47	8.73%	Jun-50	-4.92%
Jul-41	3.95%	Jul-44	2.61%	Jul-47	4.31%	Jul-50	1.13%
Aug-41	-0.63%	Aug-44	1.40%	Aug-47	-0.75%	Aug-50	6.21%
Sep-41	0.68%	Sep-44	-0.11%	Sep-47	0.48%	Sep-50	5.90%
Oct-41	-5.01%	Oct-44	5.21%	Oct-47	5.15%	Oct-50	0.99%
Nov-41	-0.86%	Nov-44	-0.80%	Nov-47	-0.96%	Nov-50	1.42%
Dec-41	-10.27%	Dec-44	1.12%	Dec-47	-2.66%	Dec-50	4.50%

Date	% Change	Date	% Change	Date	% Change	Date	% Change
Jan-51	10.50%	Feb-56	2.67%	Mar-61	4.19%	Apr-66	3.72%
Feb-51	0.69%	Mar-56	6.79%	Apr-61	-1.87%	May-66	-4.41%
Mar-51	-4.07%	Apr-56	0.88%	May-61	-0.21%	Jun-66	-1.31%
Apr-51	4.66%	May-56	-3.83%	Jun-61	-2.07%	Jul-66	-0.95%
May-51	-2.90%	Jun-56	3.16%	Jul-61	0.66%	Aug-66	-10.00%
Jun-51	-3.39%	Jul-56	7.09%	Aug-61	2.90%	Sep-66	1.18%
Jul-51	4.46%	Aug-56	-3.45%	Sep-61	0.37%	Oct-66	8.85%
Aug-51	5.13%	Sep-56	-4.41%	Oct-61	5.67%	Nov-66	1.69%
Sep-51	0.90%	Oct-56	1.14%	Nov-61	6.28%	Dec-66	2.41%
Oct-51	-5.42%	Nov-56	-0.10%	Dec-61	-0.92%	Jan-67	6.47%
Nov-51	-1.18%	Dec-56	1.37%	Jan-62	-1.22%	Feb-67	0.85%
Dec-51	1.77%	Jan-57	0.84%	Feb-62	1.96%	Mar-67	4.66%
Jan-52	3.04%	Feb-57	-3.84%	Mar-62	-0.65%	Apr-67	3.30%
Feb-52	-4.08%	Mar-57	4.00%	Apr-62	-4.62%	May-67	-0.59%
Mar-52	0.76%	Apr-57	2.61%	May-62	-16.05%	Jun-67	3.93%
Apr-52	-4.46%	May-57	0.92%	Jun-62	-7.25%	Jul-67	4.17%
May-52	2.02%	Jun-57	-0.10%	Jul-62	5.02%	Aug-67	-0.78%
Jun-52	3.36%	Jul-57	2.37%	Aug-62	1.12%	Sep-67	2.67%
Jul-52	1.42%	Aug-57	-6.65%	Sep-62	-2.92%	Oct-67	-3.32%
Aug-52	-2.02%	Sep-57	-6.01%	Oct-62	-2.50%	Nov-67	1.03%
Sep-52	-1.07%	Oct-57	-8.88%	Nov-62	12.68%	Dec-67	1.84%
Oct-52	-2.29%	Nov-57	-0.42%	Dec-62	0.96%	Jan-68	0.13%
Nov-52	4.84%	Dec-57	-4.13%	Jan-63	4.42%	Feb-68	-3.72%
Dec-52	0.33%	Jan-58	10.34%	Feb-63	-0.22%	Mar-68	-3.46%
Jan-53	2.81%	Feb-58	-4.04%	Mar-63	3.30%	Apr-68	10.38%
Feb-53	-1.63%	Mar-58	5.88%	Apr-63	3.92%	May-68	7.71%
Mar-53	-0.24%	Apr-58	0.25%	May-63	1.73%	Jun-68	4.42%
Apr-53	-3.32%	May-58	2.62%	Jun-63	0.29%	Jul-68	-1.83%
May-53	-1.04%	Jun-58	0.63%	Jul-63	-0.03%	Aug-68	2.40%
Jun-53	-2.23%	Jul-58	5.29%	Aug-63	4.35%	Sep-68	3.45%
Jul-53	3.02%	Aug-58	2.72%	Sep-63	-1.25%	Oct-68	1.48%
Aug-53	-1.23%	Sep-58	3.71%	Oct-63	1.69%	Nov-68	3.38%
Sep-53	-2.99%	Oct-58	2.95%	Nov-63	-3.02%	Dec-68	-0.23%
Oct-53	3.30%	Nov-58	1.92%	Dec-63	3.88%	Jan-69	-1.19%
Nov-53	0.56%	Dec-58	3.63%	Jan-64	2.50%	Feb-69	-5.34%
Dec-53	0.77%	Jan-59	3.38%	Feb-64	1.86%	Mar-69	-1.29%
Jan-54	6.21%	Feb-59	2.58%	Mar-64	0.91%	Apr-69	1.70%
Feb-54	1.12%	Mar-59	-2.04%	Apr-64	3.62%	May-69	0.88%
Mar-54	3.23%	Apr-59	2.75%	May-64	0.93%	Jun-69	-7.88%
Apr-54	2.16%	May-59	0.38%	Jun-64	2.09%	Jul-69	-7.30%
May-54	1.81%	Jun-59	-1.92%	Jul-64	2.62%	Aug-69	6.95%
Jun-54	1.29%	Jul-59	1.93%	Aug-64	0.26%	Sep-69	4.96%
Jul-54	6.53%	Aug-59	-0.35%	Sep-64	4.51%	Oct-69	11.40%
Aug-54	2.06%	Sep-59	-5.00%	Oct-64	1.55%	Nov-69	-1.12%
Sep-54	1.92%	Oct-59	1.03%	Nov-64	0.51%	Dec-69	-2.37%
Oct-54	0.65%	Nov-59	0.55%	Dec-64	-0.27%	Jan-70	-3.93%
Nov-54	7.41%	Dec-59	3.81%	Jan-65	8.09%	Feb-70	4.04%
Dec-54	4.01%	Jan-60	-4.21%	Feb-65	0.69%	Mar-70	-0.80%
Jan-55	0.86%	Feb-60	-0.45%	Mar-65	-2.71%	Apr-70	-16.67%
Feb-55	3.02%	Mar-60	2.02%	Apr-65	5.67%	May-70	-13.24%
Mar-55	-1.12%	Apr-60	-0.64%	May-65	-5.10%	Jun-70	2.58%
Apr-55	6.20%	May-60	-0.69%	Jun-65	-7.33%	Jul-70	4.90%
May-55	-0.21%	Jun-60	1.77%	Jul-65	2.37%	Aug-70	0.66%
Jun-55	4.32%	Jul-60	-3.83%	Aug-65	2.58%	Sep-70	6.70%
Jul-55	2.31%	Aug-60	3.83%	Sep-65	5.27%	Oct-70	-1.78%
Aug-55	-2.72%	Sep-60	-7.44%	Oct-65	0.39%	Nov-70	3.08%
Sep-55	-0.93%	Oct-60	-2.21%	Nov-65	2.36%	Dec-70	7.48%
Oct-55	-1.29%	Nov-60	5.49%	Dec-65	4.82%	Jan-71	10.22%
Nov-55	4.54%	Dec-60	5.77%	Jan-66	0.93%	Feb-71	2.61%
Dec-55	-0.20%	Jan-61	9.80%	Feb-66	-1.22%		
Jan-56	0.26%	Feb-61	3.75%	Mar-66	-4.31%		

Source: Global Financial Data. Total returns as calculated by GFD to simulate a backtested Nasdaq Composite Index; not official Nasdaq data.

APPENDIX D

Nasdaq Composite Returns

Date	% Change	Date	% Change	Date	% Change	Date	% Change
		Jan-74	2.97%	Jan-77	-2.39%	Jan-80	7.02%
		Feb-74	-0.61%	Feb-77	-1.02%	Feb-80	-2.30%
Mar-71	4.57%	Mar-74	-2.20%	Mar-77	-0.47%	Mar-80	-17.10%
Apr-71	5.97%	Apr-74	-5.86%	Apr-77	1.43%	Apr-80	6.86%
May-71	-3.61%	May-74	-7.67%	May-77	0.12%	May-80	7.47%
Jun-71	-0.42%	Jun-74	-5.29%	Jun-77	4.33%	Jun-80	4.87%
Jul-71	-2.35%	Jul-74	-7.86%	Jul-77	0.92%	Jul-80	8.89%
Aug-71	2.99%	Aug-74	-10.89%	Aug-77	-0.55%	Aug-80	5.65%
Sep-71	0.56%	Sep-74	-10.74%	Sep-77	0.75%	Sep-80	3.44%
Oct-71	-3.60%	Oct-74	17.17%	Oct-77	-3.30%	Oct-80	2.67%
Nov-71	-1.08%	Nov-74	-3.50%	Nov-77	5.77%	Nov-80	7.97%
Dec-71	9.76%	Dec-74	-4.97%	Dec-77	1.84%	Dec-80	-2.79%
Jan-72	4.16%	Jan-75	16.65%	Jan-78	-4.00%	Jan-81	-2.24%
Feb-72	5.48%	Feb-75	4.61%	Feb-78	0.61%	Feb-81	0.10%
Mar-72	2.20%	Mar-75	3.64%	Mar-78	4.66%	Mar-81	6.15%
Apr-72	2.49%	Apr-75	3.81%	Apr-78	8.46%	Apr-81	3.12%
May-72	0.91%	May-75	5.81%	May-78	4.39%	May-81	3.11%
Jun-72	-1.85%	Jun-75	4.72%	Jun-78	0.05%	Jun-81	-3.45%
Jul-72	-1.79%	Jul-75	-4.40%	Jul-78	5.00%	Jul-81	-1.91%
Aug-72	1.72%	Aug-75	-5.02%	Aug-78	6.88%	Aug-81	-7.50%
Sep-72	-0.26%	Sep-75	-5.92%	Sep-78	-1.57%	Sep-81	-8.03%
Oct-72	0.49%	Oct-75	3.58%	Oct-78	-16.38%	Oct-81	8.45%
Nov-72	2.09%	Nov-75	2.35%	Nov-78	3.21%	Nov-81	3.14%
Dec-72	0.58%	Dec-75	-1.50%	Dec-78	2.87%	Dec-81	-2.75%
Jan-73	-3.99%	Jan-76	12.15%	Jan-79	6.65%	Jan-82	-3.80%
Feb-73	-6.22%	Feb-76	3.69%	Feb-79	-2.59%	Feb-82	-4.76%
Mar-73	-2.45%	Mar-76	0.40%	Mar-79	7.51%	Mar-82	-2.11%
Apr-73	-8.18%	Apr-76	-0.60%	Apr-79	1.56%	Apr-82	5.15%
May-73	-4.83%	May-76	-2.26%	May-79	-1.79%	May-82	-3.34%
Jun-73	-1.62%	Jun-76	2.59%	Jun-79	5.11%	Jun-82	-4.06%
Jul-73	7.59%	Jul-76	1.07%	Jul-79	2.32%	Jul-82	-2.31%
Aug-73	-3.47%	Aug-76	-1.74%	Aug-79	6.45%	Aug-82	2.92%
Sep-73	6.04%	Sep-76	1.74%	Sep-79	-0.31%	Sep-82	8.95%
Oct-73	-0.93%	Oct-76	-1.00%	Oct-79	-9.63%	Oct-82	13.31%
Nov-73	-15.12%	Nov-76	0.85%	Nov-79	6.44%	Nov-82	9.26%
Dec-73	-1.41%	Dec-76	7.42%	Dec-79	4.77%	Dec-82	0.04%

Date	% Change	Date	% Change	Date	% Change	Date	% Change
Jan-83	6.86%	Jan-88	4.29%	Jan-93	2.86%	Jan-98	3.12%
Feb-83	4.96%	Feb-88	6.47%	Feb-93	-3.67%	Feb-98	9.33%
Mar-83	3.89%	Mar-88	2.10%	Mar-93	2.89%	Mar-98	3.68%
Apr-83	8.22%	Apr-88	1.23%	Apr-93	-4.16%	Apr-98	1.78%
May-83	5.35%	May-88	-2.34%	May-93	5.91%	May-98	-4.79%
Jun-83	3.23%	Jun-88	6.57%	Jun-93	0.49%	Jun-98	6.51%
Jul-83	-4.63%	Jul-88	-1.86%	Jul-93	0.11%	Jul-98	-1.18%
Aug-83	-3.80%	Aug-88	-2.78%	Aug-93	5.41%	Aug-98	-19.93%
Sep-83	1.45%	Sep-88	2.96%	Sep-93	2.68%	Sep-98	12.99%
Oct-83	-7.45%	Oct-88	-1.35%	Oct-93	2.16%	Oct-98	4.58%
Nov-83	4.05%	Nov-88	-2.88%	Nov-93	-3.19%	Nov-98	10.06%
Dec-83	-2.47%	Dec-88	2.67%	Dec-93	2.97%	Dec-98	12.47%
Jan-84	-3.65%	Jan-89	5.22%	Jan-94	3.05%	Jan-99	14.28%
Feb-84	-5.91%	Feb-89	-0.40%	Feb-94	-1.00%	Feb-99	-8.69%
Mar-84	-0.71%	Mar-89	1.76%	Mar-94	-6.19%	Mar-99	7.58%
Apr-84	-1.33%	Apr-89	5.12%	Apr-94	-1.29%	Apr-99	3.31%
May-84	-5.91%	May-89	4.36%	May-94	0.18%	May-99	-2.84%
Jun-84	2.93%	Jun-89	-2.44%	Jun-94	-3.98%	Jun-99	8.71%
Jul-84	-4.15%	Jul-89	4.26%	Jul-94	2.29%	Jul-99	-1.76%
Aug-84	10.86%	Aug-89	3.18%	Aug-94	6.02%	Aug-99	3.82%
Sep-84	-1.85%	Sep-89	0.99%	Sep-94	-0.17%	Sep-99	0.25%
Oct-84	-1.16%	Oct-89	-3.66%	Oct-94	1.73%	Oct-99	8.02%
Nov-84	-1.82%	Nov-89	0.10%	Nov-94	-3.49%	Nov-99	12.46%
Dec-84	1.99%	Dec-89	-0.28%	Dec-94	0.22%	Dec-99	21.98%
Jan-85	12.67%	Jan-90	-8.58%	Jan-95	0.43%	Jan-00	-3.17%
Feb-85	1.96%	Feb-90	2.41%	Feb-95	5.10%	Feb-00	19.19%
Mar-85	-1.75%	Mar-90	2.28%	Mar-95	2.96%	Mar-00	-2.64%
Apr-85	0.49%	Apr-90	-3.55%	Apr-95	3.28%	Apr-00	-15.57%
May-85	3.65%	May-90	9.26%	May-95	2.44%	May-00	-11.91%
Jun-85	1.86%	Jun-90	0.72%	Jun-95	7.97%	Jun-00	16.62%
Jul-85	1.72%	Jul-90	-5.20%	Jul-95	7.26%	Jul-00	-5.02%
Aug-85	-1.19%	Aug-90	-13.01%	Aug-95	1.89%	Aug-00	11.66%
Sep-85	-5.84%	Sep-90	-9.63%	Sep-95	2.30%	Sep-00	-12.68%
Oct-85	4.36%	Oct-90	-4.26%	Oct-95	-0.72%	Oct-00	-8.25%
Nov-85	7.32%	Nov-90	8.86%	Nov-95	2.23%	Nov-00	-22.90%
Dec-85	3.33%	Dec-90	4.12%	Dec-95	-0.67%	Dec-00	-4.90%
Jan-86	3.51%	Jan-91	10.80%	Jan-96	0.73%	Jan-01	12.23%
Feb-86	7.08%	Feb-91	9.38%	Feb-96	3.80%	Feb-01	-22.39%
Mar-86	4.22%	Mar-91	6.46%	Mar-96	0.12%	Mar-01	-14.48%
Apr-86	2.27%	Apr-91	0.50%	Apr-96	8.09%	Apr-01	15.00%
May-86	4.41%	May-91	4.41%	May-96	4.44%	May-01	-0.27%
Jun-86	1.34%	Jun-91	-5.97%	Jun-96	-4.70%	Jun-01	2.43%
Jul-86	-8.42%	Jul-91	5.49%	Jul-96	-8.81%	Jul-01	-6.23%
Aug-86	3.09%	Aug-91	4.71%	Aug-96	5.64%	Aug-01	-10.94%
Sep-86	-8.41%	Sep-91	0.23%	Sep-96	7.48%	Sep-01	-17.00%
Oct-86	2.88%	Oct-91	3.06%	Oct-96	-0.44%	Oct-01	12.79%
Nov-86	-0.33%	Nov-91	-3.51%	Nov-96	5.82%	Nov-01	14.22%
Dec-86	-2.99%	Dec-91	11.92%	Dec-96	-0.12%	Dec-01	1.03%
Jan-87	12.40%	Jan-92	5.78%	Jan-97	6.88%	Jan-02	-0.84%
Feb-87	8.39%	Feb-92	2.14%	Feb-97	-5.13%	Feb-02	-10.47%
Mar-87	1.20%	Mar-92	-4.69%	Mar-97	-6.67%	Mar-02	6.58%
Apr-87	-2.85%	Apr-92	-4.16%	Apr-97	3.20%	Apr-02	-8.51%
May-87	-0.30%	May-92	1.15%	May-97	11.07%	May-02	-4.29%
Jun-87	1.95%	Jun-92	-3.71%	Jun-97	2.97%	Jun-02	-9.44%
Jul-87	2.42%	Jul-92	3.06%	Jul-97	10.53%	Jul-02	-9.22%
Aug-87	4.61%	Aug-92	-3.05%	Aug-97	-0.41%	Aug-02	-1.01%
Sep-87	-2.35%	Sep-92	3.58%	Sep-97	6.20%	Sep-02	-10.86%
Oct-87	-27.23%	Oct-92	3.75%	Oct-97	-5.46%	Oct-02	13.45%
Nov-87	-5.61%	Nov-92	7.86%	Nov-97	0.44%	Nov-02	11.21%
Dec-87	8.29%	Dec-92	3.71%	Dec-97	-1.89%	Dec-02	-9.69%

Date	% Change	Date	% Change	Date	% Change	Date	% Change
Jan-03	-1.09%	Jan-04	3.13%	Jan-05	-5.20%	Jan-06	1.96%
Feb-03	1.26%	Feb-04	-1.76%	Feb-05	-0.52%	Mar-06	4.06%
Mar-03	0.27%	Mar-04	-1.75%	Mar-05	-2.56%	Apr-06	-0.74%
Apr-03	9.18%	Apr-04	-3.71%	Apr-05	-3.88%	May-06	-6.19%
May-03	8.99%	May-04	3.47%	May-05	7.63%	Jun-06	-0.31%
Jun-03	1.69%	Jun-04	3.07%	Jun-05	-0.54%		
Jul-03	6.91%	Jul-04	-7.83%	Jul-05	6.22%		
Aug-03	4.35%	Aug-04	-2.61%	Aug-05	-1.50%		
Sep-03	-1.30%	Sep-04	3.20%	Sep-05	-0.02%		
Oct-03	8.13%	Oct-04	4.12%	Oct-05	-1.46%		
Nov-03	1.45%	Nov-04	6.17%	Nov-05	5.31%		
Dec-03	2.20%	Dec-04	3.75%	Dec-05	-1.23%		

Source: Global Financial Data.

APPENDIX E

U.K. Stock Market Total Returns

Date	% Change	Date	% Change	Date	% Change	Date	% Change
Jan-26	0.44%	Jan-29	3.27%	Jan-32	2.78%	Jan-35	-0.24%
Feb-26	-0.38%	Feb-29	-0.54%	Feb-32	-0.75%	Feb-35	3.57%
Mar-26	-1.45%	Mar-29	-0.23%	Mar-32	1.51%	Mar-35	-4.14%
Apr-26	0.04%	Apr-29	-0.65%	Apr-32	-8.48%	Apr-35	-3.25%
May-26	2.19%	May-29	-0.99%	May-32	-2.56%	May-35	4.47%
Jun-26	2.39%	Jun-29	0.66%	Jun-32	-3.36%	Jun-35	3.88%
Jul-26	-0.20%	Jul-29	2.94%	Jul-32	7.58%	Jul-35	2.57%
Aug-26	2.37%	Aug-29	1.84%	Aug-32	9.90%	Aug-35	0.19%
Sep-26	1.22%	Sep-29	0.96%	Sep-32	5.05%	Sep-35	-0.98%
Oct-26	-1.07%	Oct-29	-2.45%	Oct-32	-0.17%	Oct-35	-2.57%
Nov-26	1.43%	Nov-29	-8.25%	Nov-32	0.88%	Nov-35	3.42%
Dec-26	0.25%	Dec-29	0.45%	Dec-32	-0.69%	Dec-35	5.02%
Jan-27	2.46%	Jan-30	0.12%	Jan-33	0.97%	Jan-36	1.17%
Feb-27	1.40%	Feb-30	0.11%	Feb-33	0.01%	Feb-36	4.76%
Mar-27	-0.27%	Mar-30	-0.29%	Mar-33	0.43%	Mar-36	0.54%
Apr-27	1.37%	Apr-30	2.18%	Apr-33	0.41%	Apr-36	-1.83%
May-27	1.22%	May-30	-2.49%	May-33	4.59%	May-36	1.64%
Jun-27	0.28%	Jun-30	-5.34%	Jun-33	4.99%	Jun-36	-2.07%
Jul-27	0.70%	Jul-30	1.67%	Jul-33	6.60%	Jul-36	1.78%
Aug-27	0.99%	Aug-30	-4.12%	Aug-33	6.82%	Aug-36	2.60%
Sep-27	1.26%	Sep-30	3.21%	Sep-33	3.27%	Sep-36	2.66%
Oct-27	1.60%	Oct-30	-5.25%	Oct-33	-1.76%	Oct-36	1.68%
Nov-27	0.28%	Nov-30	-0.99%	Nov-33	5.16%	Nov-36	2.80%
Dec-27	1.04%	Dec-30	-4.95%	Dec-33	-2.98%	Dec-36	1.20%
Jan-28	1.04%	Jan-31	1.04%	Jan-34	1.73%	Jan-37	-0.14%
Feb-28	0.21%	Feb-31	0.12%	Feb-34	2.13%	Feb-37	0.00%
Mar-28	3.06%	Mar-31	0.71%	Mar-34	1.25%	Mar-37	-3.43%
Apr-28	2.31%	Apr-31	-4.46%	Apr-34	1.93%	Apr-37	-0.35%
May-28	2.35%	May-31	-9.38%	May-34	1.50%	May-37	-2.32%
Jun-28	-2.90%	Jun-31	1.87%	Jun-34	-1.52%	Jun-37	1.56%
Jul-28	-0.30%	Jul-31	2.20%	Jul-34	-1.95%	Jul-37	-2.70%
Aug-28	1.99%	Aug-31	-6.41%	Aug-34	-1.86%	Aug-37	0.85%
Sep-28	1.96%	Sep-31	-8.42%	Sep-34	3.01%	Sep-37	0.86%
Oct-28	1.62%	Oct-31	12.93%	Oct-34	2.38%	Oct-37	-2.98%
Nov-28	0.80%	Nov-31	-0.76%	Nov-34	-0.02%	Nov-37	-3.45%
Dec-28	-0.04%	Dec-31	-8.37%	Dec-34	2.75%	Dec-37	-4.64%

Date	% Change	Date	% Change	Date	% Change	Date	% Change
Jan-38	0.67%	Jan-43	4.12%	Jan-48	0.69%	Jan-53	2.89%
Feb-38	0.03%	Feb-43	-0.04%	Feb-48	-9.40%	Feb-53	3.62%
Mar-38	-5.14%	Mar-43	1.04%	Mar-48	4.22%	Mar-53	0.98%
Apr-38	-5.64%	Apr-43	0.64%	Apr-48	2.94%	Apr-53	-1.92%
May-38	6.82%	May-43	1.16%	May-48	2.15%	May-53	-3.15%
Jun-38	-7.20%	Jun-43	-0.16%	Jun-48	-6.44%	Jun-53	1.78%
Jul-38	4.26%	Jul-43	2.89%	Jul-48	-0.95%	Jul-53	3.48%
Aug-38	0.96%	Aug-43	2.57%	Aug-48	2.64%	Aug-53	3.68%
Sep-38	-4.29%	Sep-43	1.00%	Sep-48	0.75%	Sep-53	3.09%
Oct-38	-8.21%	Oct-43	-0.65%	Oct-48	3.32%	Oct-53	2.92%
Nov-38	10.37%	Nov-43	-1.93%	Nov-48	2.90%	Nov-53	2.86%
Dec-38	-0.43%	Dec-43	1.68%	Dec-48	-1.09%	Dec-53	1.11%
Jan-39	-2.01%	Jan-44	1.65%	Jan-49	1.77%	Jan-54	4.02%
Feb-39	-3.44%	Feb-44	0.12%	Feb-49	-1.86%	Feb-54	3.38%
Mar-39	7.96%	Mar-44	0.62%	Mar-49	-5.78%	Mar-54	0.64%
Apr-39	-2.18%	Apr-44	1.51%	Apr-49	1.55%	Apr-54	4.63%
May-39	-3.44%	May-44	3.88%	May-49	-3.94%	May-54	5.01%
Jun-39	8.76%	Jun-44	2.78%	Jun-49	-8.32%	Jun-54	0.24%
Jul-39	-3.44%	Jul-44	2.95%	Jul-49	4.46%	Jul-54	4.75%
Aug-39	-0.15%	Aug-44	-1.16%	Aug-49	1.08%	Aug-54	6.09%
Sep-39	-5.17%	Sep-44	-1.41%	Sep-49	2.36%	Sep-54	2.72%
tct-39	0.52%	Oct-44	1.19%	Oct-49	-3.71%	Oct-54	5.38%
Nov-39	11.77%	Nov-44	2.01%	Nov-49	0.17%	Nov-54	-0.74%
Dec-39	-0.71%	Dec-44	0.46%	Dec-49	3.60%	Dec-54	-0.28%
Jan-40	-0.38%	Jan-45	0.70%	Jan-50	-2.26%	Jan-55	5.70%
Feb-40	0.84%	Feb-45	1.04%	Feb-50	1.96%	Feb-55	-6.89%
Mar-40	7.58%	Mar-45	0.58%	Mar-50	0.24%	Mar-55	-0.82%
Apr-40	-1.66%	Apr-45	1.95%	Apr-50	0.55%	Apr-55	2.80%
May-40	-1.61%	May-45	-4.29%	May-50	2.54%	May-55	5.13%
Jun-40	-14.02%	Jun-45	2.02%	Jun-50	3.02%	Jun-55	6.19%
Jul-40	-20.87%	Jul-45	-2.79%	Jul-50	-1.67%	Jul-55	1.69%
Aug-40	10.49%	Aug-45	1.33%	Aug-50	3.01%	Aug-55	-6.48%
Sep-40	5.32%	Sep-45	1.79%	Sep-50	4.76%	Sep-55	-1.40%
Oct-40	3.97%	Oct-45	4.11%	Oct-50	0.15%	Oct-55	-3.06%
Nov-40	6.88%	Nov-45	-0.90%	Nov-50	1.28%	Nov-55	2.11%
Dec-40	1.36%	Dec-45	-1.60%	Dec-50	-1.65%	Dec-55	3.14%
Jan-41	3.16%	Jan-46	2.23%	Jan-51	3.66%	Jan-56	-4.32%
Feb-41	-2.83%	Feb-46	0.81%	Feb-51	3.96%	Feb-56	-4.67%
Mar-41	-0.48%	Mar-46	-0.43%	Mar-51	-3.89%	Mar-56	0.09%
Apr-41	-0.49%	Apr-46	3.37%	Apr-51	8.66%	Apr-56	9.54%
May-41	2.82%	May-46	4.73%	May-51	3.71%	May-56	-3.47%
Jun-41	3.36%	Jun-46	-0.07%	Jun-51	0.30%	Jun-56	0.11%
Jul-41	9.00%	Jul-46	-0.10%	Jul-51	-5.74%	Jul-56	0.52%
Aug-41	4.47%	Aug-46	2.56%	Aug-51	2.99%	Aug-56	2.18%
Sep-41	2.72%	Sep-46	-2.57%	Sep-51	4.02%	Sep-56	-0.37%
Oct-41	0.09%	Oct-46	3.19%	Oct-51	0.88%	Oct-56	-1.20%
Nov-41	6.46%	Nov-46	4.02%	Nov-51	-7.60%	Nov-56	-6.38%
Dec-41	-1.22%	Dec-46	3.69%	Dec-51	-1.96%	Dec-56	5.89%
Jan-42	2.56%	Jan-47	0.04%	Jan-52	-6.04%	Jan-57	7.30%
Feb-42	-3.94%	Feb-47	-1.66%	Feb-52	-0.74%	Feb-57	1.25%
Mar-42	-0.42%	Mar-47	-0.38%	Mar-52	-3.27%	Mar-57	0.98%
Apr-42	1.45%	Apr-47	4.51%	Apr-52	5.27%	Apr-57	6.38%
May-42	2.11%	May-47	1.26%	May-52	-6.17%	May-57	1.11%
Jun-42	0.42%	Jun-47	0.66%	Jun-52	-3.68%	Jun-57	1.79%
Jul-42	3.25%	Jul-47	-5.59%	Jul-52	7.29%	Jul-57	0.86%
Aug-42	2.68%	Aug-47	-8.00%	Aug-52	5.68%	Aug-57	-2.31%
Sep-42	4.04%	Sep-47	1.74%	Sep-52	0.53%	Sep-57	-8.76%
Oct-42	5.42%	Oct-47	-1.69%	Oct-52	1.16%	Oct-57	-5.45%
Nov-42	4.44%	Nov-47	6.01%	Nov-52	0.32%	Nov-57	1.83%
Dec-42	0.51%	Dec-47	5.88%	Dec-52	1.99%	Dec-57	-1.04%

Date	% Change	Date	% Change	Date	% Change
Jan-58	-1.54%	Jan-60	-0.19%	Jan-62	0.69%
Feb-58	-4.64%	Feb-60	-1.77%	Feb-62	1.41%
Mar-58	7.18%	Mar-60	1.16%	Mar-62	-2.10%
Apr-58	5.23%	Apr-60	-5.19%	Apr-62	5.17%
May-58	1.23%	May-60	4.01%		
Jun-58	5.54%	Jun-60	-2.34%		
Jul-58	0.70%	Jul-60	0.57%		
Aug-58	6.36%	Aug-60	5.84%		
Sep-58	3.85%	Sep-60	-0.62%		
Oct-58	3.73%	Oct-60	1.74%		
Nov-58	1.44%	Nov-60	-4.58%		
Dec-58	7.03%	Dec-60	1.70%		
Jan-59	-1.44%	Jan-61	4.43%		
Feb-59	2.98%	Feb-61	5.32%		
Mar-59	1.04%	Mar-61	4.67%		
Apr-59	4.97%	Apr-61	2.56%		
May-59	3.62%	May-61	-0.89%		
Jun-59	0.62%	Jun-61	-7.65%		
Jul-59	-1.37%	Jul-61	-2.34%		
Aug-59	9.02%	Aug-61	-3.47%		
Sep-59	-1.67%	Sep-61	-0.99%		
Oct-59	14.99%	Oct-61	-2.02%		
Nov-59	2.82%	Nov-61	1.76%		
Dec-59	7.24%	Dec-61	2.02%		

Source: Global Financial Data. Total returns as calculated by GFD to simulate a backtested FTSE All-Share index; not official FTSE data.

APPENDIX F

U.K. Stock Market (FTSE All-Share) Total Returns

Date	% Change	Date	% Change	Date	% Change	Date	% Change
		Jan-65	3.91%	Jan-68	7.01%	Jan-71	0.92%
		Feb-65	-0.94%	Feb-68	-2.08%	Feb-71	-2.12%
		Mar-65	-0.44%	Mar-68	9.16%	Mar-71	7.16%
		Apr-65	1.03%	Apr-68	8.63%	Apr-71	11.94%
May-62	-11.09%	May-65	-0.14%	May-68	-0.84%	May-71	3.86%
Jun-62	-1.86%	Jun-65	-4.46%	Jun-68	5.87%	Jun-71	2.22%
Jul-62	-1.43%	Jul-65	0.38%	Jul-68	3.38%	Jul-71	7.73%
Aug-62	6.33%	Aug-65	1.40%	Aug-68	3.53%	Aug-71	0.63%
Sep-62	-1.40%	Sep-65	6.19%	Sep-68	-0.21%	Sep-71	0.42%
Oct-62	1.55%	Oct-65	5.31%	Oct-68	-0.87%	Oct-71	-1.66%
Nov-62	5.87%	Nov-65	1.56%	Nov-68	-0.14%	Nov-71	2.99%
Dec-62	1.86%	Dec-65	-1.40%	Dec-68	7.80%	Dec-71	6.26%
Jan-63	0.75%	Jan-66	3.62%	Jan-69	4.46%	Jan-72	4.65%
Feb-63	2.12%	Feb-66	1.34%	Feb-69	-9.78%	Feb-72	6.24%
Mar-63	2.60%	Mar-66	-2.35%	Mar-69	0.98%	Mar-72	2.03%
Apr-63	-2.81%	Apr-66	0.36%	Apr-69	-4.56%	Apr-72	4.28%
May-63	0.85%	May-66	4.33%	May-69	-3.64%	May-72	-3.78%
Jun-63	-0.56%	Jun-66	2.55%	Jun-69	-4.96%	Jun-72	-4.79%
Jul-63	1.38%	Jul-66	-9.68%	Jul-69	-7.24%	Jul-72	6.06%
Aug-63	3.33%	Aug-66	-8.73%	Aug-69	4.39%	Aug-72	2.23%
Sep-63	1.84%	Sep-66	3.74%	Sep-69	2.53%	Sep-72	-10.40%
Oct-63	1.89%	Oct-66	-3.51%	Oct-69	-3.81%	Oct-72	3.93%
Nov-63	1.41%	Nov-66	1.89%	Nov-69	5.48%	Nov-72	8.09%
Dec-63	1.90%	Dec-66	3.47%	Dec-69	5.18%	Dec-72	-1.61%
Jan-64	-1.81%	Jan-67	2.50%	Jan-70	1.05%	Jan-73	-9.68%
Feb-64	-2.92%	Feb-67	-1.54%	Feb-70	-4.13%	Feb-73	-3.55%
Mar-64	3.12%	Mar-67	4.56%	Mar-70	1.86%	Mar-73	0.62%
Apr-64	1.66%	Apr-67	5.22%	Apr-70	-10.01%	Apr-73	0.90%
May-64	-1.01%	May-67	-0.05%	May-70	-6.73%	May-73	1.30%
Jun-64	-1.05%	Jun-67	4.78%	Jun-70	5.15%	Jun-73	-0.03%
Jul-64	4.26%	Jul-67	0.65%	Jul-70	4.32%	Jul-73	-4.95%
Aug-64	1.36%	Aug-67	2.53%	Aug-70	0.17%	Aug-73	-3.12%
Sep-64	0.88%	Sep-67	5.21%	Sep-70	6.88%	Sep-73	3.66%
Oct-64	-2.10%	Oct-67	5.32%	Oct-70	-0.05%	Oct-73	3.33%
Nov-64	-4.25%	Nov-67	5.19%	Nov-70	-6.31%	Nov-73	-12.71%
Dec-64	-3.29%	Dec-67	-3.03%	Dec-70	6.08%	Dec-73	-7.48%

Date	% Change	Date	% Change	Date	% Change	Date	% Change
Jan-74	-4.12%	Jan-79	2.06%	Jan-84	6.96%	Jan-89	13.96%
Feb-74	4.82%	Feb-79	6.68%	Feb-84	-1.29%	Feb-89	-0.75%
Mar-74	-20.38%	Mar-79	12.60%	Mar-84	6.70%	Mar-89	3.59%
Apr-74	8.98%	Apr-79	5.37%	Apr-84	2.39%	Apr-89	1.93%
May-74	-7.89%	May-79	-6.10%	May-84	-10.41%	May-89	0.55%
Jun-74	-9.89%	Jun-79	-4.72%	Jun-84	2.60%	Jun-89	1.30%
Jul-74	-4.06%	Jul-79	-3.88%	Jul-84	-2.23%	Jul-89	7.01%
Aug-74	-11.61%	Aug-79	4.85%	Aug-84	10.08%	Aug-89	3.26%
Sep-74	-12.09%	Sep-79	3.46%	Sep-84	3.33%	Sep-89	-2.79%
Oct-74	3.56%	Oct-79	-6.27%	Oct-84	1.85%	Oct-89	-7.26%
Nov-74	-14.82%	Nov-79	-2.04%	Nov-84	3.48%	Nov-89	5.76%
Dec-74	1.37%	Dec-79	-0.10%	Dec-84	6.22%	Dec-89	6.18%
Jan-75	54.10%	Jan-80	10.18%	Jan-85	3.78%	Jan-90	-2.95%
Feb-75	24.47%	Feb-80	5.34%	Feb-85	-0.84%	Feb-90	-3.46%
Mar-75	-5.94%	Mar-80	-8.39%	Mar-85	2.24%	Mar-90	-0.01%
Apr-75	18.59%	Apr-80	4.39%	Apr-85	1.34%	Apr-90	-5.96%
May-75	4.61%	May-80	-1.79%	May-85	2.34%	May-90	11.15%
Jun-75	-11.35%	Jun-80	11.24%	Jun-85	-5.74%	Jun-90	1.86%
Jul-75	-2.72%	Jul-80	5.30%	Jul-85	2.26%	Jul-90	-1.56%
Aug-75	14.22%	Aug-80	0.66%	Aug-85	6.96%	Aug-90	-7.99%
Sep-75	3.17%	Sep-80	3.18%	Sep-85	-2.66%	Sep-90	-7.91%
Oct-75	4.38%	Oct-80	6.07%	Oct-85	7.21%	Oct-90	3.40%
Nov-75	1.87%	Nov-80	0.78%	Nov-85	4.10%	Nov-90	4.36%
Dec-75	4.25%	Dec-80	-4.46%	Dec-85	-1.70%	Dec-90	0.53%
Jan-76	9.69%	Jan-81	-0.51%	Jan-86	2.09%	Jan-91	0.62%
Feb-76	-2.81%	Feb-81	5.75%	Feb-86	8.23%	Feb-91	11.33%
Mar-76	-1.04%	Mar-81	2.34%	Mar-86	8.27%	Mar-91	4.19%
Apr-76	3.37%	Apr-81	7.73%	Apr-86	1.38%	Apr-91	1.58%
May-76	-6.42%	May-81	-4.54%	May-86	-3.05%	May-91	0.25%
Jun-76	-1.04%	Jun-81	2.07%	Jun-86	3.84%	Jun-91	-3.03%
Jul-76	-2.12%	Jul-81	0.15%	Jul-86	-5.13%	Jul-91	7.14%
Aug-76	-4.33%	Aug-81	5.23%	Aug-86	6.14%	Aug-91	2.94%
Sep-76	-5.75%	Sep-81	-16.36%	Sep-86	-5.35%	Sep-91	0.37%
Oct-76	-10.61%	Oct-81	3.36%	Oct-86	5.15%	Oct-91	-2.00%
Nov-76	8.25%	Nov-81	10.61%	Nov-86	1.30%	Nov-91	-5.33%
Dec-76	18.52%	Dec-81	-0.12%	Dec-86	2.85%	Dec-91	2.00%
Jan-77	10.12%	Jan-82	6.19%	Jan-87	8.22%	Jan-92	3.67%
Feb-77	3.02%	Feb-82	-3.82%	Feb-87	9.18%	Feb-92	0.51%
Mar-77	3.88%	Mar-82	3.60%	Mar-87	2.19%	Mar-92	-4.16%
Apr-77	3.15%	Apr-82	0.96%	Apr-87	2.74%	Apr-92	10.17%
May-77	3.32%	May-82	3.34%	May-87	7.50%	May-92	2.44%
Jun-77	2.81%	Jun-82	-3.87%	Jun-87	5.47%	Jun-92	-6.76%
Jul-77	-2.16%	Jul-82	3.96%	Jul-87	4.44%	Jul-92	-5.64%
Aug-77	11.75%	Aug-82	3.33%	Aug-87	-4.21%	Aug-92	-3.62%
Sep-77	9.13%	Sep-82	5.89%	Sep-87	5.73%	Sep-92	10.50%
Oct-77	-1.73%	Oct-82	2.61%	Oct-87	-26.51%	Oct-92	4.49%
Nov-77	-4.69%	Nov-82	2.00%	Nov-87	-9.93%	Nov-92	4.84%
Dec-77	3.38%	Dec-82	2.29%	Dec-87	9.70%	Dec-92	4.17%
Jan-78	-4.51%	Jan-83	3.78%	Jan-88	5.33%	Jan-93	0.19%
Feb-78	-4.77%	Feb-83	1.48%	Feb-88	-0.46%	Feb-93	2.48%
Mar-78	6.69%	Mar-83	3.60%	Mar-88	-0.68%	Mar-93	1.84%
Apr-78	1.99%	Apr-83	7.05%	Apr-88	4.01%	Apr-93	-1.05%
May-78	4.48%	May-83	0.03%	May-88	-0.10%	May-93	1.42%
Jun-78	-2.34%	Jun-83	5.28%	Jun-88	4.58%	Jun-93	2.29%
Jul-78	6.89%	Jul-83	-2.45%	Jul-88	0.55%	Jul-93	1.40%
Aug-78	2.92%	Aug-83	1.40%	Aug-88	-5.08%	Aug-93	6.54%
Sep-78	-0.15%	Sep-83	-0.67%	Sep-88	4.33%	Sep-93	-1.52%
Oct-78	-3.47%	Oct-83	-1.44%	Oct-88	2.32%	Oct-93	4.16%
Nov-78	1.93%	Nov-83	6.03%	Nov-88	-2.99%	Nov-93	-0.33%
Dec-78	-0.60%	Dec-83	2.27%	Dec-88	-0.27%	Dec-93	8.32%

Date	% Change	Date	% Change	Date	% Change	Date	% Change
Jan-94	3.94%	Jan-98	3.95%	Jan-02	-1.04%	Jan-06	2.91%
Feb-94	-3.80%	Feb-98	5.78%	Feb-02	-0.81%	Feb-06	1.20%
Mar-94	-6.21%	Mar-98	4.36%	Mar-02	4.19%	Mar-06	3.79%
Apr-94	1.52%	Apr-98	0.56%	Apr-02	-1.55%	Apr-06	1.06%
May-94	-4.83%	May-98	0.59%	May-02	-1.23%	May-06	-4.78%
Jun-94	-2.08%	Jun-98	-1.92%	Jun-02	-8.42%	Jun-06	2.01%
Jul-94	6.00%	Jul-98	-0.15%	Jul-02	-9.22%		
Aug-94	5.58%	Aug-98	-10.38%	Aug-02	0.33%		
Sep-94	-6.68%	Sep-98	-3.70%	Sep-02	-11.76%		
Oct-94	1.93%	Oct-98	6.98%	Oct-02	7.79%		
Nov-94	-0.28%	Nov-98	5.05%	Nov-02	3.54%		
Dec-94	-0.04%	Dec-98	1.92%	Dec-02	-5.34%		
Jan-95	-2.56%	Jan-99	0.87%	Jan-03	-8.97%		
Feb-95	0.74%	Feb-99	4.96%	Feb-03	2.62%		
Mar-95	4.32%	Mar-99	3.09%	Mar-03	-0.62%		
Apr-95	2.92%	Apr-99	4.85%	Apr-03	9.37%		
May-95	3.81%	May-99	-4.44%	May-03	4.39%		
Jun-95	-0.21%	Jun-99	2.15%	Jun-03	0.31%		
Jul-95	5.12%	Jul-99	-0.63%	Jul-03	3.95%		
Aug-95	1.40%	Aug-99	0.89%	Aug-03	1.57%		
Sep-95	1.34%	Sep-99	-3.66%	Sep-03	-1.59%		
Oct-95	0.26%	Oct-99	2.86%	Oct-03	4.95%		
Nov-95	3.40%	Nov-99	6.43%	Nov-03	1.29%		
Dec-95	1.32%	Dec-99	5.17%	Dec-03	2.92%		
Jan-96	2.47%	Jan-00	-8.16%	Jan-04	-0.86%		
Feb-96	0.17%	Feb-00	0.69%	Feb-04	2.86%		
Mar-96	0.84%	Mar-00	4.42%	Mar-04	-1.32%		
Apr-96	4.32%	Apr-00	-3.29%	Apr-04	2.06%		
May-96	-1.21%	May-00	0.68%	May-04	-1.32%		
Jun-96	-1.21%	Jun-00	0.53%	Jun-04	1.47%		
Jul-96	-0.75%	Jul-00	1.18%	Jul-04	-1.54%		
Aug-96	5.00%	Aug-00	5.18%	Aug-04	1.65%		
Sep-96	1.88%	Sep-00	-5.43%	Sep-04	2.78%		
Oct-96	0.80%	Oct-00	1.72%	Oct-04	1.57%		
Nov-96	1.67%	Nov-00	-4.19%	Nov-04	2.93%		
Dec-96	1.73%	Dec-00	1.49%	Dec-04	2.04%		
Jan-97	3.78%	Jan-01	1.61%	Jan-05	1.33%		
Feb-97	1.18%	Feb-01	-5.08%	Feb-05	2.59%		
Mar-97	0.26%	Mar-01	-5.05%	Mar-05	-0.87%		
Apr-97	2.14%	Apr-01	6.05%	Apr-05	-2.41%		
May-97	3.38%	May-01	-1.80%	May-05	4.07%		
Jun-97	-0.39%	Jun-01	-2.82%	Jun-05	3.40%		
Jul-97	5.05%	Jul-01	-2.28%	Jul-05	3.39%		
Aug-97	-0.40%	Aug-01	-2.50%	Aug-05	1.17%		
Sep-97	8.10%	Sep-01	-9.27%	Sep-05	3.42%		
Oct-97	-7.14%	Oct-01	3.24%	Oct-05	-2.89%		
Nov-97	1.53%	Nov-01	4.36%	Nov-05	3.30%		
Dec-97	5.94%	Dec-01	0.45%	Dec-05	3.94%		

Source: Global Financial Data.

APPENDIX G

Germany Stock Market Returns

Date	% Change		Date	% Change		Date	% Change		Date	% Change
Jan-26	11.50%		Jan-29	-1.01%		Jan-32	0.63%		Jan-35	4.94%
Feb-26	10.24%		Feb-29	-2.96%		Feb-32	0.64%		Feb-35	3.85%
Mar-26	6.13%		Mar-29	0.04%		Mar-32	0.63%		Mar-35	1.93%
Apr-26	9.22%		Apr-29	0.42%		Apr-32	0.63%		Apr-35	1.97%
May-26	-1.09%		May-29	-3.66%		May-32	2.50%		May-35	2.29%
Jun-26	6.55%		Jun-29	2.84%		Jun-32	-1.21%		Jun-35	3.29%
Jul-26	8.47%		Jul-29	-1.73%		Jul-32	0.96%		Jul-35	1.29%
Aug-26	10.01%		Aug-29	-0.66%		Aug-32	5.09%		Aug-35	1.18%
Sep-26	2.60%		Sep-29	-0.92%		Sep-32	13.37%		Sep-35	-2.62%
Oct-26	10.09%		Oct-29	-5.39%		Oct-32	-2.66%		Oct-35	-1.52%
Nov-26	6.42%		Nov-29	-3.49%		Nov-32	2.17%		Nov-35	-1.28%
Dec-26	-0.08%		Dec-29	-3.33%		Dec-32	6.44%		Dec-35	0.11%
Jan-27	14.75%		Jan-30	4.72%		Jan-33	4.92%		Jan-36	3.08%
Feb-27	6.68%		Feb-30	1.03%		Feb-33	0.61%		Feb-36	2.50%
Mar-27	-2.61%		Mar-30	-0.77%		Mar-33	8.92%		Mar-36	-0.14%
Apr-27	6.30%		Apr-30	3.19%		Apr-33	3.85%		Apr-36	3.47%
May-27	-3.81%		May-30	0.10%		May-33	0.99%		May-36	3.50%
Jun-27	-8.47%		Jun-30	-3.78%		Jun-33	-1.97%		Jun-36	2.76%
Jul-27	3.57%		Jul-30	-4.95%		Jul-33	-4.02%		Jul-36	1.74%
Aug-27	-1.37%		Aug-30	-5.55%		Aug-33	-2.96%		Aug-36	-0.90%
Sep-27	-3.30%		Sep-30	-0.35%		Sep-33	-5.25%		Sep-36	-1.37%
Oct-27	-2.87%		Oct-30	-5.72%		Oct-33	-0.21%		Oct-36	6.27%
Nov-27	-9.11%		Nov-30	-2.97%		Nov-33	3.37%		Nov-36	0.88%
Dec-27	6.15%		Dec-30	-4.71%		Dec-33	5.65%		Dec-36	-0.79%
Jan-28	5.50%		Jan-31	-5.62%		Jan-34	4.52%		Jan-37	1.46%
Feb-28	-2.09%		Feb-31	5.37%		Feb-34	5.61%		Feb-37	1.78%
Mar-28	-1.01%		Mar-31	7.14%		Mar-34	4.52%		Mar-37	1.44%
Apr-28	4.74%		Apr-31	2.12%		Apr-34	-2.27%		Apr-37	1.46%
May-28	3.35%		May-31	-9.56%		May-34	-2.01%		May-37	1.45%
Jun-28	1.11%		Jun-31	-7.99%		Jun-34	4.28%		Jun-37	1.24%
Jul-28	-2.44%		Jul-31	1.90%		Jul-34	2.40%		Jul-37	1.88%
Aug-28	0.19%		Aug-31	0.68%		Aug-34	3.23%		Aug-37	1.35%
Sep-28	0.62%		Sep-31	-25.09%		Sep-34	4.22%		Sep-37	-0.44%
Oct-28	-1.00%		Oct-31	1.02%		Oct-34	0.44%		Oct-37	-1.05%
Nov-28	0.22%		Nov-31	1.03%		Nov-34	-3.12%		Nov-37	-0.72%
Dec-28	1.48%		Dec-31	-12.30%		Dec-34	-0.38%		Dec-37	-0.32%

Date	% Change	Date	% Change	Date	% Change	Date	% Change
Jan-38	2.64%	Jan-43	1.44%	Jan-48	2.07%	Jan-53	1.89%
Feb-38	0.15%	Feb-43	0.41%	Feb-48	2.03%	Feb-53	-3.11%
Mar-38	0.57%	Mar-43	0.11%	Mar-48	10.00%	Mar-53	-1.22%
Apr-38	1.25%	Apr-43	0.13%	Apr-48	9.09%	Apr-53	0.00%
May-38	-1.46%	May-43	0.46%	May-48	8.36%	May-53	-1.31%
Jun-38	-1.59%	Jun-43	0.24%	Jun-48	13.22%	Jun-53	0.00%
Jul-38	-1.98%	Jul-43	0.13%	Jul-48	-92.37%	Jul-53	2.35%
Aug-38	-4.91%	Aug-43	0.12%	Aug-48	1.97%	Aug-53	4.60%
Sep-38	1.40%	Sep-43	0.30%	Sep-48	1.37%	Sep-53	7.47%
Oct-38	4.60%	Oct-43	0.27%	Oct-48	2.45%	Oct-53	4.09%
Nov-38	-1.01%	Nov-43	-0.11%	Nov-48	2.65%	Nov-53	2.81%
Dec-38	-2.31%	Dec-43	0.72%	Dec-48	2.59%	Dec-53	-0.25%
Jan-39	1.17%	Jan-44	-0.54%	Jan-49	3.02%	Jan-54	3.83%
Feb-39	1.37%	Feb-44	0.00%	Feb-49	5.13%	Feb-54	3.69%
Mar-39	-1.39%	Mar-44	0.00%	Mar-49	4.65%	Mar-54	2.08%
Apr-39	0.95%	Apr-44	0.00%	Apr-49	0.00%	Apr-54	0.35%
May-39	-0.42%	May-44	0.77%	May-49	9.11%	May-54	1.51%
Jun-39	-1.28%	Jun-44	0.00%	Jun-49	8.36%	Jun-54	6.44%
Jul-39	-0.38%	Jul-44	0.66%	Jul-49	0.00%	Jul-54	9.48%
Aug-39	2.04%	Aug-44	0.00%	Aug-49	7.70%	Aug-54	3.86%
Sep-39	-0.07%	Sep-44	0.00%	Sep-49	14.31%	Sep-54	6.64%
Oct-39	-0.10%	Oct-44	0.00%	Oct-49	12.51%	Oct-54	6.23%
Nov-39	2.82%	Nov-44	0.00%	Nov-49	11.13%	Nov-54	4.78%
Dec-39	3.95%	Dec-44	0.00%	Dec-49	15.02%	Dec-54	7.82%
Jan-40	3.64%	Jan-45	-0.30%	Jan-50	-12.21%	Jan-55	6.22%
Feb-40	2.56%	Feb-45	-0.40%	Feb-50	-0.97%	Feb-55	-0.94%
Mar-40	3.72%	Mar-45	-0.43%	Mar-50	-9.04%	Mar-55	5.00%
Apr-40	2.90%	Apr-45	-0.43%	Apr-50	3.36%	Apr-55	10.26%
May-40	3.05%	May-45	-0.40%	May-50	-1.17%	May-55	1.09%
Jun-40	0.71%	Jun-45	-0.44%	Jun-50	0.00%	Jun-55	0.27%
Jul-40	0.49%	Jul-45	-0.44%	Jul-50	2.23%	Jul-55	3.84%
Aug-40	3.11%	Aug-45	-0.44%	Aug-50	3.08%	Aug-55	1.84%
Sep-40	4.68%	Sep-45	-0.41%	Sep-50	5.11%	Sep-55	0.76%
Oct-40	3.86%	Oct-45	-0.89%	Oct-50	2.02%	Oct-55	-8.11%
Nov-40	2.98%	Nov-45	-0.86%	Nov-50	-3.84%	Nov-55	-3.29%
Dec-40	0.00%	Dec-45	-0.14%	Dec-50	2.05%	Dec-55	4.94%
Jan-41	3.03%	Jan-46	-1.19%	Jan-51	5.92%	Jan-56	1.05%
Feb-41	1.47%	Feb-46	-1.34%	Feb-51	8.16%	Feb-56	-2.73%
Mar-41	-1.16%	Mar-46	-0.90%	Mar-51	1.76%	Mar-56	0.28%
Apr-41	0.30%	Apr-46	-1.37%	Apr-51	-0.71%	Apr-56	1.70%
May-41	1.96%	May-46	-2.35%	May-51	2.56%	May-56	-3.30%
Jun-41	4.02%	Jun-46	-1.91%	Jun-51	6.48%	Jun-56	-1.98%
Jul-41	3.55%	Jul-46	0.99%	Jul-51	4.97%	Jul-56	-0.54%
Aug-41	1.29%	Aug-46	1.93%	Aug-51	15.45%	Aug-56	-2.93%
Sep-41	1.95%	Sep-46	0.45%	Sep-51	0.62%	Sep-56	2.49%
Oct-41	-6.03%	Oct-46	0.96%	Oct-51	8.92%	Oct-56	2.15%
Nov-41	-0.22%	Nov-46	2.31%	Nov-51	-2.33%	Nov-56	-2.31%
Dec-41	0.43%	Dec-46	1.36%	Dec-51	14.67%	Dec-56	2.47%
Jan-42	2.09%	Jan-47	0.88%	Jan-52	12.48%	Jan-57	0.66%
Feb-42	2.15%	Feb-47	0.46%	Feb-52	-0.95%	Feb-57	-2.01%
Mar-42	-0.11%	Mar-47	0.00%	Mar-52	-7.92%	Mar-57	1.58%
Apr-42	1.30%	Apr-47	0.00%	Apr-52	-1.66%	Apr-57	1.88%
May-42	0.43%	May-47	0.00%	May-52	-6.24%	May-57	-1.39%
Jun-42	0.59%	Jun-47	0.45%	Jun-52	-5.00%	Jun-57	-1.69%
Jul-42	-0.54%	Jul-47	1.32%	Jul-52	-1.68%	Jul-57	2.55%
Aug-42	0.21%	Aug-47	1.30%	Aug-52	0.57%	Aug-57	4.01%
Sep-42	0.26%	Sep-47	0.00%	Sep-52	4.19%	Sep-57	3.30%
Oct-42	0.86%	Oct-47	0.85%	Oct-52	-5.72%	Oct-57	-1.30%
Nov-42	0.33%	Nov-47	0.87%	Nov-52	-2.38%	Nov-57	1.54%
Dec-42	0.72%	Dec-47	1.26%	Dec-52	-1.92%	Dec-57	0.95%

Date	% Change		Date	% Change		Date	% Change		Date	% Change
Jan-58	3.20%		Jan-60	4.28%		Jan-62	-1.64%		Jan-64	6.11%
Feb-58	2.31%		Feb-60	0.73%		Feb-62	-1.30%		Feb-64	3.01%
Mar-58	-0.43%		Mar-60	-1.55%		Mar-62	-0.64%		Mar-64	4.28%
Apr-58	4.18%		Apr-60	3.40%		Apr-62	-3.16%		Apr-64	-0.26%
May-58	0.64%		May-60	6.51%		May-62	-7.45%		May-64	-1.85%
Jun-58	4.54%		Jun-60	14.29%		Jun-62	-8.84%		Jun-64	-1.49%
Jul-58	3.11%		Jul-60	7.50%		Jul-62	-2.80%		Jul-64	2.43%
Aug-58	6.92%		Aug-60	8.46%		Aug-62	-3.65%		Aug-64	2.28%
Sep-58	7.17%		Sep-60	0.23%		Sep-62	-1.23%		Sep-64	0.94%
Oct-58	5.64%		Oct-60	-5.70%		Oct-62	-8.03%		Oct-64	-3.31%
Nov-58	6.59%		Nov-60	-1.78%		Nov-62	11.52%		Nov-64	-3.23%
Dec-58	-0.68%		Dec-60	-2.14%		Dec-62	4.89%		Dec-64	0.68%
Jan-59	5.87%		Jan-61	-0.84%		Jan-63	-3.37%			
Feb-59	1.55%		Feb-61	-0.77%		Feb-63	-2.48%			
Mar-59	0.09%		Mar-61	-0.86%		Mar-63	0.17%			
Apr-59	6.24%		Apr-61	2.17%		Apr-63	2.78%			
May-59	6.90%		May-61	4.51%		May-63	9.07%			
Jun-59	10.79%		Jun-61	0.75%		Jun-63	1.91%			
Jul-59	14.24%		Jul-61	-8.08%		Jul-63	-0.20%			
Aug-59	12.62%		Aug-61	-4.48%		Aug-63	4.43%			
Sep-59	-5.68%		Sep-61	-4.42%		Sep-63	3.04%			
Oct-59	-4.24%		Oct-61	2.06%		Oct-63	-1.79%			
Nov-59	5.47%		Nov-61	6.80%		Nov-63	-2.60%			
Dec-59	4.83%		Dec-61	-3.11%		Dec-63	1.17%			

Source: Global Financial Data. Total returns as calculated by GFD to simulate a backtested DAX index; not official DAX data.

APPENDIX H

Germany Stock Market (DAX) Total Returns

Date	% Change	Date	% Change	Date	% Change	Date	% Change
Jan-65	-0.17%	Jan-68	6.22%	Jan-71	13.08%	Jan-74	5.94%
Feb-65	-1.33%	Feb-68	0.71%	Feb-71	3.80%	Feb-74	-5.78%
Mar-65	-1.89%	Mar-68	0.17%	Mar-71	1.47%	Mar-74	0.11%
Apr-65	-0.05%	Apr-68	5.10%	Apr-71	-5.44%	Apr-74	3.95%
May-65	-2.26%	May-68	0.87%	May-71	1.77%	May-74	-2.62%
Jun-65	-2.08%	Jun-68	2.28%	Jun-71	-0.50%	Jun-74	-1.97%
Jul-65	-0.98%	Jul-68	1.54%	Jul-71	3.90%	Jul-74	-1.31%
Aug-65	1.84%	Aug-68	1.43%	Aug-71	-3.79%	Aug-74	0.56%
Sep-65	0.42%	Sep-68	-1.02%	Sep-71	-4.04%	Sep-74	-4.16%
Oct-65	-2.71%	Oct-68	1.63%	Oct-71	-6.84%	Oct-74	0.69%
Nov-65	-2.19%	Nov-68	-1.79%	Nov-71	1.13%	Nov-74	5.26%
Dec-65	-1.15%	Dec-68	-1.84%	Dec-71	6.07%	Dec-74	1.49%
Jan-66	3.57%	Jan-69	3.08%	Jan-72	4.70%	Jan-75	7.68%
Feb-66	1.52%	Feb-69	1.73%	Feb-72	7.71%	Feb-75	10.34%
Mar-66	-1.11%	Mar-69	0.34%	Mar-72	3.92%	Mar-75	0.99%
Apr-66	-2.34%	Apr-69	0.16%	Apr-72	-1.92%	Apr-75	2.68%
May-66	-5.76%	May-69	4.62%	May-72	3.11%	May-75	-6.06%
Jun-66	-4.28%	Jun-69	1.00%	Jun-72	-1.87%	Jun-75	0.99%
Jul-66	-5.45%	Jul-69	-3.84%	Jul-72	6.85%	Jul-75	8.52%
Aug-66	0.97%	Aug-69	3.57%	Aug-72	-1.27%	Aug-75	-4.14%
Sep-66	3.17%	Sep-69	0.91%	Sep-72	-3.06%	Sep-75	-1.29%
Oct-66	-2.75%	Oct-69	4.13%	Oct-72	-2.57%	Oct-75	7.20%
Nov-66	-2.71%	Nov-69	5.23%	Nov-72	1.42%	Nov-75	4.58%
Dec-66	1.01%	Dec-69	-2.91%	Dec-72	-0.84%	Dec-75	0.74%
Jan-67	-0.07%	Jan-70	-3.60%	Jan-73	5.15%	Jan-76	0.95%
Feb-67	7.06%	Feb-70	-1.94%	Feb-73	-1.77%	Feb-76	0.52%
Mar-67	2.21%	Mar-70	0.48%	Mar-73	6.00%	Mar-76	2.96%
Apr-67	-0.75%	Apr-70	-5.01%	Apr-73	-4.56%	Apr-76	-5.34%
May-67	-1.60%	May-70	-9.02%	May-73	-9.19%	May-76	-1.78%
Jun-67	-1.21%	Jun-70	-2.28%	Jun-73	0.25%	Jun-76	2.30%
Jul-67	1.97%	Jul-70	6.38%	Jul-73	-7.22%	Jul-76	-1.59%
Aug-67	12.74%	Aug-70	1.06%	Aug-73	1.26%	Aug-76	-0.78%
Sep-67	4.56%	Sep-70	-2.48%	Sep-73	-9.19%	Sep-76	0.68%
Oct-67	1.42%	Oct-70	-1.18%	Oct-73	7.00%	Oct-76	-7.04%
Nov-67	4.93%	Nov-70	-3.91%	Nov-73	-10.91%	Nov-76	4.41%
Dec-67	2.27%	Dec-70	-1.66%	Dec-73	-1.15%	Dec-76	0.61%

Date	% Change	Date	% Change	Date	% Change	Date	% Change
Jan-77	0.97%	Jan-82	2.35%	Jan-87	-11.33%	Jan-92	5.30%
Feb-77	-2.27%	Feb-82	1.59%	Feb-87	-4.93%	Feb-92	4.25%
Mar-77	2.49%	Mar-82	2.71%	Mar-87	3.10%	Mar-92	-1.66%
Apr-77	6.93%	Apr-82	-0.25%	Apr-87	0.30%	Apr-92	0.64%
May-77	-0.82%	May-82	-0.78%	May-87	-0.98%	May-92	3.26%
Jun-77	-1.42%	Jun-82	-1.18%	Jun-87	6.29%	Jun-92	-3.19%
Jul-77	1.57%	Jul-82	0.51%	Jul-87	6.69%	Jul-92	-7.79%
Aug-77	2.44%	Aug-82	-0.85%	Aug-87	1.03%	Aug-92	-5.68%
Sep-77	0.55%	Sep-82	5.56%	Sep-87	-2.66%	Sep-92	-3.91%
Oct-77	2.42%	Oct-82	-0.06%	Oct-87	-22.39%	Oct-92	1.27%
Nov-77	0.97%	Nov-82	3.62%	Nov-87	-12.42%	Nov-92	2.01%
Dec-77	-1.18%	Dec-82	5.93%	Dec-87	-1.97%	Dec-92	-0.18%
Jan-78	1.59%	Jan-83	-1.13%	Jan-88	-5.98%	Jan-93	2.22%
Feb-78	0.79%	Feb-83	7.22%	Feb-88	14.93%	Feb-93	6.27%
Mar-78	-0.57%	Mar-83	11.07%	Mar-88	0.31%	Mar-93	1.70%
Apr-78	-2.47%	Apr-83	6.69%	Apr-88	-0.71%	Apr-93	-2.14%
May-78	2.41%	May-83	-4.35%	May-88	1.55%	May-93	0.62%
Jun-78	2.95%	Jun-83	4.80%	Jun-88	5.00%	Jun-93	2.48%
Jul-78	4.32%	Jul-83	3.52%	Jul-88	3.28%	Jul-93	5.99%
Aug-78	1.52%	Aug-83	-5.58%	Aug-88	-0.16%	Aug-93	7.04%
Sep-78	2.62%	Sep-83	2.40%	Sep-88	6.20%	Sep-93	-1.52%
Oct-78	-2.19%	Oct-83	7.74%	Oct-88	3.91%	Oct-93	8.11%
Nov-78	-0.92%	Nov-83	1.95%	Nov-88	-2.99%	Nov-93	-0.35%
Dec-78	0.00%	Dec-83	0.64%	Dec-88	4.10%	Dec-93	7.73%
Jan-79	2.08%	Jan-84	3.75%	Jan-89	2.08%	Jan-94	-2.51%
Feb-79	-3.19%	Feb-84	-4.37%	Feb-89	-1.75%	Feb-94	-3.08%
Mar-79	-1.82%	Mar-84	-0.24%	Mar-89	1.76%	Mar-94	1.52%
Apr-79	0.30%	Apr-84	1.48%	Apr-89	3.51%	Apr-94	4.86%
May-79	-4.07%	May-84	-2.11%	May-89	2.38%	May-94	-4.62%
Jun-79	-1.59%	Jun-84	3.24%	Jun-89	5.55%	Jun-94	-3.77%
Jul-79	3.38%	Jul-84	-6.15%	Jul-89	5.17%	Jul-94	4.28%
Aug-79	1.33%	Aug-84	5.27%	Aug-89	3.75%	Aug-94	2.60%
Sep-79	0.32%	Sep-84	6.73%	Sep-89	1.29%	Sep-94	-7.40%
Oct-79	-4.15%	Oct-84	1.14%	Oct-89	-6.77%	Oct-94	1.79%
Nov-79	0.74%	Nov-84	0.39%	Nov-89	5.29%	Nov-94	-1.21%
Dec-79	-1.78%	Dec-84	1.78%	Dec-89	10.71%	Dec-94	2.40%
Jan-80	0.68%	Jan-85	5.05%	Jan-90	1.98%	Jan-95	-4.15%
Feb-80	2.64%	Feb-85	1.86%	Feb-90	-0.75%	Feb-95	3.40%
Mar-80	-7.49%	Mar-85	0.98%	Mar-90	9.73%	Mar-95	-7.64%
Apr-80	3.47%	Apr-85	3.63%	Apr-90	-6.50%	Apr-95	4.51%
May-80	3.35%	May-85	8.21%	May-90	1.95%	May-95	3.88%
Jun-80	3.34%	Jun-85	6.47%	Jun-90	2.92%	Jun-95	0.61%
Jul-80	3.18%	Jul-85	-3.54%	Jul-90	3.93%	Jul-95	5.35%
Aug-80	-1.42%	Aug-85	8.84%	Aug-90	-14.29%	Aug-95	0.21%
Sep-80	-0.07%	Sep-85	5.19%	Sep-90	-16.36%	Sep-95	-2.07%
Oct-80	-1.26%	Oct-85	13.19%	Oct-90	7.84%	Oct-95	-1.96%
Nov-80	0.66%	Nov-85	-1.26%	Nov-90	0.21%	Nov-95	1.92%
Dec-80	-2.09%	Dec-85	10.29%	Dec-90	-2.78%	Dec-95	1.40%
Jan-81	-1.44%	Jan-86	0.75%	Jan-91	-1.06%	Jan-96	7.39%
Feb-81	0.02%	Feb-86	-2.99%	Feb-91	8.32%	Feb-96	-0.42%
Mar-81	2.77%	Mar-86	8.90%	Mar-91	-1.25%	Mar-96	-0.03%
Apr-81	4.48%	Apr-86	5.14%	Apr-91	6.09%	Apr-96	0.02%
May-81	-1.40%	May-86	-9.25%	May-91	3.45%	May-96	2.11%
Jun-81	6.41%	Jun-86	-0.33%	Jun-91	-2.51%	Jun-96	2.38%
Jul-81	1.38%	Jul-86	-5.05%	Jul-91	-1.78%	Jul-96	-3.28%
Aug-81	-2.34%	Aug-86	14.45%	Aug-91	1.19%	Aug-96	2.50%
Sep-81	-5.41%	Sep-86	-5.68%	Sep-91	-2.82%	Sep-96	3.38%
Oct-81	-0.31%	Oct-86	0.73%	Oct-91	-2.21%	Oct-96	0.03%
Nov-81	2.28%	Nov-86	3.43%	Nov-91	-1.21%	Nov-96	4.90%
Dec-81	-2.36%	Dec-86	-1.16%	Dec-91	-0.87%	Dec-96	1.60%

Date	% Change	Date	% Change	Date	% Change	Date	% Change
Jan-97	5.36%	Jan-00	-0.16%	Jan-03	-4.30%	Jan-06	5.77%
Feb-97	6.47%	Feb-00	13.72%	Feb-03	-6.89%	Feb-06	2.94%
Mar-97	4.99%	Mar-00	-1.20%	Mar-03	-4.26%	Mar-06	3.12%
Apr-97	0.38%	Apr-00	-2.40%	Apr-03	20.01%	Apr-06	0.86%
May-97	3.83%	May-00	-4.72%	May-03	1.71%	May-06	-5.61%
Jun-97	5.88%	Jun-00	-2.39%	Jun-03	7.61%	Jun-06	-0.44%
Jul-97	13.94%	Jul-00	2.67%	Jul-03	7.83%		
Aug-97	-10.21%	Aug-00	0.53%	Aug-03	0.80%		
Sep-97	5.38%	Sep-00	-5.54%	Sep-03	-5.90%		
Oct-97	-9.09%	Oct-00	1.50%	Oct-03	11.70%		
Nov-97	4.36%	Nov-00	-10.69%	Nov-03	2.17%		
Dec-97	5.94%	Dec-00	0.10%	Dec-03	5.18%		
Jan-98	4.34%	Jan-01	4.55%	Jan-04	2.93%		
Feb-98	6.14%	Feb-01	-7.26%	Feb-04	-0.44%		
Mar-98	7.61%	Mar-01	-6.13%	Mar-04	-3.70%		
Apr-98	0.54%	Apr-01	6.41%	Apr-04	3.26%		
May-98	7.49%	May-01	-1.52%	May-04	-1.47%		
Jun-98	4.11%	Jun-01	-0.98%	Jun-04	3.25%		
Jul-98	0.07%	Jul-01	-3.27%	Jul-04	-3.75%		
Aug-98	-16.29%	Aug-01	-9.64%	Aug-04	-2.91%		
Sep-98	-6.99%	Sep-01	-15.12%	Sep-04	2.87%		
Oct-98	3.77%	Oct-01	6.00%	Oct-04	1.54%		
Nov-98	6.63%	Nov-01	7.87%	Nov-04	4.09%		
Dec-98	-0.05%	Dec-01	2.46%	Dec-04	2.99%		
Jan-99	3.16%	Jan-02	0.61%	Jan-05	0.53%		
Feb-99	-3.58%	Feb-02	-1.07%	Feb-05	2.57%		
Mar-99	-1.17%	Mar-02	5.33%	Mar-05	-0.12%		
Apr-99	8.09%	Apr-02	-5.08%	Apr-05	-3.74%		
May-99	-4.56%	May-02	-3.56%	May-05	6.64%		
Jun-99	5.29%	Jun-02	-7.32%	Jun-05	3.35%		
Jul-99	-3.63%	Jul-02	-14.81%	Jul-05	6.51%		
Aug-99	2.26%	Aug-02	0.16%	Aug-05	-0.83%		
Sep-99	-2.66%	Sep-02	-23.85%	Sep-05	4.55%		
Oct-99	5.87%	Oct-02	12.95%	Oct-05	-2.75%		
Nov-99	6.42%	Nov-02	4.57%	Nov-05	5.09%		
Dec-99	14.10%	Dec-02	-12.01%	Dec-05	3.95%		

Source: Global Financial Data.

APPENDIX I

Japan Stock Market Total Returns

Date	% Change	Date	% Change	Date	% Change	Date	% Change
Jan-26	4.79%	Jan-29	1.75%	Jan-32	26.47%	Jan-35	0.17%
Feb-26	3.34%	Feb-29	3.37%	Feb-32	3.97%	Feb-35	2.65%
Mar-26	-1.74%	Mar-29	0.51%	Mar-32	-3.01%	Mar-35	0.61%
Apr-26	0.32%	Apr-29	-2.67%	Apr-32	-8.18%	Apr-35	-0.16%
May-26	0.00%	May-29	-3.63%	May-32	1.16%	May-35	-1.65%
Jun-26	-0.64%	Jun-29	0.00%	Jun-32	-4.57%	Jun-35	-2.29%
Jul-26	3.06%	Jul-29	-3.38%	Jul-32	4.10%	Jul-35	-0.46%
Aug-26	-0.63%	Aug-29	-4.22%	Aug-32	4.02%	Aug-35	5.79%
Sep-26	-1.42%	Sep-29	0.33%	Sep-32	9.79%	Sep-35	2.70%
Oct-26	0.32%	Oct-29	0.66%	Oct-32	2.95%	Oct-35	0.81%
Nov-26	0.80%	Nov-29	-0.66%	Nov-32	17.25%	Nov-35	1.19%
Dec-26	-3.55%	Dec-29	-3.15%	Dec-32	22.04%	Dec-35	0.83%
Jan-27	4.34%	Jan-30	-0.26%	Jan-33	3.61%	Jan-36	2.97%
Feb-27	3.22%	Feb-30	2.23%	Feb-33	-7.54%	Feb-36	3.39%
Mar-27	-0.84%	Mar-30	-3.10%	Mar-33	1.88%	Mar-36	-5.68%
Apr-27	-6.36%	Apr-30	-5.54%	Apr-33	1.70%	Apr-36	3.52%
May-27	-2.37%	May-30	-1.10%	May-33	3.49%	May-36	1.34%
Jun-27	-1.34%	Jun-30	-7.59%	Jun-33	5.46%	Jun-36	1.07%
Jul-27	-1.19%	Jul-30	-2.20%	Jul-33	1.40%	Jul-36	0.53%
Aug-27	0.60%	Aug-30	1.13%	Aug-33	0.18%	Aug-36	2.25%
Sep-27	2.56%	Sep-30	-6.79%	Sep-33	5.63%	Sep-36	0.86%
Oct-27	1.83%	Oct-30	-3.70%	Oct-33	1.39%	Oct-36	0.27%
Nov-27	-0.82%	Nov-30	5.87%	Nov-33	-2.77%	Nov-36	-2.04%
Dec-27	2.72%	Dec-30	6.82%	Dec-33	3.32%	Dec-36	3.88%
Jan-28	1.53%	Jan-31	-0.40%	Jan-34	5.11%	Jan-37	3.14%
Feb-28	2.37%	Feb-31	2.71%	Feb-34	3.10%	Feb-37	4.72%
Mar-28	2.01%	Mar-31	5.76%	Mar-34	0.80%	Mar-37	4.60%
Apr-28	-1.44%	Apr-31	-0.37%	Apr-34	-2.94%	Apr-37	1.45%
May-28	2.31%	May-31	-1.30%	May-34	1.17%	May-37	-1.31%
Jun-28	1.73%	Jun-31	0.38%	Jun-34	-1.00%	Jun-37	1.00%
Jul-28	1.62%	Jul-31	2.34%	Jul-34	-1.75%	Jul-37	-1.31%
Aug-28	-0.87%	Aug-31	-3.38%	Aug-34	0.32%	Aug-37	-10.95%
Sep-28	0.59%	Sep-31	-3.12%	Sep-34	-3.23%	Sep-37	4.09%
Oct-28	-2.41%	Oct-31	-8.10%	Oct-34	-1.26%	Oct-37	-0.96%
Nov-28	-0.60%	Nov-31	1.17%	Nov-34	0.49%	Nov-37	0.52%
Dec-28	-1.43%	Dec-31	8.60%	Dec-34	-1.11%	Dec-37	5.26%

Date	% Change	Date	% Change	Date	% Change	Date	% Change
Jan-38	2.95%	Jan-43	3.10%	Jan-48	2.39%	Jan-53	21.93%
Feb-38	0.56%	Feb-43	-0.73%	Feb-48	51.89%	Feb-53	-11.02%
Mar-38	-1.44%	Mar-43	-1.54%	Mar-48	18.51%	Mar-53	-16.97%
Apr-38	-4.93%	Apr-43	0.90%	Apr-48	1.37%	Apr-53	5.78%
May-38	1.54%	May-43	0.66%	May-48	-10.93%	May-53	-4.56%
Jun-38	-4.39%	Jun-43	0.38%	Jun-48	-7.10%	Jun-53	4.23%
Jul-38	0.36%	Jul-43	0.73%	Jul-48	10.81%	Jul-53	9.45%
Aug-38	4.22%	Aug-43	-0.22%	Aug-48	1.58%	Aug-53	4.92%
Sep-38	-0.43%	Sep-43	0.14%	Sep-48	-9.10%	Sep-53	11.97%
Oct-38	0.68%	Oct-43	0.37%	Oct-48	5.44%	Oct-53	-4.30%
Nov-38	-5.31%	Nov-43	0.14%	Nov-48	20.89%	Nov-53	-2.21%
Dec-38	2.05%	Dec-43	0.00%	Dec-48	-0.60%	Dec-53	-8.09%
Jan-39	4.40%	Jan-44	1.54%	Jan-49	67.39%	Jan-54	-6.34%
Feb-39	2.54%	Feb-44	-0.65%	Feb-49	-4.67%	Feb-54	-0.37%
Mar-39	-0.89%	Mar-44	-1.80%	Mar-49	25.49%	Mar-54	-5.64%
Apr-39	0.21%	Apr-44	-0.67%	Apr-49	5.73%	Apr-54	5.48%
May-39	1.92%	May-44	-0.51%	May-49	17.72%	May-54	-6.22%
Jun-39	4.06%	Jun-44	0.30%	Jun-49	-16.34%	Jun-54	7.13%
Jul-39	2.97%	Jul-44	-4.15%	Jul-49	-0.83%	Jul-54	-4.67%
Aug-39	0.60%	Aug-44	1.16%	Aug-49	21.50%	Aug-54	4.22%
Sep-39	7.27%	Sep-44	5.03%	Sep-49	-6.33%	Sep-54	2.23%
Oct-39	7.13%	Oct-44	6.14%	Oct-49	-12.81%	Oct-54	-5.96%
Nov-39	3.38%	Nov-44	-2.00%	Nov-49	-12.66%	Nov-54	0.97%
Dec-39	1.54%	Dec-44	0.84%	Dec-49	-9.87%	Dec-54	9.35%
Jan-40	-2.70%	Jan-45	0.84%	Jan-50	-15.14%	Jan-55	3.16%
Feb-40	2.09%	Feb-45	-2.62%	Feb-50	16.93%	Feb-55	1.61%
Mar-40	1.87%	Mar-45	-2.48%	Mar-50	-8.44%	Mar-55	-1.30%
Apr-40	0.58%	Apr-45	2.39%	Apr-50	2.57%	Apr-55	-0.89%
May-40	-2.67%	May-45	0.15%	May-50	-4.34%	May-55	1.92%
Jun-40	-2.90%	Jun-45	-0.85%	Jun-50	-7.73%	Jun-55	1.43%
Jul-40	-3.60%	Jul-45	1.35%	Jul-50	14.17%	Jul-55	5.13%
Aug-40	1.20%	Aug-45	1.77%	Aug-50	18.18%	Aug-55	6.61%
Sep-40	-8.93%	Sep-45	0.48%	Sep-50	-7.65%	Sep-55	2.66%
Oct-40	-2.89%	Oct-45	0.40%	Oct-50	1.93%	Oct-55	6.68%
Nov-40	8.87%	Nov-45	0.48%	Nov-50	4.34%	Nov-55	-2.93%
Dec-40	-2.88%	Dec-45	0.42%	Dec-50	-6.40%	Dec-55	9.06%
Jan-41	0.00%	Jan-46	-30.23%	Jan-51	14.28%	Jan-56	0.19%
Feb-41	2.30%	Feb-46	0.68%	Feb-51	6.41%	Feb-56	3.59%
Mar-41	3.10%	Mar-46	0.67%	Mar-51	3.05%	Mar-56	5.71%
Apr-41	1.00%	Apr-46	0.59%	Apr-51	-2.14%	Apr-56	3.80%
May-41	-1.09%	May-46	0.64%	May-51	6.33%	May-56	4.67%
Jun-41	-0.07%	Jun-46	1.83%	Jun-51	3.65%	Jun-56	2.38%
Jul-41	-6.33%	Jul-46	-21.06%	Jul-51	5.28%	Jul-56	0.81%
Aug-41	2.85%	Aug-46	4.26%	Aug-51	8.04%	Aug-56	-1.14%
Sep-41	3.72%	Sep-46	29.41%	Sep-51	7.23%	Sep-56	1.34%
Oct-41	-1.57%	Oct-46	2.64%	Oct-51	8.07%	Oct-56	3.80%
Nov-41	1.50%	Nov-46	-7.07%	Nov-51	-3.69%	Nov-56	10.75%
Dec-41	14.32%	Dec-46	-5.62%	Dec-51	6.74%	Dec-56	-0.92%
Jan-42	0.15%	Jan-47	1.77%	Jan-52	13.20%	Jan-57	3.85%
Feb-42	0.73%	Feb-47	0.64%	Feb-52	-3.98%	Feb-57	0.00%
Mar-42	-1.19%	Mar-47	5.15%	Mar-52	1.56%	Mar-57	3.32%
Apr-42	1.53%	Apr-47	22.64%	Apr-52	12.95%	Apr-57	0.68%
May-42	1.76%	May-47	10.96%	May-52	11.15%	May-57	-10.79%
Jun-42	3.17%	Jun-47	-1.51%	Jun-52	9.16%	Jun-57	-0.02%
Jul-42	-0.97%	Jul-47	-8.55%	Jul-52	3.76%	Jul-57	12.94%
Aug-42	3.21%	Aug-47	-7.90%	Aug-52	2.16%	Aug-57	4.31%
Sep-42	-1.19%	Sep-47	3.68%	Sep-52	8.04%	Sep-57	0.92%
Oct-42	3.44%	Oct-47	-7.07%	Oct-52	12.30%	Oct-57	4.85%
Nov-42	-3.33%	Nov-47	-2.60%	Nov-52	12.12%	Nov-57	3.70%
Dec-42	-1.12%	Dec-47	35.52%	Dec-52	1.33%	Dec-57	6.72%

Date	% Change	Date	% Change	Date	% Change	Date	% Change
Jan-58	-25.76%	Jan-62	5.35%	Jan-66	2.41%	Jan-70	-1.51%
Feb-58	0.62%	Feb-62	-2.27%	Feb-66	1.91%	Feb-70	1.30%
Mar-58	1.92%	Mar-62	-3.01%	Mar-66	5.04%	Mar-70	4.14%
Apr-58	4.30%	Apr-62	-3.40%	Apr-66	-0.70%	Apr-70	-12.04%
May-58	1.52%	May-62	-0.56%	May-66	-2.10%	May-70	-2.58%
Jun-58	4.02%	Jun-62	5.60%	Jun-66	-0.38%	Jun-70	1.91%
Jul-58	-2.38%	Jul-62	-1.31%	Jul-66	2.54%	Jul-70	0.29%
Aug-58	4.31%	Aug-62	0.74%	Aug-66	-1.18%	Aug-70	-0.99%
Sep-58	0.92%	Sep-62	-7.88%	Sep-66	0.70%	Sep-70	-1.06%
Oct-58	4.85%	Oct-62	-3.44%	Oct-66	-0.40%	Oct-70	1.37%
Nov-58	3.70%	Nov-62	17.14%	Nov-66	-2.00%	Nov-70	-2.79%
Dec-58	6.72%	Dec-62	-0.75%	Dec-66	4.88%	Dec-70	0.89%
Jan-59	4.57%	Jan-63	4.42%	Jan-67	1.95%	Jan-71	5.57%
Feb-59	3.20%	Feb-63	3.53%	Feb-67	1.39%	Feb-71	4.68%
Mar-59	9.12%	Mar-63	12.87%	Mar-67	-0.71%	Mar-71	8.33%
Apr-59	-2.81%	Apr-63	1.27%	Apr-67	-0.14%	Apr-71	5.25%
May-59	9.08%	May-63	-1.45%	May-67	5.16%	May-71	-0.64%
Jun-59	0.81%	Jun-63	0.03%	Jun-67	-0.67%	Jun-71	9.64%
Jul-59	4.36%	Jul-63	-11.78%	Jul-67	-0.62%	Jul-71	0.54%
Aug-59	2.62%	Aug-63	-0.40%	Aug-67	-8.13%	Aug-71	-12.77%
Sep-59	6.66%	Sep-63	-2.94%	Sep-67	-0.30%	Sep-71	2.81%
Oct-59	4.83%	Oct-63	1.72%	Oct-67	3.72%	Oct-71	-5.48%
Nov-59	3.53%	Nov-63	-5.08%	Nov-67	-5.71%	Nov-71	6.63%
Dec-59	-11.36%	Dec-63	-2.52%	Dec-67	-0.01%	Dec-71	8.60%
Jan-60	6.91%	Jan-64	8.26%	Jan-68	2.67%	Jan-72	6.11%
Feb-60	3.67%	Feb-64	-4.46%	Feb-68	1.85%	Feb-72	7.23%
Mar-60	8.46%	Mar-64	-1.01%	Mar-68	2.78%	Mar-72	4.97%
Apr-60	4.50%	Apr-64	-0.18%	Apr-68	4.59%	Apr-72	5.71%
May-60	-10.66%	May-64	8.18%	May-68	1.77%	May-72	8.58%
Jun-60	10.91%	Jun-64	3.16%	Jun-68	4.77%	Jun-72	2.76%
Jul-60	0.82%	Jul-64	-2.27%	Jul-68	5.38%	Jul-72	8.58%
Aug-60	6.27%	Aug-64	-2.53%	Aug-68	6.04%	Aug-72	2.50%
Sep-60	5.66%	Sep-64	-2.58%	Sep-68	9.79%	Sep-72	4.58%
Oct-60	-0.10%	Oct-64	-3.07%	Oct-68	-5.73%	Oct-72	3.21%
Nov-60	1.17%	Nov-64	-0.03%	Nov-68	-0.96%	Nov-72	17.50%
Dec-60	3.14%	Dec-64	2.28%	Dec-68	-0.40%	Dec-72	9.17%
Jan-61	6.43%	Jan-65	4.47%	Jan-69	5.67%		
Feb-61	0.40%	Feb-65	-0.52%	Feb-69	-2.03%		
Mar-61	3.52%	Mar-65	-4.74%	Mar-69	7.23%		
Apr-61	0.95%	Apr-65	3.01%	Apr-69	2.33%		
May-61	-0.74%	May-65	-5.33%	May-69	7.95%		
Jun-61	4.73%	Jun-65	-1.34%	Jun-69	-2.70%		
Jul-61	-1.36%	Jul-65	3.72%	Jul-69	-5.04%		
Aug-61	-8.63%	Aug-65	11.93%	Aug-69	2.73%		
Sep-61	-3.21%	Sep-65	-1.62%	Sep-69	7.75%		
Oct-61	-12.60%	Oct-65	0.76%	Oct-69	2.16%		
Nov-61	0.59%	Nov-65	7.35%	Nov-69	-13.00%		
Dec-61	8.21%	Dec-65	5.26%	Dec-69	28.01%		

Source: Global Financial Data. Total returns as calculated by GFD to simulate a backtested TOPIX index; not official TOPIX data.

APPENDIX J

Japan Stock Market (TOPIX) Total Returns

Date	% Change	Date	% Change	Date	% Change	Date	% Change
Jan-73	1.56%	Jan-76	5.76%	Jan-79	3.07%	Jan-82	2.14%
Feb-73	-5.14%	Feb-76	0.24%	Feb-79	-3.22%	Feb-82	-4.52%
Mar-73	1.07%	Mar-76	-0.91%	Mar-79	0.05%	Mar-82	-5.47%
Apr-73	-11.05%	Apr-76	0.60%	Apr-79	2.49%	Apr-82	3.24%
May-73	2.40%	May-76	0.82%	May-79	0.72%	May-82	-0.21%
Jun-73	1.66%	Jun-76	3.94%	Jun-79	-0.34%	Jun-82	-1.97%
Jul-73	5.55%	Jul-76	-2.93%	Jul-79	-0.54%	Jul-82	-2.76%
Aug-73	-3.94%	Aug-76	1.90%	Aug-79	1.88%	Aug-82	1.96%
Sep-73	-5.25%	Sep-76	0.05%	Sep-79	3.43%	Sep-82	-0.78%
Oct-73	-0.50%	Oct-76	-2.94%	Oct-79	-1.76%	Oct-82	3.76%
Nov-73	-9.00%	Nov-76	-0.31%	Nov-79	0.59%	Nov-82	7.76%
Dec-73	-5.48%	Dec-76	13.90%	Dec-79	2.10%	Dec-82	3.77%
Jan-74	6.46%	Jan-77	-4.44%	Jan-80	1.84%	Jan-83	-2.29%
Feb-74	-0.11%	Feb-77	3.10%	Feb-80	0.65%	Feb-83	0.89%
Mar-74	-2.69%	Mar-77	-2.75%	Mar-80	-2.90%	Mar-83	4.46%
Apr-74	3.22%	Apr-77	1.77%	Apr-80	3.30%	Apr-83	1.60%
May-74	4.34%	May-77	-0.56%	May-80	-0.37%	May-83	0.93%
Jun-74	-2.63%	Jun-77	-0.06%	Jun-80	1.04%	Jun-83	3.23%
Jul-74	-5.35%	Jul-77	-1.27%	Jul-80	-0.90%	Jul-83	1.91%
Aug-74	-9.60%	Aug-77	5.75%	Aug-80	2.65%	Aug-83	0.92%
Sep-74	-0.86%	Sep-77	-0.01%	Sep-80	2.58%	Sep-83	3.00%
Oct-74	-7.36%	Oct-77	-3.27%	Oct-80	2.93%	Oct-83	-1.20%
Nov-74	10.40%	Nov-77	-1.70%	Nov-80	-1.03%	Nov-83	0.40%
Dec-74	-3.78%	Dec-77	-1.25%	Dec-80	0.61%	Dec-83	7.51%
Jan-75	4.14%	Jan-78	4.90%	Jan-81	3.12%	Jan-84	6.07%
Feb-75	10.31%	Feb-78	2.69%	Feb-81	0.07%	Feb-84	-0.84%
Mar-75	4.58%	Mar-78	5.38%	Mar-81	7.22%	Mar-84	13.32%
Apr-75	0.21%	Apr-78	-0.18%	Apr-81	9.15%	Apr-84	-0.89%
May-75	-0.80%	May-78	0.28%	May-81	1.45%	May-84	-10.47%
Jun-75	3.07%	Jun-78	0.76%	Jun-81	4.65%	Jun-84	2.73%
Jul-75	-4.95%	Jul-78	2.55%	Jul-81	1.91%	Jul-84	-4.13%
Aug-75	-4.16%	Aug-78	-1.36%	Aug-81	-0.24%	Aug-84	7.45%
Sep-75	-4.73%	Sep-78	1.73%	Sep-81	-8.39%	Sep-84	1.27%
Oct-75	10.29%	Oct-78	0.59%	Oct-81	0.11%	Oct-84	4.96%
Nov-75	1.39%	Nov-78	1.68%	Nov-81	0.51%	Nov-84	1.30%
Dec-75	1.82%	Dec-78	3.12%	Dec-81	4.15%	Dec-84	5.43%

Date	% Change	Date	% Change	Date	% Change	Date	% Change
Jan-85	1.05%	Jan-90	-4.99%	Jan-95	-6.10%	Jan-00	-0.82%
Feb-85	4.98%	Feb-90	-6.28%	Feb-95	-7.87%	Feb-00	0.66%
Mar-85	2.57%	Mar-90	-12.92%	Mar-95	-2.53%	Mar-00	-0.44%
Apr-85	-3.33%	Apr-90	-0.96%	Apr-95	1.83%	Apr-00	-3.34%
May-85	3.62%	May-90	10.42%	May-95	-5.83%	May-00	-7.64%
Jun-85	3.07%	Jun-90	-3.78%	Jun-95	-4.54%	Jun-00	4.55%
Jul-85	-4.36%	Jul-90	-3.87%	Jul-95	11.63%	Jul-00	-8.70%
Aug-85	2.72%	Aug-90	-12.36%	Aug-95	6.86%	Aug-00	4.02%
Sep-85	0.94%	Sep-90	-20.21%	Sep-95	1.05%	Sep-00	-2.44%
Oct-85	0.59%	Oct-90	18.16%	Oct-95	-1.88%	Oct-00	-6.17%
Nov-85	-2.79%	Nov-90	-10.99%	Nov-95	5.04%	Nov-00	-1.25%
Dec-85	5.23%	Dec-90	4.99%	Dec-95	6.46%	Dec-00	-5.77%
Jan-86	-1.14%	Jan-91	-1.32%	Jan-96	2.25%	Jan-01	1.29%
Feb-86	4.40%	Feb-91	14.59%	Feb-96	-3.25%	Feb-01	-4.50%
Mar-86	20.05%	Mar-91	0.88%	Mar-96	5.31%	Mar-01	3.31%
Apr-86	-2.10%	Apr-91	-0.37%	Apr-96	4.62%	Apr-01	6.98%
May-86	3.26%	May-91	0.08%	May-96	-1.86%	May-01	-4.07%
Jun-86	3.64%	Jun-91	-7.40%	Jun-96	1.91%	Jun-01	-0.71%
Jul-86	6.26%	Jul-91	2.21%	Jul-96	-7.47%	Jul-01	-8.50%
Aug-86	9.49%	Aug-91	-6.82%	Aug-96	-2.57%	Aug-01	-7.26%
Sep-86	2.47%	Sep-91	6.06%	Sep-96	5.74%	Sep-01	-6.94%
Oct-86	-8.08%	Oct-91	3.02%	Oct-96	-4.73%	Oct-01	3.51%
Nov-86	5.50%	Nov-91	-8.27%	Nov-96	0.79%	Nov-01	-0.86%
Dec-86	5.93%	Dec-91	-0.93%	Dec-96	-5.86%	Dec-01	-1.72%
Jan-87	11.88%	Jan-92	-4.88%	Jan-97	-6.69%	Jan-02	-5.84%
Feb-87	1.30%	Feb-92	-4.67%	Feb-97	1.34%	Feb-02	4.35%
Mar-87	5.86%	Mar-92	-8.33%	Mar-97	-0.78%	Mar-02	5.08%
Apr-87	11.43%	Apr-92	-7.12%	Apr-97	4.95%	Apr-02	2.06%
May-87	2.06%	May-92	4.48%	May-97	3.17%	May-02	3.52%
Jun-87	-5.50%	Jun-92	-10.15%	Jun-97	4.52%	Jun-02	-8.50%
Jul-87	-1.52%	Jul-92	-1.37%	Jul-97	-0.63%	Jul-02	-5.81%
Aug-87	6.58%	Aug-92	13.65%	Aug-97	-7.50%	Aug-02	-2.41%
Sep-87	-0.57%	Sep-92	-5.09%	Sep-97	-2.47%	Sep-02	-1.83%
Oct-87	-12.58%	Oct-92	-2.42%	Oct-97	-8.01%	Oct-02	-6.38%
Nov-87	-0.58%	Nov-92	3.48%	Nov-97	-1.95%	Nov-02	3.54%
Dec-87	-6.97%	Dec-92	-1.14%	Dec-97	-6.14%	Dec-02	-5.50%
Jan-88	10.86%	Jan-93	-0.66%	Jan-98	7.88%	Jan-03	-2.61%
Feb-88	8.11%	Feb-93	-1.11%	Feb-98	0.41%	Feb-03	-0.27%
Mar-88	4.02%	Mar-93	12.00%	Mar-98	-1.12%	Mar-03	-3.12%
Apr-88	1.62%	Apr-93	13.20%	Apr-98	-2.29%	Apr-03	1.09%
May-88	-4.36%	May-93	0.98%	May-98	-0.12%	May-03	5.18%
Jun-88	2.78%	Jun-93	-3.42%	Jun-98	0.75%	Jun-03	7.88%
Jul-88	3.85%	Jul-93	5.04%	Jul-98	2.58%	Jul-03	3.98%
Aug-88	-4.81%	Aug-93	2.01%	Aug-98	-12.31%	Aug-03	6.69%
Sep-88	2.82%	Sep-93	-3.70%	Sep-98	-5.33%	Sep-03	2.02%
Oct-88	0.78%	Oct-93	0.27%	Oct-98	-0.76%	Oct-03	2.41%
Nov-88	6.24%	Nov-93	-15.73%	Nov-98	10.42%	Nov-03	-4.17%
Dec-88	3.05%	Dec-93	4.79%	Dec-98	-4.91%	Dec-03	4.44%
Jan-89	4.11%	Jan-94	13.20%	Jan-99	3.53%	Jan-04	0.37%
Feb-89	-0.70%	Feb-94	0.17%	Feb-99	-0.44%	Feb-04	3.36%
Mar-89	1.15%	Mar-94	-3.85%	Mar-99	13.66%	Mar-04	9.48%
Apr-89	0.79%	Apr-94	2.57%	Apr-99	5.52%	Apr-04	0.60%
May-89	1.96%	May-94	4.94%	May-99	-2.99%	May-04	-3.90%
Jun-89	-3.44%	Jun-94	-0.52%	Jun-99	9.18%	Jun-04	4.43%
Jul-89	7.33%	Jul-94	-2.14%	Jul-99	4.43%	Jul-04	-4.23%
Aug-89	-0.97%	Aug-94	0.19%	Aug-99	-1.47%	Aug-04	-0.84%
Sep-89	3.97%	Sep-94	-3.62%	Sep-99	3.69%	Sep-04	-2.06%
Oct-89	-0.35%	Oct-94	0.50%	Oct-99	3.79%	Oct-04	-1.51%
Nov-89	5.09%	Nov-94	-4.05%	Nov-99	4.97%	Nov-04	1.24%
Dec-89	1.85%	Dec-94	2.57%	Dec-99	4.93%	Dec-04	4.69%

Date	% Change		Date	% Change		Date	% Change
Jan-05	-0.30%		Jul-05	2.09%		Jan-06	3.70%
Feb-05	2.75%		Aug-05	5.80%		Feb-06	-2.92%
Mar-05	1.00%		Sep-05	12.77%		Mar-06	4.63%
Apr-05	-4.39%		Oct-05	1.16%		Apr-06	-0.68%
May-05	1.25%		Nov-05	6.34%		May-06	-7.95%
Jun-05	2.98%		Dec-05	7.45%		Jun-06	0.48%

Source: Global Financial Data.

APPENDIX K

Fisher Investments Global Total Return Performance

FI Fiscal Year	Net Annual Return (%)	S&P 500 Return (%)	MSCI World Benchmark Return (%)
1996	28.6%	26.0%	18.4%
1997	33.6%	34.7%	22.3%
1998	21.4%	30.2%	17.0%
1999	17.2%	22.8%	15.7%
2000	15.6%	7.2%	12.2%
2001	-10.2%	-14.8%	-20.3%
2002	-5.7%	-18.0%	-15.2%
2003	-7.3%	0.3%	-2.4%
2004	20.5%	19.1%	24.0%
2005	5.3%	6.3%	10.1%
2006	17.7%	8.6%	16.9%
Annualized Returns (ending 06/30/06)			
1 Year	17.7%	8.6%	16.9%
3 Year	14.3%	11.2%	16.9%
5 Year	5.5%	2.5%	5.7%
7 Year	4.4%	0.5%	2.4%
10 Year	9.9%	8.3%	6.9%
Since 7/01/1995	11.5%	9.8%	7.9%

Fisher Investments Private Client Group has prepared and presented this report in compliance with the Global Investment Performance Standards (GIPS®). The composite has been independently verified for the period January 1, 1995 through December 31, 2005.

Composite returns presented in the preceding table are calculated on a fiscal year basis ending June 30 for illustrative purposes. Annualized returns are presented from 1/1/95 through 6/30/06.

1. Fisher Investments (FI) is an investment adviser registered with the Securities and Exchange Commission. FI currently advises over $31 billion across two principal business units – Fisher Investments Institutional Group (FIIG) and Fisher Investments Private Client Group (FIPCG). FIPCG manages and serves all private client accounts managed by FI.

2. These results have been prepared and presented in compliance with GIPS standards for the period January 1, 1995 through June 30, 2006.

3. The composite's performance before 12/31/95 comprises equity-oriented, broad mandate FIIG accounts. Since 12/31/95, the composite comprises FIPCG accounts managed within the parameters of the Global Total Return strategy. The firm assets included in #4 below are based on FIIG before 12/31/95 and FIPCG after that date.

4. The number of accounts, dollar value (in millions), and percentage of firm assets represented by the composite as of each year end, respectively, was: 1995—1, $2, 0.2%; 1996—116, $75, 33%; 1997—461, $314, 60%; 1998—1078, $1026, 79%; 1999—2148, $2397, 85%; 2000—3845, $3488, 88%; 2001—6801, $5999, 93%; 2002—10973, $6765, 88%; 2003—13796, $11514, 89%; 2004—16265, $14059, 88%; 2005— 16795, $14947, 85%.

5. The Global Total Return composite consists of accounts following the Global Total Return strategy. This broad-mandate strategy seeks capital appreciation by investing primarily in domestic and foreign common stocks, but may from time to time invest in fixed-income securities, money market instruments and other equity-type securities as well as utilize hedging instruments such as short equity positions and options.

6. The Morgan Stanley Capital International (MSCI) World Index has been selected as the benchmark for the composite. The MSCI World is an unmanaged, capitalization-weighted stock index measuring

the performance of selected stocks in 23 developed countries and is presented net of dividend withholding taxes.

7. Valuations and returns are computed and stated in US Dollars.

8. Performance for this composite was determined using time-weighted rates of return, with valuation on at least a monthly basis and geometric linking of periodic returns. Valuations are based on trade date. Returns reflect the reinvestment of dividends, royalties, interest and other forms of accrued income.

9. Performance results reflect the deduction of advisory fees, brokerage or other commissions and any other expenses that were charged to client accounts.

10. In 2001 and 2002, eligible portfolios in the Global Total Return strategy contained a small derivatives weight, specifically index put options. The use of derivatives was primarily focused on reducing benchmark risk within a bear market strategy. The strategy also utilized market neutral strategies, fixed income and/or cash in accounts to reduce risk, and may do so again when a significant market decline is expected.

11. Fisher Investments Private Client Group current standard tiered fee schedule (also listed in Part II of Fisher Investments' Form ADV) is: 1.25% on less than $1 million, 1.125% on the next $1 million to $5 million, and 1.00% on the next $5 million and greater. If FI accepts an account under one half-million dollars, a 1.50% annual fee will supersede the aforementioned fee schedule.

12. The dispersion of annual returns is measured by the asset-weighted standard deviation across portfolio returns gross of fees represented within the composite for the full year: 1995—N/A; 1996—7.0%; 1997—3.5%; 1998—5.0%; 1999—5.0%; 2000—2.8%; 2001—1.7%; 2002—1.7%; 2003—2.0%; 2004—1.3%; 2005—1.3%.

13. Annual Returns for each calendar year since January 1, 1995 against the MSCI World Index ("MSCI") for: 1995 (Gross) 39.3%, (Net) 38.3%, (MSCI) 20.7%; 1996 (Gross) 21.6%, (Net) 20.2%, (MSCI) 13.5%; 1997 (Gross) 24.2%, (Net) 22.8%, (MSCI) 15.8%; 1998 (Gross) 29.1%, (Net) 27.7%, (MSCI) 24.3%; 1999 (Gross) 26.0%, (Net) 24.7%, (MSCI) 24.9%; 2000 (Gross) -7.4%, (Net) -8.5%, (MSCI) - 13.2%; 2001 (Gross) 4.4%, (Net) 3.2%, (MSCI) -16.8%; 2002 (Gross) -23.1%, (Net) -24.1%, (MSCI) -19.9%; 2003 (Gross) 35.3%, (Net) 33.8%, (MSCI) 33.1%; 2004 (Gross) 9.7%, (Net) 8.3%, (MSCI) 14.7%; 2005 (Gross) 8.8%, (Net) 7.5%, (MSCI) 9.5%.

14. Annualized Returns from January 1, 1995 through June 30, 2006 against the MSCI World Index ("MSCI") for: 1 Year (Gross) 19.1%, (Net) 17.7%, (MSCI) 16.9%; 3 Year (Gross) 15.7%, (Net) 14.3%, (MSCI) 16.9%; 5 Year (Gross) 6.7%, (Net) 5.5%, (MSCI) 5.7%; 7 Year (Gross) 5.7%, (Net) 4.4%, (MSCI) 2.4%; 10 Year (Gross) 11.2%, (Net) 9.9%, (MSCI) 6.9%; Since 1/1/1995 (Gross) 13.8%, (Net) 12.5%, (MSCI) 8.4%.

15. Past performance is no guarantee of future returns; investments in securities involve risk of loss. Other methods may produce different results, and the results for individual portfolios and for different periods may vary depending on market conditions and the composition of the portfolio.

16. A complete list and description of FI composites, performance results and policies regarding calculating and reporting returns are available upon request.

APPENDIX L

Ten-Year History of the *Forbes* Report Card

Year	Ken Fisher's Forbes Stock Picks	S&P 500 Price Index
1996	13.9%	12.1%
1997	23.0%	33.0%
1998	14.9%	14.9%
1999	20.5%	11.5%
2000	0.0%	-10.0%
2001	-2.5%	-11.4%
2002	-6.0%	-3.0%
2003	31.6%	17.6%
2004	12.6%	7.6%
2005	14.3%	3.4%
10 Year Annualized Return:		
	11.7%	6.8%

Disclosure

This is *Forbes* magazine's third party accounting of the results of Ken Fisher's *Forbes* picks.

Each year since 1996 *Forbes* verifies and publishes returns for each of its columnists' securities recommendations for the year before (among those who make specific recommendations in their columns). It is called the columnist's "Report Card". This is not an actual portfolio of managed money. The numbers above come directly from *Forbes* magazine annually. They are calculated solely based on calendar years. The methodology *Forbes* uses assumes readers buy $10,000 of each stock recommended and immediately subtracts a 1% hypothetical brokerage commission.

That is compared to putting $10,000 into an S&P500 index fund at the same date with no hypothetical commission and no other fees. For example, in 2004 Ken Fisher recommended 51 stocks in *Forbes* throughout the year. If $10,000 had been put into each stock the total invested would have been $510,000 which would have appreciated by yearend 2004 to $574,000, a 12.6% appreciation. The same amount of money invested in the S&P 500 at those various times without a hypothetical commission would have totaled $548,000 for a return of 7.6% at the end of 2004. Using this methodology Ken Fisher's *Forbes* stock picks tied the S&P 500 in 1998, lagged it in 1997 and 2002 and beat it in all other years and overall beat it by an average annualized 4.9% per year for calendar years 1996 through 2005.

These are not the results of Fisher Investments' actual portfolio management (see Appendix G). Nor is this accounting consistent with GIPS performance standards normally used for money management. These results also do not include the effect of a management fee that is normally charged for professional money management. There is no attempt in this methodology to account for the transaction costs of bid/ask spreads or friction which reduce returns in real money management. The stocks Ken Fisher recommends in *Forbes* are not stocks actually owned by Fisher Investments' clients which are intentionally different recommendations for regulatory reasons (see description in Chapter 9).

APPENDIX M

The United Deficits: Data

Year	US Current (millions)	US Trade Deficit (millions)	US Budget Deficit (millions)	US Gov't Debt (billions)	UK Current (millions)	UK Trade Deficit (millions)	UK Budget Deficit (millions)	UK Gov't Debt (billions)
1975	18,114	12,404	-53,242	542	-1,695	-3,333	-1,681	52
1976	4,293	-6,082	-73,732	629	-972	-3,911	-2,001	65
1977	-14,337	-27,246	-53,659	706	-286	-2,239	-1,506	74
1978	-15,143	-29,763	-59,185	777	821	-1,478	-4,056	80
1979	-290	-24,565	-40,726	829	-1,002	-3,451	-5,064	89
1980	2,316	-19,407	-73,830	909	1,740	1,329	-5,459	98
1981	5,031	-16,172	-78,968	995	4,846	3,238	-6,284	114
1982	-5,533	-24,156	-127,977	1,137	2,233	1,879	-4,231	125
1983	-38,695	-57,767	-207,802	1,372	1,258	-1,618	-4,806	133
1984	-94,342	-109,072	-185,367	1,565	-1,294	-5,409	-7,059	144
1985	-118,159	-121,880	-212,308	1,817	-570	-3,416	-5,485	157
1986	-147,176	-138,538	-221,227	2,121	-3,614	-9,617	-5,555	163
1987	-160,661	-151,684	-149,730	2,346	-7,538	-11,698	-3,906	168
1988	-121,159	-114,566	-155,178	2,601	-19,850	-21,553	5,524	167
1989	-99,485	-93,141	-152,623	2,868	-26,321	-24,724	8,736	154
1990	-78,965	-80,864	-221,147	3,206	-22,281	-18,707	4,393	152
1991	3,743	-31,135	-269,269	3,598	-10,659	-10,223	-7,948	151
1992	-47,998	-39,093	-290,334	4,002	-12,974	-13,050	-28,584	166
1993	-81,997	-70,195	-255,085	4,351	-11,919	-13,066	-39,735	235
1994	-118,031	-98,379	-203,228	4,643	-6,768	-11,126	-35,632	278
1995	-109,481	-96,265	-163,991	4,921	-9,015	-12,023	-28,561	314
1996	-120,216	-103,942	-107,473	5,181	-7,001	-13,722	-22,858	343
1997	-135,978	-108,178	-21,935	5,369	-937	-12,342	-11,608	357
1998	-209,560	-164,868	69,200	5,478	-3,972	-21,813	7,464	354
1999	-296,816	-263,252	125,541	5,606	-24,416	-29,051	14,980	353
2000	-413,454	-378,344	236,151	5,629	-24,094	-32,976	19,288	318
2001	-385,703	-362,692	128,161	5,770	-22,391	-40,648	16,267	319
2002	-473,943	-421,735	-157,799	6,198	-17,615	-46,675	-8,740	345
2003	-530,669	-496,508	-377,575	6,760	-18,571	-47,416	-21,522	375
2004	-603,224	-605,321	-412,144	7,486	-25,475	-57,629	-21,981	417
2005	-791,508	-716,729	-318,300	7,933	-26,550	-44,242	-13,695	457

Sources: The White House, Bureau of Economic Analysis, U.S. Census Bureau, U.S. Department of Treasury, National Statistics, HM Treasury.

NOTES

Preface

1. Matthew Miller and Peter Newcomb, "The Forbes 400," *Forbes* (September 22, 2005), pp. 89–320.
2. Standard & Poor's Research Insight.
3. Thomson Financial Datastream.
4. See note 3.

Chapter 1   Question One: What Do You Believe That Is Actually False?

1. Investment Company Institute and The Securities Industry Association (www.ici.org), "Equity Ownership in America" (2005), p. 7.
2. John Y. Campbell and Robert J. Shiller, "Valuation Ratios and the Long-Run Stock Market Outlook," *Journal of Portfolio Management* (Winter 1998), pp. 11–26.
3. Kenneth L. Fisher and Meir Statman, "Cognitive Biases in Market Forecasts," *Journal of Portfolio Management* (Fall 2000), pp. 72–81.
4. Alfred Cowles III and Associates, *Common Stock Indexes*, 2nd ed. (Bloomington, IN: Principia Press, 1939).
5. See note 2.
6. See note 2.
7. See note 2.
8. When Meir and I originally looked at the data from 1872 until 1999 for our aforementioned study back in 2000, we found an R-squared of 0.26—still statistically random.
9. If you're inclined to data and statistics, I refer you to another scholarly article Meir Statman and I did in the Summer 2006 issue of the *Journal of Investing* where we show the data for the United Kingdom, Germany, and Japan.

10. Daniel Kahneman and Amos Tversky, "Prospect Theory: An Analysis of Decision Under Risk," *Econometrica*, vol. 47, no. 2 (March 1979), pp. 263–292.
11. Richard H. Thaler, Amos Tversky, Daniel Kahneman, and Alan Schwarts, "The Effect of Myopia and Loss Aversion on Risk Taking: An Experimental Test," *Quarterly Journal of Economics* (May 1997), pp. 647–661.
12. Daniel Kahneman, Paul Slovic, and Amos Tversky, *Judgment Under Uncertainty: Heuristics and Biases* (New York: Cambridge University Press, 1982), pp. 480–481.
13. Bloomberg, Bloomberg Fair Market Composite 10-year BBB-rated corporate bond index, June 2006.
14. Global Financial Data, S&P 500 total return, October 9, 2002, through June 30, 2006.
15. See note 14, S&P 500 total returns, 1982 through 1989 were 22 percent, 23 percent, 6 percent, 32 percent, 19 percent, 5 percent, 17 percent, and 32 percent, respectively.
16. Office of Management and Budget, "Overview of the President's 2007 Budget," http://www.whitehouse.gov/omb/pdf/overview-07.pdf (accessed June 30, 2006).
17. U.S. Department of Commerce, Bureau of Economic Analysis, "National Economic Accounts," http://www.bea.gov/bea/dn/nipaweb/TableView.asp?SelectedTable=5&FirstYear=2005&LastYear=2006&Freq=Qtr (accessed July 28, 2006).
18. Congress of the United States, Congressional Budget Office, "The Budget and Economic Outlook: Fiscal Years 2007 to 2016," http://www.cbo.gov/showdoc.cfm?index=7027&sequence=0 (accessed May 4, 2006).
19. See note 14, S&P 500 total return.
20. Thomson Financial Datastream, MSCI World net return for calendar year 2003.

Chapter 2   Question Two: What Can You Fathom That Others Find Unfathomable?

1. Kenneth L. Fisher, "Advanced Fad Avoidance," *Forbes* (March 13, 1995), p. 180.
2. Global Financial Data, S&P 500 total return.
3. See note 2, U.S. Fed Funds Official Target Rate and S&P 500 Composite Total Return Index from January 2001 through June 2003.
4. U.S. Department of Commerce, National Bureau of Economic Research, "The NBER's Recession Dating Procedure," http://www.nber.org/cycles/recessions.html (accessed October 21, 2003).
5. See note 2.
6. See note 4, "Table C-51: Survey of Current Business," http://www.nber.org/cycles.html (accessed October 1994).
7. U.S. Department of Commerce, Bureau of Economic Analysis, "Current-Dollar and 'Real' GDP," http://bea.gov/bea/dn/gdplev.xls (accessed August 30, 2006).
8. Thomson Financial Datastream, MSCI World Index net return in calendar year 2003.
9. Ibbotson Analyst, "S&P/Barra 500 Growth Total Return Index and S&P/Barra 500 Value Total Return Index."

10. Thomson One Analytics, S&P 500 Composite 12-Month Forward P/E Ratio.

11. Global Financial Data, S&P returns.

12. See note 11.

13. Federal Election Commission, "Appendix A: 1988–2000 Presidential General Election Percentage of Popular Vote Received by State," http://www.fec.gov /pubrec/fe2000/appa.htm (accessed December 2001).

14. See note 13.

15. "Guide to U.S. Elections," *Congressional Quarterly* (1975), p. 271.

16. See note 15.

17. See note 15.

18. See note 2, S&P 500 total return.

19. *Wikipedia*, "United States House Elections, 2002," http://en.wikipedia.org/wiki /United_States_House_elections,_2002 (accessed June 29, 2006).

20. See note 2, S&P 500 total returns.

Chapter 3 Question Three: What the Heck Is My Brain Doing to Blindside Me Now?

1. Investment Company Institute, Archive of Trends releases, "Net New Cash Flow in Stock Mutual Funds," http://www.ici.org/stats/mf/arctrends/index .html#TopOfPage (accessed June 29, 2006).

2. See note 1.

3. Thomson Financial Datastream, MSCI World Index price return.

4. See note 3, MSCI World Index net return.

5. See note 3, S&P 500 return from July 17, 1998, through August 31, 1998.

6. See note 3, S&P 500 return.

7. See note 3, S&P 500 return for 1998 calendar year.

8. Richard H. Thaler, Amos Tversky, Daniel Kahneman, and Alan Schwarts, "The Effect of Myopia and Loss Aversion on Risk Taking: An Experimental Test," *Quarterly Journal of Economics* (May 1997), pp. 647–661.

9. Gina K. Logue, "Discovery Could Change Continent's History," *Middle Tennessee Record*, V14.20 (April 24, 2006), pp. 8, 7.

10. Library of Congress, Bills/Resolutions, Pension Security Act of 2002, A.H.R. 3762.14, http://thomas.loc.gov/cgi-bin/query/z?c107:H.R.3762.

11. See note 3, General Electric total return.

12. See note 3.

13. See note 3, MSCI World Index net return in 2005.

14. See note 3, Altria return, December 31, 1999, through December 31, 2005.

15. Global Financial Datastream, S&P 500 total return.

16. Standard & Poor's Research Insight, S&P 500 constituent returns 1997.

17. See note 16.

18. See note 3. Tech stocks as measured by Nasdaq 100 Index.

19. See note 3. MSCI World Index net return.

20. See note 3. Nasdaq 100 Index.
21. See note 3. MSCI World Index net return.
22. Brad M. Barber and Terrance Odean, "Boys Will Be Boys: Gender, Overconfidence, and Common Stock Investment," *Quarterly Journal of Economics*, vol. 116, no. 1 (February 2001), pp. 261–292.
23. Jonathan Weisman, "Projected Iraq War Costs Soar," *Washington Post* (April 27, 2006), p. A16, http://www.washingtonpost.com/wp-dyn/content/article/2006/04/26/AR2006042601601.html.

Chapter 4 Capital Markets Technology

1. Global Financial Data, S&P 500 Index annual total returns, 1926 through 2005.
2. National Oceanic and Atmospheric Administration, National Hurricane Center, "Retired Hurricane Names 1954–2005," http://www.nhc.noaa.gov/retirednames.shtml (accessed May 11, 2006).
3. James O'Shaughnessy, *What Works on Wall Street: A Guide to the Best-Performing Investments Strategies of All Time* (New York: McGraw-Hill, 1997).
4. Jack Hough, "Price/Sales Ratio," *Wall Street Journal* (April 13, 2006), p. D3.
5. Kenneth L. Fisher and Meir Statman, "Investor Sentiment and Stock Returns," *Financial Analysts Journal* (March/April 2000), pp. 16–23.
6. Darrell Huff, *How to Lie with Statistics* (New York: W.W. Norton & Company, 1954/1993).
7. See note 1, S&P 500 total return.
8. Kenneth L. Fisher, "Forecasting Made Easy," *Research* (September 2002), pp. 50–54.
9. See note 5.
10. Kenneth L. Fisher, "1980 Revisited," *Forbes* (March 6, 2000), p. 186.
11. Kenneth L. Fisher, "Never Say Dow," *Forbes* (November 15, 1999), p. 310.
12. As of June 14, 2006, NYSE, http://www.nyse.com/marketinfo/indexes/nya_characteristics.shtml.
13. Thomson Financial Datastream, Dow Jones as of June 30, 2006, 3M ranked #80 in list of NYSE constituents on June 30, 2006.
14. See note 13, as of June 30, 2006.
15. Standard & Poor's Research Insight as of June 30, 2006.
16. See note 15.
17. See note 13, Nasdaq 100 Index.
18. See note 13, Shanghai SE B Share return.
19. Bloomberg, IFC Global Total Zimbabwe Index, in U.S.$.
20. See note 1. China GDP.
21. See note 1. Germany GDP.
22. See note 13, DAX Index.
23. See note 13, Japan GDP.
24. See note 13, TOPIX Index.

Chapter 5   When There's No There, There!

1. Romesh Ratnesar, "Gulf Wars I and II," *Time* (March 23, 2003), http://www.time .com/time/covers/1101030331/wgw1.html, this number includes troops deployed from the United States, Saudi Arabia, Kuwait, France, Syria, and Egypt.

2. See note 1; this number includes troops deployed from the United States, the United Kingdom, Australia, and Poland.

3. U.S. Department of Energy, Energy Information Administration, "Crude Oil and Total Petrolatum Imports: Top 15 Countries" (February 2006), http://www.eia.doe .gov/pub/oil_gas/petroleum/data_publications/company_level_imports/current /import.html (accessed May 15, 2006).

4. U.S. Department of Energy, Energy Information Administration, "World Proved Crude Oil Reserves, January 1, 1980–January 1, 2006 Estimates" (January 18, 2006), http://www.eia.doe.gov/pub/international/iealf/crudeoilreserves.xls (accessed May 15, 2006).

5. Joe Barton, "Barton Releases Discussion Draft of Refinery Bill," U.S. House of Representatives, Committee on Energy and Commerce, http://energycommerce .house.gov/108/News/09262005_1661.htm (accessed June 20, 2006).

6. American Petroleum Institute, "Gasoline Taxes: July 2006," http://api-ec.api.org /filelibrary/2006-gasoline-diesel-taxes-summary.pdf (accessed August 15, 2006).

7. Society of Petroleum Engineers, "How Much Oil and Natural Gas is Left?" http://www.spe.org/spe/jsp/basic/0,,1104_1008218_1109511,00.html (accessed May 15, 2006).

8. Bureau of Labor Statistics, Maximum Monthly Unemployment Rate, January 1970–December 1979, http://data.bls.gov/PDQ/servlet/SurveyOutputServlet.

9. U.S. Department of Energy, "Strategic Petroleum Reserve Inventory," http://www .fossil.energy.gov/programs/reserves (accessed May 16, 2006).

10. John Shages, Department of Energy, Office of Fossil Energy, "Releasing Crude Oil from the Strategic Petroleum Reserve," http://www.fossil.energy.gov/programs /reserves (accessed May 16, 2006).

11. See note 10.

12. Anton Dammer, Department of Energy, Office of Fossil Energy, "Oil Shale Activities," http://www.fossil.energy.gov/programs/reserves/npr/NPR_Oil_Shale_Program .html (accessed May 16, 2006).

13. Saudi Aramco, "Quick Facts about Saudi Aramco," http://www.saudiaramco .com/bvsm/JSP/content/channelDetail.jsp?BV_SessionID=@@@@1282495389 .1147806175@@@@&BV_EngineID=cccjaddhkiehdelcefeceefdfnkdfhn .0&datetime=05 percent2F16 percent2F06+22 percent3A03 percent3A25&SA .channelID=-1073750311 (accessed May 16, 2006).

14. National Energy Board of Canada, "Canada's Oil Sands: Opportunities and Challenges to 2015" (Updated June 2006), http://www.neb-one.gc.ca/energy /EnergyReports/EMAOilSandsOpportunitiesChallenges2015_2004/EMAOiSand Opportunities2015Canada2004_e.pdf (accessed June 29, 2006).

15. Energy Information Administration, "International Energy Annual 2003" (June 29, 2006), http://www.eia.doe.gov/emeu/international/energyconsumption.html (accessed July 25, 2006).

16. U.S. Bureau of Economic Analysis, "Table 1: Percent Changes in Real Value Added by Industry Group" (April 27, 2006), http://www.bea.gov/bea/newsrelarchive/2006/gdpind05.xls (accessed August 14, 2006).

17. U.S. Bureau of Economic Analysis, "Table 1.5.5: Gross Domestic Product, Expanded Detail" (July 28, 2006), http://www.bea.gov/bea/dn/nipaweb/SelectTable.asp?Selected=Y (accessed August 22, 2006).

18. U.S. Bureau of Economic Analysis, "Current and 'Real' Gross Domestic Product," http://www.bea.gov/bea/dn/home/gdp.htm (accessed August 14, 2006).

19. Alexandra Twin, "Skidding on Oil," *CNN Money* (March 16, 2005), http://money.cnn.com/2005/03/16/markets/markets_newyork (accessed May 17, 2006).

20. Jennifer Lee, "Stocks Fall as Oil Rises," *Forbes* (July 6, 2005), http://www.forbes.com/markets/2005/07/06/video-webcast-oil-cx_jl_0706video03.html (accessed August 23, 2006).

21. Tom Van Riper, "Oil falls as Saudis up output, stocks rise" *Daily News* (May 22, 2004), http://www.nydailynews.com/business/story/195674p-169057c.html (accessed May 17, 2006).

22. Annalisa Burgos, "Stocks Rise as Oil Falls," *Forbes.com* (August 17, 2005), http://www.forbes.com/markets/2005/08/17/us-stocks-closer-cx_ab_0817video03.html (accessed May 17, 2006).

23. Energy Information Administration, "Crude Oil Price Summary," http://www.eia.doe.gov/emeu/mer/petro.html (accessed August 14, 2006).

24. Associated Press, "Site for Nuclear Plant Narrowed" (September 22, 2005), http://www.cbsnews.com/stories/2005/09/22/tech/main879414.shtml (accessed August 14, 2006).

Chapter 6 No, It's Just the Opposite

1. U.S. Treasury Department Bureau of the Public Debt, "The Debt to the Penny," http://www.publicdebt.treas.gov/opd/opdpenny.htm (accessed June 30, 2006).

2. Freddie Mac, "Weekly Primary Mortgage Market Survey," http://www.freddiemac.com/dlink/html/PMMS/display/PMMSOutputYr.jsp?year=2006# (accessed June 29, 2006).

3. U.S. Bureau of Economic Analysis, "Current-Dollar and 'Real' Gross Domestic Product," nominal current dollar GDP as of June 30, 2006, http://www.bea.gov/bea/dn/gdplev.xls (accessed August 2, 2006).

4. Standard & Poor's Research Insight.

5. See note 4.

6. See note 4.

7. Bloomberg, Fair Market 10-year BBB-rated corporate bond composite as of June 30, 2006.

8. Global Financial Data, average of annual S&P 500 total returns from 1965 to 1981.
9. Kenneth L. Fisher, *The Wall Street Waltz* (Woodside, CA: Business Classics, 1987).
10. U.S. Bureau of Economic Analysis, "Personal Saving Rate," as of second quarter 2006, http://www.bea.gov/briefrm/saving.htm (accessed August 2, 2006).
11. U.S. Bureau of Economic Analysis, "Table 2.4.5: Personal Consumption Expenditures by Type of Product," http://www.bea.gov/bea/dn/nipaweb /TableView.asp?SelectedTable=69&FirstYear=2004&LastYear=2005&Freq=Year (accessed August 2, 2006).
12. See note 11.
13. According to Microsoft's proxy statement, Bill Gates's base salary in 2005 was $600,000.
14. U.S. Bureau of Economic Analysis, "Exhibit 1: U.S. International Trade in Goods and Services," http://www.bea.gov/bea/di1.htm (accessed August 10, 2006).
15. U.S. Census Bureau, "FT900: U.S. International Trade in Goods and Services," http://www.census.gov/foreign-trade/www/index.html (accessed August 30, 2006).
16. U.S. Bureau of Economic Analysis, "Current-Dollar and 'Real' Gross Domestic Product," nominal current dollar GDP as of June 30, 2006, http://www.bea .gov/bea/dn/gdplev.xls (accessed August 2, 2006).
17. Global Financial Data, S&P 500 total returns.
18. National Statistics, "UK Trade," as of June 30, 2006, http://www.statistics .gov.uk/cci/nugget.asp?id=199 (accessed August 2, 2006).
19. Global Financial Data, FTSE All-Share total returns.
20. Hugh Rockloff, "The 'Wizard of Oz' as a Monetary Allegory," *Journal of Political Economy*, vol. 98 (August 1990), pp. 739–760.

Chapter 7 Shocking but True

1. Thomson Financial Datastream, Nasdaq Composite Index peaked on March 10, 2000.
2. See note 1, MSCI World Index troughed on October 9, 2002.
3. Kenneth L. Fisher, "That Wall of Worry," *Forbes* (May 9, 2005), p. 142.
4. Bloomberg, one day price return of MBNA on June 30, 2005.
5. See note 4, price return of MBNA from May 9, 2005, through June 30, 2005.
6. Kenneth L. Fisher, "Surprise: America Owes Too Little," *Forbes* (April 18, 2005), p. 244.
7. See note 1, CP Ships price return on August 22, 2005.
8. See note 1, CP Ships price return from April 18, 2005, through August 22, 2005.
9. Ibbotson Analyst, small-cap value stocks measured by the Fama-French Small Value Total Return Index.
10. Warren Buffet and Carol J. Loomis, "America's Growing Trade Deficit Is Selling the Nation out from under Us. Here's a Way to Fix the Problem—And We Need to Do It Now," *Fortune* (November 10, 2003), pp. 106–116.
11. Global Financial Data.

12. Global Financial Data, U.S. Federal Reserve trade-weighted dollar index as of June 30, 2006.

13. U.S. Bureau of Economic Analysis, "Current-Dollar and 'Real' Gross Domestic Product," nominal current dollar GDP as of June 30, 2006, http://www.bea .gov/bea/dn/gdplev.xls (accessed August 2, 2006). Global Financial Data, correlation coefficient of U.S. current account deficit as percentage of GDP and U.S. trade-weighted dollar from first quarter 1981 through first quarter 2006 is 0.05.

14. Chris Crotty, "iSuppli Teardown Reveals Apple's Surprising Choices for iPod Nano," *iSuppli* (September 22, 2005), http://www.isuppli.com/marketwatch /default.asp?id=316.

Chapter 8   The Great Humiliator and Your Stone-Age Brain

1. Ibbotson Analyst, annualized average of S&P 500 total returns from 1926 to 2005 is 10.4 percent. (You may have also heard the market returns an average 12 percent a year. Both figures are correct, however 12 percent is the arithmetic average while 10 percent is the annualized average and a better way to look at markets. For a review on why, flip back to Chapter 5. Note also by starting such an analysis at differing dates or picking different indexes, you can justify almost any annual average you want between 5 percent and 15 percent.)

2. Global Financial Data, S&P 500 total returns.

3. Thomson Financial Datastream, MSCI World Index net return in 2005.

4. Global Financial Data, S&P 500 total return in 2005.

5. Global Financial Data, MSCI World Index net return, January 1, 2006 through January 13, 2006.

6. Michael J. Mandel, "The New Economy: It Works in America. Will It Go Global?" *BusinessWeek* (January 31, 2000), http://www.businessweek.com/2000/00_05 /b3666001.htm.

7. Standard & Poor's Research Insight, top 30 stocks by market capitalization of the S&P 500 Index.

8. Standard & Poor's, "S&P 500 Index Description," http://www2.standardandpoors .com/servlet/Satellite?pagename=sp/Page/IndicesIndexPg&l=EN&b=4&f=1&s =6&ig=48&i=56&r=1&so=0&fd=&xcd=500&dt=30-JUN-2006 (accessed July 14, 2006).

9. Global Financial Data, Nasdaq Composite Index price return and S&P 500 total return.

10. The 1930 bear market was a loss of 86 percent to stocks and lasted 34 months. The 2000 bear market yielded 49 percent but lasted 31 months.

11. At market close on July 17, 1998, YTD performance was over +22 percent. From then through August 31, the S&P 500 corrected by 19 percent.

12. The S&P 500 Total Return Index has been positive 57 out of 80 years, from 1926 to 2005.

13. Global Financial Data.

14. See note 3, S&P 500 Composite Price Index performance.
15. Global Financial Data, S&P 500 total return.
16. U.S. Bureau of Economic Analysis, "Table 1: Real Gross Domestic Product and Related Measures," http://www.bea.gov/bea/newsrelarchive/2006/gdp106f.xls (accessed August 2, 2006).
17. Global Financial Data, S&P 500 total return.
18. See note 3, MSCI World net return.
19. U.S. Census Bureau, "State & County QuickFacts: Louisiana," http://quickfacts.census.gov/qfd/states/22000.html (accessed June 8, 2006).
20. International Monetary Fund, http://www.imf.org (accessed August 3, 2006).
21. Ned Davis Research, Inc., return on Dow Jones Industrial Average.

Chapter 9   Putting It All Together

1. Michael S. Rozeff, "Lump-Sum Investing versus Dollar-Averaging," *Journal of Portfolio Management* (Winter 1994), pp. 45–50.
2. Richard H. Thaler, Amos Tversky, Daniel Kahneman, and Alan Schwartz, "The Effect of Myopia and Loss Aversion on Risk Taking: An Experimental Test," *Quarterly Journal of Economics* (May 1997), pp. 647–661.
3. Kenneth L. Fisher and Meir Statman, "The Mean Variance Optimization Puzzle: Security Portfolios and Food Portfolios," *Financial Analysts Journal* (July/August 1997), pp. 41–50.
4. Matthew Miller and Peter Newcomb, "The Forbes 400," *Forbes* (September 22, 2005), pp. 89–320.
5. Harold Seneker, Jonathan Greenberg, and John Dorfman, "The Forbes 400," *Forbes* (September 13, 1982), pp. 100–186.
6. Ibbotson Analyst, total returns of S&P 500 and U.S. Long-Term Government Bond from 1926 to 2005.
7. See note 5.
8. See note 5.
9. Morgan Stanley Capital International as of June 30, 2006.
10. Thomson Financial Datastream, technology as measured by the Nasdaq 100 Index, health care as measured by the S&P 500 Pharmaceuticals Index, which is now discontinued. Standard deviations are of each index, 50/50 portfolio and standard deviation derived by combining both tech and health care indices and rebalancing each year.
11. Standard & Poor's Research Insight, dollar-weighted average of the S&P 500 Composite Index constituents as of June 30, 2006.
12. See note 10, there are 20 stocks in the S&P 500 Composite with market capitalizations over $100 billion. Their weights in the index range from 0.9 percent to 3.1 percent.
13. Kenneth L. Fisher, "Give It Time," *Forbes* (January 31, 2005), p. 142.
14. See note 10, total return in calendar year 2005.

15. Global Financial Data, S&P 500 Industrials sector total return in 2005.

16. See note 10, total return in 2005 for S&P 500 Composite Index and net return in 2005 for MSCI World Index.

17. See note 10, total return in 2005.

18. Office of New York State Attorney General Eliot Spitzer, press release, "Investigation Reveals Widespread Corruption in Insurance Industry" (October 14, 2004).

19. See note 10.

20. See note 18.

21. Ian McDonald and Leslie Scism, "AIG's ExChief Clears a Hurdle but Faces More," *Wall Street Journal* (November 25, 2005), http://online.wsj.com/article/SB113288840104206370.html.

22. See note 10, AIG's total return from February 11 to April 22, 2005.

23. See note 10, AIG's total return from April 22, 2005 to January 11, 2006 was 42 percent.

24. See note 10, AIG's total return from October 14, 2004 to January 11, 2006 was 19 percent.

25. See note 10, S&P 500 total return from October 14, 2004 to January 11, 2006 was 20 percent.

GLOSSARY

Accretive   Anything making a firm's value grow, particularly as reflected in *earnings per share*.

American Depository Receipt (ADR)   Receipt for a foreign firm's share, paid for in U.S. dollars and traded on U.S. exchanges. Americans trading in ADRs needn't exchange dollars for foreign currency.

Annualized average (or geometric average or mean)   Rather than an arithmetic average (or mean), an annualized average properly calculates annual investment returns. To get an annualized average, multiply 1 plus each year's return, raise it to the power of the *n*th root (where *n* is the number of years), and subtract 1.

Ask   Also known as the offer, the ask is the price a seller is willing to accept for a security. The difference between the *bid* and *ask* is known as the *bid-ask spread*. See also *bid*.

Bear   An investor who is pessimistic about future returns—usually regarding stocks—but the term can be applied to any investing category. Investors are *bearish* if they are fearful of stocks. Some investors are perma-*bears*, generally always preferring lower returns with less volatility.

Bear market   A prolonged broad market downturn exceeding 20 percent. Not to be confused with a *correction*.

Beta   A measure of a stock's (or category's) volatility relative to an index. For example, if the S&P 500's beta is 1, stocks with higher beta are more volatile, and stocks with lower beta are less volatile, than the broad market. Beta can also be used to measure relative volatility among peers.

Bid   The price a buyer offers to pay for a stock. See also *ask*.

Bid-ask spread   The difference between the *bid* and the *ask*.

Blue chip   A large, nationally recognized, financially sound firm with a long track record usually selling high-quality and widely accepted goods and services. General Electric, ExxonMobil, and IBM are all considered *blue chips*.

Bond   A debt investment. Investors lend money to an institution by buying bonds and receive fixed interest payments in return. When the bond matures, the investor receives the principal back. Municipal bonds (munis) are exempt from federal taxes and some state and local taxes if you live in the municipality where the bond is issued. U.S. Treasuries are exempt from state taxes.

Bond fund   A *mutual fund* in which the underlying investments are largely *bonds*.

Bubble   Frequently misused in reference to any category's price that has appreciated—true bubbles are rare. A bubble, normally identified after it has burst, is the rapid increase and subsequent decrease in prices for a specific category of equity or commodity (e.g., tech in 2000; energy in 1980).

Bull market   A lengthy period of time marked by overall positive broad market returns. Bull markets have occupied over 70 percent of historic periods.

Call option   The right to buy a stock (or bond or commodity) at a certain price by a certain date. A call option writer sells the right to a buyer.

Capital gain   Appreciation in value of a security, bond, commodity, or other instrument.

Capital gains tax   Tax paid on any capital gain when it's realized (sold).

Carry trade   When an investor borrows in one currency at a lower interest rate and buys a short-term bond at a higher interest rate in a different currency. As long as the higher yielding currency doesn't weaken, the spread between the interest rates is profit.

Cash flow   For investors, any cash generated by dividends, interest, coupon payments, or proceeds from the sale of stocks, bonds, or commodities. On a tax-adjusted basis, no form of cash flow is superior to any other.

Central bank   The institution in each country responsible for setting monetary policy, printing money, managing reserves, and controlling inflation. In the United States, the central bank is the *Federal Reserve System,* also known as the Fed.

Certificate of deposit (CD)   Debt instrument issued by a bank paying a fixed interest rate driven by market forces. Investors commit to a fixed period in return for a fixed interest rate. Maturities range from a few weeks to a few years.

Cognitive bias   In behavioral finance, the tendency to believe something is true that is not supported by facts but by tradition or conditioning.

Commodity   Goods traded on a commodity market in bulk, such as metals, grains, and food. Other investment vehicles may be traded on a commodity exchange, such as certain futures and options.

Confirmation bias   Cognitive error causing investors to seek evidence confirming their preset notions and reject contradictory evidence.

Consumer Price Index (CPI)   Issued by the Bureau of Labor Statistics (BLS), this figure is a popularly used measure of inflation. It measures the relative change in prices of a basket of consumer goods and services.

Contrarian   An investor who believes the likeliest outcome is the opposite of what the consensus expects.

Correction   A short, sharp downturn in prices during a longer bull market trend, usually marked by investor pessimism and a bearish story that is later deemed a nonevent. Corrections are of a lesser magnitude and lesser duration than bear markets. Bear markets have short, sharp positive corrections.

Correlation   A statistical measure between −1 and 1 demonstrating similarity between two variables' movements. A correlation close to 1 means the two variables move in a similar direction and magnitude. A correlation close to −1 means the two move in opposing directions. A correlation close to 0 means the two have no similarity.

Covered call   A covered call combines a "written" *call option* with a long stock position. Loss potential is total except for the premium, making a covered call the exact same security as a *naked put*.

Cyclical stock   A stock sensitive to business cycles moving largely with the market. A stock for which there is *elastic demand*.

Day trading   Trading with the intention of capturing short-term moves. Day-traders may buy and sell the same security within a few hours, weeks, or months.

Debt-to-equity ratio   Ratio demonstrating an institution's debt relative to its equity. Just one component used by corporations in assessing optimal capital structures. Also, used by lending institutions to determine the amount they are willing to lend an individual or corporation.

Defensive   Describing anything that counteracts big market downside. A defensive portfolio is one intended to be up slightly or flat during a bear market.

Defensive stock   A stock viewed as typically stable during economic downturns and capable of weathering bear markets well. A stock for which there is *inelastic demand*.

Deflation   A drop in average price levels, usually caused by excessive tightening of money supply. Can lead to reduced economic demand and higher unemployment. Not to be confused with *disinflation*.

Dilutive   Anything reducing the value of a firm, particularly as reflected in *earnings per share*.

Discount rate   The rate charged member banks for borrowing directly from the Federal Reserve Bank. This rate is controlled directly by the Fed.

Disinflation   The slowing of growth of average prices levels. Can be thought of as the slowing of *inflation*. Not to be confused with *deflation*.

Dividend   A taxable payment made to stock holders, usually quarterly, out of a firm's current or retained earnings. Can be paid in cash or stock.

Earnings per share (EPS)   A firm's total earnings divided by total number of shares outstanding.

Dow Jones Industrial Average (DJIA)   A price-weighted index of 30 *blue chip* U.S. stocks. Commonly referred to as the "Dow."

Earnings-to-price ratio (E/P)   Ratio of a firm's earnings per share to its share price—also known as the *earnings yield*. The reverse of the *price-to-earnings ratio*.

Earnings yield   This valuation, expressed as an interest rate, easily allows a comparison between the relative value of stocks and the going bond rates as well as borrowing costs. See also *earnings-to-price ratio*.

Efficient market   The theory that the stock market quickly and efficiently prices in all widely known information, which is why trading on known information will not yield excess returns.

Elastic demand   Demand for goods and services that is sensitive to economic cycles and expands and contracts with the economy. For example, demand for high-priced technology or consumer discretionary goods is generally *elastic*.

Excess return   Return garnered above a stated index's return.

Exchange-traded fund (ETF)   A security that tracks a specific index, equity category, or other basket of assets but is traded on an exchange like a single stock.

Expense ratio   Usually expressed as a percentage, the amount of total fund assets used to cover all expenses of managing the fund. This includes the management fee clients pay as well as trading, taxes, and other operational expenses. The expense ratio lowers the total return for the investor.

Federal funds rate   The rate banks charge each other for borrowing federal funds. This rate is also controlled by the Fed.

Federal Open Market Committee (FOMC)   A 12-member committee responsible for setting credit and interest rate policy for the *Federal Reserve System*. They set the discount rate directly and control the federal funds rate by buying and selling government securities impacting the rate. They meet eight times a year under the direction of a chairman—currently Ben Bernanke.

Federal Reserve Board   The seven members of the Board of Governors are appointed by U.S. presidents to serve 14-year terms. They serve on the *FOMC* and assist in setting *monetary policy*.

Federal Reserve System   The U.S. central banking system, responsible for regulating the flow of money and credit. Known as the Fed, it serves as a bank for other banks and the U.S. government.

Front-running   Trading based on soon-to-be public information, hoping to get a short-term run-up in price when the news disperses. An example of *insider trading* and a felony.

Fundamental analysis   A method of stock analysis focusing solely on a firm's fundamentals—financials, debt, management, operations, competition, and the like—in determining the future value of a stock.

Glass-Steagall Act   A series of laws passed in response to the stock market crash of 1929 sponsored by Senator Carter Glass (D-VA) and Henry B. Steagall (D-AL). Among other reforms, the act capped interest paid on savings deposits, established the Federal Deposit Insurance Corporation (FDIC), which insures deposits in the event of bank failure, and most notoriously separated the banking and brokerage industries—prohibiting banks from offering investment, commercial banking, and insurance services. President Clinton signed the *Gramm-Leach-Bliley Act* repealing the Glass-Steagall Act in 1999.

Gold standard   A monetary system pegging the value of currency to a fixed weight in gold. An international gold standard was established via the Bretton Woods Agreements in 1944. The United States abandoned the gold standard and the Bretton Woods Agreements fell apart in 1971.

Gramm-Leach-Bliley Act   In response to the mega-merger of Citibank (a traditional bank) with Travelers Group (an insurance firm), this act was passed in 1999 to modernize financial services laws. Most important, it repealed the Depression Era Glass-Steagall Act by allowing competition among banks, securities firms, and insurance firms, creating the all-encompassing "financial" sector.

Gross domestic product (GDP)   The monetary value of all goods and services produced in a country over a certain time period. In America, the U.S. *GDP*'s growth is a popularly used indicator of overall economic health.

Growth stock   Any stock with a P/E higher than the broad market's average. Because growth stocks have high P/Es (an after-tax measurement), they also have low E/Ps (i.e., the earnings yield, or the reverse of the P/E) and a relatively low cost of raising capital through stock issuance.

Hedge fund   A managed portfolio of investments that is generally unregulated (unlike a mutual fund or a registered investment advisor) and may invest in any highly speculative or illiquid vehicles, including options. The underlying investments can be illiquid, but so can the fund as some hedge funds require a minimum investment period.

Hindsight bias   A cognitive error causing investors to exaggerate the quality of their foresight—overestimating quality of initial knowledge and forgetting initial errors.

Hyperinflation   The rapid increase in average price levels, usually caused by excessive money supply growth.

Illiquid   Anything not converted quickly into cash.

Index fund   A mutual fund tracking a stated market index.

Individual retirement account (IRA)   A retirement account any employed person (or spouse of an employed person) can open and contribute to. Assets in the account grow tax deferred and contributions may be tax deductible, depending on the account holder's adjusted gross income. Distributions taken before age 59½ are generally subject to penalty. Distributions taken after 59½ are taxed at the account owner's income tax bracket.

Inelastic demand   Demand for goods and services that is constant, no matter the state of the economy. For example, demand for pharmaceuticals and some consumer staples is generally *inelastic,* as consumers usually won't buy more or less in an economic expansion or contraction.

Inflation   Rate of increase in average price levels. Different indexes use different baskets of goods and services to compute the average prices. A commonly cited index is the *Consumer Price Index.*

Initial public offering (IPO)   The first sale of equities to the public by a private firm. In making an IPO, a private firm has "gone public."

Insider   Any person with access to nonpublic information material to a firm, which can include officers, directors, and other key employees as well as their immediate families. *Insiders* are strictly prohibited from trading based on inside information.

Insider trading   Trading based on any nonpublic information—which is a felony. One need not be an *insider* to commit insider trading.

Laissez-faire   In French, "let it alone," referring to the theory that government interference in business should be minimal to allow maximum growth.

Large cap (or big cap)   Refers to the relative size of a firm's *market capitalization*. Traditionally, any firm with a market cap above $10 billion or $20 billion was referred to as *large cap*. However, a better guide is the dollar-weighted average of the broad market. *Large caps* are larger than the dollar-weighted average.

Long bond   A bond with a maturity of generally 10 years or longer.

Margin   Money borrowed using securities as collateral.

Market capitalization (market cap)   Value of a company as measured by the total value of outstanding shares (current share price × total number of outstanding shares).

Market index   A representation of the weighted average of companies comprising an index. The index is intended to represent a category, country, or the market as a whole (e.g., S&P 500, TOPIX, or Nasdaq).

Momentum investing   A trading strategy trying to capture short-term price movements based on the belief that stock price patterns are indicative of future results.

Monetary policy   Actions by a country's central bank impacting money supply and growth, credit conditions, and interest rates.

Mutual fund   An investment company investing in a variety of securities as dictated by the specific fund's prospectus. Investors do not own the underlying investments; they buy shares of the fund itself.

Myopic loss aversion (sometimes just *loss aversion*)   A cognitive error causing investors to act to avoid short-term loss, usually at the detriment of longer-term goals.

Naked put   A put option in which the seller (or "writer") does not own the *short* position. Loss potential is total except for the premium. The exact same security as a *covered call*.

Nasdaq 100 Index   A modified capitalization-weighted index designed to track the performance of the 100 largest and most actively traded non-financial domestic and international securities listed on *the NASDAQ Stock Market*.

Nasdaq Composite Index (or just "the Nasdaq")   A capitalization-weighted index designed to track the performance of all the securities listed on *the NASDAQ Stock Market*. Though most listed companies are technology related, the Nasdaq includes financial, bio-tech, industrial, and consumer companies.

The NASDAQ Stock Market   The National Association of Securities Dealers Automated Quotations System (NASDAQ) Stock Market is a fully electronic stock market. Listed companies include domestic and international firms in the financial, bio-tech, industrial, consumer, and technology sectors.

No-load fund   A mutual fund that does not charge an upfront commission. However, some no-load mutual funds still charge 12b-1 fees.

NYSE Composite Index   A capitalization-weighted index designed to track the performance of all common stocks listed on the New York Stock Exchange (NYSE).

Opportunity cost   Risk of missing superior returns from an alternate investment.

Order preference   A cognitive error causing investors to insist on certain things in a certain order for no other reason than societal convention. For example, order preference causes professionals to make annual forecasts in January, not April. It also causes investors to focus on individual stock or category performance rather than their whole portfolio.

Overconfidence   A cognitive error causing investors to overestimate their skill or knowledge. This may lead investors to trade too frequently, day-trade, or become overweighted in a presumed "hot" category.

Positive yield curve   A yield curve in which shorter-term rates are lower than longer-term rates. A *positive yield curve* occurs most of the time, and signals favorable credit conditions.

Price-to-earnings ratio (P/E ratio)   A ratio of a firm's share price to its earnings per share. One of the most commonly cited stock valuation ratios.

Price-to-sales ratio (PSR)   Ratio of a firm's share price to its per-share sales.

Pride   Mental process associating success with skill and repeatability.

Prospectus   A legal document accompanying a mutual fund or an annuity detailing the investment objectives, manager history, expenses, fees, and other investment details.

Put option   The right to sell a stock (or bond or commodity) at a certain price by a certain date. A put option writer sells the right to a buyer. If the option exercises, the buyer *puts* the stock to the writer, and the writer must buy it.

Random walk   The theory that stock prices follow a random, unpredictable path, and past price movements are not predictive of future movements.

Recession   A contraction in the business cycle, usually manifesting in slow or negative GDP growth.

Regression analysis   In statistics, a method for measuring the relatedness of two variables.

Regret   Mental process denying responsibility for failure.

Return on assets (ROA)   Ratio of net income to total assets.

Return on equity (ROE)   Ratio of net income to equity (net worth).

Risk   Investors typically equate risk with near-term volatility. However, simply, risk is the price of being wrong about an investment.

Russell 2000 Index   A capitalization-weighted index designed to track the performance of the 2,000 smallest (on a *market-capitalization* basis) U.S. stocks included in the *Russell 3000 Index*.

Russell 3000 Index   A capitalization-weighted index designed to track the performance of the 3,000 largest (on a *market-capitalization* basis) and most liquid U.S. stocks.

S&P 500 Composite Stock Price Index   A capitalization-weighted index designed to track the performance of the 500 stocks of the S&P 500. Stocks are included in the index based on their liquidity, market-cap (i.e., "large" cap), and sector. While not necessarily the 500 largest U.S. companies, these are generally the 500 most widely held.

Sell short (or just *short*)   When an investor sells a borrowed security with the intention of buying it back at a lower price. The difference between the price where the investor borrowed and sold it and bought it back is profit. This can be done with an individual security or an index.

Short rate   Interest rate that is monopoly set by a country's central bank. Not to be confused with a *short-term rate*.

Short-term rate   Free market-set interest rate of a shorter-term maturity (e.g., the interest rate on a 3-month *T-bill* is a *short-term rate*).

Small cap   Refers to the relative size of a firm's *market capitalization*. Traditionally, any firm with a market cap under $10 billion or $20 billion was referred to as *small cap*. However, a better guide is the dollar-weighted average of the broad market. *Small caps* are smaller than the dollar-weighted average.

Standard deviation   A measure of dispersion from the mean. In investing, standard deviation is used to measure volatility risk (e.g., a stock with a high standard deviation is understood to be very volatile).

Stop-loss (also, stop-limit)   An order placed with a broker to sell a stock when it reaches a certain price.

Supply-side economics   Championed by Art Laffer, Jude Wanniski, and Ronald Reagan (whose critics derisively called it "voodoo" economics), a theory of macroeconomics focusing on the supply side of the supply-demand equation—believing supply creates its own demand. Supply-siders believe, among other things, lowering income tax rates increases economic activity and therefore increases income tax receipts.

Tax deferral   Legally postponing the payment of taxes on gains through an investment vehicle such as an IRA, 401(k), or other retirement accounts.

Tax-loss selling   Selling stocks that are down at the end of the year to offset any taxable gains realized in the same year to reduce overall tax liability. Tax-losses may also be carried forward to offset future taxable gains.

Technical analysis   Analysis of a stock's historical price movements using charts or other tools to detect patterns while disregarding stock or market fundamentals. This strategy is based on the belief that past performance is indicative of future performance.

Terminal value   The projected value of an asset at the end of an investor's time horizon.

Time horizon   The period of time an investor needs their assets to last. For most investors, their time horizon is the life expectancy or that of a spouse or beyond.

Total return   The true rate of return of an asset, including capital gains, dividends, interest, and distributions realized over a given period.

Treasury bill (T-bill)   A U.S. debt security in maturities of less than one year.

Treasury bond   A U.S. debt security in maturities from 10 to 30 years.

Treasury note   A U.S. debt security in maturities from one year to seven years.

12b-1 fee   Part of a mutual fund *expense ratio* that reimburses the fund for marketing, promotion, and distribution costs. Reduces the investor's total return.

Underwrite   The assumption of risk. In insurance, an underwriter assesses risk and defines how much premium the insured should pay for a specified level of coverage. In investing, the underwriter assumes the risk of buying new securities in the hopes of reselling to the public at a profit.

Unrealized gain   The appreciation in value of an asset that has not been sold.

Unrealized loss   The depreciation in value of an asset that has not been sold.

Value stock   Any stock with a P/E lower than broad market's average. Because value stocks have low P/Es (an after-tax measurement), they also have high E/Ps (the reverse of the P/E and also the *earnings yield*). When borrowing costs are lower than their earnings yield, value companies will generally be more eager to raise expansion capital through borrowing rather than stock issuance.

Volatility   Generally thought to be a measure of market *risk*. Can be expressed as a statistical measure of the return variance between two securities, a security and the market, two equity categories, and so on. If something is more *volatile*, it has more return variance and is thought to be more risky.

Whipsaw   A quick, steep reversal in the direction a security, sector, or the market is heading.

Wilshire 5000 Total Market Index   A capitalization-weighted index designed to track the performance of over 6,500 U.S. stocks, including all of those listed in the NYSE and most of those in the Nasdaq and the American Stock Exchange (Amex). To be included in the index, companies need only be headquartered in the United States and traded on an American exchange.

Yield   Expressed as an interest rate, the annual income in dividends or interest an investment returns.

Yield curve   Interest rates of varying maturities plotted graphically. Generally, short-term interest rates are lower and longer-term rates are higher, creating a *positive* curve sloping up and to the right. An *inverted* yield curve means short-term rates are above longer-term rates, creating a curve sloping down and to the right. When interest rates are approximately at the same level, the curve is *flat*.

INDEX

Page numbers followed by a "t" or an "f" refer to tables and figures.